Alexander McCaul

The old paths

The Talmud tested by Scripture

Alexander McCaul

The old paths
The Talmud tested by Scripture

ISBN/EAN: 9783337127305

Printed in Europe, USA, Canada, Australia, Japan

Cover: Foto ©Andreas Hilbeck / pixelio.de

More available books at **www.hansebooks.com**

THE OLD PATHS,

OR

THE TALMUD TESTED BY SCRIPTURE;

BEING

A COMPARISON OF THE PRINCIPLES AND DOCTRINES

OF

MODERN JUDAISM,

WITH THE

RELIGION OF MOSES AND THE PROPHETS.

BY THE

REV. ALEXANDER McCAUL, D.D.,

LATE PROFESSOR OF DIVINITY, KING'S COLLEGE, LONDON;
AND LATE PREBENDARY OF ST. PAUL'S.

LONDON:
LONDON SOCIETY'S HOUSE,
16, LINCOLN'S INN FIELDS.

1880.

TO

THE RIGHT HONOURABLE AND RIGHT REVEREND

CHARLES JAMES, LORD BISHOP OF LONDON,

ETC. ETC.,

WHOSE APPROBATION OF HIS LABOURS

HAS BEEN AN ENCOURAGEMENT AND A REWARD,

THE FOLLOWING PAGES

ARE RESPECTFULLY

AND GRATEFULLY INSCRIBED, BY

THE AUTHOR.

ADVERTISEMENT TO THE SECOND EDITION.

NINE years have now elapsed since "The Old Paths" appeared as a volume. They have been translated, in the meantime, into Hebrew, German, and French; and their merits discussed by the learned and unlearned of the Jewish people, in all the countries of their dispersion. The reception has in general been favourable, and the effect upon the Jewish mind perceptible. Since their first appearance, the West London Synagogue and the Liturgies of the British Jews, both renouncing that which "The Old Paths" pronounced objectionable, have started into existence. The assembled rabbies at Brunswick and Frankfort have discussed topics similar to some treated in "The Old Paths," and in some cases come to similar conclusions respecting the value of Rabbinic Traditions. The Reform Societies of Germany have commenced a formidable attack upon the Oral Law, and a free discussion is now carried on in the numerous Jewish periodicals of that country, of which the results are easily foretold. The promised German translation of the Talmud, if ever completed, must, without any discussion, overthrow Talmudism. Its exhibition in any European language is the most fatal attack that can be made on its authority. It needs only to be seen as it is, in order to be rejected. The reader is again warned against mistaking this discussion of the merits of Rabbinism for an attack upon the Jewish people, or the rabbies of the present day. The reproach attaches not to the victims, but to the authors of tradition. The Jews are a great and a noble people, and the majority ignorant of the details of the system, by which they have been bowed down and misrepresented for centuries; so ignorant, indeed, that some zealously undertake a defence of the whole, maintain that Rabbinism is a perfect model of charity and wisdom, and regard "The Old Paths" as a mere emanation of common Anti-Jewish prejudice. Such persons are requested to compare these papers with the articles in the Jewish periodical, entitled, "Der Israelit des Neun zehnten Jahr hunderts," written by Rabbi Dr. Holdheim, and other distinguished Jewish scholars. They will there find that, had the author not been influenced by a desire to avoid all occasion of unnecessary offence, truth might have been stated with more severity.

A mistake in one number, not, however, affecting the argument, has been corrected.

ADVERTISEMENT TO THE FIRST EDITION.

THE reader will perceive, by the date at the head of each number, that the following papers were published weekly, and, from the contents, he will readily infer that they were intended for distribution amongst those Jews who still adhere to the rabbinic system. But in presenting them to the public as a volume, it may be well to state that the great object was to exhibit Judaism as it appears in its practical workings, and that, therefore, most references are made to the Jewish Prayer-book, and to the codes of law commonly in use amongst rabbinic Jews, and which are considered as authoritative. It was the Author's wish, not to ridicule any man's superstition, but to instruct those, whom Moses and the Prophets would have declared to be in error. He has therefore, carefully avoided the tone in which Eisenmenger and others have treated this subject, and, in treating the Jewish legends, has confined himself to those which are mentioned in the prayers of the

Synagogue. The materials are the result of many years' study and practical observation. Buxtorf, Majus, Edzard, Eisenmenger, Wagenseil, &c., have been carefully consulted, but the Jewish Liturgies, the Arbah Turim, the Shulchan Aruch, the Yad Hachasakah, are the principal sources, whence this view of Judaism has been drawn. The Author has only to add a hope, that these papers may not be misunderstood, either by Jew or Christian, but that all who read them will carefully distinguish between Judaism and the Jewish people—and a wish, that they may contribute to the welfare of Israel, and the promotion of truth.

CONTENTS.

	Page
I. Rabbinism not a Safe Way of Salvation	1
II. Implicit Faith not due to the Rabbies	8
III. Rabbinic Injustice to Women, Slaves, and Gentiles	16
IV. Rabbinic Intolerance towards other Nations	24
V. Talmudic Intolerance contrasted with the Charity of the Bible	32
VI. Compulsory Conversion of the Gentiles	39
VII. The Feast of Purim	47
VIII. Rabbinic Contempt for the Sons of Noah	55
IX. Christians cannot be reckoned amongst the "Pious of the Nations of the World"	63
X. Rabbinic Washing of Hands	70
XI. Rabbinic Artifices respecting Leaven at the Passover	79
XII. The Passover a Type of Future Deliverance	87

CONTENTS.

	Page
XIII. Severity of the Rabbinic Ordinances	95
XIV. Severity and Artifice	103
XV. Sabbath Mixture	111
XVI. Intolerance of Rabbinic Prayers	119
XVII. Rabbinic Legends in the Synagogue Services	127
XVIII. Rabbini Legends, continued	136
XIX. Legends in the Prayers for Pentecost	144
XX. Legends in the Prayers for Pentecost	152
XXI. Legends in the Prayers for Pentecost	160
XXII. Rabbinic Magic	167
XXIII. Astrology	175
XXIV. Amulets	183
XXV. Charms	191
XXVI. Charms, continued	199
XXVII. Sabbatic Laws	207
XXVIII. Fast for the Destruction of the Temple	215
XXIX. Sabbatic Laws, continued	223

XXX.
Sabbatic Laws, continued 231
XXXI.
Rabbinic Excommunication 239
XXXII.
New Year's Day 247
XXXIII.
New Year, continued 255
XXXIV.
New Year, continued 262
XXXV.
Justification 270
XXXVI.
Day of Atonement 279
XXXVII.
Feast of Tabernacles 287
XXXVIII.
Prayers for the Dead 295
XXXIX.
Almsgiving 302
XL.
Priests and Levites 310
XLI.
Rabbinic Ideas of the Deity 319
XLII.
Title of Rabbi 326
XLIII.
Sanhedrin 334
XLIV
Sanhedrin, continued 342
XLV.
Sanhedrin, continued 349
XLVI.
Contempt for the Female Character 357

	Page
XLVII.	
Polygamy	365
XLVIII.	
Divorce	372
XLIX.	
Rabbinic Laws concerning Meat	380
L.	
The Birth of Messiah	387
LI.	
Slaughtering of Meat, continued	396
LII.	
Laws concerning Meat with Milk	403
LIII.	
Rabbinism oppressive to the Poor	411
LIV.	
Gentile Wine	419
LV.	
Mourning for the Dead	427
LVI.	
Dispensation from an Oath	434
LVII.	
Doctrine of Oaths, continued	442
LVIII.	
Meritoriousness of Circumcision	449
LIX.	
Cruelty to the Unlearned	457
LX.	
Recapitulation	464

THE OLD PATHS.

No. I.*

RABBINISM NOT A SAFE WAY OF SALVATION.

SALVATION IS OF THE JEWS. Amongst all the religious systems existing in the world, there are but two deserving of attentive consideration, and they are both of Jewish origin, and were once exclusively confined to the Jewish nation. They are now known by the names of Judaism and Christianity; but it must never be forgotten that the latter is as entirely Jewish as the former. The Author of Christianity was a Jew. The first preachers of Christianity were Jews. The first Christians were all Jews; so that, in discussing the truth of these respective systems, we are not opposing a Gentile religion to a Jewish religion, but comparing one Jewish creed with another Jewish creed. Neither in defending Christianity, do we wish to diminish aught from the privileges of the Jewish people; on the contrary, we candidly acknowledge that we are disciples of the Jews, converts to Jewish doctrines, partakers of the Jewish hope, and advocates of that truth which the Jews have taught us. We are fully persuaded that the Jews whom we follow were in the right—that they have pointed out to us "the old paths," "the good way," and "we have found rest to our souls." And we, therefore, conscientiously believe, that those Jews who follow the opposite system are as wrong as their forefathers, who, when God commanded them to walk in the good old way, replied, "We will not walk therein." Some modern Jews think that it is impossible for a Jew to be in error, and that a Jew, because he is a Jew, must of necessity be in the right. Such persons seem to have forgotten how the majority of the people erred in making the golden calf—how the generation that came out of Egypt died in the wilderness because of their unbelief—how the nation at large actually opposed and per-

* Published originally January 15, 1836.

secuted the truth of God in the days of Elijah—how their love of error sent them into the Babylonish captivity—and how there has been some grievous error of some kind or other, which delivered them into the hands of the Romans, and has kept them in a state of dispersion for so many hundred years. But the passage from which our motto is taken sets forth most strikingly the possibility of fatal mistake on the part of the Jewish nation, and also the possibility, in such a case, of God's turning to the Gentiles. "Thus saith the Lord, Stand ye in the ways, and see, and ask for the old paths, where is the good way, and walk therein, and ye shall find rest for your souls. But they said, We will not walk therein. Also, I set watchmen over you, saying, Hearken to the sound of the trumpet. But they said, We will not hearken. *Therefore hear, ye nations*, הגוים שמעו, *and know, O congregation, what is among them. Hear, O earth; behold, I will bring evil upon this people, even the fruit of their thoughts, because they have not hearkened unto my words, nor to my law, but rejected it.*"—Jer. vi. 16—19. Who will dare to deny, after such a passage, the possibility of a Jew's being in error?

But some may ask, What is Judaism? what is Christianity? ANSWER.—Judaism is that religious system contained and acknowledged in the prayers of the Jewish synagogue, whether German or Portuguese, and professed by all who use them as the ritual of their worship. Christianity is the religious system taught in the New Testament; or, in other words, Judaism is the Old Testament explained according to the traditional law, תורה שבעל פה. Christianity is the Old Testament explained according to the New. According to this explanation, the Jewish Prayer-book teaches the divine authority of the oral law. Of this there can be no doubt, for, in the first place, the whole ritual of the synagogue service, and the existence and arrangement of the synagogue itself, is according to the prescription of the oral law, as may be seen by comparing the Jewish prayers with the Hilchoth T'phillah. If it be asked why the Jew uses these prayers, and no other—why he wears phylacteries (תפילין) and the veil (טלית)—why he conforms to certain ceremonies at the New Year, and the Day of Atonement, and the other feasts—why he repeats a certain benediction at the reading of the law—why he reads out of a parchment roll, rather than out of a printed book—why a roll of the law written in one way is lawful, and in another way unlawful, the only answer is, the oral law commands us thus to do. The whole synagogue worship, therefore, from the beginning to the end of the year, is a practical confession of the authority of the oral law, and every Jew who joins in the synagogue worship does, in so far, conform to the prescriptions of Rabbinism. But, secondly, the Jewish Prayer-book explicitly acknowledges the authority of the oral law. In the daily prayers, fol. 11, is found a long passage from the oral law, beginning,

איזהו מקומן של זבחים,

"which are the places where the offerings were slaughtered," &c. On fol. 12, we find the thirteen Rabbinical rules for expounding the law, beginning,

רבי ישמעאל אומר,

"Rabbi Ishmael says," &c. At the end of the daily prayers we find a whole treatise of the oral law, called, פרקי אבות, "the ethics of the fathers," the beginning of which treatise asserts the transmission of the oral law. In the morning service for Pentecost, there is a most comprehensive declaration of the authority and constituent parts of the oral law. "He, the Omnipotent, whose reverence is purity, with his mighty word he instructed his chosen, and clearly explained the law, with the word, speech, commandment, and admonition, in the Talmud, the Agadah, the Mishna, and the Testament, with the statutes, the commandment, and the complete covenant," &c., p. 89. In this prayer, as used, translated, and published by the Jews themselves, the divine authority of the oral law is explicitly asserted, and the Talmud, Agadah, and Mishna, are pointed out as the sources where it is to be found. For these two reasons, then, we conclude that the Judaism of the Jewish Prayer-book is identical with the Judaism of the oral law, and that every Jew who publicly joins in those prayers does, with his lips at least, confess its divine authority.

Having explained what we mean by Judaism, we now go on to another preliminary topic. Some one may ask, what is the use of discussing these two systems? May they not both be safe ways of salvation for those that profess them? To this we must, according to the plain declarations of these systems themselves, reply in the negative. The New Testament denounces the oral law as subversive of the law of God. "Then the Pharisees and scribes asked him, Why walk not thy disciples according to the tradition of the elders, but eat bread with unwashen hands? He answered and said unto them Well hath Esaias prophesied of you hypocrites, as it is written, This people honoureth me with their lips, but their heart is far from me. Howbeit in vain do they worship me, teaching for commandments the doctrines of men." (Mark vii. 5—7.) The oral law is still more exclusive. It excludes from everlasting life all who deny its authority, and explicitly informs us that Christians are comprehended in this anathema,—

ואלו הן שאין להם חלק לעולם הבא אלא נכרתין

ואובדין ונדונין על גודל רשעם וחטאתם לעולם
ולעולמי עולמים המינין והאפיקורסין והכופרים
בתורה וכו׳ :

"These are they who have no part in the world to come, but
who are cut off, and perish, and are condemned on account of the
greatness of their wickedness and sin for ever, even for ever and
ever, the heretics and the Epicureans, and the deniers of the
law," &c. Here is the general statement. But to prevent all
mistake, a particular definition of each of these classes is added,
from which we extract the following passage:—

שלשה הן הכופרים בתורה, האומר שאין התורה מעם
ה׳ אפילו פסוק אחד אפילו תיבה אחת אם אמר משה
אמרו מפי עצמו הרי זה כופר בתורה וכן הכופר
בפירושיה והיא תורה שבעל פה והמכחיש במגידיה
כגון צדוק וביתום והאומר שהבורא החליף מצוה זו
במצוה אחרת וכבר בטלה תורה זו אף על פי שהיא
היתה מעם ה׳ כגון הנוצרים והההגרים כל אחד משלשה
אלה הוא כופר בתורה :

"There are three classes of the deniers of the law. He who
says that the law is not from God, yea, even one verse or one
word: or if he says that Moses gave it of his own authority.
Such an one is a denier of the law. Thus, also, he who denies
its interpretations: that is, the oral law, and rejects its Agadoth
as Sadok and Baithos: and he who says that the Creator has
changed one commandment for another, and that the law has long
since lost its authority, although it was given by God, as the
Christians and Mahometans, each of these three is a denier
of the law."—Hilchoth T'shuvah, c. iii. 8.

In the first extract we see that those persons called "deniers
of the law," are, according to the doctrine of modern Judaism,
shut out from a hope of salvation. In the second extract we
see that Christians are by name included in that class: from
the two together it inevitably follows that modern Judaism
teaches that Christians cannot be saved. We do not find any
fault with modern Judaism for pronouncing this sentence; we
do not tax the Jews either with uncharitableness or intolerance
because of this opinion. On the contrary, we honour those who,
conscientiously holding this opinion, have the honesty and the
courage to declare it. If they consider us as deniers of the law,
they must, of course, believe that our state is far from safe; and
if this be their conviction, the best proof which they can give
of true charity, is to warn us of our danger. But, at the same
time, when a religious system condemns us by name, and pro-

nounces sentence concerning our eternal state in so decided a tone, and that simply because we dissent from some of its tenets, we not only think that we have a right to defend ourselves and our religion, but consider it our bounden duty to examine the grounds on which a system of such pretension rests, and honestly, though quietly, to avow our reasons for rejecting it. We know, indeed, that there are some Rabbinical Jews, who think this sentence harsh, and consider themselves justified in denying it, because there is another sentence in this same oral law, which says, "that the pious amongst the nations of the world have a part in the world to come." But can they prove, by any citation from the oral law, that Christians are included "amongst the pious of the nations of the world?" If they can, then they will prove that in one place the oral law denies, and in another place affirms the salvability of Christians; that is, they will prove that the oral law contains palpable contradictions, and therefore cannot be from God. If they cannot produce any such citation, then the general declaration that "the pious of the nations of the world" may be saved, is nothing to the purpose; for the same law which makes this general declaration, does also explicitly lay down the particular exception in the case of Christians, and that after it has made the general declaration. In fact, the exception follows close on the heels of the general rule. The general rule is,—

כל ישראל יש להם חלק לעולם הבא .... וכן
חסידי אומות העולם יש להם חלק לעולם הבא :

"*All Israel has a share in the world to come . . . . and also the pious of the nations of the world have a share in the world to come.*" The words which immediately follow this declaration contain the exception,—

ואלו הן שאין להם חלק לעולם הבא וכו׳

"*But these are they which have no part in the world to come,*" &c. This exception is, therefore, plainly made in order to guard against any false inference from the general statement, and, therefore, according to the oral law, Christians cannot be saved. We proceed, therefore, to inquire into the merits of this system, which makes so decided a statement respecting our eternal state. We have a standard of comparison to which no Jew will object, even that Holy Book, which contains the writings of Moses and the prophets. We reject the oral law, not because it seems in itself bad or good to our judgment, but because it is repugnant to the plain words of the Old Testament. There is not space to enter at large into the proof at present, but we subjoin one passage, which is in itself amply sufficient to disprove the divine authority of any religious system where it occurs. In the Talmud, in the Treatise Pesachim, fol. 49, col. 2, we read as follows:—

אָמַר רִבִּי אֶלְעָזָר עַם הָאָרֶץ מוּתָּר לְנָחֲרוֹ בְּיוֹם
הַכִּפּוּרִים שֶׁחָל לִהְיוֹת בְּשַׁבָּת אָמְרוּ לוֹ תַּלְמִידָיו
רַבִּי אֱמוֹר לְשָׁחֲטוֹ אָמַר לָהֶן זֶה טָעוּן בְּרָכָה וְזֶה
אֵינוֹ טָעוּן בְּרָכָה:

Rabbi Eleazar says, "It is lawful to split open the nostrils of an amhaaretz (an unlearned man) on the Day of Atonement which falls on the Sabbath. His disciples said to him, Rabbi, say rather that it is lawful to slaughter him. He replied, That would require a benediction, but here no benediction is needful." It is hardly needful to remind the reader that the law of Moses says, לֹא תִרְצָח, "Thou shalt not kill." But there is in this passage a sneering contempt for the unlearned, which is utterly at variance with the character of Him "whose mercies are over all his works," the unlearned and the poor, as well as the mighty and the learned.

Indeed the passage is so monstrous, that one is almost inclined to think that it must have crept into the Talmud by mistake; or, at the least, to expect that it would be followed by reprehension the most explicit and severe. But no, a little lower down another of these "wise men" says,—

עַם הָאָרֶץ מוּתָּר לְקָרְעוֹ כְּדָג׳

"It is lawful to rend an amhaaretz like a fish;" and, a little above, an Israelite is forbidden to marry the daughter of such a person, for that she is no better than a beast. But the whole of the preceding passage is so characteristic of the spirit of Rabbinism, that it is worth inserting—

תָּנוּ רַבָּנָן וְכוּ׳,

"Our Rabbies have taught. Let a man sell all that he has, and marry the daughter of a learned man. If he cannot find the daughter of a learned man, let him take the daughter of the great men of the time. If he cannot find the daughter of a great man of the time, let him marry the daughter of the head of a congregation. If he cannot find the daughter of the head of a congregation, let him marry the daughter of an almoner. If he cannot find the daughter of an almoner, let him marry the daughter of a schoolmaster. But let him not marry the daughter of the unlearned, for they are an abomination, and their wives are vermin; and of their daughters it is said, ' Cursed is he that lieth with any beast.' " Here, again, one is inclined to suppose that there is a mistake, or that these words were spoken in jest, though such a jest would be intolerably profane; but all ground for such supposition is removed on finding this passage transcribed into the digest of Jewish law, called the Schulchan Aruch, part 2; in the Hilchoth P'riah ur'viah, by which transcription it is stamped with all the authority of a law. Here, then, the reader is led to think, that an amhaaretz must mean something more and worse than an unlearned man—that it ought, perhaps, to be taken in its literal signification, "people of the land," and that it may refer to the idolatrous and wicked Canaanites. But the common usage of the Talmud forbids a supposition. There is a well-known sentence which shows that even a High Priest might be an amhaaretz:—

ממזר ת"ח קודם לכהן גדול עם הארץ,

"A learned man, though illegitimate, goes before a High Priest, who is an amhaaretz." Here the amhaaretz is plainly opposed to him that is learned. And so, on the page of the Talmud from which we have quoted above, we find the following words:—

עם הארץ אסור לאכול בשר בהמה שנאמר זאת תורת
הבהמה והעוף כל העוסק בתורה מותר לאכול בשר
בהמה ועוף וכל שאינו עוסק בתורה אסור לאכול
בשר בהמה ועוף:

"An amhaaretz is forbidden to eat the flesh of a beast, for it is said, 'This is the *law* of the beast and the fowl.' (Levit. xi. 46.) Every one that laboureth in the law, it is lawful for him to eat the flesh of the beast and the fowl. But for him who does not labour in the law, it is forbidden to eat the flesh of the beast and the fowl." According to this passage an amhaaretz is one who does not labour in the study of the law; and it being found on the very same page with the above most revolting declarations, it plainly shows the proud and haughty spirit of the authors of the Talmud, and their utter contempt for the poor, whose circumstances preclude them from the advantages of study. But, in reading such passages, the question naturally suggests itself, to which of the two classes does the poor Jewish population of London belong? There must be at the least hundreds, if not thousands of poor Jews in this great city who cannot possibly devote themselves to study. Amongst whom, then, are they to be classed? Amongst the learned תלמידי חכמים? or amongst the unlearned עמי הארץ? Are they, their wives, and daughters, as the Talmud says, to be called an abomination, vermin, and compared to the beasts? Or can a religion inculcating such sentiments proceed from that Holy One who is no respecter of persons? See here, ye children of Abraham, whom the providence of God has placed amongst the children of poverty, and cut off from the advantage of a learned education. You are not disciples of the wise, nor the great men of the time, nor heads of synagogues, nor almoners, nor even schoolmasters. You are quite shut out from these classes whom your Talmudical doctors favour so highly. See, then, in the above passages, what the Talmud says of yourselves, your wives, and daughters? Can you believe that this is the law of the God of Israel? Can you think for one moment, that these doctors knew " the old paths," " the good way?" If you do we must assure you that we cannot. We rather find it in that book, which says, " Blessed is the man that considereth the poor and needy." (Psalm xli. 1.) And in that other book, which speaks in the same spirit, and says that " God hath chosen the foolish things of this world to confound the wise; and the weak things of this world to confound the things which are mighty, and base things of the world, and things which are not, to bring to nought things that are; that no flesh should glory in his presence." (1 Cor. i. 27, 28)

No. II.

IMPLICIT FAITH NOT DUE TO THE RABBIES.

It appears from the undisguised acknowledgments of the New Testament, that the doctors and rabbies of the Jews, the Pharisees, and scribes, were the implacable enemies of Jesus of Nazareth, and that they were the main instruments in effecting his death. The modern Jews consider this fact as a sufficient apology for their rejection of his claims to the Messiahship. They take it for granted that the great and learned men of that day were also good men, and that they had valid reasons for their conduct. They think if Jesus of Nazareth had been the true Messiah, that the Sanhedrin, the great Jewish council of the time, would have acknowledged him, and conclude that, as they rejected him, he cannot be the true Messiah. The New Testament, on the contrary, accounts for their unbelief by plainly telling us, that they were bad men; and that they were enemies to the Lord Jesus, because he told them the truth, and exposed their hypocrisy. Now, which of these two representations accords with the truth? Were the scribes and Pharisees, those great advocates of the *oral law*, תורה שבעל פה, good men or bad men? The readers of our first number will be in some degree qualified to answer this question. Could those be good men who profanely talked of the lawfulness of killing an unlearned man, and who contemptuously compared the wives and daughters of the unlearned to "vermin and beasts?" If they could talk with levity of "rending like a fish" an unlearned man, one of their own brethren who had never done them any harm, what were they likely to do with one who exposed their wickedness, and boldly told them that they by their traditions made void the law of God? The very fact, that Jesus of Nazareth was put to death by such men, is presumptive evidence, that he was a good man, and that his claims were just. But, however that be, it is worth while to inquire into the charges which the New Testament brings against these learned men, and to see whether they are substantiated by the memorials of their character and spirit, which they themselves have left us in their laws. One of the charges preferred against them is, that they were ambitious men, covetous of worldly honour, and loving the pre-eminence. "But all their works they do to be seen of men; they make broad their phylacteries, and enlarge the borders of their garments. And love the uppermost rooms at feasts, and the chief seats in the synagogues, and greetings in the markets, and to be called of men, Rabbi, Rabbi." (Matt. xxiii. 5—7.) Now, is this charge true? Does the oral law justify this assertion, or does it prove, on the contrary, that the enemies of Jesus were humble, pious men, whose piety serves as a warrant for the uprightness of their conduct in their treatment of the Lord Jesus? Let the reader judge from the following laws which these men framed with respect to themselves. In the first place they claim for themselves more honour and reverence than is due to a man's own parents :—

כשם שאדם מצווה בכבוד אביו ובייראתו כך הוא
חייב בכבוד רבו ובייראתו יותר מאביו וכו׳:

"As a man is commanded to honour and fear his father, so he is bound to honour and fear his Rabbi more than his father; for his father has been the means of bringing him into the life of this world, but his Rabbi, who teaches him wisdom, brings him to the life of the world to come." (Hilchoth Talmud Torah, c. 5.) This general rule is bad enough, but the particulars are still worse. "If a man should see something that his father has lost, and something that his Rabbi has lost, he is first to return what his Rabbi has lost, and then to return that which belongs to his father. If his father and his Rabbi be oppressed with a load, he is first to help down that of his Rabbi, and then that of his father. If his father and his Rabbi be in captivity, he is first to ransom his Rabbi and afterwards his father unless his father be the disciple of a wise man (*i.e.*, learned), in which case he may ransom his father first." How fearful is this doctrine! A man is to see his father, the author of his existence, the guardian of his infancy, who has laboured for his support, and watched over him in the hour of sickness, he is to see this friend, to whom, under God, he owes everything, pining away in the bitterness of captivity, and yet, when he has got the means of restoring him to liberty and his family, he is to leave him still in all his misery, and ransom the Rabbi; where is this written in the Old Testament? "Honour thy father and thy mother," is there the first commandment that follows after our duty to God, and the first movement of natural affection. But this Rabbinical doctrine silences the voice of nature, and makes void the law of God. What is the doctrine of the New Testament here? "If any provide not for his own, and specially for those of his own house, he hath denied the faith, and is worse than an infidel." (1 Tim. v. 8.) The disciples of the Lord Jesus Christ never claimed for themselves any honour like this. In the passage just cited, they plainly declare that the first, in the circle of duties to men, is the duty to our own flesh and blood. And the only case in which the New Testament permits a deviation from this rule, is that where the same exception is made in the law of Moses, when love to parents would interfere with love to God. "If any man come to me and hate not his father and mother, and wife and children, and brethren and sisters, yea, and *his own life also*, he cannot be my disciple." (Luke xiv. 26.) Here father and mother, and kindred, are put in one category with a man's own life, in order to show that there is but one case in which the natural ties of blood may be overlooked, and this is when the service of God requires it. As it is also written in the law of Moses, "If thy brother, the son of thy mother, or thy son, or thy daughter, or the wife of thy bosom, or thy friend who is as thine own soul, entice thee secretly, saying, Let us go and serve other gods, which thou hast not known, thou nor thy fathers............Thou shalt not consent unto him, nor hearken unto him, neither shall thine eye pity him," &c. (Deut. xiii. 6—9.) And thus the tribe of Levi is praised, because "He said unto his father and his mother, I have not known him; neither did he acknowledge his brethren, nor know his own children." (Deut. xxxiii. 9.) But this Talmudical law is widely different. It has no saving clause to show that the case specified is an exception to the general rule. It does not pretend to suppose that the father is a bad man, or an idolater, or an apostate. It specifies but one exception, and that is, where the father is "the disciple of a wise man;" otherwise, though he be a good man, and a pious man, a loving and tender parent, still he is to be disregarded by his own son, and the Rabbi preferred before him. Is it possible to doubt that the men who conceived, sanctioned, and promulgated a law like this, had an eye to their own personal honour and interest? Is it reasonable to suppose that men who would sacrifice their own father to the honour of their Rabbi, would be very tender about the life of one who appeared, like Jesus of Nazareth, as an opposer of their pretensions? Or can the Jews, with the law and the prophets in their hands, suppose that these men pointed to "the old paths," "the good way?" This is certainly not the doctrine of Moses. He says :—

ארור מקלה אביו ואמו ואמר כל העם אמן :

"Cursed be he that setteth light by his father or his mother, and all the people shall say, Amen." (Deut. xxvii. 16.)

But these men did not stop here. They were not content with being exalted above father and mother. They did not scruple to assert, that their honour was as sacred as that of God himself:—

ואין לך כבוד גדול מכבוד הרב ולא מורא ממורא
הרב · אמרו חכמים מורא רבך כמורא שמים :

"Thou must consider no honour greater than the honour of the Rabbi, and no fear greater than the fear of the Rabbi. The wise men have said, The fear of thy Rabbi is as the fear of God."

They endeavour to prove the validity of these extravagant claims by such passages as Exod. xvi. 8, "Your murmurings are not against us, but against the Lord." But they have taken for granted what they can never prove, and that is, that every Rabbi is invested with the same office and authority as Moses. But where, in all the law of Moses, is there any warrant for such an assumption? Moses could with all propriety say, "Your murmurings are not against us, but against the Lord," for he held a special commission from God, and had proved to the people the reality of his commission by a series of miracles. But this the Rabbies never pretended to do. In this dearth of evidence the advocates of tradition flee for refuge to Deut. xvii. 8, &c. "If there arise a matter too hard for thee in judgment, between blood and blood, between plea and plea, and between stroke and stroke, being matters of controversy within thy gates; then shalt thou arise, and get thee up into the place which the Lord thy God shall choose; and thou shalt come unto the priests, the Levites, and unto the judge that shall be in those days, and inquire, and they shall show thee the sentence of judgment. And thou shalt do according to the sentence, which they of that place which the Lord shall choose shall shew thee; and thou shalt observe to do according to all that they inform thee; according to the sentence of the law which they shall teach thee, and according to the judgment which they shall tell thee, thou shalt do; thou shalt not decline from the sentence which they shall show thee to the right hand nor to the left." Here, say the traditionists, is a plain and unequivocal command. No doubt, God here plainly declares what is to be done in a difficult case. He commands the Israelites to go to the place which the Lord God chose, that is, to the place where was found the ark of the covenant; and to inquire, not of the Rabbies, but of the priests, the Levites, and the judge השופט. But this passage, instead of proving that "the fear of the Rabbi is as the fear of God," proves the contrary. It supposes first, that the Rabbies and learned men may differ in judgment, that there may be a controversy, and consequently, that one party may be in the wrong. It, therefore, effectually overthrows Rabbinical infallibility. It shows that these learned men are, after all, only poor fallible creatures like ourselves, and that, therefore, we are not to fear them as we would fear God, nor reverence their dictates, as the Word of God. It shows secondly, that in a case of difficulty, the Israelites were not to appeal to the Rabbies, but to the priests כהנים, and to the judge שופט, and even to them only in the place which the Lord should choose. There is not one word said about the Rabbies or the wise men, and, therefore, this passage completely annihilates all their lofty pretensions. For centuries the place which the Lord chose has been desolate, and there has been no priest standing to minister before the Lord. The Jews have thus lost all possibility of appeal. They have neither ministering priest nor judge, and the Mosaic law nowhere recognises the pretensions of the Rabbies. But some Jew may say, that though this passage does not prove the authority of the Rabbies, it does at least warrant the Jews in persisting to reject the claims of the Lord Jesus, for that he was condemned by the priests, and in Jerusalem, the place which the Lord chose. We confess that this objection is plausible; but can easily prove that it is nothing more. In order to this, we ask the Jews, whether the above command to abide by the sentence of the priests is in every case, and without any exception, binding? To this question there are two answers possible—Yes and No. If they say No, then they admit that the priests might sometimes be in the wrong, and we would, of course, take advantage of this admission to show that they erred in their judgment on Jesus of Nazareth. They will then, most probably, say, Yes; the sentence of the priests, the Levites, and the judges, is in every case binding, and Israel is commanded not to deviate from it, either to the right hand or to the left, upon pain of capital punishment. We beg of them then to turn to the 26th chapter of the Prophet Jeremiah, and to consider the case there set before them. We there find that Jeremiah had delivered a message from God, very similar to our Lord's prediction of the destruction of Jerusalem. "I will make this house like Shiloh, and will make this city a curse to all the nations of the earth." We find, further, that for this message the priests condemned Jeremiah to death, just as their successors condemned Jesus of Nazareth. "Now it came to pass, when Jeremiah had made an end of speaking all that the Lord had commanded him to speak unto all the people, that *the priests*, and the prophets, and all the people took him, saying, Thou shalt surely die." We find, further, that this sentence was pronounced "in the place which the Lord had chosen," in the Temple itself. "And all the people were gathered against Jeremiah in the house of the Lord." We find, further, that the sentence against Jeremiah was no rash sudden act, but the deliberate judgment of the priests. For when the princes of Judah came afterwards to inquire into the matter, "Then spake *the priests* and the prophets unto the princes and to all the people, saying, *This man is worthy to die*, for he hath prophesied against this city, as ye have heard with your ears." Now, then, we ask again, whether the people of Israel was in duty bound to abide by this sentence, and not to decline from it, either to the right hand or to the left? We fearlessly reply, that they were not bound by this sentence, and that, if they had executed it, they would have been guilty of murder, as Jeremiah himself declares: "But know ye for certain, that if ye put me to death, ye shall surely bring innocent blood upon yourselves, and upon this city, and upon the inhabitants thereof: for of a truth the Lord hath sent me unto you to speak all these words in your ears." We infer, therefore, that it was possible for the priests, assembled in solemn deliberation in the house of the Lord, to err in judgment, and to pronounce an unrighteous sentence. We infer, further, that it was possible for the priests so far to err, as to condemn to death a true prophet of the Lord. We infer, further, that in such a case the people was not bound by this mistaken judgment; but that it was their duty to decline from it, both to the right hand and to the left. We infer, lastly, that as the priests might mistake, and unjustly condemn to death a true prophet, their sentence against Jesus of Nazareth forms no more argument against the Messiahship of Jesus, than the similar sentence just considered did against the true prophetic character of Jeremiah; and that it affords just as little warrant for Jewish unbelief as the former sentence did for putting Jeremiah to death.

But it may be asked, if the judgment of the priests was not infallible, and if men were sometimes justifiable in refusing it, what use was there in the above commandment to apply to them in cases of difficulty, and to abide by their sentence? The answer to this is very simple. The priest that stood to minister before the Lord had it in his power, before the destruction of the first Temple, to inquire of the Lord and to receive a miraculous answer from God himself, which answer was, of course, infallible, and universally obligatory, without the possibility of exception. We find in the Old Testament many instances in which the Israelites availed themselves of this power, as in Judges xx. 27, "And the children of Israel inquired of the Lord (for the ark of the covenant of God was there in those days: and Phinehas, the son of Eleazar, the son of Aaron, stood before it in those days), saying, Shall I yet again go out to battle against the children of Benjamin my brother, or shall I cease? And the Lord said, Go up; for to morrow I will deliver them into thine hand." And in the history of David's life, there are several instances of his employment of this miraculous power, as 1 Sam. xxiii. 4, "Then David inquired of the Lord yet again. And the Lord answered him and said, Arise, go down to Keilah; for I will deliver the Philistines into thine hand." In all such cases where the priest first inquired of the Lord, his sentence was, of course, infallible, and the Israelites were bound to abide by it. But where they did not inquire of the Lord, their sentence was only that of fallible men, and, therefore, not binding upon the consciences of the people. Of this sort was their sentence upon Jeremiah. Being wicked men, they did not choose to ask counsel of the Lord, but pronounced sentence according to the devices of their own hearts. In the case of the Lord Jesus Christ the priests could not ask counsel of the Lord, for in the second Temple the Urim and Thummim, and the ark of the covenant, were wanting; the miraculous power, therefore, did not exist, and for this very reason the sentence of the priests, during the whole period of the second Temple, was only fallible, like that of other men, and, therefore, not binding, and consequently of no force as an argument against the Messiahship of the Lord Jesus Christ. The above passage, therefore, from the 17th of Deuteronomy, is of no use to the Rabbinical Jews, it does not prove the infallibility of the priests in the second Temple, and is still less applicable for sanctioning the traditions of the oral law, and the extravagant claims of the Rabbies. Having given this passage the consideration it deserves, we now return to the laws which the Rabbies have made in favour of themselves, and for their own honour. We consider that the two passages of the oral law already quoted, prove that the New Testament gives a fair delineation of their character. When men, without any warrant from God's Word, claim for themselves the same degree of reverence which is due to God, it must be admitted that they are vainglorious and wicked in no ordinary degree. But it is possible to descend to particulars:—For instance, our Lord says, that these men "loved greetings in the marketplaces, and to be called of men, Rabbi, Rabbi." Now one of the laws, still extant, forbids a man, when speaking of his Rabbi, to call him by name:—

אסור לו לתלמיד לקרות לרבו בשמו ואפילו שלא בפניו,

"It is forbidden to a disciple to call his Rabbi by name, even when he is not in his presence." Another law, still extant, prescribes the formula of greeting or salutation:—

ולא יתן שלום לרבו או יחזיר לו שלום כדרך שנותנים לריעים ומחזירים זה לזה אלא שוחה לפניו ואומר לו ביראה וכבוד שלום עליך רבי:

"Neither is he to salute his Rabbi, nor to return his salutation in the same manner that salutations are given or returned amongst friends. On the contrary, *he is to bow down before the Rabbi, and to say to him, with reverence and honour, Peace be unto thee, Rabbi.*" The Rabbinical Jews, who see this, must not mistake us. We do not consider it in anywise sinful, but decorous, to treat a Rabbi with all due respect. We should feel no objection ourselves to make a bow to a Rabbi, and to salute him in the prescribed formula. But we cite these laws to show that the New Testament gives a fair representation of the Pharisees: for men, who could gravely sit down and enter into all these details of the mode in which they were to be honoured, and then give out these laws as divine, and, besides all this, call in the civil power to enforce them, must have had no mean idea of themselves and their own dignity. It must never be forgotten that these laws are not the mere regulations of a religious community. When the Rabbies had the power in their own hands, they enforced them by civil sanctions. They were not satisfied with excluding despisers of Rabbinical authority from eternal life, *they prosecuted such before the tribunals, and sentenced them to a pecuniary fine and excommunication*, as may be seen from the following law:—

וכל המבזה את החכמים אין לו חלק לעולם הבא והרי הוא בכלל כי דבר יהוה בזה: אף על פי שהמבזה את החכמים אן לו חלק לעולם הבא אם באו עדים שבזהו אפילו בדברים חייב נדוי. ומנדין אותו בית דין ברבים וקונסין אותו ליטרא זהב בכל מקום ונותנין אותו לחכם. והמבזה את החכם בדברים אפילו לאחר מיתה מנדין אותו בית דין וכו'.

"Whosoever despises the wise men has no share in the world to come. But notwithstanding this, if there come witnesses to prove that he has been guilty of contempt, even in words, his sentence is excommunication, and the tribunal (house of judgment) excommunicates him publicly, and everywhere mulct him in a pound of gold, and give it to the wise man. He that despiseth a wise man in words, even after his death, is to be excommunicated by the tribunal," &c. We now ask the Jews of modern times what they think of those who made their own personal honour the subject of legislation, who required the same reverence for their words as the Word of God, and who dragged up him that refused it before a tribunal, had him sentenced to pecuniary fine, and excommunication; and, besides all this, excluded him from the hope of everlasting life? Had such men any idea of liberty of conscience?

No. III.

RABBINIC INJUSTICE TO WOMEN, SLAVES, AND GENTILES.

If any of our readers should think that the design of these papers is to represent the oral law as a system of unmixed evil, we beg to assure them that they are mistaken. We are fully aware that a system based on the law and the prophets, must and does contain much that is good and worthy of admiration. Of this nature is the general command to all Israelites to study the law, which is as follows:—" Every man of Israel is bound to study the law. Whether he be poor or rich, healthy or unhealthy, young or old, yea, though he live upon alms, and beg from door to door, and though he have a wife and children, he is bound to set apart a fixed time for the study of the law, by day and by night, as it is written, 'Thou shalt meditate therein by day and by night.'" And again, the maxim, "Every one that is bound to learn is also bound to teach;" and that, "therefore, a man is bound to teach his son and his son's son," &c., is in accordance with the plain command of God, and is therefore good. But the explanation and development of these good principles shows that the system itself is radically bad, and therefore cannot be from God. No one will deny that the Rabbies are right in asserting the obligation resting on every Israelite to study the law: but they are wrong in their explanation of what the law is. Immediately after the above good command, the oral law goes on to say, "Every one is bound to divide the time of his study into three parts: one-third to be devoted to the written law; one-third to Mishna; and one-third to Gemara:" so that the written law of God is to have only half as much attention as the traditions of men.

This is bad enough. But the Rabbies do not stop here. They go on to say, that this third of attention is only required when a man begins to study, but that when he has made progress, he is to read the law of God only at times, and to devote himself to Gemara.

בד״א בתחלת תלמודו של אדם אבל כשינדיל
בחכמה ולא יהא צריך לו ללמוד תורה שבכתב ולא
לעסוק תמיד בתורה שבעל פה יקרא בעתים מזומנים
תורה שבכתב ודברי השמועה כדי שלא ישכח דבר
מדברי דיני תורה ויפנה כל ימיו לגמרא:

"What has been said refers only to the beginning of a man's learning, but as soon as a man becomes great in wisdom, and has no need of learning the written law, or of labouring constantly in the oral law, let him at fixed times read them, that he may not forget any of the judgments of the law, *but let him devote all his days to Gemara.*" It is to be observed that "oral law" is here taken in a limited sense, as referring to the expositions of the written law, or, as Rabbi Joseph Karo* explains it, the Mishna; and Gemara signifies the legal decisions which are inferred by a process of reasoning, and to this third topic of Jewish theology the Israelites are commanded to give the chief of their time and attention, rather than to the written Word of God.

The apparent excellence of the above command to study the law is thus utterly destroyed by the Rabbinical exposition of what is to be studied. And if we go on to inquire upon whom this command is binding, the Rabbinical answer will afford just as little satisfaction. When the Rabbies say, that "every man of Israel is bound to study the law," they mean to limit the study to the men of Israel, and to exclude the women and slaves. The very first sentence of the Hilchoth Talmud Torah is

נשים ועבדים וקטנים פטורים מתלמוד תורה,

"Women and slaves and children are exempt from the study of the law." According to this declaration, women are not obliged to learn. The following extract will confirm this opinion, and at the same time show that there is no obligation on fathers to have their daughters taught.

אשה שלמדה תורה יש לה שכר אבל אינו כשכר
האיש מפני שלא נצטוית . וכל העושה דבר שאינו
מצווה עליו לעשותו אין שכרו כשכר המצווה ועושה
אלא פחות ממנו ואע״פ שיש לה שכר צוו חכמים

* Joreh Deah, sec. 246.

שלא ילמד אדם את בתו תורה מפני שרוב הנשים
אין דעתן מכוונת להתלמד אלא הן מוציאות דברי
תורה לדברי הבאי מפי עניות דעתן . אמרו חכמים
כל המלמד את בתו תורה כאלו למדה תיפלות .
בד'א בתורה שבעל פה אבל תורה שבכתב לא ילמד
אותה לכתחלה ואם למדה אינו כמלמדה תיפלות :

"A woman who learns the law has a reward, but it is not equal to the reward which the man has, *because she is not commanded to do so:* for no one who does anything which he is not commanded to do, receives the same reward as he who is commanded to do it, but a less one. But though the woman has a reward, the wise men have commanded that no man should teach his daughter the law, for this reason, that the majority of women have not got a mind fitted for study, but pervert the words of the law on account of the poverty of their mind. The wise men have said, Every one that teacheth his daughter the law is considered as if he taught her transgression.*
But this applies only to the oral law. As to the written law, he is not to teach her systematically; but if he has taught her, he is not to be considered as having taught her transgression."

According to this decision, it is absolutely forbidden to teach a woman the oral law; and the teaching of it is looked upon as the teaching of transgression תיפלות. We cannot forbear asking the advocates of the oral law, whether it does not here testify against itself that it is bad. It declares of itself that it is unfit for the perusal and study of the pure female mind, and that it is as corrupting as the teaching of transgression. We ask, then, can such a law be divine? Can it proceed from the God of Israel, who hath said, "Be ye holy, for I am holy?" What a noble testimony to the superiority of the written Word, and to the justice of the Lord Jesus Christ's opposition to the oral law! The oral law itself says, "He that teacheth his daughter the oral law, is to be considered as if he taught her transgression. He that teacheth her the written law, is not to be so considered." With such a confession, we fearlessly ask the sons and daughters of Israel, who then was in the right? Jesus of Nazareth, who opposed it, or the scribes and Pharisees who defended it?

But "the wise men" also forbid Israelites to teach women the written law, and declare that women are not bound to learn. For the prohibition they assign two reasons. First, they say that God has commanded them to teach only their sons, in proof of which they refer to Deut. xi. 19, "And ye shall teach

---

* תיפלות. In the translation of this word we follow the interpretation of the Joreh Deah, which renders it דבר עבירה. This is obviously not the place to discuss the other opinions of the Rabbies.

them your children." In the Hebrew it is בְּנֵיכֶם "your sons;" and the rabbies infer וְלֹא אֶת בְּנוֹתֵיכֶם, "and not your daughters."* Secondly, they say, as we have seen above, "that the majority of women have not got minds fitted for study," and in the Talmud† this is attempted to be proved from Scripture. "A wise woman once asked R. Eliezer, How it was that after the sin of the golden calf, those who were alike in transgressions did not all die the same death? He replied, A woman's wisdom is only for the distaff, as it is written, 'All the women that were wise-hearted did spin with their hands.'" (Exod. xxxv. 25.) We hesitate not to say, that both these reasons are contrary to Scripture. We do not deny that בְּנֵיכֶם signifies sons, but we utterly deny the conclusion of the Rabbies, that because the masculine word is used, therefore the women are not included in the command. There is an abundance of instances in which the masculine word בָּנִים is used for children generally, without any allusion to sex. Take for example Exod. xxii. 23 (in the English 24), "And my wrath shall wax hot, and I will kill you with the sword; and your wives shall be widows, and your children בְּנֵיכֶם (literally your sons) orphans." Here again the masculine word is used, so that if the Rabbinical argument be valid in the above case, it will be valid here, and consequently the daughters are excluded from this denunciation, so that the sons were to be orphans, but not the daughters, which is plainly impossible. In the same way we can prove that the daughters of Israel did not wander in the wilderness forty years, for in Numbers xiv. 33, it is said, "And your children וּבְנֵיכֶם (literally your sons, and, therefore, according to Talmudic logic, not your daughters) shall wander in the wilderness forty years." The same logic will also prove that during the three days of miraculous darkness in Egypt, the women of Israel were left in darkness as well as the Egyptians, for it is said all the children of Israel (וּלְכָל בְּנֵי יִשְׂרָאֵל, literally the sons of Israel) had light in their dwellings. And thus also it might be proved that not one oi the ten commandments is binding upon the women, for the masculine gender is employed throughout. This logic, therefore, is evidently false; and we conclude, on the contrary, that as the women are included in all these passages—as they wandered through the wilderness, and had light in their dwellings—and are bound to keep the ten commandments as well as the men, so also they are included in the command, " Ye shall teach them your children," and that, therefore, the command of the oral law not to teach women, is contrary to the Word of God. But we are not confined to argument, God has plainly commanded that the women should learn as well as the men. "And Moses

---

* See Kiddushin, fol. 29, col. 2. † Joma., fol. 66, col. 2.

commanded them, saying, At the end of every seven years, in the solemnity of the year of release in the Feast of Tabernacles, when all Israel is come to appear before the Lord thy God in the place which he shall choose, thou shalt read this law before all Israel in their hearing. Gather the people together, men *and women*, and children, and thy stranger that is within thy gates, that they may hear, and *that they may learn* ולמען ילמדו, and fear the Lord your God, and observe to do all the words of this law." (Deut. xxxi. 10—12.) Here a most beautiful order is observed, and required of women as well as men; hearing——learning—fearing—keeping the words of the law—God wills that the women should fear him and keep his commandments as well as the men; and therefore he wills that they should make use of the same means, that they should hear, and learn all the words of the law. The traditionists have, therefore, in this case plainly made void the law of God. God commands women as well as men to learn the law; the Rabbies say they are exempt from this duty. God commands that the woman should be taught. It is plain, therefore, that the oral law, which contradicts the written law, cannot be from God. The command of God is so plain that it is unnecessary to enter deeply into the second Rabbinical reason for the prohibition to teach women the law. It is evident that God did not think that the poverty of their understanding was any obstacle to their learning his will. Indeed it has pleased Him to show that He is no respecter of persons with regard to male or female, more than with regard to rich or poor. He has not only given them his law, but conferred on women as well as men the gift of prophecy, so that the names of Deborah, Hannah, and Huldah, must ever be remembered amongst the inspired messengers of God. The Rabbies seem to have forgotten that "the fear of the Lord is the beginning of wisdom," and that this fear may be implanted by God just as easily in the heart of a woman as of a Rabbi. But without inquiring further into their reasons or their motives, suffice it to say, that the oral law in thus robbing women of their right and inheritance in the law of God, and in degrading them to the same category with children and slaves, is opposed to the plain commands of the written law. But not so the New Testament. It exactly agrees with the Old in considering woman as a rational and responsible being, and a candidate for everlasting life. It, therefore, gives one general rule for the education of children, male and female. "Ye fathers, provoke not your children to wrath, but bring them up in the nurture and admonition of the Lord." (Ephes. vi. 4.) It does indeed prescribe modesty and subjection to the women in the mode of learning, but in so doing it plainly points out their duty to become acquainted with the will of God. "Let the woman learn in silence with all subjection. But I suffer not a woman to teach nor to usurp authority over the man, but to be in silence." (1 Tim. ii. 11, 12.)

In these and other passages the woman is placed in the position assigned her in the Old Testament, and not in the very subordinate rank imposed upon her by the oral law. "Women, and slaves (עבדים), and children, are exempt from the study of the law." But we think that this rule is as false with regard to slaves as to women. Here the oral law says that slaves are not bound to learn. In Hilchoth Avadim, c. viii. 18, we find that they are not to be taught.

אסור לאדם ללמד את עבדו תורה:

"It is forbidden to a man to teach his slave the law." But, alas, the passage of the Word of God which forbids it, is not referred to. It is only an inference from the passage, "Ye shall teach your *sons*;" but is evidently contrary to the whole tenour of the law of Moses. In the first place, the Israelite who had been sold by the tribunal, or who, on account of poverty, had sold himself, was still an Israelite, and did not forfeit, finally, his right to his inheritance in the land; how, then, could he forfeit his right to the law, which Moses gave as "the inheritance of the congregation of Jacob?" The law of Moses expressly provides a day of rest "for the man servant and the maid servant," that they may not only have rest for their bodies, but may have time to learn the will of God, and provide for that eternity to which they are hastening as well as their masters. Indeed, if meditation on the Word of God was more necessary for one Israelite than another, it was for the Hebrew servant. If he had been guilty of theft, and had been sold by the tribunal, he had special need of instruction in the law of God to lead him to repentance, and to teach him his duty for the future. If he had been guilty of no crime, but had been compelled by poverty to sacrifice his liberty, surely he needed the consolation which the Word of God can supply, to enable him to bear his hard lot with patience, and to prevent him from murmuring. But here the oral law steps in, and actually prohibits his master from teaching him; and instead of encouraging him in his leisure time to turn to the Word of God as his refuge and his comfort, it tells him that he is not bound to study it. Here, again, the New Testament is much more like the law of Moses, which breathes, all through, a spirit of the most tender compassion for those in servitude. Moses commands the Israelites to remember that they had themselves been bondmen in Egypt. The New Testament reminds Christian masters that they have a master in heaven. "Ye masters, do the same things unto them, forbearing threatening: knowing that your master also is in heaven;

neither is there respect of persons with him." (Ephes. vi. 9.) It also plainly teaches that the relation which exists between believing masters and servants is, before God, that of brethren. " And they that have believing masters, let them not despise them, because they are brethren ; but rather do them service because they are faithful and beloved, partakers of the benefit." (1 Tim. vi. 2.) Yea, the New Testament lays down a general principle, the very opposite of that, that " women, and slaves, and children are exempt from the study of the law." It says, " There is neither Jew nor Greek, there is neither bond nor free, there is neither male nor female, for ye are all one in Christ Jesus." (Gal. iii. 28.) It does not dispense men from their relative duties, nor deprive any of their legitimate privileges, but teaches that for all, Jew or Greek, bond or free, male or female, there is but one way of salvation. Very different is the doctrine of the oral law. We have seen that it makes a grand distinction between male and female, bond and free, we need not, therefore, be surprised if it make the line of demarcation broader still between Jew and Greek.

גוי שעסק בתורה חייב מיתה . לא יעסוק אלא בשבע
מצוות שלהן בלבד . וכן גוי ששבת אפילו ביום מימות
החול . אם עשהו לעצמו כמו שבת חייב מיתה . ואין
צריך לומר אם עשה מועד לעצמו . כללו של דבר אין
מניחין אותן לחדש דת ולעשות מצוות לעצמן מדעתן .
אלא או יהיה גר צדק ויקבל כל המצוות . או יעמוד
בתורתו ולא יוסיף ולא יגרע . ואם עסק בתורה או שבת
או חדש דבר . מכין אותו ועונשין אותו ומודיעין אותו
שהוא חייב מיתה על זה אבל אינו נהרג:

" A Gentile who employs himself in the law is guilty of death. He is not to employ himself except in the seven commandments that belong to the Gentiles. And thus a Gentile who keeps a Sabbath, though it be on one of the week days—if he make it to himself as a Sabbath, he is guilty of death. It is not necessary to add, if he appoint for himself a festival. The general rule is that they are not permitted to innovate in religion, or to make commandments for themselves out of their own heads. Either let a Gentile become a proselyte of righteousness, and take upon him the whole law: or let him remain in his own law, and neither add nor diminish. But if he employs himself in the law, or keeps a Sabbath, or makes any innovation, he is to be beaten and punished, and informed that he is for this guilty of death—but he is not to be killed." (Hilchoth Melachim, c. x. 9.) This law is taken from the Talmudical treatise Sanhedrin,*

* Fol. 59, col. 1.

where it is followed by an apparently contradictory statement, "that a Gentile who employs himself in the law is as good as a high priest;" but the contradiction is immediately removed by the explanation which there follows, and says, that "law" is to be understood of the seven commandments of the Gentiles. Now we admit liberty of conscience was not understood at the time; and that it would be unjust to expect that the compilers of the oral law (who were ignorant of, or opposed to, the New Testament, where liberty of conscience was first plainly revealed) should be at all elevated above the level of their own times. But making this admission and apology for the men, we cannot help saying that the law itself is bad, and cannot be from God. Religion is a matter between God and man. The heart, the conscience, and the understanding are all alike concerned. Instruction out of God's Word is, therefore, the only means of producing conviction. Entertaining these sentiments, we endeavour to compare the oral law with the Word of God, and to convince its advocates that they are in error. We do not wish to have the modern Jews confounded with the authors of the system. Very many Jews of the present day are ignorant of its details. Not having time to make the inquiry, they take it for granted, that their forefathers were right in preferring their own system to Christianity, and that they are bound to do the same. But even those who are learned in the oral law, and know its details, are not to be viewed in the same light as the original compilers. They have received the system from their forefathers, and view it through the medium of filial affection and national prejudice. They remember that to the Jews the law was given, and that the Jewish nation has been the original instrument in God's hand to diffuse light over the world; they have therefore hitherto taken it for granted that they must be right. The narrow prejudices of Christians for ages confirmed them in their views. But now circumstances are different. Christians begin to understand the position in which God has placed the Jewish nation, and to look forward to their restoration to the favour of God as the time of blessing for the whole world. Christians can now honour and estimate the learning, the talent, and the constancy of those very Rabbies whose system they consider as erroneous. Now, then, is the time for the Jews themselves to inquire into those religious opinions, which have been handed down to them, and to compare them with the law and the prophets. We trust that many will admit, that the laws which we have been considering are bad, and therefore cannot be from God. Let them then remember, that the originators of these laws are the men who rejected the claims of the Lord Jesus Christ. If then these men were in error in making these laws, they were in condemning Jesus of Nazareth because he opposed them; and if the laws be bad, the

Lord Jesus was right in opposing them. Yea, and where they taught error He and his disciples taught the truth. The Rabbies have taught constraint. Jesus of Nazareth and his disciples have taught that fire is not to be called down from heaven on those who differ from us; that "the servant of God must not strive; but be gentle to all men, apt to teach, patient, in meekness instructing those that oppose themslves; if God will peradventure give them repentance to the acknowledging of the truth." (2 Tim. ii. 25.)

No. IV.

RABBINIC INTOLERANCE TOWARDS OTHER NATIONS.

THE Jewish deputies, when asked by Napoleon whether they considered Frenchmen as their brethren, replied in the affirmative, and after quoting the Mosaic laws respecting the stranger said, "To these sentiments of benevolence towards the *stranger*, Moses has added the precept of general love for mankind: '*Love thy fellow-creature as thyself.*'"* And in the authorized Jewish Catechism used in Bavaria, after the explanation of the moral duties, we find the following question:— "Are these laws and duties, affirmative and negative commandments, binding with respect to a non-Israelite?" ANSWER— "By all means, for the fundamental law of all these duties, '*Love thy neighbour as thyself*,' is expressly laid down by the Holy Scriptures in reference to the non-Israelite, yea, to the heathen, as it is written, 'And if a stranger sojourn with thee in your land, ye shall not vex him. But the stranger that dwelleth with you shall be unto you as one born amongst you, *and thou shalt love him as thyself*: for ye were strangers in the land of Egypt: I am the Lord your God.'" (Levit. xix. 33—35.)† These declarations are very explicit, and, as forming part of public documents, highly satisfactory. The representatives of the Jewish people in France, and the teachers of the Jewish youth in Bavaria, declare, that in the scriptural command, "Thou shalt love thy neighbour as thyself," neighbour means *fellow-man*, without distinction of nation or religion. Where then did they learn this interpretation? From the

---

* Transactions of Parisian Sanhedrin, p. 178.
† Lehrbuch der Mosaischen Religion. München, 1826, page 150.

Talmud or from the New-Testament? The Jewish deputies say, from the former. On the page cited above they add, "This doctrine is also professed by the Talmud. We are bound, says a Talmudist, to love as brethren all those who observe the *Noachides*,* whatever their religious opinions may otherwise be." We are bound to visit their sick, to bury their dead, to assist their poor, like those of Israel. In short, there is no act of humanity which a true Israelite is not bound to perform towards those who observe the *Noachides*." The Bavarian Catechism is more cautious. It makes no such bold assertion respecting the Talmud. It only intimates that the oral law teaches this doctrine, by subjoining to the passage from Leviticus the same extract from Maimonides, alluded to by the Jewish deputies. The Catechism gives the extract a little more at length, and as follows:—" We are bound in everything to treat the non-Israelite, who sojourns with us, with justice and with love, as we would treat an Israelite. Yea, we are even bound to maintain him, as the Scripture teaches in the words, 'Thou shalt give it to the stranger that is in thy gates, that he may eat it.' (Deut. xiv. 21.) Our wise men have commanded us for the good of society, even to visit the sick of the heathen, to bury their dead, and to deal out alms to them: for of our Creator it is said, 'The Lord is good to all; and his tender mercies are over all his works.' (Psalm cxlv. 9.) (Maimonid. Hilchoth Melachim, 10, 12.)"

No doubt the passage as here given, both by the French deputies and the Bavarian Catechism, is very plausible; and if it could be found verbatim, either in the Talmud or any of its compendiums, would go far to justify the bold assertion of the former, and the cautious insinuation of the latter. But unfortunately the original passage is very different. In the above citations, it is mutilated in order to suit the purpose of the citers. In the Jad Hachasakah it stands as follows:—

וכן יראה לי שנוהגין עם גרי תושב בדרך ארץ
וגמילות חסדים כישראל . שהרי אנו מצווין להחיותן
שנאמר לגר אשר בשעריך תתננה ואכלה . וזה
שאמרו חכמים אין כופלין להם שלום . בגוים לא
בגר תושב . אפילו הגוים צוו חכמים לבקר חוליהם .
ולקבור מתיהם עם מתי ישראל . ולפרנס את ענייהם
בכלל עניי ישראל . מפני דרכי שלום · הרי נאמר
טוב ה' לכל ורחמיו על כל מעשיו ונאמר דרכיה
דרכי נועם וכל נתיבותיה שלום :

* We quote the passage as we find it. Noachides is here taken for the seven commandments of the children of Noah, contrary to the usual acceptation of the word.

"And thus it appears to me, that *the proselytes allowed to sojourn* are to be treated with the same courtesy and benevolence as the Israelites; for behold, we are commanded to maintain them, as it is written, 'Thou shalt give it to the stranger (proselyte) that is in thy gates, that he may eat it.' *As to that saying of our wise men not to return their salute, it refers to the Gentiles, not to the proselyte allowed to sojourn.* But even with regard to the heathen, the wise men have commanded us to visit their sick, and to bury their dead with the dead of Israel, and to feed their poor along with the poor of Israel, FOR THE SAKE OF THE WAYS OF PEACE: for it is written, 'The Lord is good to all, and his mercies are over all his works; and again, 'Her ways are ways of pleasantness, and all her paths are peace.'" (Prov. iii. 17.) The reader will observe that there are several striking differences between this translation and that of the Bavarian Catechism; and these differences prove that, by the word "neighbour," the oral law does not understand a fellow-man without any regard to his religious opinions. First, the Bavarian Catechism says, "We are bound in everything to treat the non-Israelite who sojourns with us with justice and with love, and as we would treat an Israelite." The original says, "And thus *it appears to me*, that *the proselytes allowed to sojourn* are to be treated with the same courtesy and benevolence as the Israelites." The Bavarian Catechism translates this passage as it if were the undisputed law of Israel thus to act; whereas Maimonides only offers his own opinion. He says, "It appears to me." Here the French deputies represent the matter more accurately, by saying, "We are bound, says *a Talmudist.*" Not the Talmud, but a Talmudist. Then, again, the Bavarian Catechism speaks generally of "non-Israelites." Maimonides speaks of only one particular class, the proselytes who had permission to sojourn in the land of Israel. That we do not misrepresent Maimonides' meaning, is plain from the words of the Jewish deputies, who also restrict the sense to that one particular class. "We are bound, says a Talmudist, to love as brethren all those who observe the *Noachides*, whatever their religious opinions may otherwise be." Here, then, on the showing of the Jewish deputies themselves, the Talmud does not teach that all men are to be loved as brethren, but only those who keep the seven commandments of Noah. How, then, are we to regard the idolater and the heathen, who have not embraced these seven commandments, and how are we to treat them? This leads us to notice,

2dly, The important *omission* made by the Bavarian Catechism. In citing the words of Maimonides, the compilers have omitted the whole sentence, "As to the saying of our wise men not to return their salute, it refers to the Gentiles, not to the proselytes allowed to sojourn." To this sentence, the French Jewish deputies have also made no allusion; and yet this sentence is found in the very middle of the passage quoted. What goes before and what follows is quoted by both, but both have with one common consent omitted this passage. Now this mere fact of omission is, in itself, sufficient to excite the suspicions of Israelites not acquainted with the oral law. The Jewish deputies in Paris, and the compilers of the Jewish Catechism in Bavaria, had one common object—they wished to prove, or to intimate, that the Talmud teaches us to love as ourselves all our fellow-men, without any respect to religious differences. In order to prove this, they both refer to one and the same passage—and from the middle of that passage they both omit one important sentence. What conclusion will be drawn by any man of common understanding? Just this, that as they both quote one and the same passage, there must be a great scarcity of proof from the Talmud: and that, as they both make the same omission, the sentence omitted must be unfavourable to that proof; and that, therefore, this one passage does not prove that the Talmud teaches any such doctrine. Such is the conclusion to which we are led by considering the facts of the case. An examination of the omitted passage will show that this conclusion is most just—"As to the saying of our wise men, not to return their salute, it refers to the Gentiles, not to the proselytes allowed to sojourn." Had this passage been inserted in its place, the Bavarian Catechism could not have been translated גרי תושב (sojourning proselytes) "non-Israelites," for from this passage it appears that these *sojourners* are different from the "Gentiles," whose salute is not to be returned. In plain English, this passage restricts "the courtesy and benevolence" to those proselytes who, by taking upon them the seven commandments of Noah, obtained the privilege of sojourning in the land of Israel; and consequently excludes "the Gentiles"—and consequently disproves the assertion that the Talmud teaches us to love as ourselves all our fellow-men without any respect to religious differences. On the contrary, this passage tells us that the salutation of the Gentiles is not to be returned. It prescribes two different lines of conduct to be pursued towards different religionists, and makes the difference of religious persuasion the basis of the rule. But some readers may say, that the difference is very small—that the command "not to return the salute of the Gentiles," is a mere matter of etiquette—whereas the command to visit the sick of the Gentiles, to bury their dead, and to feed their poor; is a substantial kindness. This we should admit, if the reason assigned for such conduct, "for the sake of the ways of peace," did not utterly remove all the apparent kindness. And this brings us to

The third misrepresentation of the Bavarian Catechism. It translates the words מפני דרכי שלום (for the sake of the ways of peace) "for the good of society." Here, then, there is an evident difference between us. But who is right? We do not ask the Israelite to believe us. Maimonides here refers to another passage of the oral law, where this expression is fully explained, and where the command "not to return the salutation of the Gentiles" is also found. We will give this passage, and then the unlearned can judge for themselves:—

מפרנסין עניי עכו״ם עם עניי ישראל מפני דרכי שלום . ואין ממחין בידי עניי עכו״ם בלקט שכחה ופאה מפני דרכי שלום . ושואלין בשלומם אפי׳ ביום חגם מפני דרכי שלום ואין כופלין להם שלום לעולם . ולא יכנס לביתו של נכרי עכו״ם ביום חגו לתת לו שלום . מצאו בשוק נתן לו שלום בשפה רפה ובכובד ראש . אין כל הדברים האלו אמורים אלא בזמן שגלו ישראל לבין האומות או שיד עכו״ם תקיפה על ישראל אבל בזמן שיד ישראל תקיפה עליהם אסור לנו להניח עכו״ם בינינו . אפילו יושב ישיבת ארעי או עובר ממקום למקום בסחורה לא יעבור בארצנו אלא עד שיקבל עליו שבע מצוות שנצטוו בני נח . שנאמר לא ישבו בארצך אפילו לפי שעה ואם קבל עליו ז׳ מצוות הרי זה גר תושב וכו׳ :

"The poor of the idolaters are to be fed with the poor of Israel *for the sake of the ways of peace.* They are also permitted to have part of the gleaning, the forgotten sheaf, and the corner of the field, *for the sake of the ways of peace.* It is also lawful to ask after their health, even on their feast-day, *for the sake of the ways of peace;* but never to return (literally, reiterate) the salutation, nor to enter the house of an idolater on the day of his festival to salute him. If he be met in the street, he is to be saluted in a low tone of voice, and with a heavy head. *But all these things are said only of the time that Israel is in captivity among the nations, or that the hand of the idolaters is strong upon Israel. But when the hand of Israel is strong upon them, we are forbidden to suffer an idolater amongst us, even so much as to sojourn incidentally, or to pass from place to place with merchandize.* He is not to pass through our land until he take upon him the seven commandments given to the children of Noah, for it is said 'They shall not dwell in thy land,' (Exod. xxiii. 33,) not even for an hour. But if he take upon himself the seven commandments, then he is a proselyte permitted to sojourn (גר תושב)." Hilchoth Accum, c. x. 5 &c.

This is the passage alluded to, and the reader may now judge whether the words, "For the sake of the ways of peace," can be interpreted as the Bavarian Catechism renders them, "for the good of society." If so, then "the good of society" is to be consulted only whilst the Jews are in captivity, and the Gentiles have got the power: but as soon as the Jews get the the power, "the good of society" may safely be disregarded. The meaning plainly is, that in the present position of affairs it is advisable to keep the peace between Jews and Gentiles, inasmuch as the Gentiles are at present the strongest. Now, then, it is expedient to visit the sick, and feed the poor, and bury the dead of the Gentiles, for this will promote that object; but when the tables are turned, and the Gentiles are the weakest, there will be no necessity "for the ways of peace," or, as the Bavarian Catechism has it, "for the good of society." In is plain, therefore, that the passage cited by the French deputies and the Bavarian Catechism, does not answer the purpose for which it is cited. It does not prove that the Talmud teaches us to love our fellow-men as ourselves, whatever be their religious opinions. On the contrary, it teaches that a wide distinction is to be made between one class of religionists and another: and that if men be idolaters, we are to show them no kindness, except for fear of the consequences that might result from betraying our real sentiments. When, therefore, the Jewish deputies and the compilers of the Bavarian Catechism asserted the true explanation of the Mosaic command, "Thou shalt love thy neighbour as thyself," it is plain that they had not learned it from the Talmud, but somewhere else. We hesitate not to say, that they learned it from the New Testament, for there it is taught plainly, repeatedly, and without any reservation. A certain lawyer once asked Jesus of Nazareth, "Who is my neighbour? And Jesus answering, said, A certain man went down from Jerusalem to Jericho, and fell among thieves, which stripped him of his raiment, and wounded him, and departed, leaving him half dead. And by chance there came down a certain priest that way; and when he saw him he passed by on the other side. And likewise a Levite, when he was at the place, came and looked on him, and passed by on the other side. But a certain Samaritan, as he journeyed, came where he was; and when he saw him, he had compassion on him, and went to him, and bound up his wounds, pouring in oil and wine, and set him on his own beast, and brought him to an inn, and took care of him. And on the morrow when he departed, he took out two-pence, and gave them to the host, and said unto him, Take care of him; and whatsoever thou spendest more, when I come again, I will repay thee. Which now of these three, thinkest thou, was neighbour to him that fell among the thieves? And he said, He that showed mercy on him. Then said Jesus unto him, Go thou and do likewise." (Luke x. 29, &c.) Here then the Lord Jesus Christ teaches us that we are to show kindness even to an idolater, for that even he is included in the class specified by the word "neighbour." Jesus of Nazareth makes no limitation "for the sake of the ways of peace," but gives a general command. And he appears to have selected this case of a man lying half dead, in order to contrast it with a similar case supposed in the oral law.

"If a Gentile, and idolater, be seen perishing, or drowning in a river, he is not to be helped out. If he be seen near to death, he is not to be delivered. But to destroy him by active means, or to push him into a pit, or such-like things, is forbidden, as he is not at war with us."* The Lord Jesus does not say that the man who went down from Jerusalem to Jericho was an idolater. He only says, "a certain man." But he evidently intimates that he was such, for if he had been a Jew, the priest and the Levite would not have passed him without rendering assistance. As he was only an idolater, according to the oral law, the priest and the Levite were not simply not to blame in leaving him to his fate, but were obeying a command. They saw him perishing—near to death. They did not use any violence to accelerate it. They only looked at him, and left him to perish. So far, then, the lawyer who asked the question thought that the priest and Levite were in the right. But then the Lord Jesus introduces a Samaritan, whom the oral law also looks upon as an idolater, and showing how he acted, he appeals to the plain common sense of the questioner, "Which of these three was neighbour to him that fell among thieves?" And the lawyer is compelled to acknowledge, "He that showed mercy." We make a similar appeal to the advocates of the oral law. We ask, which is, the oral law or the New Testament, the most like the law of God? The oral law forbids you to help a poor dying fellow-creature in his hour of need, because he is an idolater. It commands you to stifle the natural instinct of the human heart, which is indeed the voice of the God of nature—to behold the agonizing struggles, and hear the heartrending cries of a drowning fellow-sinner, and yet when you have it in your power to snatch him from the jaws of death, and from that everlasting destruction which awaits him, to leave him to his fate, without help and without pity. The New Testament, on the contrary, tells you, that though, by his idolatry, he has incurred the wrath of God, yet he is your neighbour—that it is your duty to help him, and by that very help to endeavour to lead him to the truth. Which then agrees with the law of God? We are quite sure that the language of your heart is, the New Testament is right.

* Hilchoth Accum, c. x. 1.

The oral law is wrong. Your brethren in France and Bavaria have already proclaimed that opinion to the world. In the answer of the Jewish deputies to Napoleon and in the Bavarian Catechism, they have said, "that we are to love our fellow-creature as ourselves," whatever be his religion. They have thus made an involuntary acknowledgment of the superiority of the New Testament, and of the benefit which it has been to the world. Just suppose, for a moment, that the scribes and Pharisees had succeeded in extirpating the doctrine of Jesus of Nazareth, what would have been the consequence to you and to the world? Had the doctrines of Jesus perished, the oral law would have had an undisturbed and universal domination, for the Karaites have always been few in number, and have never exerted any influence on mankind at large. The Jews in France, Bavaria, as well as in England and elsewhere, would all have known the law only according to the oral interpretation, and consequently would not have understood the command, "Thou shalt love they neighbour as thyself." They would still have held the fearful doctrine, that a perishing idolater was not to be helped. They would, moreover, have had none but idolaters around them, for all the knowledge of God that prevails amongst us Gentiles comes from Jesus of Nazareth. Jew and Gentile, then, would have lived "hateful and hating each other." You may think, perhaps, that some mighty spirit would have burst the chains of tradition, and reasserted, the simple truth of God. But such an event is altogether beyond the limits of probability. One of the mightiest intellects that ever dwelt in a tenement of clay was that of Moses, the son of Maimon; a man whose learning and industry were equal to his genius. If ever there was a Jew, who was likely to overcome the prejudices of tradition, it was he. And yet with all his genius and all his opportunities, he never was able to arrive at the true sense of the command which we have just considered. The atrocious passages, which we have above discussed, are all taken from his compendium of the oral law. You are indebted, then, to Jesus of Nazareth for your deliverance from this foul error. With respect to your duty to your neighbour, your own brethren in France and Bavaria confess, that you are right iṅ you follow Jesus of Nazareth, and that you are wrong if you follow those who rejected him. Remember, then, that your duty to your neighbour is half of the whole law of God, and examine whether the Christians, who are confessedly right in the second table of the law do not, also, possess the truth respecting the first.

No. V.

TALMUDIC INTOLERANCE CONTRASTED WITH THE CHARITY OF THE BIBLE.

ANY one who considers the circumstances of the Jewish people after the desolation of the first temple, will be inclined to make great allowances for the spirit of the Rabbinical laws against idolaters. Idolatry was not to them a mere system of religious error. It was the source of all their misfortunes; and idolaters were the destroyers of their country—the desolaters of their temple—and their own most cruel and tyrannical oppressors. Scarcely had they emerged from the horrors of the Babylonish captivity, when they were exposed to the insults and outrages as well as the persecutions of Antiochus; and hardly had they recovered from the havoc of his fury, before they were overrun by the fierce and haughty Romans, who were at last the executioners of the wrath of the Almighty. They not only saw the abominations of idolatry, but they felt the hard hand of the idolater; no wonder, then, if they hated the man as well as the system. In the Hilchoth Rotzeach there is a law which amply illustrates the misery of their situation, and the habitual treatment which they received from idolaters. According to this law, " It is forbidden to a Jew to be alone with Gentiles, for they are suspected of shedding blood; neither is a Jew to join company with them in the way; if he meet a Gentile, he is to cause him to pass on his right hand (that the Jew, as the commentary says, may be able to defend himself, in case the Gentile should make an attempt on his life); if they be ascending a height, or going down a descent, the Jew is not to be below and the Gentile above him; but the Jew above and the Gentile below, lest he should fall upon him to kill him; neither is he to stoop down before him, lest he should break his skull." What an affecting picture does this present of the Jews under heathen domination; and who can wonder if such treatment called forth the natural feelings of the human heart, and dictated laws in the same fierce and merciless spirit ? We, for our part, are quite ready to admit and to deplore the mighty provocations, which roused the spirit of retaliation in the Rabbies, and consequently, to make all due allowance for the men. But that is not the question before us. We are inquiring whether their religious system, the oral law, is or is not from God, and whether this religious system teaches Jews to love all their fellow-men as themselves? We have shown that the evidence adduced on this point by the French and Bavarian Jews, proves the contrary; and is therefore, nothing to the purpose. But we do not wish to rest the decision upon such limited proof, even though it be strong; we are willing to look at the whole system, and to compare it with the law and the prophets, which we all admit as divine authority. We say, then, that the Talmud not only does not teach us to love all our fellow-men, but that it puts idolaters altogether without the pale of humanity. We have seen already that it forbids its followers to save the life of a perishing idolater. But it goes farther still, and extends this precept even to an idolater's infant, which knows not its right hand from its left:—

בת ישראל לא תיניק את בניק של בנה של נכרית מפני
שמגדלת בן לעבודה של כוכבים ומזלות ולא תילד
את הנכרית עכו״ם אבל מילדת היא בשכר משום איבה:

"A daughter of Israel shall not suckle the son of a heathen woman, because that would be to bring up a son for idolatry; neither shall she act as midwife to a heathen idolatress. But if she should, it must be for pay, on account of the enmity (that might otherwise be excited")." (Hilchoth Accum, c. ix. 16.) What is meant by "pay, on account of the enmity," is fully explained in the following passage, which forbids a Rabbinical physician to cure a sick idolater:—

מכאן אתה למד שאסור לרפאות עובדי כוכבים
ומזלות אפילו בשכר ואם חיה מתירא מהן או
שהיה חושש משום איבה מרפא בשכר אבל בחנם
אסור:

"Hence thou learnest, that it is forbidden to cure idolaters even for pay. But if (an Israelite) is afraid of them, or is anxious on account of enmity, he may cure them for pay; but to do it gratuitously is forbidden." Hence the commonest offices of humanity are forbidden. But the Talmud goes further still, and prohibits even the giving of good advice to these outcasts.

ואסור להשיא עצה טובה לגוי או לעבד רשע . . . .
ולא נתנסה דניאל אלא על שהשיא עצה טובה
לנבוכדנצר ליתן צדקה. שנאמר לחן מלכא מלכי
ישפר עלך:

"It is forbidden to give good advice to a heathen or to a wicked slave.... Daniel was exposed to danger for no other reason than this, that he advised Nebuchadnezzar to give alms, as it is written, 'Wherefore, O king, let my counsel be acceptable unto thee.' (Dan. iv. 23, in English 27.)" * A more striking instance of the spirit of the Talmud can hardly be found. Nebuchadnezzar was the benefactor of Daniel, and had elevated

---

* Hilchoth Rotzeach, c. xii. 15. See also Bava Bathra, fol. iv. col. 1., about the middle of the page, where the punishment of Daniel is more fully discussed.

him from the situation of a captive to the first dignity of the empire; and Daniel had not refused, but voluntarily taken upon himself the duties and responsibilities of the king's chief adviser. Under such circumstances, an ordinary reader of the Bible would imagine that Daniel was bound by every tie of gratitude to his benefactor, of duty and fidelity to his sovereign, to give him the best advice in his power. No, says the Talmud. If the man be an idolater, gratitude, duty, and fidelity are out of the question; and because Daniel exercised those godlike graces, he was punished. It appears, at all events, on the Talmud's own showing, that Daniel was not a Talmudist. These extracts seem sufficient to prove, that the Talmud altogether excludes idolaters from all benefit of the command, "Thou shalt love thy neighbour as thyself." The system which makes it unlawful to save his life, to cure his sickness, to suckle his child, to help his wife in the hour of nature's trial, or even to give him good advice, can scarcely be said to teach us to love all our fellow-men, without any regard to religious differences. It may, however, be said, that the passages adduced lead to this conclusion only by inference, and that none of them expressly declares that an idolater is not our neighbour. We shall, therefore, add a few passages where this is plainly taught.

הגונב את הגוי או שגנב נכסי הקדש אינו משלם
אלא הקרן בלבד שנאמר ישלם שנים לרעהו . לרעהו
ולא להקדש ׳ לרעהו ולא לגוי :

"He that steals from a Gentile, or he that steals property *devoted* to sacred purposes, is only to pay the principal: for it is said, 'He shall pay double unto *his neighbour.*' (Exod. xxii. 8, English 9.) To his neighbour, not to devoted property. To his neighbour, and *not to a Gentile.*" (Hilchoth Genevah, c. ii. 1.) The same decision is given with respect to the law found, Levit. v. 20, in English vi. 1, "If a soul sin, and commit a trespass against the Lord, and *lie unto his neighbour,* . . . . all that about which he has sworn falsely; he shall even restore it in the principal, and shall add the fifth part more thereto." The oral law says—

הנשבע לגוי משלם את הקרן ואינו חייב בחומש
שנאמר וכחש בעמיתו :

"He that sweareth to a Gentile must pay the principal, but is not bound to add the fifth part—(why not?) because it is said, 'and lie unto his neighbour.'" (Hilchoth Gezelah, c. i. 7.) So that the reason here assigned why the Gentile is not to get the fifth part in addition, is, because he is not a neighbour. In like manner, in the 11th chapter of this same treatise, which treats

of the restoration of things found, it is expressly commanded to
restore whatever belongs to a Jew, because he is a brother; but
to keep whatever belongs to an idolater, because he is not
a brother.

השבת אבדה לישראל מצות עשה שנאמר השב
תשיבם:

'To restore to an Israelite anything that he has lost, is an
affirmative commandment, for it is said, 'Thou shalt in any
case bring them again unto thy brother.'" (Deut. xxii. 1.)

אבדת גוי עובד ע״ז מותרת שנאמר אבדת אחיך.
והמחזירה הרי זה עובר עבירה מפני שהוא מחזיק
ידי רשעי עולם. ואם החזירה כדי לקדש את השם
שיפארו את ישראל וידעו שהם בעלי אמונה הרי זה
משובח:

"Anything that a Gentile has lost is lawful, for it is said,
'With all lost things of *thy brother's.*' (Deut. xxii. 3.) And
he that restores it transgresses a transgression, for he strengthens
the hands of the wicked of the world. But if he restore it in
order to sanctify the Name, that they may think well of Israel,
and know that they are honest people, this is praiseworthy."
In these passages (and many more might be added if it were
necessary) it is plainly taught that an idolatrous Gentile is not
to be regarded as " our neighbour," or our brother. We think,
then, that we have fully proved that the Jewish deputies
in France, and the compilers of the Jewish Catechism in
Bavaria, did not learn their exposition of the command, " Thou
shalt love thy neighbour as thyself," from the Talmud; neither
in the particular passage which they quote, nor from the general
principles of the Talmudic system. We have already stated our
belief that they learned that exposition from the New Testament,
for there it is taught plainly and repeatedly. We quoted, in
proof, a parable spoken by the Lord Jesus Christ. We shall now
add a few more passages in confirmation.

As to *showing kindness* to all our fellow-men, the New
Testament teaches us to make no exception with regard to
idolaters, or others who have not the same creed, but gives the
following general rules:—" As we have, therefore, opportunity,
let us do good UNTO ALL MEN, especially unto them that are of
the household of faith." (Gal. vi. 10.) " See that no man
render evil for evil UNTO ANY MAN; but ever follow that which
is good both among yourselves, and TO ALL MEN." (1 Thess.
v. 15.) " The Lord make you to increase and abound IN LOVE
one toward another, and TOWARD ALL MEN." (1 Thess. iii. 12.)
You observe that in these general rules the New Testament

makes no reservation with respect to idolaters, or epicureans, or heretics, or any other of those unfortunate beings whom the Talmud outlaws from all the common charities of humanity. It commands us to do good to *all*—and that not to avoid enmity, nor for the sake of the ways of peace, nor because we are afraid, nor because we wish them to speak well of us, and to be thought honest people, but because it is our duty. The New Testament requires of its followers, not only to abstain " from active violence " in injuring them, but to do active good in assisting them, and the examples, which it proposes for our imitation, are of the same character as the precepts which it imposes upon our obedience. It sets before us Jesus of Nazareth, whom the traditionists crucified, praying for his murderers, and saying, " Father, forgive them ; for they know not what they do "—and Stephen, his first martyr, interceding for them that stoned him, " Lord, lay not this sin to their charge." And Paul, whose feelings to those who differed from him in religion are thus expressed, " Brethren, my heart's desire and my prayer to God for Israel is, that they may be saved." It sets before us the disciples of the Lord Jesus healing the diseases of all who applied, without reference to their religious opinions. (Acts xix. 11.) We repeat our question, then, which system is according to the truth and the will of God, the Talmud, or the New Testament ? Your brethren in France and Bavaria have declared, by adopting the New Testament exposition, that it is right; and by rejecting the intolerant principle which pervades the oral law, that the oral law is wrong. We trust that your hearts respond to their declarations. But we do not rest the decision on the natural feelings of the heart, we appeal to Moses and the prophets.

The question is, do the laws, which God gave respecting the idolatrous nations of Canaan, apply to all other idolaters, and under all circumstances ? The oral law answers this question in the affirmative, and hence the source of all those revolting laws which we have just considered. But the oral law is wrong : 1st, Because it draws a general conclusion from a particular case, which is contrary to all sound reasoning. That the command to destroy these nations was peculiar appears from the command itself—God does not speak generally of all the heathen, but only of certain nations which he specifies— " When the Lord thy God shall bring thee into the land, whither thou goest to possess it, and hath cast out many nations before thee, the Hittites, and the Girgashites, and the Amorites, and the Canaanites, and the Perizzites, and the Hivites, and the Jebusites, seven nations greater and mightier than thou ; and when the Lord thy God shall deliver them before thee ; thou shalt smite them, and utterly destroy them ; thou shalt make no covenant with, nor shew mercy unto them." (Deut. vii. 1, 2.) Here the command is precise, and is as much violated by extending it to those to whom God has not extended it, as by refusing to execute it on those whom He has here designated as the just victims of his wrath.

2dly, The oral law is wrong in this general application, for it contradicts the written law—God expressly distinguishes between these and the other nations—"When thou comest nigh unto a city to fight against it, then proclaim peace unto it. And it shall be, if it make thee answer of peace, and open unto thee, then it shall be, that all the people that is found therein shall be tributaries unto thee, and they shall serve thee......Thus shalt thou do unto all the cities which are very far from thee, which are not of the cities of these nations. But of the cities of these people, which the Lord thy God doth give thee for an inheritance, thou shalt save alive nothing that breatheth, but thou shalt utterly destroy them; the Hittites, and the Amorites, the Canaanites, and the Perizzites, the Hivites, and the Jebusites; as the Lord thy God hath commanded thee." (Deut. xx. 10, 18.) In the first case God commands mercy—in the second, extermination. And if, as in the first case, he commands merciful dealing even to a nation at war with Israel, much more does he command it towards those, with whom Israel is not at war.

3dly, The written law not only gives a general rule, but lays down exceptions founded on certain principles. "Thou shalt not abhor an Edomite, for he is thy brother; thou shalt not abhor an Egyptian, because thou wast a stranger in his land." (Deut. xxiii. 7.) Now the Egyptians were idolaters, yet God commands the Israelites not to abhor them, and gives a reason which will now apply to most nations of the earth— "Because thou wast a stranger in his land." Suppose, then, that a Rabbinist were to see an Egyptian drowning, is he to show him mercy? To say, No, will contradict the written law; and to say, Yes, will overthrow the monstrous fabric of Rabbinic legislation respecting idolaters.

4thly, The general practice of the Israelites, as described in the subsequent books of the Old Testament, directly contradicts the oral law. We have seen already that the Prophet Daniel did not hold the doctrine, that no mercy was to be shown to an idolater. When he knew of the judgment that was about to descend on Nebuchadnezzar, he was deeply distressed. "He was astonied for one hour, and his thoughts troubled him;" and instead of leaving the idolater to perish, he endeavoured to find means to ward off the calamity The prophet Elisha was of the same mind: when the idolatrous leper came to him for help, he administered it, and, contrary to the Talmudic command, he administered it *gratuitously;* and Gehazi, for acting in conformity to Talmudic ordinance, and making the idolater pay, was smitten with the leprosy. (2 Kings v. 20.) In like manner, when the Syrian host was miraculously led into Samaria, and the King of Israel proposed to act as a Talmudist and smite them, the man of God answered, "Thou shalt not smite them; wouldest thou smite those whom thou hast taken with thy sword and bow? Set bread and water before them, that they may eat and drink and go to their master." (2 Kings vi. 21, 22.) This answer is important, as it not only furnishes an example, but exhibits the principle, according to which idolatrous captives, not Canaanites, were to be treated. The prophet appeals to the general rule, "Wouldest thou smite those whom thou hast taken captive with thy sword and bow? Even then, as they are not Canaanites, they ought not to be smitten: therefore, in this case much more, they ought to be treated with mercy. We have still another instance of a prophet acting contrary to the oral law, and in conformity with the New Testament interpretation. The prophet Jonah once saw idolaters "nigh unto death," and ready to sink in the great deep, but he had mercy on them, and pointed out the means of deliverance. When he fled from the presence of the Lord, the mariners in whose ship he sailed were idolaters; for when the storm raged, it is said, "They cried every man unto his god." In their anguish they said unto him, "What shall we do unto thee, that the sea may be calm unto us?" In other words, "What shall we do to save our lives?" Now if Jonah had been a Talmudist, it would have been plainly not his duty to have told them, but to have allowed the sea to rage on until the ship went to pieces, and he had the satisfaction of seeing the idolaters go to the bottom. This would have been an act of obedience to a precise command, and could have made no difference to Jonah. For, as to himself, there are two suppositions possible, either he knew that the Lord had prepared a fish to swallow him, or he knew it not. If he knew it, then he was secure of his own safety, and would have known that the fish could find him out just as readily if the ship went to pieces, as if the idolaters threw him into the sea. It would, therefore, have been doubly his duty to conceal from the idolaters the means of deliverance. On this supposition, Jonah's counsel to them can only be accounted for on the principle that he was not a Talmudist, but considered it his duty to save the lives of perishing idolaters, even when nothing was to be feared or to be gained. If, on the other hand, he did not know of the fish, he must have expected a watery grave, whether the idolaters threw him into the sea, or whether he waited until the ship went to pieces. In this case, also, if a Talmudist, it would have been his duty to have stayed where he was, and if he perished, die in the fulfilment of the command, to show no mercy to idolaters. But he did not—he had compassion on them, and, to save their lives, relinquished his only chance of safety, by telling them to throw him into the sea. It is plain, therefore, that Jonah was not a Talmudist. We have here, then, three inspired prophets, Daniel, Elisha, and Jonah, all bearing a practical testimony against the Talmudic principle, which extends God's law against the Canaanites to all idolaters, and under all circumstances.

Lastly, We have the testimony of the God of Israel himself. He who gave the command to destroy the Canaanites on account of their exceeding wickedness, shows by his own dealings with the world, that this case is an exception to the general rule, for " The Lord is good to all, and his mercies are over all his works." He provides food and clothing for the idolater, as well as for those who worship him in truth ; or, as the New Testament says, " He maketh his sun to rise on the evil and on the good, and sendeth rain on the just and the unjust." (Matt. vi. 45.) He, then, whose conduct most resembles that of his Creator, is, beyond all doubt, the nearest to the truth. The Talmud, therefore, is wrong, and the New Testament explanation of the command, " Thou shalt love thy neighbour as thyself," is right. We ask the Jews, then, to account for this fact, that Jesus of Nazareth was right, and those who condemned him wrong, respecting one-half of the whole law. And we ask, moreover, those Jews who abhor the above Talmudic principles, how they can conscientiously join in the synagogue prayers, which ascribe to the Talmud Divine authority? We ask them why, at the very least, they have never publicly protested against these enormities ; but allow their brethren through the world to remain victims to a system, which not only contradicts the written law of God, but outrages all the better feelings of even fallen humanity?

No. VI.

COMPULSORY CONVERSION OF THE GENTILES.

WHEN, at the close of the fifteenth century, the Jews were driven out of Spain, some of the magnanimous exiles, who had preferred loss of all things to a compulsory change of religion, arrived at the frontiers of Portugal, and there sought an asylum. A permanent abode was refused, and a temporary sojourn was granted them on two conditions—1st, That each should pay a certain quantity of gold for his admission ; and 2dly, That if they were found in Portugal after a certain day, they should either consent to be baptized, or be sold for slaves.* Now Jews of every degree and shade of religious belief will agree with us, that these conditions were most disgraceful to those who imposed them. To refuse gratuitous assistance to the poor and needy, merely because they had been brought up in a different religious faith, was utterly unworthy of those professing faith in Divine revelation. To compel the unfortunate to choose between loss of liberty or of conscience was the act of a fiend. But now suppose that the Portuguese had endeavoured to persuade these poor exiles that their conduct, however base it might appear, was commanded by God himself. Suppose, further, that when called upon to prove that this command was from God, they had confessed that no such command was to be found in the written books of their religion, that it was only a tradition of their oral law, do you think that the Jewish exiles would have been satisfied with such proof, and submitted? Would they not, in the first place, have questioned the authority of a command resting merely upon uncertain tradition? And would they not have argued, from the detestable nature of the command itself, that it could not possibly emanate from the God of truth and love? We ask you then to apply these principles to תורה שבעל פה the oral law. The Portuguese refused to perform an act of humanity to the unfortunate Jewish exiles, unless they were paid for it. Your oral law, as we showed in our last number, forbids you to give medical advice to a sick idolater gratuitously. The Portuguese voluntarily undertook to convert the Jews by force. Your oral law teaches compulsory conversion as a Divine command. If the oral law could be enforced, liberty of conscience would be at an end. Neither Jew nor Gentile would be permitted to exercise the judgment, which God has given him. His only alternative would be submission to Rabbinic authority, or death. The dreadful command to kill, by any means, those Israelites who have become epicureans, or idolaters, or apostates, is well known,† and sufficiently proves that the oral law recognises no such thing as liberty of conscience in Israel. It pronounces a man an apostate if he denies its Divine authority, and demands his life as the penalty. The execution of this one command would fill the world with blood and horror ; and recall all the worst features of inquisitorial tyranny. Not now to mention those Israelites who have embraced Christianity, there are in England, and every part of Europe, many high-minded and honourable Jews, who have practically renounced the authority of the oral law. The

* Jost. volume vii. p. 91. † Hilchoth Rotzeach, c. iv. 10.

OF THE GENTILES.

Rabbinical millennium would commence by handing over all such to the executioner. Their talents, their virtue, their learning, their moral excellence, would avail nothing. Found guilty of epicureanism or apostasy, because they dared to think for themselves, and to act according to their convictions, they would have to undergo the epicurean's or the apostate's fate.

Such is the toleration of the oral law towards native Israelites, but it is equally severe to converts. It allows no second thoughts. It legislates for relapsed converts, as the Spanish Inquisition did for those Jews who, after embracing Christianity, returned to their former faith and sentences all such to death.

בן נח שנתגייר ומל וטבל. ואחר כך רצה לחזור
מאחרי ה' ולהיות גר תושב בלבד כשהיה מקודם.
אין שומעין לו. אלא יהיה כישראל לכל דבר או
יהרג:

"A Noahite who has become a proselyte, and been circumcised and baptized, and afterwards wishes to return from after the Lord, and to be only a sojourning proselyte, as he was before, is not to be listened to—on the contrary, either let him be an Israelite in everything, or let him be put to death." (Hilchoth Melachim, c. x. 3.) In this law there is an extraordinary severity. The oral law admits that a Noahite, that is, a heathen who has taken upon himself the seven commandments of the children of Noah, may be saved. It cannot, therefore, be said that the severity was dictated by a wish to deter men from error, and to restrain them from rushing upon everlasting ruin, as the Inquisition pleads. The oral law goes a little further, and not only will not permit a man to change his creed, but will not even suffer him to change his ceremonial observances. Though the man should commit no crime, and though he should continue to worship the one true God, in spirit and in truth, yet if he only alter the outward forms of his religion, modern Judaism requires that he should be put to death.

But the tender care of the oral law is not limited to the narrow confines of Judaism, it extends also to the heathen, amongst whom it directs the true faith to be propagated by the sword. First, it gives a particular rule. In case of war with the Gentiles, it commands the Jews to offer peace on two conditions—the one that they should become tributaries, the other that they should renounce idolatry and take upon them the seven precepts of the Noahites, and then adds—

ואם לא השלימו או שהשלימו ולא קבלו שבע
מצוות עושין עמהם מלחמה והורגין כל הזכרים

הגדולים . וביוזין כל ממונם וטפם ואין הורגין אשה
ולא קטן שנאמר והנשים והטף וכו' :

"But if they will not make peace, or if they will make peace but will not take upon them the seven commandments, the war is to be carried on against them, and all the adult males are to be put to death; and their property and their little ones are to be taken as plunder. But no woman or male infant is to be put to death, for it is said, 'The women and the little ones' (Deut. xx. 14), and here little ones mean male infants." (Hilchoth Melachim, c. vi. 4.) Now what difference, we would ask, is there between the conduct here prescribed, and that actually practised by the Portuguese, at the period above referred to, and thus described by a Jew:*—"At the expiration of the appointed time, most of the Jews had emigrated, but many still remained in the country. The King therefore gave orders to take away from them all their children under fourteen years of age, to distribute them amongst Christians, to send them to the newly-discovered islands, and thus to pluck up Judaism by the roots. Dreadful was the cry of lamentation uttered by the parents, but the unfortunates found no mercy." Do you condemn this conduct in the Portuguese? Be then consistent, and condemn it in the Talmud too. As for ourselves, we abhor it as much, yea more, in those calling themselves Christians. We look upon the actors in that transaction as a disgrace to the Christian name, and the deed itself as a foul blot upon the history of Christendom. But we cannot help thinking that, dreadful and detestable as this mode of conversion is, it pleased God in his providence to suffer wicked men thus to persecute Israel, that the Jews might have a practical experience of the wickedness of the oral law, and thus be led to reject such persecuting principles. The Jewish nation rejected the Lord Jesus Christ, and preferred the oral law. This law, not dictated by a spirit of retaliation upon the Portuguese, but invented by the Pharisees centuries before Portugal was a kingdom, commanded the Jews to convert the heathen by force, to murder all who would not consent to be thus converted, and to take away the children. And God suffered them to fall into the hands of men of similar principles, who took away their children, attempted to convert themselves by force, and sold for slaves the Jews who refused to be thus converted; so that the very misfortunes of the nation testify aloud against those traditions which they preferred to the Word of God. But perhaps some Jew will say that this is only a particular command, referring to the nations in the vicinity of the land of Israel. We reply, that the command to convert the heathen by

* Dr. Jost's Geschichte der Israeliten, vol. vii. p. 93.

force, is not particular, but general, referring to the whole world. If the Jews had the power, this is the conduct which they are to pursue towards all the nations of the earth.

וכן צוה משה רבינו מפי הגבורה לכוף את כל באי העולם לקבל מצוות שנצטוו בני נח . וכל מי שלא קבל יהרג :

"And thus Moses our master, has commanded us, by Divine tradition, to compel all that come into the world to take upon themselves the commandments imposed upon the sons of Noah, and whosoever will not receive them is to be put to death." (Hilchoth Melachim, c. viii. 4.)

Such is the Talmudic system of toleration, and such the means which it prescribes for the conversion of the world. We acknowledge that persons calling themselves Christians have had an oral law very similar in its principles and precepts, but we fearlessly challenge the whole world to point out anything similar in the doctrines of Jesus Christ, or in the writings of his apostles. The New Testament does, indeed, teach us to seek the conversion of the world, not by force of arms, but by teaching the truth. " Go ye, therefore, and make disciples of all nations, baptizing them in the name of the Father, and of the Son, and of the Holy Ghost; teaching them to observe all things whatsoever I have commanded you." (Matt. xxviii. 19.) In the parable of the tares and wheat, Jesus of Nazareth hath expressly taught us that physical force is not to be employed in order to remove moral error. The servants are represented as asking the master of the house, whether they should go and root out the tares that grew amongst the wheat, but the answer is, "Nay, lest while ye gather up the tares, ye root up also the wheat with them. Let both grow together until the harvest; and in the time of harvest I will say to the reapers, Gather ye together first the tares, and bind them in bundles to burn them: but gather the wheat into my barn." (Matt. xiii. 24—43.) He tells us expressly to have nothing to do with the sword, " For all they that take the sword, shall perish with the sword." (Matt. xxvi. 52.) And therefore the apostle says, " The weapons of our warfare are not carnal, but mighty through God to the pulling down of strong holds." (2 Cor. x. 4.) Here again, then, there is a great difference between the oral law and the New Testament. The former commands that the truth be maintained and propagated by the sword. The latter tells us that "faith cometh by hearing, and hearing by the Word of God." Which, then, is most agreeable to the doctrine of Moses and the prophets? We answer fearlessly, the means prescribed by the New Testament, for—

1st, No instance can be adduced from the Old Testament, in

which God commanded the propagation of the truth by the power of the sword. The extirpation of the seven nations of Canaan is not in point, for the Israelites were not commanded to make them any offer of mercy on condition of conversion. The measure of their iniquity was full, and therefore the command to destroy every soul absolute. Neither in the command referred to by Maimonides is there the least reference to conversion. It simply says, " When thou comest nigh unto a city to fight against it, then proclaim peace unto it. And it shall be if it make thee answer of peace, and open unto thee, then it shall be that all the people that is found therein shall be tributaries unto thee, and they shall serve thee. And if it will make no peace with thee, but will make war against thee, then thou shalt besiege it : and when the Lord thy God hath delivered it into thine hands, thou shalt smite every male thereof with the edge of the sword. But the women and the little ones, and the cattle, and all that is in the city, even all the spoil thereof, shalt thou take unto thyself." (Deut. xx. 10—14.) Here is not one word said about conversion, or about the seven commandments of the sons of Noah. The command itself is hypothetical, " When thou comest nigh unto a city ; " and therefore gives no colour nor pretext for setting out on a war of conversion, " to compel all that come into the world." As it stands, it is a humane and merciful direction to restrain the horrors of the then prevailing system of warfare; and beautifully exemplifies the value which God sets upon the life of man, whatever his nation or his religion. He will not suffer it to be destroyed unnecessarily ; and even in case of extremity, he commands the lives of the women and the children, who never bore arms against Israel, to be spared. There is not a syllable about forcing their consciences : that is all pure gratuitous addition of the oral law, which turns a merciful command into an occasion of bigotry and religious tyranny.

2dly, As God has given no command to propagate religion by the sword, so neither has He given any countenance to such a doctrine, by the instrumentality which He has employed for the preservation of religion in the world. He did not choose a mighty nation of soldiers as the depositories of his truth, nor any of the overturners of kingdoms for his prophets. If it had been his intention to convert the world by force of arms, Nimrod would have been a more suitable instrument than Abraham, and the mighty kingdom of Egypt more fitted for the task than the family of Hebrew captives. But by the very choice He showed, that truth was to be propagated by Divine power working conviction in the minds of men, and not by physical strength. It would have been just as easy for him to have turned every Hebrew captive in Egypt into a Samson, as to turn the waters into blood ; and to have sent them into the world to overturn idolatry by brute force; but He preferred to enlighten the minds of men by exhibiting a series of miracles, calculated to convince them of his eternal power and Godhead. When the ten tribes revolted, and fell away into idolatry, He did not employ the sword of Judah, but the voice of his prophets, to recall them to the truth. He did not compel them, as the oral law would have done, to an outward profession, but dealt with them as with rational beings, and left them to the choice of their hearts. Nineveh was not converted by Jewish soldiers, but by the preaching of Jonah. So far is God from commanding the propagation of religion by the sword, that He would not even suffer a man of war to build a temple for his worship When David thought of erecting a temple, the Lord said unto him, " Thou hast shed blood abundantly, and hast made great wars; thou shalt not build an house unto my name, because thou hast shed much blood upon the earth." (1 Chron. xxii. 8.) Thus hath God shown his abhorrence of compulsory conversion, and in all his dealings confirmed his Word, " Not by might nor by power, but by my Spirit, saith the Lord of hosts." (Zech. iv. 6.)

3dly, God has in his Word promised the conversion of the world, but not by the means prescribed in the oral law. His promise to Abraham was, " In thy seed shall all the families of the earth be blessed." (Gen. xxii. 18.) Now this can hardly mean that his descendants are to treat all nations, as the Portuguese treated the Jews. The 72nd Psalm gives rather a different view of the fulfilment of this promise. It promises not a victorious soldier like Mahomet, but one " in whose days the righteous shall flourish, and abundance of peace so long as the moon endureth. . . . . . All nations shall call HIM blessed." The prophet Isaiah tells us " that out of Zion shall go forth (not conquering armies to compel, but) the law, and the Word of the Lord from Jerusalem. And he shall judge among the nations, and rebuke many people; and they shall beat their swords into ploughshares, and their spears into pruning-hooks; nation shall not lift up sword against nation, neither shall they learn war any more." Zechariah says, " He shall speak peace to the heathen;" and declares that the conversion of the world will not be the reward of conquest, but the result of conviction. " In those days it shall come to pass, that ten men shall take hold, out of all the languages of the nations, even shall take hold of the skirt of him that is a Jew, saying, We will go with you, *for we have heard* that God is with you." (Zech. viii. 23.) Here again, then, you see that whilst the oral law differs from Moses and the prophets, the New Testament agrees with them. Account, then, for this extraordinary fact, that whilst the whole Jewish nation lost the great and glorious doctrine of liberty of conscience, it has been preserved for you and for all mankind by Jesus of Nazareth. Just suppose that the principles of the Talmud had triumphed, either amongst the Jews or the Portuguese, what would have been the consequence to the world? If the Talmudists had attained to supreme power, we should have had to choose between compulsory conversion and the sword. If the Portuguese had attained to universal dominion, both you and we should have had the alternative of compulsory conversion or the fires of the Inquisition. In either case, the noblest and most precious gift that the God of heaven ever sent down to earth, liberty of conscience, would have been extinct. But, thank God, the doctrine of Jesus of Nazareth has triumphed over the oral laws of both Jews and Portuguese, and the result is, that both you and we have the liberty of worshipping God according to the convictions of our understanding and the dictates of our conscience. Behold, then, how you are indebted to Jesus of Nazareth. Without him you would not have known religious liberty, either theoretically or practically. He is right on this all-important point, whilst those who condemned him to death and rejected his claims are wrong. If he was not the true Messiah, but only a pretender, how is it that God has made him and his doctrine the exclusive channel for preserving the truth of his Word, and conveying such blessings to you as well as to us Gentiles? If the Pharisees were right in rejecting him, how is it that God has rewarded their piety by giving them over to such gross delusions, and making them the transmitters of doctrines, which would fill the world with blood and hatred and discord, and make even the truth odious in the eyes of all mankind? For ourselves we cannot help coming to the conclusion, that He who has taught us mercy and love to all men, and delivered both you and us from such horrors—and who, in doing this, rose above all the doctrines of his nation and his times, was taught of God, and is, therefore, the true Messiah, the Saviour of the world.

Certain it is, that this doctrine has already been a blessing to the world; and that until your nation embrace its principles, at least on this one point of love and toleration, it is impossible that the promised glory and pre-eminence of the Jewish nation should come. With such principles as are inculcated in the oral law, a restoration to the land of your forefathers would be no blessing. It would only realize all the legislative and religious speculations of the Talmudists, and arm them with the power to tyrannize over their more enlightened brethren. It would be the triumph of tradition over the Word of God, and that the God of truth will not permit. It would be to instal the spirit of intolerance and persecution on the throne of love and charity, and that God will not suffer. The Talmud is, thus, a main obstacle in the way of God's fulfilling his promises to the nation, because it incapacitates Israel for the reception or the right employment of the promised blessings. Is it not, then, the duty of all Jews who desire and long for the glory and the happiness which God has promised, to lift up their voice with power, and to protest against that system which prevents the fufilment of God's promises; and by all lawful means to endeavour to deliver their brethren from the bondage of such intolerance?

No. VII.

THE FEAST OF PURIM.

THE feast of Purim now at hand, recalls to the Jewish recollection one of those miraculous deliverances, with which the history of Israel abounds. The narrative of the institution, as contained in the Bible, is a signal proof and illustration of the superintending providence of God, instructive to all the world, but calling peculiarly for the gratitude and praise of the Jewish nation, whose forefathers were then delivered. And it is much to the honour of their posterity that they have not suffered the lapse of more than twenty centuries to wear out the memory of this great event, but that to this day they observe its anniversary with alacrity and zeal. If the oral law simply contented itself with commanding the observance and prescribing the mode of worship for such an important season, we should have no fault to find; but the oral law claims for itself Divine origin and authority, anathematizes any denial of these claims as heresy, and sentences the heretic to death. We are, therefore, compelled to examine its pretensions, and to scrutinize its features, in order to see whether they really bear the stamp of divinity. We have already pointed out some, that savoured more of earth than heaven: the constitutions for the feast of Purim may be traced to the same source. The following law respecting the meal to be provided on this occasion did certainly not come to man from heaven:—

חובת סעודה זו שיאכל בשר ויתקן סעודה נאה
כפי אשר תמצא ידו . ושותה יין עד שישתכר וירדם
בשכרותו :

"A man's duty with regard to the feast is, that he should eat meat and prepare a suitable feast according to his means; and drink wine, until he be drunk, and fall asleep in his drunkenness." (Hilchoth Megillah, c. ii. 15.) The Talmud, however, is not satisfied with so indefinite a direction, but lays down, with its usual precision, the exact measure of intoxication required.

חייב איניש לבסומי בפוריא עד דלא ידע בין ארור
המן לברוך מרדכי :

"A man is bound to get so drunk with wine at Purim, as not to know the difference between Cursed is Haman, and Blessed is Mordecai." (Megillah, fol. 7, col. 2.) But perhaps some learned champion of the Talmud will fly to that sort of refuge for destitute commentators, the parabolic language of the orient, and tell us that this precept is not to be understood literally but figuratively; and that so far from recommending intoxication, it means to inculcate excess of sobriety or devotion, such abstraction of the senses, from all outward objects, as not to distinguish between cursed is Haman and blessed is Mordecai. This sort of defence is neither imaginary nor novel. In this way Rabbi Eliezer's permission to split open an unlearned man like a fish has been made to signify the spiritual opening of the understanding, and of course the overweening anxiety of the Rabbies to communicate instruction to the ignorant. But however we dull Gentiles may be enlightened by such an exposition, we much doubt whether the greatest amhaaretz in Israel will believe the interpretation. The great and learned Rabbies Solomon Jarchi and Moses Maimonides have understood literal drunkenness, and have named wine as the legitimate liquor. R. Joseph Karo has simply given the command verbatim as it stands in the Talmud, but a note in the Orach Chaiim shows, that some of the modern Rabbies were not able to swallow such a command, and, therefore, say that an Israelite does his duty, if he only drink a little more than usual. The Talmud itself admits of no such softening down, nor explaining away, for immediately after the precept it goes on to propose an example and to furnish an illustration of its meaning in the following history of the very Rabbi, on whose authority this traditional command rests;—

רבה ורבי זירא עבדו סעודת פורים בהדי הדדי .
איבסום קם רבה שחטיה לרבי זירא למחר בעא רחמי
ואחייה . לשנה אמר ליה ניתי מר ונעביד סעודת
פורים בהדי הדדי אמר ליה לאו בכל שעתא ושעתא
מתרחיש ניסא :

"Rabba and Rabbi Zira made their Purim entertainment

together. When Rabba got drunk, he arose and killed Rabbi Zira. On the following day he prayed for mercy, and restored him to life. The following year Rabba proposed to him again to make their Purim entertainment together, but he answered, 'Miracles don't happen every day.'" (Talmud, Tr. Megillah, fol. 7, col. 2.) This history of one of the men who are authorities for the above Talmudic command to get drunk, plainly illustrates its meaning, and shows that the Talmud meant and commanded its followers to drink wine to excess on this occasion. It sets before them the example of one of the greatest Rabbies committing murder in his drunkenness, and so far from reprobating this sin, it gravely tells us that God interposed by a miracle to prevent the ill-consequences; and that the Rabbi, far from being cured of his propensity, or making any declaration of his intention to amend, continued in that state of mind, that his colleague found it imprudent to trust himself at his table. Now every body that is acquainted with the Jews, knows that they are a temperate and sober people; and because they are so, we ask them whether the above command can be from God? and whether they believe that the Talmud speaks truth in giving the above narrative? It says not merely that men may get drunk with impunity, but that to get drunk is an act of piety, and obedience to a command! Here, again, the Talmud is directly at issue with the New Testament, which says, "Be not drunk with wine, wherein is excess." (Ephes. v. 18.) "Take heed to yourselves, lest *at any time* your hearts be overcharged with surfeiting, and *drunkenness*, and the cares of this life, and so that day come upon you unawares." (Luke xxi. 34.) The New Testament holds out to us no hope, that if in our drunkenness, we should commit murder, a miracle will be wrought in order to deliver us from the consequences; but tells us, that "neither murderers nor drunkards shall inherit the kingdom of God." (1 Cor. vi. 9, 10.) Now which of these two doctrines is the most agreeable to the revealed will of God? How would you desire to meet death, if death should come upon the feast of Purim? Would you wish the angel of death to find you, in obedience to the oral law, insensible from overmuch wine? or in that state of sobriety and thoughtfulness prescribed by Jesus of Nazareth? Does not the inward tribunal of the heart decide that Jesus of Nazareth is right, and that the Talmud is wrong? And does not the Old Testament confirm the sentence? Isaiah says, "Woe unto them that rise up early in the morning, that they may follow strong drink; that continue until night, till wine inflame them! and the harp and the viol, the tabret and pipe, and wine are in their feasts; but they regard not the work of the Lord, neither consider the operation of his hands. Therefore my people are gone into captivity, because they have no knowledge; and their honourable men are famished, and their multitude dried up with thirst." (Isaiah v. 11—13.) And so Moses commands the parents that should have a son "a glutton and a drunkard," to bring him to justice, and to have him stoned. (Deut. xxi. 20.) The Talmud, then, manifestly contradicts the Old Testament; it therefore cannot speak truth when it narrates that God wrought a miracle in order to save a drunkard and a murderer from that punishment, which He had himself commanded to be visited upon either of these crimes. The story of the miracle is therefore a palpable falsehood, contradictory to the law of Moses, and derogatory to the honour of God. How, then, can the Talmud be of God? If you attempt to distinguish, as some do, between the Talmud and the oral law, and say that though the Talmud contains the oral law, yet it is not all inspired, then we ask, how can you rely upon the testimony of a witness convicted of wilful, gross, and flagrant falsehood? If you do not believe in the above miracle of the drunken Rabba, you denounce it as a liar. If it lie, then, upon this solemn occasion in relating a miracle, in handing down the law of God, how can you depend upon it at all? If it does not scruple to forge miracles, what warrant have you for believing that it does not forge laws also:

But suppose, which is far more probable, that Rabbi Zira, when killed by Rabba, had not come to life again, would Rabba, in the eye of the modern Jewish law, be considered as a murderer, and guilty of death, or as an innocent person, who might safely be permitted to go at large, and pursue his usual avocations? This is a question well deserving an answer from some of your learned men, and naturally suggested by some principles asserted and implied in the following decisions of the oral law :—

קריאת המגלה בזמנה מצות עשה מדברי סופרים.
והדברים ידועים שהיא תקנת הנביאים. והכל חייבים
בקריאתה, אנשים ונשים וגרים ועבדים משוחררים.
ומחנכין את הקטנים לקריאתה. ואפילו כהנים
בעבודתן מבטלין עבודתן ובאין לשמוע מקרא
מגלה. וכן מבטלין התלמוד תורה לשמוע מקרא
מגלה, קל וחומר לשאר מצוות של תורה שכולן
נדחין מפני מקרא מגלה. ואין לך דבר שנדחה
מקרא מגלה מפניו חוץ ממת מצוה שאין לו קוברים
שהפוגע בו קוברו תחלה ואחר כך קורא:

"The reading of the Megillah (the book of Esther) in its time is an affirmative precept according to the words of the scribes, and it is known that this is an ordinance of the Prophets. The obligation to read it rests upon all, men, women, and proselytes, and manumitted slaves. Children also are to be accustomed to the reading of it. Even priests in their service are to neglect their service, and to come to hear the reading of the Megillah. In like manner the study of the law is to be omitted, in order to hear the reading of the Megillah, and *a fortiori* all the remaining commandments of the law, all of which give way to the reading of the Megillah: but there is nothing to which the reading of the Megillah gives way, except that particular class of dead person called the dead of the commandment, who has none to bury him. He that happens upon him is first to bury him, and afterwards to read." (Hilchoth Megillah, c. i. 1.) On this extract we have several remarks to make, but at present we request the attention of our readers to the reason given why the reading of the Megillah is more important than any of the commandments. It is this. According to the oral law, "the study of the law is equivalent to all the commandments, and the other commandments are to give way to this study." But according to the passage before us, the study of the law is to give way to the reading of the Megillah. The reading of the Megillah, therefore, being greater than the greatest of the commandments, is of course greater than all the inferior ones. Now apply this reasoning to the above command to get drunk, and you will prove that getting drunk at Purim feast is the greatest of all the commandments. In order to get drunk, it is plain that the study of the law must give way. The man who cannot distinguish between "Cursed be Haman and blessed be Mordecai," certainly cannot study, neither can he bury the dead. The commandment, therefore, to which the study of the law and the burying of the dead give way, must be the greatest of all the commandments; *i.e.*, the getting drunk on Purim is the greatest of all the commandments. This conclusion, which inevitably follows upon Talmudic principles, necessarily shows that those principles are false. But that is not the object for which I have exhibited this conclusion; it is with reference to the case of Rabba abovementioned. Having got drunk according as the oral law commanded, and having thereby obeyed the greatest of the commandments, and one to which all others are necessarily in abeyance, was he guilty or innocent in having murdered R. Zira? It certainly seems a very hard case to condemn him to death for an act, which resulted from his obedience to the greatest of all the commandments. He might urge that he had a great dislike to drunkenness—that he had overcome his natural aversion simply to satisfy the Rabbinical requirements—that by the time that he had arrived at the prescribed incompetency to distinguish between Haman and Mordecai, he had lost all power of distinguishing between right and wrong—that, therefore, he had not done it with malice propense; what sentence, therefore, does the Talmud pronounce against a murderer of this sort? If Rabba was allowed to go at large, as would appear from his invitation to Rabbi Zira the following year, a repetition of the same offence was possible, a repetition of the miracle in R. Zira's opinion highly improbable. Thus Rabba might go on from year to year killing one or more with impunity, and would be a far more dangerous neighbour than "the ox that was wont to push with his horn." If, on the other hand, he is to be punished capitally, then the oral law is plainly not from God; for obedience to the greatest of its commandments makes it possible for a man to commit the greatest of crimes, and to subject himself to the extremity of punishment. But we object, secondly, to *the exaltation of a mere human ordinance above the Word of God.* The reading of the book of Esther at the feast of Purim, is no doubt a very appropriate, and may be a very profitable exercise. But it is confessedly of human appointment. It is of the words of the scribes; the time and the mode are altogether Rabbinical ordinances. Why, then, "are all the remaining commandments of the law to give way to the reading of the Megillah?" The priest was to neglect the service to which God had appointed him, in order to obey a mere human institution. And the Israelites to neglect the duties of love and charity, to fulfil a mere ceremonial commandment. Here is a plain token that the oral law is not from God, but is the offspring of human invention and superstition. The human mind exalts ceremonies above moral duties. God declares that all outward observances are secondary. "I desired mercy and not sacrifice, and the knowledge of God more than burntofferings." (Hos. vi. 6.) " He hath showed thee, O man, what is good; and what doth the Lord require of thee, but to do justly, and to love mercy, and to walk humbly with thy God?" (Mic. vi. 8.) And so the New Testament says in the very same spirit, "The first of all the commandments is, Hear O Israel: the Lord our God is one Lord, and thou shalt love the Lord thy God with all thy heart, &c. This is the first commandment. And the second is like, namely this, Thou shalt love thy neighbour as thyself. There is none other commandment greater than these." (Mark. xii. 29—31.) The oral law, on the contrary, tells us that "all the commandments, except the burying of the dead, are to give way to the reading of the Megillah," to a mere ceremony; and that not even of God's appointment. God prefers mercy before the sacrifices which He himself has instituted. The Talmud prefers a human institution to all God's commandments. A more striking instance of genuine superstition, and a stronger proof of the human origin of the oral law cannot be found.

The book of Esther appears to have been a peculiar favourite of the Rabbies. The reading of it takes precedence of all other duties but one, and is considered as obligatory, even upon the women, who are declared exempt from the study of the law. It is true that it contains a very notable warning for disobedient wives, and a striking instance of the deliverance of Israel by the instrumentality of a woman; but when we consider that the name of God does not occur once in the whole book, and that the law contains the account of man's creation and fall, the ten comandments, the deliverance from Egypt, and all those events of primary interest to women as well as men, it becomes of some importance to consider why the women, who are not bound to study the law of God, are bound to read the book of Esther. The authors of the oral law appear to have attached uncommon importance to this book, as appears from this circumstance, and still more so from the following startling declaration of Maimonides:—

כל ספרי הנביאים וכל הכתובים עתידין ליבטל
לימות המשיח חוץ ממגלת אסתר. והרי היא קיימת
כחמשה חומשי תורה והלכות של תורה שבעל
פה שאינן בטלין לעולם:

" All the books of the prophets, and all the Hagiographa, except the roll of Esther, will cease in the days of Messiah. But it is perpetual as the five books of the written law, and the constitutions of the oral law, which shall never cease." (Hilchoth Megillah.) Some of the Rabbies say that this is to be taken conditionally, " although they were all to cease, yet this would not cease." But this still attributes a decided superiority to the book of Esther above all the other books. What then is there in it, that gives this book such a peculiar favour, and makes the history of Esther more important than that of the conquest of Canaan, or of the glory of Solomon, or of the restoration of the house of the Lord? Is there more devotion and piety to be found in it than in the Psalms of David? Does it contain more wisdom than the Proverbs of Solomon? Is there a sublimer flight of Divine poetry, a more heavenly afflatus than in the visions of Isaiah? A more open revelation of the mysteries of the Deity than is to be found in Job, or Daniel, or Ezekiel? Why do the Rabbies pronounce it worthy of preservation, whilst they contemplate without emotion the loss of all the other books? We cannot possibly discover, unless it be that it furnishes more gratification to the spirit of revenge so natural to all the children of Adam, whether they be Jew or Gentile. To forgive is to be like God—and God alone can teach forgiveness either speculatively or practically. But the book of Esther contains an account of the revenge which the Jews took upon their enemies, not like the destruction of the Canaanites, fulfilling the commands of God upon His enemies, but taking personal and individual revenge on their own. And this very fact may be one reason why God did not permit his most holy name to occur in the whole book—just as he did not permit David to build him a temple, so he would not have his name associated with deeds of personal revenge. But, however that be, we can discover no other reason for the decided preference which the oral law gives to the book of Esther. And we think that after the specimens which we have already given of their spirit towards idolaters we do them no injustice; especially as, in this particular case, the oral law breathes this spirit aloud.

צריך שיאמר ארור המן ברוך מרדכי, ארורה זרש
ברוכה אסתר, ארורים כל עכו״ם ברוכים כל ישראל:

"It is necessary to say, Cursed be Haman, Blessed be Mordecai, Cursed be Zeresh, Blessed be Esther, Cursed be all idolaters, Blessed be all Israel." (Orach Chaiim, sec. 690.) Why this is necessary, is not told us. It appears not to bring glory to God, nor any blessing to man. Haman and Zeresh have long since passed into eternity, and received from the just Judge the reward of their deeds. Mordecai and Esther have in like manner appeared before the God of Israel, and received according to their faith. To these, then, the voice of human praise or reproach is as nothing. But to curse a dead enemy, to pursue with unrelenting hatred those who have already fallen into the hands of the living God, is certainly not a Divine ordinance, and cannot be an acceptable act of worship in poor sinners, who themselves stand so much in need of forgiveness. To curse the dead is bad, but to curse the living is, in one sense, still worse. "Cursed be all idolaters." According to our calculation, there are 600 millions of idolaters —according to the Jewish account, there must be more. Why, then, should they be cursed? That will not convert them from the error of their ways. It will not make them more happy, either in this world or in the next. We are not aware, even if God were to hear this execration and curse the idolatrous world, that it would be productive of any blessing to Israel. Why make a day of thanksgiving for mercies received an opportunity of invoking curses upon the majority of mankind? The Word of God teaches a very different petition for the heathen. "God, be merciful to us, and bless us, and cause his face to shine upon us. That thy way may be known upon earth, thy saving health among all nations. Let the people praise thee, O God; yea, let all the people praise thee." (Ps. lxvii.)

No. VIII.

RABBINIC CONTEMPT FOR THE SONS OF NOAH.

THE noblest inquiry, to which the mental powers can be directed, is, Which religion comes from God? The most satisfactory mode of conducting such an inquiry, independently of the external evidence, is to compare the principles of one system with those of the other, and both with an acknowledged standard, if such there be, and this is what we are endeavouring to do in these papers. We by no means wish to make the modern Jews responsible for the inventions of their forefathers, but to show them that their traditional argument for rejecting Christianity, and that is the example of the high priest and the Sanhedrin, is of no force; inasmuch as these same persons, who originally rejected Jesus of Nazareth, were in great and grievous error in the fundamental principles of religion, whilst He who was rejected taught the truth. To do this we must appeal to the oral law, and discuss its merits. We have shown already that those persons did not understand at least one half of the law; that their doctrines were in the highest degree uncharitable. It has, however, been replied, that the Talmud is more tolerant than the New Testament, for it allows " that the pious of the nations of the world may be saved ; " whereas the latter asserts that " whosoever believeth not shall be damned." We must, therefore, inquire into the extent of toleration and charity contained in that Talmudic sentence. The first step in this inquiry, is to ascertain who are the persons intended in the expression "The pious of the nations of the world." The oral law tells us, as quoted in No. 6, that the Israelites are commanded to compel all that come into the world to receive the seven commandments of the sons of Noah, and adds,

והמקבל אותם הוא הנקרא גר תושב בכל מקום :

"He that receives them is called universally a sojourning proselyte." And a little lower down it says plainly

כל המקבל שבע מצוות ונזהר לעשותן הרי זה
מחסידי אומות העולם . ויש לו חלק לעולם הבא :

" Whosoever receives the seven commandments, and is careful to observe them, he is one of the pious of the nations of the world, and has a share in the world to come." (Hilchoth M'elachim, c. viii. 10.) From these two declarations, then, we learn that "the pious of the nations of the world" are the same as "the sojourning proselytes," who were allowed to reside in the land of Israel, and that their piety consisted in receiving and practising the seven commandments. What these commandments were, we are informed in the next chapter of the same treatise.

עַל שִׁשָּׁה דְבָרִים נִצְטַוָּה אָדָם הָרִאשׁוֹן. עַל ע״ז. וְעַל בִּרְכַת הַשֵּׁם. וְעַל שְׁפִיכַת דָּמִים. וְעַל גִּלּוּי עֲרָיוֹת. וְעַל הַגֶּזֶל. וְעַל הַדִּינִים. אַף עַל פִּי שֶׁכּוּלָן הֵן קַבָּלָה בְיָדֵינוּ מִמֹּשֶׁה רַבֵּינוּ. וְהַדַּעַת נוֹטָה לָהֶן. מִכְּלַל דִּבְרֵי הַתּוֹרָה יֵרָאֶה שֶׁעַל אֵלּוּ נִצְטַוָּה. הוֹסִיף לְנֹחַ אֵבֶר מִן הַחַי שֶׁנֶּאֱמַר אַךְ בָּשָׂר בְּנַפְשׁוֹ דָמוֹ לֹא תֹאכֵלוּ. נִמְצְאוּ שֶׁבַע מִצְוֹת. וְכֵן הָיָה הַדָּבָר בְּכָל הָעוֹלָם עַד אַבְרָהָם:

"The first Adam was commanded concerning six things—idolatry, blasphemy, shedding of blood, incest, robbery, and administration of justice. Although we have all these things as a tradition from Moses, our master, and reason naturally inclines to them, yet, from the general tenour of the words of the law, it appears that he was commanded concerning these things. Noah received an additional command concerning the limb of a living animal, as it is said, 'But flesh in the life thereof, which is the blood thereof, ye shall not eat.' (Gen. ix. 4.) Here are the seven commandments, and thus the matter was in all the world until Abraham." (Ibid. ix. 1.)

Now, without stopping to dispute about the command given to Noah, we cannot help saying that the above tradition is very defective, and certainly not derived from Moses, for it is opposed to the history which he himself has given us. In the first place, that command, on which, the oral law lays such stress, "Be fruitful and multiply," was originally given to Adam (Gen. i. 28), and was renewed to Noah, after the deluge. If the Rabbies reckon this as a separate command in the case of the Jews, as may be seen in the Hilchoth Priah Ureviah, it is only fair to reckon it as a separate command in the case of the Gentiles, and thus we get an eighth command. In the second place, God ordained marriage as a holy state. "The Lord God said, It is not good that man should be alone; I will make him an help meet for him." "And the rib which the Lord God had taken from man made he a woman, and brought her unto the man." Here is God's holy institution, and in the following verses we have the obligations of marriage distinctly acknowledged. "And Adam said, This is now bone of my bones, and flesh of my flesh; she shall be called Woman, because she was taken out of man. Therefore shall a man leave his father and his mother, and shall cleave unto his wife, and they shall be one flesh." Here, then, is a ninth commandment. We know, indeed, that the oral law gives a different account, but its doctrine is false and pernicious. In the face of the above plain narrative, it teaches as follows :—

קודם מתן תורה היה אדם פוגע אשה בשוק אם
רצה הוא והיא לישא אותה מכניסה לתוך ביתו
ובועלה בינו לבין עצמו ותהיה לו לאשה :

"Before the giving of the law, a man might happen to meet a woman in the street; if they both agreed on marriage, he took her to his house, and cohabited with her, and she became his wife." (Hilchoth Ishuth, c. i. 1.) Now, not to speak of profane history, there is not in the law of Moses a single passage to give colour to this statement, unless it be the following :—" And it came to pass, when men began to multiply on the face of the earth, and daughters were born unto them, that the sons of God saw the daughters of men that they were fair; and they took them wives of all which they chose." But, whatever is meant by "Sons of God," it is plain that this conduct is mentioned, not as having the sanction or approval of God, but as a proof of antediluvian wickedness, for it is immediately added, "And the Lord said, My Spirit shall not always strive with man, for that he also is flesh." But it is not simply an error of judgment, it is most pernicious as it regards both Gentiles and Jews, for it completely annuls the sanctity and obligation of the marriage tie. It teaches that as the marriage of Noahites is contracted without solemn espousals, so it may be dissolved without the formality of a divorce.

ומאימתי תהיה אשת חברו כגרושה שלנו ?
משיוציאנה מביתו וישלחנה לעצמה . או שתצא היא
מתחת רשותו ותלך לה . שאין להן גירושין בכתב .
ואין הדבר תלוי בו לבד . אלא כל זמן שירצה הוא
או היא לפרוש זה מזה פורשין :

"When is his (the Noahite's) neighbour's wife to be considered in the same light, as a divorced woman with us? From the time that he sends her forth from his house, and leaves her to herself. Or from the time that she goes forth from under his power, and goes her way; for they have no divorces in writing, neither does the matter depend upon that alone;* but whenever he or she please to separate one from the other, they separate." (Hilchoth Melachim, c. ix. 8.) We Gentiles have great reason to be thankful that Jesus of Nazareth has taught us a different doctrine, according with the original institution of marriage. What would have been

---

* Instead of לבד *alone*, there is another reading, "לבד, the tribunal.

the state of the world, if the oral law had attained supreme power, and the Gentiles had been instructed in the above law as Divine? What would result from the doctrine that every man may turn out his wife, and every woman leave her husband, whenever they like? The peace and well-being of Gentile society would be at an end. The frightful state of disorder and misery that would ensue, as well as the words of the original institution, plainly show that this doctrine is not from God. But the effect upon the believers in the oral law is still worse. With reference to them, the marriage of Gentiles is no marriage at all. The oral law says distinctly—

אין אישות לגוים.

"There is no matrimony to the Gentiles." (Hilchoth Melachim, viii. 3.) And again,

אין אישות אלא לישראל או לגוים על הגוים אבל לא לעבדים על עבדים ולא לעבדים על ישראל:

"There is no matrimony except to Israel, or to Gentiles with respect to Gentiles; but not to slaves with respect to slaves, nor to slaves with respect to Israel." (Hilchoth Issure Biah, c. xiv. 19.) Here, then, the oral law directly makes void the law of God, and pronounces that a command given to Adam in Paradise, and therefore equally binding on all his descendants, is in particular cases of no force at all. The oral law, therefore, is certainly not from God.

We have already made out nine commandments; in sacrifice we find a tenth. Cain and Abel brought sacrifices, and the only reason that can be assigned is, that they had received a command to that effect. Sacrifice was either a Divine command or the dictate of their own reason. But it was not the dictate of reason, for reason says, that the Creator of all things has no need of gifts, and, least of all, such gifts as imply the slaughter of an innocent animal. It must, therefore, have been of Divine command. The reason why the Rabbies excluded this command is plain. They did not choose that there should be acceptable sacrifices offered anywhere but amongst themselves. But that this doctrine is altogether of a recent date is plain. It was not known to Job. He says not a word about the seven commandments, and he was in the habit of offering sacrifices. "And it was so when the day of their feasting was gone about, that Job sent and sanctified them, and rose up early in the morning, and offered burnt-offerings according to the number of them all." (Job i. 5.) And the Lord himself expressly commanded Job's friends to do so likewise. "And it was so, that after the Lord had spoken these words unto Job, the

Lord said to Eliphaz the Temanite, My wrath is kindled against thee, and against thy two friends ...... Therefore, take unto you now seven bullocks and seven rams, and go to my servant Job, and offer up for yourselves a burnt-offering, and my servant Job shall pray for you, for him will I accept." (Job xlii. 7, 8.) It was not known to Elisha. When Naaman said, "Shall there not then, I pray thee, be given to thy servant two mules' burden of earth? For thy servant will henceforth offer neither burnt-offering nor sacrifice unto other gods, but unto the Lord." (2 Kings v. 17.) Elisha made no objection. He did not tell him that he had only seven commandments to attend to. Neither had Isaiah any idea that, when Judaism triumphed, the whole world was to be compelled to adhere to the seven commandments, for he plainly predicts the contrary. "And the Lord shall be known to Egypt, and the Egyptians shall know the Lord in that day, and shall do sacrifice and oblation: yea, they shall vow a vow unto the Lord and perform it." (Isaiah xix. 21.) Here again, then, the oral law contradicts the Word of God.

But the law of God points out to us an eleventh commandment, in the distinction between clean and unclean animals. The Lord commanded Noah to take of the former by sevens and of the latter by pairs. (Gen. vii. 2.) And when Noah came forth from the ark "he builded an altar unto the Lord; and took of every clean beast, and of every clean fowl, and offered burnt-offerings on the altar." (Gen. viii. 2.) It is plain, from the command, that a greater number of clean than unclean animals was required. Noah's conduct shows that the rite of sacrifice was the cause of the requirement. We have a twelfth commandment in the appointment of a priesthood. "Melchizedek was the priest of the Most High God," (Gen. xiv. 10,) which he most certainly could not have been, if he had not been Divinely appointed. From the law itself, then, we have made out twelve distinct commandments. Eight would have been sufficient to overthrow the oral tradition. But we appeal to the common sense of every Talmudist. We ask him to look over the meagre list of the seven commandments, in which neither love to God nor man is included, and to tell us whether it be at all probable that "the God of the spirits of all flesh" would leave all mankind, excepting the small company of Rabbinists, without any better rule for time, and any better guide to eternity? Is it possible that the God of love and mercy should leave the majority of his reasonable creatures in doubt as to his love, and tell them that he requires no love from them? Yet this is what the oral law says. The Gentiles are, according to it, left without any direction as to the worship of God, and are pronounced guilty of death if they study the law. Nay, they are expressly told that God does not require them to glorify him by their obedience.

בן נח שאנסו אנס לעבור על אחת ממצוותיו.
מותר לו לעבור. אפילו נאנס לעבוד ע״ז עובד. לפי
שאינן מצווין על קדוש השם:

" A Noahite who is forced to transgress one of his commandments, it is lawful for him to do so. Even if he be compelled to commit idolatry he may commit it, for they are not commanded to sanctify God." (Hilchoth Melachim, c. x. 2.) So that, according to the Rabbies, the Noahite who is compelled to commit murder, adultery, or even to deny his God, may do it with impunity; he still belongs " to the pious of the nations of the world," and may have a share in the world to come. We confess that we cannot see in this doctrine either charity or toleration. We can discover only that narrowness of heart which characterizes the oral law. In order to magnify themselves, and depreciate the other nations, the Rabbies first swell out their own commandments to 613, and reduce the commandments of the nations to seven. But not content with that, they also strive to confine the glories of martyrdom to themselves, and tell the Gentiles that God does not require them to sanctify His name. Can such doctrine come from God? Is God the God of the Rabbinists only? We grant that the Jews are his "peculiar people." We acknowledge that "they have much advantage every way"—that "they are beloved for the fathers' sakes"—that the time is coming when "all that see them shall acknowledge them that they are the seed whom the Lord has blessed." But we still think that God's heart is large enough to comprehend us Gentiles too in his love. We know that we are the work of His hand, and we trust that, as He is our Father, he requires, and is pleased to see even in Gentiles, the feelings of children, love and filial fear. And we found this our faith on your Scriptures as well as ours. The Word of God tells us that, long before there were any Rabbies in the world, He had a gracious and tender care for all mankind. He promised to our first parents a Saviour who should "bruise the serpent's head." He saved Noah and his family, not one of whom was a Rabbi, from the deluge; and when they came forth from the ark, He made a gracious covenant not with one nation only, but "with all flesh," and hung up on high a lovely and glittering arch, from one end of the heavens to the other, that all the habitants of earth might have a token of their Father's love, and learn to look up to Him with humble confidence. When he chose Abraham and his seed, it was not an act of partiality, but that in his seed all the families of the earth might be blessed. He did not leave himself without witness to the nations. He manifested himself to Job, and taught him "that his Redeemer liveth," and moved even the prophets of Israel to predict again and again the happy times when, "from the rising of the sun to the going down of the same, His name should be great among the Gentiles, and in every place incense should be offered to his name, and a pure offering; for my name shall be great among the heathen, saith the Lord of hosts." (Mal. i. 11.) Having this word, we reject the oral law which contradicts it, and would make God the God of the Rabbinists only: and we believe in the New Testament, which exactly agrees with your written law, and asks, "Is he the God of the Jews only? Is he not also of the Gentiles?"—and answers, "Yes, of the Gentiles also" (Rom. iii. 29)—and which also declares that, in the sight of God, "There is no difference between the Jew and the Greek; for the same Lord over all is rich unto all that call upon him, for whosoever shall call upon the name of the Lord shall be saved." (Rom. x. 12, 13.)

In the fixing of the commandments, then, for the sons of Noah, we have detected an intolerant and uncharitable spirit very different from that of the Old and New Testament. But we have further to inquire, what was the extent of toleration conceded to them? We do not stop to prove that they were not allowed to possess land, nor to be judges, nor members of the Sanhedrim, nor to hold any office, nor to intermarry with the Jews. From all that, they were excluded by the law of God himself. They were allowed to sojourn in the land, and hence their name "sojourning proselytes." Further, "They were to be treated with the same courtesy and benevolence as the Israelites." (See No. 4, p. 26.) But further than this the toleration did not extend. The oral law, though it commands "courtesy and benevolence," does not administer even-handed justice to the "pious of the nations of the world," as may be seen from the following specimens :—

ישראל שהרג בשגגה את העבד או את גר תושב גולה.

וכן גר תושב שהרג את גר תושב או את העבד בשגגה גולה.

גר תושב שהרג את ישראל בשגגה אף על פי שהיה שוגג הרי זה נהרג.

"An Israelite who unintentionally kills a slave, or a sojourning proselyte, is imprisoned (in one of the cities of refuge)."

"And so a sojourning proselyte who unintentionally kills a sojourning proselyte, or a slave, is imprisoned."

"A sojourning proselyte who unintentionally kills an

Israelite, although he did it unintentionally, is to be put to death." (Hilchoth Rotzeach, c. v. 3.) The written law, on the contrary, says, "These six cities shall be a refuge, both for the children of Israel and for the stranger, and for the sojourner among them: that any one that killeth any person unawares may flee thither." (Numbers xxxv. 15.) Again, the oral law says—

ישראל שהרג גר תושב אינו נהרג עליו בבית דין .
שנאמר וכי יזיד איש על רעהו:

"An Israelite who kills a sojourning proselyte, is not put to death on his account by the tribunal, for it is said, 'But if a man come presumptuously upon his neighbour.' (Exodus xxi. 14.)" The law of God says, " Whoso sheddeth man's blood, by man shall his blood be shed : for in the image of God made he man." (Gen. ix. 6.) And to this law the New Testament commands us Christians to adhere, rejecting the oral traditions; and in consequence the laws of Christian countries make no difference between the murderer of a Jew, a Christian, Turk, Infidel, or Heretic. Short as all Christian nations confessedly come of the pure morality of the New Testament, their laws direct the administration of impartial justice, and are a terror to all evil doers of every creed and sect. The liberality of the Talmud then, in allowing a share of salvation to the pious of the world is not so very great, nor its toleration of a very comprehensive character. It not only withholds justice from the pious of the world, but gives as the reason, because they are not considered as neighbours. Want of room prevents us from pursuing this subject further at present. We therefore ask, Is this law from God? Can God, in an oral law, directly contradict his written law? Can you point out anything similar in the New Testament? Is this law just or unjust? You will grant that it is unjust and erroneous. Then your fathers have been mistaken about one of the first principles of the administration of justice, for many centuries. And your brethren who adhere to this system as Divine, as on the Barbary coast, for instance, are still mistaken. Why do you not protest aloud against such error? Why not endeavour to convince your brethren that they are wrong? In England there is nothing to prevent you. There is full liberty, free toleration. You may lift up your voice like a trumpet against the errors of the Talmud. You may expunge all acknowledgment of its authority from your prayers—you may return to Moses and the prophets, and no man will say nay.

No. IX.

CHRISTIANS CANNOT BE RECKONED AMONGST THE "PIOUS OF THE NATIONS OF THE WORLD."

WE said, in our last number, that "the pious of the nations of the world" are, according to the oral law, those who have received the seven commandments of the sons of Noah. We said that of the laws laid down for their own conduct, some, as for instance that respecting divorces, are such as would introduce confusion and misery into Gentile society—and that others, referring to the administration of justice by Rabbinical tribunals, are extremely unjust. But the advocates of the oral law think, nevertheless, that it is very tolerant, more tolerant than the New Testament, because it says that "the pious of the nations of the world have a share in the world to come." Now we cannot help feeling a curiosity to know how great or how small that share will be. And this our curiosity is excited by the following information, which the oral law commands to be communicated to a Gentile who wishes to turn Jew:—

וכשם שמודיעין אותו עונשן של מצוות כך מודיעין אותו שכרן של מצוות . ומודיעין אותו שבעשיית מצוות אלו יזכה לחיי העולם הבא . ושאין שום צדיק גמור אלא בעל החכמה שעושה ויודען : ואומרים לו חוי יודע שהעולם הבא אינו צפון אלא לצדיקים והם ישראל . וזה שתראה ישראל בצער בעולם הזה טובה היא צפונה להם שאין יכולין לקבל רוב טובה בעולם הזה כאומות . שמא ירום לבם ויתעו ויפסידו שכר העולם הבא כענין שנאמר וישמן ישורון ויבעט : ואין הקדוש ברוך הוא מביא עליהן רוב פורענות כדי שלא יאבדו אלא כל האומות כלין והן עומדין וכו' :

"As they are to make known to him the punishments attached to the commandments, so they are also to inform him of the rewards for keeping them. They should inform him, that, by the doing of these commandments, he will be worthy of everlasting life; and that there is no perfectly righteous man, except that possessor of wisdom who does and knows them. And they are to say to him, Be assured that *the world to come is laid up for none but the righteous, and they are Israel:* and as to this that thou seest Israel in trouble in this world, their good things are laid up for them, *for they cannot receive an abundance of good things in this world, like the nations.* Their heart might, perchance, be lifted up, and they might go astray, and lose the reward of the world to come, as it is said, 'Jeshurun waxed fat and kicked.' The Holy One, blessed be he, brings upon them the abundance of afflictions for no other reason than this, that they may not be lost. *All the nations shall be utterly destroyed*, but they shall abide." (Hilchoth Issure Biah., c. xiv. 3—5.) To us this sounds very much like a flat contradiction to the above declaration, that "the pious of the nations of the world have a share in the world to come." Here, on the contrary, it is stated that the blessings of that state are reserved "for none but the righteous, and they are Israel;" and again, "All the nations shall be utterly destroyed." And it is even implied that the nations get their good things in this world, and do not suffer affliction, as they are not to have that blessedness, which is reserved for the righteous. How, then, are we to reconcile these two sayings? There are only two ways which occur to us, either by saying that this is not strictly true, but only a fair speech in order to catch proselytes; or, if it be strictly true, that then "the pious of the world" are to have a much smaller share in the blessedness to come. In any case the spirit is far from charitable or tolerant. It represents God as an accepter of persons, saving Israelites simply because they are Israelites, and destroying the other nations because they are not Israelites. The New Testament representation is very different, and far more worthy of "the Judge of all the earth." It does indeed say, "He that believeth shall be saved, and he that believeth not shall be damned." But in this very declaration, we have an impartial rule applied to all mankind. "He that believeth," of whatsoever nation, kindred, or tongue—Jew or Gentile, white or black—"shall be saved." "He that believeth not," whether he be called a Jew or a Christian, whether he be a son of Japhet, of Shem, or of Ham, " shall be damned." The New Testament asserts no monopoly of salvation for one favoured family. It excludes none because he had not the happiness to be descended from a privileged stock. It lays down a general and impartial rule to be applied to all the children of men. The oral law says,

כל ישראל יש להם חלק לעולם הבא :

"All Israel has a share in the world to come." The New Testament says, "Not every one that saith unto me, Lord, Lord, shall enter the kingdom of heaven, but he that doeth the will of my Father which is in heaven." (Matt. vii. 21.) The oral law says, "The world to come is laid up for none but the righteous, and they are Israel." The New Testament says, "God is no respecter of persons; but in every nation he that feareth him, and worketh righteousness, is accepted with him." (Acts x. 34, 35.) Now then we appeal to the good sense of every Jew, even of the Talmudists to tell us which of these two, statements is must just, impartial, and worthy of the Just Judge?

But the reasoning employed in the above extract from the oral law, is as false as the principles which it is intended to support, when it says, "As to this that thou seest Israel in trouble in this world, their good things are laid up for them, for they cannot receive an abundance of good things in this world like the nations," it directly contradicts the law of Moses, which everywhere promises an abundance of temporal blessings to Israel, if obedient. "It shall come to pass, if thou shalt hearken diligently unto the voice of the Lord thy God, to observe and to do all the commandments which I command thee this day, that the Lord thy God will set *thee on high above all nations* of the earth, and all these blessings shall come upon thee, and overtake thee, if thou shalt hearken unto the voice of the Lord thy God. Blessed shalt thou be in the city, and blessed shalt thou be in the field. Blessed shall be the fruit of thy body, and the fruit of thy ground, and the fruit of thy cattle, the increase of thy kine, and the flocks of thy sheep...

....The Lord shall cause thine enemies that rise up against thee to be smitten before thy face; they shall come out against thee one way, and flee before thee seven ways. The Lord shall command the blessing upon thee in thy store-houses, and in all that thou settest thine hand unto; and he shall bless thee in the land which the Lord thy God giveth thee." (Deut. xxviii. 1—8, &c.) Here, then, is temporal blessing in abundance, promised to obedience; and the afflictions which have come upon Israel are not because of their piety, but because of their disobedience. In this case, then, the oral law speaks utter falsehood. God has not two ways of dealing with nations, but one way. He gives every nation a fair trial, and if they refuse to hearken to his voice, he pours out upon them his wrath. The rise, and growth, and trial, of a nation is slower, and requires more time than the growth and trial of individual men. The life of a nation is, so to speak, longer than the life of a man. Centuries are required as the time of a nation's trial, but all history, sacred and profane, testifies the truth of the general rule given in the Old Testament, "Righteousness exalteth a nation, but sin is a reproach to any people." The only difference which God makes between Israel and the other nations, is with regard to their national existence in this world. He has crumbled the mighty empires of Assyria, Babylon, Greece, and Rome into dust, but he still preserves the independent existence of the family of Abraham, according to his covenant; and when, as a nation, they repent and return to him, He will remove the rod of his anger, and give them the temporal prosperity which He has promised by the mouth of Moses his servant. But this promise of temporal blessing will not justify any impenitent Jew at the tribunal of God's judgment. The hopes held out by the oral law are utterly fallacious, and dishonouring to God, inasmuch as he is represented as unduly favouring one nation, and unjustly condemning all others.

An advocate of the oral law may, however, find out some other way of evading the evident intolerance of the above statement, and still insist upon it, that as the Talmud says, "The pious of the nations of the world have a share in the world to come," it is a very tolerant book. We therefore proceed to inquire what pains the Rabbies have taken to add to the number of those who are to be saved. They believe, as we are told, that every one, who receives and observes the seven commandments of the sons of Noah, will be saved; they believe that all others must be lost; have they then taken any pains to make known this important information to the world? Or, if that was not to be expected during the captivity, did they during the days of their power and dominion? Or, at least, did they offer every facility to those Gentiles who might come to renounce idolatry, to receive the necessary instruction? Did they command all their disciples to be ready day and night to open their doors at the knock of the penitent idolater, and by receiving rescue him from everlasting destruction? Not one of all these things. They commanded that, when there was no jubilee, such converts should be refused, and that if they did not choose to be circumcised and observe the whole Mosaic law, they should be left to perish.

אי זה הוא גר תושב זה גוי שקבל עליו שלא
יעבוד עכו"ם עם שאר המצוות שנצטוו בני נח ולא
מל ולא טבל הרי זה מקבלין אותי והוא מחסידי
אומות העולם. ול מה נקרא שמו תושב לפי שמותר
לנו להושיבו בינינו בארץ ישראל כמו שבארנו
בהלכות עכו"ם. ואין מקבלין גר תושב אלא בזמן
שהיובל נוהג:

"What is meant by a sojourning proselyte? Such an one is a Gentile, who has taken upon himself not to commit idolatry, together with the remaining commandments given to the sons of Noah, but is not circumcised nor baptized. Such an one is received, and is of the pious of the nations of the world. And why is he called *a sojourner?* Because it is lawful for us to let him dwell amongst us in the land of Israel, as we have explained in the laws concerning idolatry. *But a sojourning Proselyte is not received* WHEN THE JUBILEE CANNOT BE OBSERVED." (Hilchoth Issure Biah., c. xiv. 7, 8.) At all other times the unfortunate heathen might perish, if they did not choose to become Jews altogether. Now what will be thought of the charity of this law if we add, that there has been no jubilee, and consequently no pious amongst the nations for two thousand seven hundred years and more? Yet this is what the oral law tells us.

משגלו שבט ראובן ושבט גד וחצי שבט מנשה
בטלו היובלות שנאמר וקראתם דרור בארץ לכל
יושביה . בזמן שכל יושביה עליה . והוא שלא יהיו
מעורבבין שבט בשבט אלא כולן יושבים כתקונן:

"Since the time that the tribe of Reuben, and the tribe of Gad and the half-tribe of Manasseh were led away captive, the jubilees have ceased, for it is said, 'And ye shall proclaim liberty throughout the land unto all the inhabitants thereof' (Lev. xxv. 10); that means, when all its inhabitants are upon it, and, moreover, when the tribes are not mixed one with another, but all dwelling according as they were appointed." (Hilchoth Shemitah, c. x. 8.) We have the account of this captivity in the following words, "In those days the Lord began to cut Israel short: and Hazael smote them in all the coasts of Israel: from Jordan eastward, all the land of Gilead, the Gadites, and the Reubenites, and the Manassites." (2 Kings x. 32, 33.) That was, according to the common chronology about 884 years before the Christian era. If to this we add 1836, we have 2720 years since the time that there could be a jubilee, and consequently 2720 years since any Gentiles were converted from the errors of idolatry to the religion of the sons of Noah. What is it then but solemn mockery, in any one acquainted with the oral law, to tell us that the Talmud is tolerant, and admits " that the pious of the nations of the world may be saved;" when according to that same book seven-and-twenty centuries have elapsed, since any such converts were received? We believe that those who make this defence are unacquainted with the principles of the system which they undertake to defend. The truth is, that the authors of the oral law, finding that they could not altogether deny salvation to the pious of other nations, were determined not to add to their number, and therefore limited the possibility of this mode of conversion to times that had elapsed long before they were born. But in their own times they would not receive any one who was not willing to be circumcised and to receive the whole law. And hence we see how exactly the New Testament represents the state of the case, when Christianity was first propagated amongst the Gentiles, and free salvation was proclaimed to all who believed, without becoming Jewish proselytes. The Rabbinists opposed with all their might. " And certain men which came down from Judea taught the brethren and said,

Except ye be circumcised after the manner of Moses, ye cannot be saved." And again, " There rose up certain of the sect of the Pharisees which believed, saying that it was needful to circumcise them, and to command them to keep the law of Moses." (Acts xv. 1—5.) There was no year of jubilee, and therefore renunciation of idolatry was not sufficient in the eyes of these traditionists, who believed that at such a time there was no salvation except for those who observed the whole law. But how is it now? If a Gentile should desire now to become one of the pious of the nations, could the Jews receive him? According to the above general principles, certainly not. The tribes are still scattered and mixed up together. The land has not got " all its inhabitants." There can be no jubilee, and therefore those that wish to be saved, must, according to the oral law, turn Jews, or take their chance of living to a year of jubilee. But we are not necessitated to argue from the principles. The thing is expressly laid down in the oral law. After explaining, as we have quoted above, who are the pious of the world, and that when the jubilee is possible, is the only time for receiving them, it adds—

אבל בזמן הזה אפילו קבל עליו כל התורה כולה
חוץ מדקדוק אחד אין מקבלין אותו :

" But in the present time, though a man should be willing to take upon him the whole law, with the exception of only one of its least requirements, he is not to be received." Now then what becomes of the boasted toleration of the Talmud? It says, that " the pious of the nations of the world may be saved." But it says, first, that such converts can only be received when the jubilee can be celebrated. It says, secondly, that this only opportunity has not occurred for the last 2,700 years; and, lastly, it positively forbids the Jews in the present time to give the Gentiles a chance of salvation, unless they are willing to receive the whole law. What use is it then to talk of the pious of the world, or to say that people of other religions may be saved? According to the Talmud, there are no pious of the nations, unless perchance there may be some descendants of those who were received 2,700 years ago. But all history that we have ever seen is silent on the subject. We do not know of a single congregation of Noahites in the whole world. The forefathers of the Christians were not received during the usage of jubilee. They were idolaters received against the wishes of the Rabbinists. The Britons and the Saxons were converted to Christianity long after the final dispersion of the Jews, that is, at a time when, according to the Talmud, it was unlawful to add to the pious amongst the nations. Neither were they received according to the Talmudic condition, in the presence of three learned Jews.

THE "PIOUS OF THE NATIONS OF THE WORLD." 69

וצריך לקבל עליו בפני שלשה חברים :

"And it is necessary for such an one to take the seven commandments on him in the presence of three learned men, who are qualified to be Rabbies." (Hilchoth Melachim, c. viii. 10.) According to the oral law, then, there are no such persons now existing as "the pious of the nations of the world." It is, therefore, idle to talk of the liberality with which they would be treated, were they forthcoming. Thus the only appearance of an argument in favour of the Talmud vanishes into thin air, and mocks our grasp, as soon as we endeavour to lay hold of it. Those who caught at this phantom of charity, no doubt meant it sincerely. They thought that the oral law was misrepresented. They were told that it was charitable, and they therefore nobly came forward in its defence. If they had known its true principles, they would have renounced them. Their advocacy went on a false supposition. But now that we have set forth the true bearings of the case, and given them chapter and verse to which they may refer, and convince themselves, we call upon them to do so: and then, as they hate intolerance, to join with us in protesting against it, even though it should be found in that system, which hitherto they have believed, on the testimony of others, to be Divine. At the same time we would seriously ask of them to compare this system, which has been for more than 1,700 years the religion of the majority of the Jewish nation, with the system laid down in the New Testament, and to decide which is most agreeable to the character of God, as revealed in the law and the prophets, and most beneficial to the world. The oral law says, that God has commanded the heathen to be left for 2,700 years without the means of instruction, and that when the days of Israel's prosperity come, the nations are to be converted by force; but that even then, they will not be raised to the rank of brethren, but only be sojourning proselytes. The oral law looks forward to no reunion of all the sons of Adam into one happy family. The New Testament has, on the contrary, commanded its disciples to afford the means of instruction " to every creature." It speaks to us Gentiles, who were once regarded as poor outcasts, in the language of love, and says, "Now, therefore, ye are no more strangers and foreigners, but fellow-citizens with the saints, and of the household of God." (Ephes. ii. 19.) It takes nothing from you. It asserts your privileges as the peculiar people of God; but it reveals that great, and to us, most comfortable truth, "That the Gentiles should be fellow-heirs, and of the same body;" and it promises a happy time, when there shall be one fold and one Shepherd. It does, indeed, tell us not to forget what we once were, "aliens from the commonwealth of Israel, and strangers from the covenant of promise, having no hope, and without God in the world." (Eph. ii. 12.) It reminds us that the olive-tree is Jewish, and that you are the natural branches, and warns us against all boasting. (Rom. xi. 16—24.) And we desire to remember these admonitions, and to acknowledge with thankfulness, that all that we have received, is derived from the Jewish nation. We ask you not to compare the oral law with any Gentile speculations, or systems, or inventions, but with doctrines essentially and entirely Jewish. Christianity has effected great and glorious changes in the world, but we take not the glory to ourselves. We give it to God, who is the author of all good, and under Him, to the people of Israel. We ask you, then, to compare these two Jewish systems, Rabbinism, which has done no good to the Gentiles, and perpetuated much error amongst the Jews; and Christianity, which has diffused over the world the knowledge of the one true God—disseminated the writings of Moses and the prophets, and increased the happiness of a large portion of mankind. The comparison may require time, and ought to be conducted with calmness and seriousness. But we think that, even without instituting that comparison, you must acknowledge that the principles of the oral law, discussed in this paper, are contrary to the law of Moses; and that, therefore, a decided and solemn protest against these Rabbinical additions, is an immediate and imperative duty.

No. X.

RABBINIC WASHING OF HANDS.

THERE are various marks by which a religion of man's making may be detected. It is usually intolerant, superstitious, and voluminous. It limits the love of God to a particular class. It exalts ceremonial observances above the worship of the heart; and so multiplies its laws and definitions, as to put the knowledge of it beyond the reach of any but the learned. Any one of these marks would go far towards shaking the claims of a religious system. For instance, if it lay down as religious duties so many and such subtle laws, as it is impossible for the unlearned to attain a knowledge of, it is plainly the invention of the learned, who have thought only of themselves, and have not that tender regard and consideration for the ignorant, which the Creator has. His religion must be for all, the poor as well as the rich, and the ignorant as well as the wise of this world. We fear that the oral law of the Rabbies will not stand any one of these tests: it is, at all events, a religion for the learned, and the learned only. There is scarcely one of its commandments that is not so encumbered with distinctions and definitions, as to make the right interpretation of it the sole property of the educated. Take, for example, one of the first and most frequent of the commandments, in the Rabbinist's daily practice, נְטִילַת יָדַיִם (the washing of hands.) The command appears very simple. It says—

יִרְחַץ יָדָיו וִיבָרֵךְ עַל נְטִילַת יָדָיִם:

" Let him wash his hands, and pronounce the benediction for the washing of hands." (Orach Chaiim., § 4.) But out of this short command arise endless distinctions, according to which the act performed is regarded as a valid or invalid fulfilment of the command.

כָּל הַנּוֹטֵל יָדָיו צָרִיךְ לְהִזָּהֵר בְּאַרְבָּעָה דְּבָרִים. בְּמַיִם עַצְמָן שֶׁלֹא יְהוּ פְּסוּלִין לִנְטִילַת יָדַיִם וּבְשִׁעוּר שֶׁיְהֵא בָהֶן רְבִיעִית לְכָל שְׁתֵּי יָדַיִם. וּבְכֵלִי שֶׁיְהוּ הַמַּיִם שֶׁנּוֹטְלִין בָּהֶן בִּכְלִי. וּבְנוֹטֵל שֶׁיְהוּ הַמַּיִם בָּאִין מִכֹּחַ נוֹתֵן:

" Every one who washes his hands must attend to four things. 1st, To the water, that it be not unlawful for the washing of hands. 2d, To the measure, that there be a quartern for the two hands. 3d, To the vessel, that the water, wherewith the washing is performed, be in a vessel. 4th, To the washer, that the water come with force from him that pours." (Hilchoth Berachoth, vi. 6.) Each of these four limitations requires new explanations and definitions of its own, as for example, there are four things that make water unlawful for the washing of hands; one of these is, if any work be done with it. This necessarily requires fresh definitions of what is and is not work. Then come the directions as to how far the washing is to reach, the position of the hands, whether they are to be held up or down, the drying of the hands. A perfect and accurate knowledge of all these conditions can be attained only by the learned. And after all the care which these things require, the Israelite may after all fall short of Talmudic requirement, for there is still another condition, that involves another host of Rabbinic definitions, the non-observance of which will invalidate the merit of his washing.

כל החוצץ בטבילה חוצץ בידים וכו' :

"Every thing that is an impediment in baptism is an impediment in washing of hands." (Hilchoth Mikvaoth, xi. 2.) This, of course, leads to a new inquiry, what constitutes an impediment.

אלו חוצצין באדם . לפלוף שחוץ לעין . ולד
שחוץ למכה . והדם היבש שעל גבי המכה . והרטיה
שעליה . וגלדי צואה שעל בשרו . ובצק או טיט
שרחת הצפורן . והמלמולין שעל הגוף וטיט היון .
וטיט היוצרים וכו' :

"These are the impediments in human beings. The film that is outside the eye. The incrustation outside a wound. Dry blood that is on a wound. The plaster that is on it. Filth upon the flesh. The impurity or dirt under the nails. Dirt upon the body, mud, potter's clay, &c." (Ibid., c. ii. 1.) Every one of these can give rise to endless questions in casuistry, which are evidently beyond the powers of the unlearned, and must draw him, if he be a conscientious man, to the Rabbi to solicit his advice. Thus, one of the very first commandments with which the Jew begins the day, requires for its accurate fulfilment a degree of knowledge which is far beyond the attainment of the multitude. This one commandment involves scores of others. Nay, we doubt not that an accurate Talmudist might make 613 constitutions out of this one alone; and we appeal to the conscience of the great majority of Jews in London to decide whether they possess the knowledge here required, and consequently whether it is possible for them to keep this one commandment. If they transgress any one of these Rabbinic distinctions, their hands are not washed, and consequently they are unfit for prayer. But this is not a command for the morning only. It must be repeated through the day.

כל האוכל הפת שמברכין עליו המוציא צריך
נטילת ידים תחלה וסוף . ואף על פי שהוא פת
חולין ואף על פי שאין ידיו מלוכלכות ואינו יודע להן
טומאה לא יאכל עד שיטול שתי ידיו . וכן כל דבר
שטיבולו במשקה צריך נטילת ידים תחלה :

"Every one who eats that sort of bread, for which the benediction is, 'Blessed art thou, O Lord our God, King of the universe! who bringeth forth bread from the earth,'* is bound to wash his hands at the beginning and end. And although

---

* Jewish Prayer-book, p. 152.

the bread be common, and although his hands have not been
defiled, and he is not aware of any uncleanness upon them, he
is not to eat until he wash both his hands. And thus, also,
with regard to anything that is dipped in fluid, the washing of
hands is necessary at the beginning." (Hilchoth Berachoth,
vi. 1.) Here, again, it is necessary to know the different sorts
of bread, and the compounds that may be made with the
different sorts of flour, and the various forms of benediction,
and out of these again may arise as many doubts and questions
as out of the former, for the solution of which learning,
acuteness, and practice are required; and the want of these
may lead to transgression, and, according to the Rabbies, to
most fatal consequences. For instance, neglect of this command after the meal may cause blindness.

כל פת שהמלח בו צריך נטילת ידים באחרונה
שמא יש בו מלח סדומית או מלח שטבעו כמלח
סדומית ויעביר ידיו על עיניו ויסמא. מפני זה חייבין
ליטול ידים בסוף כל סעודה מפני המלח. ובמחנה
פטורים מנטילת ידים בתחלה. מפני שהם טרודים
במלחמה וחייבין באחרונה מפני הסכנה:

"All bread that has salt in it requires washing of hands after
it; lest perhaps it might be the salt of Sodom, or salt of the
same nature, and a man might pass his hand over his eyes and
become blind. On this account all are bound to wash their
hands at the end of every meal, because of the salt. But in a
camp they are exempt from washing at the beginning, because
they are oppressed with the fatigues of war, and are bound to
wash after meal on account of the danger." (Ibid., 3.) Suppose,
then, that a poor ignorant man, with the best intention in the
world, set about this washing, and made a mistake with regard
to the water, or the vessel, or the pouring, or the position
of his hands; or suppose that a soldier, in the hurry of a camp,
were to make this mistake, or omit the washing altogether, and
then have the ill luck to put his hands to his eyes, according to
the oral law, blindness would be the consequence. Any neglect
or defect in the morning ablution would be more fatal still.

יידקדק לערות עליהן ג' פעמים מפני שרוח רעה
שורה על חידים קודם נטילה ואינה סרה עד שיערה
עליהן של"ש פעמים. ועל כן צריך למנוע מהגיע
בידו קודם הנטילה לפה. ולחוטם. ולאזנים. ולעינים.
מפני שרוח רעה שורה עליהם:

"A man must be very careful in pouring water on his hands
three times for an evil spirit rests upon the hands before

washing, and does not depart until water be poured on them three times. Therefore it is necessary, before washing, to abstain from touching the hand to the mouth, and the nose, and the ears, and the eyes, because an evil spirit rests upon them." (Orach Chaiim., § 4.)

Now, is this the religion of the God of love, and mercy, and justice? Is it at all like Him to give laws so subtle and multifarious in their distinctions, that it is next to impossible for the unlearned man to obey them aright, and then to attach to this non-observance such calamitous consequences? If it be replied that the punishment is visited only on those who transgress wilfully, then there are thousands of Jews, perhaps in this very city, who live in the habitual and wilful omission of this precept, and who have the use of their eyes, just as well as the strictest Rabbinist. This fact, which no one will dispute, proves beyond doubt, that the oral law has spoken falsehood, and therefore throws utter discredit upon its testimony respecting the tradition of the commandment itself. It is confessedly not a commandment from God, but from the scribes.

כבר ביארנו שנטילת ידים וטבילתן מדברי סופרים :

"We have explained long ago, that the washing and bathing of the hands are derived from the words of the scribes." (Hilchoth Mikvaoth, xi. 1.) That they had no Divine authority for the command is evident from the subtilty and superstition of its ordinances; for we presume that few will question the superstition of the threat of blindness to the disobedient, or of the fable of the evil spirit resting upon the hands. One such command, then, will go far to discredit the whole story of an oral law, and to invalidate the character of its witnesses. They were evidently superstitious men, no way elevated above the vulgar prejudices of the times, not at all scrupulous in adding to the law of God, and evidently aiming at a complete domination over the consciences of their followers. It is hardly possible to believe that they were not aware of the necessary result of the system, the complete subjugation of the consciences of the multitude. The mass of mankind has no leisure for the study of juristic distinctions, they must, therefore, if they believe such to be Divine, cast themselves upon the mercy of the learned, and there can be no doubt that those who have the keys of salvation, will also possess no small degree of influence and power in this world. But, whatever was the motive, there can be no doubt about the severity with which the Rabbies enforced this command. They exacted even from the poor unfortunate, whom circumstances left only enough water to slake his thirst, that he should sacrifice a part of it to this Rabbinical purification.

RABBINIC WASHING OF HANDS.

אפילו אין לו מים אלא כדי שתייה נוטל ידיו
במקצתן ואח"כ אוכל ושותה מקצתו :

"Though he should only have enough water to drink, he is to wash his hands with a part of it, and then to eat, and to drink the remainder." (Hilchoth Berachoth, vi. 19.) And not content with this harsh requirement, they sentence the despiser of their commands to excommunication.

וצריך ליזהר בנטילת ידים שכל המזלזל בנטילתם
חייב נדוי :

"It is necessary to be very careful in washing of hands, for every one who despises the washing of hands is guilty of excommunication." (Orach Chaiim., § 158.) And this same book confirms this decision by a case which actually occurred of a man thus excommunicated, and who dying in his excommunication had the usual indignities offered to his corpse.

את מי נדו את אלעזר בן חצר שפקפק בנטילת
ידים וכשמת שלחו בית דין והניחו אבן גדולה על
ארונו ללמדך שכל המתנדה ומת בנדויו בית דין
סוקלין את ארונו :

"Whom did they excommunicate? Eleazar ben Chatzar, who despised the washing of hands; and when he was dead, the tribunal sent, and had a great stone laid on his coffin, to teach thee that of every one who is excommunicated and dies in his excommunication, the coffin is stoned by the tribunal." (Talmud, Berachoth, fol. 19, col. 1.) When they had the power they employed it to the full, and now that they have it not, the oral law still threatens poverty and extirpation to every transgressor

כל המזלזל בנטילת ידים בא לידי עניות : ואמר
ר׳ זריקא אמר ר׳ אלעזר כל המזלזל בנטילת ידים
נעקר מן העולם :

"Every one who despises washing of hands sinks into poverty. R. Zerika says, in the name of R. Eliezer, Every one that despises the washing of hands is rooted out of the world." (Orach Chaiim., ibid.) Such is the toleration of the oral law towards Jews, accused of no breach of God's commandment, convicted of no denial of God's Word, guilty of no crime. And yet these same men, who are strict even to persecution about one of their own institutions, allow that which they consider the Word of God to be transgressed with impunity, if it be expedient. They assert their belief, that the law of Moses forbids the Jews to have clothing, like that of the Gentiles, to shave or to wear their hair like the other nations, and yet they say the transgression of this Divine command is lawful under the following circumstances:—

ישראל שהיה קרוב למלכות וצריך לישב לפני מלכיהם והיה. לו גנאי לפי שלא ידמה להם הרי זה מותר ללבוש במלבושיהן ולגלח כנגד פניו כדרך שהן עושין:

"An Israelite who is near to Royalty, and is obliged to sit before Gentile kings, and for whom it would be disgraceful not to be like them, is allowed to dress and to shave as they do." (Hilchoth Accum., xi. 3.) But it is not to be wondered at, that those should lightly esteem the Word of God, who are capable of confounding the guilt of transgressing a mere human ceremony with the guilt of transgressing a Divine command. The Talmud makes the sin of neglecting this command as great as that of gross immorality.

כל האוכל לחם בלא נטילת ידים כאלו בא על אשה זונה וכו׳:

"Every one who eats bread without washing of hands, is as guilty as if he had committed fornication." (Sotah, fol. iv., col. 2.)

The sum of all that has been said is, that the scribes and Pharisees added a commandment not given by Moses, that they so refined upon the conditions of its fulfilment as to make it almost impossible for the unlearned not to transgress it, and yet denounced such heavy penalties upon the transgressor as to make it an intolerable burden to the conscientious; that when they had the power, they persecuted all that refused obedience, and did not scruple to pronounce the guilt of transgression as great as that of breaking one of the moral commandments. They have presented as the religion of Moses a system which is voluminous, superstitious, and intolerant; difficult to the comprehension of the unlearned, terrific to their consciences, and cruel to their persons. But when the poor were ground down and oppressed under this weight of superstition and tyranny, God sent them a deliverer in Jesus of Nazareth, who asserted the revealed truth of God, and protested against this mental bondage. "Then came together unto him the Pharisees, and certain of the scribes which came from Jerusalem. And when they saw some of his disciples eat bread with defiled (that is to say, with unwashen) hands they found fault. . . . He answered and said unto them, Well hath Esaias prophesied of you hypocrites, as it is written, This people honoureth me with their lips, but their heart is far from me. Howbeit in vain do they worship me, teaching for doctrines the commandments of men. . . . . And when he had called all the people unto him, he said unto them, Hearken unto me every one of you and understand: there is nothing from without a man that, entering into him, can defile him: but the things which come out of him, those are they that defile him. . . . . For from within, out of the heart of men, proceed evil thoughts, adulteries, fornications, murders, thefts, covetousness, wickedness, deceit, lasciviousness, an evil eye, blasphemy, pride, foolishness: all these things come from within, and defile the man." (Mark vii. 1—23.) Here the Lord Jesus asserts what is alike the truth of God, and agreeable to the dictates of sound sense. So Samuel said in the Old Testament.

האדם יראה לעינים ויהוה יראה ללבב :

"Man looketh on the outward appearance, but God looketh on the heart." (1 Sam. xvi. 7.) But the scribes and Pharisees treated the Lord Jesus in the spirit of the laws which we have adduced above. They persecuted him unto death, and to the death He willingly went a martyr for the truth, and a sacrifice for the sin of the world. The authors of the oral law had but a short triumph. He rose from the dead, and his doctrine spread through the world, and everywhere announced freedom from the bondage of superstition as well as a hope of everlasting life. And the Jewish nation is at this hour enjoying the fruits of His death and doctrine in their liberty from Rabbinic domination. Many of you now hold some of those principles, the assertion of which was the cause of His death. You believe that moral duties are far beyond ceremonial observances. You believe, many of you, that to eat with unwashen hands is no sin, and have given up the practice. You transgress this commandment of the scribes, and yet you are not excommunicated nor persecuted. For all this you are indebted to Jesus of Nazareth. If the oral law had triumphed, and the doctrine of Jesus been silenced, you would still be living the victims of superstition or persecution. You would have been afraid of being struck with blindness, or haunted with an evil spirit, or even of being rooted out of the world. If a ray of Divine light had visited your understanding, and you had protested against these traditions, you would have had to feel the weight of Rabbinical persecution, like Jesus of Nazareth. You would have been excommunicated like Eleazar, and if God had given you strength to remain faithful, would have died excommunicated, and have had a stone upon your coffin. How is it that now you are free, that you can think and act without any such fear? Is it because the Talmud has altered? No, it is just what it was. The conscientious believers in the Talmud are just the same as their fathers, and as conscientious men, if they had the power, they would think it their bounden duty to treat you, as their predecessors treated Eleazar. But the doctrine of Jesus of Nazareth delivers you; and the followers of Jesus of Nazareth are your protectors against the rigour of the oral law, and the intolerance of your brethren. Should not this fact, then, lead you to examine into the claims of that same Nazarene? How is it that if the principles of Jesus of Nazareth should ever become universal, the world will be universally happy; whereas if the principles of those who rejected him become universal, the whole world will groan under superstition and cruelty? What stronger testimony can there be to the justice of his claims, and the injustice of his condemnation? Examine, then, into the other evidence, and in the meanwhile protest against the principles of the Talmud, and endeavour to deliver your brethren. There are multitudes of Jews who still groan under the superstitious laws respecting the washing of hands. In the book of daily prayer published here in London, the ordinance of washing of hands is acknowledged as Divine. On the 151st leaf, col. 2, you will find the following blessing:—

ברוך אתה ה׳ אלהינו מלך העולם אשר קדשנו במצותיו וצונו על נטילת ידים:

"Blessed art thou, O Lord our God! King of the universe! who hath sanctified us with his commandments, and commanded us to cleanse our hands." Now this is a positive untruth; God has not given the commandment respecting the washing of hands. And yet here your prayer-book solemnly tells him that he has. And this prayer-book has also put a rubric to this benediction, "When the children wash their hands in the morning, they are taught to say the following blessing." From which it appears that the Jewish children in England are still taught to acknowledge the Divine authority of the Talmud, for the only way in which that benediction can be defended, is by saying that the oral law is Divine, and that its commandments were given by God. It is therefore a holy and imperative duty on all those Israelites who reject Talmudic superstition and intolerance to have this benediction erased from their prayer-book, and to preserve the children from the infection of that law which persecutes the living and insults the dead.

No. XI.

RABBINIC ARTIFICES RESPECTING LEAVEN AT THE PASSOVER.

ONE of the many bright features in the national character of Israel is the devoted constancy, with which they have, in the most troublous times and under the most disastrous circumstances, celebrated the anniversary of their first great national deliverance. More than three thousand years have now rolled away since Israel's God heard the cries of the first-born in Egypt, and by slaying the first-born of their enemies, effected their salvation with a mighty hand and an outstretched arm. And yet the memory of that great event is still fresh in the hearts of the nation, and the children of Israel, wherever scattered, in the wilds of Poland, the coasts of Africa, or the torrid regions of India, as well as amongst ourselves, are now making consentaneous preparation for the approaching festival. Such constancy and such devotion bespeak minds of no ordinary mould, and naturally lead us to ask, how is it that the Lord does not now hear Israel's cries and prayers, which ascend from every region under heaven, and restore them to that place in His dispensations and that rank amongst the sons of men, which his Word assigns to them? A Christian would give the answer suggested by the New Testament, but we waive that at present. The oral law gives a reply the same in substance. It tells us that the mass of the nation has obscured the light of Divine revelation by the admixture of human inventions, that, therefore, a restoration would only be the establishment of error, and is consequently impossible. We have already given some proofs of this assertion, the Rabbinical laws relating to the Passover furnish us with many more, and to these the season of the year now naturally refers us.

Amongst the first directions relating to the Passover, the Word of God gives this plain command, "Even the first day shall ye put away leaven out of your houses." (Exod. xii. 15.) This is intelligible to the most illiterate, and easy to be obeyed, but the Rabbies have superadded a mass of explanations and observances, which tend only to perplex and to burden the conscience. In the first place they are not satisfied with the honest endeavour of an Israelite to obey the command of God, unless he does it according to the form and manner which they prescribe.

ומה היא השבתה זו האמורה בתורה היא שיבטלו
בלבו ויחשוב אותו כעפר ויטים בלבו שאין ברשותו
חמץ כלל. ושכל חמץ שברשותו הרי הוא כעפר
ודבר שאין בו צורך כלל:

" What is meant by the putting away (of leaven) mentioned in the law? It is this, that a man annul it in his heart, and count it as dust, and intend in his heart to have no leaven whatever in his possession, and that all the leaven in his possession shall be as dust, and of no necessity whatever." (Hilchoth Chometz Umatzah, c. ii. 2.) Here, then, they require a formal intention, but they have also prepared a form of words in which to clothe it.

כל חמירא וחמיעא דאיכא ברשותי דחמיתיה ודלא חמיתיה דבערתיה ודלא בערתיה לבטל ולהוי כעפרא דארעא :

" All manner of leaven that is in my possession, which I have seen, and which I have not seen ; which I have removed, and which I have not removed, shall be null, and accounted as the dust of the earth." (Levi's Prayers for the Passover, fol. 2, col. 1.) And to this form a rubric is added, " If the master is not at home, he annuls the leaven wherever he is." Now this may at first sight appear as a very innocent ceremony, but God warns us against all additions to His Word and commandments. It is in itself presumptuous, and as connected with the Rabbinical doctrine of merit, must have an injurious tendency upon the minds of the multitude. They will argue that by observing this form, they have fulfilled a commandment, and that consequently there is an additional sum of merit to be put to the credit side of their account, as a set off against their transgressions. And on the other hand, if they forget to go through this form at the right hour, and afterwards any leaven be found in their houses, the Rabbies bring them in guilty of transgressing two negative commandments, which they say is a more heinous offence than disobeying the affirmative precepts.

לפיכך אם לא בטל קודם שש ומשש שעות ולמעלה מצא חמץ שהיה דעתו עליו והיה בלבו ושכחו בשעת הביעור ולא בערו הרי זה עבר על לא יראה ולא ימצא שהרי לא בער ולא בטל :

" Therefore, if a man does not annul (the leaven) before the sixth hour, and afterwards from the sixth hour and onwards should find leaven, which was on his mind and in his heart, but he forgot it at the hour of removal, and did not remove it ; Behold, such an one has transgressed the command, ' It shall not be seen with thee' (Exod. xiii. 7), and also the command, It shall not be found in your houses' (Exod. xii. 19), for he neither removed it nor annulled it." (Hilchoth Chometz, c. iii. 8.) Now, can you believe that this decision is from God who

searcheth the heart? Can you believe that a man who had it
in his mind and heart to remove a piece of leaven according to
God's commandment, but whilst removing the rest forgot this
one piece, is to be brought in guilty, simply because he did not
observe a mere form, which God has nowhere commanded?
Or that he would not have been guilty, if he had repeated
some half dozen words prescribed by men, sinners like himself?
Very different is the declaration of God himself, יַעַן אֲשֶׁר הָיָה,
עִם לְבָבֶךָ "Because it was in thine heart" (1 Kings viii. 18):
he accepted the intention, and gave it the blessing of obedience.
The Rabbinic decision is, therefore, not of God, and goes far
towards overthrowing the claims of the whole oral law. But
the Rabbies were not satisfied with this invention of בִּטּוּל
חָמֵץ annulling the leaven, they have imposed upon the consciences of their followers another observance, utterly unknown
to Moses, and that is בְּדִיקַת חָמֵץ, the searching for leaven.

אוֹר לְאַרְבָּעָה עָשָׂר בְּנִיסָן קוֹדֶם צֵאת הַכּוֹכָבִים
בּוֹדְקִין אֶת הֶחָמֵץ לְאוֹר הַנֵּר שֶׁל שַׁעֲוָה הַיְחִידִי.
וּמִשֶּׁהִגִּיעַ זְמַנּוּ אָכוּר לַעֲשׂוֹת שׁוּם מְלָאכָה וְלֹא לֶאֱכוֹל
וְלֹא לִלְמוֹד :

" On the evening before the 14th of Nisan, before the coming
out of the stars, they are to search for the leaven by the light
of a single wax taper : and when the time draws near, it is unlawful to do any work, or to eat, or to study." (Passover
Prayers, fol. 1, col. 2.) For this command there is evidently
no foundation in the law of Moses. It is confessedly מִדִּבְרֵי
סוֹפְרִים of the words of the Scribes, and yet the most minute
directions are given, and the greatest attention required, as if it
had been from God himself, and various cases supposed where
a second search is necessary, as for instance :—

אִם רָאָה עַכְבָּר שֶׁנִּכְנַס לַבַּיִת וְחָמֵץ בְּפִיו אַחַר בְּדִיקָה
צָרִיךְ לִבְדּוֹק פַּעַם שְׁנִיָּה אַף עַל פִּי שֶׁמָּצָא פֵּרוּרִין
בְּאֶמְצַע הַבַּיִת אֵין אוֹמְרִין כְּבָר אָכַל אוֹתָהּ הַפַּת
בִּמְקוֹם זֶה וַהֲרֵי הַפֵּירוּרִין אֶלָּא חוֹשְׁשִׁין שֶׁמָּא הִנִּיחָהּ
בְּחוֹר אוֹ בְּחַלּוֹן וְאֵלּוּ הַפֵּירוּרִין שָׁם הָיוּ וּלְפִיכָךְ חוֹזֵר
וּבוֹדֵק. אִם לֹא מָצָא כְּלוּם הֲרֵי זֶה בּוֹדֵק כָּל הַבַּיִת
וְאִם מָצָא אוֹתָהּ הַפַּת שֶׁנָּטַל הָעַכְבָּר וְנִכְנַס אֵין צָרִיךְ
בְּדִיקָה :

" If, after the search, he see a mouse come into the house with
leaven in his mouth, it is necessary to search a second time.
And although he should find the crumbs about the house, he is
not to say, the mouse has eaten the bread long since, and these
are the crumbs, but, on the contrary, he must fear lest it should

have left the leaven in a hole or a window, and these crumbs were there before; he must therefore search again. If he find nothing, then he must search the whole house; but if he find the bread with which the mouse went off, then no further search is necessary." Another case of equal importance, and more ingenuity, is the following:—

נכנס עכבר לבית וככר בפיו ויצא עכבר משם
וככר בפיו אומרים הוא הראשון שנכנס הוא האחרון
שיצא ואינו צריך לבדוק . היה הראשון שנכנס שחור
וזה שיצא לבן צריך לבדוק . נכנס עכבר וככר בפיו
ויצאה משם חולדה וככר בפיה צריך לבדוק . יצאה
משם חולדה ועכבר וככר בפיה אינו צריך לבדוק
שזה הככר הוא שהיה בפי העכבר:

"If a mouse enter a house with bread in his mouth, and a mouse also go out of the same house with bread in his mouth, one may conclude that this is one and the self-same mouse, and it is not necessary to search. But if the former that entered was black, and the latter that went out white, a search is necessary. If a mouse went in with bread in his mouth, and a weasel come out with bread in her mouth, it is necessary to search. If a mouse and a weasel both go out, and bread in the weasel's mouth, there is no search required, for this is the identical bread that had been before in the mouse's mouth." (Hilchoth Chometz, c. ii.) We do not mean to say that this sort of wisdom was never found in Christians. We are well aware that the scholastic divines display much of the same perverse ingenuity, and the achievements of mice have figured in Gentile theology too, but we have renounced that whole system as contrary to the Word of God. You still adhere to the theology of the Scribes, and are now about to keep a solemn festival according to their ordinances. And yet you see how poor their view of true piety, and how perverse the application of their time and their ingenuity. The most unlearned Israelite who has read the law of Moses in its simple dignity, will know very well that when God commanded the Israelites to remove leaven from their houses, he did not mean that they should go and rummage out the mouse-holes, or spend their time looking after mice and weasels. If, instead of the oral law, you had read this in the New Testament, would you not have taken it as complete evidence against the claims of that book? and if St. Paul or St. Peter had given such commands to the Gentile converts, would you not have said, these men were either fools or knaves? But in the New Testament nothing like it is to be found. The precepts there given, and the instruction there conveyed, is all of a noble and dignified character, whilst the trifling and the folly still exist in the oral law handed down by those who rejected Jesus of Nazareth. If the testimony of men at all depends upon the wisdom of him who gives it, the testimony of the Scribes is not worth much. But the trifling is exceeded by the presumption. These men have said, as we have quoted above from your prayer-book, " that when the time for the search draws near, it is unlawful to do any work, or to eat, or to study;" so that the poor man is to give up his lawful business, the hungry man to abstain from his lawful food, and all to neglect even the reading of God's holy Word, in order to go and search into holes and corners, for that which they know is not to be found, or to find that which was laid in their way intentionally and for that very purpose. We ask you can this be from God, or, are the men who make the reading of God's Word give way to this ceremony, to be depended upon as teachers of the true religion?

But the oral law not only adds human inventions, but lays down principles which involve considerable difficulties, the solution of which requires no small share of ingenuity. For instance—

חמץ שעבר עליו הפסח אסור בהנאה לעולם :

" It is for ever unlawful to have any profit from leaven, that has existed during the season of the Passover." This is understood of leaven belonging to Israelites, and according to this all Israelites are obliged to sell, or give away, or lose all the leaven which they may have at the commencement of Passover, and of course, if they have much, the loss would be very serious. But the Rabbies who have made the difficulty, have also found various ways of evading it. One is by pledging the leaven with a certain form of words—

ישראל שהרהין חמצו אצל הגוי אם אמר לו אם
לא הבאתי לך מעות מכאן ועד יום פלוני קנה חמץ
זה מעכשיו הרי זה ברשות הגוי ואותו החמץ מותר
לאחר הפסח :

" An Israelite who has pawned his leaven to a Gentile, if he says to him, in case I do not bring thee the money from this time to a certain day, you have purchased this leaven from the present time; then this leaven is considered as in the possession of the Gentile, and it is lawful after the Passover." (Hilchoth Chometz, c. iv.) If, therefore, an Israelite, who has a large quantity of leaven, wishes to keep the commandment of removing all leaven from his possession, and at the same time to be able to resume the possession after the Passover; and to have the worldly gain too, as well the spiritual profit, he has nothing to do but to pawn it with this form of words. Now we ask every Jew of common sense, whether this be not a mere trick, an attempt to cheat one's own conscience, an unworthy artifice to serve God, and yet to avoid the loss which would result from a simple observance of the command? It is plain that a man who acts thus has no real intention of renouncing the possession of the leaven. And this is not a single case; the oral law is rich in such cases, as it allows a mock pawning, so it allows a mock sale or gift.

אעפ״י שהישראל מכירו לעכו״ם ויודע בו שלא
יגע בו כלל, אלא ישמרנו לו עד לאחר הפסח
ויחזור ויתננו לו מותר:

"Although the Israelite knows that the Gentile will not touch the leaven at all, but keep it for him until after the Passover, and will then return it to him, it is lawful." Of course a learned Israelite, acquainted with this provision of the oral law, will select a Gentile of this description to whom to sell or give his leaven, fully aware that after Passover it will be his again, and he may enjoy the profit. But suppose a Jew had lent money to a Gentile, and received the interest every week in bread, what is he to do? It is evident that at Passover he cannot make use of the bread on account of the leaven, neither after the Passover can he receive that bread nor money for it, as according to the oral law he must have no profit from leaven which has witnessed the Paschal week. This is a difficult case, but it is not of our making. The oral law which has proposed the difficulty, has also provided a solution.

ישראל שמקבל מגוי ככרות ברבית בכל שבוע
כתב אבי העזרי שיאמר לו קודם הפסח שיתן לו
בשבוע של פסח קמח או מעות ואז אפילו אם באו
אחר כך לחשבון מותר לקבל ממנו מה שלא קבל
בתוך הפסח:

"An Israelite who receives bread from a Gentile every week as interest, is, according to Avi Haezri, to tell him before the Passover, that in the Passover week he must give him flour or money, and then when they come to make up their accounts, he may receive from him that which he did not receive during the Passover." (Arbah. Turim. Orach Chaiim, sec. 450.) According to this simple device, merely by saying a few words, he can make that lawful, which before would have been a great sin. It is not needful even to intend to have money or flour, he may intend to have the leaven after the Passover; the words have the transforming efficacy. The same book gives Rashi's solution of another similar difficulty.

שאלה לרש״י, ישראל וגוי שיש להם תנור בשותפות

כיהו לומר לגוי טול אתה של פסח ואני אטול אחר
כך והשיב שיתנה קודם הפסח ויטול דמים מאות
שבוע :

"A question proposed to Rashi—Suppose that an Israelite
and a Gentile had an oven in partnership, shall he say to the
Gentile, Take thou the profit during the Passover, and I
will take afterwards? He replied, Let him make a bargain
before the Passover, and take the price of that week." (Ibid.)
A man of common sense will see that here, as in the other
cases, the Jew does really receive the profit from leaven in
existence during the Passover, and that whether he receive
the money or the profit before or afterwards, there is no real
difference in the circumstances of the transaction; one principle pervades all these decisions, and that is, evasion of what
is considered a Divine command. The man who gives away
the leaven with the full intention of resuming possession after
the Passover, and the man who sells only for the week, in full
persuasion that his right and interest remain, does in reality
neither give nor sell. There may be an outward appearance
of the thing, but God does not judge according to the
appearance; he looks on the intention of the heart. He is
not satisfied with the form of giving or selling, but looking
at the inmost thoughts of the soul, He sees that the man
does not wish nor intend to do either one or the other, and
marks him as a deliberate, and wilful transgressor. But we
appeal to every unsophisticated mind in Israel, would such a
system of evasion be considered as honourable, even according
to the maxims of this world? Or can that conduct, which
men would call dishonourable, be considered as an acceptable
service before God? But, above all, can it be the law given
to Moses by the God of truth? This it is which gives this
discussion all its importance. If the Talmud and all its
decisions were retained merely as a curious remnant of antiquity, as the effusions of a perverse ingenuity, or the waking dreams of scholastics, we might both pass it by with a
smile. But it is proposed as the law of God. It is the religion of the great majority of the Jewish people, and no
doubt at this very time, many an Israelite in Poland and
elsewhere, if not in England, is preparing a mock sale, or
drawing up a contract for the imaginary disposal of the
leaven in his possession, in obedience to the above directions.
They do it in simplicity, with a mistaken devotion. They
are misled; but does not a fearful load of responsibility rest
upon those Israelites who know better, and yet leave their
brethren in this grievous error, yea, and confirm them in it
by joining in all the ceremonies which that system prescribes?
Because of this system, the nation is still exiled from the land

of Israel. Because of this system, the anger of the Lord is not turned away, but His arm is stretched out still. If then you love your people—if you desire their national exaltation, and their eternal welfare, lift up your voice and protest against the oral law. Condemn the Scribes and Pharisees as the inventors of the system, and the first authors of that moral captivity in which the people has been held for so many centuries. Now when you remember the mercies of the Lord in delivering you from the house of bondage, make an effort to deliver your brethren from the more degrading chains of error and superstition. At the same time we would ask you to consider the case of so many of your nation, who, when these chains were rivetting, gloriously maintained their freedom, and have left us a collection of writings, entirely free from every trace of this mistaken ingenuity. We mean the disciples of Jesus of Nazareth. They, too, were Jews, children of Abraham, and of the stock of Israel. How is it then, that they who were condemned by the Talmudists as heretics, and propagators of a false religion, have left us the principles of a healthy, manly, and rational piety, whilst their judges and accusers have fallen headlong into error and even absurdity? If Jesus and his disciples were deceivers or fanatics, how is it that they were preserved from inculcating such false doctrines: and if the Scribes and Pharisees were right in condemning and persecuting them—were actually serving God in resisting false pretensions, how is it that they were given over to such delusions, and to such a system of trifling? That they were not infallible, the above extracts from the oral law prove beyond all controversy. They have altogether erred in the first element of acceptable worship, simplicity of intention and uprightness of heart. They have confounded the form with the reality of obedience to God's commands. And in all these things where they have erred, Jesus and his disciples have asserted and maintained the truth. Account for this fact. The Talmud tells you to light a taper and search for leaven in a mousehole, and to get rid of all in your possession by a fictitious contract. The New Testament says, "Purge out the old leaven, that ye may be a new lump, as ye are unleavened. For even Christ our Passover is sacrificed for us: therefore let us keep the feast not with old leaven, neither with the leaven of malice and wickedness; but with the unleavened bread of sincerity and truth." (1 Cor. v. 7, 8.)

No. XII.

THE PASSOVER A TYPE OF FUTURE DELIVERANCE.

THIS year, the Jewish and the Christian times for celebrating the Feast of the Passover nearly coincide ; and the coincidence ought to remind us both of that happy period, when all the children of man, so long divided, shall again be united into one great, holy, and happy family ; all rejoicing in the mercy and favour of their Heavenly Father, and all loving each other in sincerity and truth. To that period we look forward, and even now we use our humble endeavours to accelerate its approach. Yea, one of the reasons, why we endeavour to lead Israel to a rejection of the oral law, is because we firmly believe that it is one of the main hindrances in the way of their happiness and that of the nations of the world. We have no wish to rob you of any one blessing promised in the Word of God. We would not deprive you of one hope founded upon God's promises. On the contrary, we rejoice to think that notwithstanding all the vain traditions of the Scribes and Pharisees, it has pleased God to keep alive in your hearts the memory of his past mercy, and the hope of his future goodness. To the consideration of these two points, the law of Moses and your appointed prayers lead you at this season, and through the mercy of God, and the love of some of your brethren, we of the Gentiles have been brought to rejoice in similar considerations. Let us then endeavour to anticipate the future, and rejoice together even now, omitting on this solemn occasion a special discussion of the oral law. If God's mercy were all past, and only a matter of history, we might and ought to feel grateful for the benefits bestowed upon our fathers : our joy would, however, suffer a considerable diminution. But this is not the case. In the midst of your grateful acknowledgment for the wonders in Egypt, you can mingle a prayer for the future, and say,

לשנה הבאה בירושלים :

" Next year in Jerusalem."

רחם נא יי אלהינו על ישראל עמך ועל ירושלים
עירך ועל מזבחך ועל היכלך ׳ ובנה ירושלים עיר
הקודש במהרה בימינו והעלנו לתוכה ושמחנו בה :

" O Lord our God, have mercy, we beseech thee, upon Israel thy people, and upon Jerusalem thy city, and upon thine altar, and upon thy temple ; and build Jerusalem, the holy city, speedily, in our days, and bring us up into the midst of it, and make us glad therein." (Haggadah Shel Pesach.) And to this prayer we can say, "Amen" with all our hearts. The future restoration and blessedness of Israel is one of our fondest expectations; and whilst we contemplate the circumstances and the glory of the first Exodus, the Word of the living God leads us to look forward to that which is to come.

כימי צאתך מארץ מצרים אראנו נפלאות :

"According to the days of thy coming out of the land of Egypt will I show unto him marvellous things," is the promise by the mouth of Micah the prophet (c. vii. 10).

והחרים יהוה את לשון ים מצרים והניף ידו על
הנהר בעים רוחו והכהו לשבעה נחלים והדריך
בנעלים . והיתה מסלה לשאר עמו אשר ישאר מאשור
כאשר היתה לישראל ביום עלותו מארץ מצרים :

"And the Lord shall utterly destroy the tongue of the Egyptian sea, and with his mighty wind shall he shake his hand over the river, and shall smite it in the seven streams, and shall make men go over dry shod. And there shall be a highway for the remnant of his people, which shall be left from Assyria; like as it was to Israel in the day that he came up out of the land of Egypt," is the declaration of the Prophet Isaiah (xi. 15, 16). Seeing that neither of these declarations was fulfilled at the return from Babylon, nor at any period since, we firmly believe that they shall be fulfilled in the time to come, and that therefore the compilers of the Haggadah were fully warranted in intermingling, with their Passover thanksgivings, a prayer for the fulfilment of the promised mercies; and we do not scruple to say that in this respect, the Jewish Rabbies have been right, whilst many Christian interpreters have been wrong; though they might have known and given a true explanation of all similar passages, if they had only followed the plain words of their master, Jesus of Nazareth, "Think not that I am come to destroy the law or the prophets." (Matt. v. 17.) We make this remark to show that we do not condemn the Rabbies inconsiderately; but that we are willing to do them all justice, where their opinions agree with the Word of God. Their expectation of the future restoration of Israel is well founded, and their faith in the promises relating to it worthy of all imitation. Oh, that the whole nation had more of it—that their hearts were more directed to the land of their forefathers—that their thoughts were more full of the Divine promises. Then they would cry more earnestly to God, and He would "hear their groaning, and remember his covenant with Abraham, Isaac, and Jacob," as he did at the deliverance from Egypt. The careless and the ungodly deceive themselves

A TYPE OF FUTURE DELIVERANCE.   89

with the idea, that when God's time comes, the deliverance will
take place without any endeavour of theirs. Let them read the
law of Moses, and they will find that though God had promised
to bring their fathers out of Egypt, the deliverance itself was
preceded by a time of prayer and crying unto God. To
Abraham he had said.

יָדוֹעַ תֵּדַע כִּי גֵר יִהְיֶה זַרְעֲךָ בְּאֶרֶץ לֹא לָהֶם
וַעֲבָדוּם וְעִנּוּ אוֹתָם אַרְבַּע מֵאוֹת שָׁנָה... וְדוֹר רְבִיעִי
יָשׁוּבוּ הֵנָּה וגו׳ :

"Know of a surety that thy seed shall be a stranger in a land
that is not theirs, and shall serve them; and they shall afflict
them four hundred years..... But in the fourth generation they
shall come hither again," &c. (Gen. xv. 13, 16.) But this
promise was no warrant for their remaining careless, and at
ease; it was on the contrary a basis for earnest prayer and
supplication, and a plea for mercy. And, therefore, when the
time drew near, we read,

וַיֵּאָנְחוּ בְנֵי יִשְׂרָאֵל מִן הָעֲבוֹדָה וַיִּזְעָקוּ וַתַּעַל
שַׁוְעָתָם אֶל הָאֱלֹהִים מִן הָעֲבוֹדָה :

"And the children of Israel sighed by reason of the bondage,
and they cried, and their cry came up unto God, by reason of the
bondage." And God himself gives this as one reason why he
came to deliver them.

וְעַתָּה הִנֵּה צַעֲקַת בְּנֵי יִשְׂרָאֵל בָּאָה אֵלָי :

"Now, therefore, behold the cry of the children of Israel is
come unto me." (Exod. iii. 9.) Here, then, all Israelites, who
desire the fulfilment of God's promises should learn that state
of mind, which is a pre-requisite to the interposition of their
great deliverer. Israel can no more be delivered now than of
old, unless they earnestly desire deliverance. To what purpose
should He deliver and restore those, who care nothing about
the land of their forefathers, nor about the glory of the nation—
who say, We are very comfortable and happy here, and all we
desire is to be like the other nations (נִהְיֶה כַגּוֹיִם)—what good
would it do to us to return to the land of Israel? God's promises
are not to such grovelling and unbelieving spirits. Along with
his promise of mercy, he gives a command for continual supplication,

הַמַּזְכִּירִים אֶת יְהֹוָה אַל דֳּמִי לָכֶם . וְאַל תִּתְּנוּ דֳמִי
לוֹ עַד יְכוֹנֵן וְעַד יָשִׂים אֶת יְרוּשָׁלַיִם תְּהִלָּה בָּאָרֶץ :

"Ye that make mention of the Lord, keep not silence, and give
him no rest, till he establish, and till he make Jerusalem a praise

in the earth." (Isaiah lxii. 6, 7.) And in Ezekiel, after the declaration, "This land that was desolate is become like the garden of Eden; and the waste, and desolate and ruined cities, are become fenced, and are inhabited," &c., he adds—

כה אמר אדני יהוה עוד זאת אדרש לבית ישראל
לעשות להם :

"Thus saith the Lord God, I will yet for this be inquired of by the house of Israel, to do it for them." (Ezek. xxxvi. 37.) Upon which Rashi remarks—

אתפתה להם בתפלתם בדרשם אותי על זאת :

"I will be made favourable to them through their prayer, when they seek me with regard to this." Hence prayer is commanded; in Hosea we are told, that without prayer deliverance is impossible.

אלך אשובה אל מקומי עד אשר יאשמו ובקשו פני :

" I will go and return to my place, till they acknowledge their offence, and seek my face." (Hosea v. 15.) Let the children of Israel return then, and seek the Lord their God, and David their King, then they shall fear the Lord and His goodness in the latter days. (Hosea iii. 5.)

In the consideration of the deliverance from Egypt there is, however, one circumstance which should teach the Israelites to rejoice with trembling, and that is, that the majority of those, who went forth from Egypt, never entered the land of Israel, but died in the wilderness on account of their sin and unbelief. That which has happened, may happen again. Israel might be delivered again from the lands of their dispersion, and be led forth with a mighty hand, and outstretched arm, and with great signs and wonders, and yet after all die in their sins. Indeed, it is not merely a legitimate deduction from the past, but an express prophecy of the future. "As I live, saith the Lord God, surely, with a mighty hand, and with a stretched out arm, and with fury poured out, will I rule over you; and I will bring you out from the people, and will gather you out of the countries wherein ye are scattered, and with a mighty hand, and with a stretched out arm, and with fury poured out. And I will bring you into the wilderness of the people, and there will I plead with you face to face. Like as I pleaded with your fathers in the wilderness of the land of Egypt, so will I plead with you, saith the Lord God. And I will cause you to pass under the rod, and I will bring you into the bond of the covenant."

וברותי מכם המורדים והפושעים בי מארץ מגוריהם
אוציא אותם ואל אדמת ישראל לא יבוא :

"And I will purge out from among you the rebels, and them that transgress against me ; I will bring them forth from the country where they sojourn, and they shall not enter into the land of Israel." (Ezek. xx. 33—38.) Here then we see, whether we consider the past or the future, that a mere temporal deliverance is not sufficient—that God's greatest temporal blessings, and even his mighty signs and wonders, may lead us in the more dreadful and fatal captivity of sin. Surely if a miraculous deliverance could deliver the soul, those that saw the miracles in Egypt, and experienced the Lord's mercy in their preservation from the destroying angel, and in the passage through the Red Sea, ought to have been perfect in holiness. Yet we find, after all that they saw and heard, that they were a disobedient and faithless generation, and that they perished in the wilderness. The history, then, of this great deliverance reminds us in the most forcible manner of the bondage of sin, and the necessity of a more noble and gracious emancipation. Israel was in bondage in Egypt, and the Lord had compassion and delivered them. All mankind, Jews and Gentiles, are born slaves to sin, and dreadful is the misery which they have suffered, and hopeless the prospect for the future, unless God have provided a way of escape. Now is it likely that that God who had compassion on the Israelites in their temporal affliction, should look, unmoved and unpitying, upon the temporal and spiritual wretchedness of the whole human race? Is it conceivable that those gracious ears, which heard the cries of Israel in Egypt, should be deaf to the groans and lamentations of all the sons of men ? Is it consistent with the Bible-character of God to provide a remedy for temporal sorrow, and yet furnish no means of deliverance from everlasting woe ? Is it like our Heavenly Father to stretch out his hand to save a few of his children from Egypt, and yet leave the great majority to perish in ignorance and sin? Blessed be God, who, in his great mercy, sent Jews to our forefathers to tell us of the blood of another and greater passover, which can preserve Gentiles as well as Jews from the wrath to come.

משיח פסחנו נזבח בעדנו :

"Messiah, our passover, is sacrificed for us ;" and therefore we too keep the feast, and join in the hymn of thanksgiving, "Blessed be the Lord God of Israel, for He hath visited and redeemed his people." You remember the paschal lamb of Egypt. We can say—

הנה שה אלהים הנושא את חמאות כל העולם :

"Behold the Lamb of God, that taketh away the sin of the world." You remember the sprinkling of blood that delivered your fathers from temporal death. We rejoice because,

דם יֵשׁוּעַ הַמָּשִׁיחַ יְטַהֲרֵנוּ מִכָּל חֵטְא׃

"The blood of Jesus, the Messiah, cleanseth us from all sin."
You remember how, four days before the Passover, it was necessary to select a lamb without spot and without blemish. We think of the true Paschal Lamb, the Messiah, how, four days before the great sacrifice, he came up to Jerusalem, and was examined before the tribunals, and declared to be without sin. Pilate's testimony was, "Ye have brought this man unto me, as one that perverteth the people; and, behold, I, having examined him before you, have found no fault in this man touching those things whereof ye accuse him: no, nor yet Herod: for I sent you to him; and lo, nothing worthy of death is done unto him." (Luke xxiii. 14, 15.) You remember how the destroying angel passed over the houses where the blood was sprinkled: we look forward to that more dreadful time, when he shall come as the Psalmist describes:—

יָבֹא אֱלֹהֵינוּ וְאַל יֶחֱרַשׁ אֵשׁ לְפָנָיו תֹּאכֵל וּסְבִיבָיו
נִשְׂעֲרָה מְאֹד׃ יִקְרָא אֶל הַשָּׁמַיִם מֵעָל וְאֶל הָאָרֶץ
לָדִין עַמּוֹ׃ אִסְפוּ לִי חֲסִידָי כֹּרְתֵי בְרִיתִי עֲלֵי זָבַח׃

"Our God shall come, and shall not keep silence: a fire shall devour before him, and it shall be very tempestuous round about him. He shall call to the heavens from above, and to the earth, that he may judge his people. Gather my saints together unto me: those *that have made a covenant with me by sacrifice.*" (Ps. l. 3—5.) And we hope to be found amongst that number, and that the blood of the true Sacrifice will then deliver us. It is evident that the Psalmist here is not speaking of the sacrifices of the temple, for immediately after we read—

שִׁמְעָה עַמִּי וַאֲדַבֵּרָה יִשְׂרָאֵל וְאָעִידָה בָּךְ אֱלֹהִים
אֱלֹהֶיךָ אָנֹכִי׃ לֹא עַל זְבָחֶיךָ אוֹכִיחֶךָ וְעוֹלוֹתֶיךָ לְנֶגְדִּי
תָמִיד׃ לֹא אֶקַּח מִבֵּיתְךָ פָר מִמִּכְלְאֹתֶיךָ עַתּוּדִים׃

"Hear, O my people, and I will speak; O Israel, and I will testify against thee: I am God, even thy God. I will not reprove thee for thy sacrifices or thy burnt offerings, to have been continually before me. I will take no bullock out of thy house, nor he goats out of thy folds." Here God plainly excepts the offerings of bulls and goats, and thereby overthrows the exposition of Rashi and others, who say that the covenant and sacrifices here alluded to are the same as those described at the giving of the law, when Moses said, "Behold the blood of the covenant," &c. (Exod. xxiv. 8.) The sacrifices then offered were "burnt-offerings and peace-offerings of oxen," which God here declares that he will not accept. Besides, God is not speaking of many sacrifices, but of one sacrifice עֲלֵי זָבַח

He is moreover speaking of one great sacrifice, by virtue of which sinful men may stand before him as saints at the great day of judgment, and obtain mercy. This certainly cannot mean the sacrifices of the Mosaic covenant at Sinai, for by reason of that sacrifice, they will appear as guilty sinners who have broken God's covenant, as he himself says—

אשר המה הפרו את בריתי :

"Which my covenant they brake." (Jer. xxxi. 32.) At that solemn hour the Mosaic covenant will only condemn, and therefore cannot be meant here. Indeed the rabbies appear to have felt the untenableness of this exposition, and therefore invented another figurative one—

ויש דרש כי על ברית מילה שהחזיקו בה ישראל בגלות :

"There is also an allegorical interpretation referring it to the covenant of circumcision, which Israel has faithfully adhered to in the captivity." (Kimchi, in loc.) But this exposition is as unfounded as the former. Circumcision is never called a sacrifice in Scripture. Neither will it serve a man in the day of judgment. What then is the sacrifice which is here intended? We answer, the true Passover, the blood of the Messiah, whereby the new covenant is ratified. Some object that the shedding of blood is altogether unnecessary—that if God will forgive at all, he can forgive without atonement or sacrifice. But this objection will equally affect the sacrifice of the first Passover. On the very same grounds, we may say, What necessity was there for killing a lamb, and sprinkling its blood upon the door-posts? The directions given by Moses are very striking—"Kill the passover. And ye shall take a bunch of hyssop, and dip it in the blood that is in the bason, and strike the lintel and the two side posts with the blood that is in the bason; and none of you shall go out at the door of his house until the morning. For the Lord will pass through to smite the Egyptians; and when he seeth the blood upon the lintel, and on the two side posts, the Lord will pass over the door, and will not suffer the destroyer to come in unto your houses to smite you." (Exod. xii. 21—23.) Surely the blood was not necessary to make known to him which house belonged to an Israelite. He could have saved them as well without the blood as with it. Why then destroy the life of a lamb, and give them all this trouble? Suppose that an Israelite had thus argued at that time, had refused to kill the passover, or having killed it, had neglected to sprinkle the blood, or having done both, was not content to abide in his house, but had gone forth before the morning, what would have been the consequence? Certain punishment. God was indeed determined to save Israel, but only in a certain way: and he that did not choose to submit to God's method, would naturally lose the benefit of his appointment. Our business is not to argue with God, but having ascertained His will, to submit to it. Inquire, then, what God means by "his saints who have made a covenant with Him by sacrifice;" and endeavour to enter into that covenant, that when He appears to judgment, ye may be gathered unto Him. If the Christian view be not the true one, then since the destruction of the temple there has been no sacrifice, and no way of entering into that covenant with Him. You observe the season—you abstain from leaven —but there is no sacrifice. The main, yea the essential, element of the Passover is wanting. The lamb cannot be slain. And even if it could be, if you had again a temple and a high-priest, and all the service of a sanctuary, still the sacrifice of the Passover would only be a memorial of mercies long since gone by. It would be no real atonement for your sins, and when you had slain it, and eaten of it, the question would still remain, How am I, a sinner, to appear in the presence of the righteous Judge?

The first part of this paper will have shown you, that we are firm believers in the future glory and blessedness of Israel; that we do not, therefore, in offering you our hope for eternity, wish to deprive you of your own hopes for time. No, we wish you every blessing which God has promised by the mouth of Moses and the prophets, and can affectionately join in the words—

לשנה הבאה בירושלים :

If it should please God to spare us all to see the re-union of all the families of the earth, we should rejoice to unite with others in acknowledging "that ye are the seed whom the Lord has blessed." But we should rejoice a thousandfold more to meet you in the heavenly Jerusalem, and to mingle our voices with yours in singing,

"Worthy is the Lamb that was slain to receive power, and riches, and wisdom, and strength, and honour, and glory, and blessing." Amen.

No. XIII.

SEVERITY OF THE RABBINIC ORDINANCES.

THE feast of the Passover, ordained as a memorial of past mercies, has at the same time served to remind us of another deliverance necessary both for Jew and Gentile, and also of a happy time when "there shall be one fold and one shepherd"—"One LORD and His name One." But the blessed anticipations of the future cannot, and ought not, withdraw our thoughts from the reality of the present. That happy time is not yet come. Jews and Christians are not yet agreed as to the articles of faith; and this feast of the Passover especially directs our attention to the cause and origin of the difference. At this solemn season of the year, Jesus of Nazareth was condemned by the Scribes and Pharisees, and by them delivered to the Roman power to be executed as a malefactor. One portion of the Jewish nation, and that the majority, concurred in the judgment of the rulers. Another portion, at first small, but ultimately considerable in number and station, arraigned the justice of the sentence, and professed their faith in His Messiahship. The question between Jews and Christians at present is, which of these two portions of the Jewish nation was in the right. In these papers we have taken up this simple position, that the religious system of those who rejected Jesus of Nazareth is contrary to the law and the prophets, and is therefore false; whilst the doctrines of Him, that was rejected, are in conformity with those writings, and must therefore be true. When we say that the rabbinical system is false, we do not mean that the Pharisees held no truth. On the contrary, we showed in our last number that some of their expectations were agreeable to the Word of God, and therefore true. All we intend is, that the peculiarities of Rabbinism of which the system is composed are erroneous. The laws relating to the present festival furnish us with abundant proof of our assertion. The Divine commands relating to it exhibit the care, consideration, and condescension of God in providing an opportunity of instruction, a time of relaxation, and a season of joy for the poor as well as the rich. The rabbinical laws, on the other hand, are burdensome, oppressive, and hurtful, especially to the poor and unlearned.

We take our first proof from one of the laws relating to the ארבע כוסות "the four cups"—God has given a simple command to Israel to make known to their children the reasons for the feast. והגדת לבנך וגו׳ "And thou shalt declare unto thy son in that day, saying, This is done because of that which the Lord did unto me, when I came forth out of Egypt." (Exod. xiii. 8.) In order to fulfil this command, a sort of liturgy has been composed, much of which is solemn and beautiful: and a ceremonial appointed, of which one ordinance is, that there should be four cups or glasses of wine.

וכל אחד ואחד בין אנשים בין נשים חייב לשתות
בלילה הזה ארבע כוסות של יין ואין פוחתין לו מהן:

"All persons, whether men or women, are obligated on this night to drink four cups (or glasses) of wine, and this number is not to be diminished." (Hilchoth Chometz, c. vii.) As to the ceremony of the four cups, the circumstances connected with them evidently show that they are not for the purpose of revelry, but part of a solemn religious observance.

כל כוס וכוס מארבע כוסות הללו מברך עליו
ברכה בפני עצמה. כוס ראשון אומר עליו קידוש
היום. כוס שני קורא עליו את ההגדה. כוס שלישי
מברך עליו ברכת המזון. כוס רביעי גומר עליו את
ההלל ומברך עליו ברכת השיר:

"Over each of these four cups a benediction is to be pronounced. Over the first cup is said the consecration of the day. Over the second cup the Haggadah is read. Over the third cup the benediction for food is pronounced. And over the fourth the Hallel is completed, and the benediction for the song pronounced." (Ibid.) With a solemn religious ordinance it is not for us to find fault. On the contrary, in these and their other prayers, we earnestly wish the Jews the blessing of God, and the spirit of grace and supplication. But when we find this human institution imposed as a burden upon the conscience, and the observance of it exacted from those who have not the means of gaining their daily bread, we must protest against it as harsh and oppressive. Now in the oral law this requirement is made.

מי שאין לו יין עבר אדרבנן דאמרי ולא יפחתו
לו מארבע כוסות, וצריך למכור מה שיש לו לקיים
מצות חכמים ולא יסמוך על הפת שאם קיים כוס
אחד לא קיים השלשה לכן ימכור מה שיש לו ולהוציא
הוצאות עד שימצא יין או צמוקים:

"Whosoever has not got wine transgresses a command of the Rabbies, for they have said, that there is to be no diminution from the four cups. And it is necessary to sell what he has in order to keep the command of the wise men. He is not to depend upon the bread, for if he fulfil the command concerning one cup, he has not fulfilled that respecting the three. Therefore let him sell what he has, and furnish the expense, until he

SEVERITY OF THE RABBINIC ORDINANCES.

procure wine or raisins." (Arbah Tur. Orach Chaiim, 483.) It may be replied, that the congregation furnishes those who have not the means. But what is to become of those who have displeased the dispensers of the congregation's bounty, or what is a Jew to do, who is living alone in the midst of Gentiles, as is frequently the case, particularly in this country? If he be a conscientious Rabbinist he must either grieve his conscience by transgression, or sell what he may not be well able to spare. The same may also be said of the unleavened cakes. The Rabbies have given so many directions about the lawful mode of preparing them, as to make it almost impossible for a Jew, living at a distance from a congregation, to keep the command, and to keep the poor in a state of perpetual bondage to the synagogue, if they wish to be supplied by the bounty of the congregation.

But this utter want of consideration for the poor is more strikingly displayed in the institution and exaction of a second holy day, where God has required the observance of only one, as the Rabbies themselves acknowledge in the following passage:—

ששת ימים האלה שאסרן הכתוב בעשיית מלאכה
שהן ראשון ושביעי של פסח וראשון וח'· של חג
הסוכות וביום חג השבועות ובאחד לחודש השביעי
הן הנקראים ימים טובים. ושביתת כולן שוה שהן
אסורין בכל מלאכת עבודה חוץ ממלאכה שהיא לצורך
אכילה שנאמר אך אשר יאכל לכל נפש וכו':

"These are the six days on which the Scripture has forbidden the doing of work. The first and seventh day of Passover: the first and eighth day of the Feast of Tabernacles: the day of the Feast of Weeks, and the first day of the seventh month; and these days are called holy days. The sabbatism of all is alike; it is unlawful on them to do any manner of work, excepting that which is necessary for the preparation of food, as it is said, 'Save that which every man must eat.' (Exod. xii. 16.)" (Hilchoth Jom. Tov., c. i. 1.) Here is an express recognition of what God has commanded. And yet the Scribes were not content with this ordinance of God, but have appointed the observance of a second day on all these occasions, and have annexed the sentence of excommunication to any transgression of their command.

ואנו שעושים שני ימים טובים כל מה שאסור בראשון
אסור גם בשני. ומנדין עליו למי שמזלזל בו. ואם
הוא צורבא מרבנן אין מחמירין לנדותו אלא מלקין
אותו:

"To us, who observe two days, every thing that is forbidden on the first day, is also forbidden on the second day; and whosoever makes light of it, is to be excommunicated. But if he be an acute Talmudist the excommunication is not to be severe, only he is to be beaten." (Orach Chaiim, 496.) In the Yad Hachasakah we find the same severity, and the same exception.

יום טוב שני אף על פי שהוא מדברי סופרים כל
דבר שאסור בראשון אסור בשני . וכל המחלל יום
טוב שני ואפילו של ראש השנה בין בדבר שהוא
משום שבות ובין במלאכה בין שיצא חוץ לתחום
מכין אותו מכת מרדות או מנדין אותו אם לא יהיה
מן התלמידים :

"Although the second holy day is only of the words of the Scribes, every thing that is forbidden on the first day, is forbidden on it also. And every one who professes the second holy day, even that of the new year, whether it be in a matter relating to the sabbatism, or by work, or by going beyond the Sabbath limit, is to receive the beating denounced against rebellion, or to be excommunicated, unless he be a learned man." (Hilchoth Jom. Tov., c. i. 24.) The hardship, oppression, and severity of this ordinance are apparent at first sight, and are severely felt by many a poor Jew in this city, who hardly knows how to get bread for himself and his children. In every case it robs him in one week of two days, on which God has allowed him to work, and to endeavour to gain a livelihood. But if the first day of a festival happen on a Thursday, then that day, Friday, and Saturday, he dare not do anything to earn the means of subsistence for his family. Sunday is the Christian Sabbath, so that in one week four successive days are lost, and in the following week four more. What, then, is the poor man to do? If he does not work, his children may starve; if he makes use of the time allowed him by his merciful God, and pursues his daily occupations, he transgresses a command of unmerciful men, and renders himself obnoxious to his more bigoted brethren. True that they cannot now beat him with the stripes awarded to the rebellious, and that they would hardly dare, in the present state of things, to excommunicate him; yet there are other ways and means of persecution more secret, but equally sure. But whatever be the present circumstances, the cruel and oppressive spirit of the oral law remains the same. If the Rabbinists had the power, they would soon proceed to excommunicate and flog all the profaners of the second holy day. We appeal, then, to the common sense of every Jew, and ask him, What right have men to rob the poor of that time which God hath given them? or to sentence a man who only goes to get bread for his children, and in so doing transgresses none of God's commandments, to excommunication or flogging, especially to that severe species of flogging here specified?

The flogging here spoken of is called מכת מרדות, "the flogging of rebellion," and is altogether different from that merciful punishment prescribed in the law. God says, "And it shall be, if the wicked man be worthy to be beaten, that the judge shall cause him to lie down, and to be beaten before his face, according to his fault by a certain number. Forty stripes he may give him, and not exceed; lest, if he should exceed, and beat him above these with many stripes, then thy brother should seem vile to thee." (Deut. xxv. 2, 3.) Here, as everywhere else, in the midst of judgment, God remembers mercy. The Rabbies, never satisfied unless they can add to, or diminish from, God's commandments, have reduced the number to thirty-nine, lest they should make any mistake. But to compensate for this diminution, they have invented "the flogging of rebellion," which is without number and without mercy, as may be seen from the following explanation of the Baal Aruch:—

מי שעובר על מצות עשה שאמר לו עשה סוכה
עשה לולב ואינו עושה מכין אותו עד שתצא נשמתו
בלא אומד ובלא מכח משולשה וכן מי שעובר על
דברי חכמים מכין אותו בלא מספר ובלא מנין ובלא
אומד ולמה קורין אותו מכת מרדות שמרד בדברי
תורה ובדברי סופרים:

"Whosoever transgresses an affirmative commandment, for instance, he was commanded to make a tabernacle, or a lulav, and did not, he is to be beaten until his soul go out, without any consideration of his strength, and without dividing the flogging into three. And, in like manner, whosoever transgresses the words of the wise men, he is to be beaten without number, and without consideration. Why is this called the flogging of rebellion? Because he has rebelled against the words of the law and against the words of the Scribes." (Baal Aruch, in voc.) This, then, is the punishment denounced against those who try to get bread for their children on the second holy day; a punishment invented by the Rabbies themselves, not against the immoral or the irreligious, but against the transgressors of their own commandments. What could have been the spirit, the temper, the religious feeling of such men? Had they any perception of the merciful character of the law, or any resemblance to the compassionate nature of the God of Israel? Can you put any confidence in the religious instruction of those who would excommunicate or flog a fellow-creature to death because he obeyed the instincts of nature, because he could not stay at home and listen to the cries of his famishing children, but went forth, to procure them food in the manner, and on the day which God had permitted him to do so? These are the men who condemned Jesus of Nazareth to death, and this is the religion of the oral law, which you prefer to the mild and merciful doctrines of Christianity. If Rabbinism had continued in its power, you would have been exposed to all the severity of this intolerance. The triumph of Christianity has, in this respect, also been a blessing to the Jewish nation, and the power of the followers of Jesus of Nazareth protects you from excommunication and corporal chastisement.

The cruelty and hardship of the imposition of a second holy day, with such a punishment annexed appears not only from the circumstance of its being altogether a human institution, but further, that the original object of its institution has long since ceased. The Scribes appointed the observance of two days at a time, when the feast-days were fixed by the appearance of the moon, lest those at a distance from Jerusalem should keep a wrong day, but now that they are fixed by calculation, this is altogether unnecessary.

בזמן הזה שאין שם סנהדרין ובית דין של ארץ
ישראל קובעין על חשבון זה היה מן הדין שיהיו
בכל המקומות עושין יום טוב אחד בלבד אפילו
המקומות הרחוקות שבחוץ לארץ כמו בני ארץ
ישראל שהכל על חשבון אחד סומכין וקובעין אבל
תקנת חכמים הוא שיזהרו במנהג אבותיהם שבידם:

"In the present time, when there is no Sanhedrin, nor house of judgment in the land of Israel, the feasts are fixed by calculation, and therefore all places, even those that are remote from the land of Israel, ought properly to observe only one day as a holy day, as well as the inhabitants of that country, for all depend on and fix the feast by one and the same calculation; but it is an ordinance of the wise men to adhere diligently to the custom of their forefathers." (Hilchoth Kiddush Hachodesh, c. v. 5.) There is, therefore, no excuse for this burden imposed upon the poor, and much less for the cruel punishments, denounced against those who cease to observe what is confessedly an useless custom. How different is the doctrine of Christianity with respect to such days. No excommunication, no flogging, no imposing of burdens upon the consciences of our brethren. The New Testament condemns even all rash judgment in such matters. It says, "Who art thou, that judgeth another man's servant? To his own master he standeth or falleth. Yea he shall be holden up, for God is able to make him stand. One man esteemeth one day above another; another esteemeth every day alike. Let every man be fully persuaded in his own mind. He that regardeth the day, regardeth it to the Lord; and he that regardeth not the day, to the Lord he doth not regard it. He that eateth, eateth to the Lord, for he giveth God thanks; and he that eateth not, to the Lord he eateth not, and giveth God thanks. For none of us liveth to himself, and no man dieth to himself. For whether we live, we live unto the Lord, and whether we die, we die unto the Lord; whether we live, therefore, or die, we are the Lord's." (Rom. xiv. 2—8.) Here is the spirit of love and mercy, and therefore the spirit of God. How is it, then, that Jesus and his disciples were able to overcome the prejudices of their times, and to stem the torrent of authority and learning, which was altogether in favour of the opposite opinions? How is it, if they were impostors and deceivers that they have left a tolerant and merciful system, whilst the Scribes and Pharisees, who, according to that supposition, were the true servants of God, have left a religion of oppression and cruelty? "Ye shall know them by their fruits. Do men gather grapes of thorns, or figs of thistles? Even so every good tree bringeth forth good fruit, and every evil tree bringeth forth evil fruit. A good tree cannot bring forth evil fruit, neither can a corrupt tree bring forth good fruit." (Matt. vii. 16—18.) This is certainly true in nature. Now the Pharisees have brought forth evil fruit, Jesus of Nazareth and his disciples have brought forth good fruit. What is the conclusion from such premises?

But we have hitherto spoken only generally of the Institution of a second holy day, we have yet to consider the details of the commandment, which will show still more clearly that "The Scribes and Pharisees bind heavy burdens, and grievous to be borne, and lay them on other men's shoulders." (Matt. xxiii. 4.) They are, as usual, most exact in defining what is and is not work. They say,

כל שאסור בשבת בין משום שהוא דומה למלאכה
או מביא לידי מלאכה בין שהוא משום שבות הרי
הוא אסור ביום טוב אלא אם כן היה צורך אכילה
וכיוצא בה . או דברים שהם מותרים ביום טוב כמו
שיתבאר בהלכות אלו . וכל שאסור לטלטלו בשבת
אסור לטלטלו ביום טוב אלא לצורך אכילה וכיוצא
בה וכל שמותר בשבת מותר ביום טוב :

" Every thing that is unlawful on the Sabbath, either because it has the appearance of work, or because it leads to work, or on account of sabbatising, is unlawful on a holy day, unless it be necessary for the preparation of food, and the like, or such things as are allowed on the holy day, as will be explained in these constitutions. And every thing that it is unlawful to move on the Sabbath, is also unlawful to be moved on the holy day, unless it be necessary for food : and every thing that is lawful on the Sabbath is lawful on a holy day." (Hilchoth Jom. Tov., c. i. 17.) This law effectually ties up the hands of the poor Rabbinist. He not only dare not pursue his trade, but he dare not make any domestic arrangement, that might promote order in his house, or conduce to his comfort. He must not write a letter to his friends, nor even extinguish a fire, though it be to save his property.

אף על פי שהותרה הבערה ביום טוב שלא לצורך אסור לכבות את האש אפילו הובערה לצורך אכילה. שהכבוי מלאכה ואין בו צורך אכילה כלל. וכשם שאין מכבין את האש כך אין מכבין את הנר ואם כבה לוקה כמי שארג או בנה ... אין מכבין את הדליקה כדי להציל ממון ביום טוב כדרך שאין מכבין בשבת אלא מניחה ויוצא :

" Although it has been pronounced lawful to kindle fire on the holy day, even where not absolutely necessary, yet it is unlawful to extinguish fire, even though it had been kindled for the preparation of food; for the extinguishing of fire is work, and is not at all necessary for the dressing of food. And as fire is not to be extinguished, so neither is a candle to be extinguished and whosoever extinguishes is to be flogged, just as he that weaves or builds. .... Fire is not to be extinguished, in order to save property on a holy day, no more than on the Sabbath. On the contrary, one lets it burn and goes away." (Ibid., c. iv. 2, 4.) In the Arbah Turim this law is laid down with still more precision.

אסור לכבות את הדליקה ביום טוב אפילו רואה את ביתו שנשרף. אסור לכבות הבקעת בין אם מכבה מפני שחס עליה שלא תשרף בין אם מכבה שלא תתעשן הקדרה. ודוקא כשאפשר לו להצילה מעישון בלא כבוי כגון שיסירנה מאש זה ויתננה על אש אחר אבל אם אין לו אש אחר ואם לא יכבנה תתעשן הקדרה מותר לכבותה כדי שלא תתעשן הקדרה :

" It is unlawful to extinguish fire on a holy day, even though a man should see his house burning. It is unlawful to extinguish split wood, either for the sake of saving it from being burned, or to keep a pot from being smoked, that is to say, if he can keep it from being smoked without extinguishing the fire, as by removing it from one fire to another. But if he has not got another fire, and if the pot must be smoked unless he extinguish it, then the extinguishing is lawful, that the pot may not be smoked." (Orach Chaiim, 514.) Now we put it to the common sense of every Jew, whether in these laws there be justice, mercy, and religion; or hardship, inconsideration, and absurdity?

No. XIV.

SEVERITY AND ARTIFICE.

THE oral law says, as we saw in our last, that, on a holy day, it is unlawful to extinguish a fire in order to save a man's house and property, but that it is lawful, on the same day, to do the very same thing to keep a pot of cookery from being smoked. This sentence may perhaps appear wise and pious to those who have got more houses than one, or the means of procuring them; but with respect to the poor man, who in such a case loses his all, and must see his family left without a roof over their heads or a bed to lie on, this decision is as cruel as it is senseless. There is, however, a tyranny more dreadful than that which affects only the temporal condition of men. The spiritual despotism, which burdens and fetters the conscience and enslaves the soul, is more intolerable still. Under temporal losses a man's mind may be supported by a sense of religion; but when his religion, by the multiplicity and rigour, and intricacy of its requirements, becomes his tormentor, man is bereft of his last consolation. The religion of the oral law appears to us to be of this character, and its enactments with regard to the holy days will serve to justify this our opinion. We have seen already, that it requires two days' cessation from business, where God requires only one, and that the general rule is, Whatsoever is unlawful on the Sabbath, is unlawful on the holy day, with one exception. The Scribes, however, were not content with this, they have contrived to invent something, which, though lawful on the Sabbath, is on these days unlawful. They say, that there is a certain class of things which, if not deliberately destined the day before for the use of the holy day, are unlawful. To this class they give the name of מוּקְצָה *Muktzeh*, which literally signifies "separated or cut off," but which, for shortness' sake and for want of a better word in English, we shall call "*undestined*."

ויש ביום טוב מה שאין בשבת איסור מוקצה
שהמוקצה אסור ביום טוב ומותר בשבת מפני שיום
טוב קל משבת אסרו בו המוקצה שמא יבואו לזלזל בו :

"There is on the holy day one thing which is not found on the Sabbath, and that is, the forbidding of the *undestined*, for the *undestined is* unlawful on the holy day, and is lawful on the Sabbath. Because the holy day is less sacred than the Sabbath, they forbade the *undestined* on that day, lest persons should be led to make light of it." (Hilchoth Jom. Tov. c. i. 17.)

כיצד תרנגולת העומדת לגדל ביצים ושור העומד
לחרישה ויוני שובך ופירות העומדין לסחורה כל
אלו וכיוצא בהן מוקצה הן ואסור לאכול מהן ביום
טוב עד שיכין אותה מבערב ויחשוב עליהם לאכילה :

"For instance, a hen that is kept for the purpose of hatching eggs, and an ox that is kept for ploughing, pigeons in a pigeon house, and fruits that are kept for sale, all these and the like are *undestined*, and it is unlawful to eat of them on a holy day, unless a man destine them on the eve preceding, and form an intention to eat them." (Ibid.) By this law a numerous class of things is forbidden, which God has no where forbidden, and fresh chains are forged for the conscience. An unlearned man can hardly tell what does or does not belong to the class, and if he be in doubt must first go to the rabbi, before he can eat or make use of any thing doubtful; for this definition extends not only to eatables, but to other things, as for instance, fuel. Suppose, for example, that a man or a family had eaten nuts or almonds on the eve of the holy day, is it lawful or unlawful to burn the shells on the holy day itself? The Word of God leaves the Jew at perfect liberty to do as he pleases, but the oral law tells him that he may by doing either commit a great sin. If he cannot resolve his scruples in this matter, he must be content to go to the rabbi or some learned man, and submit to his decision, and thus every unlearned and devout Jew is brought into complete captivity to the decisions of the learned. Another very similar law, and tending to the same bondage, is that which makes any thing that is born or comes into existence on the holy day, unlawful.

וכשם שהמוקצה אסור ביום טוב כך הנולד אסור .
חול מכין לשבת וחול מכין ליום טוב אבל אין יום
טוב מכין לשבת ולא שבת מכינה ליום טוב . לפיכך
ביצה שנולדה ביום טוב אחר השבת אסורה :

"And as the undestined is unlawful on the holy day, so also what is born is unlawful. On a common day a man may destine things for the Sabbath, and also for the holy day. But on a holy day things may not be destined for the Sabbath, nor on the Sabbath for the holy day, therefore an egg that is laid on the holy day after the Sabbath is unlawful." (Ibid.) Now not to speak of the minute trifling of this law, there are cases where it may become very oppressive. Suppose that by some means an unlawful egg should get amongst a number of lawful eggs, they would all become unlawful.

ואפילו נתערבה באלף כולן אסורות :

"Yea, though it should be mixed up amongst a thousand, they are all unlawful." It is true that the rabbies endeavour to guard against such an accident, by forbidding the removal of such an egg on the holy day; but a Gentile or a child might, through inadvertently putting such an egg amongst others, produce great inconvenience or even loss, and to this the poor man must submit, or burden his conscience with a wilful transgression. But this law forbidding to eat or move whatsoever comes into existence on the holy day extends beyond the class of eatables. Wood accidentally broken on this day belongs to this class, and it is therefore unlawful to use it as fuel, or to move it. In like manner, ashes of wood that has been burnt on the holy day, is considered as having come into existence, and it is a sin to move it, when once it has cooled. And again, if a fire should go out on the holy day, it is a grave question whether the fuel that remains may be kindled again.

Thus the conscience is burdened with definitions of unlawful, but the directions about things lawful are quite as numerous and perplexing. For instance, it is lawful to make a fire on a holy day, and to put on the pot for cooking, but an unlearned man or woman may commit a sin in the mode of doing it, and, therefore, the Baal Turim says,

כשעושה האש ונותן עליה קדירה צריך ליזהר
בסדור העצים ובנתינת הקדירה עליהם שלא יחיה
דומה לבנין דאמר רב יהודה מדורתא מלמעלה
למטה שרי . ממטה למעלה אסור :

"When one makes a fire and puts on a pot, it is necessary to be very careful in the arranging of the wood, and the mode of setting the pot upon it, so that there should be no resemblance to building, for Rav Judah has said, every pile of wood begun from the top to the bottom is lawful, from the bottom to the top is unlawful." (Orach Chaiim, 502.) For this reason very minute directions are given for the performance of each of these operations. The fire is to be made in the following manner:—

העושה מדורה ביום טוב כשהוא עורך את העצים
אינו מניח זה על זה עד שיסדר המערכה מפני
שנראה כבונה . ואף על פי שהוא בנין עראי אסור
אלא או שופך העצים בערבוב או עורך בשנוי . כיצד
מניח עץ למעלה ומניח אחר תחתיו ואחר תחתיו
עד שהוא מגיע לארץ :

"He that makes a pile of fire on a holy day, when he is arranging the wood, is not to lay one piece upon another, so as to make an orderly arrangement, for that looks as if he were building; and although it be an accidental building it is unlawful. But either he is to scatter the wood in confusion, or to arrange them with some variation. How so? He is to lay one piece at the top, and another piece under it, and another under that, until it reaches the ground." (Hilchoth Jom. Tov. c. iv. 14.) In like manner the pot is not to be placed upon stones, or whatever else is to support it, but is to be held up, and the support placed under it; and so with other things. The great principle is, that some difference is to be made between the work done on the holy day and on a common day, and therefore in the carrying of wine, or wood, or other things, they are not to be carried in a basket, nor as usual, but on the shoulder or in some extraordinary way. Now, as the speculations of men who had not much to do, or who chose to devote the powers that God had given them to such minutiæ, these things hardly appear as harmless; but when imposed as a burden upon the consciences of others, they are utterly unjustifiable, and if they were found in the New Testament, they would furnish abundant matter for Jewish wit and ridicule. They would naturally say, what, is this the religion that the Messiah came to teach? Had he nothing better to do than to look after the making of fires, and the putting on of pots? But this is not the religion of Jesus of Nazareth, nor of his apostles. There is nothing similar in the New Testament. This is the religion, and these the laws of those who reject him.

But this system of minute legislation has another and a worse consequence; it leads to difficulty, and the difficulty leads to artifice, and thus the mind, instead of being improved and benefited, is actually corrupted by the practice of this rabbinical religion. Thus the oral law says, that it is unlawful on a holy day to cook food for the following day,

SEVERITY AND ARTIFICE. 107

especially for a common day, but that if any of the food remain it is lawful. What is the consequence? Naturally that more food is prepared than is necessary for the holy day because they know that this may be eaten the day after. And this is no imaginary deduction of ours, it is a case propounded most fully, and allowed by the rabbies.

ממלאה אשה קדירה בשר אף על פי שאינה צריכה
אלא לחתיכה אחת. ממלא נחתום הבית של מים אף
על פי שאינו צריך אלא לקיתון אחד. ממלאה אשה
תנור פת אף על פי שאינה צריכה אלא לככר אחד
שבזמן שחפת מרובה בתנור היא נאפת יפה. ומולח
אדם כמה חתיכות בשר בבת אחת אף על פי שאינו
צריך אלא לחתיכה אחת וכן כל כיוצא בזה:

"A woman may fill a pot with meat, though she wants only one piece. A cook may fill a boiler with water, though he wants only the least quantity. A woman may fill an oven with bread, though she want only one loaf, for when the oven is full, the bread bakes better. A man may salt a great many pieces of meat at once, although he require only one piece; and so with similar things." (Hilchoth Jom. Tov. c. i. 10.) Now this is plainly an evasion of what is considered a Divine command. In like manner the oral law forbids the preparing of food for Gentiles.

אין אופין ומבשלין ביום טוב כדי להאכיל גוים או
כלבים שנאמר הוא לבדו יעשה לכם לכם ולא לגוים
לכם ולא לכלבים:

"It is unlawful to bake or to cook on a holy day, in order to feed Gentiles or dogs; for it is said, 'That only may be done for you.' (Exod xii. 16.) 'For you,' and not for Gentiles. 'For you,' and not for dogs." (Ibid.) The principle of this decision may lead to several difficulties: first, a Jew may have Gentiles in his employ and service whom he boards, what is he to do then? This difficulty he may get over in the manner just mentioned, by having more cooked than he wants, then it is lawful for the Gentile to eat of the surplus. But suppose a Gentile and a Jew had a beast in partnership, and either wished to have it slaughtered on the holy day, is it lawful for a Jew to slaughter it? According to the above decision, it would appear not, for it is preparing food to feed a Gentile; but the rabbies have found out a reason for evading the command.

בהמה שחציה של גוי וחציה של ישראל מותר
לשחטו ביום טוב שאי אפשר לאכול ממנה כזית בשר
בלא שחיטה:

"A beast which partly belongs to a Gentile and partly to an Israelite, may lawfully be slaughtered on a holy day, for it is impossible to eat the size of an olive of the meat, if it be not slaughtered by a Jew." (Ibid.) This, also, is nothing more nor less than an evasion. But now suppose that a Jew finds on a holy day, and after he has eaten his meals, that a beast belonging to him is likely to die, and that therefore he is likely to lose it altogether, what is he to do? The oral law lays it down that it is unlawful to slaughter for the following day, and yet if it die without slaughtering, it must be totally unlawful to eat. In this case there is a saving clause which removes the difficulty.

מי שהיתה לו בהמה מסוכנת לא ישחוט אותה ביום טוב אלא אם כן יודע שיוכל לאכול ממנה כזית צלי מבעוד יום. כדי שלא ישחוט ביום טוב מה שיאכל בחול:

"He that has a beast near unto death must not slaughter it on a holy day, unless he knows that he can eat of its flesh the size of an olive, roasted, whilst it is still day, that he may not slaughter on a holy day what is to be eaten on a common day." (Ibid.) Here the evasion is palpable. The man has already eaten his meals, he knows that it is not for the holy day, that it is simply to save himself from loss, and yet the oral law obliges him to be guilty of deceit, and to eat a minute particle of it, that the appearance may be kept up. If it were intended mercifully to save the poor from loss, why not make it lawful at once, without any such condition? Here the mercy of the enactment is quite destroyed by the encouragement of deceit. In the same way the oral law forbids open, straightforward buying and selling on a holy day, and yet prescribes a method of evasion.

לא יאמר אדם לטבח תן לי בדינר בשר אלא תן לי חלק או חצי חלק ולמחר עושין חשבון על שוויו:

"A man must not say to a butcher, Give me meat for so much money, only, Give a portion, or half a portion, and on the morrow they settle the account as to its value." (Ibid. c. iv. 20.)

הולך אדם אצל חנוני או רועה חרגיל אצלו או אצל הפטם חרגיל אצלו ולוקח ממנו בהמות ועופות וכל מה שירצה והוא שלא יזכור לו שום דמים ולא סכום מנין:

"A man may go to his accustomed shopkeeper, or shepherd, or grazier, and take from him cattle, fowls, and whatsoever he pleases; only he must not mention to him any money, nor any number." (Ibid.) To take any thing from a shopkeeper by weight or measure is also forbidden, if it be done openly and honestly, but allowed if it be done cunningly and deceitfully.

וכן לא יקח מבעל החנות במדה או במשקל אלא
כיצד הוא עושה אומר לחנוני מלא לי כלי זה ולמחר
נותן לו שוויו ואפילו היה כלי המיוחד למדה ימלאנו
והוא שלא יזכור לו שם מדה:

"And thus a man must not take any thing from a shopkeeper by weight or measure, only let him say to the shopkeeper, Fill this vessel for me; and on the morrow he gives him the value. And even though the vessel should be one set apart for the purpose of measuring, he may fill it, provided that the name of a measure be not mentioned." (Ibid.) In all these cases it is plain that a real transaction of buying and selling takes place, and on the showing of the rabbies themselves, contrary to the Word of God. Those men who would flog a fellow-creature for not keeping their own commandment of a second holy day, make no scruple of devising and prescribing a system of fraudulent evasion of God's commands. Perhaps some may think that we use too strong language when we apply the words cunning and deceit to those devices of the oral law, but this language was suggested by the oral law itself, which does not scruple to use similar words, and to pronounce that, in similar cases, cunning or deceit is lawful.

אותו ואת בנו שנפלו לבור מעלה את הראשון על
מנת לשחטו ואינו שוחטו. ומערים ומעלה את השני
על מנת לשחטו ושוחט אי זה מהן שירצה משום
צער בעלי חיים התירו להערים:

"If a first-born beast and its offspring fall into a pit, the first is to be helped out on condition of slaughtering it, but it is not slaughtered. Then guile is to be used, and the second also helped out on condition of slaughtering it, and then they slaughter which of the two they please. On account of the affliction of the animals, it has been pronounced lawful to use guile." (Ibid. c. ii.) Here the oral law speaks plainly, it fairly says that guile may be used. It is no defence to say, that this guile was suggested by compassion for the animals. If it be lawful to help the animals out of the pit at all, it is lawful to do it without any guile, openly and honestly. And if it be unlawful to help them out, it is doubly unlawful to do so through guile and deceit, as if God was ignorant of the thoughts and designs of their hearts, and could be satisfied with false and fictitious conditions. But there is another case, where this same word is also used, and where the excuse of compassion is altogether out of the question.

חמפשיט עור בחמה ביום טוב לא ימלחנו שזה
עיבוד הוא ונמצא עושה מלאכה שלא לצורך אכילה
.... ומותר למלוח בשר לצלי על גבי העור ומערימים
בדבר זה . כיצד מולח מעט בשר מכאן ומעט מכאן
עד שימלח העור כולו :

"He that takes off the hide of a beast on a holy day, must not salt it, for this is work, and he would be guilty of doing work that is not necessary for the preparation of food. . . . But it is lawful to salt meat for roasting on the top of the hide, and in this matter guile is employed. How so? Thus. A little meat is salted on one part, and then a little on another part, until the whole hide be salted." (Ibid. c. iii. 4.) Here no defence whatever can be offered. The oral law confesses that to salt a hide is unlawful, its compilers therefore set to work to find out a method of doing what was forbidden, and yet have the appearance of keeping the law, and they sagaciously discovered the above solution of the difficulty. Thus the law of God is made null by the traditions of men. The commandments of the Scribes are enforced by flogging and excommunication, but full permission given to violate God's commands, if only an appearance of obedience can be preserved. No wonder that Jesus of Nazareth, whose characteristic is mildness and gentleness, used such harsh language to the authors of this system. His general address to them was, " Woe unto you, Scribes and Pharisees, hypocrites." They professed the utmost anxiety to have the law of God observed. This was the professed object of their commandments. They were invented as a hedge to keep off every Israelite from even an approach to transgression; and they enforced the observance of this defence by the severest punishments. But where the law of God interfered with their worldly interest, their profit or their gain, they fearlessly made void the law, and inculcated a system of guile and evasion. And this is perhaps the most deadly element in the Talmudic potion. The human heart is ever ready to imbibe what is bad, and the human mind most quick in generalizing the principles of evil. The only efficient remedy for this disease of head and heart is the inculcation of those pure and holy principles, which God has graciously revealed. But when these principles are themselves adulterated, and a system of guileful evasion taught as the religion of Moses and the prophets, what are the results to be expected? The cruel oppression of the poor is bad enough. The enslaving the consciences of the weak is worse; but the corrupting the minds of the simple by such pernicious doctrines, is the worst of all. Yet this is the work of the Jewish religion, as taught in the oral law, and as recognized in the prayers of the synagogue. We do not mean to say that there is anything peculiar in the system. We know that the Provincial Letters develop a Gentile system as corrupt and corrupting. But that system has nothing to do with the Christianity of the New Testament. Our forefathers renounced it long ago. The Jews still adhere to the oral law, and in their prayers and observances still acknowledge its Divine authority; and wherever Judaism exists in vigour, these are the doctrines instilled into the minds of the young, and to which the flower of the Jewish nation devote the vigour of their manhood and the judgment of their old age. That there are Jews who abhor this system, and have adopted the purer principles of the New Testament, even though they do not profess Christianity, we well know. But how is it that there are none who have courage to protest against it? How is it that there is not one who comes forward to emancipate his brethren from moral slavery and the galling chain of superstition and error? "There is none to guide her among all the sons whom she hath brought forth: neither is there any that taketh her by the hand of all the sons that she hath brought up." (Isaiah li. 18.)

No. XV.

SABBATH MIXTURE.

IN discussing the substance and tendency of the oral law, the very nature of our design compels us to dwell upon its peculiarities, and to notice those traits which appear as its essential characteristics. Our object is not, primarily, to show its defects and faults, but to prove that it is not of Divine authority. In proving this, it is absolutely necessary to show, by a comparison with the law and the prophets, as the unerring standard of right and wrong, that the system is bad. We know, and have more than once admitted, that as it is not a mere human invention, but a corruption of a divinely revealed religion, it must contain much that is good. But this admission no more justifies the system, than a small quantity of gold in a mixed metal would prove that the whole mass is gold. And this comparison may be well illustrated by the holy day constitutions, which have lately occupied our attention. The concluding paragraph of these constitutions contains several beautiful and pious precepts; as, for example, after the

command to rejoice on such days, and to provide nuts and
such-like things for the children, new clothes and ornaments
for the women, and good eating and drinking for the men, we
read as follows :—

וכשהוא אוכל ושותה חייב להאכיל לגר ליתום
ולאלמנה עם שאר העניים אבל מי שנועל דלתי ביתו
ואוכל ושותה עם בניו ואשתו ואינו מאכיל ומשקה
לעניים ולמרי נפש אין זו מצוה אלא שמחת כרסו
ועל אלו נאמר זבחיהם כלחם אונים להם כל אוכליו
יטמאו כי לחמם לנפשם וגו' :

"And when he eats and drinks, he is bound to feed the stranger,
the orphan, and the widow, with the other poor. But he that
bolts the doors of his house, and eats and drinks with his
children and his wife, but does not furnish meat and drink to the
poor and afflicted, is not to be regarded as having fulfilled the
commandment; on the contrary, his joy is that of a glutton,
and of such persons it is said, 'Their sacrifices shall be unto
them as the bread of mourners; all that eat thereof shall be
polluted : for their bread for their soul shall not come into the
house of the Lord.' (Hos. ix. 4.)" (Arbah Turim, 529.) This
makes a merciful provision for the poor, and as teaching all
who partake of the good things of this world to remember their
poorer brethren, is worthy of praise and imitation. We know
also that this charity is practised by all devout Jews in every
part of the world, and that they are on this account entitled to
the respect of all who can appreciate benevolence. But the
reason why every believer in revelation will approve this
commandment is, because it accords with the Word of God.
Moses has made this precept a part of his law : " The stranger,
and the fatherless, and the widow, which are within thy gates,
shall come, and shall eat and be satisfied ; that the Lord thy
God may bless thee in all the work of thine hand which thou
doest." (Deut. xiv. 29.) And in the New Testament there is
found a similar command : " When thou makest a dinner or a
supper, call not thy friends, nor thy brethren, neither thy
kinsmen nor thy rich neighbours ; lest they also bid thee again,
and a recompense be made thee. But when thou makest a
feast, call the poor, the maimed, the lame, the blind ; and thou
shalt be blessed; for they cannot recompense thee; for thou
shalt be recompensed at the resurrection of the just." (Luke xiv.
12—14). But excellent as this rabbinical commandment is in
itself, it loses considerably when interpreted according to the
system. A person acquainted only with the law of Moses, or
the doctrine of Jesus of Nazareth, would say, that one of the
most lovely features in the command is the universal love

inculcated towards the stranger as well as the Israelites. But an acquaintance with the oral law would compel him to retract this commendation, for there universally the stranger is interpreted to mean, "a proselyte to Judaism," as for instance—

אהבת הגר שבא ונכנס תחת כנפי חשכינה שתי
מצוות עשה . אחת מפני שהוא בכלל רעים . ואחת
מפני שהוא גר והתורה אמרה ואהבתם את הגר:

"To love the stranger who comes, and is gathered under the wings of the Shechinah, is to fulfil two affirmative precepts; one, because he is included in the number of those considered 'neighbours,' and a second, because the law says, 'Ye shall love the stranger.'" (Hilchoth Deoth. c. vi. 4.) Here, then, that comprehensive word "stranger" is narrowed down to the signification "religious proselyte," and abundance of similar passages have already been given in Nos. 4 and 5. But even with this great drawback we admit that there is much to be commended in the above commandment. We are quite willing to recognize all the good which we can, and therefore add another passage or two which deserve notice.

מדת החסידים אשר השם לנגדם תמיד ובכל
דרכיהם ידעוהו בעת שמחתם אז יותר ויותר מברכים
ומשבחים להקב״ה אשר שמחם . ויאמר האדם בלבו
בעת שמחתו והנאתו אם כך היא שמחת העולם הזה
אשר הוא הבל כי יש אחריה תוגה וצער אם כן מה
תהיה שמחת העה״ב התמידה שאין אחריה תוגה:

"It is a characteristic of the pious, who set the Lord always before them, and in all their ways acknowledge him, that in the time of their joy they multiply still more the blessings and praises of the Holy One, blessed be He, who makes them to rejoice. At such a season, too, a man ought to think, if such be the joy of this world, which is vanity, for it is followed by sorrow and trouble, what will be the joy of the world to come, which is everlasting, and to which no sorrow can succeed." (Arbah Turim, ibid.) This passage also, as resting upon the unsophisticated Word of God, must receive unqualified assent. The character of the pious is here beautifully described by the union of two passages of Scripture. They are those "who set the Lord always before them," (Ps. xvi. 8,) and who "in all their ways acknowledge him." (Prov. iii. 6.) God grant that all, both Jews and Christians, may earnestly endeavour to realize this character. The piety of this passage is equalled by the prudence of one of their police regulations for the three great feasts.

חייבין ב"ד להעמיד שוטרים ברגלים שיהיו שוטטים
ומחפשים בגנות ופרדסים ועל הנהרות שלא יתקבצו
שם לאכול ולשתות אנשים ונשים ויבואו לידי עבירה:

"The tribunal is bound, at the three feasts, to appoint officers for the purpose of going about and inspecting gardens, and parks, and rivers, that men and women may not congregate in such places to eat and drink, and be led to commit sin." If the authors of the oral law had confined themselves to such commandments as these, there would be but little to blame. But unfortunately the good and useful precepts bear but a small proportion to the whole, and are often directly counteracted by the peculiar principles of the system. The above general description of piety is unexceptionable, but the detail of the requirements, even for the holy day alone, is such as must effectually pervert and distort the features there delineated. How can a man have a just idea of setting the Lord always before him, who thinks that a cunning evasion of God's commandments is permitted, as was shown in the last number? Or how can a man be said to acknowledge God, when his mind is filled and occupied with the manifold and perplexing ceremonies of man's institution? Of these inventions many have already been given, but more remain, and the Jewish Prayer-book for the passover especially reminds us of one.

דיני עירוב תבשילין:

"The laws of the mixture for the cooking of victuals." The oral law has made it unlawful on the holy day to prepare food for the Sabbath.

יום טוב שחל להיות ערב שבת אין אופין ומבשלין
ביום טוב מה שהוא אוכל למחר בשבת:

"When a holy day falls on the eve of the Sabbath, it is unlawful to bake or to cook on that day what is to be eaten on the morrow, *i.e.* on the Sabbath." (Hilchoth Jom. Tov. c. vi. 1.) This law may of course create a great inconvenience, for if nothing remains after the meals of the holy day, there will be no food for the Sabbath, and on that day the law of Moses forbids all cooking. And, strange to say, the evasion which is allowed at other times is here forbidden. A man is not permitted to cook a surplus of victuals under the pretence that it is for the holy day. Another and more solemn mode of evasion has been invented, and is thus prescribed in the Jewish Prayer-book—

אם חל ערב פסח ביום ד' אז צריכין לעשות ערוב
תבשילין קודם י"ט. וכך מעשהו. לוקחין מצה שלימה

וכזית תבשיל או בשר או ביצה צלויה ומניחין אותה
על המצה . ובעל הבית וכו׳ :

Of which D. Levi gives the following translation, which though not very literal, is preferable to a new one, as occurring in an authorized edition of the Jewish prayers :—

"If the first day of the festival happens on the Thursday, the following ceremony is observed. On the day preceding the festival, the master of every family takes a whole cake and a piece of meat, fish, or a roasted egg ; and having delivered them to one standing by, to denote that all the other Jews in the city that may have forgotten to make the mixture shall, nevertheless, have the benefit of the said mixture, so as to be able to prepare on the festival what is necessary for the Sabbath, he then says the following :—

ברוך אתה יי אלהינו מלך העולם אשר קדשנו
במצותיו וצונו על מצות ערוב :
בהדין ערובא יהא שרי לנא למיפא ולבשלא ולאטמנא
ולאדלקא שרגא ולמעבד כל צרכנא מיומא טבא
לשבתא . לנו ולכל ישראל הדרים בעיר הזאת :

"Blessed art thou, O Lord, our God! King of the universe, who has sanctified us with thy commandments, and commanded us concerning the mixture."

"By this mixture it shall be allowable for us to bake, boil, and to keep the victuals warm : to light up lights, and to do, and prepare all things necessary, on the festival for the Sabbath ; we, and all Israel that dwell in this city." (Levi's Prayers, vol. v. pp. 4, 5.) Now, against this ceremony several and serious objections may be made. First, if it be absolutely unlawful on the holy day to cook for the Sabbath-day, how is the unlawfulness removed by going through a trifling ceremony, and repeating a few words? The cooking is, in the sight of God, either lawful or unlawful. If lawful, then this ceremony is utterly useless, and the solemn calling upon God is only a solemn profanation. If unlawful, then nothing but a dispensation from Israel's great lawgiver, God himself, can make it lawful. Any thing short of this must, by every honest man, be regarded either as an evasion, or a bold and wilful transgression. Secondly, the unlawfulness on which this ceremony is founded, is altogether of man's making—God has nowhere forbidden the Jews to prepare for Sabbath on the holy day. The Scribes have here as elsewhere dared to add to the law of God.

ואיסור זה מדברי סופרים כדי שלא יבוא לבשל

מיום טוב לחול . שקל וחומר הוא לשבת אינו מבשל כל שכן לחול :

"This prohibition is of the words of the Scribes, that a man may not be led to prepare on a holy day for a common day. For if he feel it unlawful to cook for Sabbath, still more will he feel this for a common day." (Hilchoth Jom. Tov. vi. 1.) Here it is plainly confessed that the prohibition is not from God but from man. A reason is assigned for this addition, which is unsatisfactory, and shows that the Scribes thought the law imperfect, and themselves wiser than God. They were afraid, if men got into a habit of cooking on the holy day for the following day, when that day was the Sabbath, they might get into the habit of cooking generally for the following day, and thus cook for common days. But did not God foresee this possibility, and know the frailty of human nature just as well as the rabbies? why then did he not take this precaution himself? If this precaution be absolutely necessary, as it was not given by God, it will necessarily follow that God did not give that which was necessary, and therefore that the law of God was imperfect until it was mended by the rabbies. If the law, as given by God, be perfect, and who can deny it without blasphemy, then this precaution of the rabbies is useless, and they are proved guilty of making additions to the law of God, and of imposing needless burdens on the consciences of their brethren. If this ceremony were left to the free will of every individual, it would be very different, but it is imposed as an indispensable duty, and a man pronounced a sinner if he does not comply.

מי שאיפשר לו לערב ואינו מערב אלא שרוצה לסמוך על עירובו של גדול העיר נקרא פושע ואינו יוצא בו :

"He who can make the mixture, and does not, but chooses to depend on the mixture made by the great men of the city, is called a sinner, and has not fulfilled his duty." (Arbah Turim, 527.) Here then his conscience is burdened, but further, he may be exposed to considerable inconvenience, to escape from which he is driven again to a prescribed exercise of artifice and guile.

מי שלא הניח עירוב תבשילין ולא הניחו לו אחרים כשם שאסור לו לבשל ולאפות כך קמחו ומאכלו אסור . ואסור לאחר שהניח לעצמו לבשל ולאפות לזה שלא הניח עד שיקנה לו . שנמצא זה

מבשל ואופה שלו שהרי קנהו ואם רצה יתן אחר
כך לזה שלא הניח במתנה:

"He that has not performed the ceremony of the mixture for himself, and for whom others have not done it, as it is unlawful for him to boil or to bake, so his flour and food are unlawful; and it is unlawful for another, who has performed the ceremony for himself, to boil and bake for such an one until he buy for himself. Then he may boi. and bake of his own, for he has bought it, and if he please may make a present of it to the other." Here of course the purchase is fictitious. In like maner it is unlawful for him to light the Sabbath candle. This would be a great misfortune, and a learned rabbi has accordingly found out a remedy of the same kind.

כתב הר׳ מאיר מרוטנבורק שיכול לחפש בחדר
שום חפץ בנר אפילו מבעוד יום ולהניחנו דולק עד
הלילה:

"Rabbi Meyer, of Rothenburg, has said in his writings, that a man may seek for something in the room by the light of a candle, yea though it be still day, and then leave it lighting until night." (Arbah Turim, 527.) We ask the Jews seriously to consider this specimen of rabbinical wisdom and conscientiousness. A man who has not performed the ceremony of the mixture dare not do what God has allowed him to do, he dare not light the candle for Sabbath, that is, if he does it honestly and openly, he would, according to the oral law, commit a sin. But then he may do this same thing by using guile and deceit, which God has forbidden, and then according to these same teachers, the act is lawful. He may light a candle under pretence of searching for something, even though he has the daylight, and therefore evidently does not want it for that purpose, and then he can leave it lighting. Thus the oral law teaches that the neglect of a mere human invention is a greater sin than guile and deceit. Is not this to strain at a gnat and to swallow a camel? But some Rabbinist may say, if the oral law encourages guile and deceit, why does it forbid the employment of guile in the preparation of food for the Sabbath, as has been stated above? This is a curious point, and deserves attention. The oral law says, if food be left after the meals of the holy day, it is lawful to eat it on the Sabbath, provided that no guile be used; but if guile be used, it is unlawful. Whereas, if a man wilfully neglect the ceremony of the mixture, and cook notwithstanding for the Sabbath he may lawfully eat what he has prepared. This has at first sight, the appearance of wishing to discourage guile, but the reasons, given for this decision, show that this is far from being the case.

ולמה החמירו ואסרו על המערים ולא אסרו על
המזיד שאם חתירו למערים נמצאו הכל מערימין
וישתקע שם ערובי תבשילין . אבל המזיד אינו מצוי
ואם עבר היום לא יעבור פעם אחרת :

"What is the reason that they were more severe upon him that used guile than upon the wilful transgressor, and made it unlawful for the former, but not for the latter? The reason is this, if they had pronounced it lawful for him that uses guile, all would use guile, and the very name of mixture for food would perish. On the other hand, a wilful transgressor is rare, and if he transgresses to-day, he will not transgress again." The employment of guile, then, is not forbidden because it is odious in the sight of God and man, but simply from the fear that it might operate prejudicially upon the observance of a rabbinic command. Such is and must be the effect of multiplying religious ceremonies, and imposing them upon the conscience as necessary to salvation. The conscience becomes burdened, and beset with difficulties, and is glad of any refuge or relief, even though it should be derived from artifice and deceit. Artifice is at last made lawful, or even prescribed, as we have seen in many intances, and then religion, which God intended as a remedy for our moral disease, becomes itself a new source of infection. But if any burdened conscience should awake and become sensible of the cheat that has been put upon it by the oral law, the probability is that it will cast off religion altogether, and mistake Moses too for a companion of the Scribes and Pharisees; and thus many a rabbinical Jew has been led to utter infidelity.

But there is still a third objection to be urged against this ceremony of the mixture, and that is, that it prescribes a form of thanksgiving to God for appointing that which he never appointed: "Blessed art thou, O Lord our God! King of the universe! who has sanctified us with thy commandments, and commanded us concerning the mixture." Where has God commanded the mixture? Where, from one end of the law to the other, or in the prophets, is there one word about this ceremony? It is from first to last a pure invention of the Scribes. God never appointed it. This prayer, then, contains a positive untruth, and thus the ignorant and unlearned are deceived, and taught even in the solemn act of public worship to believe that God has commanded what he never commanded.

The minds of children, too, are thus imbued with the commandments of men, and taught in the language of prayer to stamp the divine authority upon the invention of the Scribes and Pharisees. And this is done not only in the forests of Poland, or on the uncivilized coasts of Barbary, but here in England. This ceremony and this prayer are prescribed in the two editions of the Jewish prayer-book, published by Levi and Alexander. In this country, where full liberty of conscience prevails, the language of the synagogue is just the same as in the darkest and most oppressed regions of the habitable globe. The Jewish children are still taught to bless God for giving what he never gave, and the sacred voice of prayer still consecrates the intolerance, the errors, and the absurdities of the oral law. In other countries, where the circumstances were not so favourable, the Jews have made more than one attempt to renounce and repudiate the errors of the Talmud. But in England, whether from listlessness or from a love to these Talmudic doctrines, we do not presume to say, nothing has been done either by the German or the Portuguese Jews. In England the Talmud still maintains its empire of error and uncharitableness, and spiritual tyranny, and not one individual has dared publicly to protest against it. We ask the Jews seriously to consider this matter, and to compare the extracts which we give with Moses and the prophets; if the oral law agrees with that which is confessedly the Word of God, then we beg of them to explain the lawfulness of using guile, of inventing new commandments, and enforcing them with the severest punishments. But if they decide that these things are altogether forbidden by God, then we call upon them to protest aloud against these adulterations of revealed truth.

No. XVI.*

INTOLERANCE OF RABBINIC PRAYERS.

IN our last number we ventured to say, that in the English synagogues "The sacred voice of prayer still consecrates the intolerance, the errors, and the absurdities of the oral law;" and we gave an instance in proof of our assertion. But to some

* The British Jews of Burton-street Synagogue have expunged from their prayers the intolerance here complained of.

Israelites, who have overlooked the contents of their Prayer-book, this assertion may require more proof; we therefore, proceed to give it, and first of all with regard to intolerance. In the ceremonial for the first two evenings of the Passover, in the midst of the rejoicings and thanksgivings, which the memory of their great deliverance naturally calls forth, we suddenly find the following prayer:—

שפוך חמתך אל הגוים אשר לא ידעוך ועל
ממלכות אשר בשמך לא קראו : כי אכל את יעקב
ואת נוהו השמו . שפוך עליהם זעמך וחרון אפך
ישיגם . תרדף באף ותשמידם מתחת שמי ה' :

" Pour out thy wrath upon the heathen that have not known thee, and upon the kingdoms that have not called upon thy name. For they have devoured Jacob, and laid waste his dwelling place. (Psalm lxxix. 6, 7.) Pour out thine indignation upon them, and let thy wrathful anger take hold of them. (Psalm lxix. 24.) Persecute them in anger, and destroy them from under the heavens of the Lord." (Lament. iii. 66.) Here are three passages of Scripture, taken from their context, and joined together to make one prayer. In their context, and with reference to the times for which those portions of Scripture were given by God, they are intelligible. After the destruction of Jerusalem by the Romans, whilst the Jewish mind was still in a state of violent excitement against the authors of that calamity, such an imprecation may appear natural. During the persecutions of the Crusaders or the Inquisition it might be excusable, but in the present time and circumstances it is indefensible. Who are the heathen and the kingdoms, whom the offerers of these petitions wish to be pursued with God's wrath, and to be destroyed from under the heavens? Are they the Christians, or the heathen idolaters of Africa and India? The Mahometans profess a faith in the Unity very similar to that of the later rabbies: they, therefore, cannot be intended. If it be said that the idolatrous heathen are here intended, we must still protest against the intolerance of this imprecation; why should the Jews wish for their destruction? What evil did these poor ignorant people ever do to the Jews in England, that they should pray for their destruction rather than their conversion? If it be said, that nobody at all is intended in the present day, why, we would ask, is it still made a part of the Passover ceremonial? We have before us several copies of the Haggadah, some printed very lately, and it occurs in them all.

If this were the only passage of the kind to be found in the liturgies of the synagogue, it might perhaps admit of palliation or excuse, but it is only one of a similar class, all breathing the same spirit. In the morning service for the second day of the Passover, as translated by D. Levi, we find another more fearful still.

ברח דודי אל לבך ועיניך שם . ואם זנחנו טוב
מדשם . אנא שמע שאנת קול צורריך ורגשם . רוח
מדם גושם . ועפרם מחלב ידשם . ופגריהם יעלה
באשם :

"Hasten, O my beloved, to where thy heart and eyes are; and though we have cast off that that is good and pleasant, yet hear the roaring raging *voice* of those that oppress thy people; satiate the clods with their blood; manure the earth with their fat; and let the stench of their carcasses ascend." (Levi's Prayers, vol. 5, fol. 142.) The translation is D. Levi's, so that it cannot be said, that the sense has been misrepresented or distorted for polemical purposes. It is the translation of a Jew, and of a Jew in England, and the title-page tells us that it is the second edition "carefully revised and corrected, and illustrated by Isaac Levi." The title-page also says, "As read in their synagogues and used in their families." Is not this prayer intolerant? Is there any thing like it in the New Testament, or in our Christian Prayer-books? And yet we are told that modern Judaism is more tolerant than Christianity, and that it teaches charity to all men. Let not the Jews think that we impute this spirit to the whole nation. No such thing. This passage is quoted as a specimen of the spirit of the oral law and its authors, who not only were possessed of this spirit of resentment, but so overwhelmed with it, as to transfuse it into their addresses to the God of mercy, and to prescribe it as a part of the public worship of the congregation. Whenever introduced, there it still remains, as a testimony to the spirit of the first opposers of Jesus of Nazareth, and as a portion of the liturgic service of the synagogue. In these passages, however, it does not appear what nations are intended; no name or particular characteristic is given, though the allusion, in the last quoted prayer, to Isaiah xxxiv., naturally leads the reader to think of Edom; but in other places a more definite form is prescribed, from which we find that Edom is the great object of hatred.

ליל שמורים אל חצה . בחצות לילה בתוך מצרים
כיצא . גבור על אדום יחצנה כחצה :

"God divideth the night of preservation, when in the midst of the night he went forth through the *land* of Egypt: may the mighty God also divide it concerning Edom." (Levi, ibid. fol. 7.) This is a petition that God would do to Edom as he did unto Egypt. Again, a little further on we read,

פסח חרב חדה על אדום . ביד צח ואדום . כימי
חג פסח :

"On the Passover, a sharp sword shall fall on Edom, by the hand of him who is white and ruddy, as in the days of the feast of Passover." (Ibid. fol. 10.) And so throughout the prayers there are frequent allusions to this subject, as for instance—

שם יקרא ככתיבתו . מחציו תתמלא תיבתו . עוד
תתנשא מלכותו . וכסאו יכון במלאתו . נכדי שעיר
בהכותו . באויביו יתן נקמתו :

"Then will his name be pronounced as it is written: when the other half will complete the word; his dominion also will be greatly exalted, and his throne be completely established; when he shall smite the descendants of Esau, and take vengeance on his enemies." (Ibid. fol. 214.) But these are sufficient to show that Edom is the great object of antipathy, and of course the great question is, whom do the Jews understand by Edom? Let the most famous of their rabbies instruct us in this matter, and first let us hear Maimonides :—

אדומים עובדי עכו"ם הם ויום ראשון הוא יום
אידם לפיכך אסור לשאת ולתת עמהם בא"י יום
חמישי ויום ששי שבכל שבת ושבת ואצ"ל יום ראשון
עצמו שהוא אסור בכל מקום :

"The Edomites are idolaters, and the first day of the week is the day of their festival; therefore it is forbidden to have commerce with them in the land of Israel, on the fifth and sixth day of every week. It is not necessary to say that the first day itself is every where unlawful." (Hilchoth Accum. c. ix. 4.) There is but one class of religionists who observe the first day of the week as sacred. Now let us hear Kimchi. In his commentary on Joel iii. 19, "Egypt shall be a desolation, and Edom shall be a desolate wilderness, for the violence against the children of Judah, because they have shed innocent blood in their land:" he says,

זכר מצרים בעבור ישמעאלים ואדום בעבור מלכות
רומי . ואלה שתי האומות הנה הגוברות זה ימים
רבים ותהיינה עד עת הגאולה והיא חיותא רביעאה
במראות דניאל .... ואמר זה בעבור כי מלכות רומי
רובם אדומים ואעפ"י שנתערבו בהם עמים רבים כמו
שנתערבו גם כן במלכות ישמעאלים נקראים על
העיקר :

INTOLERANCE OF RABBINIC PRAYERS. 123

" The prophet mentions Egypt and Edom : Egypt, on account of the Turks, and Edom, on account of the Roman empire; and these two have now had dominion for a long time, and will continue until the redemption. This is the fourth beast in the visions of Daniel. . . . . And this is said, because the majority of the Roman empire is composed of Edomites. For although many other nations are mixed among them, as is also the case with the Turkish empire, they are called after the root." Kimchi then fixes Edom upon the Roman empire, in which he evidently includes the Greek empire, for he wrote in the 12th century, long before the Constantinopolitan dynasty was overturned. Aben Esra gives a similar interpretation on the blessing of Esau.

ורומי שהנחלתנו היא מזרע כתים וכן אומר המתרגם
וצים מיד כתים והיא מלכות יון בעצמו כאשר
פירשתי בספר דניאל והיו אנשים מתי מספר שהאמינו
באיש ששמוחו אלוה וכאשר האמינה רומי בימי
קונסטאנטין שחדש כל הדת ושם על דגלו צורת
האיש. ולא היו בעולם שישמרו התורה החדשה חוץ
מאדומים מעטים על כן נקראה רומי מלכות אדום :

" Rome, which led us away captive, is of the seed of Kittim, and so the Targumist has said, in Numbers xxiv. 24, ' And ships shall come from the coast of Kittim.' And this is the same as the Greek monarchy, as I have explained in the book of Daniel ; and there were very few who believed on the man of whom they made a god. But when Rome believed in the days of Constantine, who changed the whole religion, and put an image of that man upon his standard, there were none in the world who observed the new law except a few Edomites, therefore Rome is called the kingdom of Edom." (Comment. on Gen. xxix.) We do not now stop to refute the false statements which Aben Ezra here makes. Every one that knows anything of history, knows that in less than a century after the time of Jesus of Nazareth, the Christian religion had made great progress in the whole Roman empire, and that the propagation of the new law, as Aben Ezra calls it, before the time of Constantine, was more rapid and more extensive than after his conversion. Our business at present is with his interpretation of the word Edom; he says plainly that Edom and Edomites mean the Christians. Now let us hear Abarbanel :—

ומזה תדע שלא לבד על ארץ אדום הסמוכה
לא"י נבא הנביא כ"א גם על האומה שנסתעפה משם
ונתפשטה בכל העולם והיא אומת הנוצרים היום הזה
שהם מבני אדום :

"From this you may learn that the prophet (Obadiah) did not prophesy only against the land of Edom, which is in the neighbourhood of the land of Israel, but also against that people which branches off from thence, and is spread through the whole world, and that is the people of the Christians in this our day, for they are of the children of Edom." (Comment. on Obadiah.) Here, then, we have Maimonides, Kimchi, Aben Ezra, and Abarbanel, all giving the same interpretation, and all asserting that Edom means the Christians. According to this interpretation, then, the above dreadful imprecations are for the destruction of the Christians. Is this tolerant or charitable? Is this in accordance with Moses' account of the Divine character—"Merciful and gracious, long-suffering, and abundant in goodness and truth?" Are these the petitions that poor sinful creatures ought to offer when they assemble for the worship of the Creator of all flesh? Above all, are they suitable in an English synagogue, and in the present day? You may say that Kimchi and those other commentators, lived in the times of Popery, and that Edom only means the Roman Catholic Christians. But what will those Jews say who live in Rome itself, and France, and Bavaria, and other Roman Catholic countries? You may think them in error, so do we, but we cannot for that pray that God "would satiate the clods with their blood, manure the earth with their fat, and cause the stench of their carcases to ascend." We could not utter such an imprecation against the cannibals of New Zealand, nor the man-stealers of Africa. But if you say that you do not offer up these petitions against the Christians, whether Protestant or Romanist, may we ask against whom then are they directed? And what are your thoughts when you hear these petitions read, and join in them in the synagogue? The literal Edom was destroyed long since; the children of Edom have long since been utterly lost. Where are their posterity now to be found? The above-named rabbies say the Romans were descended from Edom, but where is their proof, either from the Bible or from profane history? But suppose it was so, how will that prove that the Greeks, the French, the Germans, or the inhabitants of the British isles are thus descended? The truth is, there is no historical evidence whatever to give even a colour to this assertion respecting Rome. The rabbies found dreadful denunciations of wrath against Edom in the prophets, particularly in Obadiah and the thirty-fourth of Isaiah, and they thought that Rome and the Christians deserved such punishment more than any one else; they therefore applied them to these objects of their antipathy. As far as authentic history will carry us, the descendants of the Edomites are to be sought for rather amongst the Jews themselves, than amongst any other people; for the last that we read of the Edomites is, that they were subdued by John Hyrcanus, and converted to Judaism at the point of the sword.* Amongst the Jews, then, their descendants have ever since continued, and strange enough some of them may now be offering in the synagogue these imprecations against themselves. But, however that be, the prophecies against Edom do certainly not apply to the Christian religion, which was not Edomitical, but altogether Jewish in its origin. Jesus of Nazareth was a Jew, and his apostles and first disciples from a province of Judea as remote as possible from Edom. And even if the rabbies could prove that Rome is Edom, still this will have nothing to do with the other nations who are no wise descended from, or connected with that city or people.

We are not ignorant of the many prophecies against Edom, but, however many or severe, they form no justification of these prayers, even if the rabbies know who is intended. God is a merciful God, as well as a just Judge, and when he arises to judgment, or when he utters a denunciation of wrath, we may be sure that he does all in truth and righteousness. But that furnishes no excuse for the sons of men who presumptuously take upon themselves to call down God's wrath by prayer, or to offer themselves as the executioners of his anger. The Word of God contains many denunciations of wrath against the Jews, but this does not justify the nations who have persecuted and oppressed them. What would the Jews think of us if we collected all the fearful passages in the twenty-sixth chapter of Leviticus, and the twenty-eight of Deuteronomy, and wove them into a prayer to call down God's wrath upon the people of Israel? What would they say if we appointed this form for the most solemn days, and for the time of our festivity? Yet this is what the rabbies have done, and what the oral law prescribes, and therefore we say, that such teaching is not from God. And we say this, not simply because reason leads to this conclusion, but because such prayers are directly contrary to the express command of God. When he sent the Jews into captivity to Babylon, he did not tell them to pray that " he might pour out his wrath" upon that city, and much less to " satiate the clods with the blood" of its inhabitants. On the contrary, he said—

" And seek the peace of the city whither I have caused you to be carried away captives, and pray unto the Lord for it : for in the peace thereof shall ye have peace." (Jerem. xxix. 7.) Now how does this command agree with the above prayers? Suppose even that the rabbies were right, and that Edom does mean Rome, how can the Jews there pray for its peace and for its utter destruction at the same time? Those prayers are

* See Jost's Geschichte, vol. i. 70 and 153.

utterly irreconcileable with this command of God, and therefore furnish another proof of the error as well as the intolerance of the oral law. This was the object which we had peculiarly in view. We do not wish to burden every Israelite in London with this intolerance. Many are perhaps ignorant that such prayers are offered in the synagogue—many overlook them through inattention, and many others disapprove of them. But in those who do know and disapprove, it is exceedingly inconsistent to join in them, or to remain silent. The spirit of these prayers is thus countenanced, and the intolerance handed down from generation to generation. Children go to the synagogue, and hear these prayers offered; they think as it is the language of prayer, of public prayer, of the prayers of the people of Israel, it must be right. What other conclusion can they form? Thus they imbibe the same spirit, and thus the people of Israel are kept in bondage to the intolerance of by-gone generations. But some will say, We acknowledge that these prayers are contrary to the Bible. Remember, then, that in making this acknowledgment, you admit that the synagogue—yea, the whole nation of Jews, has been in error for many centuries. And if the Jewish nation has been universally mistaken upon so simple, yet essential, a point of religion as true charity, it is highly probable that they are mistaken on other points too, especially those that are more difficult and less obvious to human reason. But above all, remember that whilst the whole system of the oral law, in its precepts and prayers, has taught you to curse your enemies, Jesus of Nazareth has taught us to bless. "Ye have heard that it hath been said, Thou shalt love thy neighbour, and hate thine enemy: but I say unto you, Love your enemies, bless them that curse you, do good to them that hate you, and pray for them which despitefully use you, and persecute you." (Matt. v. 43, 44.) "Bless them which persecute you: bless, and curse not." (Rom. xii. 14.) But some Israelites may still think that it is unfair to judge the oral law by this one service for the Passover. Such an one we would remind of the blessing of the Epicureans, as it is called, which he is bound to say—

בכל תפלה שבכל יום :

"in every prayer, every day." (Hilchoth T'phillah, c. ii. 2.)

ולמלשינים אל תהי תקוה וכל עושי רשעה כרגע
יאבדו והזדים מהרה יכרתו ותכניעם במהרה בימינו .
ברוך אתה ה' שובר אויבים ומכניע זדים :

"O let the slanderers have no hope: all the wicked be annihilated speedily, and all the tyrants be cut off quickly; humble thou them quickly in our days. Blessed art thou, O Lord, who destroyed our enemies." (Daily Prayers, fol. 36.) Here is the same utter want of mercy. No desire for their amendment, no prayer for their conversion, but an invocation of sudden wrath and destruction. And this the synagogue prescribes, not on its feasts only, but every day; yea, and every time of prayer is to be marked by the voice of malediction. There is also another command relating to this daily malediction, which illustrates still farther the spirit of the oral law.

שליח צבור שטעה ונבהל ולא ידע מהיכן יתחיל
ושהה שעה יעמוד אחר תחתיו. ואם טעה בברכת
האפיקורסין אין ממתינין לו אלא מיד יעמוד אחר
תחתיו שמא אפיקורסות נזרקה בו :

" If the reader in the synagogue should make a mistake, or be confused and not know where to begin, and delay for an hour, then let another rise up in his stead. But if he made the mistake with regard to the blessing of the Epicureans, he is not to be waited for, but let another instantly rise up in his stead, for perhaps he is infected with Epicureanism." (Ibid. c. x. 3.) According to this law, if the reader go wrong in invoking a blessing, or offering up an intercessory prayer for mercy, such a petition may be delayed for a whole hour. But if this malediction should be the place of his mistake, there is to be no delay and no postponement. If the reader cannot offer it in time, another is to rise up immediately, and cry to heaven for a curse.

No. XVII.

RABBINIC LEGENDS IN THE SYNAGOGUE SERVICES.

WE have just considered the extraordinary command of the oral law, which provides, that, if the reader in the synagogue should make a mistake in reading the prayers, the congregation shall wait for him for an hour: except the mistake occur in cursing the Epicureans, for then, " He is not be waited for, but let another instantly rise up in his stead, for he is, perhaps, infected with Epicureanism." The special notice of this case is as honourable to the Jews as it is condemnatory of the oral law. It would appear from this that such mistakes had occurred. Readers in the synagogues have sometimes stumbled and stammered when they came to this fearful malediction. And truly we are not surprised, if a man of piety, acquainted with God's Word, should be overwhelmed in publicly cursing his fellow-men, and be unable to bring the words of imprecation over his lips. The care which the Scribes took to legislate for such an occurrence, implies an honourable testimony to the good feeling of the nation, though it strongly marks their own intolerance, and forms a striking contrast to the spirit inculcated in the teaching of Jesus of Nazareth. When his disciples asked him to teach them to pray, he taught them a short form; but short as it was, it contained the petition, " Forgive us our trespasses, as we forgive them that trespass against us," and was followed by this admonition, " For if ye forgive men their trespasses, your heavenly Father will also forgive you. But if ye forgive not men their trespasses, neither will your Father forgive your trespasses." (Matt. vi. 14, 15.)

The intolerance which we have noticed, proves sufficiently that the religious ideas of the oral law have not been drawn from Moses and the prophets; and this will appear still further from the absurd legends which are alluded to in the prayers of the synagogue, as if they were acknowledged verities. In the Liturgy for the feast of Pentecost, which is now approaching, we find more than one such allusion, to which we would most earnestly call your attention. And first of all, those prayers recognise the legend of Leviathan and Behemoth. In the morning service for that day the Jews repeat the following words:—

מנת דילן דמלקדמין פרש בארמותא . טלולא
דלויתן ותור טור רמותא . וחד בחד כי סביך ועביד
קרבותא . בקרנוהי מנגח בהמות ברברבותא . יקרטע נון
לקבליה בציצוי ובגבורדא . מקרב ליה בריה בחרביה
ברברבותא . ארסטון לצדיקי יתקן ושרותא . מסחריו
עלי תכי דכדכוד וגומרתא . נגידין קמיחון אפרסמון
נהרתא . ומתפנקין ורוי בכסי רויתא . חמר מרת
דמבראשית נטיר ביה נעורתא :

Which D. Levi thus translates:—" He will certainly *bestow on* us the portion which he hath promised us of old. The sporting of Leviathan with the ox of the high mountains,* when they shall approach each other and engage in battle. With his horn he thrusts at the mightiest beasts, but the Leviathan will leap towards him with his fins and great strength. His Creator will then approach him with his great sword, and will prepare him for an entertainment (or a banquet) for the righteous; who will be seated at a table formed of jasper and carbuncle, with a

* This alludes to בהמות. See Job xl. 15, &c. D. Levi.

river of balm flowing before them. When they will delight themselves and be satiated with the bowls of wine prepared at the creation, and reserved in the wine-press." In this portion of the Liturgy of the synagogue, there is a very plain reference to the battle between Behemoth and Leviathan. The felicity of the righteous in the world to come is also described, and a part of it is said to consist of the banquet which God will prepare for them from the flesh of Leviathan, when he shall have killed him. It is true that D. Levi has the following note on this banquet: "All this is to be understood in a figurative sense, and by no means literally, as several Christian commentators have done, and thus cast undeserved reproach on the Rabbinical writers." But he has neither given us his authority, nor his reasons for this assertion; nor has he explained the meaning of the figure. We should be glad to know what ninety-nine out of every hundred Jews understand when they hear this read in the synagogue. What do they understand by the name Behemoth? What by Leviathan? What by God's killing him? What by preparing him as a banquet for the righteous? But however Jews in the present day may explain it away, there can be little doubt how the authors of this hymn and the Jews of old understood it. In the Talmud we have the following account of these two great beasts:—

אמר רב יהודה אמר רב כל שברא הקב״ה בעולמו
זכר ונקבה בראם. אף לויתן נחש בריח ולויתן נחש
עקלתון זכר ונקבה בראם ואלמלא נזקקין זה לזה
מחריבין כל העולם :כולו . מה עשה הקב״ה ׳סירס
את הזכר והרג את הנקבה ומלחה לצדיקים לעתיד לביא
שנאמר והרג את התנין אשר בים . ואף בהמות בהררי
אלף זכר ונקבה בראם ואלמלא נזקקין זה לזה מחריבין
כל העולם כולו מה עשה הקב״ה סירס הזכר וציגן
חנקבה ושמרה לצדיקים לעתיד לבוא :

"R. Judah said, Rav said, Everything that God created in this world he created male and female. And thus he did with Leviathan the piercing serpent, and Leviathan the crooked serpent, he created them male and female. But if they had been united, they would have desolated the entire world. What, then, did the Holy One do? He took away the strength of the male Leviathan, and slew the female and salted her for the righteous for the time to come, for it is said, 'And he shall slay the whale (or dragon) that is in the sea.' (Isaiah xxvii. 1.) In like manner with regard to Behemoth upon a thousand mountains, he created them male and female, but if they had been united they would have desolated the entire world.

What then did the Holy One do? He took away the strength of the male Behemoth, and made the female barren, and preserved her for the righteous for the time to come."—(Bava Bathra, fol. 74, col. 2.) In this narrative there are no marks of allegory. The creation of the world is not an allegory, but a fact. The creating of living creatures male and female is another fact. The weakening of the male and the salting of the female to prevent the desolation of the world, does not look like a figure. The Jewish commentators certainly take the matter very seriously, and speak of the creation of Leviathan, not as of an allegory, but as of a real occurrence. Thus R. Moses, the son of Nachman, in his commentary on the words, "And God made great whales," after describing the great size, adds,—

ורבותינו אמרו כי התנינים הגדולים הוא לויתן
ובת זוגו שבראם זכר ונקבה והרג הנקבה ומלחה
לצדיקים לעתיד לבוא. אפשר כי מפני זה לא היה
ראוי שיאמר בהם ויהי כן כי לא עמדו עוד:

"And our rabbies have said that 'the great whales' mean Leviathan and his mate, for God created them male and female, but slew the female, and salted her for the righteous for the time to come: and perhaps this is the reason why the words, 'And it was so,' are not added, for they (the race of Leviathan) did not continue." (Com. in Gen. i. 21.) From this it is evident that the famous rabbi knew nothing of an allegory, for he makes this legend the reason why certain words used after the other works of creation are not here applied. In like manner Abarbanel speaks of this same pair of living creatures as real, and as possibly belonging to the class of great whales.

ואם כלל הכתוב השרץ והדגה כאחד יאמר הכתוב
שברא השם בהם מינים מתחלפים כי יש מהם תנינים
גדולים וכמו שאמרו בפרק הספינה אמר רבה בר בר
חנא זמנא חדא הוה קא אזלינא בספינתא וחזינא
להההיא כוורא דיתבא ליה חלתא על גביה וקרח
אגמא עלויה. סברינא די יבשתא היא וסלקינן ויתבינן
ובשלינן הם גביה דכוורא ואיתהפיך ואי לא דהוה
ספינתא מקרבא לון הוה מטבע לון. וכיוצא בזה
יספרו גם היום יורדי הים באניות. ואולי לויתן ובת
זוגו שזכרו רבותינו מאלה חיו עם היות שהפילוסופים
מבני עמנו ייחסו לאותה הגדה ענינים עמוקים
מהחכמה ואין צורך להם במקום הזה:

"But if the Scripture class creeping things and fish together, then this verse tells us that God created various species, for some of them are great whales, as is said in the 5th chapter of Bava Bathra, 'Rabbah Bar Bar Channa says, Once upon a time we were sailing in a ship, and we saw that fish upon whose back the sand remains and rushes grow; we thought it was terra firma, and landed, and remained there and cooked. But when the fish's back grew warm, he turned round, and if the ship had not been at hand we must have been drowned.' They that go down to the sea in ships in the present time tell similar stories: and perhaps the Leviathan and his mate, mentioned by our rabbies, belonged to this species. However, the philosophers of the children of our people attribute to this chapter matter deeper than philosophy, but which we do not want in this place." (Com. in Gen. i. 21.) It is true that Abarbanel here distinctly admits the existence of mysteries in that chapter of the Talmud. But it is equally plain, that he considered the Leviathan, mentioned by the rabbies, not as an allegory, but a real creation; and therefore assigned it to the same class as the wonderful fish seen by Bar Bar Channa, unless we take his words as a sly insinuation, that the story of Leviathan is about as true as that narrated by the veracious rabbi.

These two great rabbies, then, did not take the legend of Leviathan figuratively; and we might add some other similar testimonies, but that Behemoth also claims a share of our attention, and an inquiry into his nature will contribute evidence to the same effect, that this legend was not taken figuratively but literally. In the first place, D. Levi himself refers us to Job xl. 15, and there we read, "Behold now Behemoth, which I made with thee; he eateth grass like an ox." Here there certainly is no allegory. The words speak of a living creature, and so they are interpreted by all the Jewish commentators, whom we have an opportunity of consulting. Ralbag says—

בהמות הוא בעל חיים שמו כן :

"Behemoth is an animal, and that is his name." (Com. in loc.) Aben Esra, on the words, "Behold now Behemoth, which I made with thee," says—

בהמות שם בהמה גדולה אין בישוב גדולה ממנה
וטעם עמך לפי שהיתה ביבשה כי באחרית יזכור
הלויתן שהוא בים ויש אומרים כי טעם עמך שהבהמות
נולדו ביום אחד עם אדם הראשון וזה דרך דרש :

"*Behemoth* is the name of a great beast. In the habitable world there is not a greater than it. The reason why the words '*with thee*' are added, is, that it is a land animal, and at the end he mentions Leviathan, which is an animal of the sea. But some say the meaning of 'with thee' is, that the beasts were created on the same day with the first Adam; but this interpretation is after the manner of a drash." (Aben Esra in loc.) This passage not only gives Aben Esra's opinion as to the real existence of Behemoth, but shows that other commentators, to whom he alludes, were of the same mind. Rashi not only asserts the existence, but says plainly, בהמות מוכן לעתיד, "Behemoth, that is prepared for the time to come." And again, in his commentary on Psalm l. 10, he takes the words בהמות בהררי אלף, which we translate, "The cattle upon a thousand hills," as referring to "Behemoth upon a thousand hills," and says—

הוא המתוקן לסעודת העתיד שהוא רועה אלף
חרים ליום וכל יום ויום צומחים :

"This is he that is prepared for the banquet of the time to come, for he eats up the produce of a thousand hills in one day, and every day they grow again." The context of these words evidently show that Rashi, the most popular, and the most read of all the Jewish commentators, looked for a real, not an allegorical, feast upon the flesh of the Leviathan and Behemoth. The preceding and following words speak not of allegorical, but of real cattle and fowls. According to Rashi, the whole passage would read thus:— "I will take no bullock out of thy house, nor he-goats out of thy folds. For every beast of the forest is mine, and Behemoth upon a thousand hills. I know all the fowls of the mountain," &c. Here, then, Behemoth is introduced amongst real animals all fit for food, so that it is impossible to take it figuratively. This animal is also suitable in size for so great an entertainment; he consumes the produce of a thousand mountains every day. This was also the opinion of Jonathan, for in his Targum on the fiftieth Psalm he has paraphrased the tenth verse as follows:—

ארום דילי כל חיות חורשא ועתדת לצדיקיא בגן
עדן בעיריא דכין ותור בר דרעי בכל יומא בטורין
אלפא :

"For every beast of the wood is mine, and I have prepared for the righteous in Paradise pure cattle, and the wild ox, that feeds every day upon a thousand mountains." All these testimonies (and many more might be added) plainly prove, that the Jews, in times past, looked for a real and substantial feast upon Leviathan and Behemoth; and when we remember that the commentary of Rashi is the first that is put into the hands of the Jewish youth all over the world, and that it is generally regarded as almost, if not altogether, inspired, it is easy to conclude what is the opinion of the great majority of Jews, even in the present day, as to this entertainment. Maimonides, indeed, denies that there will be any eating and drinking in the world to come. He says—

העולם הבא אין בו גוף וגויה אלא נפשות הצדיקים
בלבד בלא גוף כמלאכי השרת. הואיל ואין בו גויות
אין בו לא אכילה ולא שתיה:

"In the world to come there is neither body nor corporeality, but only the souls of the righteous without a body, like the ministering angels. So neither is there eating and drinking." (Hilchoth T'shuvah, c. viii. 2.) But this is a solitary opinion, as is evident from the note on the passage by Abraham ben Dior, who says—

דברי האיש הזה בעיני קרובים למי שאומר אין
תחיית המתים לגופות אלא נשמות בלבד וחיי ראשי
לא היה דעת חז״ל על זה:

"The words of this man are, in my eyes, very near to those of him who says, that there is no resurrection to the body, but only to the soul; and I swarc by my life that this was not the opinion of our wise men of blessed memory." Indeed Maimonides himself acknowledges, in his Commentary upon the Mishna, that the majority of the Jews thought very differently of the world to come. He there enumerates five classes of opinions, amongst which one is, that at that time the earth will bring forth clothes ready made, and bread ready baked; but in every one of the five, good eating and drinking is a main article. Of the fifth class he says—

וכת חמישית והם הרבה מחברים העניינים האלה
כולם ואומרים כי התוחלת הוא שיבא המשיח ויחיה
המתים ויכנסו לגן עדן ויאכלו שם וישתו ויחיו בריאים
כל ימות עולם:

"And the fifth class (and they are numerous) include all these things, and say that the great hope is, that Messiah shall come and raise the dead, and they shall be gathered into Paradise, and there shall eat and drink and be in good health to all eternity." (Sanhedrin, fol. 119, col. 1.) This, then, Maimonides gives as the general expectation of the majority, and this expectation exactly agrees with the above description of the feast to be prepared from Leviathan and Behemoth.

We have, therefore, not only the testimony of the most celebrated rabbies to prove that this feast is not allegorical but literal, but we have the still stronger evidence of the general expectations of the nation as enumerated by Maimonides. D. Levi ought, therefore, to have said that *he* understood it allegorically, but we have seen that this is not the opinion of the nation, nor of the most celebrated rabbies. We are therefore warranted in saying that the prayers of the synagogue not only consecrate the intolerance of the Talmud, but also stamp its absurd legends with authority. It is surely not exceeding the bounds of soberness and modesty to call this story of the battle between Leviathan and Behemoth, and the feast to be prepared of their flesh, and the salt meat of the female Leviathan, an absurd legend. David Levi evidently thought it was such, and was therefore glad to betake himself to allegory. In the Bible there is not one word about the killing or salting of the female Leviathan, nor about the capacious stomach of Behemoth, which requires a thousand mountains daily to satisfy it. This is all the pure invention of the rabbies, and we ask the Jews whether such legends form fit subjects for the prayers or praises of the synagogue, or whether they can be acceptable in the eyes of the God of Israel? We do not mean to conceal the fact, that Christian prayer-books may be found with legends as fabulous, and as foolish. But they are the prayer-books of former generations, or of those who still adhere to traditions of men. With them we have nothing to do. Three hundred years have now elapsed since our forefathers cleared out all such follies. But the Jewish prayer-books still remain unchanged, and unless the Jews make some vigorous effort, the legend of Leviathan and Behemoth will be read with all solemnity in the synagogues of England at the coming Feast of Pentecost. It is grievous to think that that nation which once held up the torch of Divine truth to enlighten the world, should still abide in the darkness and superstitions of the Talmud. And yet this is, beyond all doubt, the condition of Israel, so long as the Divine authority of the Talmud is recognised in their public prayers. Individuals may say, that they do not believe in its follies, nor cherish its intolerance, but this cannot be said of the majority. The synagogue, in its public worship, still pronounces the maledictions, and recites the legends of the oral law, and thus declares, in the most solemn manner that can be devised, that the religion of the Talmud is the religion of the congregation. A mere confession of faith is nothing to such a declaration as this. A man may trifle with his fellow-men, but sentiments addressed to God in prayer or praise must justly be considered as the language of the heart.

How different is the doctrine of the New Testament. There all these monstrous fables are utterly rejected; there is not even an allusion to them. Mahomet, confessedly the author of a false religion, has incorporated not a few of the Talmudic legends into the Koran. But the disciples of Jesus of Nazareth, though they lived at a time when the patronisers of these fables had power, were altogether preserved from such absurdity. They have transmitted no such distorted view of God's dealings in creation, nor of the joys which he has prepared for his people in eternity. Their doctrine is, that, "Known unto God are all his works from the beginning of the world." (Acts xv. 18.) He is "The Father of lights, with whom is no variableness nor shadow of turning." (James i. 17.) They also give us an account of the felicity of the blessed, but a feast upon Leviathan or Behemoth is not one of its features. " Behold, the tabernacle of God is with men, and he will dwell with them, and they shall be his people, and God himself shall be with them, and be their God. And God shall wipe away all tears from their eyes; and there shall be no more death, neither sorrow, nor crying; neither shall there be any more pain: for the former things are passed away." (Rev. xxi. 3, 4.) "Beloved, now are we the sons of God, and it doth not yet appear what we shall be; but we know that, when he shall appear, we shall be like him, for we shall see him as he is." (1 John iii. 2.) These are the hopes and expectations which that body of Jews, who rejected the oral law, have taught us to entertain and to cherish. Yes, brethren of the house of Israel, our hope is altogether Jewish. We do not mean to charge upon "the peculiar people of God" the folly of the Talmud. Some of the nation forsook the pure Word of God, and adopted the doctrine of an oral law. The natural consequence was, that they advanced gradually farther and farther in the mazes of error; and there all their followers continue. But we never forget that it was another portion of the Jewish nation which taught us to worship the true and living God. Our only wish is, that you would forsake Jewish error, and embrace Jewish truth.

No. XVIII.

RABBINIC LEGENDS CONTINUED.

THAT the traditions of the Talmudists abound with the most absurd and incredible stories, is a matter of notoriety. But when a Talmudist is pressed with any one of these, as a proof that the oral law is not from God, he has a ready answer. It is an allegory, and contains the most profound and mysterious wisdom. It would be very easy to show from the books printed in Jewish-German, for the edification of the women and the unlearned, and where the legends are related as undoubted matter of fact, that this is a mere evasion. But we have other evidence that is indisputable. The Liturgy of the synagogue alludes to many as to authentic history, and we would not believe any one who should dare to assert, that the Rabbinists, in prayer, utter with their lips, what they do not believe in their heart. In the Pentecost prayers, from which we have already quoted, we find allusion to an anecdote recorded of Adam,

תכלית כל פועל רום ותחתונים . שביעי לימים
חנמנים . ראשון למקראי זמנים. קדוש לאדוני האדונים .
צבי קודש שבת שאננים . פדה מדין יציר מלפנים .
ענתה שירה וכפרה פנים :

Which D. Levi thus translates, "It (the Sabbath-day) is the end of all work above and beneath; it is accounted the seventh among the days; the first convocation of seasons; holy to the Lord of hosts; a glorious holy Sabbath to those who rest thereon; it redeemed the first created man from judgment; he chanted a song, and appeased the wrath of God." (fol. 81.) Here two important circumstances, not mentioned by Moses, are alluded to. First, that the Sabbath redeemed Adam from judgment, and secondly, that his song appeased the wrath of God. They are found in the traditions of the rabbies at full length, and are related as follows:—

בשבע שעות ביום בערב שבת נכנס אדם הראשון
בגן עדן והיו מלאכי השרת מקלסין אותו ומכניסין
אותו לגן עדן ובין השמשות בערב שבת גורש ויצא
והיו מלאכי השרת קוראין עליו ואומרין אדם ביקר
בל ילין נמשל כבהמות נדמו . כבהמה נדמה אין
כתיב אלא כבהמות נדמו שניהם . בא יום השבת
ונעשה סניגור לאדם הראשון אמר לפניו רבון העולמים
בששת ימי דזמעשה לא נהרג הרג בעולם ובי אתה

RABBINIC LEGENDS CONTINUED. 137

מתחיל זו היא קדושתי וזו היא ברכתי שנאמר ויברך
אלהים את יום השביעי ויקדש אותו . ובזכות יום
השבת ניצל אדם מדינה של גיהנם וראה אדם כחה
של שבת אמר לא לחנם ברך הקב״ה את השבת וקדש
אותו התחיל משורר ומזמר ליום השבת. שנאמר מזמור
שיר ליום השבת . ר' ישמעאל אומר המזמור הזה
אדם הראשון אמרו ונשכח בכל הדורות עד שבא
משה וחדשו וגו' :

"At the seventh hour of the day, on the eve of the Sabbath, the first Adam was introduced into Paradise; and the ministering angels were engaged in lauding and introducing him. But between the suns, on the eve of the Sabbath, he was driven out, and went forth; and the ministering angels were calling to him, and saying, 'Adam being in honour abideth not: he is like the beasts that perish.' It is not written, 'like a beast that perishes,' but 'like the beasts that perish;' *i.e.*, they both. The Sabbath-day came, and became an advocate for the first Adam. It said before God, Lord of the world, in the six days of the creation, nothing in the world was killed, and wilt thou begin with me? Is this my sanctification, and is this my blessing, as it is said, 'And God blessed the seventh day, and sanctified it.' Therefore by the merit of the Sabbath-day Adam was delivered from the judgment of hell; and when Adam saw the power of the Sabbath, he said, It was not for nothing, that the Holy One, blessed be He, blessed and sanctified it, so he began singing and chanting to the Sabbath-day, as it is said, 'A psalm or song to or for the Sabbath-day.' (Psalm xcii. 1.) Rabbi Ishmael says, This psalm was said by the first Adam, but was forgotten in all the generations, until Moses came and restored it." (Pirke Eleazar, fol. 13, col. 3.) The Yalkut Shimoni gives the story substantially the same, excepting that when Adam said, "A psalm or song to the Sabbath-day," the Sabbath reproved him, and said, "Dost thou sing hymns to me? Come and let us both sing hymns to the Holy One, blessed be He, 'It is a good thing to give thanks unto the Lord.'" (Ps. xcii. 1.) This, then is the story which the prayer-book of the synagogue authenticates, by interweaving, in its addresses to the God of Israel, the above-quoted words concerning the Sabbath, "It redeemed the first created man from judgment; he chanted a song, and appeased the wrath of God." From first to last it bears the plain marks of mendacity. It misrepresents the merciful character of God, as if he would have destroyed Adam, had it not been the Sabbath-day. It ascribes a certain degree of merit to Adam, who had been guilty of the most inexcusable ingratitude to his Divine Benefactor. And it directly contradicts the narrative of Moses, who ascribes the mercy vouchsafed to the spontaneous overflowings of the grace of God. Besides all this, it is perfectly ludicrous to imagine that Adam, just driven out of Paradise for his disobedience, with the curse of the Almighty resting upon him, goaded by the pangs of a guilty conscience, and his whole frame undergoing the mighty transition from immortality to corruption—it is perfectly ludicrous to imagine that he could be in a fit mood to sit down and compose a poem. Indeed the rabbies themselves have not left this story a fair appearance of credibility, for on the very same page of the Yalkut, where this origin of the ninety-second Psalm is described, another equally veracious incident in the life of Adam, is assigned as the occasion of its composition.

אמר ר׳ לוי המזמור הזה אדם הראשון אמרו פגע
אדם הראשון בקין אמר ליה מה נעשה בדינך אמר
ליה עשיתי תשובה ונתפשרתי התחיל אדם הראשון
מטפח על פניו אמר כך הוא גדול כחה של תשובה
ולא הייתי יודע מיד עמד אדם הראשון ואמר מזמור:

"Rabbi Levi says, this hymn was said by the first Adam. Adam happened to meet Cain, and said to him, What has been done in the matter of thy judgment? He replied, I have repented, and been reconciled. Adam began to strike his forehead with his hand, and said, So great is the power of repentance, and I did not know it! Immediately the first Adam stood, and said this Psalm." Thus, on the showing of the traditions themselves, this legend, formally adopted in the prayers of the synagogue, is a falsehood. Can this be acceptable worship? Is it reasonable worship? Is the legend itself, in any of its features, worthy of that great people, that received the law of God at Sinai? This is the religion of the High-priests and Pharisees who rejected Jesus of Nazareth, and this the wisdom of those who condemned Him, and that fully accounts for their conduct. Men, who had let loose their imaginations into the regions of romance and fiction, were not likely to love the sober truth inculcated by Jesus and his disciples. Their appetites were vitiated, and they were not satisfied with the unadorned narrative of Moses. They had 'ost all relish for the simple majesty of the "oracles of God." We appeal to the native acuteness, and unsophisticated feeling of every right-minded Jew, and ask whether it is not a melancholy spectacle to behold the wise men of Israel thus trifling with the sin of Adam, that sad event, the source of all our woes? Very different is the tone in which the New Testament speaks both of it, and of the mind of God in reference to it. "Wherefore, as by one man sin entered into the world, and death by sin; and so death passed upon all men, for that all have sinned: for until the law sin was in the world; but sin is not imputed when there is no law. Nevertheless death reigned from Adam to Moses, even over them that had not sinned after the similitude of Adam's transgression, who is the figure of Him that was to come. But not as the offence, so also is the free gift. For if through the offence of one many be dead, much more the grace of God, and the gift by grace, which is by one man, Jesus Christ, hath abounded unto many." (Romans v. 12—15.) But whatever the Jews may think of the New Testament representation, we have here shown that their Liturgy contains an absurd legend, borrowed from tradition ages ago, and which remains there to this day. But, alas! the very next sentence of the prayer, from which we have quoted, contains two more.

קיימה לאות ולעד בין אב לבנים, נצור יציאותיה
כהורו נבונים. משא בלי להוציא מבפנים. למחלליה
מיתות דנים. כרת ורגימת אבנים. ידועה היא לך
במן מימים קדמונים. טעמו לא רד בה ממעונים.
חוברי אוב בה לא נענים. זכור כי בה ישבות נהר
צפונים:

" It (the Sabbath) is noted as a sign and a witness between the heavenly Father and his children: observe its removals, as taught by the wise men, not to bring out a load from within; death is pronounced against those that profane it, either by excision or stoned with stones; by the manna it was well known unto thee in ancient days, for on the Sabbath that food did not descend; *the necromancers were not answered on it; remember that on it the incomprehensible river[b] resteth.*" Amongst the other honours of the Sabbath-day, and the other testimonies to its sacredness, this prayer recounts two miracles. The one, that necromancers could not bring up the dead on that day; the other, the weekly Sabbatarian rest of the river Sambation. The first of these miracles has been left by D. Levi without notice or explanation. He thought, perhaps, that it would not do in English. But to the second, the resting " of the incomprehensible river[b]" he has attached the following note :—

"[b] This denotes the river סמביון, said to rest on the Sabbath from throwing up stones, &c., which it does all the week. See Sanhedrin, fol. lxv. 2; Yalkut on Isaiah, fol. lii. 1; Pesikta, Tanchuma, sect. כי תשא. See also Shalsheleth Hakkabala, and Juchsin."

D. Levi himself thus acknowledges, that no allegory is here intended, but that the Rabbinists do really believe that there is a river that throws up stones all the week, and rests on the Sabbath-day. Many and various are the accounts which the rabbies give of it, but we shall confine ourselves to one or other of D. Levi's references, which also throw light upon the subject of the necromancers.

ואף שאלה זה שאל טורנוס רופוס הרשע את ר״ע
אמר לו ומה יום מיומים אמר לו ומה גבר מגוברין
א״ל דמרי צבי שבת נמי דמרי צבי. אמר ליה הכי
קאמינא לך מי יימר דהאידנא שבהא. אמר לו נהר
סמבטיון יוכיח בעל אוב יוכיח קברו של אביו יוכיח
שאין מעלה עשן בשבת:

"Turnus Rufus, the wicked, also proposed this question to R. Akiva, saying, Why is the Sabbath-day better than other days? He replied, Why art thou greater than other men? He answered, So is the will of my Master. The rabbi said, So is it with the Sabbath, such is the will of God. Turnus Rufus said, But I mean to say, who will prove to me that this day is the Sabbath-day? The rabbi answered, The river Sambation will prove this;—a necromancer will prove this;—the grave of thy father will prove this, for the smoke is not made to ascend from it on the Sabbath." (Sanhed. fol. 65, col. 2.) In his commentary upon this passage, Rashi says of the Sambation,

נהר אחד של אבנים ובכל ימות השבת שוטף
והולך וביום השבת שוקט ונח:

"The Sambation is a certain river of stones, which rolls along all the days of the week, but on the Sabbath-day it is perfectly still." He also explains to us what is meant by the smoke not ascending from the grave on the Sabbath-day, in the following note:

קברו של אביו דטורנוס רופוס כל ימות השבת
היה מעלה עשן שחיה נדון ונשרף ובשבת פושעי
גיהנם שובתין:

"On all the other days of the year a smoke was made to ascend from the grave of the father of Turnus Rufus, for he was suffering the judgment of burning, but on the Sabbath-day, the sinners in hell have rest." Whether Turnus Rufus saw the smoke or not, the Talmud does not inform us, but the Bereshith Rabba, another work of equal credibility in such matters of fact, tells the story a little more at length, and informs us that he was not satisfied with the argument drawn from the river Sambation. R. Akiva therefore advised him to cite his father from the dead on the Sabbath and the other days, and that this

experiment would convince him. To this Turnus Rufus
consented, and the results are described in the following
words :—

וסלק כל יומי דשבתא ובשבתא לא סלק בחד
בשבא אסקיה אמר ליה מן דמיתת איתעבדית יהודי
אתמהא מפני מה עלית כל ימות השבת ושבת לא
עלית אמר ליה כל מי שאינו משמר את השבת
אצלכם ברצונו כאן הוא משמר אותו בעל כרחו.
אמר לו וכי עמל יש לכם שאתם עמלים כל ימות
השבת ובשבת אתם נוחין אמר לו כל ימות השבת
אנו נידונין ובשבת אנו נוחין :

"His father came up every day of the week, but on the
Sabbath-day he did not come up. On the first day of the week
he brought him up again, and said to him, Father, hast thou
been made a Jew since thy death; why is it that thou comest
up on all the other days of the week, but not on Sabbath? He
replied, Whosoever will not keep the Sabbath voluntarily in
your world, must keep it here in spite of himself. He then
said, Father, have you then got work on the other days of the
week, and rest on the Sabbath? The father replied, On the
other days of the week we are judged, but on the Sabbath we
are at rest." (Bereshith Rabba, fol. 9, col. 4.) Such are the
legends which the Jewish Prayer-book, on the solemn feast of
Pentecost, stamps with all the authority of authentic history.
Is it necessary to prove to the Jews of England that both these
stories are utterly untrue? Is it necessary to say, that there is
not, and never was, such a river as the Sambation? Within a
century the world has been explored in every direction. From
Cooke to Kotzebue the globe has been many times circumnavi-
gated, but none has brought us any tidings of the Sambation.
Since the times of Benjamin of Tudela, and Abraham Peritsol,
there has been a host of adventurous travellers, but none had
the luck to behold the miraculous torrent of the Sambation. In
this very city Jews are occasionally found from every part of
the world, but from the banks of the Sambation no messenger
has yet arrived. The whole account is a fiction, and is unworthy
of a place in the prayers of the Jews of England. The same
may be said of the necromancers, who obtain no answer on the
Sabbath-day. It is nothing more than a clever fiction. By
the law of Moses necromancy is forbidden to the Jews, and
therefore the inventor well knew that no pious Jew would ever
make the experiment, either on the Sabbath or the other days.
The story of Turnus Rufus, and his father, as told in the
Bereshith Rabba, is plainly contrary, even to the assertions of
the oral law itself. The father is made to say, "Whosoever

will not keep the Sabbath voluntarily in your world, must keep it here, in spite of himself;" which implies that all, who do not keep the Jewish Sabbath, must be punished in the flames of hell; whereas the oral law says that the observance of the Sabbath is not required of the sons of Noah. When this prayer was introduced into the Liturgy of the synagogue we know not, but there it now stands, and in one short paragraph contains three downright falsehoods. David Levi himself points us to R. Akiva as the author of the last two; and accordingly the Talmud records the original reference to the business of the necromancers and the river Sambation, as proceeding from the mouth of that great Rabbi. This brings us back to the time immediately succeeding the rejection of Jesus of Nazareth, and shows us the superstition and the falsehood of those who rejected him. Either R. Akiva invented these things himself, and then he is guilty of deliberate falsehood, or he received these accounts from others who went before him, and then he was a superstitious man, and the guilt of inventing falsehood is thrown back on the earlier rabbies. What is to be thought then of the wisdom of those men who were weak enough to believe, or wicked enough to invent, such absurd fables? Yet these are the men who opposed Christianity, and this is the system which a large portion of the Jewish nation has preferred for 1700 years. That the Rabbinical Jews have firmly believed these legends is plain. They occur in the Talmud, whose authority is regarded as divine. They are repeated by Rashi, Ramban, Bechai, and a whole host of the most esteemed Jewish writers. They have formed a part of the synagogue service for centuries, and are still found in the Prayer-books of the English Jews, to testify that they are not yet emancipated from the chains of superstition. If they had been, if any considerable number of Jews had been convinced of the falsehood of these stories, they would never have suffered them to remain in the worship of God. It is utterly impossible to suppose that men would sanction the solemn propagation of falsehood, and yet whenever the Pentecost prayers are read or printed, there the fables of Behemoth and Leviathan, Adam and the Sabbath, Turnus Rufus and the Sambation, are solemnly accredited to the world as worthy of all belief and honour. The fact that they constitute a part of a solemn address to Almighty God, and that not from an individual, but from the congregation of Israel, gives them a sanction that nothing else could confer. The foreign Jew who comes to England from some country where there is not so much light, might, if he found such fables struck out of the English synagogue service, obtain a little light, and go back to his countrymen with the news, that the enlightened English Jews have rejected all these absurdities; and thus the moral emancipation of the nation might be prepared throughout the world. But no; the superstitious Talmudist from Turkey, or from Barbary, or the North, arrives in England, goes to the synagogue, and finds the same fables and the same superstitions that he had learned in his less favoured native land, and returns as he came. Perhaps he takes with him a copy of the synagogue prayers, printed in London, and exhibits to his countrymen Behemoth and Leviathan, the necromancers and the Sambation, adorned with all the beauty of English printing, paper, and binding. There is surely a great and solemn responsibility resting on those Israelites who do not believe these fables, to protest against their admission into the prayers of the synagogue. The honour of the nation, the welfare of their brethren, and the glory of God, all call for such a public protestation. The Jewish nation is a great and intellectual people, highly gifted by God with those powers that adorn and dignify humanity. But this is not the estimate formed by the world at large. Why not? Because the world at large knows only the fables and absurdities of the Talmud, but is ignorant of the real monuments of Jewish genius. What can be said, then, by an advocate for the Jews, to one who holds the Jewish mind cheap? All arguments will prove powerless as long as these instances of superstition and folly are contained in the Jewish prayers. The objector will still point to them, and say, If you want to know what men really believe, do not look at their controversial works, or their apologetic writings, but examine their Prayer-book. Consider not what they say to man, but listen to what they say to God. There they are sincere. What can we answer to this argument? Can we say that all the follies and intolerance of former generations are expunged? No; whether from love or from listlessness, there they abide to this day.

But the honour of the nation is but of small weight compared with its spiritual and temporal prosperity. The English Jews might, by erasing all such passages, and thoroughly reforming their Prayer-book, prove a blessing to their brethren scattered through the world. Do the intelligent and enlightened part of the nation really wish to raise their brethren in the moral scale? It must be done by purifying their religious notions. There is an inseparable bond of union between religion and moral virtue. Superstition degrades and enfeebles the mind; but zeal for the glory of God calls still more loudly upon every devout Israelite to vindicate the honour of that revelation which God consigned to their care, and which is obscured by these fabulous additions.

No. XIX.

LEGENDS IN THE PRAYERS FOR PENTECOST.

One of the most glorious circumstances in the national history of Israel, as well as one of the most extraordinary facts in the records of mankind, is the descent of the Lord God upon Mount Sinai to proclaim the law. Glorious it is for Israel, for never did nation hear the voice of the Lord, speaking out of the midst of the fire, as Israel heard. The display of God's grace and favour is the glory of his people, and here they were both displayed pre-eminently. The grandeur and awfulness of the scene we cannot now enter upon, except to remark, that the grandeur of the reality is equalled by the dignity of the narrative, which Moses has left us in the 19th and 20th chapters of Exodus. None but an inspired historian could have treated an event so honourable to his nation, with such majestic simplicity. The style and tone furnish an irresistible evidence to the truth of the relation. And perhaps this evidence is much strengthened by the contrast presented in the writings of the rabbies. There is no part of the Scripture history which they have more amplified by additions of their own; as plainly stamped with falsehood, as the other with truth. We have here a wide field before us, but shall confine ourselves to those legends which are authenticated in the synagogue prayers for the anniversary of that great event. In the morning service for the second day is found an account of the giving of the law, in which the following wonderful passage occurs:—

צבאות קודש אחזום בעתה . צלע כגיגית עליהם
כפפת . צרופה קבלו במנוד ואימתה :

"Dread seized the holy hosts, when thou didst turn the mountain over them as a tub: they received the pure law with fear and tremor." (D. Levi's Pentecost Prayers, fol. 150.) Here is a circumstance in the giving of the law, which few readers of the Pentateuch will remember. All will grant that to see Mount Sinai hanging over them, like a tub or an extinguisher, was a very dreadful sight, if it really happened. But surely every reasonable Israelite will inquire upon what evidence it rests? In all the previous history God appears as a merciful Father, visiting his children in their affliction, redeeming them from bondage, and exhibiting miracle after miracle as their safety or their necessity required; how is it, then, that He appears so suddenly in the character of a tyrant or a destroyer, ready to drop the mighty mountain upon the heads of his people, and cover them up for ever under the rocky mass? Moses throws no light upon the subject. The oral law, the Talmud, must explain the mystery.

ויתיצבו בתחתית ההר אמר ר׳ אבדימי בר חמא
בר חסא מלמד שכפה עליהם הקב״ה את ההר כגיגית
ואמר להם אם תקבלו את התורה מוטב ואם לאו שם
תהא קבורתכם, אמר ר׳ אחא בר יעקב מכאן מודעא
רבה לאורייתא וכו׳ :

"And they stood at the nether part of the mountain (or beneath the mountain). (Exod. xix. 17.) R. Avdimi, the son of Chama, the son of Chasa, says, These words teach us that the Holy One, blessed be He, turned the mountain over them like a tub, and said to them, If ye will receive the law, well; but if not, there shall be your grave. R. Acha, the son of R. Jacob, says, This is a great confession for the law." (Shabbath, fol. 88, 1.) From this extract it appears that the whole foundation of the fable is a sort of pun upon the words בתחתית ההר, "beneath the mountain," or as the English translators rightly have it, "at the nether part of the mountain." R. Avdimi thought that these words meant, as Rashi says, תחת ההר ממש, "under the mountain in the strictest sense of the words." But then the puzzle was, how the Israelites got into that situation. R. Abdimi's imagination supplied the rest. But in the first place, the word תחתית occurs often enough in both the singular and plural, but never has this signification. In the second place, this fable directly contradicts the Mosaic account. God had already sent notice to inform the people of the giving of the law, and they had replied, "All that the Lord hath spoken we will do." (Ver. 8.) In the third place, if the mountain was turned over them like a tub, how did Moses get up to the top, and what necessity was there for the command, "Go down, charge the people, lest they break through?" &c. (Ver. 21.) And lastly, if the law was forced upon the Israelites contrary to their wish, cannot they make this an apology for disobedience? Is not this what R. Acha, the son of Jacob, actually does, when he says, "This is a great confession for the law?" So at least Rashi explains his words.

מודעא רבה שאם יזמינם לדין למה לא קיימתם
מה שקבלתם עליכם יש להם תשובה שקבלוה באונס :

"A great confession, for if he call them to judgment, saying, Why have ye not kept that which ye took upon yourselves, they have an answer, that they were forced to receive it." (Rashi Comment. in loc.) And this fable, contrary to the narrative of Moses, derogatory to the mercy of God, and subversive to the principle of human responsibility, the rabbies have introduced into the prayers of the synagogue, and there it still stands as an evidence of the absence of God's Spirit from those who rejected Jesus of Nazareth, and imposed the oral law upon Israel. But this want of wisdom appears not only in the nature of the additions which they have made to the Word of God, but also in the conflicting statements which these additions contain. In the legend just given Israel is represented as having been unwilling to receive the law, and yet in the morning service for the first day of Pentecost, we have an allusion to another legend, which describes the great reward bestowed upon them, because they received it with such a ready mind.

הם קבלו עול תורה עלימו, ונעשה לנשמע הקדימו,
טרם נשמע נעשה נמר, וצדקה בה נחשבֽה למו,
ולשני כתרים סוימו, למלוכה וכהונה וללויה אוימו:

"They willingly took the yoke of his law upon them, and caused the expression, 'We will do,' to precede, 'We will hearken;' before they heard it they said, 'We will do,' and which was accounted for righteousness to them; and they were dignified with two crowns; and rendered awful with the sovereignty of the priesthood, and the Levitical institution." (Pentecost Prayers, fol. 86.) At first sight it would appear as if this were a mere figurative expression to denote either the priesthood and the Levitical institution, or the monarchy and the priesthood. But then a difficulty occurs, why are only two crowns mentioned? Every one knows that in a figurative sense the oral law says that Israel is crowned with three crowns, as it is said,

בשלש כתרים נכתרו ישראל כתר תורה וכתר
כהונה וכתר מלכות:

"Israel is crowned with three crowns, the crown of the law, and the crown of the priesthood, and the crown of the kingdom." (Hilchoth Talmud Torah, chap. iii. 1.) Why then does this prayer only mention two? It is because it refers to a totally different circumstance. The number of the crowns, and the reason assigned for their bestowal, "because they caused the expression 'We will do,' to precede 'We will hearken,'" both identify the allusion as being made to the following Talmudic legend:—

בשעה שהקדימו ישראל נעשה לנשמע באו ששים
ריבוא של מלאכי השרת לכל אחד ואחד מישראל
קשרו לו שני כתרים אחד כנגד נעשה ואחד כנגד

נשמע וכיוון שחטאו ישראל ירדו מאה ועשרים רבוא
מלאכי חבלה ופרקום שנאמר ויתנצלו בני ישראל את
עדים מהר חורב:

"In the hour when Israel caused, 'We will do,' to precede 'We will hearken,' there came six hundred thousand ministering angels, one to each Israelite, and invested him with two crowns, one answering to 'We will do;' and the second answering to 'We will hearken.' But when Israel sinned, there descended twelve hundred thousand evil angels, and took them away: as it is said, 'The children of Israel stripped themselves (or were stripped) of their ornaments by the mount Horeb.'" (Ex. xxxiii. 6.) (Shabbath, fol. 88, 1.) Here, then, is no allegory, no allusion to the allegorical crowns of Israel, but a narrative of a supposed fact, which occurred in the history of each of the six hundred thousand Israelites who went forth from Egypt. The commentary in the Talmud evidently treats this as a grave and authentic history, for it tells us the material of which the crowns were composed.

שני כתרים של הוד היו לפיכך כשנטלם משה
קרן עור פניו:

"The two crowns were crowns of glory, therefore, when Moses wore them the skin of his face shone." From this it is evident that the Rabbinists considered this legend to be as authentic as the fact recorded in the Bible (Exod. xxxiv. 30), that the skin of Moses' face shone. They were not satisfied with the honour conferred upon Moses, but were led, by a vainglorious feeling, to extend it to every individual Israelite, and to add what is not said of Moses, but what increases the marvellousness of the narrative, that six hundred thousand angels descended for the purpose of crowning Israel, and that twice that number was necessary for the removal of the crowns once conferred. But how does this story agree with the former? If the Israelites were compelled to receive the law against their will, by the terrors of the mountain hanging over their heads, what great merit was there to deserve these two crowns? If the Israelites were so willing, and received such a glorious reward, what necessity was there for turning the mountain over them like a tub? These stories are inconsistent in themselves, without foundation in the Word of God, and are therefore unworthy of a place in the prayers of Israel. But this prayer has other particulars equally wonderful, to which we proceed. A sentence or two farther on, this prayer describes the effect which the delivery of the ten commandments produced upon Israel.

ואחת בדברו החריד עולמו, ועשרים וארבעה מיל
מחלך נעו עמו, שתים זו כהשמיעו נואמו:

"When he spoke the first word, his world was terrified, and when they heard two commandments, they moved backward the space of twenty-four מִיל miles." (Pentecost Prayers, fol. 87.) To understand this, we must again refer to the Talmud, which gives us the particulars.

אמר ר׳ יהושע בר לוי כל דבור ודבור שיצא מפי
הקב״ה חזרו ישראל לאחוריהן י״ב מיל והיו מלאכי
השרת מדדין אותן שנאמר מלאכי צבאות ידודון ידודון
אל תקרא ידודון אלא ידדון :

"Rabbi Joshua, the son of Levi, says, as each commandment proceeded from the mouth of the Holy One, blessed be He, Israel retreated twelve miles, and the ministering angels led them back, as it is said, 'the angels of the host did flee apace.' (Ps. lxviii. 13.) Do not read יִדֹּדוּן 'they fled;' but יְדַדּוּן, they led.'" (Shabbath, fol. 88, 2.) In this short passage we have two deliberate alterations of the Word of God, in order to square it with this absurd tradition. In the first place, מלאכי צבאות "Kings of hosts" is changed into מלכי צבאות "angels of hosts," and in the second place, "They fled," is changed into "they led." These alterations do of themselves throw discredit upon the story which requires them, and not only upon this story, but upon the whole oral law, which allows such trifling with the Word of God. But our business is at present with the legend, and as it is told a little more circumstantially in the Jalkut, it will be well to give that version of it also.

ויעמדו מרחוק חוץ לשנים עשר מיל מגיד שהיו
ישראל נרתעין לאחוריהן שנים עשר מיל וחוזרין
לפניהם שנים עשר מיל הרי עשרים וארבעה מיל על
כל דבור ודבור נמצאו מחלכין באותו היום מאתים
וארבעים מיל באותה שעה אמר הקב״ה למלאכי השרת
רדו וסייעו את אחיכם שנאמר מלכי צבאות ידודון
ידודון ידודון בהליכה ידודון בחזרה :

"'They removed and stood afar off' (Exod. xx. 18)—a distance of twelve miles. This shows us that Israel retreated backwards twelve miles, and then advanced forwards twelve miles, altogether twenty-four miles, as each commandment was delivered. Thus they travelled in that day two hundred and forty miles. At that time the Holy One, blessed be He, said to the ministering angels, Descend and help your brethren, for it is said, 'The Kings of hosts did lead, did lead.' (Ps. lxviii. 13.) That is, they led when they went, and they led them when they returned." (Jalkut Shimoni, part

i. fol. 53, 1.)   It is hardly needful to point out the absurdity
of this narration.   Just think of the Israelites running away
twelve miles, when they heard a commandment, and then
brought back again, and then running away again.   How unlike the simple and dignified narrative which Moses has left!
We ask every intelligent Israelite what he thinks? Is this story
a falsehood? If so, why is it left in the prayers of the synagogue? If it stood alone, we might suppose that by some over-
sight or other it had crept in, but we have already noticed
many like it, and the very next sentence of this same prayer
contains another.

בְּרִדְתּוֹ לְדַבֵּר לְעַם עוֹלָם, רָעֲשׁוּ אוּמוֹת הָעוֹלָם,
פַּחַד קְרָאָם וְרַעַד הֶחִילָם, חִיל כְּיוֹלֵדָה הִבְהִילָם,
סָעֲרוּ וְחָרְדוּ וְסָר צִלָּם, וְאֵצֶל קְמוּאֵל בָּאוּ כֻלָּם, לְנַחֵשׁ
בְּקִסְמֵי קִלְקוּלָם, וְשָׁאֲלוּ לוֹ מַה זֶּה בָּא לָעוֹלָם, שֶׁמָּא
הַיּוֹם לִימֵיו חוֹזֵר הָעוֹלָם:

" When he came down to speak to the immortal people, the
people of the world were moved, dread seized them, and
trembling laid hold on them ; pain troubled them as a woman
in travail : they were shaken and disturbed, and their shadow
departed from them ; they all came to Kemuel, to divine with
their erroneous divinations, and asked him, What is this that
hath happened to the world ? Perhaps the world is this day to
return to its chaos."   The preceding story told us what
happened to Israel, the allusion in this sentence tells us
of the terror which came upon the Gentiles; but to understand
the allusion, we must again refer to the Talmud.

וַיִּשְׁמַע יִתְרוֹ כֹּהֵן מִדְיָן מַה שְׁמוּעָה שָׁמַע וּבָא
וְנִתְגַּיֵּיר ר׳ יְהוֹשֻׁעַ אוֹמֵר מִלְחֶמֶת עֲמָלֵק שָׁמַע שֶׁהֲרֵי
כָּתוּב בְּצִדּוֹ וַיַּחֲלוֹשׁ יְהוֹשֻׁעַ אֶת עֲמָלֵק וְאֶת עַמּוֹ לְפִי
חָרֶב, ר״א הַמּוֹדָעִי אוֹמֵר מַתַּן תּוֹרָה שָׁמַע שֶׁכְּשֶׁנִּתְּנָה
תּוֹרָה לְיִשְׂרָאֵל קוֹלוֹ הוֹלֵךְ מִסּוֹף עוֹלָם וְעַד סוֹפוֹ וְכָל
אוּמוֹת הָעוֹלָם אֲחָזָתַן רְעָדָה בְּהֵיכְלֵיהֶן וְאָמְרוּ שִׁירָה
שֶׁנֶּאֱמַר וּבְהֵיכָלוֹ כֻּלּוֹ אוֹמֵר כָּבוֹד נִתְקַבְּצוּ כֻּלָּם אֵצֶל
בִּלְעָם הָרָשָׁע וְאָמְרוּ לוֹ מַה קוֹל הֶהָמוֹן הַזֶּה אֲשֶׁר
שָׁמַעְנוּ שֶׁמָּא מַבּוּל בָּא לָעוֹלָם אָמַר לָהֶם ה׳ לַמַּבּוּל
יָשַׁב וַיֵּשֶׁב ה׳ מֶלֶךְ לְעוֹלָם, כְּבָר נִשְׁבַּע הקב״ה שֶׁאֵינוֹ
מֵבִיא מַבּוּל לָעוֹלָם אָמְרוּ לוֹ מַבּוּל שֶׁל מַיִם אֵינוֹ
מֵבִיא אֲבָל מַבּוּל שֶׁל אֵשׁ מֵבִיא שֶׁנֶּאֱמַר כִּי הִנֵּה בָאֵשׁ
ה׳ נִשְׁפָּט אָמַר לָהֶם כְּבָר נִשְׁבַּע שֶׁאֵינוֹ מַשְׁחִית כָּל
בָּשָׂר, וּמַה קוֹל הֶהָמוֹן הַזֶּה אֲשֶׁר שָׁמַעְנוּ אָמַר לָהֶן
חֶמְדָּה טוֹבָה יֵשׁ לוֹ בְּבֵית גְּנָזָיו שֶׁהָיְתָה גְּנוּזָה אֶצְלוֹ

תתקע"ד דורות קודם שנברא העולם ובקש ליתנה
לבניו שנאמר ה' עוז לעמו יתן פתחו כולם ואמרו
ה' יברך את עמו בשלום :

"'And Jethro the priest of Midian heard.' (Exod. xviii. 1.) What was it that he heard which induced him to come and be a proselyte? R. Joshua says, he heard of the war with Amalek, for immediately before it is written, 'And Joshua discomfited Amalek and his people with the edge of his sword.' (Exod. xvii. 13.) R. Eliezer, the Modite, says, he heard the giving of the law, for when the law was given to Israel, his voice went from one end of the world to the other, and all the nations of the world were seized with trembling in their temples, and they repeated a hymn, as it is said, 'In his temple doth every one speak of his glory.' (Psalm xxix. 9.) They gathered themselves together to Baalam the wicked, and said to him, What is the voice of the tumult which we have heard? Perhaps a flood is coming upon the world. He replied, 'The Lord sitteth upon the flood;' yea, the Lord sitteth King for ever.' (Verse 10.) The Holy One, blessed be He, has sworn long since that He will not bring a flood upon the world. They replied, He will not bring a flood of waters, but He will bring a flood of fire! for it is said, 'By fire will the Lord plead.' (Isaiah lxvi. 16.) He answered them, He has sworn long since that he will not destroy all flesh. What, then, is the voice of the tumult which we have heard? He said to them, God has had a most desirable good in the house of his treasures, which has been treasured up with him for nine hundred and seventy-four generations before the creation of the world, and he now seeks to give it to his children, for it is said, 'The Lord will give strength to his people.' Then they all began and said, 'The Lord will bless his people with peace.'" (Ps. xxix. 11.) (Zevachin, fol. 116, 1.) This is the fable to which your prayers refer, and which all Israel throughout the world is taught to believe, and to commemorate in the solemn act of public worship. That it is a mere fable is very easy to prove. First, it contradicts the narrative given by Moses. This fable says that the tremendous noise made at the giving of the law, brought Jethro to Moses—that this was what he heard. But if you will read the whole verse, from which the Talmud quotes a few words, you will find that there was no occasion for asking what Jethro heard, for Moses himself expressly tells us what he heard, and why he came. "When Jethro, the priest of Midian, Moses' father-in-law, heard of all that God had done for Moses, and for Israel his people, and that the Lord had brought Israel out of Egypt, then Jethro," &c. (Exodus xviii. 1—5.) If you will read the whole chapter, you will find that Jethro was come and gone before the law was given, and consequently before the tremendous noise was made; so that it is certainly false that this was the cause of his coming. Secondly, that all the nations heard the voice of God is false, for it also contradicts the language of Moses, who makes it the peculiar privilege of Israel, that they alone heard the voice. "Did ever people hear the voice of God speaking out of the midst of the fire, as thou hast heard, and live?" (Deut. iv. 33.) Lastly, this story is palpably absurd. The Talmud represents Balaam and his Gentile contemporaries quoting Scripture like two rabbies, and that, hundreds of years before the portions which they quote were written! They both quote the 29th Psalm, a Psalm of David, about 500 years before he was born, and the Gentiles quote the 66th of Isaiah above 700 years before it was written! And your rabbies have not been content to keep this absurd and foolish story in the Talmud, but have inserted it in the prayers for the solemn festival of Pentecost. According to these prayers, you are taught to believe that, at the giving of the law, God turned Mount Sinai over the people of Israel like a tub, and compelled them to receive the law against their will; and yet that, for their ready obedience, six hundred thousand angels were sent down to crown each man with two crowns. You are taught to believe that when the commandments were given, Israel walked backwards and forwards two hundred and forty miles. And that the voice of God was so loud that it was heard by all the nations of the world, who all went to Balaam, and all knew and quoted the Psalms and the prophets, centuries before they were written. This is what you have got by following the oral law. It is in vain for you to say that you do not believe these things—there they stand in your Prayer-book. If you do not believe them, why do you leave them there? But whatever individuals may say, it is evident that the compilers of the Jewish Liturgy heartily believed every word of them, and therefore introduced them into their prayers. And it is equally certain that, wherever the Talmud maintains its authority, these fables form part of the faith of Israel. But some will say, We do not believe them. Why not; Do you disbelieve them because they are true? No, but because they are false. Then you confess that the oral law contains downright palpable falsehoods, and that in many of its narrations it is not worthy of credence. Of what value, then, is the oral law, and what credit can we give to the authors of it, who did not scruple to invent these foolish stories?

No. XX.

LEGENDS IN THE PRAYERS FOR PENTECOST.

NEARLY eighteen centuries have now elapsed since a large portion of the Jewish nation deliberately chose Rabbinism in preference to Christianity. The great question between Jews and Christians is, whether those persons made a right choice. The means of answering the question are within our reach. The oral law exists, diffused through the volumes of the Talmud, and compressed in the prayers of the synagogue. There we can look for it, and judge of its spirit and its intrinsic excellence and evidence. The Rabbinists say, that the oral law was given to Moses on Mount Sinai, and that the oral law which they now possess, is identically the same as that then received; and they appeal in proof of this assertion to the continuity of its transmission from father to son down to the present day. The Christian objects that this oral law is full of fables. The Talmudist replies by making a distinction between the דינים the laws and the Agadah, or legendary part: and the Christian is satisfied or silenced until he opens the Jewish Prayer-book, and finds that the most absurd and improbable of all the Talmudic legends are there recognised as undoubted verities, and integral parts of modern Judaism. Many of these, and sufficient to annihilate all claims which the oral law can make to truth, have been examined, but as this part of the subject is important, two more must be considered before we can at present take leave of them. In the sentence immediately following our last extract from the Jewish prayers we read as follows:—

וכל דור ודור ומנהיגיהם, אשר עמדו לפניהם,
והעתידים לעמוד אחריהם, כולם העמידם בסיני
עמהם, להודיעם כי דור דע נחשק מכולהם, טוב
טעם ודעת להשכילהם, וכל מום לא היה בהם, כי
שלמים ומושלמים היו כולהם:

Which D. Levi thus translates, "And every generation, and its governors that existed before them, and those that rose after them, were all placed at Mount Sinai with them, to let them know, that the intelligent generation was more acceptable than them; to make them understand good judgment and knowledge: there was no blemish in them, for they were entirely perfect." (Pentecost Prayers, p. 87.) The assembling of the living nation of Israel, to hear the voice of the Creator, was not grand enough for the rabbies, they have therefore added that the souls of all the unborn generations were present to hear and receive the law. The comparison of this tradition with some already considered suggests several interesting topics for inquiry. For instance, whether these souls were under the mountain or not when it was turned over them—whether they performed the journey of two hundred and forty miles backwards and forwards at the giving of the ten commandments, &c.? But the authority, which this tradition confers on the oral law, demands our more immediate attention, and is particularly manifest in that version of the story, which is found in Medrash Rabba.

וידבר אלהים את כל הדברים האלה לאמר, אמר
ר' יצחק מה שהנביאים עתידין להתנבאות בכל דור
ודור קבלו מהר סיני שכן משה אומר להם לישראל
כי את אשר ישנו פה עמנו עומד היום ואת אשר
איננו פה עמנו היום, עמנו עומד היום אין כתיב כאן
אלא איננו עמנו היום אלו הנשמות העתידות להבראות
שאין בהן ממש שלא נאמרה בהן עמידה שאע"פ
שלא היו באותה שעה כל אחד ואחד קבל את שלו
וכן הוא אומר משא דבר ה' אל ישראל ביד מלאכי,
בימי מלאכי לא נאמר אלא ביד מלאכי שכבר היתה
הנבואה בידו מהר סיני ועד אותה שעה לא נתנה לו
רשות להתנבאות, וכן ישעיה אומר מעת היותה שם
אני, אמר ישעיה מיום שנתנה תורה בסיני שם הייתי
וקבלתי את הנבואה הזאת אלא ועתה ה' אלהים
שלחני ורוחו עד עכשיו לא נתן לי רשות להתנבאות,
ולא כל הנביאים בלבד קבלו מסיני נבואתן אלא אף
החכמים העומדים בכל דור ודור כל אחד ואחד קבל
את שלו מסיני וכן הוא אומר את הדברים האלה
דבר ה' אל כל קהלכם:

" 'And God spake all these words, saying.' (Exod. xx. 1.) R. Isaac says, that all those things, which the prophets were to prophesy in every generation, they received from Mount Sinai, for so Moses says to Israel, 'But with him that standeth here with us this day, and also with him that is not here with us this day.' (Deut. xxix. 15.) Here in the latter clause, it is not said, 'That *standeth* with us this day,' but 'With him that *is not* here with us this day.' These are the souls that were to be created, who had no corporeal existence, and of whom therefore it could not be said they *stood* there. But although they did not exist in that hour, every one of them received his own, and so it is written, 'The burden of the Word of the Lord to Israel in the hand of Malachi.'

(Mal. i. 1.) Here it is not said in the days of Malachi, but in the hand of Malachi, for this prophecy had been long since in his hand, even from Mount Sinai: but up to that time permission had not been given him to prophesy. In like manner Isaiah says, 'From the time that it was, there am I.' (Isaiah xlviii. 16.) Isaiah means to say, From the day that the law was given there was I, and I received this prophecy, only 'Now the Lord God and His Spirit hath sent me;' that is, until then permission had not been given him to prophesy. But it was not the prophets only who received their prophecy from Sinai, but also the wise men in every generation, each one of them received his own from Sinai, and so it is said, 'These words the Lord spake unto all your congregation.' (Deut. v. 22.)" (Shemoth Rabba Parashah, 28.) The object of this fable is very plain, it is to clothe the rabbies with infallible authority. It is here asserted that the rabbies of every generation were all present at the giving of the law, and each received immediately from Sinai those legal decisions and doctrines which he was to communicate to the world, and consequently every thing, that a rabbi teaches, is infallibly right and true, and as authoritative as the words of Moses and the prophets, for " God spake all these words," as this legend interprets this verse. The rabbies of every generation are included, so that, according to this tradition the wise men of Israel, even in this degenerate time, still deliver infallible instructions which they received more than three thousand years ago from the mouth of God himself. But this fable avers too much. If all Israel was present at Sinai, and each individual, whether prophet, or rabbi, or layman, received the law at that time, what use was there in the transmission from father to son, from the time of Moses down to us? Nay, more, what use is there in teaching at all, for every man then received his own? Nay, further, what use is the written law, for if every man was taught at Sinai, there is no need for him to read and learn now? But this is a matter which every Israelite can decide for himself. Let him ask himself, how much he remembers of this wonderful event in his existence, his presentation at Sinai, and his reception of the law from the Lord himself. The Scripture proofs which are here given are evidently nothing to the purpose. The first proof is, " God spake all these words, saying." (Exod. xx. 1.) But every one who will take the trouble of reading the chapter will see, that " all these words" cannot apply to the prophecies, nor to the decisions of the rabbies, but to the ten commandments and to them only. So far from delivering all the decisions and comments since taught by the rabbies, God spake only the ten commandments to the people, and when they heard these, " they said unto Moses, Speak thou with us and we will hear; but let not God speak with us, lest we die." (Verse 19.) To say, therefore, that God's speaking "all these words" includes the whole oral law and all the rabbinical comments, is gross perversion of the text, and direct contradiction of Moses' account.

The next and most usual verse adduced to prove this fable is Deut. xxix. 14, 15, where it is said, "Neither with you only do I make this covenant and oath; but with him that standeth here with us this day, before the Lord our God, and also with him that is not here with us this day." But this verse plainly proves the contrary, that the other generations of Israel were there in no sense whatever. The Hebrew words are as strong as they can be.

ואת אשר איננו פה עמנו היום :

Those with whom the covenant is made are divided into two classes, "Him that standeth here," and "Him that is not here." If the word standeth had been repeated, if the verse said, "With him that standeth here, and with him that standeth not here," there might have been some colour for this fable: the rabbies might have urged that though the unborn generations did not stand there, they stood somewhere else; but the present wording of the verse utterly excludes all possibility of existence, either corporeal or incorporeal. "With him that is not here, איננו" shows that they were there in no sense.

The proof taken from Malachi, "The burden of the word of the Lord to Israel in the hand of Malachi," is nonsense. Every one, that knows anything of Hebrew, knows that ביד signifies "by," "by means of." But even taken literally, it will not prove that Malachi was at Sinai; there is nothing in the words to inform us when Malachi received the prophecy. The proof from Isaiah is more unhappy still. The whole context shows that it is God who speaks in that verse, and not the prophet. Indeed we might ask, if Isaiah had already received all his prophecies at Sinai, what was the use of the vision of the Lord sitting upon his throne, and the commission which is there given? (Isai. vi.) And so we might ask concerning most of the prophets. The case of Samuel is here particularly worthy of consideration. According to the above tradition cited in the Jewish prayers, Samuel had been at Sinai, and there received all that he was to deliver during his sublunary existence. And yet when the word of the Lord came to him, he did not recognise the Divine call, and three times went to Eli, and it was Eli who at last told him that it was God. Now how is this written history to be reconciled with the above tradition? The tradition says that Samuel had heard the voice of God at Sinai, that there all the prophetic words which he was ever to deliver were made known to him, and yet the Bible says, "Now Samuel did not yet know the Lord, neither was the word of the Lord yet revealed unto him." (1 Sam. iii. 7.)

The last proof, taken from Deut. v. 22, if considered in its context, also proves the contrary. The tradition quotes only a part of the verse, "These words the Lord spake unto all your congregations;" but if you read on you will find, "And he added no more," which words plainly limit the first sentence to the ten commandments. This tradition, then, as being contrary to Scripture, to the law of Moses, is a falsehood, and is therefore unworthy of a place in the prayers of that people, whom God selected from all the nations of the earth to be his witnesses, and the depositories of his truth. But this tradition is objectionable not only as a fable, though that is a very strong objection to any thing proposed as an article of faith, but on account of the purpose which it was intended to serve. It was invented for the purpose of strengthening the spiritual tyranny of the Scribes and Pharisees over the minds of the people. It is not therefore merely an erroneous interpretation of Scripture, nor the dream of a fanatic imagination, but the deliberate invention of men who knew what they were about, and had an object which they were endeavouring to compass, and for the attainment of which they did not stick at deliberate falsehood. They were, however, too wise to confine all the advantages of this appearance at Sinai to themselves; they asserted that the whole people of Israel obtained an advantage which makes them superior to all other nations. The prayer which we have quoted above alludes to this, when it says, "There was no blemish in them, for they were all entirely perfect." This sentence rather puzzles an ordinary reader of the Bible, who thinks of the conduct and character of Israel as there described; the Talmud, however, helps us to understand this eulogy:—

מפני מה גוים מזוחמין שלא עמדו על הר סיני
שבשעה שבא הנחש על חוה הטיל בה זוהמא,
ישראל שעמדו על הר סיני פסקה זוהמתן גוים שלא
עמדו על הר סיני לא פסקה זוהמתן, אמר ליה רב
אחא בריה דרבא לרב אשי גרים מאי אמר ליה אע״ג
דאינהו לא הוו מזליהו הוו, דכתיב את אשר ישנו
פה עמנו עומד היום לפני ה׳ אלהינו ואת אשר איננו
פה וגו׳:

"Why are the Gentiles defiled? Because they did not stand upon Mount Sinai, for in the hour that the serpent came to Eve, he communicated a defilement, which was taken away from Israel when they stood on Mount Sinai: but the defilement of the Gentiles was not removed, as they did not stand on Sinai. Rav Acha, the son of Rabba, said to Rav Ashai, how, then, does it fare with proselytes? He replied, although they went not there, their good fortune (or star) was there, as it is written, ' With him that standeth here with us this day, before the Lord our God, and also with him that is not here with us this day.' (Deut. xxix. 15.)" (Shabbath. fol. 145, col. 2, at the bottom of the page.) The commentary on this passage quotes still further particulars from Siphri, and says—

כל שעמדו על הר סיני נתקדשו ונטהרו, ונתרפאו
מכל מום ואף עורים ופסחים שהיו בישראל כדתניא
בספרי :

"All that stood on Mount Sinai were sanctified and purified, and were healed from every blemish, even the blind and the lame that then happened to be in Israel, as is taught in Siphri." In this part of the fable the inventors of the oral law endeavour to flatter the vanity of the Israelites, and thus to engage their affections in behalf of that tradition which was to secure their own power. The Scribes understood well the deceitfulness of the human heart, and knew that men love to hear and are ready to believe any thing that tends to their own personal aggrandizement. But in thus flattering the people, they were turning their backs upon that example which Moses set them; and contradicting the whole current of Scripture testimony. Moses and the prophets, as the servants of God, told the people of their sins and their evil deeds, that they might repent and be saved. Their object was not to secure popular favour, nor to advance their own selfish purposes; they therefore could afford to be honest and to speak truth. The inventors of the oral law, on the contrary, were endeavouring to erect a fabric of personal honour and power: they were therefore obliged to address themselves to the weak side of the human heart; and in doing so, were compelled to run counter to the plainest declarations of God's Word. All men and every nation like to be told that they are superior to the rest of the world, and are distinguished by moral endowments from the mass of mankind. The inventors of the oral law, therefore, told Israel that they were far elevated above all other nations, for they had been cleansed at Sinai from that innate defilement which still contaminates all the rest of the children of men. But is this true—is this what Moses and the prophets say? Moses says, "Understand, therefore, that the Lord thy God giveth thee not this good land to possess it for thy righteousness : for thou art a stiff-necked people." "Ye have been rebellious against the Lord from the day that I knew you." (Deut.

ix. 6, 24.) Isaiah says of Israel, " From the sole of the foot even unto the head there is no soundness in it, but wounds, and bruises, and putrifying sores." " Ah! sinful nation!—a people laden with iniquity; a seed of evil-doers—children that are corrupters." (Isaiah i. 4—6.) And again he says, " Woe is me, for I am undone: because I am a man of unclean lips, and I dwell in the midst of a people of unclean lips." (Isaiah vi. 5.) Jeremiah says, " Can the Ethiopian change his skin and the leopard his spots? Then may ye also do good that are accustomed to do evil." (Jer. xiii. 23.) And again, " All these nations are uncircumcised, and all the house of Israel are uncircumcised in the heart." (Jer. ix. 26.) The Lord himself says to Ezekiel, " Son of man, I send thee to the children of Israel, to a rebellious nation that hath rebelled against me: they and their fathers have transgressed against me to this very day. For they are impudent children and stiff-hearted." (Ezek. ii. 3, 4.) And again, " Thou art not sent to a people of a strange speech and of an hard language, but to the house of Israel: not to many people of a strange speech and of an hard language, whose words thou canst not understand; surely had I sent thee to them, they would have hearkened unto thee. But the house of Israel will not hearken unto thee: for they will not hearken unto me; for all the house of Israel are impudent and hard-hearted." (Ezek. iii. 4, 7, &c.) We do not quote these passages to show that the Gentiles have a more favoured constitution of moral nature. Far from it; in reading these accounts given by the prophets, we recognise the features of our own picture. Far be it from us to glory; we cite these passages to show you how miserably your oral law endeavours to blind and delude you by flattering your vanity. It tells you that you have been purged from every stain; Moses and the prophets teach you the truth—that you are just like the other sons of men, and have no moral superiority or advantage whatever. We wish to point out to you how the system of rabbinism is diametrically opposed to Moses and the prophets, and above all, to impress upon you that the authors of this oral law are not worthy of your confidence, for they have, for their own private interests, invented narratives and doctrines which contradict that Word of God, which ought to be Israel's glory. We wish to show you how certain principles of evil pervade every part of that system, not even excepting those prayers which are offered up in the public worship of God. There these fables also occur, and we ask every Israelite who loves the law of Moses or hopes in the promises of God by the prophets, how he can conscientiously stand by in the synagogue and hear the words of Moses and the prophets openly contradicted? How can he remain silent when the reader declares of Israel that there is no blemish in them, for they are all entirely perfect, when he knows and feels that he and all his brethren are just as frail, as sinful, and as imperfect as the other sons of men? How can they expect the return of God's favour to their nation so long as these fictions are made a part of public worship? Moses teaches very different doctrine. He says, "If they shall confess their iniquity, and the iniquity of their fathers, with their trespass which they have trespassed against me, and that also they have walked contrary unto me; and that I also have walked contrary unto them, and have brought them into the land of their enemies: if then their uncircumcised hearts be humbled, and they then accept of the punishment of their iniquity: then will I remember my covenant with Jacob, and also my covenant with Isaac, and also my covenant with Abraham will I remember: and I will remember the land." (Levit. xxvi. 40—42.) Here Moses makes a conviction and acknowledgment of guilt, an indispensable preleminary to the return of God's favour to the nation. Israel must feel that, so far from being cleansed from all impurity, their heart is uncircumcised, and this uncircumcised heart must be humbled; but how is this possible, so long as the oral law and the prayers of the synagogue teach that the Israelites are the most righteous of mankind, because they received the law, which the other nations rejected—and the most pure, or rather the only pure, of mankind, inasmuch as they were cleansed from every taint at Sinai? These doctrines harden the heart against true humility, prevent true repentance, and thereby retard the happiness and the glory of Israel.

No. XXI.

LEGENDS IN THE PRAYERS FOR PENTECOST.

If Moses or the prophets had any where recorded, that God had, along with the written law also given an oral law, our duty would then be to find out where it is: and to inquire whether that oral law, which now forms the keystone of modern Judaism, is the one which was given by God. But neither Moses nor any other prophet has said one word on the subject. The words תורה שבעל פה "oral law" are no where to be found in the Bible, nor is there any mention of the thing itself. If the Bible had plainly alluded to the existence of the thing, we should not quarrel about the name, which might have been invented for the sake of brevity and convenience. But it is remarkable that when Moses commanded the law to be read publicly in the ears of all the people, he says not a syllable about the oral explanation, which if it existed must at least have been of equal importance; and still more so that the succeeding prophets should have observed such a profound silence about that, which now constitutes the main substance of Israel's religion, and is the key to the observances and prayers of the synagogue. This silence is in itself suspicious, and compels us to examine the evidence of its transmission. The first step here is to ascertain the character of the witnesses, who say that they received the oral law from their fathers and transmitted it to their posterity. If it appear that, in their general testimony, they were disinterested and truth-loving persons, who have never been convicted of distorting truth for their private advantage, nor of receiving and circulating fables as authentic history, their testimony in this particular matter will be of considerable value. But if it can be proved that either from a deliberate desire to deceive, or from an incapacity to weigh evidence and to distinguish between fact and fiction, they have transmitted a huge mass of foolish fables as authentic history, then their testimony is worth nothing, and the story of an oral law having no other evidence must be classed amongst the other fables which have come down to us on their authority. That the account of the giving and transmission of the oral law rests solely and exclusively on the testimony of the rabbies is clear from the account itself, as it is found in the Jad Hachasaka.

כל המצוות שנתנו לו למשה בסיני בפירושן נתנו
שנאמר וארגה לך את לוחות האבן והתורה והמצוה,
תורה זו תורה שבכתב, והמצוה זו פירושה, וצונו

לעשות התורה על פי המצוה ּ ומצוה זו היא
הנקראת תורה שבע״פ :

"All the commandments which were given to Moses were given with their explanation, for it is said, 'I will give thee the tables of stone and the law and the commandment.' (Exod. xxiv. 12.) 'The law,' this is the written law, 'And the commandment,' this is the explanation thereof. And he has commanded to fulfil 'the law' according to '.the commandment.' And the commandment is that which is called *The oral law*." Truly the rabbies must have been hard set when they chose this passage to prove the existence of an oral law. The keen and clear mind of the sagacious Rambam evidently felt the difficulty; he, therefore, to give some plausibility to the proof, omitted the concluding part of the sentence which he quotes from the Bible. He says, "As it is written 'I will give thee tables of stone and the law and the commandment,'" and there he stops, but let every Israelite open his Pentateuch and read the remainder, and he will find the whole sentence to be this, "I will give thee tables of stone, and the law and the commandment which *I have written*, to teach them." Not one word here about an oral law, but about that which God had written. It is true that the passage of the Talmud from which Rambam derived this doctrine gives the whole passage, but it appears from the process of abbreviation which he has applied, as if he were ashamed of the explanation there given and thought it more prudent to omit it. But as it is one of the main passages which support the doctrine of an oral law, it must be considered.

ואמר ר׳ לוי בר חמא אמר ר׳ שמעון בן לקיש
מאי דכתיב ואהנה לך את לוחות האבן והתורה
והמצוה אשר כתבתי להורותם , לוחות אלו עשרת
הדברות תורה זו מקרא והמצוה זו משנה אשר
כתבתי אלו נביאים וכתובים להורותם זו גמרא מלמד
שכולם נתנו למשה מסיני :

"R. Levi bar Chama says, R. Simon ben Lakish says, what is that that is written 'I will give thee tables of stone, and the law and the commandment which I have written to teach them?' '*The tables*' are the ten commandments. '*The law*' is the written law. '*The commandment*' is the Mishna. '*Which I have written*' means the prophets and sacred writings. '*To teach them*' means the Gemara. It teaches us that they were all given to Moses from Sinai." (Berachoth, fol. 5, col. 1.) Can any man of common understanding receive this interpretation, which throws all grammar and context to the winds, and gravely asserts that not only the law and its explanation, but the prophets and the whole Talmud, were given to Moses at Sinai? Will he give up his own reason and the word of the living God to the authority of R. Simon ben Lakish? There cannot possibly be any argument which would prove the falsehood of the narrative concerning the oral law so completely as this interpretation, which is regarded as one of its main foundations. The words of Moses which are here perverted plainly speak of that which God had written. "I will give thee tables of stone, and the law and the commandment which I have written to teach them." Did God write the oral law, and give it to Moses? What became of it then? If it was written, how did it become oral? These words "Which I have written," have sadly puzzled the rabbinical commentators, who know not how to reconcile the plain and obvious sense of the words, with that interpretation which had been already put upon them in the Talmud. Rashi seemed to think that the difficulty might be got over by saying—

כל שש מאות ושלש עשרה מצוות בכלל עשרת הדברות הן :

"All the six hundred and thirteen commandments are comprehended in the ten commandments." (Com. in Exod. xxiv. 12.) But this, though true in one sense, will not obviate the difficulty. God promises to give Moses the law and the commandment which he had written. If the oral law had not been written, it was not included. Saadiah Gaon, as quoted by Aben Ezra, proposes another solution:—

אמר חגאון כי אשר כתבתי דבוק עם לוחות האבן לא עם התורה והמצוה כי השם לא כתב רק עשרת הדברים :

"The Gaon says that the words, 'Which I have written,' are to be connected with 'The tables of stone,' and not with 'The law and the commandment,' for God wrote only the ten words." But unfortunately Moses has so connected them, and we have no warrant for reversing his order. Aben Ezra himself, after giving the Talmudic exposition, gives it as his own opinion, that these words refer to the ten commandments. He says—

ולפי דעתי כי התורה הדבור הראשון והחמישי והמצוה השמונה הדברים :

"But in my opinion, 'The law' refers to the first and fifth commandment; and 'The commandment' to the other eight." (Aben Ezra, Com. in loc.) This is about the truth. God gave Moses the law and the commandment which he had written; but as Saadiah admits, God wrote only the ten words, therefore the ten words are the same as "the law and the commandments." Some will say there is tautology here, that when God says, "I will give thee tables of stone," he means the ten commandments, and that therefore the additional promise "of the law and the commandment" is only an unnecessary repetition. But this is not true. By "tables of stone," God meant tables of stone. He might have given to Moses the ten commandments without giving him stone tables, or he might have given him the tables of stone without giving him the ten words; but as he intended to give him both, He says, "I will give thee tables of stone, and the law, and the commandment." Neither is there any difficulty in the circumstance that these ten words are called both "law and commandment." Inasmuch as they were a revelation of God's will, they are justly denominated "law," תורה; and as they were proposed as a rule of life, obedience to which was required, they are entitled, המצוה "The commandment." The simple meaning, therefore, is, that God promises to give the ten commandments which he had written. Every thing else, and therefore the oral law, is excluded. This passage, therefore, gives no support to the doctrine that Moses received an oral as well as a written law on Mount Sinai. Indeed, the desperate perversion to which this text has been subjected, throws discredit upon the whole; and the necessity for such perversion shows that there was no plain text in the writings of Moses, to which the inventors of the oral law could appeal.

The authority, then of the oral law must rest altogether upon the character of those witnesses who handed it down. But this is a very sandy foundation, for we have already seen that these men were guilty of inventing or propagating the most absurd fables; their testimony, therefore, is of no value. This has been proved abundantly already; but there is one story for which we had not room in our last number, and which, as being immediately connected with the giving of the law, must now be considered. Like the others, it comes before us authenticated by its introduction into the prayers of the synagogue, in which the following plain allusion is made:—

ויקרא לציר ולמרומו העלו, וביגו לבין עם שלישי
עלו, והעמידו וננש אל עו׳פלו, ופנים בפנים
דבר לו, וקרנים מידו לו, ידודון ידודון רעשו למולו,
ודברו לפני צור ואמרו לו, מה אנוש כי תגדלו, ומה
תחשבהו למקומנו להעלו, קנין שעשועים להנחיל לו:

"When he called the messenger (Moses) and made him ascend to heaven, and appointed him as the third person between him and his people, and caused him to approach and stand in the thick darkness, and spake to him face to face, and rays streamed from his hand to him, the angels were moved, and rushed towards him; and in the presence of the Creator they spake, saying thus to him, What is man that thou shouldest exalt him? and wherefore make such an account of him as to bring him up to our place and cause him to inherit the delightful possession (the law)?" (Pentecost Prayers, fol. 88.) Here it is plainly said, that the angels remonstrated with God at the favour shown to Moses. This circumstance is not to be found in the writings of Moses, but it is recorded in the Talmud, and the particulars are thus given:—

בשעה שעלה משה למרום אמרו מלאכי השרת
לפני הקב״ה רבונו של עולם מה לילוד אשה בינינו,
אמר להם לקבל תורה בא, אמרו לפניו חמדה גנוזה
שגנוזה לך מששת ימי בראשית תשע מאות ושבעים
וארבעה דורות קודם שנברא העולם אתה מבקש
ליתנה לבשר ודם, מה אנוש כי תזכרנו ובן אדם כי
תפקדנו ה׳ אדונינו מה אדיר שמך בכל הארץ אשר
תנה הודך על השמים, אמר לו הקב״ה למשה חזור
להן תשובה אמר לפניו רבונו של עולם מתיירא אני
שמא ישרפוני בהבל שבפיהם, אמר לו אחוז בכסא
כבודי וחזור להן תשובה שנאמר מאחז פני כסא פרשז
עליו עננו ואמר ר׳ נחום מלמד שפירש שדי מזיו
שכינתו וענגו עליו אמר לפניו רבונו של עולם תורה
שאתה נותן לי מה כתיב בה אנכי ה׳ אלהיך אשר
הוצאתיך מארץ מצרים אמר להם למצרים ירדתם
לפרעה השתעבדתם תורה למה תהא לכם, שוב מה
כתיב בה לא יהיה לך אלהים אחרים בין ערלים
אתם שרויין שעובדין ע״ז שוב מה כתיב בה זכור
את יום השבת לקדשו כלום אתם עושין מלאכה
שאתם צריכין שבות, שוב מה כתיב בה לא תשא
משא ומתן יש ביניכם שוב מה כתיב בה כבד את
אביך ואת אמך אב ואם יש לכם שוב מה כתיב בה
לא תרצח לא תנאף לא תגנוב קנאה יש ביניכם יצר
הרע יש ביניכם מיד הודו לו להקב״ה:

"In the hour when Moses ascended up on high, the ministering angels said before God, O Lord of the world, what business has he that is born of a woman amongst us? He replied, He is come to receive the law. They answered, This most desirable treasure, which has been treasured up from the six days of creation, six hundred and seventy-four generations before the world was created, dost thou now wish to give it to flesh and blood—what is man that thou art mindful of him, and the son of man that thou visitest him? O Lord, our Lord, how excellent is thy name in all the earth, who hast set thy glory above the heavens. The Holy One said to Moses, Give them an answer. He replied, O Lord of the world, I am afraid, lest they burn me with the breath of their mouth. He said, Lay hold on the throne of my glory and give them an answer, for it is said, 'He that holdeth the face of his throne, he spreadeth his cloud over him.' (Job xxvi. 8, 9.) Rabbi Nahum says, This teaches us that the Almighty spread some of the glory of the Shechinah and his cloud over him. He then said, Lord of the world, what is written in the law that thou art about to give me? 'I am the Lord thy God that brought thee out of Egypt.' He then said, Did ye ever go down into Egypt and serve Pharaoh—why, then, should ye have the law? Again, what is written therein? 'Thou shalt have none other God.' He then asked them, Do ye then dwell amongst the uncircumcised, that ye should commit idolatry? Again, what is written? 'Remember the Sabbath-day to sanctify it.' Do ye, then, do any work, so as to need rest? Again, what is written? 'Thou shalt not take the name of the Lord,' &c. Have ye, then, any business that would lead to this sin? Again, what is written? 'Honour thy father and mother.' Have ye, then, got any father and mother? Again, what is written? 'Thou shalt not kill, thou shalt not commit adultery, thou shalt not steal.' Have ye, then, got envy or the leading principle that would lead to these sins? Immediately they praised the Holy One, blessed be He," &c. (Shabbath, fol. 88, col. 2, &c.) It is not necessary to prove that this account is a fiction. The absurdity of the whole scene is too palpable. To what purpose should the angels wish for the law of Moses, or be envious of men to whom it was given? Is it possible that the spirits that minister before the throne of God, were not able to see the unsuitableness of the law for them, until Moses pointed it out to their consideration? We think that if this scene had ever taken place, Moses might have given them other passages of the law much more to the purpose; but it is plainly a fable invented by the designing, and propagated by the credulous. These two stories then, that Moses received the oral law, and that he disputed with the angels in heaven, come to us upon one authority; they are both circumstances in one event; and the fabulousness of the one takes away all credit from the other. The oral law rests solely upon the testimony of its transmitters, but here these persons are convicted of transmitting palpable falsehood : their testimony to the oral law is therefore useless, and the whole fabric of tradition falls. This one fable is sufficient, but the readers will remember that this is only one of a considerable number selected from the Jewish Prayer-book. To extract all similar stories from the Talmud would be to make some folio volumes. The Prayer-book, however, gives enough to invalidate the testimony of the Scribes and Pharisees, and to incapacitate them for ever from appearing as witnesses. Perhaps some one will say, But they are also the witnesses for the written law, and therefore, if we reject their testimony, we must give up the written law also. But this is not so. For *that* we have other testimony—we have that of the Jewish nation, of which the Scribes and Pharisees were at first only an inconsiderable portion. We have the testimony of Jesus and his disciples, the great opposers of the oral law. We have the testimony of the predictions, which we behold still accomplishing. We have the whole internal evidence, so that if there never had been Pharisees, the evidence for the written law would be just as valid. As it is, the contrast which the written law presents, when compared with the oral law, furnishes in itself a strong evidence of its truth and authenticity. The written law is simple, sober, dignified. The oral law is multifarious, extravagant, absurd. The oral law is poison—the written law is the antidote. The oral law is a counterfeit, which proves the existence of the genuine coin. Men who receive both on the sole authority of the rabbies may, when they find the falsehood of the one, reject the other also, but this can never be the case with those who calmly compare and weigh the two in the balance of right reason.

We now dismiss these Talmudic fables for the present. We have proved by instances that the oral law abounds with such. We have proved by extracts from the Prayers of the synagogue, that these fables form a part of the faith of all rabbinical Jews. We have, therefore, proved that the inventors of these fables attained their object. They have succeeded in deceiving the great majority of their countrymen. It is for the Jews of the present day to consider whether these extravagant fictions are still to be handed down to unborn generations—still to appear as a reproach upon Israel's understanding—still to disfigure and dishonour the public worship of the chosen people. Former generations may have handed them down in ignorance, and be therefore partly excusable. But in the present day there is a large body of Jews here in England who are fully convinced that these legends are false : it is the duty, the sacred duty, of all such to protest against their further propagation. If they do not, they make themselves accomplices in the guilt of those who invented them, and responsible for all the injury, temporal and spiritual, which the propagation of such error may inflict upon their brethren and their posterity. But whatever course they may pursue, the existence of these fables shows that the oral law itself is altogether an invention of men, and proves that Jesus of Nazareth conferred a great and substantial benefit on the nation and on mankind, by vindicating and preserving for us the unadulterated truth of God's written Word.

These fables prove further, that there is neither weight nor value in the sentence which these men pronounce against the Lord Jesus Christ. It is the sentence of those who did not scruple to falsify and pervert the law of God; it is the testimony given by the notorious inventors and propagators of fables, and cannot be received by any one competent to weigh evidence. Fables of any kind will invalidate testimony, but religious fables utterly incapacitate their inventors and propagators from being admitted as witnesses at all. The man who will venture to tamper with sacred history, either by adding to, or diminishing from, its records, clearly shows that he has lost all reverence for truth, and all sense of the divine character, as a vindicator of truth and a punisher of falsehood. The man who trifles with sacred facts, cannot be regarded as a witness at all in those which he considers profane or common. When, therefore, the Talmudists, or the wise men of his time, bear witness against Jesus of Nazareth, whom they hated, we must remember that they have been convicted of false witness again and again in the case of Moses, whom they professed to love. Their testimony is therefore a nullity, and if we wish to examine the claims of Jesus of Nazareth, we must look elsewhere for the data which are to form the basis of our judgment.

No. XXII.

RABBINIC MAGIC.

MODERN Judaism is the religion of the oral law. The dogmas, rites, ceremonies, and prayers, all rest upon its authority. If, therefore, the oral law can be proved to be an invention of men, the whole fabric of modern Judaism crumbles into dust. It then follows that the Jews have been more than eighteen centuries the disciples of error, and that, if they now desire to believe and profess the true religion, revealed by God to their forefathers, they must renounce their present Talmudic system, and return to the law and the prophets. But the oral law is a human invention. It has been proved, on the authority of the Jewish Prayer-book, that it abounds with the most absurd fables, which cannot be the Word of God, but are evidently and obviously the invention of man. It appears, therefore, that the Jewish nation has been for centuries deluded by the traditions of the Scribes and Pharisees—that they have been utterly mistaken in their faith, taking the fictions of men for the truth of God—and have thereby sunk from the honourable position, in which God placed them as depositories of the truth, to the unenviable situation of the credulous and superstitious. Such is the result of an inquiry into the contents of prayers of the synagogue. An examination of the traditional commandments will show in like manner, that the oral law is every where inseparably mingled with fables, which throw discredit upon the whole. One of the most important parts of the oral law is that which relates to the constitution of the great tribunal the Sanhedrin, for, as is asserted, that council fixed the authority of all traditions, and even examined into the claims, and decided upon the divine mission of the prophets. If it appear, therefore, that the oral law teaches what is manifestly fabulous with respect to that tribunal, the main pillar of tradition is taken away. Now without entering into the whole subject at present, the following specimen will show what degree of credit can be given to the traditional accounts respecting it:—

אמר ר׳ יוחנן אין מושיבין בסנהדרין אלא בעלי קומה ובעלי חכמה ובעלי מראה ובעלי זקנה ובעלי כשפים ויודעים בשבעים לשון שלא תהא סנהדרין שומעת מפי התורגמן :

"Rabbi Johannan says, none were allowed to sit in the Sanhedrin, who were not men of stature, men of wisdom, men of good appearance, aged, skilled in magic, and acquainted with the seventy languages, so that the Sanhedrin might not be obliged to hear through an interpreter." (Sanhedrin, fol. 17, col. 1.) In this short extract there are several fables—first, that all the members of the Sanhedrin should be skilled in magic, or magicians, is plainly contrary to the express command of God, who says, "There shall not be found among you any one that maketh his son or his daughter to pass through the fire, or that useth divination, or an observer of times, or an enchanter, or a witch מכשף—for all that do these things are an abomination unto the Lord: and because of these abominations the Lord thy God doth drive them out from before thee."

(Deut. xviii. 10—12.) This command of God makes no exception in favour of the members of the Sanhedrin. It absolutely forbids any such in Israel for any purpose. The commentary indeed tells us, that this magical skill was required in self-defence.

להמית מכשפים הבוטחים בכשפיהם להנצל מידי
בית דין :

" In order to kill the magicians who trusted in their magical arts to deliver them out of the hands of the tribunal." But this explanation does not mend the matter. Magic is a thing absolutely unlawful and expressly forbidden by God. It was therefore unlawful either to learn or to practise it, even for the purpose of killing a magician. If the plea of self-defence or necessity made it lawful for the Sanhedrin to learn magic, the same argument would justify it doubly in the case of the people, who were more likely to be the objects of the magician's attacks; for surely these persons would be careful to avoid all contact with the members of the Sanhedrin, whom they knew to be more than a match for them in the black art. According to this method of arguing all Israel might have been skilled in magic, though the law requires that not one such person should be found among them. Either then this account is absolutely false, or the members of the Sanhedrin were bad men, who learned what was expressly forbidden by the law of God; and in either case, the Talmudic accounts of this tribunal are unworthy of credit.

But it may well be doubted whether the members of this great council confined their magical excrcitations to the killing of magicians. We find elsewhere, if the Talmud speak truth, that the rabbies at least made other magical experiments, and have even recorded the means which they employed, for the benefit of posterity.

אבא בנימין אומר אלמלא נתנה רשות לעין לראות
אין כל בריה יכולה לעמוד מפני המזיקין אמר אביי
אינהו נפישי מינן וקימי עלן כי כסלא לאוגיא, אמר
רב הונא כל חד וחד מינן אלפי משמאליה ורבבתא
מימיניה אמר רבא האי דוחקא דהוה בכלה מיניהו
הוי הני ברכי דשלהי מיניהו, הני מאני דרבנן דבלי
מחופיה דידהו הני כרעי דמנקפא מיניהו האי מאן
דבעי למדע להו ליתי קיטמא נהילא ונהדר אפורייה.
ובצפרא חזי כי כרעי דתרנגולא האי מאן דבעי למחזינהו
ליתי שליתא דשונרא אוכמתא בר אוכמתא בוכרתא
בת בוכרתא ולקליה בנורא ולשחקיה ולימליה עיניה

I

מיניה וחזי להו ולשדייה בנובתא דפרזלא ולהתמיה
בגושפנקא דפרזלא דילמא גנבי מיניה ולחתום פומיה
כי היכי דלא ליתזק רב ביבי בר אביי עבד הכי
ואתזק בעי רבנן רחמי עליה ואתסי:

"Abba Benjamin says, if permission had been given to see them, no creature could stand before the hurtful demons. Abbai says, They are more than we, and stand against us like the trench round the garden-bed. Rav Huna says, Every one of us has a thousand on his left hand, and ten thousand on his right hand. Rabba says, The want of room at the sermon is caused by them—the wearing out of the rabbies' clothes is caused by their rubbing against them—the bruised legs are caused by them. Whosoever wishes to ascertain their existence, let him take ashes that have been passed through a sieve, and let him strew his bed, and in the morning he will see the marks of a cock's claws. Whosoever wishes to see them, let him take the interior covering of a black cat, the daughter of a first-born black cat, which is also the daughter of a first-born, and let him burn it in the fire, and pulverise it, and let him then fill his eyes with it, and he will see them. But let him pour the powder into an iron tube, and seal it with an iron signet, lest they should steal any of it, and let him also seal up the mouth thereof, that no injury may arise. Rav Bibi bar Abbai did thus, and received an injury. But the rabbies prayed for mercy upon him, and he was cured." (Berachoth, fol. 6, col. 1.) Here, then, is magic for the people, and all Israel is instructed in the means to see demons. It is not for us to decide whether those, who might use these means, would ever see men again, but this is certain, that the oral law here gives a magical recipe to those who are not members of the Sanhedrin, sets before us one of the Talmudic doctors as an example, and moreover encourages to do as he did, by holding out the possibility of a miraculous cure, if any injury should arise. If, then, this story be true, the oral law permits magic, which the law of God forbids; if it be false, then the oral law is convicted of another monstrous falsehood, and is altogether unworthy of credit. How long will the people of Israel suffer themselves to be deluded by a system, of which the striking characteristic is, that it has no regard for truth? The Jews object against Jesus of Nazareth, that he leads them away from the law of Moses, but where does he, or his disciples, inculcate the study of magic, or prescribe rules for facilitating intercourse with demons, contrary to the express command of God? Just suppose that this whole extract, instead of being found in the Talmud, had formed a portion of the New Testament, how would the Jews have laughed at this prescription for its folly, and argued against its wickedness, how triumphantly would they have shown that a law that teaches and encourages magic could not have been given by God? The existence of one such passage would have been sufficient, in their eyes, to condemn the whole Christian system. Let, then, the Jews deal with the oral law in the same way. Let them judge it and its fables by an appeal to Moses and the prophets. But let them remember that in this, as in many other instances, the New Testament agrees with the law of Moses, whilst the oral law differs from both. The New Testament classes witchcraft along with idolatry, and other sins which exclude from the joys of eternal life. "The works of the flesh are manifest, which are these: adultery, fornication, uncleanness, lasciviousness, *witchcraft*, hatred, variance, emulations, wrath, strife, seditions, heresies, envyings, murders, drunkenness, revellings, and such like; of the which I tell you before, as I have also told you in times past, that they which do such things shall not inherit the kingdom of God." (Galat. v. 19—21.) In this case, then, where the oral law leads you away from the doctrine of Moses, the religion of Jesus of Nazareth brings you back again.

This is, however, not the only fable contained in that short law concerning the members of the Sanhedrin. We are told, besides, that no one was allowed to sit in that council "unless he understood the seventy tongues." Now we would ask every disciple of the oral law calmly to consider this statement, and then say what he thinks of its veracity. Did he ever hear or know of scholars in the present times acquainted with seventy languages, and that so perfectly as to be able to converse with and examine witnesses, and form a judgment upon their evidence, without the aid of an interpreter? Surely, the study of languages is as much cultivated in the present day as it was then, and there are at least as many facilities for their acquisition. The system of grammar is now fully developed. The art of printing has made it easy to obtain foreign books. Lexicons and other apparatus may be procured, and yet, with all these facilities, we much doubt whether there be, in the whole world, one single person possessing that knowledge of languages here ascribed to every individual member of the Sanhedrin. According to the oral law, there always had been, in Israel, seventy-one such persons at least, but probably more; for as a member died, or became superannuated, another was found ready to succeed him. But the wonder is here made still more wonderful, for there were not only seventy-one persons acquainted with seventy languages, but those persons were also acquainted, as Rambam tells us, with medicine, astronomy, and all the existing systems of idolatry, and moreover skilled in magic. And, besides all this, all these persons were fine handsome fellows, "Men of stature, men of good appearance."

Is this credible—can all Israel, or all the world, furnish one such person at present, handsome or ugly, tall or short? or can there be found amongst that intelligent people the Jews, one man, woman, or child, so silly as to believe so manifest a falsehood? We can tell them that their great rabbi, Rambam, did not believe it, and therefore in his Compendium took the liberty of altering this Talmudic statement. Instead of seventy languages, he says simply—

ושידעו ברוב הלשונות :

"And that they should be acquainted with most languages." It was too much for him. Being a learned man himself, he knew the impossibility of such universal knowledge; and he therefore softened down the Talmudic hyperbole to the limits of what he considered possibility. This is not merely our conclusion from Rambam's alteration, the commentator has expressly said the same:—

וכתב רבינו יודעין ברוב הלשונות משום דדבר זר
להמצא מי שידע בכל ע׳ לשון :

"Our rabbi has written, 'Acquainted with most languages,' because it is a rarity to find a person acquainted with all the seventy languages." (Hilchoth Sanhedrin, c. 2.) Rambam himself, then, is here a witness against the fabulous exaggerations of the Talmud.

But perhaps some one will say, that seventy is only a round number to signify many, that we must not, therefore, be too strict in its exposition. This subterfuge, however, will not serve here. The authors of the Talmud said seventy, because they believed that, by giving this number, they included all the languages in the world. They believed that there were seventy nations, and therefore they said seventy languages. This article of Jewish faith is found everywhere in the Talmud, and in the commentaries, as for instance—

אמר ר׳ יוחנן מאי דכתיב יתן אומר המבשרות
צבא רב כל דבור ודבור שיצא מפי הגבורה נחלק
לשבעים לשונות :

R. Johannan says, What is the meaning of that Scripture, 'The Lord gave the Word: great was the company of those that published it?' It teaches, that as each commandment proceeded from the mouth of God, it was divided into seventy languages." (Shabbath, fol. 88, col. 2.) The foundation of this opinion is an arbitrary interpretation of a verse in the song of Moses. "When the Most High divided to the nations their inheritance, when he separated the sons of Adam, he set the bounds of the people according to the number of the children of Israel.' (Deut. xxxii. 8.) Upon which Rashi thus comments :—

בשביל מספר בני ישראל שעתידין לצאת מבני שם
ילמספר שבעים נפש של בני ישראל שירדו למצרים
הציב גבולות עמים שבעים לשון:

"On account of the number of the children of Israel who were to proceed from the sons of Shem, and according to the number of the seventy souls of the children of Israel who descended into Egypt, he set the bounds of the people, that is, the seventy languages. That this latter clause is altogether arbitrary, and a mere gratuitous addition, is plain from an inspection of the text, where not one syllable is said about the seventy souls, nor about the number of the nations, but about the fixing the bounds of their habitations. Rashi himself did not trust in this exposition, and he has therefore given another:—" On account of the number of the children of Israel who were to proceed from the children of Shem." Aben Esra also passes by the seventy nations altogether, and says that, "According to the number of the children of Israel," means, that the bounds of the nations were so set as to leave sufficient room for the Israelites. His words are—

אמרו המפרשים על דור הפלגה שנפצה כל הארץ
כי אז גזר השם להיות ארץ ז׳ גוים לישראל והיא
שתספיק למספרם ועל כן למספר בני ישראל:

"The commentators have interpreted this of the generation of the dispersion, when all the earth was scattered, for then God decreed that Israel should have the land of the seven nations, which would be sufficient for them, therefore it is said, 'according to the number of the children of Israel.'" This verse, then, gives no colour to the opinion that there are only seventy nations and seventy languages. Fact proves that the number is much greater, for the Bible exists already in twice that number of languages, and the work of translation is not yet accomplished. The oral law, therefore, fails altogether in attaining the object which it had in view in telling this extraordinary story. It wished to say, that in the Sanhedrin there never was need of an interpreter, for that every member understood every language in the world, and believing that there were only seventy languages, it stated this number. But now we know that even if each member understood seventy languages, yet to be able to decide cases for all the nations of the earth, they would have required to know as many more. The oral law then, betrays here an utter ignorance of the state of the world, which shows that it is not from that God who confounded the languages of the earth, and therefore knows how many there are; but from men who desired to magnify the acquirements of the nation far beyond the sober truth. The men who could deliberately say, that the Sanhedrin was composed of seventy-one persons, all handsome, all men of stature, all skilled in magic, and all so perfectly acquainted with seventy languages, as to need no interpreter, would have said seven hundred, or seven thousand, or any thing else that suited their purpose. They are evidently wilful exaggerators, whose word is therefore not to be trusted. The motive here is vain glory. The object is simply to give all the honour to men, to the Rabbies whose learning and genius were so marvellous. There is no intimation that God gave the members of the Sanhedrin this knowledge, which far exceeds the power or the life of man to attain by ordinary means. No, all the glory of these marvellous acquirements is ascribed to man alone. This forms a striking contrast to a narrative recorded in the New Testament. We are there told that on a certain occasion the disciples of Jesus of Nazareth addressed in their own language, "Parthians, and Medes, and Elamites, and the dwellers in Mesopotamia, and in Judea, and Cappadocia, in Pontus and Asia, Phrygia, and Pamphylia, in Egypt, and in the parts of Lybia about Cyrene, and strangers of Rome, Jews and proselytes, Cretes and Arabians," that is, the inhabitants of sixteen countries. Now, the small number here stated is a presumptive evidence of the truth of the fact. If an impostor, a Rabbinist who wished to make a good story, had written this account, he would, beyond all doubt, instead of sixteen, have specified all the seventy languages. To his countrymen, who believed in the acquirements of the Sanhedrin, this would have appeared no wise incredible. Indeed, if a man of that time had wished to invent a miracle, the number seventy would have been absolutely necessary for his purpose. For if every member of the Sanhedrin could speak seventy languages, to say that other men spoke sixteen would have been no miracle at all. The small number, therefore, here given, shows that the authors of the narrative had no wish to invent a miracle, but to state the sober truth. But then consider the entire absence of vain-glory. The praise and the power of speaking even this small number of languages is given altogether to God. The men were Galileans, and had not acquired this by their own labour and genius. "They were all filled with the Holy Ghost, and began to speak with other tongues, as the Spirit gave them utterance." (Acts ii. 1—11.) Here then is a striking difference between the narratives of the Talmud and those of the New Testament. The former exalts men. The latter gives glory to God.

No. XXIII.

ASTROLOGY.

THE favourite Jewish objection to the claims of Jesus of Nazareth is that passage at the beginning of the thirteenth chapter of Deuteronomy: "If there arise among you a prophet, or a dreamer of dreams, and giveth thee a sign or a wonder, and the sign or the wonder come to pass, whereof he spake unto thee, saying, Let us go after other gods, which thou hast not known, and let us serve them, thou shalt not hearken unto the words of that prophet, or that dreamer of dreams." In citing this passage, the Jews take for granted that the religion of Jesus is essentially different from that of Moses; that it leads to the worship of strange gods: and that it is in fact a species of heathenism, whilst the religion of the oral law, which they now profess, is utterly free from all heathen elements, and identical with the religion of their prophets. All this they take for granted; but the subject is capable of being inquired into. The oral law and the New Testament are both extant, and a little examination will enable us to decide, on rational grounds, whether Judaism or Christianity savour most of heathenism. In our last number, we saw that Judaism contains magic for the Sanhedrin and magic for the people, whilst the New Testament utterly forbids it: in this respect then Judaism resembles the heathen religion. Our business in this number shall be to point out, in astrology, another feature of resemblance. The Talmud and its doctors all agree in asserting the influence of the stars over the fates and fortunes of men. In the first place, the Talmud lays down these general maxims:—

חיי בני ומזוני לאו בזכותא תליא מלתא אלא
במזלא תליא מלרא:

"Life, children, and a livelihood depend not on merit, but on the influence of the stars." (Moed Katon, fol. 28, col. 1.)

מזל מחכים ומזל מעשיר:

"The influence of the stars makes wise, the influence of the stars makes rich." (Shabbath, fol. 156, col. 1.) But it also tells us the following particulars:—

האי מאן דבחד בשבא יהי גבר ולא חדא ביה....
האי מאן דבתרי בשבא יהי גבר רגזן מ״ט משום
דאיפליגו ביה מיא, האי מאן דבתלתא בשבא יהי גבר

עתיר וזנאי מ״ט משום דאיברו ביה עשבים, האי מאן
דבארבעה בשבא יהי גבר חכם ונחיר מ״ט משום
דאיתלו ביה מאורות. האי מאן דבחמשא בשבא יהי
גבר גומל חסדים מ״ט משום דאיברו ביה דגים ועופות,
האי מאן דבמעלא שבתא יהי גבר חזרן אמר ר׳ נחמן
בר יצחק חזרן במצוות, האי מאן דבשברא יהי בשבתא
ימות עלי דאחילו עלוהי יומא רבא דשבתא אמר רבא
בר רב שילא וקדישא רבה תקרי:

"He that is born on the first day of the week, will be a
man excelling, but in one quality only.* . . . He that
is born on the second day of the week will be an angry
man. What is the reason? Because on it the waters were
divided. He that is born on the third day of the week
will be a rich and profligate man. What is the reason?
Because on it the herbs were created. He that is born on
the fourth day of the week will be a wise man and have
a powerful memory. What is the reason? Because on that
day the lights were hung up in the heavens. He that is
born on the fifth day of the week will be a benevolent man.
What is the reason? Because on it were created the fishes
and the fowls. He that is born on the eve of the Sabbath
will be a man who makes a circuit. Rav Nachman bar
Isaac says, who makes the circuit in the commandments.†
He that is born on the Sabbath, on the Sabbath also he
shall die, because on his account they profaned the great
day of the Sabbath. Rabba bar Rav Shila says, he shall
possess an eminent degree of holiness." (Shabbath, fol. 156,
col. 1.) Here is completely the heathen doctrine of fate.
Not only the external circumstances of fortune, but the
moral qualities of the soul are made to depend upon the
day of a man's nativity. Whether a man be profligate or
holy, according to this doctrine, does in no wise depend
upon himself, his own choice, or conscience, but simply on
the circumstance of his birth happening on a Tuesday or a
Saturday. There is indeed a difference of opinion amongst
the Talmudic doctors, as to the nature of the sidereal influence, but all agree in the fact, as may be seen further
from the opinion of R. Huna:—

לא מזל יום גורם אלא מזל שעדה גורם האי מאן
דבחמה יהי גבר זיותן יהי אכל מדליה ושתי מדליה
ורזוהי גלן אם גניב לא מצלח. האי מאן דבכוכב

* According to Rashi.
† According to Rashi, one who goes from house to house to get alms.

ASTROLOGY. 177

נוגה יהי גבר עתיר וזנאי יהי מאי טעמא משום דאיתיליד
ביה נורא, האי מאן דבכוכב יהי גבר נהיר וחכים
משום דספרא דחמא הוא, האי מאן דבלבנה יהי גבר
סביל מרעין בנאי וסתיר ובנאי אכל דלא דיליה
ושתי דלא דיליה ורזוהי כסן אם גנב מצלח, האי מאן
דבשבתי יהי גבר מחשבתיה בטלין ואית דאמר כל
דמחשבין עלוהי בטלין, האי מאן דבצדק יהי גבר
צדקן אמר רב נחמן בר יצחק וצדקן במצוות, האי
מאן דבמאדים יהי גבר אשיד דמא אמר רב אשי אי
אומנא אי גנבא אי מהולא אמר רבה אנא במאדים
הואי אמר אביי מר נמי עניש וקטיל וכו':

"These things do not depend upon the sidereal influence of the day, but on the sidereal influence of the hour. He that is born under the influence of the sun will be a splendid man, eating and drinking of that which belongs to himself, and will reveal his secrets: if he be a thief he will not prosper. He that is born under Nogah (Venus) will be a rich and profligate man. What is the reason? Because on it the fire was created. He that is born under Kochav (Mercury) will be a man of strong memory, and wise, for Mercury is secretary to the sun. He that is born under the influence of the moon, will suffer much, building and destroying, destroying and building: eating and drinking what does not belong to him, and a keeper of his own secrets. If a thief he will prosper. He that is born under Shabthai (Saturn) will be a man whose thoughts come to nought, but some say those, that think against him, shall come to nought. He that is born under Tsedek (Jupiter) will be a righteous man. Rav Nachman bar Isaac says, righteous in the commandments.* He that is born under Maadim (Mars) will be a shedder of blood. Rav Achai says, either a letter of blood, or a thief, or a circumciser. Rabbah said, I was born under Mars. Abbai answered, Therefore, you are fond of punishing and killing." (Shabbath, ibid.) In this passage the heathenism is still more apparent. It is notorious that the ancient Greek and Roman idolaters considered Venus as the patroness of profligacy, Mercury as the god of eloquence and learning, Mars as the god of war, and behold! here in the oral law you have the very same doctrine. "If a man be born under Venus, he will be a rich and profligate man; if under Mercury, a man of strong memory and wise; if under Mars, a shedder of blood." The habits of the mind are here also expressly attributed

---

* Rashi says a man who is liberal in almsgiving.

to the influence of the planets, and a thief has got the promise of success, if his nativity happened under the influence of the moon. What then becomes of human responsibility, and how does this doctrine agree with the words of Moses, "Behold I have set before you life and death, blessing and cursing, therefore choose life, that both thou and thy seed may live?" (Deut. xxx. 19.) It will be replied by Talmudists, that the oral law also says:—

אין מזל לישראל :

"Israel is not under the influence of the stars." We shall, therefore, consider that passage in its context which immediately follows:—

ר׳ חנינא אומר מזל מחכים מזל מעשיר ויש מזל
לישראל ר׳ יוחנן אמר אין מזל לישראל ואזדא ר׳ יוחנן
לטעמיה דאמר ר׳ יוחנן מניין שאין מזל לישראל
שנאמר כה אמר ה׳ אל דרך הגוים אל תלמדו ומאותות
השמים אל תחתו כי יחתו הגוים מהמה יחתו הגוים
ולא ישראל אמר רב אין מזל לישראל דאמר רב יהודה
אמר רב מניין שאין מזל לישראל שנאמר ויוצא אותו
החוצה אמר אברהם לפני הקב״ה רבונו של עולם בן
ביתי יורש אותי אמר לו לאו כי אם אשר יצא ממעיך
אמר לפניו רבונו של עולם נסתכלתי באיצטגנינות
שלי ואיני ראוי להוליד בן אמר לו צא מאיצטגנינות
שלך שאין מזל לישראל:

"Rabbi Chanina says, the influence of the stars makes wise, the influence of the stars makes rich, and Israel is under that influence. Rabbi Jochanan says, Israel is not under the influence of the stars, and Rabbi Jochanan helped his argument, for Rabbi Jochanan says, From whence is it proved that Israel is not under the influence of the stars? Because it is said, 'Thus saith the Lord, Learn not the way of the heathen, and be not dismayed at the signs of heaven; for the heathen are dismayed at them.' (Jer. x. 2.) The heathen but not Israel. Rav says, Israel is not under the influence of the stars, for Rabbi Judah says, Rav says, From whence is it proved that Israel is not under the influence of the stars? From that which is said, 'And he brought him forth abroad.' (Gen. xv. 5.) Abraham said before God, Lord of the world, One born in my house is my heir.' God replied not so, but 'He that shall come forth out of thine own bowels.' Abraham replied, I have consulted my astrology, and am not fit to beget a son. God said, Go forth from thy astrology, for Israel is not under the influence of the stars." (Shabbath, ibid.) Now this passage, if taken in the most favourable point of view, proves only that Israel is not under the influence of the stars; but this exception proves to demonstration that the oral law teaches, that all other nations are under that influence. According to this doctrine, all the Gentiles, and of course Christians among the number, are given up to unchanging and unchangeable fate. They are good and bad, rich and poor, happy and unhappy, according to the sidereal influence at their nativity, and consequently are utterly irresponsible for their actions. A Gentile thief, or murderer, or adulterer, is not so, because he yielded to temptation, or to evil dispositions, but because he happened to be born under the influence of the Moon, or of Mars, or of Venus. This is the religion of the oral law, on the most favourable view of the case, and consequently God is represented first as a partial governor, who gives constitutional advantages to one favourite nation, which He withholds from all others; and then, secondly, as an unjust judge, who punishes the Gentiles for doing what the irresistible influence of the stars compelled them to do. This doctrine is of itself sufficient to prove that the oral law is not of God, and that as a religion it stands upon a line with the heathen and Mahometan systems of fate, and is consequently infinitely below Christianity. The New Testament recognises no system of favouritism, but represents God as a just judge, "who will render to every man according to his deeds" (Rom. ii. 6); and all men as responsible for the evil which they commit. "There is no respect of persons with God. For as many as have sinned without law, shall also perish without law; and as many as have sinned in the law, shall be judged by the law." (Ibid, 11, 12.) This is a view worthy of the Divine character, whereas the astrological system of the oral law, which represents God as giving up all nations to the influence of the stars, and then punishing them for following that influence which He himself ordained, is nothing short of blasphemy, and is much more akin to heathenism than to the doctrine of Moses and the prophets. But, secondly, this passage of the Talmud contains two statements directly contradicting each other. Rabbi Chanina says, Israel is under the influence of the stars—the others say, Israel is not under the influence of the stars; whichever statement we receive as true, the other is necessarily false, and therefore the oral law contains falsehood, and therefore is unworthy of credit. Thirdly, the story which is here given of Abraham has falsehood on the face of it, and after all does not disprove, but rather confirms the doctrine that Israel, as well as the other nations, is under the influence of the stars; for as Rashi tells us, Abraham and Sarah escaped from their sidereal destiny only by changing their names. Rashi's words are—

אמר לו צא מאיצטגנינות שלך שראית במזלות
שאינך עתיד להעמיד בן אברם אין לו בן אבל אברהם
יש לו בן שרי לא תלד אבל שרה תלד אני קורא
לכם שם אחר וישתנה המזל :

"God said to Abraham, Go forth from thy astrology, for thou hast seen in the stars that thou art not to have a son. *Abram* is not to have a son, but *Abraham* is to have a son. *Sarai* is not to bear a child, but *Sarah* shall bear a child. I call you by another name, and thus the influence of the stars will be changed." (Com. in Gen. xv. 5.) Here it is plainly intimated, and that in the name of God himself, that Abraham and Sarah were both under the influence of the stars, and that if they had not changed their names, they never could have had a child. This was evidently Rashi's opinion; and when we remember that the majority of the Jews in the world implicitly follow Rashi's interpretation, we may conclude that this is the prevailing doctrine. And perhaps some of the readers of this paper may even know instances of Jews who, led by this interpretation, have actually changed their name, in the hope of bettering their luck, or even of escaping from death. But however that be, it is easy to show that the Talmud and the rabbies generally believe in the astrological influence of the heavenly bodies. In addition to the passages already cited, the Talmud says expressly—

בזמן שהחמה לוקה סימן רע לאומות עולם לבנה
לוקה סימן רע לשונאיהם של ישראל מפני שישראל
מונין ללבנה ואומות העולם לחמה לוקה במזרח סימן
רע ליושבי מערב וכו' :

"An eclipse of the sun is an evil sign to the nations of the world. An eclipse of the moon is an evil sign to Israel; for Israel reckons by the moon, the nations of the world by the sun. When the eclipse happens in the east, it is an evil sign to the inhabitants of the east. When it happens in the west, it is an evil sign to the inhabitants of the west," &c., &c. (Succah, fol. 29. col. 1.) The rabbies who have lived since, teach the same doctrine. For instance, Saadiah Gaon, speaking of the manner in which the influence of the stars is modified by the signs of the zodiac, says—

ופעמים שמקצת כוכב יהלוכו במזל טוב ומקצתו
האחר במזל רע , ולאדם שיהיה לו אותו מזל יהיה
לו בראשונה טוב ולאחריהו רע :

"Sometimes the course of a star is partly in a good sign and

partly in a bad sign. The man born under this will first
prosper and then suffer adversity. (Comment. in Sepher
Jetsirah, fol. 98, col. 1.) He also explains, there, how it is
possible for astrologers to foretell sickness and death ; but this
is enough to shew his opinion, and what he had learned from
the Talmud. The writings of Aben Esra bear the same
testimony. For instance, in his commentary on the ten commandments, he says—

והדבור הרביעי דבור השבת כנגד גלגל שבתי כי
חכמי הנסיון אומרים כי לכל אחד מן המשרתים יש
יום ידוע בשבוע שבו יראה כחו והוא בעל השעה
הראשונה ביום וכן מי שהוא בעל השעה הראשונה
בלילה ואומדים כי שבתי ומאדים הם כוכבים המזיקים
ומי שיחל מלאכה או ללכת בדרך באחד משניהם
כשהם מושלים יבוא לידי נזק על כן אמרו קדמונינו
שנתן רשות לחבל בלילי רביעיות ובלילי שבתות
והנה לא תמצא בכל ימי השבוע לילה ויום זה אחר
זה שימשלו אלו שני המזיקים בהם רק ביום הזה על
כן אין ראוי להתעסק בו בדברי העולם רק ביראת
השם לבדו :

"The fourth commandment is that respecting the Sabbath,
and answers to the orb of Saturn; for the experimental
philosophers say, that each one of the ministering servants has
a certain day of the week in which he exhibits his strength,
and he is master of the first hour in the day, and thus it is also
with him who is master of the first hour in the night. They
say, also, that Saturn and Mars are the two hurtful stars, and
whosoever begins a work, or to walk in the way, when either
of these two is in the ascendant, is sure to fall into harm.
Therefore our ancients have said, that permission is given to do
injury on the nights of the fourth and seventh days of the week.
And behold, thou wilt not find, in all the days of the week, a
night and a day, one after the other, on which these two hurtful stars rule except on this day; therefore it is not suitable on
it to engage in worldly affairs, but to devote it entirely to the
fear of God." This exposition shows that Aben Esra believed
in astrology, and that the power of the stars extended to Israel
as well as to the other nations, nay the power of the stars to
do harm is here made the foundation of the command respecting
the Sabbath-day. A man, whose mind was not thoroughly
imbued with faith in astrology, could never have been led even
to entertain such an opinion, when God himself has assigned
another and entirely different reason for the institution of the

Sabbath. But indeed it is not necessary to go to the rabbies to prove that modern Judaism teaches astrology. That common wish which one so often hears amongst the Jews, even at the present day, מַזָּל טוֹב, *mazzal tov*, or good luck, has its origin in the doctrine of the Talmud, and shows how universally it has been received. And thus we see the influence which the oral law has had in leading away both learned and unlearned from the Word of God, and of spreading amongst them, as a tradition from Moses, what is merely one of the numerous errors of heathen idolatry. The heathen worshipped the host of heaven. The sun, and the moon, and other heavenly bodies, they considered as deities; it was, therefore, natural for them to suppose that they exercised an influence over the affairs of men. The Chaldeans were especially devoted to this doctrine, and had almost exalted it to the rank of a science. From them, probably during the Babylonish captivity, the Jews learned this system; and though altogether idolatrous in its origin, and learned from idolaters, it was congenial to the minds of the superstitious rabbies, and was, therefore, introduced into the oral law, where it has ever since continued. The oral law has, therefore, in this respect, adopted heathen doctrine, and teaches heathenism. Every Jew who wishes his neighbour מַזָּל טוֹב, *mazzal tov*, uses a heathen idolatrous expression—sanctioned, indeed, by the Talmud, but utterly repugnant to the doctrine of Moses. But where will he find in the New Testament any warrant either for such a doctrine or such a wish? The New Testament is entirely free from all shadow and tincture of this heathenism. Your oral law has taught you that the course of events depends upon the stars. Jesus of Nazareth has taught us, that the ordering of all events, even the minutest, proceeds from our Heavenly Father. He says, " Are not two sparrows sold for a farthing? and one of them shall not fall on the ground without your Father. But the very hairs of your heads are all numbered." (Matt. x. 29, 30.) Jesus of Nazareth, therefore, whom you are afraid to follow, lest he should lead you after other gods, directs all his followers to the one living and true God, the Creator, Preserver, and Redeemer of all things. Those men, on the contrary, who crucified Jesus of Nazareth, and that oral law, which you prefer to Christianity, have led you away from the doctrines of Moses and the prophets to the principles of heathenism. The general doctrine, that the moral nature, the weal and wo of men, are altogether dependent upon the stars, is not Mosaic, it is heathen; and the particular details concerning the influence of Venus, Mars, and Mercury, are plainly the offspring of the worst part of heathen mythology. If, then, Jews believe in this Talmudic astrology, they approach very nearly to heathenism, and such has been the case with the majority and the most learned of the nation for the last eighteen hundred years. If from the unavoidable influence of Christian knowledge, they now reject this portion of the oral law, they declare that all their most learned rabbies have been in gross error, and that the oral law, which led them astray, is not from God, but, on the contrary, in one of its most important features, a mere copy of idolatrous heathenism.

No. XXIV.

AMULETS.

In magic and astrology we have discovered two features common to idolatrous heathenism, and to the religion of the oral law. We have seen that it pervades the Talmud and the writings of the subsequent rabbies, and that it has tinctured the language of every-day life. It occurs, therefore, as might be expected, incidentally, when the oral law treats of other things; and we are induced to notice one passage of this kind, not only because it proves that faith in astrology is an essential element in the religion of the oral law, but because it sets before us another feature of resemblance to heathenism. In treating of the virtues of amulets, and of the tests, whereby to try them and those that write, the following passage occurs—

אמר רב פפא פשיטא לי תלת קמיעא לתלת גברי
תלתא תלתא זימני אתמחי גברא ואתמחי קמיעא
תלתא קמיעי לתלתא גברי חד חד זימני גברא אתמחי
קמיעא לא אתמחי חד קמיעא לתלתא גברי קמיעא
אתמחי גברא לא אתמחי בעי רב פפא תלתא קמיעי
לחד גברא מאי קמיעא ודאי לא אתמחי גברא אתמחי
או לא אתמחי מי אמרינן הא אסי ליה או דילמא
מזלא גברא הוא דקא מקבל כתבא היקו וכו׳ :

"Rav Papa says, I am certain in the case of three amulets for three men; where three copies of one amulet have cured three times, then both the writer and the amulet are approved. In the case of three amulets for three men, where each performs only one cure, then the writer is approved, the amulet is not approved. In the case of one amulet for three men, then the amulet is approved, the writer is not approved. But Rav Papa asks, What is to be the decision when there are three amulets for one man? The amulet is certainly not approved, the writer may or may not be. Shall we say that he cured him? Or was it perhaps the influence of the stars, belonging to that man, that had an affinity for that which was written? That must remain undecided." (Shabbath, fol. 61, col. 2.) Here we have the influence of the stars again, and that not in the case of the heathen, but in the case of Israelites. The whole passage refers to none but Israelites. The question, from which this digression about amulets arose, was whether it is lawful to wear amulets on the Sabbath-day, a question concerning the Jews, and them only. In this question, then, we find the doctrine of sidereal influence mixed up, or rather so certainly pre-supposed as to prevent the solution of a doubt. A case is supposed where a man has been cured by the help of three amulets, and thence arises a doubt as to whether the maker may be considered as an approved writer of amulets; and upon this case R. Papa does not venture to decide, because it is possible that the cure may be owing to the influence of the stars. How can there be a stronger proof of faith in the power of the stars over Israelites as well as over other persons?

This passage proves incontrovertibly that the heathen notion of astrology is inseparably interwoven with the religious system of the oral law, but it also presents to our consideration another circumstance equally startling, and that is, that the oral law sanctions the use of amulets or charms, as a cure for, or defence against, sickness and other evils. What, is it possible, that the Jews who think that their religion is the true religion revealed by God to Moses, and whose chief objection to Christianity is the fear lest it should lead them to strange gods, is it possible that this people should still entertain the old heathen notion concerning amulets? Yes, whilst the followers of Jesus of Nazareth have learned from him to renounce this superstitious and wicked practice, the Jews, taught by those who rejected and crucified him, still believe in the oral law which teaches the manner of making and using charms. But perhaps some one will say, it occurs only in the Gemara, but not in the Mishna. This is at all times but a poor apology for the oral law, or rather an open confession that the greatest part of that law is indefensible, but it will not serve here. The doctrine of amulets proceeds from the Mishna, which says,—

ולא בקמיע בזמן שאינו מן המומחה:

"It is not lawful to go forth on the Sabbath-day with an amulet, unless it be from an approved person." The Gemara then takes up this commandment, and comments thus upon it,—

אמר ר׳ פפא לא תימא עד דמומחא גברא ומומחא
קמיע אלא כיון דמומחא גברא אע״ג דלא מומחא קמיע

AMULETS. 185

דיקא נמי דקתני ולא בקמיע בזמן שאינו מן המומחה,
ולא קתני בזמן שאינו מומחה ש״מ, ת״ר איזה וקמיע
מומחה כל שריפא ושנה ושלש אחד קמיע של כתב
ואחד קמיע של עקרין אחד חולה שיש בו סכנה
ואחד חולה שאין בו סכנה לא שנכפה אלא שלא
יכפה וכו׳:

" Rav Papa says, do not think that it is necessary that both the man and the amulet must be approved; it is enough if the man be approved, even though the amulet be not approved. The proof is, that the Mishna says, ' Unless the amulet be from an approved person,' but does not say, ' Unless the amulet be approved,' from which it is plain. Our rabbies have taught thus, What is an approved amulet? Any amulet that has effected a cure, and done so twice or thrice. The doctrine holds good, whether the amulet be a written one, or made of roots—whether the man be dangerously ill or not—not only if he be epileptic, but that he may not become epileptic." (Shabbath, fol. 61, col. 1.) From this it appears that there are two sorts of amulets, one containing some written words, the other made of roots of various kinds, and it is equally plain that the object of wearing them was either to prevent sickness or to effect a cure. On the Sabbath those only are lawful, which have been manufactured by a man, who has already established his character for making efficacious amulets, or which have been already tried and proved to be so. This is the doctrine of the Talmud, and let every Jew remember that this doctrine is not extracted from the legendary part, but from those laws which are binding upon the consciences of all who acknowledge an oral law. And this is not any private opinion of our own, as may be seen by referring to any compilation where the laws are collected, as for instance the Jad Hachazakah, where this law is thus expressed:—

ויוצאין בקמיע מומחה ואי זה הוא קמיע מומחה
זה שריפא לשלשה בני אדם או שעשהו אדם שריפא
שלשה בני אדם בקמיעין אחרים:

" It is lawful to go out with an approved amulet. What is an approved amulet? One that has cured three persons, or has been made by a man who has cured three persons with other amulets." (Hilchoth Shabbath, c. xix. 14.) The Arbah Turim enters more at length into the subject, thus—

אין יוצאין בקמיע שאינו מומחה ואם הוא מומחה
יוצאין בו לא שנא אתמחי גברא ולא קמיע כגון שכתב
לחש אחד בג׳ אגרות ורפאו שלשתן דאתמחי גברא

לאותו לחש בכל פעם שיכתבנו אבל לא שאר לחשים
וגם אין הקמיע מומחה אם יכתבנו אחר, ולא שנא
אתמחי קמיע ולא גברא כגון שכתב לחש אחד באגרת
אחת וריפא בו שלשה פעמים שאותה אגרת מומחה
לכל אדם וכ"ש אתמחי גברא וקמיע כגון שכתב לחש
אחד בג' אגרות וכל אחד הועילה לג' אנשים או לאדם
אחד שלשה פעמים אתמחי גברא ללחש זה בכל
אגרות שיכתוב ואתמחו אגרות הללו לכל אדם, אבל
אם כתב ג' קמיעים לאדם אחד ורפאו ב' פעמים. לא
אתמחי גברא ולא קמיע, ומותר לצאת בקמיע מומחה
לא שנא הוא של כתב או של עקרין בין בחולה שיש
בו סכנה בין שאין בו סכנה, ולא שנכפה כבר ותולהו
לרפואה אלא אפילו לא אחזו חחולי אלא שהוא
ממשפחת נכפין ותולחו שלא יאחזנו שרי:

"It is not lawful to go out in an amulet, which is not approved, but if it be approved, it is lawful. Whether it be the man or the amulet which is approved, makes no difference; for instance, if a man have written one and the same charm in three copies, and all three have affected a cure, the man is approved with respect to that charm every time that he writes it, but not with respect to other charms; neither is the amulet approved if written by another. There is also no difference in the case, when the amulet is approved but the man not so; for instance, if a man write one charm, and only one copy, and has with it effected a cure three times, then that copy is approved for every man. A third case is, when both the man and the amulet are approved; for instance, if a man write one charm in three copies, and each has been of use to three men or to one man three times, then the man is approved with respect to this charm in every copy which he may write, and these copies are considered as approved for the use of all men. But if he have written three different amulets for one man, and have cured him three times, then neither the man nor the amulet is approved. Further, it is lawful to go out with an approved amulet, whether it be a writing or one made of roots, and whether the man be dangerously ill or not. Neither is it necessary that he should have been already epileptic, and now makes use of it for a cure. On the contrary, if he be of an epileptic family, and wear it as a preventive, it is lawful." (Orach Chaiim. sec. 301.) There can be no mistake here. This is Jewish law binding upon all who acknowledge tradition. Neither is it a doubtful or passing notice; on the contrary, the different cases are all enumerated, and every particular specified. The oral law here gives the most unqualified sanction to the use of amulets or charms, and that even on the Sabbath-day. That such charms are near akin to magic or witchcraft is plain from the nature and purpose of the manufacture, and from the undisguised use of the word לחש " charms ;" but there is a passage in Rashi's commentary on another Talmudic treatise, which puts this beyond all doubt; we therefore give both the text and the commentary—

תנו רבנן שמונים תלמידים היו להלל הזקן שלשים
מהן ראוים שתשרה עליהם שכינה כמשה רבינו
שלשים מהם ראוים שתעמוד להם חמה כיהושע בן
נון עשרים בינוניים גדול שבכולן יונתן בן עוזיאל קטן
שבכולן ר' יוחנן בן זכאי אמרו עליו על ר' יוחנן בן
זכאי שלא הניח מקרא משנה גמרא הלכות והגדות
דקדוקי תורה ודקדוקי סופרים וקלין וחמורין וגזרות
שוות ותקופות וגמטריאות ומשלות כובסים ומשלות
שועלים שיחת שדים ושיחת דקלים מלאכי שרת וכו' :

"Our rabbies have handed down the tradition that Hillel the elder had eighty disciples, of whom thirty were as worthy as Moses our master to have the Shechinah resting upon them. Thirty others were as worthy as Joshua the son of Nun that for them the sun should stand still. Twenty were in the middle rank, of whom the greatest was Jonathan the son of Uziel; and the least of all was Rabbi Johanan ben Zachai. Of this last-named rabbi it is said, that he did not leave unstudied the Bible or the Mishna, Gemara, the constitutions, the Agadoth, the niceties of the law and the Scribes, the argument, *a fortiori*, and from similar premises, the theory of the change of the moon, Gematria, the parables taken from grapes and from foxes, the language of demons, the language of palm-trees, and the language of the ministering angels," &c. (Bava Bathra, fol. 134, col. 1.) This was pretty well, considering that he was the least of the eighty ; what then must have been the knowledge of the others? This tradition alone, from its gross exaggeration, would be sufficient to mark the character of the rabbies as false witnesses. It is plainly a fable, such as one might expect in the "Arabian Nights' Entertainments," but not in a law that professes to have come from God. It is another proof that the account of the oral law is a mere fiction. But our object in quoting the passage here, is to point out its connexion with charms and amulets. It tells us, that this rabbi understood the language of the ministering angels? Now what use was this? Rashi tells us in his commentary, להשביעם to conjure or to adjure them: that is, to compel them to serve him, when he adjured them; that is, by their means to act the part of a conjuror. It may perhaps be said, these were the good angels, with whom a holy man might hold converse, but we are also told that he understood " the language of demons." What was the object of this? Rashi answers again—

לחשביעם ונפקא מיניה לעשות קמיע לרפואה :

" For the purpose of adjuring them : and hence it follows that amulets may be made in order to effect cures." From this it appears that the Talmud allows a man to have converse with evil spirits, and that this precedent establishes the lawfulness of amulets. And this is the religion of the oral law, these the doctrines and practices of the men who rejected Jesus of Nazareth! Here is real heathenism, not one shade of which appears in the New Testament. Oh! how different is this from the doctrine of Moses and the prophets. The oral law sends sick men to seek help in amulets and charms, but not to the God of Israel. Now what difference is there between this and the conduct of Ahaziah, when he fell down through the lattice in his upper chamber in Samaria, and was sick? " He sent messengers, and said unto them, Go inquire of Beelzebub the god of Ekron, whether I shall recover of this disease. But the angel of the Lord said to Elijah the Tishbite, Arise, go up to meet the messengers of the King of Samaria, and say unto them, Is it not because there is not a God in Israel, that ye go to inquire of Beelzebub, the god of Ekron?" (2 Kings i. 2, 3.) And so it may still be said to Israel, Is it not because there is not a God in Israel, that ye go to amulets and charms in order to get cured of your diseases? Moses points to God as the great physician; he says, " Wherefore it shall come to pass, if ye hearken to these judgments, and keep and do them, that the Lord thy God shall keep unto thee the covenant and the mercy which he sware unto thy fathers. And the Lord will take away from thee all sickness." (Deut. vi. 12—15.) God himself says—

אני ה׳ רופאך :

" I am the LORD that healeth thee." (Exod. xv. 26.) But the oral law leads men away from God, and tells them to go to an approved man and to get an approved amulet, and for this allows to learn the language of demons, and to compel them by adjuration to be subservient. Where, in all the Old Testament, is there any thing like this? When the widow's son was sick, Elijah did not give her an amulet to make him well, and yet, if there were such things, it might be supposed that he knew of them, and knew how to make them ; in short, that he was an approved man and could make an approved amulet; but Elijah's trust was not in such heathen nonsense, but in the

God of Israel. Before Him he prostrated himself, and said, "O Lord my God, I pray thee, let this child's soul come into him again." (1 Kings xvii. 22.) When Hezekiah was sick, we read not that he sent for an approved amulet, but that "He turned his face towards the wall, and prayed unto the Lord." Not charms, but faith and prayer, are the amulets of the Old Testament, and also of the New. The Lord Jesus Christ wrought many miracles of healing, and multitudes of sick people applied to him for relief, but he never directed them to amulets in order to attain it. His direction is, "Be not afraid, only believe." (Mark v. 36.) His disciples also wrought great miracles on the sick, but not by amulets. Their confession is "His name, through faith in his name, hath given him this perfect soundness in the presence of you all." (Acts iii. 16.) And their command is, not to wear amulets, but to pray. "Is any sick among you? Let him call for the elders of the Church; and let them pray over him, anointing him with oil in the name of the Lord; and the prayer of faith shall save the sick, and the Lord shall raise him up; and if he have committed sins they shall be forgiven him. The effectual fervent prayer of a righteous man availeth much. Elias was a man subject to like passions as we are, and he prayed earnestly that it might not rain, and it rained not on the earth by the space of three years and six months. And he prayed again, and the heaven gave rain, and the earth brought forth her fruit." (James v. 13—18.) This is the doctrine of the New Testament, exactly agreeing with that of Moses and the prophets, so that you need not fear that Christianity will lead you to heathenism: on the contrary, it will lead you back from the heathenism of magic and astrology, and amulets, to the God of Israel.

But there is another feature in this doctrine concerning amulets, which must not be overlooked, and that is that the manufacture of amulets may be made a mere trade for collecting the money of the credulous. If a man get a reputation as an approved manufacturer, the believers in the oral law will naturally apply to him in case of sickness, or other circumstances, where amulets are of service, and of course the remedy is not to be had for nothing. We have known and heard of such things both in the west and in the east. And thus the poor Israelites are led away from the God of Israel, and induced, as the prophet says, "To spend their money for that which is not bread, and their labour for that which satisfieth not." But what a testimony does this whole doctrine furnish to the conduct and the doctrine of Jesus of Nazareth? His great endeavour was to show the apostacy of the oral law, and to lead the people back from tradition to the Holy Scriptures. Was he right or was he wrong? Which is the religion, of the oral law or of the New Testament, most agreeable to the religion revealed to

Moses and the prophets. Is the practice of magic a Mosaic doctrine? Is permission to hold converse with evil demons a Mosaic doctrine? Is astrology a Mosaic doctrine? Is the manufacture of amulets and charms a Mosaic doctrine? No; they are all directly opposed to the doctrine and commandments of Moses, and the practice of all the holy men of old. Are these things doctrines of the oral law? Yes. Are they the doctrines of the New Testament? No. Christians are taught to abstain from all such things. Then in this, at least, Christianity is more like Mosaism. How long will the Jews suffer themselves to be thus deluded and imposed upon? Many are perhaps ignorant of the details of that system which they profess, but such ignorance is highly culpable. If men profess a religion they ought to know what it is, and what are its doctrines, and what the practices which it prescribes. Modern Judaism teaches, as the truth of God, all these heathenish notions and practices; it is time, then, for the Jews to inquire whether this be the true religion in which they have continued for so many centuries, and if not, to stand in the ways and ask for the old paths. It is a vain thing for a few individuals of the nation to attempt to deny that these superstitions are an essential portion of modern Judaism. As long as the oral law is acknowledged to be of Divine authority, that oral law must itself be taken as the witness for its own doctrines, and the standard of the modern Jewish religion. There is no possible middle course: either Jews must altogether and publicly renounce the Talmud as false, superstitious, and heathenish, or they must be content to be regarded in one of two characters, either as its faithful disciples, who believe all it says, or as timid men-pleasers, who are afraid to confess the truth of God, or to protest against the errors of man, lest they should suffer some worldly loss or inconvenience. But is it possible that cowards, in the cause of God, should be found amongst the people of Gideon, who stood boldly against the idolatry of a whole city, and overthrew the altar of Baal, or amongst the offspring of Hananiah, Mishael, and Azariah, who dared a fiery furnace, or amidst the countrymen of Daniel who trembled not at the view of the lion's den? No, we will rather believe that all the Jews are still bigoted Talmudists, and that when they cease to be, they will come forward with the spirit of their fathers and the strength of their God to vindicate the truth.

No. XXV.

CHARMS.

BOTH Jew and Gentile will agree that true religion is the fear of the Lord, but the difficulty is how are we to know it, and what are the marks that will help us to distinguish the true from the false? The Word of God gives many, of which at present we select this one :—

ראשית חכמה יראת ח׳ :

"The fear of the Lord is the beginning of wisdom." (Psalm cxi. 10.) True religion, as the Bible teaches, does not only better the heart, but also improves the understanding; whereas false religion not only corrupts, but also makes its votaries foolish. This is the uniform representation of the Bible, and thus we read of true religion, " The law of the Lord is perfect, converting the soul: the testimony of the Lord is sure, making wise the simple." (Psalm xix. 7.) And again, the wisest of men says, " Then shalt thou understand righteousness, judgment, and equity; yea, every good path. When wisdom entereth into thine heart, and knowledge is pleasant to thy soul, discretion shall preserve thee, understanding shall keep thee." (Prov. ii. 9—11.) The votaries of false religion are, on the contrary, described as devoid of all wisdom. " They are altogether brutish and foolish; the stock is a doctrine of vanities." (Jer. x. 8.) And again, " None considereth in his heart, neither is there knowledge nor understanding to say, I have burned part of it in the fire; yea, also, I have baked bread on the coals thereof; I have roasted flesh and eaten it; and shall I make the residue thereof an abomination? Shall I fall down to the stock of a tree? He feedeth on ashes; a deceived heart hath turned him aside, that he cannot deliver his soul, nor say, Is there not a lie in my right hand?" (Isaiah xliv. 19, 20.) According to these passages of Scripture, wisdom is a test of true religion, and folly of a false one, let us then apply this test to the religion of the oral law, does it commend itself to the understanding by its wisdom, and the wisdom of its teachers? It is true, that it speaks well oi itself, and calls all its doctors חכמים " Wise men," but the chapter on amulets, quite fresh in the memory of our readers, excites some doubts upon the subject, though of these we consider only the theory. The histories, which the Talmud gives of the Rabbinical practice with regard to such charms, lead to the inevitable conclusion that wisdom is not one of the characteristics of the oral law. Take for example the following direction to stop a bleeding at the nose :—

לדמא דאתי מנחירא ליתי גברא כהן דשמיה לוי
ולכתוב ליה לוי למפרע ואי לא ליתי איניש מעלמא
ונכתוב ליה אנא פפי שילא בר סומקי למפרע ואי לא
ניכתוב ליה הכי טעם דלי במי כסף טעם דלי במי
פגם ואי לא ליתיה עקרא דאספסתא ואשלא דפורייא
עתיקא וקורטסא ומוריקא וסומקא דלוליבא ונקלינהו
בהדי הדדי וליתי גבבא דעמרא וניגדול תרתי פתילתא
ולטמיש בחלא וניגדבל בקיטמא הדין וניתיב בנחירא
ואי לא ליחזי אמת המים דאזלא ממזרח כלפי מערב
וניפסע וניקום חד כרעא להאי גיסא וחד כרעא להאי
גיסא ונישקל טינא בידיה דימינא מתותי כרעא דשמאליה
ובידיה דשמאלא מתותי כרעא דימיניה ונגדול תרתי
פתילתא דעמרא וניטמיש בטינא וניתיב בנחיריה ואי
לא ליתיה תותא מרזבא וניתי מיא ולישדי עליה
ולימרו כי היכי דפסקי הני מיא ליפסק דמיה דפלניא
בר פלניתא :

"For a bleeding at the nose, let a man be brought who is a priest, and whose name is Levi, and let him write the word Levi backwards. If this cannot be done, get a layman, and let him write the following words backwards :—'Ana pipi Shila bar Sumki;' * or let him write these words, 'Taam dli bemi keseph, taam li bemi paggan;' † or let him take a root of grass, and the cord of an old bed, and paper and saffron, and the red part of the inside of a palm tree, and let him burn them together, and let him take some wool, and twist two threads, and let him dip them in vinegar, and then roll them in the ashes, and put them into his nose. Or let him look out for a small stream of water that flows from east to west, and let him go and stand with one leg on each side of it, and let him take with his right hand some mud from under his left foot, and with his left hand from under his right foot, and let him twist two threads of wool, and dip them in the mud, and put them into his nostrils. Or let him be placed under a spout, and let water be brought and poured upon him, and let them say, 'As this water ceases to flow, so let the blood of M., the son of the woman N., also cease.'" (Gittin, fol. 69, col. 1.) Now we ask any Jew of common sense, whether this passage savours most of wisdom or folly?

---

* The only explanation which Rashi gives of these words is לחש הוא "It is a charm."

† לחש הוא "It is a charm."—Rashi.

Vinegar and water may be very useful in such a case, or even mud, if used in sufficient quantity, might stop up the nose, and therefore stop the bleeding too, but what manner of benefit can proceed from the word Levi written backwards, or from those words which Rashi pronounces to be magical? Why is the mud of water flowing from east to west more efficacious, and why is it to be taken with the right hand from under the left foot, and with the left hand from under the right foot? Plainly because the authors of this passage thought there was some charm or magic power, and their minds were so overpowered by superstition, as to lead them to disregard the plain words of Moses forbidding all magic. It cannot be pretended that this is a rare case, the Talmud abounds in such remedies, all equally wise. For instance, take the following mode of treatment for the scratch or bite of a mad dog :—

תנו רבנן חמשה דברים נאמרו בכלב שוטה פיו
פתוח ורירו נוטף ואזניו סרוחות וזנבו מונח לו על
ירכותיו ומהלך בצדי דרכים ויש אומרים אף נובח
ואין קולו נשמע, ממאי הוי רב אמר נשים כשפניות
משחקות בו, ושמואל אמר רוח רעה שורה עליו,
מאי בינייהו איכא בינייהו למקטליה בדבר הנזרק
תניא כותיה דשמואל כשהורגין אותו אין הורגין אורו
אלא בדבר הנזרק דחייף ביה מסתכן דנכית ליה מיית
דחייף ביה מסתכן מאי תקנתיה נישלח מאניה ונירהוט
רב הונא בריה דרב יהושע חף ביה חד מינייהו
בשוקא שלחינהו למאניה ורחיט אמר קיימתי בעצמי
והחכמה תחיה בעליה דנכית ל'יה מאית מאי תקנתיה
אמר אביי ניתי משכא דאפא דדיכרא וניכתוב עליה
אנא פלניא בר פליניתא אמשכא דאפא דדיכרא כתיבנא
עלך כנתי כנתי קלירוס ואמרו לה קנדי קנדי קלורוס
יה יה ה' צבאות אמן אמן סלה ונשלחינהו למאניא
ולקברינהו בי קברי עד תריסר ירחי שתא ונפקינהו
ונקלינהו בתנורא ונבדרינהו לקטמיה אפרשת דרכים
והנך תריסר ירחי שתא כי שתי מיא לא לשתי אלא
בגובתא דנחשא דלמא חזי בבואיה דשידא וליסתכן
כי הא דאבא בר מרתא הוא אבא בר מניומי עבדי
ליה אימיה גובתא דדהבא:

"The rabbies have handed down the tradition, that there are five things to be observed of a mad dog: his mouth is open, his saliva flows, his ears hang down, his tail is between his legs, and he goes by the sides of the ways. Some say also, that he barks, but his voice is not heard. What is the cause of his madness? Rav says, it proceeds from this, that the witches are making their sport with him. Samuel says, it is an evil spirit that rests upon him. What is the difference? The difference is this, that in the latter case he is to be killed by some missile weapon. The tradition * agrees with Samuel, for it says, In killing him no other mode is to be used but the casting of some missile weapon. If a mad dog scratch any one, he is in danger; but if he bite him he will die. In case of a scratch there is danger; what then is the remedy? Let the man cast off his clothes and run away. Rav Huna, the son of Rav Joshua, was once scratched in the street by one of them; he immediately cast off his clothes and ran away. He also says, I fulfilled in myself those words, 'Wisdom giveth life to them that have it.' (Eccles. vii. 12.) In case of a bite the man will die; what then is the remedy? Abai says, He must take the skin of a male adder, and write upon it these words, 'I, M., the son of the woman N., upon the skin of a male adder, I write against thee, Kanti, Kanti, Klirus.' Some say, 'Kandi, Kandi, Klurus, Jah, Jah, Lord of Hosts, Amen, Amen, Selah.' Let him also cast off his clothes, and bury them in the grave-yard for twelve months of the year; then let him take them up and burn them in an oven, and let him scatter the ashes at the parting of the roads. But during these twelve months of the year, when he drinks water, let him drink out of nothing but a brass tube, lest he should see the phantom-form of the demon and be endangered. This was tried by Abba, the son of Martha, who is the same as Abba, the son of Manjumi. His mother made a golden tube for him." (Joma, fol. 83, col. 1.) This is a very plain case of the use of an amulet and of magic, but whether it be a proof of profound wisdom we leave to the judgment of the reader. What good can the poor man get from certain words written on the skin of a male adder? or from first burying and then burning his clothes, and scattering the ashes on the cross-roads? It cannot be pretended that this is medical treatment, and still less that it is the treatment commanded by the Word of God. If it had pleased God to command all this, we should not only submit, but gladly recommend this recipe in every similar case. To God Almighty no man can prescribe. He chooses what means he pleases, and may do so because his omnipotence can render them effectual. He healed the Israelites bitten by the fiery serpents by the sight of the brazen image, and he cured Naaman's leprosy by bathing in the waters of Jordan. Whatever then be the means which He prescribes, our highest wisdom is to make use of them. But as he has not prescribed the means recommended by the Talmud, but

* The Bareitha.

forbidden them in his general prohibition of magic, we must say that the man who uses them has bid adieu to all true wisdom. No wonder, then, if his own inventions are stamped with folly. But what will our readers think of the cause of the canine madness here assigned? "Rav says, It proceeds from the witches who are making their sport with him. Samuel says, It is an evil spirit that rests upon him." Rav believed, then, that God, whose mercies are over all his works, allows wicked women to torment his creatures, and to inflict upon them a dreadful malady to make sport for themselves. Is this wise, is it according to Scripture? This is the doctrine of the oral law; and if Jesus of Nazareth had not protested against it, and taught a true doctrine by asserting the truth of Scripture, this would be the universal doctrine and practice of the Jews. Whoever believes the Talmud, must believe in this and all the other follies which it contains. Whoever rejects these things, confesses that the Talmud contains what is false and foolish, and thereby shakes or rather overthrows its authority. Some person will perhaps say that similar superstitions and follies have been found amongst Christians. We grant that this has been the case wherever Christians have departed from the written Word of God, but can anything similar be found in the New Testament? That book is our standard of Christianity. As you say that the oral law is of divine authority, we say that the New Testament is of divine authority. We point out to you these follies, not in individual Jews, but in your book of authority. If you would make out a parallel case, you must do the same. But you cannot. The New Testament has nothing of the kind; and it is for you to explain how this happens that the New Testament, which you believe to be false, is entirely free from every thing of the kind.

Further, we ask every right-minded Israelite, whether he is not shocked at that profanation of the reverend and holy names of God which is here not only countenanced but prescribed. What can a devout Jew think either of the man or the book that tells us to write the names,

יה יה יהוה צבאות :

"Jah, Jah, the Lord of Hosts," by the side of such nonsense as Kanti, Kanti, Klurus? Would he say that this is consistent with true religion? And yet this profane use of the name of God for magical purposes, is not rare in the Talmud. The following is another instance :—

אמר רבה אשתעו לי נחותי ימא, האי גלא דלא דמטבע
לספינה מיתחזי כי צוציתא דנורא חיוורתא ברישא
ומחינן ליה באלוותא דחקיק עליה אהיה אשר אהיה

יה ה׳ צבאות אמן אמן סלה ונייה אמר רבה אשתעו
לי נחותי ימא בין גלא לגלא תלת מאה פרסי זמנא
חדא הוה אזלינן באורחא ודלינן גלא עד דחזינן בי
מרבעתא דכוכבא זוטא והויא בי מבזר ארבעין גריוי
בזרא דחרדלא, ואי דלינן טפי מקלינן מהבלי, ורמי
ליה גלא קלא לחברתה חברתי שבקת מידי בעלמא
דלא שטפתיה דניתי אנא ונאבדיה א״ל פוק חזי גבורתא
דמריך מלא חוטא חלא ולא עברי שנאמר האותי לא
תיראו נאום ה׳ אם מפני לא תחילו אשר שמתי חול
גבול לים חק עולם ולא יעברנהו:

"Rabbah says, They that go down to the sea have told
me, that when a wave is going to overwhelm a ship, sparks
of white light are seen on its head. But if we strike it
with a staff on which are graved the words, 'I am that I
am, Jah, Lord of Hosts, Amen, Amen, Selah,' it subsides.
They that go down to the sea have told me, that the distance
between one wave and another, is three hundred miles. It
happened once that we were making a voyage, and we raised
a wave until we saw the resting-place of the least of all
the stars. It was large enough to sow forty bushels of
mustard seed, and if we had raised it more we should have
been burned by the vapour of the star. One wave raised its
voice and called to its companion, O, companion, hast thou
left anything in the world that thou hast not overflowed?
Come, and let us destroy it. It replied, Come and see the
power of thy Lord. I could not overpass the sand even a
hair's-breadth, for it is written, 'Fear ye not me? saith the
Lord: will ye not tremble at my presence, which have
placed the sand for the bound of the sea, by a perpetual
decree that it cannot pass it?' (Jer. v. 22.)" (Bava Bathra,
fol. 73, col. 1.) Here is the same profanation of the peculiar
and holy names of God? it is to be engraved on a staff
either to lay or to raise the waves. But besides the profanity, just consider the folly of this whole story. In the
first place, it ascribes to men, no matter whether they are
good or wicked, absolute power over the waves of the sea.
Anybody can engrave those names of God upon a staff,
anybody can use the staff to strike the sea, and thus a
wicked man, without either faith, fear, or love of God, may
make and use an instrument which almost invests him with
omnipotence. Is it possible that any son of Israel can be so
credulous as to believe such manifest absurdity? But this
story reminds us again of the utter disregard of truth which
characterises the Talmud. Here we are told that, by power
of this magic staff, a wave was raised so high as to enable

those travellers to see the resting-place of the smallest of all the stars, and that so distinctly, too, as to be able to make a good guess at its measure. The slightest knowledge of modern astronomy is sufficient to show not only the improbability, but the utter impossibility of anything of the kind. The least of the stars visible to the naked eye is at an almost immeasurable distance from the earth, so as to make it perfectly ludicrous to talk of a wave being raised to such a height. All the water on the face of the globe would be far from sufficient for the formation of one such wave. But the Talmud intimates that they had the power of raising it still higher, and were prevented only by the fear of being scorched. But the Talmud is not satisfied with these wonders, it goes on to describe a conversation between two waves. The commentator, who evidently believed every word of the story, suggest that this conversation was carried on by the angels presiding over the waves.

ורמי ליה גלא נתן קולו כלומר צעק כדוגמא תחום
אל תחום קורא , ושמא מלאכים הממונים עליהם הם:

"The wave lifted up his voice, that is, it cried, and so we find, ' Deep calleth unto deep.' And perhaps this means the angels who were set over them." The commentator, it appears, had no doubt of the truth of the story, and how should he have, if he believed in the Divine authority of the Talmud? But we ask our readers do they believe this story—and if they do not, why not? Because it is too absurd, and too far beyond the bounds of possibility. Can, then, a book that swarms with similar accounts be from God? By what means did all these things about magic, astrology, amulets, magical cures, and staves, get into the Talmud? No doubt they were put in by the authors. Either, then, the authors believed in all these things, or they did not. If they did not believe in them, then they were evidently bad men, who deliberately wrote falsehood. But if they did believe these things, then, though not guilty of wilful falsehood, they were credulous, superstitious persons, who had no clear idea of the religion of Moses and the prophets; and in either case they are most unsafe guides in religion. It is for the Jews of the present day to consider whether they will still adhere to a system that involves the belief of so many incredibilities and sanctions the profanation of the names of God for the purposes of magic. Eighteen centuries are surely long enough to have remained in such thick darkness. Those who have been brought up in such a system ought now, at least, to arise and ask what have they and their forefathers been about all this while? And how it is that the New Testament, which they have rejected, is entirely free from such deformities? Something has been decidedly wrong, or the chosen people of God could not have remained so long in captivity, unheeded and unhelped by the Holy One of Israel. An exhibition of the doctrines of the oral law explains the cause. Israel has departed from the religion of Moses, and pertinaciously adhered to a system compounded of human inventions, and idolatrous heathenism. They call Moses their master, and say that the oral law is derived from him, but if we may from the work, form a conjecture about the author, it is much more probably a tradition from the magicians of Egypt or the witch of Endor. And if it had been handed down as such—if the Israelites had presented the Talmud to the world and their posterity as part of the heavy yoke of Egypt, we should not have been astonished at the universality of its reception. But that Israel should ever have been so far imposed upon, as to believe that Moses or the prophets ever had anything to do with the oral law appears almost inexplicable. However unwilling one may be to apply to fellow-sinners any prophecy that contains a denunciation of God's wrath, one cannot help asking, was it of this that the prophet said, "The Lord hath poured out upon you the spirit of deep sleep, and hath closed your eyes; the prophets and your rulers the seers hath he covered. And the vision of all is become unto you as the words of a book that is sealed, which men deliver to one that is learned, saying, read this, I pray thee; and he saith, I cannot, for it is sealed: and the book is delivered to him that is not learned, saying, Read this, I pray thee, and he saith, I am not learned." (Isaiah xxix. 10—12.) This question is, however, far more important to Israel than to us, and to them we leave the answer. Some will still persist in the assertion that this heathenish compound is the highest wisdom. The great majority of the nation is devoted to the Talmud, which is still the cistern whence the synagogues endeavour to draw the waters of life. The multitude does it in ignorance, they are, therefore, not so culpable. But there are many that know better, what then is the reason that they do not strain every nerve to deliver their brethren? These few do not suffer the oral law to interfere either with their business or their convenience. They profane the Sabbath, eat Gentile food, carry on their business on feasts and festivals. If they do all this on principle, why not protest against error? Is it because they are indifferent to the welfare of their brethren? If indifference be the only fruit of this intellectual progress, instead of rising above, they have sunk below superstition itself.

No. XXVI.

CHARMS CONTINUED.

IF men would only employ in religion a little of that common sense and earnestness, which they find so necessary for the affairs of this life, they would by God's blessing soon arrive at the truth. For example, if the father of a family should find, that by following the advice of a physician, sickness and death were constant guests, he would soon look out for another; and he would be much quickened in his measures, if this physician's counsel had produced the same results in the house of his father and his grandfather. He would not think it any shame, under such circumstances, to change his father's physician for another; on the contrary, he would think, and most men would agree with him, that it would be both a sin and a shame to retain him. Now let Israel make the application to their spiritual physicians, the Scribes, Pharisees, and Rabbies. For many centuries they have punctually followed their advice, and the consequence has been one misfortune after another, and centuries of exile from the land which God gave to their fathers; the very contrary of that which God has promised. God has said, if the Jews will obey the religion of Moses, that they shall be restored to their land. " It shall come to pass . . . if thou shalt return unto the Lord thy God, and shalt obey his voice according to all that I command thee this day, thou and thy children, with all thy heart and with all thy soul; that then the Lord thy God will turn thy captivity, and have compassion upon thee, and will return and gather thee from all nations," &c. (Deut. xxx. 2, 3.) The Jews have obeyed the commands of the rabbies, and have not been gathered; what is the conclusion? Either that God's promise has failed, which is impossible, or that the religion of the rabbies is not the religion of Moses. Such is the inevitable conclusion from the words of Moses and the facts of the case; let it then lead the sufferers to examine the religion which they have hitherto professed. A very little examination will convince any reasonable man, that it is a fearful corruption of divine truth, a compilation made by men who professed to be astrologers and magicians. Let not the Jews think that our opinion is the result of prejudice. It has been deliberately formed on evidence furnished by the oral law itself. If we are wrong, let the rabbies prove the contrary. Let them, for example, explain the following law of modern Judaism.

מי שנשכו עקרב או נחש מותר ללחוש על מקום

הנשיכה ואפילו בשבת כדי לישב דעתו ולחזק לבו
אף על פי שאין הדבר מועיל כלום הואיל ומסוכן
הוא התירו לו כדי שלא תטרף דעתו עליו:

"If any person be bitten by a scorpion or a serpent, it is lawful to charm the place of the bite, even on the Sabbath-day, in order to quiet his mind, and to encourage his heart, although it is a thing utterly profitless. Because the man is in danger, they have pronounced this lawful for him that his mind may not be distracted." (Hilchoth Accum. c. xi. 11.) Here the rabbies have allowed what God has absolutely forbidden. The men who profess such reverence for the Sabbath allow it to be profaned by magic, which is one of the works of the devil. Rambam, whose words we have just quoted, felt that it was both wicked and foolish, and has therefore endeavoured to furnish an excuse, saying that it is of no use, and is only allowed to quiet the mind of the sufferer. But that does not alter the unlawfulness. Besides, what sort of opinion could Rambam and the rabbies have had of the Jews, when they say that magic is permitted in order to quiet their minds? They evidently supposed that the Jews were a weak and superstitious people, who believed so firmly in charms, that the use of them would quiet the mind; and so ignorant or careless about God's commandments, that they could be comforted by their transgressions. The excuse, therefore, only makes the case worse. It takes for granted that the professors of the oral law are ignorant and superstitious; and then to quiet their minds allows the transgression of the law of Moses, and that on the Sabbath-day. But this excuse is altogether Rambam's invention. The original passage in the Talmud says nothing about quieting the man's mind, it simply says—

ולוחשין לחישת נחשים ועקרבים בשבת:

"It is lawful to charm serpents and scorpions on the Sabbath-day." (Sanhedrin, fol. 101, col. 1.) And Rashi's commentary on the passage—

בשביל שלא יזיקו:

"That they may not do injury." This man, then, who spent his life in the study of the Talmud, knew nothing of Rambam's apology. He plainly believed that by charming serpents on the Sabbath, they might be prevented from doing harm, and that on this account, and not for the purpose of quieting the mind, they were permitted so to do. This was also the opinion of that famous expounder of Jewish law, the Baal Turim, for after quoting Rambam's words, he adds:—

CHARMS CONTINUED.

מי שרודפים אחריו נחש או עקרב מותר לחבר
ללחש כדי שלא יזיקוהו כתב הרמב״ם הלוחש על
המכה והקורא פסוק מן התורה וכן הקורא על התינוק
שלא יבעת או מניח ס״ת או תפילין על הקטן לא די
להם שהם בכלל חברים ומנחשים אלא שהם בכלל
הכופרים בתורה שעושין דברי תורה רפואת הגוף
ואינן אלא רפואת הנפש ור״י פירש דוקא בלוחש על
המכה ומזכיר שם שמים ורוקק אותו הוא שאין לו
חלק לעולם הבא אבל אם אינו רוקק לא חמיר כולי
האי ומיהו איסורא איכא בלוחש פסוק על המכה
אפילו בלא רקיקה ובלא הזכרת שם שמים, ואם יש
בו סכנת נפשות הכל מותר ומותר לקרוא פסוק להגן
כגון בלילה על מטתו:

"If any person be pursued by a serpent or a scorpion, it is lawful to charm it to prevent it from doing injury. Rambam has written, He that charms a wound, or reads a verse from the law (as a charm), and also he that reads over an infant that it may not be afraid, or who lays a roll of the law or phylacteries upon a child, are not only to be accounted as one of the charmers and magicians, but as of the deniers of the law, for they use the words of the law as medicine for the body, whereas it is only a medicine for the soul. R. Isaac says absolutely, that he who charms a wound, mentioning at the same time the name of God and spitting, is the charmer of whom it is said that he has no share in the world to come: but if he does not spit, the matter is not so grave. It is, however, forbidden to use a verse as a charm over a wound, even though there will be no spitting nor mentioning the name of God. *But if life be in danger, every thing is lawful;* and it is lawful to read a verse as a defence, for instance at night in bed." (Joreh Deah. § 179.) From this it is pretty plain that the charming of serpents was allowed, not as Rambam says to quiet the mind of him that had been bitten, but to prevent injury, for it is allowed before the man is bitten at all, if he be only pursued by a serpent or a scorpion. But what a picture does this whole passage give us of the religious state of the Rabbinic Jews, both rabbies and people. Here you have the people described, not by Christians, but by the rabbies themselves, as sunk in the depths of superstition, using a sepher torah, a roll of the law, or phylacteries as a sort of charm for the benefit of children, and you have the rabbies forbidding this at one time, but allowing what is equally forbidden by God, to charm serpents: and, in case of danger, declaring that "Every thing is lawful," that is, allowing them to do what will make them, according to Rambam's opinion, charmers, magicians, and deniers of the law. And this is the Jewish religion, and this is what the Jews have gained by rejecting Christianity. We, poor Gentiles, who cannot trace our pedigree to Abraham, Isaac, and Jacob, should be ashamed of such follies. And if such wicked heathenish practices were to be found in our religious books, we would not let an hour pass over until we had lifted up our voice and protested against them, and should use every lawful means to deliver our children from such ungodliness and error.

We have now given quotations from the two great digests of Jewish law on the subject of using charms, but it is worth while to consider the context of the original passage, upon which these laws are based, as that will prove that the Talmud has not been misrepresented by its compilers.

תנו רבנן סכין וממשמשין בבני מעיין בשבת ולוחשין
לחישת נחשים ועקרבים בשבת ומעבירין כלי על גב
העין בשבת אמר רבן שמעון בן גמליאל במה דברים
אמורים בכלי הניטל אבל בכלי שאינו ניטל אסור ואין
שואלין בדבר שדים בשבת ר' יוסי אומר אף בחול
אסור אמר רב הונא אין הלכה כר' יוסי ואף ר' יוסי
לא אמרה אלא משום סכנה כי הא דרב יצחק בר
יוסף דאיבלע בארזא ואתעביד ליה ניסא פקע ארזא
ופלטיה:

"Our rabbies have handed down the tradition that it is lawful to anoint and rub the stomach (of a sick man) on the Sabbath, also to charm serpents and scorpions on the Sabbath: also to pass an instrument across the eye on the Sabbath. R. Simeon, the son of Gamaliel, says, that this only applies to an instrument which may be moved,* but with one that may not be moved, it is unlawful. But it is unlawful on the Sabbath to make inquiry of demons. R. Jose says, this is also unlawful on week-days. Rav Huna says, the decision is not according to R. Jose: and R. Jose himself said this only on account of danger, for that is what occurred in the case of R. Isaac, the son of Joseph, who was swallowed up in a cedar tree, but a miracle was wrought for him—the cedar opened and cast him out." (Sanhedrin, fol. 101, col. 1.) We have here, first, the charming of serpents; we ask, then, could the Talmudic doctors really believe in such folly or allow such wickedness on the Sabbath? Is there any misunderstanding, or does the context show, that they were men of that superstitious turn of mind to justify this idea? The context is all of a piece, for after

---

* Such as a key, a ring, or a knife.—Rashi.

permitting the charming of serpents, it goes on to discuss the lawfulness of asking counsel of demons, and here Rashi shall explain what this means :—

בדבר שדים שכן עושין כשאובדין שום דבר שואלין
במעשה שדים והם מגידים להם ואסור לעשות בשבת
משום ממצוא חפציך :

"To make inquiry of demons, is what they do when any thing is lost. They make inquiry by the work of demons, and they tell them, and this is forbidden on the Sabbath, on account of the words, 'Not finding thine own pleasure.' (Isaiah lviii. 13.)" This is plainly a magical operation, but yet the rabbies do not say that it is unlawful because it is magical, but because it would be attending to one's own concerns. In like manner, they say, it is unlawful on week-days, only on account of the danger. And an instance is given in Rabbi Isaac of what might happen; and here, again, we ask counsel of Rashi, in order to understand what Rabbi Isaac was about. This commentator tells us :—

היה שואל במעשה שדים ובקש השד להזיקו ונעשה
לו נס ובלעו הארז :

"He was asking counsel, by means of a demoniacal operation, and the demon sought to do him an injury, but a miracle was wrought for him, and a cedar tree swallowed him." Such, then, is the context, those men who permit the charming of serpents, also teach the doctrine of asking advice of demons, and give us a practical example in one of their friends. There can, therefore, be no mistake; the one feature of their religious system exactly agrees with the other: and the authors of the oral law represent themselves as patrons and practisers of charms and magic, and therefore to every lover of the Mosaic law, as unwise and ungodly men. It is, however, curious to see how they endeavoured to quiet their own conscience, and that of the people, in a matter so evidently repugnant to the plain words of Scripture. They pretended that there was a holy sort of magic in the practical Cabbala, which men might learn, and then perform the greatest miracles.

אי בעו צדיקי ברו עלמא שנאמר כי עונותיכם היו
מבדילים וגו' רבא ברא גברא שדריה לקמיה דר' זירא
הוה קא משתעי בהדיה ולא הוה קא מהדר ליה אמר
ליה מן חבריא את הדר לעפריך רב חנינא ורב אושעיא
הוו יתבי כל מעלי שבתא ועסקו בספר יצירה ומיברו
להו עיגלא תילתא ואכלי ליה :

"If the righteous wished, they might create the world, for it is written, 'But your sins separate, &c.' Rabba created a man, and sent him to Rabbi Zira. He spoke with him, but when the other did not answer him, he said, Thou art from the magicians, return to thy dust. Rav Chanina and Rav Oshaia used to sit every Sabbath eve and study the book of Jetzirah, and then created for themselves a three-years-old calf, and ate it." (Sanhedrin, fol. 65, col. 2.) The second miracle is here ascribed to the study of a certain book. In Rashi the first miracle performed by Rabba is ascribed to the same source.

ברא גברא ע״י ספר יצירה שמלמדו צרוף אותיות
של שם:

"He created the man by means of the book of Jetzirah, for it taught him the combination of the letters of the name of God." According to this account, these rabbies were much greater men than Moses or any of the prophets, for in the whole Old Testament there is not one such miracle recorded. Moses never created any thing, neither did he perform any of his miracles without the help of God. Either the Lord immediately commanded him, or he sought the Lord's help. But these rabbies acquired the power of omnipotence by studying a particular book, and exercised it either for their amusement or their profit. Rabba created a man, and sent him to Rabbi Zira, not as it appears to do any good, or to glorify God, but simply to show his power, or to act a little bit of waggery; and the other two created a fat calf for themselves every Sabbath eve, that they might have a good dinner. The difference between these miracles and those recorded in Scripture is obvious. The Scripture miracles are either for the glory of God, or the good of man. The rabbinical miracles are altogether for the glory of man, and the gratification of self. Moses smote the rock, and supplied all Israel with water. The rabbies create a calf, and eat it themselves. No doubt there were many poor people in Israel at the time of Rabbies Oshaia and Chanina, who would have been very glad of a calf for their Sabbath dinner, why did they not create a calf or two for them? This selfish falsehood betrays itself, and bears on its front its own condemnation. The whole doctrine of the combination of the letters in the name of God is a pure invention of men, whose minds have been debased by superstition. There is not a word about it in the whole Bible, and it is derogatory to the honour of God, who is the only Creator.

The whole Talmudic doctrine of magic does, however, explain the reason why the Scribes and Pharisees were so little moved by the real miracles of Jesus of Nazareth and his disciples. Their minds were fully possessed with faith in the power of cabalistic magic, they therefore were insensible to the real displays of divine power. They were in the same state of mind as Pharaoh and his magicians, who looked on the miracles of Moses as a mere proof of magical skill, and hardened their hearts. Even when they confessed " This is the finger of God," they were not converted. Pharaoh still persisted in his resistance. And so it was with the Scribes and Pharisees. When the Lord had raised Lazarus from the dead, "then gathered the chief priests and the Pharisees in council, and said, What do we? for this man doeth many miracles." They acknowledged the fact of the miracles, but did not receive their evidence, for they believed that the study of the book of Jetzirah would enable them to do greater. No miracle, therefore, could convince them. But besides this, their hearts were corrupt, and they had apostatized from the law of Moses; they therefore did not love the truth. They had turned aside to charms and magic, and asking counsel of demons; and when men do this, the understanding becomes darkened, so that it is rendered impervious to the light. Their unbelief, therefore, becomes an evidence to the truth of Christianity. If such transgressors of the law of Moses, and such unblushing relaters of falsehood had believed, it would have cast a shade of suspicion over the whole Gospel history. If the men, who say that Rabba created a man, and the two other worthies created a calf every week, had appeared as witnesses for the truth of Christianity, the miracles of the Gospel would have appeared in one category with these most absurd fictions. But when such men appear as the enemies and persecutors of Jesus, it testifies that He was not one of them, and that as they were bad men, and loved a false system, his doctrine must necessarily have had something good in it, or they would not have opposed it.

But this doctrine explains still more clearly the cause of God's wrath against Israel. The Jews boast that since the Babylonian captivity, they have been free from idolatry, but this is not true. They have not made images, that is, they have avoided the form, but they have retained all the substance of idolatrous heathenism. The man who charms a serpent is an idolater, and the religion which permits it is idolatrous and heathenish. The man who asks counsel of demons is an idolater of the worst class, for he does homage to unclean spirits. He turns his back upon the allwise God, who ought to be the counsellor of all his children, and by making demons his advisers, makes them his gods, and yet this is also allowed in the religion of the rabbies if it can be done without danger. Those Jews, therefore, who believe in the oral law—that is, all

Jews who make use of the synagogue prayers, have departed from the law and the God of Moses, and have chosen for themselves the doctrines and the gods of the rabbies. How then can God have compassion upon them and gather them? The thing is impossible, until they utterly renounce all these delusions, confess their sin in having followed them so long, and "return and seek the Lord their God and David their king." A long trial has been made of the rabbinical medicine, and it has altogether failed. Wherever the religion of the oral law has been or is predominant, its sway has been marked by the misery of the people. And the first dawn of a happier day has appeared only since the time that a part of the nation burst the fetters of rabbinic superstition. Compare the state of the German Jews with that of their brethren in Turkey or on the coast of Morocco. Some of the former have abandoned the oral law, and the latter still cling to it with a bigoted devotion; and yet the former have had a blessing in the improvement of their temporal and intellectual condition, and the latter still remain in mental and corporeal slavery. The mere renunciation of Rabbinism has produced these beneficial effects, and if the Jews of Europe go on from the renunciation of error to the attainment of truth, that is, if they return to the religion of Moses and the prophets, the promises of God will be fulfilled, and the nation will be restored to the land of their fathers.

The Rabbinic Jews comfort themselves with the idea, that they cannot have this world and the world to come too; but they confound two things which are perfectly distinct, God's mode of dealing with individuals, and his mode of dealing with nations. Individuals have not only an existence in time, but for eternity. Worldly misfortune to an individual is, therefore, no proof of God's displeasure, because the world is only a part, and that the smallest part, of his existence. But the case of nations is different. They exist only in time, and therefore the rewards and punishments must be temporal, and so God has uniformly promised to the Jewish people temporal prosperity, in case of national obedience, and temporal calamity in the former case. Whenever, therefore, we see Israel exiled from their land and scattered among the nations, we must infer, if Moses has spoken the truth, that it is because they have departed from the God of their fathers.

No. XXVII.

SABBATIC LAWS.

How little the oral law has hitherto done to promote the peace and happiness of Israel, we considered in our last number. It may, however, be replied, that it has not had a fair trial, and that the failure is to be attributed rather to the people than to the law. This possible reply naturally leads us to think, what then would be the state of Israel and of the world at large, if the oral law were universally and exactly observed, and its disciples had supreme dominion in the world? Suppose that all the kingdoms of the world were melted into one vast and universal monarchy, and the sceptre swayed by a devout and learned rabbi, and all the magisterial offices filled by able and zealous Talmudists, would the world be happy? This is a fair question, and well deserves consideration, for there can be no doubt that true religion was intended by its Divine Author to promote the happiness of his creatures:—

דרכיה דרכי נועם וכל נתיבותיה שלום:

"Her ways are ways of pleasantness, and all her paths are peace." (Prov. iii. 17.) And that not of a few, but of all without exception.

הלא אב אחד לכלנו, הלא אל אחד בראנו:

"Have we not all one father? Hath not one God created us?" (Mal. ii. 10.) That religion, therefore, cannot be of God, which would make the greatest portion of his creatures miserable, and confer happiness on a very limited number. The religion that came from heaven, wherever it exists, must contain the elements of happiness for all nations, and include all the families of man. It must exclude none but the wilfully and obstinately wicked, who carry the torments of hell in their own bosom, and would be necessarily unhappy even in heaven itself. A religion, whose principles, if triumphant, would effect so desirable a consummation, must be true. The question is, whether modern Judaism, if it had full and free scope for the realization of all its principles, would bear such blessed fruit? Our late inquiries about amulets and magic led us to consider some of the laws about the Sabbath-day, and as when true religion prevails, this ought to be the happiest day of the week, the laws respecting it shall furnish materials for our answer. That a rabbinical Sabbath would be the happiest day in the week we much doubt, for, in the first place, to keep the rabbinical Sabbath aright, it is necessary to be perfectly acquainted with all the laws relating to it, which are very many and very intricate, occupying even in Rambam's compendium, including the notes, above one hundred and seventy folio pages.* That any conscientious man can be happy with such a load of law about his neck appears impossible. He must be in continual fear and trembling lest he should through forgetfulness or inadvertence be guilty of transgression, and the continued watchfulness and anxiety would be more intolerable than the hardest labour. But if Rabbinism wielded the supreme power, he would have to dread the most severe and immediate punishment:—

שביתה בשביעי ממלאכה מצות עשה שנאמר וביום
השביעי תשבות, וכל העושה בו מלאכה ביטל מצות
עשה ועבר על לא תעשה שנאמר לא תעשה כל
מלאכה, ומהו חייב על עשיית מלאכה אם עשה
ברצונו בזדון חייב כרת ואם היה שם עדים והתראה
נסקל ואם עשה בשגגה חייב קרבן חטאת קבועה:

"To rest on the seventh day from work is an affirmative precept, for it is said, 'On the seventh day thou shalt rest. Whosoever, therefore, does any work, annuls an affirmative, and transgresses a negative precept, for it is said, 'Thou shalt do no manner of work.' What is meant by being guilty on account of doing work? If it be done voluntarily and presumptuously, the meaning is, that he is liable to excision, and if there were witnesses and a warning, he is to be stoned. If he did it in error, he must bring a certain sin-offering." (Hilchoth Shabbath, c. i. 1.) This sounds something like the law of Moses, but is in reality far more severe. The whole force depends upon the meaning of the word "work," and the rabbinical sense would entirely destroy the peace of society. If, for instance, a poor man could not afford to have his Sabbath lamp burn all day, and should extinguish it to save the oil; or if a humane man should see burning coals in some place likely to do injury to others, and should extinguish them, they would both be guilty, and if some zealous Talmudists happened to be present, and first remonstrated with them on the unlawfulness of the act, they would both be tried, found guilty, and stoned to death:—

כל העושה מלאכה בשבת אע״פ שאינו צריך לגופה
של מלאכה חייב עליה, כיצד הרי שכבה את הנר
מפני שהוא צריך לשמן או לפתילה כדי שלא יאבד
או כדי שלא ישרף אי כדי שלא יבקע חרס של נר
מפני שהכבוי מלאכה והרי נתכוון לכבות ואע״פ שאין

* Hilchoth Shabbath and Hilchoth Eruvin extend from fol. 140 to fol. 226.

SABBATIC LAWS.

צריך לגוף הכבוי ולא כבה אלא מפני השמן או מפני
החרס או מפני הפתילה הרי זה חייב, וכן המעביר
את הקוץ ד׳ אמות ברה״ר או המכבה את הנחלת
כדי שלא יזוקו בו רבים חייב ואע״פ שאינו צריך לגוף
הכבוי או לגוף החעבירה אלא להרחיק החיזק הרי
זה חייב וכן כל כיוצא בזה:

"Whosoever does any work on the Sabbath, even though he does not do it for the sake of the work itself, is nevertheless guilty. How so? If, for instance, a man extinguishes a lamp, because he wants the oil or the wick, and wishes that it should not waste, nor be burned, or that the earthenware part of the lamp should not be cracked; inasmuch as the extinguishing is work, and his intention was to extinguish it: although the mere act of extinguishing it was not the ultimate object, but on the contrary, the saving of the oil or the wick, or the earthen lamp, he is, nevertheless, guilty. And in like manner, whosoever, removes thorns a distance of four ells in a public place, or whosoever extinguishes coals to prevent the public from being injured, is guilty: although the ultimate object was not the extinguishing nor the moving, but he simply intended to prevent the injury, he is guilty, and so in all similar cases." (Ibid.) If this were the law of the land, and the executive were in the hands of Talmudistic zealots, the peace of the world would be at an end. The poor man could not be happy, when he saw his little property wasting; and the humane man would either be made miserable at the thought of being able to prevent much injury, and yet not doing it, or would have to expose himself to the danger of a cruel and ignominious death. We know enough of the general character of the Jewish nation to believe that there are amongst them those who would brave the danger, whose generous hearts would rise above personal considerations, but how dreadful would be the consequences! A man of a tender heart, the father of a family, would be induced, by the best of feelings, to save his fellow-men from injury. He would return to his family, and tell them how God had given him an opportunity of doing good. The family worthy of such a father would rejoice to hear the information, but the sequel of his story would turn their joy into mourning. He would have to tell them that ignominious death would be the consequence, and that because he dared to do an act of charity, and to love his brother as himself, the morrow would see his wife a widow and his children orphans. But suppose, that when he performed the act, he had been attended by two of his sons, now grown up, and zealots for the oral law—that they had warned him, and then became his accusers, as they must, if firm believers in Talmudic religion, he would have the additional pangs of seeing his own flesh and blood as the foremost of his executioners. This one law would clothe the world with mourning, and make the light of the Sabbath sun the curse of mankind. Though men might be found at first to brave the danger, the course of time and the inflexible severity of the law would soon annihilate all generous feeling. Children would be trained up with the idea that humanity is not a Sabbath virtue, and the constant resistance of the tender feelings would harden the heart, and mankind in time become totally insensible on week-days as well as Sabbath-days; and thus the enforcement of this one law would produce universal selfishness, and this would certainly not promote the happiness of the world. But take another case of a man, who leaves his home on the Friday morning to go a short distance into the country, intending to return before the commencement of the Sabbath; he meets with an accident, and breaks a limb; on the Sabbath he is sufficiently restored to think of the anxiety of his family, and writes a short note to inform them of his state, this act of common love and kindness would cost him his life; nay, if he had only begun the letter, and then overcome by fear or weakness, had left it unfinished, a rabbinic tribunal would condemn him to be stoned.

כל המתכוון לעשות מלאכה בשבת והתחיל בה
ועשה כשיעור חייב אע״פ שלא השלים כל המלאכה
שנתכוון להשלימה, כיצד הרי שנתכוון לכתוב אגרת
או שטר בשבת אין אומרים לא יתחייב זה עד שישלים
חפצו ויכתוב כל השטר או כל האגרת אלא משיכתוב
שתי אותיות חייב.

"Whosoever intends to do any work on the Sabbath, and begins it, and does a certain measure, is guilty, although he does not finish all that he intended. How so? Suppose he intended to write a letter, or a contract on the Sabbath, it is not to be thought that he will not be guilty until he finish his business, and write the whole contract or the whole letter. On the contrary, as soon as he shall have written two letters (of the alphabet) he is guilty." (Ibid.) And consequently, if it can be proved, must be stoned. Every one's daily experience will tell them of the many similar cases where a letter may be necessary for the peace or well-being of an individual or a family, and where the delay of a day would be a serious injury. If rabbinism held the reins of power, the anxiety, the sorrow, the injury must all be endured; the Sabbath-day must be made a burden and a curse, instead of a blessing, or life itself must be exposed to danger. But this would not be the only misery. These sanguinary laws would, as religious laws, bind the consciences of the weak and superstitious. A man's domestics, or his children, or even his wife, would become spies over all his Sabbath doings, and the denouncers of every transgression; and thus domestic confidence, without which not even the shadow of happiness can exist, would be destroyed, and a man's foes would be those of his own household. Much has lately been thought and said about the sanguinary nature of the laws of England, but the laws of Draco himself were merciful when compared with the religious enactments of the rabbies. Draco only sentenced to death men convicted of a crime. The oral law condemns to stoning the man, woman, or child who will venture to write two letters of the alphabet, or even who will extinguish fire to prevent a public injury. Nay, in some cases, where it actually pronounces a man innocent, it nevertheless commands him to be flogged.

נתכוון ללקוט תאנים שחורות וליקט לבנות או
שנתכוון ללקוט תאנים ואחר כך ענבים ונהפך הדבר
וליקט הענבים בתחלה ואח״כ תאנים פטור אע״פ
שליקט כל מה שחשב הואיל ולא ליקט כסדר שחשב
פטור שבלא כוונה עשה שלא אסרה התורה אלא
מלאכת מחשבת:

" If a man intended to gather black figs, but gathered white figs, or if he intended to gather figs and afterwards grapes, but the matter has been inverted, and he gathered the grapes first, and afterwards the figs, he is not guilty. Although he have gathered all that he thought of gathering, yet, because he did not gather them in the intended order, he is not guilty, for he did what was unintentional, and the law forbids only intentional work." (Ibid.) We pass by the manifest absurdity of this decision, which is, however, sufficient to prove that this law is not of God, because it is more important to consider what is to be done with a man not guilty. The law of England, or any other civilized country, would say, of course, that he is to go free; but not so the oral law. it commands that the man should be flogged.

וכל מקום שנאמר שהעושה דבר זה פטור, הרי
זה פטור מן הכרת ומן הסקילה ומן הקרבן אבל
אסור לעשות אותו דבר בשבת ואיסורו מדברי סופרים
והוא הרחקה מן המלאכה והעושה אותו בזדון מכין
אותו מכות מרדות:

" Wherever it is said, he that doeth anything is not guilty, the meaning is, that he is not liable to excision, nor stoning, nor a sacrifice, but that thing is unlawful to be done, and the prohibition is of the words of the Scribes, and is intended as a removal from the possibility of work : and he that does it presumptuously, is to be flogged with the flogging of rebellion." (Ibid.) Here, then, we have a whole class of crimes which the oral law itself allows are no crimes according to the law of Moses, but which it thinks fit to punish with that dreadful and degrading infliction. Are the professors of this traditional religion really acquainted with its ordinances ? or can any man believe that a religion which, if it had full scope and power, would become the torment of the human race, can emanate from God ?

If ever this religion attains supreme power, its adherents will be reduced to a state of the most deplorable bondage, but what would be its effect upon the other nations of the world ? It would, in the first place, deprive all other nations of a Sabbath ; for we have already quoted the law (No. 3, p. 22), which decides, " That a Gentile who keeps a Sabbath, though it be on one of the week-days is guilty of death," and though not to be executed, is yet to be flogged. This would be a very serious diminution from the happiness of millions of human beings. The Gentile—who, like the Jew, must earn his bread by the sweat of his brow, and devote six days to the concerns of the world—requires a day of rest from secular labours, and cares, and thoughts, to relieve his body and to refresh his soul, and hold communion with his God. Of this the oral law would deprive him, or, if his conscience compelled him to sanctify one day in seven, he would have to purchase his spiritual enjoyment by corporeal suffering. Many would, no doubt, be terrified at the thought of the punishment, and all trace of a Sabbath would in time cease amongst the Gentiles. The multitude would soon be left destitute of religious instruction, and general vice and misery be the consequence. This religion, then, of the oral law, would certainly not promote the happiness of the Gentiles, and they are the overwhelming majority of mankind: it therefore cannot be of God. But the violent deprivation of a holy day of rest would be far from producing kindly feelings towards the Jews. Mankind would rebel against such oppression; and the religion which commanded it instead of obtaining their reverence, as it ought to do if true, would become their detestation. This unhappy feeling would be increased by other similar laws, equally wanting in charity. For instance—

אין מילדין את הגויה בשבת ואפילו בשכר ואין
חוששין לאיבה ואע״פ שאין שם חילול השם אבל
מילדין את בת גר תושב מפני שאנו מצווין להחיותו
ואין מחללין עליה את השבת :

" A Gentile woman is not to be delivered upon the Sabbath,

not even for payment, neither is the enmity to be regarded. It is not to be done, even though no profanation of the Sabbath should be implied. But the daughter of a sojourning proselyte may be delivered, for we are commanded to preserve the life of such, but the Sabbath is not to be profaned on her account." (Ibid. chap. ii. 12.) We ask every Jew who has got the heart of a man, whether such a law can be from God? or whether the religion of which it forms a part can be true? A poor woman, in the hour of her extremity, is to be left to her fate, simply because she is an idolatress. The mother and the child are both to be left to perish, because, either through her own fault, or through the circumstances of her birth, she has remained ignorant of the true God. But grant, for the sake of argument, that the mother is so hardened a sinner as to be beyond the mercies of sinful men, what has the child done, that its life is to be given as a sport to chance? Is that the way to convert a sinner from the error of her ways, or to recommend the true religion? The most besotted of idolaters, who believes at all in a Divine and merciful being, would pronounce such religion false. A few such cases would soon spread through the world, and Judaism become the aversion of every heart that can sympathize with suffering. And thus, if true, it would confirm all mankind in error. But it cannot be: the religion that comes from God bears the impress of its author, and teaches such love and kindness that the practice of it softens, where it does not convert. Its bitterest enemies must confess that its practical principles are worthy of all admiration. But there is here a second case, the daughter of a sojourning proselyte, towards whom the oral law is a little more lenient, it allows such an one to be delivered, but does not permit the Sabbath to be profaned on her account. Suppose then that such an one found herself in the midst of Jews, and after her delivery required the comfort of a fire or warm food for herself or her infant, or any other assistance that would imply a breach of the Sabbath, it could not be done, but for an Israelitess it may be done; can this proceed from Him who seeks the happiness of all his creatures? It cannot be said that this is a rare case, for it is easy to show that this is the general spirit of the oral law :—

היתה חצר שיש בה גוים וישראלים אפילו ישראל
אחד ואלף גוים ונפלה עליהם מפולת מפקחין על
הכל מפני ישראל, פירש אחד מהם לחצר אחרת
ונפלה עליו אותו חצר מפקחין עליו שמא זה שפירש
היה ישראל והנשארים גוים, נעקרו כולן מחצר זו
לילך לחצר אחרת ובעת עקירתן פירש אחד מהם
ונכנס לחצר אחרת ונפלה עליו מפולת ואין ידוע מי

הוּא אֵין מְפַקְחִין עָלָיו, שֶׁכֵּיוָן שֶׁנֶּעֶקְרוּ כוּלָם אֵין כָּאן
יִשְׂרָאֵל, וְכָל הַפּוֹרֵשׁ מֵהֶן כְּשֶׁהֵן מְהַלְּכִין הֲרֵי הוּא
בְּחֶזְקַת שֶׁפֵּירֵשׁ מִן הָרוֹב:

"If Gentiles and Israelites live together in one court, even if there be only one Israelite and a thousand Gentiles, and a ruin fall on one of them, the rubbish is to be cleared away, on account of the Israelite. If one of them had gone by himself to another court, and that court fell upon him, the rubbish is also to be cleared away, for perhaps this one was the Israelite, and the rest were Gentiles. But if they all set out to go from this court to another court, and during the time of their moving, one of them separated and went to another court, and a ruin fell upon him, and it is not known who he is, the rubbish is not to be cleared away. For as they all moved together, it is certain that the Israelite was not amongst them; and every one who separated from them, whilst going, is to be reckoned as belonging to the majority." (Ibid. 20, 21.) Here the same utter recklessness of Gentile life or comfort is displayed, and no one will pretend that such laws, if carried into effect, would promote the happiness of mankind. Accidents, like births, happen on the Jewish Sabbath as well as on the other days, but if the oral law had power, the Gentiles to whom any accident happened, might wait until the Sabbath was over, and must thus lose the only comfort which is possible on such an occasion. When a man is suffering from severe bodily injury, there are but two sources of consolation; the one is the kind and benevolent attentions of man, the other the remembrance of God's mercy and goodness, but the oral law cuts off both from the suffering Gentile. It forbids its disciples to help him, and says at the same time that this is the law of God. But could the Jews themselves be happy on that Sabbath, where such an accident occurred, and where they had left a poor Gentile buried under the ruins of a building? Could they enjoy peace in the bosom of their family, or could they find holy pleasure in the prayers of the synagogue when they had left one of God's creatures, a fellow-man, to perish in his misery? But this law would affect more than the individual sufferer, and the few surrounding spectators. It would prevent all brotherly love between Jews and Gentiles, and until all men learn the reality of charity, the world cannot be happy. If it be true that the religion given by God, wherever it is carried into practice, makes men happy, then the religion of the oral law cannot be true, for, if practised, it would make all men miserable.

No. XXVIII.

FAST FOR THE DESTRUCTION OF THE TEMPLE.

ALL who believe the Bible look forward, in full assurance of hope, to that happy period, when Israel shall be gathered from the four corners of the earth, and restored to the land of their forefathers and the favour of their God. The days of their mourning shall then be ended, and their fasts, now observed on account of the misfortunes of the nation, shall be turned into joy and gladness :—

כה אמר ה' צבאות צום הרביעי וצום החמישי וצום השביעי וצום העשירי יהיה לבית יהודה לששון ולשמחה ולמועדים טובים והאמת והשלום אהבו :

"Thus saith the Lord of hosts, the fast of the fourth month, and the fast of the fifth, and the fast of the seventh, and the fast of the tenth, shall be to the house of Judah joy and gladness, and cheerful feasts: therefore love the truth and peace." (Zech. viii. 19.) At that time, the prophet goes on to tell us, Jerusalem shall be the metropolis of the world, and the common centre to which all the nations of the earth shall flow "to seek the Lord of hosts and to pray before him." We Christians believe this as fully, and long for the happy accomplishment as ardently as the Jews. It would give us unspeakable pleasure to behold the Jews on that height of moral dignity and glory for which God destined them, from the first hour that he chose their father Abraham to be His friend. We desire the arrival of this happy period, for the sake of the Jews themselves, but surely no Jew will feel offended with us if we say that we desire it also for our own sakes and for the sake of all the families of men. We should wish to see Divine truth triumphant, sin and misery banished, and brotherly love universal, but we see all these things connected with the restoration of Israel, and the establishment of the kingdom of God upon earth, and therefore we join with all our heart in the the most ardent aspirations of the Jewish people, and say, "Amen" to every prayer that God "would remember his covenant with Abraham, Isaac, and Jacob, and that he would also remember the land." But, alas! these prayers and wishes and anticipations all remind us that that happy day is still future. Israel is still scattered among the nations, and instead of having days of joy and gladness, is about to observe another solemn day of mourning in remembrance of the desolation of their city and temple. The ninth of the month of Av is still a fast, and Rambam thus describes the causes of mourning on that day:—

וט׳ באב ה׳ דברים אירעו בו , נגזר על ישראל
במדבר שלא יכנסו לארץ , וחרב הבית בראשונה
ובשניה , ונלכדה עיר גדולה וביתר שמה , והיו בה
אלפים ורבבות מישראל , והיה להם מלך גדול ודמו
כל ישראל וגדולי החכמים שהוא מלך המשיח , ונפל
ביד הגוים ונהרגו כולם והיתה צרה גדולה כמו חורבן
בית המקדש ובו ביום המוכן לפורענות חרש טורנוס
רופוס הרשע את ההיכל ואת סביביו לקיים מה
שנאמר ציון שדה תחרש :

"On the ninth of Av five things happened. It was decreed in the wilderness that Israel should not enter into the land. The temple was destroyed, both the first and second time. The great city named Bither was taken, and there were in it thousands and tens of thousands of Israel, and they had a great king, whom all Israel and the greatest of the wise men imagined to be the King Messiah. But he fell into the hands of the Gentiles, and the Israelites were all slain, and there was a great affliction similar to the desolation of the temple. On this same day, destined for punishment, the wicked Turnus Rufus ploughed up the sanctuary and the adjacent parts, to fulfil that which is said, 'Zion shall be ploughed as a field.' (Mich. iii. 12.)" (Hilchoth Taanioth, c. v.) The mere enumeration of all these dreadful inflictions of the Almighty suggest many and grave topics for reflection, but the most important of all is, the cause of the last desolation of the temple, and the present long captivity. To mourn over past misfortunes and to humble ourselves for past sins, is indeed good and wholesome ; but if it does not teach us how to remedy the one and to avoid the other, it can only terminate in despair. Every Israelite, therefore, who weeps for the desolation of the holy and beautiful house where his fathers worshipped, should also set himself earnestly to inquire into the cause and remedy of this great calamity. Why was it that the God of mercy desolated his own house, the only temple that He had in the world built by his own express command? The idolatry of the nation was the cause of the destruction of the first temple.

גם כל שרי הכהנים והעם הרבו למעול מעל ככל
תועבות הגוים ויטמאו את בית ה׳ אשר הקדיש
בירושלים , וישלח ה׳ אלהי אבותיהם עליהם ביד
מלאכיו השכם ושלוח כי חמל על עמו ועל מעונו ,
ויהיו מלעיבים במלאכי האלהים ובוזים דבריו ומתעתעים

DESTRUCTION OF THE TEMPLE. 217

בנביאיו עד עלות חמת ה' בעמו עד לאין מרפא,
ויעל עליהם את מלך כשדים ויהרוג בחוריהם בחרב
בבית מקדשם, ולא חמל על בחור ובתולה זקן וישש
הכל נתן בידו... וישרפו את בית האלהים וינתצו
את חומת ירושלים וכל ארמנותיה שרפו באש וכל
כלי מחמדיה להשחית:

"Moreover, all the chief of the priests, and the people, transgressed very much, after *all the abominations of the heathen*, and polluted the house of the Lord which he had hallowed in Jerusalem. And the Lord God of their fathers sent to them by his messengers, rising up betimes and sending; because he had compassion on his people, and on his dwelling-place: but they mocked the messengers of God, and despised his words, and misused his prophets, until the wrath of the Lord arose against his people, till there was no remedy. Therefore he brought upon them the King of the Chaldeans, who slew their young men with the sword in the house of their sanctuary, and had no compassion upon young man or maiden, old man or him that stooped for age: he gave them all into his hand—and they burned the house of God and broke down the wall of Jerusalem, and burned all the palaces thereof with fire, and destroyed all the goodly vessels thereof." (2 Chron. xxxvi. 14—19.) Here, then, obstinate idolatry is represented as the cause of the first desolation. Israel learned and practised the abominations of the heathen, and thus polluted the temple, and therefore God destroyed the temple and sent them into captivity. There were no doubt many and other great sins in Israel, but they are not mentioned, as if to show that nothing short of wilful and obstinate departure from God could have led him to adopt so severe a measure. As long as they retained their allegiance to God and rejected the abominations of the heathen, there was a hope and a possibility that they might repent of other sins, but when men obstinately turn away from God, and will not hearken to his warnings, all hope of repentance is at an end, and there is no alternative but just judgment. But was this the case in the second temple? Were the Jews then obstinate idolaters? Had they images amongst them, and did they pollute the second temple with such abominations of the heathen? No, rather than bow down to images, they willingly endured every torture, and offered up even their lives as a sacrifice to the truth, and when the second temple was destroyed, there was not amongst Israel a single vestige of idolatry. Never, in the whole course of their history, from the going forth out of Egypt to that day, was there such an apparently scrupulous observation of the letter of the law, and never had Israel had so many learned men devoted to the study

L

of the commandments. What then could be the cause of the second desolation? It was not idolatry, but it must have been something equally odious in the sight of God, and it must have been a sin committed equally by the priests and the people. You observe that in the above description of the first destruction, it is said, "All the chief of the priests, and the people transgressed very much." If the priests had remained faithful to their God, He would not have destroyed their temple, for there would have been hope, that, by their exertions and teaching, the people might be brought to a better mind. Or, if the people had remained faithful, God would not have punished the people for the sins of the priests; he would have cut off the wicked priests and raised up others according to his own heart. Nothing short of the unanimous wickedness of priests and people could have brought on so great a calamity. In like manner we infer that the cause of the second destruction was not any partial wickedness, but some sin, of which both priests and people were guilty, that drew down that calamity. And, further, it must have been a sin against which they were warned by special messengers of God. When the priests and the people fell into idolatry, God did not immediately destroy the first temple. He first tried whether they would listen to his warnings and repent, and therefore "he sent to them by his messengers, rising up betimes, and sending; because he had compassion on his people, and on his dwelling-place." Now, surely, when we see that God showed such compassion, when He was about to send so small a calamity as the seventy years' captivity, we may safely infer that he would not bring the more tremendous judgment of eighteen hundred years' desolation, without exhibiting a compassion proportionate to the coming infliction. In the former case he sent special messengers and prophets to warn them, he must also have acted similarly before the second destruction. Who, then, were the messengers and the prophets that warned the Jews of their sin? The Jews say, that during the second temple there was no prophecy; but is it possible to imagine that the God of Israel would shut up his bowels of compassion, and pity neither his people nor his dwelling-place, but give them both over to the most dreadful visitation that ever descended on a nation without one word of warning? When he was about to destroy Nineveh he first sent Jonah to call them to repentance, and when his judgments were about to descend upon Babylon, the words of warning were miraculously written on the wall; can we suppose, then, that God would not have as much mercy on Jerusalem and the Jews as on Babylon and Nineveh? The supposition is utterly inconsistent with God's character and dealings. There must have been prophets who announced the coming judgment and warned the people of their sin. Who were they, then, and

DESTRUCTION OF THE TEMPLE. 219

what was that sin equal to idolatry which priests and people committed and obstinately persevered in, despite of all warning, and in which their descendants still persevere? Idolatry is a departure from the true God, and the setting up a false system of religious worship. Now it is granted that the Jews did not make images, but did they set up a false system of worship and religion contrary to the religion of Moses and the prophets? Let the oral law and the Jewish Prayer-books answer that question. We have shown in these papers that the oral law, sanctioned by the Jewish Prayer-books, is directly at variance with the written Word of God. It teaches the Jews to put trust in amulets, charms, and magic, which are mere heathenism. It teaches a cruel and unmerciful system for the Jews, gives false ideas of the character of God, and actually forbids the Jews to love their Gentile brethren as themselves. The setting up of this system was the great sin which priests and people all joined in committing, and in which their posterity still continue. They were warned against this sin: God sent them extraordinary messengers, He sent them Jesus of Nazareth, the prophet like unto Moses, and the Messiah. The great burden of his preaching was against this false religion, the oral law, but they would not hearken to his words. Priests and people conspired together to reject and crucify him. Here, then, was the result of the false system which they adopted. The oral law was the tree, the rejection of the Messiah the fruits. But still the Lord had compassion upon his people, and upon his dwelling-place, he spared them yet for forty years, and in the meanwhile sent his apostles to warn them and testify against their iniquity; "but they mocked the messengers of God, and despised his words, and misused his prophets, until the wrath of the Lord arose against his people, till there was no remedy," and he gave them into the hands of the Romans. Because they rejected Jesus of Nazareth and his disciples, the temple and city were desolated. The Jews have been taught to think that Jesus and his disciples were deceivers, but let them consider this fact, that, if they were, God himself has sealed the truth of their assertions by the acts of His Providence. The preservation of the temple and city to this day would have been incontestable evidence that they were deceivers. Had no judgments followed upon the crucifixion of Jesus, it would have been evident to all mankind, that he was not what he pretended to be. But if he was indeed the Messiah, the strongest possible attestation that God could give, was the exemplary punishment of those who crucified him, and this God has given. They crucified Jesus, and God destroyed the temple and scattered the people. Without this, the religion of Jesus never could have triumphed as it has done. If the temple were still standing, and the Jews in their land, they could point to the temple and say, " See that temple, the monument of God's favour and presence, it is still amongst us, and shows that Jesus could not have been the Messiah. If he had been the Messiah, God would not have left us this unequivocal testimony of his favour." But this proof of their righteousness God has taken away, and that within forty years after the crucifixion of Jesus; so that God himself has given the strongest possible attestation to the truth of his claims. Let any reflective Israelite calmly consider this, that, if Jesus was not what he claimed to be, his crucifixion was the most meritorious act that the Jews ever performed. They thereby did what they could to stay the progress of a false religion that was to overrun the world, and to uphold the truth; can they, then, suppose that God would punish them for doing that which was right, and give the sacred sanction of His providence to him that was doing wrong? When Phinehas, the son of Eleazar, slew the Israelite and the Midianitish woman with his spear, the plague was stayed from Israel, and can we imagine that the high priests who condemned Jesus would have had a less reward if his claims had been false? If Christianity be not true, then God himself has interposed to crush the truth, and to build up falsehood. If Christianity be true, then God could do nothing more to attest its truth than he has done by the destruction of the temple. There was but one unanswerable argument against Christianity, and that was the existence of the temple; but God himself has answered that argument by taking away the temple, and therefore we infer that as God has done all that he could to establish the truth of Christianity, it must be true.

The Jews think that if Jesus had been the Messiah, it is impossible that the priests and learned men of his time could have rejected him. But the events which they commemorate on the ninth of Av show the untenableness of this argument. On this day the Jews commemorate, first of all, the decree that the Israelites should die in the wilderness. And why did they die in the wilderness? Because they would not believe in Moses. "And all the children of Israel murmured against Moses and against Aaron: and the whole congregation said unto them, Would God that we had died in the land of Egypt! or would God that we had died in this wilderness! And they said one to another, Let us make a captain, and let us return into Egypt." (Numbers xiv. 2.) Yet they had seen the plagues of Egypt, and they had passed through the Red Sea, and were at that moment supplied miraculously with food, but for all that they did not believe, and that "The whole congregation." Will any Jew say, that this unbelief proves that Moses was a false prophet? If not, why not? Every argument, that will prove that the unbelief of that generation is no argument against the claims of Moses, will equally demonstrate that the unbelief of the Jews in the time of Jesus is no argument against his Messiahship. If it was possible for them to disbelieve the word of Moses, after all that they had seen, it is equally possible that they should have rejected Christ.

But remark here, it was only the old generation that God sentenced to die in the wilderness. The children who did not participate in the unbelief of their fathers entered into the land. Now if anything similar had happened to the Jews since the destruction of the second temple, that is, if after a few years' captivity they had returned to their land *without becoming Christians*, they might then argue that the rejection of Jesus was not the sin for which they were exiled. They might say, we have not become Christians, and yet God has restored us; it is plain therefore that this was not the cause of the second desolation. But God's dealings have been just the reverse. The Jewish nation have gone on from century to century, fasting and humbling themselves before the God of their fathers, and yet he does not restore them, a plain token that they still participate in the sin of their fathers. And a plainer proof still of the truth of Christianity, for God still continues the providential act, whereby he originally proved that Christianity was true. Israel still rejects Christianity, and therefore Israel still continues in dispersion. The only argument, that could even appear to prove that the rejection of Jesus was not the cause of the second desolation, would be the restoration of the Jews in an unconverted state. But that argument God refuses to grant, and has refused it to his beloved people for many centuries. If Judaism be true, why should he thus continue to declare against it? If Christianity be false, why should he from century to century stamp it with the seal of truth?

But, in the next place, the Jews commemorate the destruction of the first temple, that is, they commemorate the idolatry of the chief priests and the people. They remember that the learned and the unlearned of the nation rejected the true God and turned to dumb idols. How then can the Jews say that it is impossible for a nation, that openly rejected the God of their fathers, to reject the Messiah? There can be no greater proof of folly and wickedness than to reject God and worship a stock or a stone; but of this Israel has been guilty, and because of this sin the first temple was destroyed. The man who rejects the true God will also reject his messenger. But Israel has done the one, why then should it be denied that they could do the other? The only possible answer that can be given is, that the priests and the people were a great deal wiser and better in the days of Jesus than in those of the first temple. But if this be true, why was the temple destroyed? why were those who were so much wiser and better, punished with a more dreadful punishment than those who were so much more foolish and wicked? If we are to judge of the comparative wisdom and piety of the two by the measure of punishment, then we must say, that the idolatrous priests and people of the first temple were a great deal wiser and better than the priests and people of the second temple, for the former escaped, after a captivity of seventy years, the latter have been exiled for seventeen centuries. The tremendous nature of the punishment would show, that the priests and people, who rejected Jesus, were more wicked than their idolatrous forefathers, and if so, their testimony against Jesus is of no value.

But the Jews also commemorate on this day the destruction of the city of Bither, that is, they commemorate the folly of all their greatest rabbies in following an impostor, and believing in him as their Messiah. There Bar Kochav took refuge with those whom he deluded. Rambam says, "All Israel, and the greatest of their wise men, imagined him to be the Messiah," and we know that the famous Rabbi Akiva was amongst the number. Here, then, we have practical proof that the judgment of those rabbies, who rejected Jesus, was not to be depended upon. If they had succeeded in their efforts, they would have taught all Israel to believe in an impostor; but the providence of God gave them all over to destruction in the very act of following a false prophet. And yet these are the men who have handed down the oral law, and compiled the precepts of rabbinic religion; men, whom the Jews themselves tell us, were the followers of a false prophet and the dupes of an impostor. How can they possibly believe in a system which has such men for its authors; men who seduced thousands and tens of thousands of Israel to plunge themselves into ruin? If Rabbi Akiva, and his colleagues, had not espoused the cause of Bar Kochav, he could never have succeeded in deluding such numbers of Israelites; they, therefore, are answerable for that dreadful calamity. But when the Jews of the present day commemorate that sore affliction, should they not remember also that it is high time to give up that religious system that was the cause of it, and of all the evils that have since followed; or at least seriously and carefully investigate a religion, fidelity to which is compatible with the departure of God's favour, the destruction of the temple, and a long and awful captivity?

No. XXIX.

SABBATIC LAWS CONTINUED.

IN our last number but one the Bible-doctrine, that true religion must necessarily promote the happiness of man, was laid down as the basis of our reasonings. The truth of the principle is admitted by every thinking man, whether Jew or Christian; but plain as it is, it is frequently overlooked, and a large portion of mankind is accustomed to look on religion and its ordinances, not as blessings in themselves, nor as a course of moral discipline devised by the wisdom of God for the good of man, but as a system of arbitrary enactments instituted to give men an opportunity of treasuring up a store of merit, and of earning an eternal reward. Hence in all the superstitions, which man has invented, we perceive an undue regard for the mere external act; and an expectation that the performance of the act will ensure the Divine favour. Thus the modern Hindoo stands on a sharp spike, or suspends his poor body by an iron hook, or offers it to be crushed under the wheels of the idol's chariot, and thinks thereby to purchase eternal felicity. And thus also the more ancient idolaters, the worshippers of Baal, in the time of their need, wounded themselves with knives and lances, and expected that for such meritorious religious observances their prayers should be heard and that they should have a blessing. But it is possible, without professing a totally false religion, to view God's true commandments in the same light, and overlooking the spirit and the object of his institution, to fix the whole attention upon the letter or outward act, and the quantum of reward which it may purchase. This the rabbies have done, particularly, in reference to the institution of the Sabbath-day. They appear to have forgotten altogether that the Sabbath was made for man as a blessing and means of grace, and have therefore in their attempts to promote the observance of the day, entirely sacrificed the peace, comfort, and happiness of man to the mere appearance of preserving the letter of the command inviolate. Their fundamental idea of keeping the Sabbath-day is, that it is an act of obedience whereby something may be purchased.

גרסינן בפ׳ כל כתבי אמר ר׳ יוחנן משום ר׳ יוסי כל המענג את השבת נותנין לו נחלה בלי מצרים, רב נחמן בר יצחק אומר אף ניצול משיעבוד מלכיות, אמר רב יהודה אמר רב כל המענג את השבת נותנין לו משאלות לבו, ואמר ר׳ חייא בר אבא אמר ר׳

יוחנן , כל המשמר שבת כהלכתה אפילו עובד ע"ז
כאנוש מוחלין לו , אמר רב יהודה אמר רב אלמלא
שמרו ישראל שבת ראשונה כהלכתה לא שלטה בהם
אומה ולשון אמר ר׳ שמעון בר יוחי אלמלא משמרים
ישראל שתי שבתות מיד נגאלין :

"We read in the sixteenth chapter of the treatise Shabbath, R. Johanan says, in the name of R. Jose, that to every one who makes the Sabbath a delight, an infinite inheritance is given. Rav Nachman, the son of Isaac says, He shall, besides, be delivered from serving the monarchies. R. Judah says, Rav says, To every one who makes the Sabbath a delight, the desires of his heart are given. R. Chiia, the son of Abba, says, in the name of Rabbi Johanan, whosoever keeps the Sabbath according to its constitutions, even though he were an idolater like Enosh, he shall be forgiven. R. Judah says, Rav says, If Israel would keep the first Sabbath according to its constitutions, no nation nor tongue should rule over them. R. Simeon, the son of Jochai, says, If Israel would keep two Sabbaths, they should be immediately delivered." (Arbah Turim. Orach Chaim, § 242.) Thus the rabbies sanction the false and superstitious notion, that an external act can purchase the favour of God, and even atone for the most atrocious violation of the divine law. The Israelites are taught to believe that if they would only observe the Sabbath according to the rabbinic constitution, all their other transgressions would immediately be forgiven, and they themselves restored to the land of their fathers, and in the meanwhile the individual sinner is told not to be uneasy, for that if he had committed idolatry, the most heinous offence against God, the observation of the rabbinical precepts respecting the Sabbath will wipe away the score. What then will he think, who has ever kept himself outwardly from this capital offence, and only been guilty, as he thinks, of sinning against his neighbour? He will make sure that the Sabbath observance will wipe out the week's reckoning, and commence his sinful career again the following week with the assurance that if he only live until the Sabbath-day, he can make all good again. And thus the Sabbath-day, ordained by God for the purpose of nurturing true religious feeling, is by the oral law turned into the means of eradicating all religious principle out of the heart. The end for which the external observance was instituted, is not only forgotten, but misrepresented. The holy affections which it was meant to produce and nourish as a preparation for eternity are overlooked, and the mere outward form held up as the price which men are to pay for eternal felicity.

That the rabbinical laws are almost altogether occupied

with the merest external observances will be plain to any one who will take the trouble to read them through. Take, for instance, some of the laws which refer to the keeping food warm on the Sabbath-day :—

מניחין קדרה על גבי האש או בשר בתנור או על
גבי גחלים וחם מתבשלים והולכין כל השבת ואוכלין
אותו בשבת ויש בדבר זה דברים שהם אסורים גזירה
שמא יחתה בגחלים בשבת, כיצד תבשיל שלא בשל
כל צרכו וחמין שלא הוחמו כל צרכן או תבשיל
שבישל כל צרכו וכל זמן שמצטמק הוא יפה לו אין
משהין אותו על גבי האש בשבת אע״פ שהונח מבעוד
יום, גזירה שמא יחתה בגחלים כדי לחשלים בשולו
או כדי לצמקן, לפיכך אם גרף האש או שכסה את
הכירה באפר או בנעורת הפשתן הדקה או שעממו
הגחלים שהרי הן כמכוסין באפר או שהסיקוה בקש
או בגבבה או בגללי בהמת דקה שהרי אין שם גחלי
בוערות הרי זה מותר לשהות עליה שהרי הסיח
דעתו מזה ואין גוזרין שמא יחתה באש :

"It is lawful to leave a pot on the fire, or meat in the oven or upon the coals, and although the cooking thus continues, it is lawful to eat them on the Sabbath. But in this matter there are some things forbidden, and the cause of the prohibition is lest any man should stir the fire on the Sabbath. For example, food that has not been cooked as much as it requires, or hot water that has not been sufficiently heated, or food which has had the requisite cooking, but which improves all the time that it is left to stew, must not be left on the fire on the Sabbath, even though it may have been placed there, whilst it was yet day on the Friday. This has been decreed, lest one should stir the coals in order to finish the cooking thereof, or to stew it. Therefore, if the fire be swept up, or covered with ashes, or with the coarse part of flax, or if the coals have ceased to glow, for then they are looked upon as covered with ashes, or if the fire had been made with straw or stubble, or with the dung of small cattle, then, as there are no burning coals, it is lawful to leave the food there on the Sabbath, for in this case the man's mind will be turned away from the cooking, and the only object of the decree is, lest the fire should be stirred." (Hilchoth Shabbath, c. iii. 3.) No one can deny that this passage prescribes the merest outward observances. The general principle is that it is not lawful to stir the fire on the Sabbath, for that would be doing work, and from this follow those other prohibitions of all things which might tempt a man to be guilty of this grave offence. But they all refer to outward acts, from which it is easy for any one, without any great exertion of self-denial, or any advance in moral discipline, to abstain, and yet he has all the merit and satisfaction of the most self-denying piety, and thinks that he is thereby paying a part of the price of his salvation, and making atonement for the gravest moral transgressions of which he may have been guilty during the week. Take, again, the following precepts, and say whether they be not of the very same character:—

מי שהחשיך לו בדרך בערב שבת ועמו כיס אם
יש עמו נכרי וחמור יתן כיסו לנכרי אף לאחר שתחשך
ולא יניחנו על החמור, אבל אם מצא מציאה אינו
יכול ליתנה לנכרי אלא אם כן באה לידו מבעוד יום
דהשתא חויא ככיסו, אין עמו נכרי יניחנה על החמור
כשהוא הולך ויזהר ליטול ממנו בכל שעה שיעמוד,
וכשיחזור וילך יניחנו עליו, היה עמו חמור וחרש
שוטה וקטן יניחנו על החמור ולא יתננה לאחד
מאלה כיון שהם אדם כמותו, היה עמו חרש ושוטה
יתננו לשוטה לפי שאין לו דעת כלל, שוטה וקטן
יתננו לשוטה שהקטן יבוא לכלל דעת, חרש וקטן
יתננה למי שירצה, אין עמו לא זה ולא זה יטלטלנו
פחות פחות מארבע אמות:

"If a man travelling on the Sabbath-eve be overtaken by night,* and has with him a purse, and there be also with him a Gentile and an ass, let him give his purse to the Gentile, even after it be dark, but let him not lay it on the ass.† But if he find anything, he may not give it to the Gentile, unless it came into his hand whilst it was yet day, for then it is a similar case to that of his purse. If there be no Gentile with him, then let him lay it on the ass, whilst he is moving, but let him take great care to take it off every time he stands still. But when he begins to move again, then let him lay it on. If there be with him an ass, and a deaf and dumb person, an idiot and a child, then let him lay it on the ass, but let him not give it to one of these, for they are human beings like himself. If there be with him a deaf and dumb person and an idiot, let him give it to the idiot, as he has no understanding at all. If an idiot and a child, let him give it to the idiot, for the child will be reckoned amongst those that have understanding. If a deaf and dumb

* That is, if the Sabbath commence before he can get to a resting-place.

† חמור אתה מצווה על שביתתו ולא דנכרי:
For thou art commanded respecting the resting of the ass, but not respecting that of the Gentile.

person and a child, let him give it to whichever he pleases. If there be with him neither one nor the other, let him move it along gradually, each time less than four ells." (Orach Chaim, sec. 266.) Here again the great concern is to observe the form and letter of the rabbinical command, which represents the carrying of a purse on the Sabbath-day as work, and therefore unlawful. The law of Moses says nothing either one way or the other, but leaves it to every man's conscience. The rabbies who made it unlawful soon found that serious inconvenience might arise, as in the case of a man on a journey overtaken by the Sabbath, before he could get to a resting-place. What is he to do, is he to leave his purse behind rather than profane the Sabbath? That alternative the Pharisees did not like, and therefore set their wits to work to devise some plan, whereby the outward form might be observed, and yet the purse be safely conveyed along with its proprietor. In the first place, they allow it to be given to a Gentile, but every man of common sense will see that this only saves the outward appearance, for it be unlawful to carry the purse, it must be equally unlawful to cause it to be carried, for he who commands or causes work to be done is really and in the sight of God the doer, just as he who hires a man to murder a third person is in reality the murderer. If, therefore, the Jew dare not carry the purse himself, neither may he give it to a Gentile, nor an idiot, nor a child, nor even lay it upon his ass. This case only shows the insincerity of the Scribes and Pharisees, and their love of money rather than of God's commandment. In other cases they lay it down as a law that no Jew is to ask a Gentile to do work for him on the Sabbath:—

אסור לומר לנוי לעשות לנו מלאכה בשבת אע״פ
שאינו מצווה על השבת ואע״פ שאמר לו מקודם השבת
ואע״פ שאינו צריך לאותה מלאכה אלא לאחר השבת
ודבר זה אסור מדברי סופרים כדי שלא תהיה שבת
קלה בעיניהן ויבואו לעשות בעצמן:

"It is unlawful to tell a Gentile to do work for us on the Sabbath, although the Sabbath command is not binding upon him, and although he told him before the Sabbath, and even though he should not require that work until after the Sabbath. This prohibition is of the words of the Scribes, and was made to prevent Israelites from thinking lightly of the Sabbath, and thus coming at last to do the work themselves." (Hilchoth Shabbath, c. vi. 1.) Here, then, the very thing which is allowed above, is expressly forbidden on the authority of the Scribes, and consequently a transgression would make a man liable to be flogged, as is expressly stated in this chapter:—

ישראל שאמר לנוי לעשות לו מלאכה זו בשבת
אע״פ שעבר ומכין אותו מכת מרדות, מותר לו ליהנות
באותה מלאכה לערב אחר שימתין בכדי שתעשה :

"An Israelite who tells a Gentile to do a certain work for
him on the Sabbath, although he has transgressed, and is to be
flogged with the flogging of rebellion, yet he may lawfully
make use of that work when the Sabbath is over, if he wait as
long as it would take to accomplish the work." (Ibid. 8.)
These two passages, then, plainly contradict each other. The
one says it is unlawful to tell a Gentile to do work on the
Sabbath, and that he who does so is to be flogged. The other
permits a Jew to give a Gentile his purse to carry, and this is
work, or else the Jew might carry it himself. Now if the
latter case be lawful, then the former is also lawful; and it is
most cruel and tyrannical to flog a man for doing what is
lawful. On the other hand, if, according to the general rule,
it be unlawful, then it is plainly unlawful in this particular
case; and it is plain that the Scribes, with all their pretensions,
thought it better to transgress what they considered a Divine
command, then to lose their money. But if the traveller has
got neither an ass, nor an idiot, nor a Gentile with him, then
there is apparently no way of escape, for it is unlawful,
according to the oral law, to carry any burden more than a
distance of four ells on the Sabbath-day; and one would
naturally expect, that those who punish a profanation of the
Sabbath with stoning or flogging—that is, who spare neither
human blood nor life—would tell him to leave his purse, rather
than transgress the Divine command. But no, they tell him
to carry it less than four ells, then to lay it down, take it up
and carry it again a distance of less than four ells, and thus,
bit by bit, carry it to the first inn. Here, again, there is an
appearance of preserving the letter of the rabbinical command;
but no man in his senses can see that there is any real difference between carrying it at one turn, or at five hundred short
turns of less than four ells, the whole distance is just the same,
and the work just the same in the sight of God. Either it is
altogether lawful, and then the rabbinical precepts appear as
folly and tyranny, or it is altogether unlawful, and then these
precepts appear as a mere evasion and a trick. But, in every
case, a cheap way is presented for purchasing salvation, and
atoning for past sin. There is no great exertion of moral principle necessary to make the traveller let another person, or an
ass carry his purse to an inn.

Another part of the rabbinical mode of observing the
Sabbath, the preparation of the Sabbath table, has just the same
tendency to direct the mind to the mere external act:—

ויסדר שלחנו ויציע המטות ויתקן כל עניני הבית
כדי שימצאנו ערוך ומסודר בבואו מבית הכנסת,
דאמר ר׳ יוסי בר חנינא שני מלאכי השרת מלוין לו
לאדם בערב שבת מבית הכנסת לביתו אחד טוב
ואחד רע כשבא לביתו מצא נר דלוק ושלחן ערוך
ומטה מוצעת מלאך טוב אומר יהי רצון שיהא כן
לשבת הבאה ומלאך רע עונה אמן בעל כרחו ואם
לאו מלאך רע אומר יהי רצון שיהא כן לשבת הבאה
ומלאך טוב עונה אמן בעל כרחו:

"Let a man arrange his table and spread the couches, and order all the affairs of his house, that he may find it ready and ordered when he returns from the synagogue; for Rabbi Jose says, in the name of Rabbi Chanina, That two angels accompany a man on the Sabbath eve, on his return from the synagogue, the one good, the other evil. When he comes to his house, if the Sabbath lamp be found lighted, and the table prepared, and the couch spread, the good angel says, God grant that it may be so the next Sabbath; and the evil angel must say Amen, in spite of himself. But if this be not the case, then the evil angel says, God grant that it may be so on the next Sabbath, and then the good spirit must say Amen, in spite of himself." (Orach Chaiim, § 262.) Let not the Israelite think that we object to the decent and reverential preparation of the house for the Sabbath, that is all right and proper; but to exalt this into a command, and represent obedience to it as a meritorious act, is to turn the mind to trivial outward performances, and to teach men to rest on them as on the great duties of religion. And here the mere putting of the house into order is represented as so grave a matter, that two angels are sent home with every Israelite on the Sabbath eve, to take cognizance of the matter. The story of the angels is evidently a fable, and is another proof of the fictitious character of the oral law; but it shows how the rabbies wandered from the substance of religion to the mere shadow of external observances. The Sabbath lamp here mentioned is another instance of the same kind:—

ויהא זהיר לעשות נר יפה דאמר רב הונא הרגיל
בנר שבת להשתדל בו לעשותו יפה הוין ליה בנים
תלמידי חכמים:

"Let a man be careful to have a handsome lamp, for Rav Huna says, He that is accustomed to take great care in trimming his Sabbath lamp well, will have children who shall be disciples of the wise, i.e. learned men." No one can deny that this is a mere external act, but yet it is represented as

meritorious, and payment is promised : but the mode in which
the performance is required is still more calculated to promote
the idea, that this external act is of great importance :—

ואחד אנשים ואחד נשים חייבין להיות בבתיחן נר
דלוק בשבת אפילו אין לו מה יאכל שואל על הפתחים
ולוקח שמן ומדליק את הנר שזה בכלל עונג שבת
וחייב לברך קודם הדלקה ברוך אתה יי אלהינו מלך
העולם אשר קדשנו במצוותיו וצונו להדליק נר של
שבת :

"Men and women are equally obligated to have a lighted
lamp in their house on the Sabbath. Yea, though a man have
nothing to eat, he must beg from door to door, and get oil, and
light the lamp, for this is an essential part of the Sabbath
delight. He is also bound to pronounce the benediction, Blessed
art thou, O Lord, King of the world! who has sanctified us by
his commandments, and commanded us to light the Sabbath
lamp." (Hilchoth Shabbath, c. v. 1.) Of course every Jew,
who thinks that a Sabbath lamp is as necessary as food, and
that God requires it even from him that has no food, must
think that it is of great value, and that obedience to this command is a most meritorious act. And yet all must confess that
it is a mere outward performance, which may be observed by
him who has neither the fear nor the love of God. The tendency
of all these laws is the same, that is, to draw the mind away
from the solemn duties of religion, and to persuade the
impenitent sinner that these observances will atone for his
transgressions. When conscience reminds him of sins, not those
which he has committed long since, of which he has repented,
and which he has forsaken, but of those which he has been
committing the past week, and intends to commit again, as soon
as the Sabbath is over, it is silenced by an enumeration of the
various acts of obedience, which are to be set down at the other
side of the account. He remembers that he has never left a
pot of victuals on a forbidden fire, nor carried his purse on the
Sabbath-day a distance of more than four ells, nor asked a
Gentile to do work for him. That, on the contrary, he has
always prepared his table, and lighted his Sabbath lamp, and
pronounced the benediction; or, in other words, that he has
kept the Sabbath according to its constitution, and that,
therefore, though he had been guilty of idolatry, he shall
obtain forgiveness. Thus these rabbinic precepts have a
direct tendency to mislead the multitude, to harden them in sin,
and thus to make and keep them unfit for that great Sabbath,
which yet remains for the people of God.

No. XXX.

SABBATIC LAWS CONTINUED.

That religion, which is true, and has God for its author, is, like the light of the sun, the common property of all who will only open their eyes, and gaze upon the gift of God. It is not a religion for the rich or the studious only, but is equally open to the understanding and the hearts of the poor and unlearned. And therefore the Bible describes the heavenly wisdom thus— "She standeth in the top of high places, by the way in the places of the paths; she crieth at the gates at the entry of the city, at the coming in at the doors: Unto you, O men, I call; and my voice is to the sons of man. O ye simple, understand wisdom; and, ye fools, be of an understanding heart." (Prov. viii. 2—5.) And so God invites men of every class by the mouth of the prophet—" Ho, every one that thirsteth, come ye to the waters, and he that hath no money; come ye, buy and eat; yea, come, buy wine and milk without money and without price." (Isa. lv. 1.) Every religion of man's making, presents, on the contrary, peculiar advantages to the rich and the learned. It offers salvation either as the purchase of almsgiving, or as the reward of religious study, or it makes religion so difficult and intricate as to put it out of the poor labouring man's power to acquire any competent knowledge of its requirements. And any system that does so must necessarily be false. Religion is as necessary to the soul as daylight is to the corporeal eye, and it would be a hard case, indeed, if the poor, who want it most, should be excluded from the possibility of acquiring its consolations; or if, in the day of judgment, the man who devotes his life to books should have a better chance, than he who labours hard to get an honest living for himself and his family; yet this is the case with the labouring classes of the Jews. The religion of the oral law has so perplexed even the simplest commandments, that an unlearned man has no chance of being able to keep them. If nothing more were required for salvation than the rabbinic sanctification of the Sabbath-day the majority of the Jewish people must despair of attaining it; for the accurate knowledge of the innumerable precepts and distinctions, which is indispensable to obedience, requires time and study, which no labouring man can bestow. And we are convinced that a considerable portion of the Jewish population of this city live in continual profanation of the Sabbath-day, if the rabbinic explanations be true. Either they move something which they ought not to move, or they carry something which they ought not to carry; and, if they do it wilfully, render themselves liable to the utmost severity of the law. For instance, the rabbies have determined that in one place it is lawful to move or carry certain things on the Sabbath-day, but in another place the very same act is unlawful, and calls down extreme punishment. They distinguish between these places thus—

ארבע רשויות לשבת, רשות. היחיד ורשות הרבים
כרמלית ומקום פטור, רשות היחיד הוא המקום המוקף
מחיצות גבוהות עשרה ויש בו ארבעה טפחים על
ארבעה ואפילו אם יש בו כמה מילין אם מוקף לדירה
ודלתותיו נעולות בלילה הוי רשות היחיד, ודיר וסחר
וחצר. וכן חריץ עמוק עשרה ורחב ד' על ד' או יותר
וכן תל גבוה י' ורחב ארבעה על ארבעה, וכותלים
המקיפין רשות היחיד על גביהן וחוריהן רשות
היחיד, ואויר רשות היחיד הוא רשות היחיד עד
לרקיע ואפילו כלי אם גבוה י' ורחב ד' על ד' כגון
תיבה או כוורת או מגדל הוי רשות היחיד, ורשות
היחיד הוא רחובות ושווקים הרחבים י' אמה על י'
אמה ומפולשים משער לשער וששים רבוא עוברין בו,
וכל דבר שהוא ברשות הרבים ואינו גבוה ג' טפחים
חשוב כקרקע והוא רשות הרבים אפילו קוצים או צואה
שאין רבים דורסין עליהם, ואם הוא גבוה ג' ומג'
עד ט' ולא ט' בכלל אם הוא רחב ד' על ד' הוי
כרמלית פחות מכאן הוי מקום פטור:

In reference to the Sabbath, places are distinguished into four sorts of jurisdiction. 1st, the private jurisdiction; 2d, the public jurisdiction; 3d, the place called Karmelith; 4th, the place which is free.

By a *private jurisdiction* is meant a place surrounded by walls, ten handbreadths high, and in which there is a space of four handbreadths by four. But even though it should contain many miles, if it be inclosed for habitation, and its gates be bolted at night, it is a private jurisdiction. A lodging-place, an inclosed space, and a court, are considered as in the same class. And thus, also, a pit which is ten handbreadths deep, and whose breadth is four by four, or more; and a raised place which is ten handbreadths high, and whose breadth is four by four. The top of the walls, also, by which a private jurisdiction is surrounded, and the openings in them, are considered as private jurisdiction. The air of a private jurisdiction, up to the firmament, is also considered; and even a vessel like a chest, if it be ten handbreadths high, and in breadth four by four. A hollow vessel, or a tower, is also considered as a private jurisdiction.

SABBATIC LAWS CONTINUED.

The term *public jurisdiction* includes roads and streets, if their breadth be sixteen ells by sixteen, and they be open from gate to gate, and six hundred thousand persons pass thereon. And everything in a public jurisdiction, which is not three handbreadths high, is reckoned as the ground, and is public jurisdiction: even thorns and filth upon which the public does not tread.

But if it be from three to nine handbreadths high, but not nine entirely, and its breadth be four by four, it is called a *Karmelith*.

"If it be less, it is called a *free place*." (Orach Chaiim, 344.)

Now it may well be doubted, concerning many Jews in this city, whether they are acquainted with even this portion of the Sabbath laws, but it is quite certain that they are ignorant of the innumerable modes of possible transgression which arise from these distinctions; for the oral law then goes on to define what is lawful concerning each. In a public jurisdiction he may move anything four ells:—

כל אדם יש לו ד' אמות ברשות הרבים שיכול
לטלטל בהם:

"Every man has got four ells within which he may move things." Or, as Rambam expresses it—

רשות היחיד ומקום פטור מותר לטלטל בכולן
אפילו היה אורך כל אחת משתיהן כמה מילין מטלטל
בכולה, אבל רשות הרבים והכרמלית אין מטלטלין
בהן אלא בארבע אמות:

"In a private jurisdiction, and in a free place it is lawful to move things the whole length of the place, even though the length of each should be many miles. But in a public jurisdiction or a Karmelith things may not be moved more than four ells." (Hilchoth Shabbath, c. xxiv. 11.) Now, it may well be asked, upon what passage of the law of Moses these distinctions are grounded, and what there is in a public jurisdiction which converts an act lawful in a private jurisdiction, into a sin to be expiated only by stoning the offender? For instance, in a private jurisdiction a man may carry certain matters for miles without violating the Sabbath commands, but if he venture out into a public jurisdiction with a pocket-handkerchief, or a snuff-box, or a half-crown in his pocket, and carry it only five ells, he is guilty of death; and if the Talmudists held the reigns of power, would be led out as soon as the Sabbath was over, and stoned. Reason revolts against such doctrine, the act is the very same in both cases, and is therefore in both cases a sin, or in both cases lawful.

Humanity shudders at the thought of stoning a man for carrying a pocket-handkerchief, and the Bible teaches us that a religion, teaching such inexorable and wanton cruelty, cannot be from God. It is true that at present the power of Christianity protects Israelites from such harsh treatment; but wherever the Talmud has any degree of influence, Israel groans under its bondage. Many a time have we seen Jews with their pocket-handkerchief tied round their knee like a garter, for this is lawful, though to carry it in his pocket would be a grave and capital offence. And we once knew an Israelite who was taking a walk on the Sabbath-day, and being addressed by a Gentile beggar, put his hand into his pocket and gave the poor man a small coin. He was observed by some Talmudists, who immediately attacked him for his profanation of the Sabbath. Afraid of losing his character, and being at that time more anxious for the praise of man than that which cometh of God, he defended himself by saying, that he had unintentionally taken out the money in his pocket, but had remembered it when addressed by the beggar, and therefore took the opportunity of getting rid of that which it was not lawful to carry. The Talmudists were satisfied, and their wrath changed into profound admiration for his piety. These cases exemplify the practical working of the rabbinic system. It burdens the consciences of the sincere, and makes the unscrupulous hypocrites. It may be replied that such things could not happen in England, and that here the Jews are too enlightened to observe such distinctions. But every one who makes this reply condemns modern Judaism as a religion unfit for the observation of the enlightened, and if he be a conscientious man, should protest against doctrines which he believes to be false, and laws which he abhors as cruel. These Sabbatic laws are a part, an essential part, of modern Judaism. There is not any part of the oral law upon which Talmudists lay more stress. The man, therefore, who does not observe them has changed his religion. He has got a new faith, as really, as if he had been baptized and professed Christianity. Every Israelite who carries a pocket-handkerchief in his pocket through the streets of London on the Sabbath-day, has apostatized from that Jewish religion, which has been professed for near two thousand years, and practically declares that the religion of the synagogue is false. How then can he, without hypocrisy, profess to believe in the religion of the Jews? or how can he, as an honest man, uphold a system which he regards as false, and which would have him executed as a criminal if it had the power? If such persons, who live in the habitual transgression of all the Sabbatic laws, have any regard for truth and for Divine revelation, they should openly declare their sentiments, announce to the world that they have forsaken the religion of their fathers, and assert that religion which they regard as true. The blindest and most bigoted Talmudist is a far more respectable man, and more acceptable in the sight of God, than he who pretends to profess a religion in which he does not believe, and whose precepts he regards as fanatical and superstitious.

But to return. From the above laws it appears that it is a sin to carry anything in a public jurisdiction a distance of more than four ells. But suppose, then, that there was something which the Talmudists might find it convenient or desirable to move to a greater distance, is there no provision to effect its conveyance? Yes. These scrupulous persons, who would stone a man to death for carrying anything five ells, have an expedient for conveying it a hundred miles if necessary :—

לפיכך מותר לאדם לעקור החפץ מרשות הרבים
וליתנו לחברו שאצלו בתוך ד' אמותיו וחברו לחברו
שאצלו אפילו ק' מילין אע״פ שהחפץ הולך כמה
מילין ברשות הרבים שכל אחד לא יטלטלנו אלא
בתוך ד' אמותיו :

"Therefore it is lawful for a man to move a matter from the public jurisdiction, and to give it to his neighbour, who is within a distance of four ells; and his neighbour to his neighbour again, and so on, even for a hundred miles. For although the thing itself go many miles, each person has only moved it his four ells." (Orach Chaiim, 348.) We have often heard of the wonderful effects of division of labour, but never knew before that it could convert a capital offence into an innocent employment. Surely it is not necessary to prove that if it be unlawful for one person to do a particular act, it is equally unlawful for a hundred persons to combine for its performance. This law really has more the appearance of a caricature devised by some enemy of the oral law, than the grave decision of religious men in a matter of life and death. But if we examine a little further, we shall find that it is unlawful to move this same thing, whatever it be, from one jurisdiction to another, though that other be close at hand :—

כשם שאסור לטלטל בכל הכרמלית כן אסור להוציא
ממנה לרשות היחיד או לרשות הרבים או להכניס
לכרמלית מרשות היחיד או מרשות הרבים, ואם
הוציא או הכניס פטור :

"As it is unlawful to move anything in the place called Karmelith, so it is unlawful to carry anything out of it into a public or private jurisdiction, or, vice versa, to introduce anything from either of these into the Karmelith. But if any one does either he is not guilty," that is, he is only to get a flogging, but not to be stoned. An unlearned man who had already seen something conveyed by the above expedient, might easily be led to commit an offence of this kind. His untutored mind might not perceive why the one should be sinful, if the other was lawful; but such an assertion of common sense would draw down certain chastisement. At all events, he might be tempted to put his head from one jurisdiction into another, especially if he was standing in the street, and was offered a drink by a friend in a house, he might put his head into the window and take what was offered, but would soon find, to his cost, that he had broken one of the Sabbatic laws:—

לא יעמוד אדם ברשות היחיד ויוציא ראשו לרשות
הרבים וישתה שם או איפכא אלא אם כן יכניס ראשו
ורובו למקום שהוא שותה דכיון שהוא צריך לאלו
המים אנו חוששין שמא יביאם אליו אבל מותר לעמוד
ברשות היחיד או ברשות הרבים ולשתות בכרמלית:

"A man may not stand in a private jurisdiction, and put forth his head into a public jurisdiction, and then drink, or *vice versa*. But if he does so, let him introduce his head and most of his body into the place in which he drinks, for as he wants the water, we fear lest he should take it to himself (into the place where he is standing). But it is lawful to stand in a private or public jurisdiction and drink in that which is called Karmelith." (Orach Chaiim, 349.) It is evident that no unlearned man can stand a fair chance with laws like these. He could not hope even to escape corporal punishment. But if the accurate observance of such laws was the condition of salvation, he would have reason to despair. The most honest desire to yield obedience and the utmost exertion of his understanding will not help him, nor compensate for his ignorance. If, for instance, he should conclude, because it is unlawful for himself to have his head in one jurisdiction and his body in another whilst he is drinking, that it would be equally unlawful for cattle in the same predicament to get food, he would be mistaken:—

בהמה שהיתה רובה בחוץ וראשה בפנים אובסין
אותה:

"A beast that has got most of its body outside, and its head inside, may be fed." And if he should take this as the general rule of his conduct, he would be mistaken again, for long-necked animals form an exception:—

ובגמל עד שיהא ראשו ורובו בפנים הואיל וצוארו
ארוך:

case of the camel, he must have his head and
ly inside, because his neck is long." (Hilchoth
:v. 1.) And so with endless cases which arise
istinction of places into four classes. Judaism
s a religion for the studious, and for them only.
led man to keep the Sabbath, as the oral law
iolutely impossible. And after all, what good
upon those who spend their life in the study?
: the heart, or open more abundant views of the
or fill the soul with love to man? That it
it and subtlety, we do not doubt, but that is but
man in general. The criminal law of any
) the same, and in truth the oral law is very
the rabbinical criminal code. Its great subject
it guilty. And even in this it does not address
science, and lead a man to consider the workings
l the wanderings of the thought, and shew him
ain-head. It is a mere dry detail of external
may be seen from the numerous specimens
e papers, and as might be shown more fully by
whole. If real devout feeling and improvement
the fear of God and the love of man be true
;ht expect it, if anywhere, in the Sabbath laws.
that holy day which God has set apart to raise
from earth to heaven. It is that period of
n on which even the poor and the unlearned
icir worldly cares and occupations, and meditate
id will of God, and that eternity to which he is
the laws, then, respecting the observance of this
naturally expect the spirit of devotion to be
: in the oral law we look in vain for anything
directions about the Sabbath are one continued
:ternal observances, which to a conscientious
with them, must constitute a load upon his
;ient to make the Sabbath the most unhappy
ven. But as to the poor and labouring classes,
ne for study, it is impossible that they should
:h more that they should keep, all that is
e right observation of the rabbinic Sabbath.
oral law were true, the poor must lose a large
)lessings, and even be in danger of perdition.
ie, then we must believe that God has given a
)le to be observed by the poor, and offering great
e rich and learned, that is that He is a respecter
;h Moses and the prophets teach the contrary.
ik our readers, what use is it to them to profess
hich they can never attain a competent know-
iture to affirm that the majority of Israelites do

not know enough of the oral law to help them to keep the Sabbath, much less to observe the six hundred and thirteen commandments; can it be said, then, that they possess a religion with which they are not even acquainted? If the knowledge and practice of the oral law be necessary to constitute a true Jew, ninety-nine out of every hundred must give up their claims to the Jewish name. But then what is to become of the Jewesses, who are not even obligated to learn? Every rabbi will be willing to confess that the women at least are ignorant of the oral law. Can they then have a portion in the world to come? If the knowledge and practice of the oral law be necessary to salvation, they cannot. But if they can be saved without it, then it follows that God has given a law, the knowledge of which is not necessary to salvation. Let every Jew ask himself this question, Am I acquainted with all the precepts of the oral law? If not, can I be saved without this knowledge? If I cannot, then the Jewish religion is one which makes it impossible for the poor to be saved. If I can, then the Jewish religion is of no real use, for I can be saved even without knowing it. Such a religion cannot be from God. His religion is necessary to be known by every man, woman, and child in the world, and the knowledge of it is just as easy to be acquired by the poor and unlearned as by the rich and studious. Let then the poor and the unlearned consider the folly of professing a religion, with which they can never hope to become acquainted, and let them return to the religion of Moses and the prophets, which, by the help of the God of Israel, every one can understand, at least so far as is necessary to salvation. The Bible, like everything that has God for its author, has beauties discoverable by the eye of the poor, at the same time that it has perfections to exercise the observation and skill of the most learned. And this holy book is the heritage of Israel, which the oral law can never be. The oral law may be the heritage and religion of the rabbies who know it, but it has no more to do with the religion of those who know it not, than the laws of the Chinese. The great majority of the Jewish people might just as well call themselves followers of Confucius. No man can be said to believe in doctrines which he does not know, and can never hope to know: and this is the case with nine-tenths of the oral law.

No. XXXI.

RABBINIC EXCOMMUNICATION.

It is a fact, that the religion of the oral law has hitherto done but little to promote the temporal welfare of the Jewish people, and it is equally certain that, if supreme, it would destroy the happiness both of Jews and Gentiles. Its endless definitions would necessarily produce transgression. Its severity and readiness in excommunication would be the source of constant trouble to individuals and families, and the sanguinary spirit of its criminal code would make the Jews a nation of mourners. Indeed, we seriously doubt, whether any, but a few fanatics, wish to see the oral law vested with supreme power, and ruling over the lives and properties of the Jewish nation. Every reflecting Israelite must know that the Sanhedrin, wielding the absolute power ascribed to it in the rabbinic traditions, would be the most oppressive tribunal that ever lorded it over the consciences of men. But we must remember that it would not be with the Sanhedrin and other tribunals alone, that the Israelites would have to do. Every rabbi, and every disciple of a wise man, would have the right of excommunicating any one who offended them. After determining that the tribunals can and ought in certain cases to excommunicate, the oral law adds—

וכן החכם עצמו מנדה לכבודו לעם הארץ שהקפיד
בו ואין צריך לא עדים ולא התראה, ואין מתירין לו
עד שירצה את החכם, ואם מת החכם באין שלשה
ומתירין לו. ואם רצה החכם למחול לו ולא לנדהו
הרשות בידו:

" And in like manner the wise man himself may, on account of his honour, excommunicate an unlearned man who has treated him with contumely, and there is no need of witnesses nor admonition. And the excommunicate person is not to be absolved until he appease the wise man. But if the wise man die, three persons come and absolve him. If, however, the wise man wish to pardon, and not excommunicate him, the power is in his own hand." (Hilchoth Talmud Torah, c. vi. 12.) From this law we see that the restoration of rabbinic power would be the most oppressive system of government ever devised. Every learned man would be a petty tyrant, constituting both judge and jury in his own person, and able, at his own caprice, to inflict a severe punishment. The most absolute aristocracy of the feudal times never dared to assume or exercise a power so monstrous and so oppressive. No priesthood, even

in the darkest times, ever claimed such personal authority as is
here given to every individual rabbi. It is true that he may,
if he please, forgive the unfortunate offender, but it is much to
be feared that such absolute power would in most cases be too
strong a temptation to the frail sons of men. And at all
events the principle is utterly inconsistent with wise legislation,
and most dangerous to the liberty of the poor and unlearned;
for the reader will observe that it is only an unlearned man, an
"am-haaretz," who may be dealt with in this summary manner.
And this is another proof that the religion of the oral law is a
religion devised for the advantage of the rich and learned, but
regardless of the spiritual and temporal welfare of the lower
classes. For the learned and the great the law is very
different:—

חכם זקן בחכמה וכן נשיא או אב ב״ד שסרח אין
מנדין אותו בפרהסיא לעולם אלא אם כן עשה כירבעם
בן נבט וחביריו אבל כשחטא שאר חטאות מלקין
אותו בצנעה שנאמר וכשלת היום וכשל גם נביא עמך
לילה אע״פ שכשל כסהו בלילה, ואומרים לו הכבד
ושב בביתך וכן כל ת״ח שנתחייב נידוי אסור לב״ד
לקפוץ ולנדותו במהרה:

"A wise man, old in wisdom, or a prince, or a president
of a tribunal, who has sinned, is never to be excommunicated
publicly, unless he have done as Jeroboam, the son of Nebat,
and his companions. But when he commits other sins, he is
to be flogged in private. For it is said, 'Therefore shalt thou
fall in the day, and the prophet also shall fall with thee in
the night,' (Hos. iv. 5,) *i.e.*, although he fall, cover him as
it were with the night. And they say to him, 'Honour thyself, and abide in thy house.' (2 Kings xiv. 10.) In like
manner, when a disciple of a wise man makes himself guilty of
excommunication, it is unlawful for the tribunal to be too quick,
and to excommunicate him hastily." (Ibid. c. vii. 1.) The
rabbies have endeavoured to justify this different legislation for
the learned and unlearned by a verse of the Bible, but their
interpretation of that verse is quite erroneous. When God
says, "Therefore shalt thou fall in the day, and the prophet
shall also fall with thee in the night," he is not speaking of the
learned and unlearned, nor of the different way in which their
sins were to be punished, but of the destruction which was
coming upon Israel, as may be seen in Kimchi's Commentary.
He interprets the verse thus—

וכשלת היום אמר כנגד ישראל בעבור מעשיך
תכשל ותפול, היום ר״ל הזמן הזה בקרוב הבוא

RABBINIC EXCOMMUNICATION. 241

מפלתך, וכן וחרה אפי בו ביום ההוא, ביום ההוא
שורש ישי והדומים להם, ענינם עת וזמן, וכשל גם
נביא עמך לילה נביא שקר חמתעה אותך יכשל עמך
כמו האדם נכשל בלילה בחשכה וכן תרגם יונתן:

"*Therefore shalt thou stumble in the day.*" This refers to
Israel, and means on account of thy deeds thou shalt stumble
and fall. *This day;* that is, in this time; thy fall shall soon
come. And so we read, "Then my anger shall be kindled
against them in that day." (Deut. xxxi. 17.) And again, "In
that day there shall be a root of Jesse," (Isaiah xi. 10,) where
day means time and period. *And the prophet also shall fall
with thee in the night,* that is, the false prophet who deceiveth
thee shall stumble with thee, as men stumble in the night
in darkness; and so the Targum of Jonathan has it. (Kimchi,
Comment. in Hos. iv. 2.) Kimchi and Jonathan, then, both
testify that the oral law gives a false interpretation of this
verse. This is in itself rather awkward for a law that professes to have been given by God, but still more so when
it is made the basis of most unjust and partial legislation,
to save the learned from the punishment which an unlearned
man would have in similar circumstances to suffer. No one
can deny that the learned and unlearned are here placed on
very unequal terms. If an unlearned man provoke a rabbi, he
may be excommunicated by that individual without either
judge or jury, or even the form of a trial. But if a learned
man makes himself liable to the same punishment, even a
court of justice has not the power to pronounce the sentence.
Who can doubt that the rabbies made these laws for their
own convenience? Can any one believe that God has given
this law, which makes the learned a privileged class of
persons, who, though guilty of the same offence as the working
classes, is to be spared, whilst they are to be punished? God is
no respecter of persons, and therefore no such law can be from
him.

The extreme injustice of this mode of legislation will appear
still more from considering the nature of the punishment:—

מהו המנהג שינהג המנודה בעצמו ושנוהגין עמו,
מנודה אסור לספר ולכבס כאבל כל ימי נידויו, ואין
מזמנין עליו, ולא כוללין אותו בעשרה לכל דבר
שצריך עשרה, ולא יושבין עמו בארבע אמות, אבל
שונה הוא לאחרים ושונין לו, ונשכר ושוכר, ואם
מת בנדויו בית דין שולחין ומניחין אבן על ארונו,
כלומר שהן רוגמין אותו, לפי שהוא מובדל מן הציבור
ואין צריך לומר שאין מספידין אותו ואין מלוין את

מטתו ... מי שישב בנידויו שלשים יום ולא בקש
להתירו מנדין אותו שנייה ישב שלשים יום אחרים
ולא בקש להתירו מחרימין אותו :

"How is an excommunicate person to conduct himself, and how are others to conduct themselves towards him ? It is unlawful for an excommunicate person, as for a mourner, to trim his beard or hair, or to wash all the days of his excommunication ; neither is he to be associated in pronouncing the benedictions ; neither is he to be reckoned as one of ten, wherever ten persons are required ; neither may any one sit within four ells of him. He may however teach others and be taught. He may hire and be hired. But if he die in his excommunication, the tribunal send and lay a stone upon his coffin to signify that they stone him because he is separated from the congregation. And it is unnecessary to say that he is not to be mourned for, and that his funeral is not to be attended. .... Whosoever remains thirty days in his excommunication without seeking to be absolved, is to be excommunicated a second time. If he abide thirty days more without seeking absolution, he is then to be anathematized." (Hilchoth Talmud Torah, ibid.) This, then, is the punishment which a learned man has it in his power to inflict at will. He may deprive him of the comforts of cleanliness and perhaps injure his health. He may hold him up to the public scorn by separating him by four ells from all decent people. He may heap obloquy upon his death and deprive him of a respectful burial, or if the man survive under the public contempt, and refuse to give the rabbi satisfaction, he will be anathematized, and his prospects for this world, at least, irretrievably ruined. The law respecting the anathematized person is this :—

אינו שונה לאחרים ואין שונין לו אבל שונה הוא
לעצמו שלא ישכח תלמודו ואינו נשכר ואין נשכרין
לו, ואין נושאין ונותנין עמו, ואין מתעסקין עמו
אלא מעט עסק כדי פרנסתו :

"He is not to teach others nor to be taught, but may learn by himself that he may not forget the learning. He is not to be hired, nor to hire. Men may have no dealings with him, nor any business except a little that he may get a livelihood." Now then suppose that an unlearned man does or says something, which a rabbi interprets as contempt, he is first excommunicated. If, in the consciousness of innocence, he refuses to ask for the rabbi's forgiveness, he is at last anathematized, and all his business stopped, and all this is done to him because he is an unlearned man. He is himself to be dishonoured, his business ruined, and he himself to die of a broken heart, not because he has committed some grievous crime, but because he has been wanting in respect either to the rabbi's person or his words. The most absolute autocrat never made a law more despotic.

But some one will say, that the rabbi has the power of forgiving if he please, and that the oral law recommends him to do so. It is true that if the affront be given in private, he has this power, and is told to forgive, but not so if it be offered in public, he has then no choice. He is bound to excommunicate the offender. That we may not appear to act unfairly, we will give the whole passage :—

אף על פי שיש רשות לחכם לנדות לכבודו אינו
שבח לתלמיד חכם להנהיג עצמו בדבר זה אלא
מעלים אזניו מדברי עם הארץ ולא ישית לבו להן
כענין שאמר שלמה בחכמתו גם לכל הדברים אשר
ידברו אל תתן לבך, וכן היה דרך חסידים הראשונים
שומעים חרפתם ואינן משיבין ולא עוד אלא שמוחלים
למחרף וסולחים לו, וחכמים גדולים היו משתבחים
במעשיהם הנאים ואומרים שמעולם לא נידו אדם
ולא החרימוהו לכבודן, וזו היא דרכם של תלמידי
חכמים שראוי לילך בה, במה דברים אמורים כשבזוהו
או חרפוהו בסתר אבל תלמיד חכם שבזהו או חרפו
אדם בפרהסיא אסור לו למחול על כבודו ואם מחל
נענש שזה בזיון של תורה אלא נוקם ונוטר הדבר
כנחש עד שיבקש ממנו מחילה:

" Although a wise man has the power to excommunicate on account of his honour, yet it is not to be praised in the disciple of a wise man who does so. On the contrary he ought to shut his ears against the words of an unlearned man (am-haaretz), and not to attend to them, according as Solomon has said in his wisdom, ' Take no heed to all the things that are spoken.' (Eccles. vii. 21.) And such was the custom of the saints of old, who heard their reviling, but did not answer; and not only so, but they pardoned the reviler, and forgave him. The greatest of the wise men used to glory in their good deeds, and say, that they had never excommunicated nor anathematized any man on account of their honour, and this is the way in which the disciples of the wise men ought to walk. In what case is this to be applied? When they have been despised or reviled in secret. *But if the disciple of a wise man be despised or reviled by any man publicly, it is unlawful for him to forgive any affront to his honour, and if he forgive he is to be punished, for this is a contempt of the law. He is on the contrary, to avenge and keep the thing in mind, like a serpent, until the offender entreat to be forgiven.*" (Ibid. c. vii. 13.) The great object of these laws is plainly to uphold the power and dignity of the rabbies, and to make it impossible for the people to shake off their yoke. The care which is taken to punish every offence against the wise men betrays a lurking consciousness of error, and a fear lest the common people should compare their precepts with Scripture, assert the plain unsophisticated truth, and thus shake off the galling chains of rabbinism. To prevent this, the very first semblance of disobedience is to be punished with excommunication. But for the poor and unlearned, if insulted by a learned man, there is no satisfaction. He cannot thunder out an excommunication or an anathema in return. For him the oral law makes no provision, except for his punishment. If Judaism, therefore, should ever attain the supreme power, the working and unlearned classes will be placed in the power and at the mercy of the learned, and every disciple of a wise man will wield the absolute power of an autocrat.

But some one may say, that if the disciple of a wise man should excommunicate any one hastily that the people would not regard his excommunication. But if they did not, they would do it at their peril, for the oral law expressly declares that they are bound to observe the excommunication not only of a rabbi, but of one of his disciples :—

הרב שנידה לכבודו כל תלמידיו חייבין לנהוג בו
נדוי במנודה אבל תלמיד שנידה לכבוד עצמו אין
הרב חייב לנהוג בו נדוי אבל כל העם חייבין לנהוג
בו נדוי :

"When a rabbi excommunicates on account of his honour, all his disciples are bound to treat the excommunicate person as such. But when a disciple excommunicates on account of his own honour, the rabbi is not bound to treat that person as excommunicate, but all the people are bound." (Ibid. c. vi. 13.) Nothing can more clearly prove the injustice of such excommunication. If the rabbi be not bound to regard the disciples' excommunication, why should all the people be bound? If the offence committed against the disciple be a sin before God, and such it ought to be to require such severe punishment, the excommunication ought to be as binding upon the rabbi as upon the people. But if it be not binding upon the rabbi, then the offence for which it was inflicted cannot be a sin in the sight of God, it is therefore an arbitrary and unjust punishment, and it is both wicked and cruel to require the people to obey it. But the principle itself is monstrous, that the disciple of a rabbi should be constituted both judge and jury in his own case, and have the power of lording it over those, whose circumstances do not permit them to devote their time to study, and who, therefore, cannot be enrolled in the privileged class. Just suppose that the clergy of this land, or the professors and students at our Universities, were to claim such power, and to excommunicate and anathematize all who treated them with disrespect, and that without any trial or conviction before a legal tribunal, and that the unfortunate victims were to be separated from society, ruined, and then their dead bodies treated with dishonour, would not this be regarded as a monstrous and insupportable tyranny? Yet this is what the oral law claims for the rabbies and their disciples, and what they would possess and exercise if Judaism ever attains to supreme power. Would the Jews wish such a power established? Do they desire to live under such a government? If they do not, if they prefer the personal liberty and the even-handed justice secured to them by Christian laws, then they confess that the Christian principles are better than those of their own religion, and they must be charged with inconsistency in professing and asserting the truth of a religion, which they hope may never triumph. Every man who believes his religious principles to be Divine, must wish that they should triumph, and that they should have free scope for their development. Any man who dreads the triumph of his religion must have secret misgivings that it is false. We therefore ask every Jew whether he desires that the oral law should attain that absolute power which it claims, and that every rabbi and his disciples should have the power of excommunicating and anathematizing all who affront them? One of the most perfect tests of a religion, is to consider what would be its effects if supreme. At present there are various systems of religion in the world, some of which, as directly contradicting others, must be decidedly false. The hope of all reflecting men is, that the truth will ultimately triumph, that God himself will at last interpose, and establish the dominion of truth and eradicate all error. Each hopes that his own system will then prevail, but let him follow out that system, and see how it will work, when all resistance shall be vain. Let the Jews calmly consider the state of things, when the rabbies and their disciples shall be masters of the world, as they must one day be, if Judaism be true. The unlearned will then be completely at their mercy, their servants and their bondmen. Will this be a happy condition, or is this state of things desirable? In the first place, there will be no personal liberty. Any man who may chance to differ from a rabbi, and treat him with disrespect will immediately be excommunicated. In the second place, there will be no liberty of conscience or of thought. Every man must then let the rabbies think for him, and he must be content to receive their decisions without any appeal. The body will scarcely have the appearance of being free, and the intellect will be bound in fetters of adamant. It will no doubt be a glorious period for the wise men and their disciples, but they will always form a small minority, compared with the bulk of mankind. The majority of Israel, not now to speak of the Gentiles, will then be degraded into poor, crouching, submissive servants of the learned, afraid to use their reason, and always having the fear and dread of excommunication before their eyes. Do they then honestly wish for such a state of things, to be tied hand and foot, and given into the hands of their learned men? If they do not, if they see the horror and the injustice and degradation of such a state of things, why do they profess a religion which will inevitably lead to it, if it be true? If such laws be unjust, and such a consummation dreadful, instead of desirable, the religion of the oral law must necessarily be false; and it is the duty of every Israelite to consider what he is doing in upholding it. The present state of things will not continue always. The Jewish nation cannot always wish to be wanderers in foreign lands. They look forward to a restoration to the land of their fathers, and they wish in that land to be happy and prosperous. But happiness and prosperity will be unknown words, if they are then to be governed according to the principles of the oral law. That law gives the learned a monopoly of power and happiness, but leaves the mass of the nation in bondage. Do they then, in contemplating the re-establishment of the kingdom of Israel, expect another than the oral law, and other principles of religion and justice? If they do, they confess that the oral law is false, and if it would be false and hurtful, and destructive of all happiness, if supreme, it is equally false and hurtful now. The Israelite, therefore, who upholds it, is upholding a false system. He may do it in ignorance, and we believe that this is the case with the majority; but it is most unbecoming in any reasonable man to profess a religion of which he is ignorant. He may answer, I have no time to acquire an accurate knowledge of my religion. The books in which it is contained are too voluminous to admit of my acquiring an acquaintance with them. I must work for my bread. We grant that this is the fact, but then this brings us back to our original position, that Judaism is only a religion for those who have leisure, that is, for the rich and the learned, and we conclude, on that very account, that it cannot be from God, who looks neither at riches nor learning, but considereth the welfare, and above all, the religious welfare of the poorest of his creatures. The especial character of the Messiah is, that he will care for the poor. " He shall judge the poor of the people, he shall save the children of the needy." (Psalm lxxii. 4.) He, therefore, cannot have the religion of the oral law. He will not be a rabbi, nor a rabbi's disciple.

No. XXXII.

NEW YEAR'S DAY.

THE season of the Jewish year, which we are now approaching, naturally leads us to the consideration of some subjects more important than those which we have lately discussed, the oral law teaches that the festival of the new year is nothing less than a day of judgment, on which God pronounces sentence respecting the state of every individual:

וכשם ששוקלין זכיות אדם ועוונותיו בשעת מיתתו
כך בכל שנה ושנה שוקלין עוונות כל אחד ואחד
מבאי עולם עם זכיותיו ביום של ראש השנה, מי
שנמצא צדיק נחתם לחיים ומי שנמצא רשע נחתם
למיתה, והבינונים תולין אותו עד יום הכפורים אם
עשה תשובה נחתם לחיים ואם לאו נחתם למיתה:

"As the merits and the sins of a man are weighed at the hour of his death, so likewise every year, on the festival of New Year's Day, the sins of every one that cometh into the world are weighed against his merits. Every one who is found righteous is sealed to life. Every one who is found wicked is sealed to death. But the judgment of the intermediate class is suspended until the Day of Atonement. If they repent, they are sealed to life, but if not, they are sealed to death." (Hilchoth T'shuvah, c. iii. 3.) This naturally leads us to consider the rabbinic doctrine of justification, and to inquire how far it agrees with Moses and the prophets. And here our first business must be to state the doctrine as it is found in the oral law.

This law teaches, first, that he whose merits are more than his sins is accounted a righteous man :—

כל אחד ואחד מבני אדם יש לו זכיות ועוונות, מי
שזכיותיו יתרות על עוונותיו צדיק, ומי שעוונותיו
יתרות על זכיותיו רשע, מחצה למחצה בינוני:

"Every one of the children of man has merits and sins. If his merits exceed his sins, he is righteous. If his sins exceed his merits, he is wicked. If they be half and half, he is a middling or intermediate person." (Ibid. 1.)

It teaches, secondly, that in estimating the comparative state, respect is had not only to the number but to the quality of the actions :—

ושקול זה אינו לפי מנין הזכיות והעוונות אלא לפי גדלם, יש זכות שהיא כנגד כמה עוונות שנאמר יען נמצא בו דבר טוב, ויש עוון שהוא כנגד כמה זכיות, שנאמר וחוטא אחד יאבד טובה הרבה:

"And this weighing is made, not with respect to the number of the merits and the sins, but according to their greatness. There is a merit which may outweigh many sins, as it is said, 'Because in him there is found some good thing.' (1 Kings xiv. 13.) And there are sins which may outweigh many merits, for it is said, 'One sinner destroyeth much good.'" (Ecclesiast. ix. 18.)

It teaches, thirdly, that it is possible by transgression or obedience to turn the scale :—

חטא חטא אחד הרי הכריע את עצמו ואת כל העולם כולו לכף חובה וגרם לו השחתה, עשה מצוה אחת הרי הכריע את עצמו ואת כל העולם כולו לכף זכות וגרם לו ולהם תשועה והצלה שנאמר וצדיק יסוד עולם זה שצדק הכריע את כל העולם לזכות והצילו, מפני ענין זה נהגו כל בית ישראל להרבות בצדקה ובמעשים טובים ולעסוק במצוות מראש השנה ועד יום הכפורים יתר מכל השנה:

"If a man sin one sin, he gives the preponderance for himself and for all the world to the scale of guilt, and causes destruction. But if he perform one commandment, he gives the preponderance both for himself and all the world to the scale of merit, and causes salvation and deliverance to himself and them, as it is said, 'The righteous is the foundation of the world' (Prov. x. 25), which means that righteousness gives the world a preponderance in the scale of merit and delivers it. And on this account all the house of Israel are accustomed to abound in almsgiving, and in good deeds, and to be diligent in the commandments in the interval between New Year's Day and the Day of Atonement more than in all the year besides." (Ibid. 4.) This then is the doctrine which we have to consider.

The first great principle is that "Every one of the children of men has merits and has sins." That every man has sins we readily admit; but that any man, or any angel, or any of God's creatures, has any merit in the sight of God we deny. First, because the idea of merit is utterly inconsistent with the idea of the relation in which the creature stands to the Creator. Every created being is bound by the very fact of his creation to love God with all his heart and soul, and mind and strength, and to do all his will. Whatsoever, therefore, he does, he can never exceed the limit of his bounden duty, and can therefore never lay any claim to merit. If created beings were free from all obligation to love God or to do his will—if they were independent and masters of themselves, then by loving God or doing his will they might have merit, for they would be doing him a service which He has no right to require. Just as a man that is free may hire himself to do work for another man, which he is not bound to do, and thereby earn wages. But not so the slave, who is his master's property. He can only do his duty, and if he toil all the day and be diligent and faithful in his master's service, he still can lay no claim to wages or to merit; he has only done what he is bound to do. To lay any claim to merit, we must stand on equal terms, and confer what the other has no right to expect. But this no created being can ever do. He is a debtor overwhelmed with such an amount of debt, that all that he has or can raise only goes in part payment, and who therefore will never be able to confer anything which is not already due. And therefore it is said, "Can a man be profitable unto God?" and again, "Is it gain to him, that thou makest thy ways perfect?" (Job xxii. 2, 3.) The unfallen angels themselves have no merit before God, and much less fallen and rebellious man.

But, secondly, the assertion that man has merits is contradicted by the plain testimonies of Scripture. If man have merits, however few, then so far as those merits are concerned, his nature must be good and holy, but God declares the contrary: "Behold, he putteth no trust in his saints; yea the heavens are not clean in his sight: how much more abominable and filthy is man, which drinketh iniquity like water." (Job xv. 15, 16.) Such language cannot be applied to any creature capable of meriting anything in the sight of God. Again, if man have merits, his merits must proceed from the good things which he has done. He that does nothing good cannot be meritorious, but yet God says, "There is none that doeth good, no, not one. They are all gone aside, they are all together become filthy; there is none that doeth good, no, not one." (Ps. xiv. 1—3.) If this be true, then no man has merits. If man have merits, they must proceed from an inherent good principle in his nature, but God says even of Israel that there is no such principle of good: on the contrary, he declares that "the whole head is sick, and the whole heart faint. From the sole of the foot, even unto the head, there is no soundness in it: but wounds, and bruises, and putrifying sores." (Isaiah i. 5, 6.) Here God describes Israel, and the description is generally true of mankind, as totally corrupt. There is no soundness in it. The intellect is corrupt, for "the whole head is sick." The affections are corrupt, for "the whole heart is faint." How, then, can he that has a perverted intellect and a corrupt heart have merits? Again, if man have merits, his good deeds, whatever they be, must be such as to deserve the approbation of God; but the confession of the prophet is—

ונהי כטמא כלנו וכבגד עדים כל צדקותינו׃

"But we are all as an unclean thing, and all our righteousness as filthy rags." (Isa. lxiv. 6.) Either, then, the oral law or the Bible says what is false. The Bible says that the very best of man's deeds, "all his righteousnesses," are no better in the sight of God than filthy rags: if this be true, then man has no merit whatsoever.

But again, the assertion that every man has merits and sins, is based upon a false principle. It takes for granted that God judges men by their individual acts, and not by the state of their hearts; that is, that he judges as we do. When we consider a man's conduct, we can only look at his acts, and to us some of them appear good and others bad. In our sight, therefore, he may have some merits and some demerits. But God looks at the heart, and sees whether a man loves him or not, and by the whole habit of his mind and affections judges the man's state and all his actions. We short-sighted creatures judge a man's heart by his actions; but God judges his actions by his heart, and where the heart is wrong, he is so far from counting any actions as meritorious, that he looks upon the whole conduct as one mass of abominable sin.

The next assertion of the oral law is, that "If a man's merits exceed his sins, he is righteous." This pre-supposes, first, that a man's merits may exceed his sins; and asserts, secondly, that in this case he is accounted righteous. But where is the man whose "merits exceed his sins?" Where is the man who keeps any one of God's commandments perfectly? In all our best deeds and efforts there is sin of admixture or of imperfection. Often, when by the help of God, a good thought or an honest intention is conceived in the heart, before it can be realized in action, some selfish and unworthy motive associates itself with it, and spoils the whole. And in every case the obedience is imperfect, so that all our best acts become occasions of committing sins either of infirmity or imperfection, and thus our sins are certainly as many as our good deeds, for each one of them has a sin as its associate. But how many are our sins of thought, word, and deed, which are mere sins without any admixture of good, and which in themselves are "more than the hairs of our head?" And even if we should admit that the final result depends not upon number, but upon magnitude, then there is one sin that extends from the moment of our birth to the latest hour of our existence, and that is, want of perfect love to God. This he requires at every moment, but yet how many hours of every day do we pursue our business or our pleasures without a single remembrance of him? And how few, how hasty, and how interrupted are our grateful recollections of the love and mercy of God! Here then is a sin which in magnitude far exceeds the aggregate of all our gratitude and all our services, and which in itself would sink the scale of guilt down to the lowest hell. But by the side of it there is another equally immense, and that is our continued transgression of the commandment, "Thou shalt love thy neighbour as thyself." The very best of all God's saints makes, at the most, but a feeble struggle against the love of self. He admits the extent of his duty to his neighbour, he knows it—he desires to fulfil it. He watches against himself, and yet, with all his care, self-love creeps in again and again, and asserts the mastery over his thoughts and actions. These two sins would outweigh a thousand times all the six hundred and eleven remaining commandments of which Israel boasts, even if they kept them all without a single transgression or a shade of imperfection. With these two sins on our consciences, it is perfectly absurd to talk of our merits exceeding our sins. There is not, and never was in the world, a mere child of Adam, whose sins did not far exceed his good deeds. If, therefore, it be necessary, in order to be accounted just, that our merits should exceed our sins, we must give up all hope of being justified before God.

But let us suppose for a moment that such a thing were possible, that there was a man whose merits exceeded his sins, would such an one be accounted just before God? First let us ask Moses, let us hear what he says. Does he promise that if your merits exceed your sins, ye shall be considered just? and does he promise life, as the oral law does, to imperfect obedience? Hear the words of Moses himself:—

ושמרתם לעשות כאשר צוה ה׳ אלהיכם אתכם
לא תסורו ימין ושמאל, בכל הדרך אשר צוה ה׳
אלהיכם אתכם תלכו למען תחיון וטוב לכם והארכתם
ימים בארץ אשר תירשון:

"Ye shall observe to do therefore as the Lord your God hath commanded you: ye shall not turn aside to the right hand or to the left. Ye shall walk in ALL the ways which the Lord your God hath commanded you, that ye may live, and that it may be well with you, and that ye may prolong your days in the land which ye shall possess." (Deut. v. 32, 33.) Here Moses requires perfect obedience as the condition of life, and does not allow a single deviation either to the right hand or to the left. It is not a single declaration, nor a sentiment wrested from its context. Moses repeats the same again and again. In the very next verses to those just quoted, he says—

וְזֹאת הַמִּצְוָה הַחֻקִּים וְהַמִּשְׁפָּטִים אֲשֶׁר צִוָּה ה׳
אֱלֹהֵיכֶם לְלַמֵּד אֶתְכֶם לַעֲשׂוֹת בָּאָרֶץ אֲשֶׁר אַתֶּם עוֹבְרִים
שָׁמָּה לְרִשְׁתָּהּ, לְמַעַן תִּירָא אֶת ה׳ אֱלֹהֶיךָ לִשְׁמֹר אֶת
כָּל חֻקֹּתָיו וּמִצְוֹתָיו אֲשֶׁר אָנֹכִי מְצַוֶּךָ אַתָּה וּבִנְךָ וּבֶן
בִּנְךָ כֹּל יְמֵי חַיֶּיךָ וּלְמַעַן יַאֲרִכֻן יָמֶיךָ:

"Now these are the commandments, the statutes, and the judgments, which the Lord your God commanded to teach you, that ye might do them in the land whither ye go to possess it; that thou mightest fear the Lord thy God, to keep ALL his statutes and his commandments, which I command thee; thou and thy son, and thy son's son, all the days of thy life: and that thy days may be prolonged." (vi. 1, 2.) Here again Moses requires perfect obedience to the whole law. He requires it of every individual of Israel. "Thou and thy son, and thy son's son;" and this universal obedience he exacts not at some stated period of the year, but every day of a man's whole life. "All the days of thy life." Moses leaves no room for some merits and some sins. If a man does what Moses requires, he can have no sins. If a man have any sins whatever, he does not fulfil what Moses requires as the condition of life. We might quote several other similar passages, but content ourselves with one, where Moses expressly declares that universal obedience is necessary to righteousness:—

וַיְצַוֵּנוּ ה׳ לַעֲשׂוֹת אֶת כָּל הַחֻקִּים הָאֵלֶּה לְיִרְאָה אֶת
ה׳ אֱלֹהֵינוּ לְטוֹב לָנוּ כָּל הַיָּמִים לְחַיֹּתֵנוּ כְּיוֹם הַזֶּה,
וּצְדָקָה תִּהְיֶה לָּנוּ כִּי נִשְׁמֹר לַעֲשׂוֹת אֶת כָּל הַמִּצְוָה
הַזֹּאת לִפְנֵי ה׳ אֱלֹהֵינוּ כַּאֲשֶׁר צִוָּנוּ:

"And the Lord commanded us to do ALL these statutes, to fear the Lord our God always, that he might preserve us alive, as it is at this day. *And it shall be our righteousness, if we observe to do* ALL *these commandments before the Lord our God, as he hath commanded us.*" (Deut. vi. 24, 25.) This is Moses' idea of righteousness, and if Moses be right the oral law is wrong. It says, "If a man's merits exceed his sins, he is righteous." Moses says, If a man keep all the commandments all the days of his life he is righteous. The oral law promises life to him who confessedly has sins. Moses requires perfect and universal obedience as the condition of life. It becomes, therefore, an important, an awfully important, consideration for every Israelite, whether he will rest his soul's salvation on the word of Moses, or on that of the oral law. If he rests upon the oral law, than he will be satisfied that a partial obedience is sufficient to secure everlasting salvation, and in this hope he will die. But if he is to be judged according to the law of Moses, he will, at the hour of God's judgment, find himself awfully mistaken. Moses knows of no righteousness, but that of universal obedience every day of a man's life, and promises life to none but those who have this righteousness. He that has it not, therefore, must be condemned. And let every Israelite mark well that Moses has not left us to draw this just conclusion from the premises which he has laid down, but has himself stated, in the distinctest and plainest terms, That he who does not yield this universal obedience is accursed. And that no man may mistake his meaning, he sums up all that he has said upon this subject, and repeats, that he who keeps ALL God's commandments shall be blessed, and that he who does not keep ALL God's commandments shall be accursed:—

והיה אם שמוע תשמע בקול ה׳ אלהיך לשמור
לעשות את כל מצותיו אשר אנכי מצוך היום ונתנך
ה׳ אלהיך עליון על כל גויי הארץ, ובאו עליך כל
הברכות האלה וגו׳ :

" And it shalt come to pass, if thou shalt hearken diligently unto the voice of the Lord thy God, to observe and to do ALL his commandments which I command thee this day, that the Lord thy God will set thee high above all nations of the earth; and all these blessings shall come on thee," &c. And then, after enumerating the blessings, he adds—

והיה אם לא תשמע בקול ה׳ אלהיך לשמור לעשות
את כל מצותיו וחקותיו אשר אנכי מצוך היום ובאו
עליך כל הקללות האלה והשיגוך, ארור אתה בעיר
וארור אתה בשדה וגו׳ :

" But it shall come to pass, if thou wilt not hearken unto the voice of the Lord thy God, to observe to do ALL his commandments and his statutes which I command thee this day, that all these curses shall come upon thee, and overtake thee. Cursed shalt thou be in the city, and cursed shalt thou be in the field," &c. (Deut. xxviii. 1—15.) Here Moses plainly says, that he who is perfectly obedient is blessed, and that he who is not perfectly obedient is cursed. And it is to be noted that Moses knows nothing of an intermediate state of man, the בינוניים

who are neither righteous nor wicked. He divides all Israel into two classes, the blessed and the cursed. He who keeps ALL God's commandments belongs to the former; he who does not keep ALL God's commandments to the latter. In this matter, then, the most important that can employ the mind of man, the oral law contradicts the plain words of Moses. One of the two is certainly in error. It is for the Israelites to choose whether they will believe Moses, or that oral law which contradicts his words. If they believe in Moses, then no one is accounted just before God, but that man who has all the days of his life kept all God's commandments without one deviation. Every other person is so far from being just, that he is accursed. If there were a human being who had all his life kept all the commandments, and only once been guilty of transgression, that one transgression makes him unjust and accursed. But there is no such person. Every man's conscience tells him that his sins far exceed his obedience, and therefore if Moses speak truth he is accursed. Oh, let no one endanger his salvation by trusting to the oral law. Let him take up the law of Moses, let him investigate the conditions which Moses lays down. We ask not now, that the Israelites should read the New Testament, or that they should listen to our arguments or any reasoning of man. We simply point out to them the words of Moses, and we show other passages of the oral law which teaches an entirely different doctrine. We ask, then, whether the man who rebels against the law of Moses can hope for salvation? Yet this is what every one who follows the oral law is doing. If his temporal welfare only were concerned, it would not be of such moment. But here his eternal interests are at stake. If the oral law be mistaken, and mistaken it is if Moses spoke truth, their eternal salvation is forfeited by every one who follows it. We therefore entreat every reader of this paper to take up the law of Moses, and to investigate this question:—
"What are the conditions of blessing and cursing, of life and death, according to the declarations of Moses? Does he promise life to that man whose merits exceed his sins, or does he require universal obedience?" To Moses himself we appeal, and him we constitute the arbiter of our differences.

No. XXXIII.

NEW YEAR, CONTINUED.

WE showed in our last number that the first axiom of the oral law respecting the mode of justification is false. Moses requires perfect and universal obedience to all the commandments as the condition of justification and life, whereas the oral law says it is sufficient if a man's merits exceed his sins. One of the two, then, has spoken falsehood. It is for the Jews to consider which of them they will brand with the character of liar. As for ourselves, we believe that Moses spoke the truth, and by his standard of right and wrong we proceed to examine the second and third principles of Rabbinic justification. The oral law tells us, further, that when God weighs the merits and the offences, "This weighing is made not with respect to the number of the merits and the sins, but according to their greatness. There is a merit which may outweigh many sins, as it is said, 'Because in him there is found some good thing.' (1 Kings xiv. 13.) And there are sins which may outweigh many merits, for it is said, 'One sinner destroyeth much good.' (Ecclesiast. ix. 18.)" And for this reason we are told that " In the ten days between the New Year and the Day of Atonement, Israel abounds in almsgiving and good works more than in all the year besides." Such is the hope which the oral law holds out to Israel. It first tells a man, that if his merits exceed his sins, he is safe. Then feeling that none but a fool or madman can dream of his merits exceeding his sins, it tries to quiet the conscience by assuring the guilty, that the quality of the deeds is regarded more than their number, and that there may be one meritorious act which will outweigh many sins. It endeavours to prove this by a citation from the Book of Kings. This is in itself suspicious. Why did it not bring one or more plain passages from the Books of Moses? They contain the law of God, and the great principles of God's judgment. In determining a case like this, an appeal to the letter of the law is absolutely necessary. Let every Israelite, then, before he trusts his salvation to the oral law, find out one passage in the law of Moses, where Moses himself declares that "one merit may outweigh many sins." We know not of one similar declaration, and therefore hesitate not to say, that whosoever rests his salvation on this hope, has apostatized from the religion of Moses.

But the passage itself, which the oral law cites, proves nothing in support of the above principle. The words were spoken of the son of Jeroboam. " He only of Jeroboam shall come to the grave, because in him there is found some good thing towards the Lord God of Israel in the house of Jeroboam." (1 Kings xiv. 13.) There is not one word said here about his being justified by that one good thing, whatever it was. It did not save the child from his sickness. It did not change the sentence of death into life. All it did was to procure him a peaceable burial. How, then, can any reasonable man argue, because the son of Jeroboam had a peaceable burial, that therefore some meritorious act will save him from the punishment due to his offences? To warrant such a conclusion, he ought first to show that the son of Jeroboam had been a grievous sinner like his father, which the Bible does not say; and, secondly, that this one meritorious act had obtained pardon of his sins, and restored him to life; and moreover it ought to be expressly said, that God considered him as just. The very circumstance that the rabbies were obliged to have recourse to such a passage, and that they could find nothing better in the law or the prophets, shows that they were hard pushed to find anything that would even bear a faint resemblance to their doctrine.

The law of Moses gives no countenance to this doctrine, and can give none, because it is directly subversive of all the principles of law and justice. The stern principle of justice is, that every transgression of the law should be followed by punishment without any reference whatever to the good deeds or merits of the transgressor. Even before an earthly tribunal, there is no deviation from this principle. If a murderer or a robber be convicted, no degree of previous or subsequent merit can be listened to as a plea against the just sentence of the law. He may in all other respects be an unexceptionable character, he may feed the poor and clothe the naked, and give all his goods in alms, but none of these things can change the sentence of guilty into not guilty, or cause him to be considered as a just or innocent person. And shall we suppose that God is less just than man? The law of Moses gives us no reason for such a supposition. It says distinctly—

ולא תקחו כופר לנפש רוצח אשר הוא רשע למות כי מות יומת:

"Moreover, ye shall take no satisfaction for the life of a murderer, which is guilty of death; but he shall surely be put to death." (Num. xxxv. 31.) According to this declaration, the good deeds or merits of a murderer are not to be regarded, and there is nothing which he can do which can avert the sentence of the law. And shall we suppose that God himself will do what he forbids men to do? If so, why did he forbid it to be done? The plain reason of this prohibition is, because it is contrary to the eternal principles of right and wrong, which God himself cannot violate without detracting from his holiness. But it is not with respect to murder only that God has laid down these stern principles of justice. He says generally—

והנפש אשר תעשה ביד רמה מן האזרח ומן הגר
את ה׳ הוא מגדף ונכרתה הנפש ההיא מקרב עמה,
כי דבר ה׳ בזה ואת מצותו הפר הכרת תכרת הנפש
ההיא עונה בה:

"But the soul that doeth ought presumptuously, whether he be born in the land, or a stranger, the same reproacheth the Lord, and that soul shall be cut off from among his people. Because he hath despised the Lord, and hath broken his commandment, that soul shall utterly be cut off; his iniquity shall be upon him." (Numb. xv. 30, 31.) There is here no promise that his merits shall be weighed against his offences. One presumptuous sin will outweigh all his supposed merits, and for that one he shall die in his iniquity. The doctrine of the prophets is just the same:—

הנפש החוטאת היא תמות:

"The soul that sinneth it shall die."

ובשוב צדיק מצדקתו ועשה עול ככל התועבות
אשר עשה הרשע יעשה וחי כל צדקתיו אשר עשה
לא תזכרנה במעלו אשר מעל ובחטאתו אשר חטא
בם ימות:

"But when the righteous turneth away from this righteousness, and committeth iniquity, and doeth according to all the abominations that the wicked man doeth, shall he live? *All his righteousness that he hath done shall not be mentioned:* in his trespass that he hath trespassed, and in his sin that he hath sinned, in them shall he die." (Ezek. xviii. 20—25.) When one reads this passage, it appears as if God had dictated it on purpose to contradict the doctrine of the oral law. There is here no mention of weighing merits against sins, and no promise that some few extraordinary merits may outweigh many sins. On the contrary, it is distinctly stated, that when the righteous man turneth away from his righteousness, "All his righteousness that he hath done shall not be mentioned." If this be true, the doctrine of the oral law is necessarily and totally false. But some one may object that there is a similar declaration made respecting the wicked:—

והרשע כי ישוב מכל חטאתיו אשר עשה ושמר את

כל חקותי ועשה משפט וצדקה חיה יחיה לא ימות, כל פשעיו אשר עשה לא יזכרו לו בצדקתו אשר עשה יחיה :

"But if the wicked man will turn from all his sins that he hath committed, and keep all my statutes, and do that which is lawful and right, he shall surely live, he shall not die. All his transgressions that he hath committed, they shall not be mentioned to him, in his righteousness that he hath done he shall live." But this verse is as strongly against the doctrine of the oral law as the others already cited. In the first place, it does not say, that he whose sins exceed his merits is wicked, but that he who commits sin is wicked. In the second place, it does not say that, by causing his merits to exceed his sins, he can become righteous, but by turning away, "from ALL his sins that he hath committed," and by keeping "ALL my statutes." It confirms the doctrine laid down already from the law of Moses, that to be righteous in the sight of God, a man must commit no sin, and keep all God's commandments. It therefore directly contradicts the oral law, and overturns the doctrine that some merits may outweigh many sins.

If more proof be needful, we have it in the case of Moses himself. Very few, if any, even of the most devoted friends of the oral law, can imagine that he has so many merits as Moses his master ; and yet the merits of Moses did not outweigh one apparently trifling transgression. Because of one sin, he was sentenced to die with the disobedient generation in the wilderness, and not permitted to enter into the land of Israel. If Moses' merits, then, could do nothing for him, how vain must be the hope of others, who think that, by abounding in almsgiving and good works for ten days, they can turn the scale of God's righteous judgment? Neither the law nor the prophets know of any intermediate class between the righteous and the wicked. They specify only the two classes, the righteous and the wicked. Those who fulfil all God's commandments belong to the one, and those who transgress any of God's commandments belong to the other. Let every man, then, examine his own heart and life, and it will not require much time nor trouble to ascertain to which class he belongs. A very little reflection will convince him that he has been, and is, a transgressor of God's commandments ; that he has no merits and no righteousness ; and therefore belongs to that class of whom Moses says, that they are accursed. Such a conclusion may appear dreadful, and so it ought to be; but the grand question is, Is it true? Let every man ask himself, "Have I kept, or do I keep, ALL God's commandments?" If he can say, Yes: then, according to the law of Moses, he is righteous, and has the promise of life. But if he must say,

No: then he is unrighteous, and the curse of God is hanging over him, ready to descend and destroy him :—

ארור אשר לא יקים את דברי התורה הזאת לעשות אותם ואמר כל העם אמן :

"Cursed be he that confirmeth not all the words of this law to do them. And all the people shall say, Amen." (Deut. xxvii. 26.) Moses holds out no hope, except to those who yield a perfect and universal obedience.

But some one will reply, if this be true, then no man can be accounted righteous, on account of his deeds :—

כי אדם אין צדיק בארץ אשר יעשה טוב ולא יחטא :

"For there is not a just man upon earth, that doeth good, and sinneth not." (Eccles. vii. 20.) And this is the truth, no man can be justified because of his good works. We must renounce all our pride, and appear at the bar of God as miserable sinners, looking only for mercy, and not for payment. We must come to the same conclusion as Job did—

אמנם ידעתי כי כן ומה יצדק אנוש עם אל , אם יחפוץ לריב עמו לא יעננו אחת מני אלף :

"I know it is so of a truth: but how should man be just with God? If he will contend with him, he cannot answer him one of a thousand." (Job ix. 2, 3.) Job had no idea that his merits exceeded his sins, but knew well that if God entered into judgment with him, he could not answer respecting even the thousandth part of his transgressions. David, the man after God's own heart, had the same conviction, and had therefore, no wish that his merits should be weighed with his sins. His prayer was—

אל תבוא במשפט את עבדך כי לא יצדק לפניך כל חי :

"Enter not into judgment with thy servant: for in thy sight shall no man living be justified." (Ps. cxliii. 2.) And when Daniel prayed, he did not venture to prefer his petitions on the score of merits, or to expect an answer as the reward of righteousness, but cast himself simply on the mercy of God:

כי לא על צדקותינו אנחנו מפילים תחנונינו לפניך כי על רחמיך הרבים :

"For we do not present our supplications before thee for our righteousnesses, but for thy great mercies." (Dan. ix.18.) How, then, can the modern Jews hope to stand at the tribunal of a heart-searching God, and not only escape condemnation, but obtain a reward because their merits exceed their sins? Are they more pure than Job, more holy than David, more righteous than Daniel? or were those three most holy men mistaken, or ignorant of the way of salvation? Certain it is that there must be some mistake somewhere. Either the rabbies were right, and then Job, David, and Daniel were mistaken, or these three men were right, and then the rabbies are fearfully and awfully mistaken. If the law requires perfect obedience, and denounces a curse against all disobedience, then the former were right in deprecating God's judgment, and casting themselves upon his mercy. But if the law requires only that a man's merits should exceed his sins, and says that all deficiencies can be made up by almsgiving and good works in the ten days between the New Year and the Day of Atonement, then they were wrong. Job was utterly mistaken when he said, "How should man be just with God?" for the rabbies say, Only be careful for the first ten days of the year, and you will be just and sealed unto life. David was utterly mistaken when he said, "In thy sight shall no man living be justified;" for the rabbies say that a man's merits may exceed his sins, and that such an one is just before God. Daniel was mistaken in not offering his prayers on the score of righteousness, but on the plea of mercy. But still, notwithstanding the certainty with which the rabbies speak, we would rather trust our own salvation to the word of Moses, of Ezekiel, of Job, David, and Daniel, than to that of the rabbies. We would rather kneel as supplicants, than claim the reward of our deeds with the rabbies.

But we cannot pass this subject without observing here also how the religion of the rabbies exhibits itself at every turn as a religion for the rich and the learned, rather than for the poor and laborious class of mankind. It teaches that almsgiving and good works, at a certain season of the year, will turn the wicked into righteous men, and transform the sinner into the saint. So the rich sinner puts his hand into his pocket, and lavishes his gold to the poor and needy, and buys what is wanting to make up his deficit of merit. The learned man sets to work at his books; for the oral law says:—

אין לך מצוה בכל המצוות כולן שהיא שקולה
כנגד תלמוד תורה, אלא תלמוד תורה, בנגד כל
המצוות כולן שהתלמוד מביא לידי מעשה לפיכך
התלמוד קודם למעשה בכל מקום :

"Amongst all the commandments, there is not one that is equivalent to the study of the law. Whereas the study of the law is equivalent to all the commandments : for study leads to practice. Therefore, study always goes before good deeds." (Hilchoth Talmud Torah.) The one with his money, therefore, and the other with his books, can effect a balance in his favour; but what is to become of the poor labouring classes, who have no money to buy righteousness, and no time for study, which is equivalent to all the other commandments? For them to turn the balance is impossible—they have not the means; and therefore, according to the oral law, they stand but a poor chance when the final account comes to be made up. This of itself would prove that the doctrine of the oral law cannot be true. God is a righteous judge, and he accepts no man's money and no man's learning. He takes no bribes, and will not wrest the judgment of the poor. The true mode, therefore, of appearing just before God, is some other than that pointed out by the oral law, and one according to which the poor sinner will stand on equal terms with his rich brother.

There is, however, another point to which we wish to direct attention. The oral law says, if a man's merits exceed his sins, he is just and sealed unto life; but if his sins exceed his merits, then he is sealed unto death: what then are we to think of all who die in each succeeding year? It is plain that they have not been sealed unto life, for then they could not have died. Then they were sealed unto death; then we must conclude that their sins exceed their merits; and as all die, then we must conclude, further, that all die in their sins—that their sins are more than their merits; and so, after all, this rabbinical doctrine comes to nothing. It tells a man that by having his merits greater than his sins, he is righteous, and will be sealed unto life; and yet, after all his almsgiving and good works, he dies like other men, and it turns out that he is not a just man, nor even one of the intermediate class, but one of the wicked. How can any rational man put his faith in such a system, which promises a great deal, but does not keep its promise? Above all, how can he trust his soul's everlasting welfare upon a promise which each successive year proves to be false? Many an one has passed into eternity already before the New Year, and of all such the oral law says they have died in their sins. Many more may pass into eternity between the New Year and the Day of Atonement. If the oral law be true, all such belong to the decidedly wicked who did not deserve the ten days' grace. Their friends and relations must, therefore, stamp their memory with the brand of the impenitently wicked, or if they entertain a hope that such persons have not died in their sins, they must declare of the oral law that it is false. If they would have a promise that will not and cannot deceive, let them take up the law and the prophets. The reader of this paper is still alive, but who can tell how soon his turn must come, and come it will, and that soon in every case. What consolation, then, will he have on his dying bed? Will he begin to balance his account of merit and sin? Alas! there is no use in that. If the oral law be true, it was balanced on the last Day of Atonement, and the sins were found to outweigh the merits, as his approaching death testifies. Where then will he flee for refuge or for consolation? In the agony and feebleness of a death-bed hour there is no time for doing good works, and poverty may cut off the rabbinic hope of purchasing salvation. In the oral law there is no hope. Can he find it, then, in the law of Moses? That law requires perfect and universal obedience, and pronounces the sinner accursed. As an accursed sinner, then, he must stand at the bar of God, unless there be some other way and some other hope. When Jacob was on his death-bed he had another hope. He could say—

לישועתך קויתי ה׳ :

"I have waited for thy salvation, O Lord." (Gen. xlix. 18.) Oh! let the reader seek this salvation in time, that when his last hour comes, he may be as calm, as happy, and as full of hope as his pious forefather. He died in a foreign land, but he died happy, trusting not in his own righteousness, but in the salvation of God. He had learned by experience that man cannot deliver himself from mere temporal trouble, but that even there God is his only refuge and his hope, and still more so in the hour of death and the day of judgment. But he had learned also to believe in המלאך הגואל the Angel who had redeemed him from all evil, and was persuaded that He would not forsake him in the great transition from time to eternity. He had not put off the consideration of salvation to the last. He could say, "I *have* waited for thy salvation, O Lord," and therefore when the awful moment arrived, he could in perfect tranquillity gather his children about him, and tell them of Shiloh who was to come, and of the salvation which he had expected.

No. XXXIV.

NEW YEAR, CONTINUED.

ALL who believe in Divine Revelation look forward to a great day, when the secrets of all hearts shall be revealed, and a righteous sentence pronounced upon all the sons of men. The most important thing in the world, then, for us to know is, the way of acceptance with God, at that solemn hour. And if men are bound as rational beings to examine the grounds of their opinions and belief on other subjects, they must be considered as altogether devoid of reason, who do not thoroughly examine and weigh the doctrines which have been taught them with regard to justification at the bar of God. A mistake on other subjects may be endured, but a mistake here is fatal and irreparable. What will be the horror of those who find that they have through their own want of consideration been trusting in a delusive hope, and have rejected, wilfully rejected, that way of acceptance which God has appointed. If there be any one point of difference between Jews and Christians, which requires profound and attentive consideration, it is this. We Christians believe that, on this all-important point, the oral law is utterly mistaken, and that all who trust their salvation to the hope which it holds out, will find themselves awfully mistaken if Moses and the prophets speak truth. We have endeavoured to show that the hope of justification by merits is contrary to the Word of God. But we shall now proceed to show that the oral law by this doctrine contradicts itself, and that therefore it is most unsafe to rest our salvation upon any of its assertions. In that law, which teaches that if a man's merits exceed his sins, he is justified, we also find the following parable, intended to explain God's dealings in the judgment of the New Year:—

משל למדינה שחייבת מס למלך ולא נתנה לו בא
אליה בחיל לגבותו, כשנתקרב אליה בי׳ פרסאות
יצאו גדולי המדינה לקראתו ואמרו לו אין לנו מה
ליתן לך הניח להם שליש, כיון שנתקרב יותר יצאו
בינוני העיר לקראתו הניח להם שליש השני, כשנתקרב
יותר יצאו כל בני העיר לקראתו הניח להם הכל,
כך המלך זה הקב״ה, בני המדינה אלו ישראל
שמסנלין עוונות כל השנה ערב ראש השנה הגדולים
מתענין ומוותר להם שליש עוונותיהם, בי׳ ימים
בינונים מתענין ומוותר להם שני שלישים, ביום
הכפורים הכל מתענין ומוותר להם הכל:

"A parable. There was a certain city, which owed tribute to the king, but did not pay it, whereupon he came upon it with an army to collect it. When he came within ten leagues of it, the great men of the city went forth to meet him, and said to him, We have nothing wherewith to pay thee, so he forgave them one-third. When he approached nearer still, the middle classes of the city went forth to meet him, and he forgave them a second-third. When he approached still nearer, all the population of the city went forth to meet him, and he forgave them all. The King here is the Holy One, blessed be He. The inhabitants of the city are Israel, who accumulate sins all the year. On the eve of the New Year, the great men fast, and one-third of their sins is remitted to them. In the ten days, the intermediate class fast, and two-thirds are remitted. On the Day of Atonement all fast, and all is remitted to them." (Orach Chaiim, 581.) Now this representation is quite at variance with the doctrine that those are justified whose merits exceed their sins. This parable, in the first place, represents all as in debt, and secondly, that they have nothing to pay, and thirdly, that the King forgives them freely and for nothing. Now this statement is directly contrary to the notion of merit. If a man has more merits than sins, and is on that score accounted just, he cannot be said to be in debt, and he needs no remission. But if it be true of the great men as well as the middle class, that they are in debt and have nothing wherewith to pay, then it is certain that they have no merits, and cannot be considered as just, but as sinners. Merit and forgiveness are as essentially opposed as payment and debt. The man who has paid his creditor all his demands can have no debt, and so the man who has kept God's commands so as to have merit, needs not forgiveness. But he who has nothing to pay, that is, he who has no merits, must either be condemned, or he must have a free forgiveness of all; and this the parable says is the case of Israel. They have nothing to pay, and God forgives them all. Merit is therefore altogether out of the question, and if this statement be true, then the doctrine of justification by merits is false, and therefore the oral law contradicts itself. How then can the Israelite trust his everlasting welfare to a system at variance with itself?

The prayers for the New Year are equally decisive against the doctrine of justification by merits. Out of many passages which deny the existence of merit, and asserts the necessity of a free forgiveness, we cite the following:—

קהלות ורבבות ואלפים , אשר לפנינו עברו חלופים ,
ולא יכלו להצטדק היות חפים , הן שמים בעיניו לא
זכו , וכל לניוני שחק כפשתה דועכו , ונתעב ונאלח
מה יזכו , קובץ מרמה ומסתתר בעיניו , אם יאמר
בלבו מי יעידני לפניו , קורותיו ורהיטיו ועציו ואבניו ,
טהור עינים ברע מראות , הצלל חטאינו בעמקי
מחבואות , ועשה עמנו לטובה אות :

"Thousands and ten thousands of congregations, which have persecuted us and are vanished, were not able to justify themselves in purity. Lo! the heavens are not pure in his sight, and all the heavenly angels are as beaten flax: how then can he that is filthy and abominable be pure? He gathereth riches by deceit; and working in secret, he says in his heart, Who can bear witness against me before him? Even the beams, rafters, planks, and stones of his house. O Thou who art too pure of sight to view evil, sink our sins in the deepest recesses, and work the good sign for us." (Prayers for the New Year, p. 149.) Here is an express acknowledgment that the congregations of old could not justify themselves by merit, an assertion in the words of the Psalm, that all men are filthy and abominable, and a prayer, not for payment of deserts, but for forgiveness of sins. If this prayer contain the sentiments of truth, and be offered in sincerity, then Israel has no merits, and the doctrine, that any man is justified by the superabundance of his merits, is a mere fiction. The man who will venture to offer this prayer, and yet hope to be saved by his good deeds, is a hypocrite, or is not right in his mind. Here again, then, the oral law is inconsistent with itself: for here it places the hope of salvation not in merit, but in the free and undeserved mercy of God. It is the duty of every Israelite, therefore, to ascertain which of the two ways is in accordance with the declaration of Moses and the prophets. It is impossible that they should both be true. The fact appears to be, that the authors of the oral law, like all other men, loved the honour and glory of personal righteousness, and hoped that all those deeds, and fasts, and almsgiving, which were so lovely in their own eyes, and gained them so much credit amongst men, would also be duly acknowledged at the bar of God's judgment. At the same time their conscience was continually awakened and terrified by the plain declarations of the Word of God, and therefore, to quiet their conscience, they were driven even against their wills to acknowledge their guilt, and to seek for a quietus. This they partly found in the hope of free mercy, but partly in inventions of their own. They placed no small dependence upon fasting and almsgiving, but their troubled conscience was not satisfied with these, and they have therefore fled for refuge to observances the most trivial, and hopes the most childish. By blowing the horn the whole month of Elul, they hope to deceive Satan, so that he may not know which is the first day of the new year, and may not be able to accuse them :—

לכן התקינו חז״ל שיהיו תוקעין בר״ח אלול בכל שנה ושנה וכל החודש כדי להזהיר את ישראל שיעשו

תשובה שנאמר אם יתקע בשופר וגו' וכדי לערבב
השטן :

"Therefore our wise men of blessed memory have ordained that the horn should be blown on the first day of the month of Elul every year, and during the whole month, to warn Israel to repent, as it is said, 'Shall a trumpet be blown in the city, and the people not be afraid?' (Amos iii. 6), and also to confuse Satan." How can any man of understanding believe that a law teaching such absurdity is from God? We are told in Zechariah and Job, that Satan does accuse the people of God: but how can any one, who has been taught by the Word of God, imagine that Satan is to be deceived by blowing the horn at a wrong time, or that even if he did not accuse at all, that God is ignorant of man's sins, or that he will judge unjustly unless he is reminded by Satan? In accusing sinners, Satan gratifies his own malignity, but his accusation is not wanted at the bar of God to convict man of sin. When men appear there they will be seen as they are. All their transgressions will be as visible as is now their bodily presence. The eye of God will penetrate every secret recess of the soul, and the conscience itself will testify and condemn the impenitent. It is therefore most absurd and irrational to hope to escape by confounding the accuser; and it is to us serious matter of astonishment how such an absurdity could have been tolerated for so many centuries, and how a people of such intellect as the Jews confessedly are, should remain the disciples of such senseless superstition.

But the rabbies expect not only to confound Satan by blowing the horn at the wrong time, but to obtain God's mercy by blowing it at the right time. Thus we are told in Vaijikra Rabbah—

בשעה שישראל נוטלין את שופריהן ותוקעין לפני
הקב"ה עומד מכסא הדין ויושב בכסא רחמים דכתיב
ה' בקול שופר ומתמלא עליהם רחמים ומרחם עליהם
והופך עליהם מדת הדין לרחמים אימתי בחודש
השביעי :

"At the hour in which Israel take their horns, and sound before the Holy One, blessed be He, He rises from the throne of judgment and sits on the throne of mercy, as it is written, 'The Lord with the sound of the trumpet' (Ps. xlvii. 5); and he is filled with mercy towards them, and has pity upon them, and changes the attribute of judgment which was against them into mercy. When does this happen? In the seventh month." (Vaijikra Rabbah, sect. 29.) This then is one of

NEW YEAR CONTINUED. 267

the means whereby the rabbies try to quiet a guilty conscience. If true, it would no doubt be very convenient for a man who has spent the year in iniquity, and who has not repented, and does not intend to repent, to get rid of all his sins by blowing a horn on the new year, and thus turning God's wrath into mercy. But it is a statement altogether opposed to the Word of God, and derogatory to his character for mercy and for justice. No mere ceremonial act can atone for sin, neither does God need the blowing of a horn to remind him of mercy. To suppose, that such a miserable ceremony can stop God in his course of justice, and make him reverse his determinations, is to deprive him of all the attributes of Deity, and to represent him as exceeding in imbecility the weakest of all the sons of men that ever occupied the judgment-seat. And yet this most absurd and unscriptural hope is not merely a rabbinic legend, or an allegory, but is in the prayers of the synagogue gravely inserted as a devout petition :—

תחנה לתוקע לפני התקיעה , יהי רצון מלפניך יי
אלהי ואלהי אבותי אלהי השמים ואלהי הארץ אלהי
אברהם אלהי יצחק ואלהי יעקב האל הגדול הגבור
והנורא שתשלח לי המלאכים הקדושים והטהורים
נאמנים משרתים ונאמנים בשליחותם חפצים ורוצים
לזכות את ישראל ואת המלאך הגדול פצפציה הממונה
להוציא זכיותיהן של ישראל בעת שהם תוקעין בשופר
ואת המלאך הגדול תשבש הממונה להשמיע זכיותיהן
של ישראל ולהבעית השטן בתקיעתם ואת השרים
הגדולים הממונים על השופר אנקתם פסתם ומלאכים
הגדולים הדרניאל וסנדלפון הממונים על תקיעתנו
המעלים תקיעתנו לפני כסא כבודך ואת המלאך
שמשיאל הממונה על התרועה ואת המלאך פרסטא
הממונה על קשר״ק להיותם מזומנים בשליחותם
להעלות תקיעתנו לפני הפרוכת ולפני כסא כבודך
והמלא על עמך ישראל ברחמים ותכנס להם לפנים
משורת הדין ותתנהג עם בניך במדת רחמים ותעלה
תקיעתנו לפני כסא כבודך וכו' :

The following prayer is said by the person who sounds the cornet, before he begins:—"May it be acceptable in thy presence, O Lord, my God, and the God of my fathers, the God of heaven, and the God of the earth; the God of Abraham, the God of Isaac, and the God of Jacob; the great God, mighty and tremendous; to send me the holy and pure angels, who are faithful ministers, and faithful in their message; and who are desirous and willing to justify Israel; and also the great angel Patzpatziah, who is appointed to present the merits of Israel, when they sound the cornet this day; and likewise the great angel Tashbach, who is appointed to declare the merits of Israel, and confound Satan with their sound of the cornet; and the great princes, who are appointed over the cornet, Enkatham and Pastam, and the great angels, Hadarniel and Sandalphon, who are appointed over our sounding, who introduce our sounding before the throne of thy glory; and also the angel Shamshiel, who is appointed over the joyful sound; and the angel Prasta, who is appointed to superintend קש״רק that they may all be expeditious in their errand; to introduce our soundings before the veil, and before the throne of thy glory; and mayest thou be filled with mercy over thy people Israel; and lead us within the temperate line of strict justice; and conduct thyself towards thy children, with the attribute of mercy, and suffer our soundings to ascend before the throne of thy glory." (Prayers for the New Year, p. 81.) Here, then, we have, in the language of solemn prayer, the very same monstrous doctrine, that the sounding of the cornet on the new year can change God's determinations; and we have it in even a more objectionable form, for it is connected with other most unscriptural superstitions. This prayer asserts what is nowhere found in Holy Scripture, that there is a certain number of angels whose express office it is to superintend the blowing of the horn, and to bear the soundings thereof before the throne of God, and at the same time to advocate their merits. In the first place, this is a pure invention, and a fond superstition. In the Word of God, not one word is mentioned of anything of the kind. We should be sorry to treat any religious tenet of any people, but especially of the Jews, with ridicule, but we cannot help asking the good sense of every reader, whether the representation here given is not in the highest degree ridiculous? The angels are to be sent down from heaven. For what purpose? Is it to warn men of the impending wrath of God, or to announce the coming redemption of Israel, or to execute God's judgments? No, but to attend to the blowing of a ram's horn, and to carry up the sounds before the throne of God, that they may turn his attribute of judgment into that of mercy. Is it necessary, then, for the angels to interfere in this matter? cannot God hear the sounding of the cornet, unless it be conveyed to him by angels? or do the movings of his compassion depend upon the blowing of a cornet? What would Elijah have said to such doctrine as this? When the priests of Baal only cried aloud, he mocked them, and said, " Cry aloud, for he is a God; either he is talking, or he is pursuing, or he is on a journey, or peradventure he sleepeth, and must be awaked." (1 Kings xviii. 27.) And yet the priests of Baal were not sounding a cornet, that they might rouse their pretended Deity to compassion. If we had not read this prayer with our own eyes, we could scarcely have believed that even Rabbinism itself could have fallen into such manifest absurdity. But the subject is far too grave to be treated with levity. Upon this absurdity, the rabbies teach Israel to rest their hope of salvation. Conscious that the hope of justification by merit is fallacious, and yet unwilling to give up what is so palatable to the pride of man, they seek about to find something that will compensate for the deficiency, and in the eagerness of desperation grasp at any thing. The trivial ceremony of blowing the cornet was therefore turned into a mystery, and a suitable apparatus of angels invented to meet the apprehensions of the superstitious and unenlightened, and in some degree to take off the apparent irrationality of believing that an act so insignificant should effect a change so great in the purposes of the Almighty. But whatever was the motive or the origin of this fable, there it now stands in the prayers of the synagogue, to lead the ignorant away from the true means of justification, and the true ideas of God's justice and God's judgment. Let no man say it is an innocent error. No error is innocent. Error in every form is pernicious; in religion it is deadly. And the most mischievous of all religious errors are those which confirm men in the idea, that external ceremonies will atone for moral delinquencies; and this is precisely the tendency of the fable here noticed. An ignorant and superstitious man, and there are many such in every religion, finds in his Prayer-book that the blowing of the cornet can change the attribute of judgment into the attribute of mercy: he believes it to be true, not only because of the book where he finds it, but because every man is glad to hear of a way of acceptance, which will save the trouble of repentance and thorough change of heart and life. He therefore perseveres through the year in the practice of those things which his heart condemns, trusting that the blowing of the cornet will set all straight, and thus he goes on from year to year until death overtakes him hardened and impenitent, and he finds too late at the bar of God, that he has been in fatal error. Upon whom then will the guilt of such person's destruction be charged? Not only upon those who invented the falsehood, but on those also who sanction it, who leave it in the Prayer-book, and thus practically teach the people superstition. Every Jew who attends the worship of the synagogue is responsible in his station and calling, for the error and falsehood which its prayers propagate amongst the people. But at all events every person who disbelieves this story of the angels carrying up the sounding of the cornet, must grant that a system teaching such a method of salvation is very unsafe; and that, as it grossly errs in this one article it is suspicious in all. But besides the absurdity of this doctrine, we must notice its inconsistency. The Prayer-book states that the blowing of the cornet is necessary to the procuring of pardon; it therefore implies that pardon is necessary, and therefore that Israel is guilty; what, then, becomes of merits? If Israel can be justified by merits, the blowing of the cornet is superfluous; for, in that case, all they want is justice. Where a man can claim salvation because of all his good deeds, he need not fear the attribute of righteousness, הדין מדת, and does not want the attribute of mercy. But the moment that he acknowledges his need of forgiveness, he confesses that he has no merits. If, therefore, the Prayer-book be right in acknowledging sin and praying for pardon, the oral law is wrong in teaching justification by merits. One contradicts the other, and therefore they cannot both be from God; and the man who believes both is guilty of renouncing his reason. But the man who trusts his salvation to a system so inconsistent with itself, is utterly devoid of wisdom. He is hazarding his eternal welfare on the testimony of a witness who contradicts himself; who says at one time, that a man can be saved by his merits, and at another time that he has no merits that can stand the scrutiny of God's righteous judgment.

No. XXXV.

JUSTIFICATION.

THE doctrine of justification by merits is agreeable, and seems very reasonable, so long as a man can theorize, that is, so long as he is not in earnest. But so soon as the prospect of death, or any other similar circumstance, compels him to realize the act of Divine judgment upon himself, it loses all its beauty and plausibility; the conscience is unsatisfied by its consolations, and reason pronounces that the hope built on merits is insecure. A solemn and earnest review of our past years soon convinces, that our good deeds are but few, that our best deeds are defiled by mixed motives; and, above all, that the love of God has not been the heart's dominant principle, and that, therefore, some other mode of justification is absolutely necessary. The truth of this statement is confirmed by the inconsistency of the oral law with itself. The great principle of the oral law is, that the observance of any one of its commands, purchases a certain quantity of merit, and that an accumulation of these merits will, at last, constitute a sufficiency; but when the solemn season of the New Year and the Day of Atonement arrives, this sufficiency is found to be insufficient, and the alarmed conscience eagerly looks round to find something, that may compensate for the deficiency of merit. We have already noticed some of the rabbinic inventions for this purpose, and now proceed to consider another, and that is, *the merit of their progenitors*. One of the main props of rabbinic hope is the righteousness of their forefathers, as may be seen almost on every page of the Jewish Prayer-book, and as is apparent in the following extracts:—

קשת רוח אשר הועקרה׃ רופאה לקץ תשעים כנתבקרה׃ שלחה פארות ולא שקרה׃ תפן בנצרים אשר חוללו כהיום׃ ושלש עקרות שהפקדו בזה יום׃ תצדיק בצדקתם מיחליך איום:

"She who was sorrowful when barren, was made to rejoice with good tidings when ninety years of age; she then sent forth shoots that failed not. Regard the merit of your ancestors who were born on this day, and the three barren ones, who were visited on this day: justify, through their righteousness, those who hope in thee, O Thou, who art tremendous." (Levi's Prayer for the New Year, p. 61.)

And again—

את חיל יום פקודה׃ באימיו כל לחום לשקדה׃ גשים בו ברך ליקודה׃ דעם לישר כעל מוקדה׃ היוצר יחד כסל נשפט׃ ושוע ודל בפלוס יושפט׃ זכר לא יעשה משפט׃ חין ערכו יזכר במשפט׃ טרם כל מפעל חצב׃ יום במחשבת צור חוצב׃ כאחור וקדם בתוך נחצב׃ ליהב עליו כל המחצב׃ מנתו כהיום כח דושנה׃ נצר להחנוט לתשעים שנה׃ סוימה אות חיות לשושנה׃ עבור לפניו בזה ראש השנה׃ פולצו פרחיה בזה יום׃ צגהם פני כס איום׃ קול דבובם ירחישו כהיום׃ רוגשים להריע למצוא פדיום׃ שעונים עליה בח לחפקדה׃ שואגים בלהק דלהות לשקדה׃ תמוכים בדשן שה עקידה׃ תשר אשר בו נפקדה:

"The fearful day of visitation is come, its dread goads all flesh; they present themselves with bended knees; O may their repentance be accounted as a burnt-offering. Thou who hast formed them judgest all their thoughts: the rich and poor are all weighed in the balance; *remember the merit of him* who said, 'Shall he not do justice?' O, remember the tenor of his prayer in judgment. Ere ought was created didst thou purpose to ordain him the rock from whence the nation was to spring; he was as the centre, the support of all creatures. His wife was on this day endued with youth, to cause the branch to put forth at ninety years of age; she was appointed as a sign to those who are likened to the rose, who are to pass before thee in judgment on this New Year's-day. Her posterity tremble this day; when they stand before thy terrible throne; they utter the voice of prayer this day; they assemble to sound the cornet, that they may obtain redemption. *They depend on her merit* to be visited like her; their assemblies cry aloud and hasten to enter into thy doors. They depend on the ashes of him who was bound as a lamb,* with whom she was visited in the month Tishri." (Ibid., p. 57.) The offering of Isaac is regarded as particularly meritorious, and constantly urged as a plea for merit. Thus—

והסתכל באפרו של יצחק הצבור על גבי המזבח
וזכור לנו עקדתו היום לזרעו של יצחק:

"Attentively view the ashes of Isaac, heaped upon the altar;† and remember this day unto his seed, his being bound on the altar." (Ibid., p. 81.) And again—

סמוכים בצדקת אב היה אחד, נשענים בסבך יחיד
ומיוחד, מובטחים בתם וביושר אב אחד:

"They depend on the righteousness of the first patriarch, and rest on the merit of the only peculiar Son, and are secure in the perfection and rectitude of the father of the nation." (Ibid., p. 105.)

These passages show plainly that, after all, the rabbies felt their own doctrine of justification by merits very unsafe ground on which to build their hope of salvation; and that they were glad to flee to merits more adequate, which they hoped to find in the righteousness of their ancestors. The modern Jews, who still adopt these prayers, profess to entertain the same hope, and we therefore proceed to inquire, whether it be built on a better foundation than that which they are compelled to relinquish. We think that it is not; for, in the first place, the saints of old, Abraham, Isaac, and Jacob, though we revere them as pious and holy men, were after all only sinful men like ourselves. They did not, and could not, save themselves by their own righteousness, and if they did not save themselves, it is folly to think that they can save us.

---

* Isaac.
† "Alluding to Isaac's being bound; and thus considered as if he had been offered, and his body burnt to ashes on the altar." (Levi's note.)

Abraham, though by the grace of God, the father of the faithful, was yet in himself so weak in faith, and so distrustful in the goodness and mercy of God, as to endeavour to save himself from the Egyptians by means of a deliberate falsehood. Sarah had so little faith as to laugh within herself at the promise of God, and then to defend herself by a lie. Isaac was guilty of similar conduct, and Jacob's sin in deceiving his brother plainly shows, that he also was a poor sinful creature. Where then are their superabundant merits, whereby they are to justify all their posterity? The Word of God says expressly,—

אח לא פדה יפדה איש לא יתן לאלהים כפרו :

"No man can by any means redeem his brother, nor give to God a ransom for him." (Ps. xlix. 8.) How then are these three men to redeem all their posterity? If they have got merits sufficient to compensate for the unrighteousness of their children, then they have a ransom; and then the Word of God, which says that no man has a ransom, is not true. But if the words of the Psalm be true,—and he is no Jew who thinks them false,—then the patriarchs have no superabundant merits, and no ransom to offer for their children, and then the hope built on their righteousness is deceitful, and those that lean on it will find themselves mistaken in the hour of judgment. Nay, more, they will find themselves accursed for departing from the Lord. He that trusts in the righteousness of Abraham, Isaac, and Jacob, to deliver him from the wrath to come, is evidently trusting in man, and making flesh his arm. If the merits of the patriarchs can save their children from the wrath of God, then God is not the Saviour of Israel, but the patriarchs are Israel's redeemers, and poor mortal men are their hope and their trust: but the Prophet says,—

ארור הגבר אשר יבטח באדם ושם בשר זרועו ומן ה׳ יסור לבו :

"Cursed be the man that trusteth in man, and maketh flesh his arm, and whose heart departeth from the Lord." (Jer. xvii. 5.) So far, then, from being secure by trusting in the righteousness of Abraham, Isaac, and Jacob, this trust increases the sinner's guilt, and draws down upon him a double curse. But it has pleased God himself to argue this question at large with the Jews, to suppose the case of a righteous father who has an unrighteous son, and to declare that the son cannot be saved by the righteousness of the father. In the Prophet Ezekiel, God says, "If a man be just, and do that which is lawful and right——he is just, he shall surely live, saith the Lord God. If he beget a son that is a robber, a shedder of blood, and that doeth the like to any of these things, and that doeth not any of those duties, but even hath eaten upon the mountains, and defileth his neighbour's wife, hath oppressed the poor and needy, hath spoiled by violence, hath not restored the pledge, and hath lifted up his eyes to the idols, hath committed abomination, hath given forth upon usury, and hath taken increase: shall he then live? he shall not live: he hath done all these abominations: he shall surely die; his blood shall be upon him." (Ezek. xviii. 5—13.) Here God sets the matter at rest, and decides that the righteousness of a father is of no use to an unrighteous son, and cannot deliver him from the punishment due to his evil deeds. The doctrine, then, of justification by the merits of ancestors, is directly opposed to the plain declaration of God himself, and, therefore, in this case also the Jewish prayers and the oral law teach error, and seduce the Jews to their everlasting destruction, by teaching them to trust in that which can do them no good. It is an awful and melancholy spectacle to see God's ancient people thus misled. At this season of the year, the devout amongst them endeavour to turn to God, fast and pray, and yet neither the one nor the other is accepted, because they put their trust in the merits of men, and their heart is turned away from God their Saviour. The prayers of the synagogue, instead of drawing down a blessing, only help to accumulate wrath, by seducing them from the Redeemer of Israel to refuges of lies. And hence it happens that all the fasts and the prayers of Israel for these seventeen centuries have been disregarded by God, and that Israel still continues in captivity. But as every lie and every error is built upon some truth as its foundation, it will be well to inquire what truth it was that gave rise to this error of justification by the merits of ancestors? The principle is *that the guilty may be saved by the merits of another person, who is righteous:* how, then, did this principle become current among the Jews? It was certainly not the invention of human reason, for reason can discover no necessary connexion between the merits of one righteous man and the pardon of another who is guilty. The principle does not hold in the ordinary judicial proceedings of this world: a robber or a murderer is not and cannot be pardoned because another member of the community, or of his family, is a good and righteous man. We must therefore look elsewhere for the origin of the principle, and we find it in the revealed will of God. We see it in the appointment of sacrifice and atonement, according to which a guilty man was pardoned by the suffering of an innocent animal. Here is at once the principle of substitution of the innocent for the guilty; and human reason, when it once has the substratum, can easily proceed to erect the superstructure. In the present case it naturally argued, if the death of one of the brute creation could effect so much, how much more would the merits of a righteous man avail, if such an one could be found? The error, then, is not in the principle, but in its application. According to the Scripture, it is true that the innocent may be substituted for the guilty; but the rabbies were wrong in applying this truth to the case of Abraham, Isaac, Jacob, and other men, who were only sinners as themselves. The Word of God, which gave the principle, also directs us to the right application. It tells us of one for whose righteousness' sake the Lord will forgive sin:—

ה׳ חפץ למען צדקו יגדיל תורה ויאדיר:

"The Lord is well pleased for his righteousness' sake; he will magnify the law and make it honourable." (Isa. xlii. 21.) Who, then, is this person? The preceding verses tell us that it is the servant of the Lord. Who, then, is the servant of the Lord? Kimchi says, on this verse, that the servant of the Lord is the prophet; but this cannot possibly be true, for the prophet was not righteous, but a sinner, as he himself tells us in the sixth chapter—" I am a man of unclean lips." The servant mentioned in the nineteenth verse is the same person as he who is called "My servant," in the first verse of the chapter—" Behold my servant, whom I uphold, mine elect, in whom my soul delighteth: I have put my spirit upon him: he shall bring forth judgment to the Gentiles." But here Kimchi says,—

זה הוא מלך המשיח כמו שפירשנו:

"This is the King Messiah, as we have interpreted." If then, in the first verse, "The servant of the Lord" means the Messiah, it must mean the same through the chapter, and the Messiah is the person for whose righteousness' sake the Lord is well pleased.

This same prophet tells us again, concerning this servant,—

בדעתו יצדיק צדיק עבדי לרבים ועונותם הוא יסבול:

"By his knowledge shall my righteous servant justify many; for he shall bear their iniquities." (Isa. liii. 11.) That the Messiah is here intended no Jew can doubt, who uses the Synagogue Prayers; for on the Day of Atonement and at the Passover, this chapter is applied to him.* Here, then, it is expressly stated, that the Messiah, by his righteousness, shall justify the guilty. And, therefore, the prophet calls the Messiah יהוה צדקנו "THE LORD OUR RIGHTEOUSNESS." (Jer. xxiii. 6.) That the Messiah is here intended there can

* See the Machsor for the Day of Atonement, in אאן מלשני בראשית, and for the Passover, in ברח דודי.

be no doubt, for he is described as "the righteous branch" of David, and thus all the commentators explain it. In these three passages, then, of the Word of God, sinners are pointed to the Messiah as their hope and their righteousness. He is God's righteous servant, and his sufferings and his merits are all-sufficient to do that which Abraham, Isaac, and Jacob cannot do. The great mistake of the oral law is to point to wrong persons, who have no righteousness, and almost totally to pass by Him whom God hath set forth as the hope of sinners. But it may here be asked, if Messiah be a man, how can he have merits more than Abraham, or any other of the children of Adam? The answer is, that though very man, he is not a sinful man as we are, neither is he a mere man. If he were a man like us, he could have no merits, and therefore could not justify us any more than we could justify him. The declaration, therefore, that he is the Lord's righteous servant, and that he is appointed for the justification of sinners, necessarily implies that he is more than a man, and the title given him by the Prophet Jeremiah puts this beyond doubt. Jeremiah calls him by the incommunicable name of God יהוה, concerning which God himself says:—

אני יהוה הוא שמי וכבודי לאחר לא אתן :

"I am the LORD: that is my name, and my glory will I not give to another." (Isa. xlii. 8.) If then יהוה be the name of God, then that Being who is called by that holy name must be God. Some of the modern rabbies reply, that this holy name is also given to the city of Jerusalem, both by Jeremiah and Ezekiel. But even if we admit this, still this is no answer to our argument. There is no fear that a city which, however great or noble, is only a mass of stones and mortar, should be mistaken for the living God, the Creator of the Universe. When, therefore, the name of God is attributed to the city, God's honour is not given to it. But when we are told of the Messiah, first that he is righteous, secondly that his righteousness is so great as to justify the guilty, and lastly that his name is יהוה, "THE LORD our Righteousness;" that is when we see that the attributes and the name of God are attributed to him, then we must conclude either that he is God, or that God has done what he has declared that he would not do, and given his honour to another. Righteousness is the attribute of God alone, and so Daniel says:—

לך ח' הצדקה ולנו בושת הפנים כיום הזה :

"O Lord, righteousness belongeth unto thee, but unto us confusion of faces, as at this day." (Dan. ix. 7.) But, in the above passages, righteousness is said to belong to the Messiah, and that in such an immeasurable degree as to be sufficient to justify the guilty sons of men; if then he have this attribute of God, he must also have the nature of God. Again, another prophet says, that of God men will say that they have righteousness in him:—

אך בה׳ לי אמר צדקות ועוז :

"Surely shall one say, in the Lord have I righteousness and strength." (Isa. xlv. 24.) And again:—

בה׳ יצדקו ויתהללו כל זרע ישראל :

"In the LORD shall all the seed of Israel be justified, and shall glory." Here it is said that God is our righteousness, and that in Him we shall be justified; but in the passages quoted above, it is said that the Messiah is our Righteousness, and that in Him we shall be justified; the person then intended in these different passages must be one and identical. Thus the difficulties are all removed, and we have one in whose righteousness we may safely trust, without making ourselves liable to the curse denounced against those who put their trust in sinful men. This is the Christian's hope. Many Jews think, and speak, and argue too, as if Christians had departed from the living God and put their trust in a man; but that of which they accuse us, they have done themselves. We have not departed from the living God. Our hope and trust and confidence is in יהוה צדקנו, The LORD our Righteousness. You have departed from the Lord, for in your prayers you say that your hope and trust is in the merits of sinful men. Our confidence is based upon the Word of God, and your hope is taught you by the rabbies, who are fallible men. Your doctrine is the doctrine of men, and your hope is in the merits of men. You have, therefore, doubly departed from God, both from his word and his righteousness. Our desire is that you would return to Him, not to us,—to his word, and not to ours. You have no merits more than we have. Your forefathers have no more than either of us, and the blowing of a ram's horn is but a poor foundation on which to build our hope of salvation; and yet these are the things on which your rabbies have taught you to depend. Examine your prayers, and compare them with the Word of God, and you will find, that as long as the Jewish nation continues to offer such petitions, their cry cannot be heard; and that if they wish for salvation, they must forsake their arm of flesh, and return to Him who was the hope of their fathers.

It was not by his own merits, nor the merits of his forefathers, nor by any ceremonial observance, that Abraham was justified, but by faith in the LORD, יהוה, as it is written:—

והאמין בה׳ ויחשבה לו צדקה :

"And he believed in the LORD, and it was counted to him for righteousness." (Gen. xv. 6.) David the King did not expect to be forgiven and justified on account of Abraham's or his other ancestors' merits; neither did he say, Blessed is the man who puts his trust in the righteousness of the patriarchs, but—

אשרי נשוי פשע כסוי חטאה , אשרי אדם לא יחשב ה' לו עון ואין ברוחו רמיה :

"Blessed is he whose transgression is forgiven, whose sin is covered. Blessed is the man unto whom the LORD imputeth not iniquity, and in whose spirit there is no guile." (Ps. xxxii. 1.) Every one, then, who desires to have this blessing, must renounce all pretensions to merit, and acknowledge himself a sinner needing forgiveness; and for this forgiveness he must look not to anything that man has done, or can do, but to the mercy of God in passing by transgression and sin. And therefore the Prophet Habakkuk lays it down as a general rule—

וצדיק באמונתו יחיה :

"The just shall live by his faith." (Habak. ii. 4.) This is the Scriptural mode of justification, and this the hope of Abraham, David, and Habakkuk. Will the Jews, then, cast in their lot with their father Abraham, and trust to that way of justification in which he walked? or will they refuse to be justified as he was, and still persist in following the inventions of men, which are not even consistent with themselves? If the oral law pointed out one way of justification, and then consistently adhered to it, there would at least be an appearance of reason in following its directions. But it points out two ways as opposite as east and west. It says a man may be justified by his own merits, and then it tells him he is to be justified by the merits of another. Both cannot possibly be true. It is the duty, then, of every man earnestly to inquire which is the true way of Salvation, and to decide, whether he is to be saved by his own merits, or the merits of his forefathers, or the merits of "THE LORD OUR RIGHTEOUSNESS."

No. XXXVI.

DAY OF ATONEMENT.

THE law and the prophets both abound with plain declarations entirely subversive of the rabbinic doctrine of human merit. But it has pleased God, besides these plain and repeated declarations, to ordain a public and solemn act to instruct even the most ignorant, and to convince the most obstinate, that by human merit there is no salvation. He commanded that, once every year, an atonement should be made by the high-priest, for himself, and for all the people of every class and degree.

וכפר את מקדש הקודש ואת אהל מועד ואת המזבח
יכפר ועל הכהנים ועל כל עם הקהל יכפר:

" And he shall make an atonement for the holy sanctuary, and he shall make an atonement for the tabernacle of the congregation, and for the altar; and he shall make an atonement for the priests and for all the people of the congregation." (Levit. xvi. 33.) Now this ordinance implies, that all Israel, the high-priest, the priests, and the people, are all sinners, all need an atonement; and, therefore, utterly annihilates all idea of justification by merits. If Israel could have been justified either by their own merits, or by the merits of their forefathers, the solemn act of annual atonement would have been superfluous. But if this atonement be necessary,—and if it were not, why did God appoint it—then there is no room for the assertion of human merits. But the truth is, as we have already seen, that the rabbies felt that their doctrine was insufficient to quiet the awakened conscience, and gladly fled to any refuge that they could discover; it is no wonder then that they have clung with uncommon tenacity to the shadow of that hope that was held out in the law of Moses. In spite of their doctrine of merit, they are glad to have even the appearance of a day of atonement to reconcile them to the Almighty. It is true they have no high-priest and no sacrifice, yet so convinced are they of the need of an atonement, that rather than confess that they have absolutely none, they teach that repentance and the day itself will atone for all sin:—

בזמן הזה שאין בית המקדש קיים ואין לנו מזבח
כפרה אין שם אלא תשובה, התשובה מכפרת על
כל העבירות אפילו רשע כל ימיו ועשה תשובה
באחרונה אין מזכירין לו שום דבר מרשעו, שנאמר
רשעת הרשע לא יכשל בה ביום שובו מרשעו, ועצמו

של יום הכפורים מכפר לשבים שנאמר כי ביום הזה
יכפר עליכם:

"At this time, when there is no temple, and we have no altar, there is no atonement but repentance. Repentance atones for all transgressions, yea, though a man be wicked all his days, and repent at last, none of his wickedness is mentioned to him, for it is said, 'As for the wickedness of the wicked, he shall not fall thereby, in the day that he turneth from his wickedness.' (Ezek. xxxiii. 12.) The Day of Atonement itself also atones for them that repent, for it is said, 'For on that day he shall make an atonement for you.' Lev. xvi. 30." (Hilchoth T'shuvah, c. i. 2.) This is the last refuge of Jewish hope, and we, therefore, propose to consider, whether it is a refuge on which a reasonable man may hazard his hope of salvation? No man of sense would hazard his life or his property upon a statement, of which one part contradicted the other; and such is the statement which we have just read. It first tells us, that in this present time "There is no atonement but repentance," and that "Repentance atones for all transgressions;" and yet, immediately after, it adds, that "The Day of Atonement itself atones for them that repent." Now the latter assertion contradicts the former. If the Day of Atonement, as is here asserted, be necessary to atone for the penitent, then it is not true, that repentance atones for all sins. But if repentance atones for all sins, then when a man repents, his sins are forgiven, and then the Day of Atonement is not necessary. There is here, therefore, a palpable contradiction, and it cannot be safe to trust to a hope at variance with itself. But, secondly, as the two parts of which this statement is composed, contradict each other, so each of them is contrary to the law of Moses. The first of them is, that "Repentance atones for all tansgressions;" but if so, then the atonement prescribed by Moses is useless, in fact, it is no atonement at all. Moses says, that the two goats were appointed by God for the atonement, but here it is said, that repentance is, in itself, sufficient. If this be true, if repentance can now atone for sins, without any sacrifice, why did Moses appoint such an useless, and even cruel rite, as the taking away the lives of poor innocent animals? If repentance be sufficient now, it was sufficient always, and then it follows, that God commanded what was useless. But if the appointment, the slaying of one goat, and the sending the other, laden with the sins of the people, into the wilderness, was necessary formerly to procure forgiveness of sins, it must be equally necessary now: unless the rabbies will take upon them to assert, that God is an arbitrary and changeable master, who, to forgive sins, at one time, requires what at another time he does not require. That the slaying of one goat, and the sending away of the other was once absolutely necessary, no man can deny. Moses prescribes it so plainly, that if there be one thing more plain than another, it is this, that when the Jews were in their own land, repentance was not a sufficient atonement for sins. Indeed, Rambam himself says :—

שעיר המשתלח מכפר על כל עבירות שבתורה
הקלות והחמורות בין שעבר בזדון בין שעבר בשגגה
בין שהודע לו בין שלא הודע לו הכל מתכפר בשעיר
המשתלח והוא שעשה תשובה אבל אם לא עשה
תשובה אין השעיר מכפר לו אלא על הקלות:

"The goat that was sent away atoned for all the transgressions mentioned in the law, whether light or grave. Whether a man transgressed presumptuously or ignorantly, consciously or inconsciously, all was atoned for by the goat that was sent away, if a man repented. But if a man did not repent, then the goat atoned only for the light offences." (Hilchoth T'shuvah, ibid.) We do not agree with the whole of this doctrine, but we cite it to show, that formerly repentance was not a sufficient atonement for sins, but that besides repentance, the goat, as appointed by God, was also necessary. And we infer, that as an atonement, besides repentance, was once necessary, it is necessary still, unless the rabbies will affirm that God has changed his mind, and abrogated the law of Moses. If repentance without any atonement be now sufficient to procure forgiveness of sins, then, beyond all doubt, the law of Moses is abrogated or changed. If the law of Moses be not abrogated and not changed, then repentance alone cannot atone for sins; and, therefore, this assertion of the oral law is false.

But the oral law endeavours to prove its assertion, by a citation from Ezekiel, "As for the wickedness of the wicked, he shall not fall thereby in the day that he turneth from his wickedness." And it might be further urged, that Ezekiel here mentions repentance only, and omits all notice of sacrifice and the Day of Atonement. But the answer is easy. Either Ezekiel meant, in this declaration, to repeal the law of Moses, or he did not. If he meant to repeal the law of Moses, then the law is repealed, and a new way of obtaining forgiveness, not taught by Moses, has been introduced, and then the whole Jewish nation is, on their own showing, palpably in the wrong in adhering to that which is repealed. But if he did not mean to repeal the law of Moses, then he made this assertion with that implied restriction which the law of Moses required; that is, he implied the necessity of sacrifice: and then this passage does not prove what the oral law asserts. But in every case, this first assertion is contrary to the law of Moses.

It is, however, evident, that the rabbies themselves were dissatisfied with their own assertion, for they immediately add to it a second, "That the Day of Atonement itself atones for them that repent, as it is said, 'For on that day he shall make an atonement for you.'" Notwithstanding the confidence of their assertion about repentance, they did not feel easy without some appearance of an atonement, and as they had no priest and no victim, they say, that the day itself atones, and endeavour to prove this assertion by a citation from Moses. But, unfortunately, this citation entirely overthrows their assertion. Moses does not say :—

היום הזה יכפר עליכם :

"This day will atone for you," but he says :—

ביום הזה יכפר עליכם :

"On that day he (the priest) shall atone for you." Moses ascribes no virtue whatever to the day itself, but only to the rites on that day to be observed, and the person by whom they were performed. Moses prescribes, first, a high-priest; secondly, a goat, whose blood was brought into the Holy of holies; and thirdly, a goat to be sent away: so that where these three are wanting, nay, where any one of the three is wanting, the conditions prescribed by Moses are not fulfilled, and there is, therefore, no atonement. Without these three things the day itself has no virtue, and is nothing different from the commonest day in the year; and now, therefore, as they are all wanting, Israel has no atonement. The assertion about the day itself, is a mere invention of the rabbies, the only value of which is to show how deeply they felt the insufficiency of repentance, and the necessity of a real atonement, in order to procure remission of sins.

But the rabbies always betray themselves by adding something to make up for the deficiency, of which they are sensible. We have seen this in their assertion about merits, and so we find it here in their assertion about atonement. They assert, that "The Day of Atonement itself atones for the penitent," but in spite of this, they have felt the need of something more, which would a little better resemble real sacrificial atonement; and hence has arisen the custom of sacrificing a cock on the eve of that solemn day. The following account of this custom is given in the קהלה שלמה, of which we have before us an edition published at Breslau, so late as the year 1830; and it is selected, partly on account of its recent publication, and partly because the directions how to act are given in Jewish-German, which shows that they are intended even for the most illiterate, and that the custom is not confined to a few speculators, but is general amongst the people :—

סדר כפרות :

אן ערב יום כפור איז דער מנהג כפרות לו מאכען , מאן נעמט
איין האן לו איינעם מאן און מאן הען לו איינער פרויא , און לו
איינער פרויא דיא מעוברת איז נעמט מאן איין הען און איין האן
פון דאס קינד וועגען , דער בעל הבית מאכט לו ערטט דיא כפרה
פאר זיך , דען דער כהן גדול האט ערטט מכפר גיווענן פאר זיך און
דער נאך אום זיין הויז געזינד דער נאך פאר כל יטראל , און דער
סדר פון דיא כפרות איז וויא אין לטון הקודט טטעהט :

ער נעמט דען האן אין דער האנד און נאגט דיא פסוקים .

בְּנֵי אָדָם יֹשְׁבֵי חֹשֶׁךְ וְצַלְמָוֶת אֲסִירֵי עֳנִי וּבַרְזֶל,
יוֹצִיאֵם מֵחֹשֶׁךְ וְצַלְמָוֶת וּמוֹסְרוֹתֵיהֶם יְנַתֵּק, אֱוִילִים
מִדֶּרֶךְ פִּשְׁעָם וּמֵעֲוֹנוֹתֵיהֶם יִתְעַנּוּ, כָּל אֹכֶל תְּתַעֵב
נַפְשָׁם וַיַּגִּיעוּ עַד שַׁעֲרֵי מָוֶת, וַיִּזְעֲקוּ אֶל יְיָ בַּצַּר לָהֶם
מִמְּצוּקוֹתֵיהֶם יוֹשִׁיעֵם, יִשְׁלַח דְּבָרוֹ וְיִרְפָּאֵם וִימַלֵּט
מִשְׁחִיתוֹתָם, יוֹדוּ לַייָ חַסְדוֹ וְנִפְלְאוֹתָיו לִבְנֵי אָדָם, אִם
יֵשׁ עָלָיו מַלְאָךְ מֵלִיץ אֶחָד מִנִּי אָלֶף לְהַגִּיד לְאָדָם יָשְׁרוֹ,
וַיְחֻנֶּנּוּ וַיֹּאמֶר פְּדָעֵהוּ מֵרֶדֶת שַׁחַת מָצָאתִי כֹפֶר :

ווער פאר זיך דיא כפרה אום טלונגט נאגט דאס :

זֶה חֲלִיפָתִי, זֶה תְּמוּרָתִי, זֶה כַּפָּרָתִי, זֶה הַתַּרְנְגוֹל
יֵלֵךְ לְמִיתָה וַאֲנִי אֶכָּנֵס וְאֵלֵךְ לְחַיִּים טוֹבִים אֲרוּכִּים
וּלְשָׁלוֹם :

דער נאך הייבט מאן ווידער אן בני אדם און אנוי דריי מאל :

"ORDER OF THE ATONEMENTS.—On the eve of the Day of Atonement, the custom is to make atonements. A cock is taken for a man, and a hen for a woman ; and for a pregnant woman a hen and also a cock, on account of the child. The father of the family first makes the atonement for himself, for the high-priest first atoned for himself, then for his family, and afterwards for all Israel." The order is as follows:

He takes the cock in his hand and says these verses:

"The children of men that sit in darkness and the shadow of death, being bound in affliction and iron ; he brought them out of darkness and the shadow of death, and brake their bands in sunder. Fools, because of their transgression, and because of their iniquities, are afflicted. Their soul abhorreth all manner of meat; and they draw near unto the gates of death. Then they cry unto the Lord in their trouble ; and he saveth them out of their distresses. He sendeth his word, and healeth them, and delivereth them from their destructions. O, that men would praise the Lord for his goodness, and for his wonderful works, to the children of men? (Psalm cvii.) If there be for him an angel, an intercessor, one among a thousand, to show unto man his uprightness, then he is gracious unto him, and saith, Deliver him from going down to the pit; I have found a ransom." (Job xxxiii. 23.)

Whilst moving the atonement round his head, he says,

"This is my substitute. This is my commutation. This cock goeth to death, but may I be gathered and enter into a long and happy life, and into peace."

He then begins again at the words, "The children of men," and so he does three times.

Then follow the various alterations that are to be made, when the atonement is made for a woman or another person, &c., and is added:—

אזוי באלד אלט מען סדר הכפרות גיאאכט גוט מען דיא הענד
דרויף לייגען , ווי מען דיא הענד גילייגט האט אויף איין קרבן און
תיכף דער נאך לו דער שחיטה נעמען:

"As soon as one has performed the order of the atonement, he should lay his hands on it, as the hands used to be laid on the sacrifices, and immediately after give it to be slaughtered." This custom, extensively prevalent amongst the Jews, proves abundantly the internal dissatisfaction of the Jewish mind with their own doctrines, and the deeply-rooted conviction of their heart, that without shedding of blood there is no remission of sin. If they really believed that repentance, or the Day of Atonement itself, or almsgiving, or merits, either their own or their forefathers', atoned for sin, they would never have devised such a custom as this. But the spirit of the Mosaic law has taken too deep a hold on the nation to suffer them to rest satisfied with anything short of actual sacrifice; and as they have no high-priest and no altar now, they make a sad and desperate attempt to tranquillize the mind with this invention. The custom then, proves, that the rabbinical doctrine respecting the atoning power of repentance is not believed nor heartily received, even by the Rabbinists themselves, how, then, can a Jew hazard his salvation on a doctrine which is contrary to the law of Moses, and which its professors do not consider satisfactory? Will he rest upon the self-devised sacrifice of a cock? God nowhere promises pardon to this observance; and how can any man of sense be satisfied without a sure promise of the unchanging and unchangeable Creator? This trust is as unsatisfactory as any of those that we have already considered. Every one of the rabbinic hopes has proved unsafe on examination. Personal merit, the merit of ancestors, the blowing of the ram's horn, repentance, the present observance of the Day of Atonement, the sacrifice of a cock, all are either directly opposed to, or unwarranted by, the Word of God. How, then, is a Jew to obtain pardon for his sins? The custom which we have just considered, speaks the sense of the Jewish nation upon this subject, and plainly declares, that an atoning sacrifice is the only real hope. It expresses, in the first place, the heartfelt conviction, that every human being is guilty and needs an atonement. It prescribes a victim for man, woman, and child, yea, even for the unborn babe, thereby teaching that the nature of man is corrupt, and that the hereditary guilt, even where there is no actual transgression, must be washed away by the blood of atonement. It expresses, further, the Jewish opinion as to the nature of sacrifice, that the sins are laid upon the victim, and that the victim is substituted for the guilty. Nothing can be plainer than the prescribed formulary, "This is my substitute. This is my commutation. This is my atonement." It declares, further, that he who offers an atonement for another, must himself be free from guilt, for it requires the father of the family first to atone for himself, and then for those of his house. These are the recorded sentiments of the Jewish nation, expressed not only in words, but embodied in a solemn religious observance on the eve of their most sacred season. By this act the Jews declare that an atonement by blood is absolutely necessary. The law of Moses makes the same declaration, by the appointment of all the rites for the Day of Atonement. Is it, then, likely that the God of Israel would leave his people without that which their hearts desire, and his law declares to be necessary for salvation? Judaism says, Yes. It affirms, by an act repeated every year, that sacrifice is necessary, and yet confesses, in its solemn prayers, that they have none. It asserts, therefore, that God has left them without that which is indispensable to procure forgiveness. Christianity presents a more merciful view of the Divine character. It does, indeed, acknowledge the necessity of atonement, but it presents a victim and a high-priest, whose one offering is sufficient for the sins of the whole world. It says, that God has left neither his own people nor the Gentiles without the means of forgiveness, but sent his righteous servant, the Messiah, to bear our sins in his own body upon the tree. The Priest after the order of Melchisedek needed no atonement to take away his own sins first, for he had none. Born in a miraculous manner, by the power of God, his humanity inherited nothing of the guilt of Adam, and as the Lord our Righteousness, he could contract no taint of sin. He is, therefore, every way qualified to make an atonement for us all. Our Christian hope, therefore, is not in a cock, the sacrifice of which God never commanded, but in that great atonement which He appointed. Our faith, our hope, our trust, are all built upon God's promise, and cannot be better expressed than in his most holy words :—

והוא מחולל מפשעינו מדכא מעונותינו מוסר
שלומנו עליו ובחברתו נרפא לנו:

"But he was wounded for our transgressions, he was bruised for our iniquities: the chastisement of our peace was upon him, and with his stripes we are healed."

It cannot, therefore, be said, that we Christians rest our hope upon an invention of our own. Our hope rests, not upon the dictates of our priests or rabbies, but upon the words which God himself spake by the mouth of his prophet. We can, therefore, confidently appeal to the Jews themselves to decide, which of the two hopes is the most reasonable. Both agreeing that an atonement, by the shedding of blood, is necessary for the remission of sins, Rabbinism tells its disciples to trust to a species of sacrifice nowhere mentioned in the Word of God. Christianity tells us to trust in the sacrifice of that great Redeemer, for whose salvation Jacob waited, whose atonement the Mosaic rites prefigured, and the Jewish prophets predicted. Their hope rests upon the unwarranted words of men; ours is built upon the Word of the living God, and is involuntarily confirmed by the rabbies themselves in the very custom which we have just considered. Even the nature of the victim is pointed out in the selection of the animal. גבר (gever) signifies both "a man" and "a cock," and thereby signifies, that a righteous man must be the sinful man's substitute: and so some of the rabbies say, that this animal, "a cock," was selected,—

כיון ששמו גבר תמורת גבר בגבר:

"Because, as its name signifies 'a man,' there is a substitution of a man for man." (Orach Chaiim, 605.) The principles exactly agree, but Christianity is directed in their application by the Word of God, to Him who is, indeed, very man, but also THE LORD OUR RIGHTEOUSNESS, יהוה צדקנו.

No. XXXVII.

FEAST OF TABERNACLES.

THE progress of the year brings with it again that season, in which God commanded his people to observe THE FEAST OF TABERNACLES; and the constancy with which Israelites in every part of the world still observe the rites and customs handed down by their forefathers, necessarily commands respect and admiration. When we remember the many centuries during which their dispersion has continued, the universal oppression which they have been compelled to suffer, and the unmerited contempt with which they have had to contend, we cannot but honour the strength of moral courage which they have displayed, in thus observing and handing down to their children a religion, which has been the cause of their misfortunes. But this very constancy, and the respect which it begets, naturally leads us to inquire whether the religious system itself be true, and, therefore, worthy of that fidelity with which it has been preserved; and, above all, whether this constancy is such as at the last great day to meet the approbation of Him who judgeth not as man judgeth. The professors of this system think, of course, that it is, and that by observing these rites and ceremonies, they are keeping the commands of God, and thereby ensuring his favour; and with regard to the observance of the Feast of Tabernacles in particular, they are taught to believe that they alone are so important, as at the day of judgment, to prove Israel's obedience, and the disobedience of the other nations. We will first state the doctrines of modern Judaism on this subject, and then examine whether they be well founded. In the Synagogue Prayers for this feast we find it stated, that the construction of a tabernacle according to rabbinic prescription, is a work of merit:—

חשובה ארבע אמות על ארבע י פסולה פחותה
מארבע י כדי לזכות עם רובע :

"It must be four cubits long, and four cubits broad: but if it be less, it is profane; that it may render the people of Israel meritorious." (P. 116.) And a little lower down, after describing the feast in Paradise on the salted Leviathan and Behemoth, it adds, that this one precept will form the last trial vouchsafed to the Gentiles, and that their unwillingness to keep it will prove the cause of their final condemnation:—

נכנסין כל האומות לדין י פני יושב על כסא דין י

וּבְצֶדֶק אוֹתָנוּ יָדִין, סֵדֶר מִצְווֹתֶיךָ תֵּן לָנוּ וּנְקַיְּמָה,
וְנִזְכֶּה עִם אֵלּוּ בְּנֶחָמָה, שַׂגִּיא כֹחַ שׁוֹכֵן רוֹמָה, עֶלְיוֹן
הַשּׁוֹפֵט כֹּל בֶּאֱמוּנָה, יַשְׁמִיעַ לָהֶם בִּתְבוּנָה, יֵשׁ לִי
מִצְוָה קְטַנָּה, פֵּירוּשׁ סוּכָּה וּשְׁאֵלִיהָ, אַרְבַּע דְּפָנוֹת
וְצֵל עָלֶיהָ, אַל תְּרַחֵק מֵאֵלֶיהָ, צְלָלִים לַעֲשׂוֹת בָּהּ
יַעְטוּ, וְחַמָּה קָדְחָה עֲלֵיהֶם וְלוֹהֲטוּ, וּבְרַגְלֵיהֶם יִבְעֲטוּ,
קָדוֹשׁ יִשְׁפּוֹךְ עֲלֵיהֶם חֵימָה, וְיַפִּילֵם בְּגֵיהִנָּם בְּלִי
רְחִימָה, בְּמַדְרֵגָה הַתַּחְתּוֹנָה בִּמְהוּמָה:

"All nations will come to be judged in the presence of Him who sitteth upon the throne of judgment; in righteousness will he judge us. *The nations will then say*, Give us the order of thy precepts, and we will perform them, that we may be equal with those in happiness, O Thou, who art great in power, dwelling on high. The Most High, who judgeth all in truth, will cause them to hear, and understand his words, saying, I have one small precept; its name, tabernacle, and its ordinations: four sides, and a shade over it: fail ye not to observe it. They then will make the shadowy booths to abide under, but the sun will shine so hot as nearly to burn them, when they will spurn at it with their feet. The Holy One will then pour out his wrath upon them, and cast them into gehinnom [hell] without mercy, into the lowest part with confusion." (Ibid.) This extraordinary account of the day of judgment, and the condemnation of the Gentiles, has been adopted from the Talmud, where it is given at great length, and all the particulars fully detailed. To give the whole would occupy too much of our space; but as parts of it are necessary to the full consideration of this subject, we give the following extracts:—

לֶעָתִיד לָבוֹא מֵבִיא הַקָּבָּ"ה סֵפֶר תּוֹרָה בְּחֵיקוֹ וְאוֹמֵר
כָּל מִי שֶׁעָסַק בָּהּ יָבוֹא וְיִטּוֹל שְׂכָרוֹ מִיָּד מִתְקַבְּצִין
וּבָאִין אוּמוֹת הָעוֹלָם בְּעִרְבּוּבְיָא שֶׁנֶּאֱמַר כָּל הַגּוֹיִם נִקְבְּצוּ
יַחְדָּו, אָמַר לָהֶם הַקָּבָּ"ה אַל הִכָּנְסוּ לְפָנַי בְּעִרְבּוּבְיָא
אֶלָּא תִּכָּנֵס כָּל אוּמָה וְאוּמָה וְסוֹפְרֶיהָ:

"In the time to come, the Holy One, blessed be He, will bring a roll of the law in his bosom, and say, Let every one, who has occupied himself herein, come and receive his reward. Immediately the nations of the world will gather themselves together, and come in promiscuous crowds, as it is said, 'Let all the nations be gathered together.' (Isaiah xliii. 9.) The Holy One, blessed be He, will then say, Come not before me promiscuously, but let each nation come by itself along with its learned men." Then follows an account of the appearance of each nation, and of the vain attempts

FEAST OF TABERNACLES.

which they make to justify their conduct. After which the narrative thus proceeds:—

אומרים לפניו רבונו של עולם ישראל שקבלוה היכן
קיימוה אמר להם הקב״ה אני מעיד בהם שקיימו את
התורה, אומרים לפניו רבונו של עולם כלום יש אב
שמעיד על בנו דכתיב בני בכורי ישראל אמר להם
הקב״ה שמים וארץ יעידו בהם שקיימו את התורה
כולה, אומרים לפניו רבונו של עולם שמים וארץ
נוגעין בעדותן שנאמר אם לא בריתי יומם ולילה
חוקות שמים וארץ לא שמתי, ואמר ר׳ שמעון בן
לקיש מאי דכתיב ויהי ערב ויהי בוקר יום הששי,
מלמד שהתנה הקב״ה במעשה בראשית ואמר אם
ישראל מקבלין את תורתי מוטב ואם לאו אחזיר
אתכם לתוהו ובוהו והיינו דאמר חזקיה מאי דכתיב
משמים השמעת דין ארץ יראה ושקטה אם יראה למה
שקטה ואם שקטה למה יראה אלא בתחלה יראה
ולבסוף שקטה, אמר להם הקב״ה מכם יבואו ויעידו
בהן בישראל שקיימו את התורה כולה, יבוא נמרוד
ויעיד באברהם שלא עבד ע״ז יבוא לבן ויעיד ביעקב
שלא נחשד על הגזל הבוא אשת פוטיפרע ותעיד
ביוסף שלא נחשד על העבירה יבוא נבוכדנצר ויעיד
בחנניה מישאל ועזריה שלא השתחוו לצלם יבוא
דרייוש ויעיד בדניאל שלא ביטל את התפלה יבוא
בלדד השוחי וצופר הנעמתי ואליפז התמני ואליהו
בן ברכאל הבוזי ויעידו בהן בישראל שקיימו את
התורה כולה שנאמר יתנו עדיהן ויצדקו, אמרו לפניו
רבונו של עולם תנו לנו מראש ונעשה אמר להם
הקב״ה שוטים שבעולם מי שטרח בערב שבת יאכל
בשבת מי שלא טרח בערב שבת מהיכן יאכל בשבת
אלא אע״פ כן מצוה קלה יש לי וסוכה שמה לכו
ועשו אותו, ומי מצית אמרת הכי והא אמר ר׳ יהושע
בן לוי מאי דכתיב אשר אנכי מצוך היום היום לעשותם
ולא למחר לעשותם היום לעשותם ולא היום ליטול
שכר אלא שאין הקב״ה בא בטרוניא עם בריותיו ואמאי
קרי ליה מצוה קלה משום דלית ביה חכרון כיס
מיד כל אחד נוטל והולך ועושה סוכה בראש גגו
והקב״ה מקדיח עליהם חמה בתקופת תמוז וכל אחד
ואחד מבעט בסוכתו ויוצא וכו׳:

"The Gentiles will then say before him, O Lord of the world, the Israelites received the law, but how did they keep it? The Holy One, blessed be He, will reply, I bear them witness that they have kept the law. The Gentiles will say, O Lord of the world, is it fair that a Father should be a witness for his children? For it is written, 'Israel is my son, even my first-born.' (Exod. iv. 22.) The Holy One, blessed be He, will then say to them, Let the heaven and the earth bear witness to them, that they have kept the whole law. The Gentiles will answer, O Lord of the world, the heavens and the earth are interested witnesses, for it is said, 'If my covenant be not with day and night, and if I have not appointed the ordinances of heaven and the earth.' (Jer. xxxiii. 25.) R. Simon Ben Lakish says, What is the meaning of the words 'And it was evening and it was morning, the sixth day?' They show us that the Holy and Blessed One, made a condition with the creation, and said, If Israel will receive my law, all is well; but if not, then I will turn you back into chaos. Hezekiah also teaches this same truth, saying, What is the meaning of the words, 'Thou didst cause judgment to be heard from heaven; the earth feared, and was still?' (Ps. lxxvi. 9, Eng. 8.) If it feared, how could it be still; and if it was still, how could it fear? The answer is, at first it feared [that Israel would not receive the law, and it should be turned into chaos]; but afterwards it was still. God will then say to the Gentiles, Then let some of yourselves come, and bear witness to Israel that they have kept the whole law. Nimrod shall then come forth and testify of Abraham that he did not commit idolatry. Laban shall come forth and testify of Jacob that he was not suspected of dishonesty. Potiphar's wife shall come forth and testify of Joseph that he was not suspected of the transgression. Nebuchadnezzar shall come forth and testify of Hannaniah, Mishael, and Azariah, that they would not worship the image. Darius shall come and testify of Daniel that he did not neglect prayer. Bildad the Shuhite, and Zophar the Naamathite, and Eliphaz the Temanite, and Elihu the son of Berachcel, shall come forth and testify of Israel that they have kept the whole law, as it is said, 'Let them bring forth their witnesses, that they may be justified.' (Isaiah xliii. 9.) The Gentiles will then say, O Lord of the world, give us the law from the beginning, and we will do it. To this the Holy One will reply, O fools, he that works on the eve of the Sabbath shall eat on the Sabbath. He that will not work on the Sabbath eve, from whence should he eat on the the Sabbath? Nevertheless, I have one easy commandment, Tabernacle is its name, go, therefore, and do it. But how is it possible to affirm that God will do this, when R. Joshua, the son of Levi, says, What is the meaning of the words, 'Which I command thee this day?' And says, the meaning is, they are to be observed to-day [*i.e.*, in this world], and not tomorrow [*i.e.*, in the world to come].* To-day they are to be observed; but the reward is not to be received to-day. The answer is, that God does not deal with his creatures in a tyrannical manner. But why is this called an easy commandment? Because it is not attended with any pecuniary loss. Immediately every one of the Gentiles will hasten away, and make a tabernacle on the roof of his house. But the Holy One, blessed be He, will cause the sun to pierce them with an extraordinary heat at that season, and then every one of them will kick down his tabernacle and go forth," &c. (Avodah Zarah, fol. 2, 3.) Such is the doctrine of the Talmud, adopted, and therefore sealed with the most solemn sanction, by the public worship of the synagogue. In the first place it is perfectly false; it has not even the merit of plausibility. It is only astonishing how an imagination so absurd should ever have found its way into the prayers of Israel; and stranger still that the Jews of England should suffer such a foul blot still to remain on their public services. It certainly represents Judaism in the most unfavourable point of view, as a religion of the grossest and most inconsistent superstition; and proves, beyond all controversy, first, that the synagogue receives, as of divine authority, even the fables of the Talmud; and, secondly, that the authors of the oral law, who could either invent or believe so absurd a statement, cannot be depended upon as faithful transmitters of the religion of the prophets.

Further, it totally misrepresents the character of God. It describes Him, first, as bearing witness to the obedience of Israel, whilst in His Word he bears constant testimony to their disobedience. Here he is represented also as calling upon heaven and earth to attest their innocence and righteousness, whilst in His Word he calls upon them to be the witnesses of their rebellion. " Hear, O heavens; and give ear, O earth; for the Lord hath spoken: I have nourished and brought up children, and they have rebelled against me." (Isaiah i. 2.) And again, " Be astonished, O ye heavens, at this, and be horribly afraid, be ye very desolate, saith the Lord. For my people have committed two evils; they have forsaken me, the fountain of living waters, and hewed them out cisterns, broken cisterns, that can hold no water." (Jer. ii. 12.) These passages of the word of God are directly opposed to the above statement of the oral law. But further, it misrepresents the Divine Being as an unmerciful and unjust judge, who pretends to give the guilty Gentiles another and easy trial by giving them the commandment respecting the tabernacles, and then employs his omnipotence so to plague them with the heat of the sun, as to render it impossible for them to yield obedience. Such a

* חיים לעשותם בעולם הזה ׳ ולא למחר דאינו יכול לעשותם לעולם הבא:

representation is altogether unworthy of the Judge of all the earth, who will deal justly by the Gentiles as well as the Jews.

But besides misrepresenting the divine character, it misleads the unlearned and superstitious to believe that, at the day of judgment, God will not render to every man according to his deeds, but will pass by their sins and their impenitence, if only they be Israelites. It therefore begets a false confidence, and is eminently calculated to lull men asleep in their sins. The man who believes this fable of the Gentiles bearing witness to the righteousness of Abraham, Joseph, Daniel, &c., and thinks that this is sufficient for his acquittal at the bar of judgment, can have no motive for personal repentance or righteousness. Neither does this fable tend to produce good will and respect towards his Gentile fellow-sinners. Few men will elevate themselves above their notions of the Deity. When, then, the Rabbinists see that, according to the oral law, God treats the Gentiles with injustice and cruelty, is it natural to suppose that he will treat them differently? This and similar passages well merit the serious consideration of all influential Israelites. It is imperative upon all such to determine, whether such passages of their prayers and their law are of divine authority or not; and if they are convinced of their falsehood, to use their unceasing exertions to expunge them from their religious system. As long as they exist, and are publicly read in the synagogue, men can only come to one conclusion, and that is, that the characteristics of the Rabbinical religion are superstition and uncharitableness. Nothing but a public protest against the error, and an erasure from the prayer-book, will satisfy the mind, or wipe away the reproach from Israel. The private professions of individuals can be of no avail in this matter. Men will go to the authorized books, especially to the prayer-book of every class of religionist, in order to judge of his principles; and no one will believe that any man can be so careless or so presumptuous as to address the Divine Being in the language of acknowledged falsehood. But above all, let every Jew compare this account of the day of judgment with that contained in our Christian books. Judaism teaches that at that great day God will appear as a partial and cruel judge. Christianity gives us the following account of the same period:—" When the Son of man shall come in his glory and all the holy angels with him, then shall he sit upon the throne of his glory; and before him shall be gathered all nations and he shall separate them one from another, as a shepherd divideth his sheep from the goats: and he shall set the sheep on his right hand, but the goats on the left. Then shall the King say unto them on his right hand, Come, ye blessed of my father, inherit the kingdom prepared for you from the foundation of the world: for I was an hungred, and ye gave me meat: I was thirsty, and ye gave me drink: I was a stranger, and ye took me in: naked, and ye clothed me: I was sick, and ye visited me: I was in prison, and ye came unto me. Then shall the righteous answer and say, Lord, when saw we thee an hungred, and fed thee? or thirsty, and gave thee drink? when saw we thee a stranger, and took thee in? or naked, and clothed thee? or when saw we thee sick, and in prison, and came unto thee? And the King shall answer and say unto them, Verily I say unto you, Inasmuch as ye have done it unto one of the least of these my brethren, ye have done it unto me. Then shall he say also unto them on the left hand, Depart from me, ye cursed, into everlasting fire, prepared for the devil and his angels: for I was an hungred, and ye gave me no meat: I was thirsty, and ye gave me no drink: I was a stranger, and ye took me not in: naked, and ye clothed me not: sick, and in prison, and ye visited me not. Then shall they also answer him, saying, Lord, when saw we thee an hungred, or athirst, or a stranger, or naked, or sick, or in prison, and did not minister unto thee? Then shall he answer them, saying, Verily I say unto you, Inasmuch as ye did it not to one of the least of these, ye did it not to me. And these shall go away into everlasting punishment: but the righteous into life eternal." (Matt. xxv. 31—46.) Such is the view which Christianity sets before us of the day of judgment, and the principles according to which that judgment shall be conducted. You will observe that the whole account is essentially different from that given by the Talmud. In the first place it represents God as a just Judge, altogether overlooking nationality; taking no notice of the temporary distinctions of Jew and Gentile: but fixing his eyes on the eternal features of moral character, and according to these fixing the eternal destinies of each individual. In the second place it tends to promote good will and charity between man and man, for it represents charity or the want of charity as the main points of inquiry, and the distinctions according to which the eternal portion of each is assigned. We ask, then, every impartial and candid Jew to tell us, which of these two accounts are most worthy of the great God whom we worship? We Christians believe that the synagogue-worshippers are in error, and they again think us in error; but we have now before us the doctrines of the two systems on the most important point in all theology—the principle of final judgment; by their respective statements, then, on this subject let each system be judged. Judaism says, that one class of men is to be saved by the partiality of the Judge, and the other class condemned simply because they are Gentiles. Christianity says, that all men shall be tried impartially by one rule, and that neither prepossession nor prejudice, but justice alone, shall influence the decision. Which, then, Judaism or Christianity, is most agreeable to the character of Him of whom the Psalmist says, "He cometh to judge the earth: with righteousness shall he judge the world, and the nations with equity?"

We are sure that the good sense of the Jewish nation must decide, that the impartial justice of the New Testament-representation is most in accordance with the spirit of the law and the prophets. Nay, we believe that every devout and thinking Israelite will feel that the Talmudic picture of God's judgment misrepresents the God of Israel as much as any graven image ever deified by heathen idolaters. To suppose that God would make a mock overture of mercy, or offer a mock trial to any of his creatures, is to strip him of the attributes of Deity, and to exhibit a blind and senseless bigot as the object of Israel's worship. A statement so abhorrent even from human reason, and so inconsistent with the Word of God, proves that its authors were not moved by the Spirit, and that the religion of which it forms a part cannot be divine. But here, as in many cases which we have already pointed out, the New Testament avoids the error of the Talmud, and teaches the doctrine conformable to the law, and in accordance with right reason. Let the advocates of the oral law explain the fact.

But this Talmudic representation of the day of judgment is not only opposed to reason and Scripture, but also seems to contradict other statements of the oral law. Here the Gentiles appear to be marked out for destruction; whereas, we are told elsewhere, that the pious of the nations of the world are to have a part in the world to come: and that obedience to the seven commandments of the sons of Noah, is all that is required from a Gentile. If this be true, what need is there of giving them the command to keep the Feast of Tabernacles? But, above all, if they are to be cast down into the lowest hell, as the Prayer-book says, how can they have a part of the blessings of the world to come? It is at the very least, the duty of those who advocate the oral law, to explain this matter to us Gentiles. We cannot persuade ourselves that a religion, which makes so little provision for the eternal welfare of the great bulk of the human race, can possibly proceed from Him who is the God of the spirits of all flesh, the Creator and Preserver of all mankind. Living daily by his bounty, and receiving all we have at his most gracious hands we believe that if he makes such provision for our bodies, He has made still more for our immortal spirits; and therefore, amongst other reasons, we believe in Christianity; for if it be not true, there is no spiritual provision for the Gentiles, and God has left the majority of his rational creatures without any proof of his paternal affection.

No. XXXVIII.

PRAYERS FOR THE DEAD.

To the fool, who hath said in his heart, There is no God it is a matter of little consequence, whether the religion of his forefathers afford a reasonable ground of hope or not. He may therefore consistently neglect all inquiry into the nature and evidences of that religion in which he happened to be born. He does not believe in it, whatever it may be, and such an inquiry could have no interest for him. Not so with the Jew or the Christian, who honestly believes, as he has been taught, that there is, in another world, an abode of bliss, and another of woe. His earnest desire must be to know how he may attain to the one and escape the other; and if his religion does not afford him a hope, a reasonable, well-grounded hope of salvation, it is not worth the having. We say a reasonable hope, for as it has pleased God to endow us with reason and understanding, and to give us his Word to guide our reason, no other hope can or ought to satisfy us. In examining, then, the modern Jewish religion, one great test of its value is, whether it affords a hope on which a reasonable man can rely, and upon which he can hazard his eternal welfare. We think not, and we have already given some reasons for this opinion. The inconsistency and contradictory nature of the rabbinic doctrines respecting justification and atonement appear to us so glaring as to destroy all confidence in the hope which they propose: and *the custom, which prevails at this and other festivals, of praying for the dead, proves, beyond a doubt, that the rabbinic hope is a mere delusion*. Amongst the prayers of the Feast of Tabernacles, we find the following declaration and prayer:—

נוהגים בתפוצות ישראל להזכיר נשמות אבותיו ביום כפור ובשלש רגלים ביום מתנת יד לאחר הפטורה י יזכור אלהים נשמת אבא מורי פלוני בר־ פלוני שהלך לעולמו בעבור שאני נודר צדקה בעדו בשכר זה תהא נפשו צרורה בצרור החיים עם נשמת אברהם יצחק ויעקב שרה רבקה רחל ולאה ועם שאר צדיקים וצדקניות שבגן עדן ונאמר אמן : יזכור אלהים נשמת אמי וכו' :

"It is customary among the dispersions of Israel, to make mention of the souls of their departed parents, &c., on the day of atonement, and the ultimate days of the three festivals; and to offer prayers for the repose of their souls.

"May God remember the soul of my honoured father, A. B.

who is gone to his repose; for that I now solemnly vow charity for his sake; in reward of this, may his soul be bound up in the bundle of life, with the souls of Abraham, Isaac, and Jacob; Sarah, Rebekah, Rachel, and Leah, with the rest of the righteous males and females that are in Paradise; and let us say, Amen."

"May God remember the soul of my honoured mother," &c. (Prayer for the Feast of Tabernacles, p. 156.) Now this custom and this prayer show that the Jews themselves do not believe in their own doctrines, nor put any trust in the hopes held out by the oral law; for if they did, they would never observe this custom nor offer this prayer. If they believed that their departed parents were already safe — that their merits, or the merits of their ancestors, or the Day of Atonement, &c., had procured for them pardon and eternal life, why should they offer alms, and pray that God would accept the alms as a ransom for the deceased? The fact of making such a vow and offering such a prayer proves, that the Rabbinical Jew has no ground for believing in the salvation of even his own father and mother; that on the contrary his belief is, that they have not been bound up in the bundle of life, and that they are not in paradise with Abraham and the other saints; but that they are in some other place, whence he hopes, by his prayer and his almsgiving, to ransom them. Here, then, we see that the rabbinical hope is a mere delusion. After all his fasting and ceremonial observances, he has no hope after death of going to the mansions of the blessed. His sad prospect is, that when he goes hence, he must go to the place of punishment, and there abide until the prayers and almsgiving of his children purchase his liberation. According, then, to this doctrine, every Jew and Jewess dies without pardon, for if they were pardoned, they would not go to the place of punishment, and if they did not go to the place of punishment, there would be no necessity to offer alms in order to deliver their souls. So then, after all the pretensions and promises of the rabbies, they here fairly confess that all the hopes which they have held out are a mere lie and a delusion; that none of their observances can deliver the soul, and that even after the dread hour of death, the survivors have still to undertake the work of saving the deceased.

This inference follows inevitably from the custom and the prayer which we have just considered; but it does not rest solely on these. The oral law furnishes other adequate proof, that the Jewish survivors of a departed parent do not believe that he is safe, and that therefore a dying Jew can have no hope of his own salvation; for it requires the surviving son to repeat a certain prayer for his departed parent, and that for many months, in order to procure his release, as we read in the *Joreh Deah*:—

עַל כֵּן נָהֲגוּ לוֹמַר קָדִישׁ עַל אָב וָאֵם בְּהִיּוֹת י"ב
חוֹדֶשׁ, וְכֵן נָהֲגוּ לְהַפְטִיר בְּנָבִיא וּלְהִתְפַּלֵּל עַרְבִית
בְּמוֹצָאֵי שַׁבָּת שֶׁהוּא הַזְּמַן שֶׁחוֹזְרִין הַנְּשָׁמוֹת לְגֵיהִנָּם,
וּכְשֶׁהַבֵּן מִתְפַּלֵּל וּמְקַדֵּשׁ בָּרַבִּים פּוֹדֶה אָבִיו וְאִמּוֹ
מִגֵּיהִנָּם:

"Therefore the custom is for twelve months to repeat the prayer called Kaddish, and also to read the lesson in the prophets, and to pray the evening-prayer at the going out of the Sabbath, for that is the hour when the souls return to hell; but when the son prays and sanctifies in public, he redeems his father and his mother from hell." (376.) Now every child who observes this custom, makes a public confession, that his deceased parent is not enjoying the bliss of paradise, but suffering the torments of hell. This is but a poor hope for a child respecting his parent, the very utmost limit of which is, that he is not one of the notoriously wicked, and that he may perhaps, by his prayers, get him out of the place of torment. But if he believes in the oral law, he must be convinced that his father or mother, with all their exertions, and notwithstanding the merits of their forefathers, and the benefits of the Day of Atonement, died in sin, sunk into perdition, and that he must now undertake the work of their salvation. The dying Jew, therefore, has no hope when he dies of being admitted to a state of happiness; he cannot die with the peace of one who knows that his sins are forgiven, but must look forward with horror to at least eleven dreary months of punishment in the abodes of the damned. The doctrine of the Talmud is, that those who die in communion with the synagogue, or who have never been Jews, are punished for twelve months, but that Jewish heretics and apostates are doomed to eternal punishment.

פּוֹשְׁעֵי יִשְׂרָאֵל בְּגוּפָן וּפוֹשְׁעֵי אוּמּוֹת הָעוֹלָם בְּגוּפָן
יוֹרְדִין לְגֵיהִנָּם וְנִדּוֹנִין בָּהּ שְׁנֵים עָשָׂר חוֹדֶשׁ לְאַחַר
שְׁנֵים עָשָׂר חוֹדֶשׁ גּוּפָן כָּלָה וְנִשְׁמָתָן נִשְׂרֶפֶת וְרוּחַ
מְפַזַּרְתָּן תַּחַת כַּפּוֹת רַגְלֵי הַצַּדִּיקִים שֶׁנֶּאֱמַר וְעַסּוֹתֶם
רְשָׁעִים כִּי יִהְיוּ אֵפֶר תַּחַת כַּפּוֹת רַגְלֵיכֶם אֲבָל הַמִּינִין
וְהַמּוֹסְרִין וְהָאֶפִּיקוֹרְסִין שֶׁכָּפְרוּ בַתּוֹרָה וְשֶׁכָּפְרוּ בִּתְחִיַּית
הַמֵּתִים וְשֶׁפֵּירְשׁוּ מִדַּרְכֵי צִבּוּר וְשֶׁנָּתְנוּ חִתִּיתָם בָּאָרֶץ
חַיִּים וְשֶׁחָטְאוּ וְהֶחֱטִיאוּ אֶת הָרַבִּים כְּגוֹן יָרָבְעָם בֶּן
נְבָט וַחֲבֵרָיו יוֹרְדִין לְגֵיהִנָּם וְנִדּוֹנִין בָּהּ לְדוֹרֵי דוֹרוֹת:

"Israelites who sin with their body, and also Gentiles, descend into hell, and are judged there for twelve months. After the twelve months their body is consumed and their soul is burnt, and the wind scatters them under the soles of the feet of the righteous, as it is said, 'Ye shall tread down the wicked, for they shall be ashes under the soles of your feet.' (Mal. iv. 3.) But heretics, and informers, and Epicureans, who have denied the law or the resurrection of the dead, or who have separated from the customs of the congregation, or who have caused their fear in the land of the living, who have sinned, or caused many to sin, as Jeroboam, the son of Nebat, all such go down to hell and are judged for ever." (Rosh Hashanah, fol. 17. 1.) According to this, the dying Israelite ought to expect twelve months of torment, and his surviving son ought to repeat the prescribed prayer for twelve months; but the rabbies have commanded that the prayer should be repeated only for eleven months, to intimate that the deceased was not so wicked as to be obliged to remain all the time of torment :—

ונהגו שאין אומרים קדיש ותפלה רק י״א חדשים
כדי שלא יעשו אביהם ואמם רשעים כי משפט רשע
י״ב הודש :

"'The custom is, not to say Kaddish more than eleven months, so as not to cast a reproach on the character of the deceased father and mother as if they were wicked, for twelve months are the term appointed for the wicked." (Joreh Deah, 376.) From this it is clear that a dying Jew's expectation must be to endure the torments of hell for at least eleven months; and when he is dead, his son confesses, in the most public manner, and the appointed prayers of the synagogue confess, of every departed Jew, that he died in sin, and was not worthy to enter into the bliss of paradise; and express, moreover, their conviction that his portion is actually with the damned. Thus it is evident that Judaism holds out no hope of the forgiveness of sins, and that all its prescribed observances are of no avail in the hour of need. A Jew's sad contemplation on his death is, then, that he is going down to hell, and his hope of liberation is based upon the prayers of his son, or upon the fact of his being an Israelite. But is this a reasonable ground of hope? No hope of salvation can be reasonable which is not built upon a plain promise of God. Our reason can tell us nothing about either heaven or hell; and therefore no speculations of our own can satisfy us respecting either one or the other. The only satisfactory testimony can come from God's revealed will; but in the whole volume of the Old Testament, there is not one promise declaring that an Israelite shall be delivered from hell after twelve months' punishment, or that the son's public prayers in the synagogue shall deliver the father. This is all the mere invention of the rabbies, without the least warrant from the Word of God. It is, therefore, not a hope on which any reasonable man can rest in peace. The sum of the whole matter is, that every Jew expects to go to hell, and that he has no promise of God to assure him that he shall be redeemed thence. Judaism is not, therefore, a religion which affords a rational hope of salvation. In asserting that every Israelite must go down to hell, it teaches that sin is not forgiven by God, but must be atoned for by the personal suffering of the offender; and that happiness cannot be enjoyed until personal satisfaction has been yielded by twelve months' torments. Now if this principle were true, there could be no salvation at all. Sin, as being an offence against an infinite Being, is infinite in magnitude, and therefore, requires infinite punishment. The justice of God is also infinite, and requires an infinite satisfaction; so that if this satisfaction is to be rendered by the personal suffering of the offender, that suffering must be infinite, that is, it must endure for ever and ever, and thus salvation is altogether out of the question. The Jewish hope is, therefore, unwarranted by Scripture, and contrary to reason, and, we may add, inconsistent with itself. In the custom and doctrine which we have just considered, a dying Jew is taught to hope that he shall be delivered from that place of torment, whither he is going, either on account of his son's prayers, or on account of his Jewish origin. But on his death-bed he is taught to believe that his death will be an atonement for his sins, for in his dying confession, these words are put into his mouth :—

ואם קרבה עת פקודתי למות, תהא מיתתי כפרה
לכל חטאותי ולכל עוונותי ולכל פשעי שחטאתי
ושעויתי ושפשעתי מיום היותי :

"But if the time of my visitation to death be near, O let my death be an expiation for all my sins, iniquities, and transgressions, wherein I have sinned, offended, and transgressed against thee, from the day of my existence." These two doctrines are plainly contrary the one to the other. If death be an atonement for all sins, then, when it is once suffered, all these sins are forgiven, and there is no need of further punishment in hell for twelve months. But if this further punishment be inflicted, then the death of the individual is not an atonement for his sins. The Jew may choose which of these hopes he pleases; but whichever he may assert to be true, the other is necessarily false; and if one be false, then the oral law teaches falsehood, and cannot be depended upon with respect to the other. There is, then, in these two statements, a glaring inconsistency, which makes them both suspicious in themselves: and the Word of God is as opposed to this last statement, as to the former. The Bible represents death as a consequence and punishment of Adam's sin, not as an atonement: and hence it is that infants die, who have never committed actual sin, and do not need an atonement on that account. Death is, therefore, a punishment, and that which is a punishment can never be an atonement. The dying Jew, then, if he be a reasonable man, has no hope that can yield him peace and consolation in that solemn hour. He prays that his death may atone for his sins, and yet believes the very contrary—that he is going down to the place of the damned, and that his son will have to undertake the work of his redemption. How any thoughtful man, especially how any Israelite who has read the Law and the Prophets, can be content with such a religion, we cannot comprehend. The very essence of religion, the very consideration that gives it any value, is the comfort which it affords to the departing sinner. If it cannot soothe, support, and comfort him in the hour of death, it is not worth the having. The Christian faith is very different, and, in our opinion, far more in accordance with the Old Testament. We believe, in the first place, that there is a full and perfect pardon for all sins by the atonement of the Messiah, so that the sinner who dies in repentance and faith, is delivered from all punishment and other consequences of sin, and enters at once into the abodes of the blessed, there to await the morning of the resurrection. The Old Testament promised that Messiah should bear our sins. The New Testament tells us that He has borne them, and that therefore we can "now be justified from all things from which we could not be justified by the law of Moses." (Acts xiii. 38, 39.) It tells us that "God made Him to be sin for us, who knew no sin; that we might be made the righteousness of God in him" (2 Cor. v. 21); and "that if any man sin, we have an advocate with the Father, Jesus, the Messiah, the Righteous; and he is the propitiation for our sins: and not for ours only, but also for the sins of the whole world." (1 John ii. 1, 2.) We believe, therefore, that Messiah has borne all that we ought to have borne, as the prophet says—

מוסר שלומנו עליו ובחבורתו נרפא לנו :

"The chastisement of our peace was upon him, and with his stripes we are healed," (Isaiah liii. 5,) and that now we are delivered. There is no twelvemonth of torment awaiting those whom Messiah has redeemed, neither do we trust in our own death as a possible atonement. Our hope is firmly fixed, and, therefore, though sinners, we can die in peace, resting on the salvation which God himself has wrought, in no fear of the torments of the damned, but humbly expecting, for the Messiah's sake, to be admitted into the mansions of the blessed. Resting on this hope, the Christian can say, "To me to live is Christ, and to die is gain." (Philip. i. 21.) He can look forward from death to the glorious consummation, as St. Paul did, who, when the hour of his martyrdom approached, was enabled to say, " I am now ready to be offered, and the time of my departure is at hand. I have fought a good fight; I have finished my course; I have kept the faith : henceforth there is laid up for me a crown of righteousness, which the Lord, the righteous Judge, shall give me at that day ; and not to me only, but unto all them also that love his appearing." The Christian expects after death not to spend twelve dreary months in hell, " For we know that if our earthly house of this tabernacle were dissolved, we have a building of God, an house not made with hands, eternal in the heavens. For in this we groan, earnestly desiring to be clothed upon with our house which is from heaven : if so be, that being clothed, we shall not be found naked. For we that are in this tabernacle do groan, being burdened : not for that we would be unclothed, but clothed upon, that mortality might be swallowed up of life." (2 Cor. v. 1—4.) Such is the hope which Christianity holds out, and it is hardly necessary to prove that it is more satisfactory, and more calculated to convey peace to the conscience of a dying believer, than the dread prospect, of twelve months' sojourn in the place of torment. This in itself proves, that Christianity is greatly superior to Judaism, and even affords a presumption that Christianity is true. Reason tells us, that if God has given a revelation at all, that revelation must contain the way of obtaining pardon for sins, and be able to administer consolation to the dying. In this respect Judaism fails. It promises forgiveness and justification to a thousand ceremonial observances, but in the hour of man's extremity, it tells him that there is no way of pardon, but that he must go down into torment, and expiate his sins by actual suffering. This system cannot, therefore, be of God. Christianity, on the contrary, has the first great essential in religion ; it informs man how he can obtain forgiveness, and tells him how to die in peace ; and the system of pardon and consolation which it proposes, is in exact accordance with the doctrine of Moses and the prophets. Moses promises pardon to an atoning sacrifice. Isaiah says, that Messiah is to be the true atonement; and Christianity rests upon these two principles. The Jew himself must admit, that our hope has at least a strong appearance of truth, and that we have the letter of the Old Testament in our favour. We have, therefore, more reason to trust to Christianity, than he has for resting on Judaism, which has not even a semblance of proof, and is as far from the letter as from the spirit of the Old Testament. We would earnestly request of every Jew to consider what is his hope in death, and what is his prospect after it? Can he be content with that which Judaism offers? Can he be happy in the prospect of twelve months' torment? Or, can the repetition of Kaddish afford him any hope of liberation from that place, whither his sins have brought him?

He cannot pretend to have any warrant from Scripture. Where does Moses tell a Jewish child to say Kaddish for his deceased parent, or that the saying of it will deliver the soul from the grasp of Divine justice? And reason does not offer a greater measure of consolation. Reason says plainly, either that the deceased is guilty or not guilty; either, therefore, justice demands that he should be punished or delivered. In the one case the prayer is unavailing, in the other unnecessary. Reason says that God either pardons or punishes; but that there is no middle way. Judaism then offers a hope equally unwarranted by reason and Scripture, and thus, forsaking a poor sinner in the hour of his extremity, is not worthy of the profession of any one who uses his reason, or reveres the Word of God.

No. XXXIX.

ALMSGIVING.

THE object of our late numbers has been to point out the inconsistency and precariousness of the various hopes, which the oral law holds out to its advocates, and the consequent inadequacy of a religion which leaves its professors without a reasonable hope of eternal happiness. In the course of our observations, the subject of almsgiving twice presented itself prominently to our notice; first, as a means of compensating for the sins and omissions of the past year; and secondly, as a means of promoting the repose of departed souls; from which it appears that the oral law considers this duty as most important and beneficial both to the living and the dead. The object of the present paper shall therefore be, to inquire into the rabbinic doctrine of almsgiving, and to compare it with the law and the prophets. The duty and extent of almsgiving are thus defined:—

מצות עשה ליתן צדקה לעניי ישראל כפי מה
שראוי לעני אם היתה יד הנותן משגת, שנאמר פתח
תפתח את ידך לו, ונאמר והחזקת בו גר ותושב
וחי עמך ונאמר וחי אחיך עמך, וכל הרואה עני

מבקש והעלים עיניו ממנו ולא נתן לו צדקה עבר בלא תעשה שנאמר לא תאמץ את לבבך ולא תקפוץ את ידך מאחיך האביון; לפי מה שיחסר העני אתה מצווה ליתן לו, אם אין לו כסות מכסים אותו, אם אין לו כלי בית קונין לו, אם אין לו אשה משיאין אותו, ואם היתה אשה משיאין אותה לאיש, אפילו היה דרכו של זה העני לרכוב על הסוס ועבד רץ לפניו והעני ירד מנכסיו קונין לו סוס לרכוב עליו ועבד לרוץ לפניו שנאמר די מחסורו אשר יחסר לו, מצווה אתה להשלים חסרונו, ואין אתה מצווה להעשירו. יתום שבא להשיאו אשה, שוכרין לו בית ומציעים לו מטה וכל כלי תשמישו ואחר כך משיאין לו אשה, בא העני ושאל די מחסורו ואין יד הנותן משגת נותנין לו כפי השגת ידו וכמה עד חמישית נכסיו מצוה מן המובחר ואחד מעשרה בנכסיו בינוני, פחות מכן עין רעה:

"It is an affirmative precept to give alms to the poor of Israel, according as the poor have need, if in the power of the giver; for it is said, 'Thou shalt open thine hand wide to him' (Deut. xv. 8); and again, 'Thou shalt relieve him' a proselyte* or a sojourner, that he may live with thee;' and again, 'That thy brother may live with thee.' (Lev. xxv. 35, 36.) Whosoever sees a poor man begging, and shuts his eyes against him, and does not give him alms, transgresses a negative precept: for it is said, 'Thou shalt not harden thine heart nor shut thine hand from thy poor brother.' (Deut. xv. 7.) According as the poor hath need, thou art commanded to give. If he has no clothing, he is to be clothed; if he has no furniture, it is to be bought for him; if he has no wife, he is to be helped to marry one; if a woman, she is to be assisted in getting a husband: yea, if it had been the poor man's custom to ride upon a horse, and to have a servant running before him—but he is now come down in the world,—it is a duty to buy him a horse to ride, and a servant to run before him, for it is said, 'Sufficient for his need, in that which he wanteth' (Deut. xv. 8); and thou art commanded perfectly to relieve his want, but not to make him rich. If an orphan apply for assistance in order to marry, it is a duty to hire a house for him, and to provide all necessary furniture, and afterwards to help him to marry. If a poor man come and ask for relief, and the giver has not as much as he wants, he

* Literally, "a stranger."

ought to give what his means afford. How much? He that gives a fifth of his property fulfils the commandment well. He that gives one part in ten fulfils it in a middling manner. He that gives less must be regarded as a person with an evil eye." (Hilchoth Matt'noth Aniim, cvii. 1—5.) In this definition of the nature and extent of the duty of almsgiving, there is much that is good and worthy of our admiration, especially in this selfish and money-loving age, when poverty is regarded, if not punished, as a crime, and the poor are, by many, considered as unworthy of all domestic comfort. Without binding ourselves to the approval of all the details here specified, we must acknowledge, that the spirit of this passage is agreeable to the idea of true charity, and, if universally acted upon, would do more for the happiness of mankind than some theories now afloat. But though ready to admire and to acknowledge the general beauty and excellence of this passage, we must also remark that the main feature of charity is, by the rabbinical system, excluded. God commands that this help should extend beyond the narrow limits of selfishness and nationality, to "the stranger and the sojourner," but the oral law neutralizes the mercifulness of God's commandment by making the word stranger signify a proselyte to Judaism. The original Hebrew word גר (Ger) plainly means a stranger, as may be seen in the words of Moses—

ואהבתם את הגר כי גרים הייתם בארץ מצרים :

"Love ye therefore the stranger; for ye were strangers in the land of Egypt." (Deut. x. 19.) It is certain that the Israelites were not proselytes, but strangers; this word, Ger, therefore, signifies stranger, not proselyte; and yet the oral law says that no one can be a Ger without sacrifice, circumcision, and baptism, or now, that there is no temple, without the two last requisites:—

ובזמן הזה שאין שם קרבן צריך מילה וטבילה
וכשיבנה בית המקדש יביא קרבן, גר שמל ולא טבל
או טבל ולא מל אינו גר עד שימול ויטבול :

"At the present time when there is no sacrifice, circumcision and baptism are necessary, and when the temple is rebuilt, he must bring a sacrifice. A Ger who is circumcised but not baptized, or baptized but not circumcised, is not a Ger, until he be both baptized and circumcised. (Hilchoth Issure Biah, c. xiii. 5, 6.) This rabbinical definition of what is meant by Ger, restricts the exercise of charity within a much narrower limit than that prescribed by God, and does, in fact, destroy one of the most beautiful features of the Mosaic law, namely, the merciful provision which it makes for the relief of the stranger. The law of Moses has the spirit of its divine Author. He calls himself "a jealous God," and it may well be called a jealous law, watching carefully over every departure from truth, and punishing it rigorously: and yet, like God himself, this just jealousy is tempered with mercy, and beams with love. The oral law, on the contrary, is an envious and vindictive code, and its zeal degenerates into narrow-hearted bigotry. It would not only punish the idolater, but exclude every stranger from the pale of charity, unless he be a proselyte; and an Israelite too, if he had in any wise dared to transgress the rabbinical commands. A remarkable instance of this hatred, to those whom it considers apostates, occurs in these laws respecting almsgiving. The oral law says, that the most meritorious exercise of charity is, the ransoming of captives:—

פדיון שבוים קודם לפרנסת עניים ולכסותם, ואין
לך מצוה גדולה כפדיון שבוים:

"The ransoming of captives goes before the feeding and clothing of the poor, and there is no commandment so great as this." (Hilchoth Matt'noth Aniim, c. 8.) And yet if a brother Israelite should deviate from the rabbinical commands, the oral law makes it unlawful to ransom him, at the same time that it enjoins the ransom of a slave if he be a proselyte:

עבד שנשבה הואיל שטבל לשם עבדות וקבל עליו
מצוות פודין אותו כישראל שנשבה, ושבוי שהמיר
אפילו למצוה אחת כגון שהיה אוכל נבלה להכעיס
וכיוצא בזה אסור לפדותו:

"A slave who is in captivity because he has received the baptism of slaves, and taken upon himself the commandments, is to be redeemed. But as to a captive who has altered even one commandment, if for instance he has eaten forbidden food in order to vex, it is forbidden to ransom such an one." (Ibid.) Thus the oral law forbids all compassion even to an Israelite, if he is not of the rabbinic religion. The conduct which it prescribes towards poor Gentiles, "for the sake of the ways of peace," מפני דרכי שלום, we have considered long since; but the prohibition to receive alms of the Gentiles, deserves notice here, as it furnishes another proof of the contracted views of the rabbies, and the falsehood of the oral law:—

אסור לישראל ליטול צדקה מן הגוים בפרהסיא
ואם אינו יכול לחיות בצדקה של ישראל ואינו יכול
ליטלה מן הגוים בצנעה הרי זה מותר, ומלך או שר
מן הגוים ששלח ממון לישראל לצדקה אין מחזירין

אוֹתוֹ מִשּׁוּם שְׁלוֹם מַלְכוּת אֶלָּא נוֹטְלִין מִמֶּנּוּ וְיִנָּתֵן
לַעֲנִיֵּי גוֹיִם בְּסֵתֶר כְּדֵי שֶׁלֹּא יִשְׁמַע הַמֶּלֶךְ׃

"It is unlawful for an Israelite to receive alms from the Gentiles openly. But if he cannot live by the alms of Israel, and cannot receive it from the Gentiles privately, then it is lawful. If a king or prince of the Gentiles sends money to Israel as alms, it is not to be returned, on account of the peace of the kingdom. On the contrary, it is to be received, but it is to be given to the poor of the Gentiles privately, so that the king may not hear of it." (Ibid.) Here the oral law endeavours to pervert that kindly feeling which should exist between all the families of man, and spurns a demonstration even of love, because it comes from a man of a different religion. At the same time its authors had not the moral courage to do this openly and honestly, and if need be, suffer for conscience sake. They command that the proffered alms should be taken from the king, as if they intended to devote it to the object for which he gave it, and then privately to apply it to a totally different purpose. This want of good faith shows abundantly that the oral law does not come from the God of truth. The narrow bigotry of the system thus neutralizes all the individual trials of excellence which the oral law contains. They appear beautiful only when viewed apart from their context; but the moment we view them in relation to the other parts of Rabbinism, their beauty is gone. Thus the duty and extent of almsgiving, as prescribed by the oral law, at first sight appears admirable; but the narrow spirit of bigotry by which it is circumscribed, totally destroys its moral value in the sight of God and man. Almsgiving is lovely only when it is the offspring of charity. God looks not at the mere outward act of giving money, but at the heart, and if there be no love there, almsgiving is valueless in his sight. And how can any one pretend that there is a grain of true God-like charity in a system which turns stranger into proselyte, prohibits to help a brother because he is not of our own religious sentiments, and refuses even to receive a kindness from one of a different religion? Just contrast this with the Christian doctrine, "Love your enemies, bless them that curse you, do good to them that hate you, and pray for them which despitefully use you, and persecute you; that ye may be the children of your Father which is in heaven: for he maketh his sun to rise on the evil and on the good, and sendeth rain on the just and the unjust. For if ye love them which love you, what reward have ye? Do not even the publicans the same? And if ye salute your brethren only, what do ye more than others? Do not even the publicans so? Be ye therefore perfect, even as your Father which is in heaven is perfect." (Matt. v. 44—48.)

ALMSGIVING.

But the oral law not only perverts and falsifies the true doctrine concerning charity, but also misleads its followers by teaching them to think that almsgiving is a peculiarly meritorious act, and will atone for other transgressions. Thus it is said—

חייבין אנו להזהר במצות צדקה יותר מכל מצות
עשה, שהצדקה סימן לצדיק זרע אברהם אבינו שנאמר
כי ידעתיו למען אשר יצוה את בניו לעשות צדקה,
ואין כסא ישראל מתכונן ודת אמת עומדת אלא
בצדקה שנאמר בצדקה תכונני, ואין ישראל נגאלין
אלא בצדקה שנאמר ציון במשפט תפדה ושביה בצדקה:

"We are bound to be more careful respecting this commandment of alms than about any other of all the affirmative precepts, for almsgiving is a characteristic of the righteous seed of our father Abraham, as it is said, 'I know him that he will command his children to do alms.' (Gen. xviii. 19.) By almsgiving alone it is that the throne of Israel is established, and that the law of truth standeth, for it is said, 'by alms (literally in righteousness) thou shalt be established.' (Isaiah liv. 14.) By alms alone it is that Israel shall be delivered, for it is said 'Zion shall be redeemed with judgment, and her converts with alms (righteousness).'" (Isaiah I. 27.) (Ibid. c. x. 1.) According to this doctrine, the man who gives alms has the merit of upholding truth in the world and helping to deliver Israel from captivity. But the following passage tells us that it will deliver from the punishment which he deserves, and which is already impending over his head:—

הצדקה דוחה את הגזירות הקשות וברעב תציל
ממות כמו שאירע לצרפית:

"Almsgiving annuls the evil decrees, and in famine it delivers from death, as happened to the widow of Sarepta." (Joreh Deah, 347.) And hence it is that, as we have seen, at the approach of the New Year the Rabbinists practise almsgiving abundantly, and also, that the survivors offer for the repose of the souls of their deceased relations. The tendency of this doctrine is obviously pernicious, for it encourages men to persist in sin, under the idea that almsgiving will compensate for all other deficiencies. The doctrine itself is positively false. Where does the law of Moses say that almsgiving can purchase forgiveness? Moses requires obedience to all the commandments, and he enjoins the practice of charity to the poor, but he denounces wrath against all transgression. The doctrine of Moses is not that obedience to one command will compensate for disobedience to another, but that disobedience to one command will make obedience to others of none effect. The doctrine that the giving of money to the poor can change the course of God's judgment, or alter this sentence, is very little short of blasphemy: for it represents him as an unjust judge who can be bribed, whose severity can be bought off, and whose favour can be purchased with money. A more degrading view of the Divine character can scarcely be imagined. Such conduct in a human judge would stamp him with infamy, and cannot possibly be true of Him who is a God of truth and justice. This one feature of rabbinic religion is sufficient to prove that it is the invention of men, and of men too without any very exalted notion of justice and equity.

Besides, this view of almsgiving takes away all the virtue of obedience and love to God, and turns it into a mere mercenary transaction. The great beauty of almsgiving is that it proceeds from love to God and man, and that its motives be mercy and obedience. But the man, who gives alms in order to atone for other transgressions, or to avert the punishment which he deserves, is not performing an act either of obedience or charity, he is simply making a purchase and driving a bargain which is much to his advantage. He has got money, and with that money he can buy a house, or a horse, or deliverance from punishment. It is, therefore, a simple question of interest. He considers which will be the most profitable investment of his money, and if he decide that deliverance from God's wrath is the most advantageous, he lays it out in almsgiving. Obedience, or love to God or man, is here altogether out of the question. Can any one, who has got the law and the prophets in his hands, imagine that such a doctrine can come from God? or can any reasonable being suppose, that escape from God's wrath, or the enjoyment of his favour depends not upon man's moral worth, but upon his ability to give alms: in a word, that his salvation depends not upon the state of his heart, but the laying out of his money? This one doctrine, if thoroughly believed and acted upon, would overturn the whole law of Moses, and offer life not to the obedient, but to the moneyed.

In this doctrine of almsgiving, however, the oral law errs at the very foundation. It has chosen the Hebrew word צדקה to stand for "almsgiving," whereas its true signification is "righteousness," as may be easily proved by reference to passages where it cannot possibly signify "almsgiving," as for instance—

וצדקה תהיה לנו כי נשמור לעשות את כל המצוה
הזאת לפני ה׳ אלהינו כאשר צונו :

"And it shall be our *righteousness* (not our almsgiving), if we observe to do all these commandments before the Lord our

God as he hath commanded us." (Deut. vi. 25.) Here צדקה cannot possibly signify almsgiving. And again,

והאמין בה' ויחשבה לו צדקה :

"And he believed in the Lord; and he counted it to him for righteousness (not for almsgiving)." (Gen. xv. 6.) And again,

לך אדני הצדקה ולנו בושת הפנים :

"O Lord, righteousness belongeth unto thee, but unto us confusion of face" (Dan. ix. 7), where it is impossible to say that "Almsgiving belongeth unto the Lord." The oral law is therefore guilty of perverting the meaning of one of the plainest and most commonly repeated words in the Bible, and of course of thereby giving an erroneous sense to the passage where it occurs. Thus it says, as we have seen above, "that by almsgiving the throne of Israel is established and the law of truth standeth," and it proves this assertion by referring to a verse of Isaiah, where the word צדקה occurs, and which signifies "by righteousness shalt thou be established," but which it perverts to mean "by almsgiving thou shalt be established." Here then the oral law is plainly convicted of falsifying the Word of God, and perverting its meaning in order to serve its own purposes and favour its own false doctrine. To teach false doctrine is bad enough, but to pervert the plain sense of Scripture is a great deal worse. Either charge, if proved, would be sufficient to prove that the oral law is a false religion, but here both charges are proved together. The oral law here teaches that almsgiving can do that which it cannot do, namely, bribe God to have mercy; and it supports its false doctrine by interpreting צדקה to signify "almsgiving," whereas it plainly signifies "righteousness." A religion guilty of such error cannot be from God. It is for the Jews, then, to consider whether they will persist in upholding the truth of a system which opposes the doctrines of Moses and the prophets, and perverts the Word of God. The great boast of the Jews is, that they are faithful to Moses and to the religion of Moses: but this boast is vain so long as they profess Judaism. If Moses were to rise from the dead, and get the oral law into his hands, he would not be able to recognise it as the religion which he left to Israel. And, as to the commands about almsgiving, he would not be able even to translate them, for in his time צדקה signified righteousness.

The prophet Isaiah would feel equal astonishment if he were to return and learn, that the oral law quoted him as an authority for the assertion, that Zion is to be redeemed, not with righteousness, but with almsgiving. And we doubt not that both Moses and Isaiah would protest as earnestly as we do against a doctrine based upon perversion. But it is extraor-

D

dinary, if the Rabbinists really believe their own doctrine, that Israel can be delivered from captivity by almsgiving, that they should set any bounds to their liberality, or ever stop giving, until the desired redemption be effected. If their doctrine be true, then all that they so earnestly pray for, is entirely in their own power. They know the means, and they possess the means of terminating this long captivity. They need only to give a sufficiency of alms, and, according to the oral law, even Zion itself shall be delivered. How extraordinary then, that they should have suffered so many centuries of misery to pass over their heads, and left their brethren to endure such calamities, when liberality in almsgiving could have put a period to all their sorrows. We think too highly of Israel's charity to suppose for a moment that they would hesitate to make the sacrifice, if they were persuaded of its efficacy. We must therefore infer, that they do not believe in the doctrine, and ask them, why do they profess a religion in which they do not believe?

No. XL.

PRIESTS AND LEVITES.

THE great test of a man's faith in, and love to, his religion is his practice. If a man live in open and perpetual transgression of its commands, no profession can satisfy us that he is in earnest, or that he really believes what his creed confesses. Now let the advocates of the oral law examine themselves by this test. They profess to believe in, and to love the law of Moses; and their great boast is, that Moses is their master, and that they are his disciples, but do they prove the reality of their faith by their obedience? They sometimes tax Christians with inconsistency in professing to believe in Moses, and yet in neglecting the observance of certain ceremonial observances; but are they themselves more careful and less guilty in this matter? We do not mean to allude to the weightier matters of the law, love to God and man: that is a question for the conscience, not a subject for controversy, but we refer to some mere external matters, easy of observance, and open to the cognisance of every man. Moses and the prophets have commanded that the priests, the Levites, הכהנים הלוים, should be the teachers of the law, and that from them the people

PRIESTS AND LEVITES. 311

should learn. Moses does not say one word about rabbies or wise men, חֲכָמִים, but restricts the office of teaching to the priests, the Levites : now, do the modern Jews obey Moses in this respect ? Who are their teachers of religion, and from whom do they learn ? Are the priests and the Levites the teachers of Israel, as Moses commanded, or are they taught by their rabbies and Chachamim, of whom Moses does not say one syllable ?

We assert, that Moses has commanded that the priests, the Levites, should be the religious teachers in Israel, and in proof we refer to the words of Moses himself. In the tenth chapter of ויקרא, Leviticus, he thus writes :—

וידבר ה׳ אל אהרן לאמר . יין ושכר אל תשת
אתה ובניך אתך בבאכם אל אהל מועד ולא תמותו
חקת עולם לדורותיכם . ולהבדיל בין הקודש ובין
החול ובין הטמא ובין הטהור . ולהורות את בני
ישראל את כל החקים אשר דבר ה׳ אליהם ביד משה :

"And the Lord spake unto Aaron, saying, Do not drink wine nor strong drink, thou nor thy sons with thee, when ye go into the tabernacle of the congregation, lest ye die : it shall be a statute for ever throughout your generations : and that ye may put difference between holy and unholy, and between unclean and clean ; and that ye may teach the children of Israel all the statutes which the Lord hath spoken unto them by the hand of Moses." Here the nature of the priest's office is clearly defined. It is, in the first place, to go into the tabernacle of the congregation, and there to serve before the Lord : and secondly to instruct the children of Israel in the difference between holy and profane, clean and unclean, and especially to teach the children of Israel "ALL THE STATUTES," which the Lord had given to Moses. The commission is not only very comprehensive, but very exclusive. If the priests were to teach "all the statutes," there is no room left for rabbies, or Chachamim, or any other description of teacher. The priests are the only divinely-accredited religious teachers in Israel.

If this passage stood alone, it would be quite sufficient to establish the doctrine; but it does not. Moses was particularly anxious to impress upon the Israelites the nature of the priestly office, and therefore repeats the instruction again and again. Thus in the law respecting a dead body found lying in a field, after commanding that the elders and judges should come forth, he adds—

ונגשו הכהנים בני לוי כי בם בחר ה׳ אלהיך
לשרתו ולברך בשם ה׳ ועל פיהם יהיה כל ריב וכל
נגע :

"And the priests, the sons of Levi, shall come near: for them the Lord thy God hath chosen to minister unto him, and to bless in the name of the Lord: and by their word shall every controversy and every stroke be tried." (Deut. xxi. 5.) One should have thought that the elders and judges were enough in such a case. But not so. God had determined that the priests were to teach Israel "all his statutes," and therefore commands that they should be present in this case, that they should give the decision.

Again, when Moses was about to part from Israel, and to leave them his dying benediction, he was directed by the spirit of prophecy to impress upon them the same great truth, and in the most solemn manner:—

וּלְלֵוִי אָמַר תֻּמֶּיךָ וְאוּרֶיךָ לְאִישׁ חֲסִידֶךָ אֲשֶׁר נִסִּיתוֹ
בְּמַסָּה תְּרִיבֵהוּ עַל מֵי מְרִיבָה, הָאוֹמֵר לְאָבִיו וּלְאִמּוֹ
לֹא רְאִיתִיו וְאֶת אֶחָיו לֹא הִכִּיר וְאֶת בָּנָיו לֹא יָדָע כִּי
שָׁמְרוּ אִמְרָתְךָ וּבְרִיתְךָ יִנְצֹרוּ. יוֹרוּ מִשְׁפָּטֶיךָ לְיַעֲקֹב
תּוֹרָתְךָ לְיִשְׂרָאֵל וגו׳:

"And of Levi he said, Let thy Thummim and thy Urim be with thy Holy One, whom thou didst prove at Massah, and with whom thou didst strive at the waters of Meribah: who said unto his father and mother, I have not seen him; neither did he acknowledge his brethren, nor knew his own children: for they have observed thy word, and kept thy covenant. *They shall teach Jacob thy judgments, and Israel thy law.*" (Deut. xxxiii. 8—10.) And as this doctrine forms a part of Moses' last words, so also it is found in the last prophetic message which God vouchsafed to Israel. Malachi, the last of the prophets, reminds Israel—

כִּי שִׂפְתֵי כֹהֵן יִשְׁמְרוּ דַעַת וְתוֹרָה יְבַקְשׁוּ מִפִּיהוּ
כִּי מַלְאַךְ ה׳ צְבָאוֹת הוּא:

"That the priest's lips should keep knowledge, and they should seek the law at his mouth: for he is the messenger of the Lord of hosts" (Mal. ii. 7): so that if there be any one thing more plain than another in the Old Testament it is this, that the sons of Levi are the divinely-appointed religious teachers of Israel, and that it is the duty of all Israelites to seek instruction from them.

It cannot be said that the priests are not now well known, and that on this account these commands have lost their force; for those who believe in the oral law, profess to know the family of Levi, and in the synagogue, at the reading of the law, the priest and the Levite are called up in a certain order:

בְּכָל קְרִיאָה וּקְרִיאָה מֵאֵלּוּ כֹּהֵן קוֹרֵא רִאשׁוֹן וְאַחֲרָיו

לוי ואחריו ישראל, ומנהג פשוט הוא היום בישראל
שאפילו כהן עם הארץ קודם לקרות לפני חכם גדול
ישראל:

"At every time of reading, the priest reads first, and after him the Levite, and after him the Israelite. And the simple custom of the present time is, that a priest, even though he be an unlearned man (amhaaretz), takes precedence in reading before the most learned, who is only an Israelite." (Hilchoth T'phillah, c. xii. 18.) And as the priests are thus supposed to be known, so the oral law expressly maintains that they still retain their priestly office, and are bound to discharge the duties of it, so far as is possible, in the captivity: and therefore requires them to bless the people as Moses commanded. Indeed the firm conviction of the Talmudists on this subject is strikingly exhibited in their assertion, that a priest, although unlearned, or even notoriously wicked, is still not exempted from his obligation to perform this duty:—

כהן שלא היה לו דבר מכל אלה המונעין נשיאת
כפים אע״פ שאינו חכם ואינו מדקדק במצוות או שהיה
חבריו מרננים אחריו או שלא היה משאו ומתנו בצדק
הרי זה נושא את כפיו ואין מונעין אותו, לפי שזו
מצות עשה על כל כהן וכהן שראוי לנשיאת כפים
ואין אומרים לאדם רשע הוסף רשע והמנע מן המצוות,
ואל תתמה ותאמר מה תועיל ברכת הדיוט זה, שאין
קבול הברכה תלוי בכהנים אלא בהקב״ה שנאמר ושמו
את שמי על בני ישראל ואני אברכם, הכהנים עושים
מצוה שנצטוו בה והקב״ה ברחמיו מברך את ישראל
כחפצו:

"A priest who has none of these disqualifications for the lifting up of hands, even though he be not learned, nor accurate in the commandments; and although his companions make a mock of him, or his dealings should not be righteous, still he is to lift up his hands [to bless], and is not to be prevented, for this is an affirmative precept binding upon every priest, who is otherwise qualified; and we must not say to a wicked man, Away, thou wicked man, be thou disqualified from keeping the commandments. Do not ask, saying, What profit can there be in the blessing of this simple fellow? for the receiving of the blessing does not depend upon the priests, but upon the Holy One, blessed be He, for it is said, 'They shall put my name upon the children of Israel, and I will bless them.' The priests perform the duty commanded them, and God, in his mercy, blesses Israel according to his pleasure."

(Ibid. c. xv. 6.) The existence, then, of the priests, and their continued obligation to perform such official duties as are now possible, are fully acknowledged, yea, it is even asserted that a wicked priest is by no means to be prevented from doing his duty: it has also been plainly proved, from the words of Moses and the prophets, that it is the duty of the priests to teach, and of the Israelites to be taught by them: and no man can deny that the performance of this duty is possible. The destruction of the temple has prevented the priest from sacrificing, but it has made no difference with regard to the possibility of teaching: it is, therefore, a fair question to propose to those who boast in their obedience to the law of Moses, *How is this Mosaic command respecting the teaching of the law fulfilled?* Are the priests, the Levites, the religious teachers in all Jewish congregations? or have they been excluded from the office assigned to them by Moses? and is it occupied by others to whom Moses did not give it? Every Jew must answer that this command of Moses is utterly disregarded—that the office of the priesthood, as established by Moses, has now scarcely the shadow of an existence amongst the Jews—that the rabbies, Chachamim, and the Melamm'dim are universally the religious teachers—and that hundreds, if not thousands, of the priests are left in utter obscurity, and not a few in destitution. Jeremiah complained of the heathen—

פני כהנים לא נשאו :

"They respected not the persons of the priests" (Lam. iv. 16); but it is equally applicable to the adherents of the oral law. Here and there a son of Levi may be a rabbi, and then he has the honour attached to the rabbinical office; but the Mosaic institution of the priesthood, as the appointed order of religious teachers to Israel is utterly disregarded. Moses declares, as we have seen above, that it is the priest's office "to distinguish between holy and unholy, and between clean and unclean;" but if a Jew has got a שאלה, a question or a difficulty, it is to the rabbi that he goes to get the decision. Moses says that the priests are appointed by God "to teach Israel all the statutes which the Lord hath spoken to them;" but now men are made rabbies and Melamm'dim who do not pretend to be of the family of Levi: and there are congregations even where there is no Levite nor priest at all, and where, therefore, this command is utterly despised. But the worst feature in this disobedience is, that it is systematic. It is not one of the casualties of the captivity, but it is the deliberate aim of the oral law to degrade the priesthood, as established by Moses, and to set up above it another office, that of rabbi, of which Moses does not say one word. The oral law, instead of deprecating the possibility of an Israelite congregation existing without a priest a son of Levi, quietly layeth down the law for doing without them. When prescribing the order in which persons are to be called up to the reading of the law, it says—

אין שם כהן עולה ישראל ולא יעלה אחריו לוי כלל :

"If there be no priest there, then an Israelite is to go up, but no Levite is to follow him." (Ibid., c. xii. 19.) And again,

ואם אין להם כהן כלל כשיגיע שליח צבור לשים
שלום וכו׳ :

"But if the congregation has no priest at all, when the reader comes to that part of the prayers he is to say," &c. (Ibid., c. xv. 10.) Now if the oral law were anxious to maintain the institution of Moses it could make no such supposition. On the contrary it would urge upon every congregation the indispensable necessity of having a priest of the family of Levi. The supposition shows that its authors cared but little about the commands of Moses, for where there is no priest it is plainly impossible for the people to obey that often-repeated precept to learn the law from the sons of Levi. And yet the authors of the oral law, who care so little for this commandment of Moses about the priests, command the appointment of Melamm'dim, or schoolmasters, under pain of utter destruction:—

מושיבין מלמדי תינוקות בכל מדינה ומדינה ובכל
פלך ופלך ובכל עיר ועיר , וכל עיר שאין בה תינוקות
של בית רבן מחרימין את אנשי העיר עד שמושיבין
מלמדי תינוקות ואם עוד לא הושיבו מחרימין את
העיר :

"Teachers of children are to be established in every province and district and city. And every city in which there are not school children the men of that city are to be visited with the Cherem, and if they still neglect, the city itself is to be devoted." (Hilch. Talm. Torah, c. ii.) When we see them enforce this commandment of their own with such zeal and severity, and yet appear so careless and negligent about the commandment of Moses, we justly infer that this neglect was intentional, and that the object was to exalt themselves, and to depress that office which God himself had ordained. And this inference is abundantly confirmed by הלכות כבוד רבו, the numerous and minute laws respecting the honour due to a rabbi, whilst the respect due to the family of Levi is almost entirely disregarded, and his office evidently depreciated below that of the former. As, for instance, in establishing the order in which captives are to be redeemed, the oral law says the priest is to be redeemed before the Levite, and the Levite before the Israelite, but then adds—

במה דברים אמורים כשחיו שניהם שוין בחכמה ,
אבל אם היה כהן גדול עם הארץ וממזר תלמיד חכם
תלמיד חכם קודם :

"In what case does this hold good? In case that they were both equal in wisdom. But if the high priest be an unlearned man, and an illegitimate child be the disciple of a wise man (chacham), the latter is to have the precedence." (Hilchoth Matt'noth Aniim, c. viii. 17.) Here the office of the priesthood and even of the high priesthood itself is put below that of the rabbi or chacham, and the intention of the Rabbinists to exalt themselves, and their utter disregard for the law of Moses and his commandments, is especially apparent. The high priest was the chief person in the whole Mosaic dispensation. Without him the blood of the offering could not be carried into the holy of holies on the Day of Atonement, and yet the oral law says, that if he and an illegitimate child, that is, the least honoured person in Israel, be both in captivity, and the latter be the disciple of a rabbi, he is to be redeemed first. It is needless to add any further proof of the fact that the command of Moses, respecting the family of Levi, is systematically and intentionally transgressed by the authors and adherents of the oral law. The priests, the Levites, have been thrust out of that office which God gave them, and others have been made the religious teachers of Israel who have no right at all to this appointment. How then can the modern Jews pretend to be zealous for the law of Moses? They are living in plain and systematic violation of one of his plainest commands. It will not do *to say* that the office of rabbi is also of divine appointment. An assertion which nullifies a Mosaic institution must have the most unexceptionable evidence. Its proof must be at least as clear as the original appointment. To persuade any real lover of the Mosaic law that the rabbies have a right to thrust out the family of Levi from their office, and to take it upon themselves, the express declaration of God is absolutely necessary. And if the rabbies could prove, which they cannot, that they are the lawful teachers of Israel, it would necessarily follow that the Mosaic law has been changed, and then one of the chief dogmas of modern Judaism, the immutability of the Mosaic law, is entirely overthrown. When Moses gave the law the priests were the religious teachers of Israel. Since the dominion of the oral law, not the priests, but the rabbies have been the teachers. Here then is an important, yea, an organic change in the Mosaic constitution. This change then is either unlawful or lawful. If it be unlawful, then the rabbies have no right to be the teachers of Israel. If it be lawful, then to change and alter the Mosaic law is lawful, and then modern Judaism, which teaches that there can be no change, is false. This is the only alternative which modern Jews can adopt,—they must either maintain the immutability of the law at the expense of the rabbinic office, or they must assert the legitimacy of the rabbinic office at the expense of the law. In either case the oral law is convicted of teaching falsehood; and in neither case can the modern Jews make a boast of loyalty to the law of Moses. They charge Christians with disregarding and transgressing the Mosaic law, but let them point out, even in the practice of Gentile Christians, any one apparent transgression more heinous than the expulsion of the family of Levi from the office to which Moses appointed them. The fact is notorious. This family is every where neglected and in obscurity, struggling with the cares and business of the world, instead of occupying the station given to them by Moses. Let all the lovers of modern Judaism consider this fact, and then ask themselves how they can pretend to be keeping the law of Moses? Let them remember that they have themselves made a change in the law by appointing rabbies instead of the priests, and that, if they defend this change, they teach the very same doctrine which they blame in Gentile Christians, namely, the mutability and abrogation of the Mosaic law. Of course we do not mean to dictate to Israel in this matter. If they are conscientiously persuaded that the institutions of Moses have been abrogated, they can then consistently maintain the appointment of rabbies, but let them give up their common, though mistaken, argument against Christianity. But if they believe what they so commonly profess, that the law of Moses is not, and cannot be abrogated, then let them act consistently, renounce the oral law, and restore the family of Levi to the office from which modern Judaism has excluded them for so many centuries. To follow the oral law, and at the same time to obey the written law of Moses in this matter, is plainly impossible. The oral law is for the rabbies and the Chachamim—the words of Moses are for the family of Levi. The Jews may, and of course will, choose as they think best; but, if they determine upon maintaining the rabbinical system, let them not pretend to be followers of Moses. Let them honestly confess that they do not like Moses and his laws, and that they prefer the new and modern religion of the rabbies. The subject is important to all Israel, but especially so to the sons of Levi themselves. God gave them the important charge of instructing the house of Israel in his laws, are they then at liberty to resign their sacred office into the hands of others? Has God dispensed them from obedience to his command? If so, what obligation rests upon them to bless the people? By lifting up their hands and blessing the people, they confess that their office still continues; and, if so, the obligation to perform all its duties continues also. Either the law of Moses is abrogated, or the priests are still the appointed religious teachers of Israel.

The priests have the same alternative as the people, *i.e.*, either to assert the rights and perform the duties of their priestly office, or honestly to acknowledge that they do not believe in Moses, nor care for his religion, but that their religion is that of the rabbies. The responsibility is however much heavier on the family of Levi than on Israelites of another tribe. To the sons of Levi, God committed the honourable office of instructing Israel. They have been set as the watchmen in Israel, and are therefore answerable, not only for their own neglect, but for the error and destruction of the people. It is then high time for them to remember their duty and the zeal of their forefathers in extirpating error, and to show themselves worthy of their high origin, and of their divine appointment, by opposing the errors of the oral law.

No. XLI.

RABBINIC IDEAS OF THE DEITY.

It is an indisputable fact, that the modern Jews have entirely cast off the laws of Moses respecting the priests of the family of Levi, and have chosen and appointed to themselves other teachers, of whom Moses says nothing. What the cause was of such extraordinary conduct in those who profess a great zeal for the law of Moses, we do not now profess to inquire; but we think that every Jew ought to have a very good reason for thus wilfully, systematically, and continually transgressing the commandments of God. He ought, at the very least, to be able to show that the doctrines of these new teachers are far superior to those of the religious teachers appointed by Moses; and that the superabundant excellence and wisdom of rabbinic teaching does, at least, justify the change which they have made in the Mosaic law. We have had occasion in these papers to consider the nature of the new doctrine chosen instead of the law of Moses, and to us it certainly appears that "The Old Paths" were better. To-day we propose to illustrate the rabbinic notions of the Deity, and do not intend by any means to select the most objectionable representations contained in the rabbinical writings, but shall confine ourselves to a few well-known passages, which are intended to explain to us the mode in which God spends his time. Concerning the day, the rabbies say that it is spent in the following manner:—

שתים עשרה שעות הוי היום , שלש הראשונות הקב״ה יושב ועוסק בתורה , שניות יושב ודן את כל העולם כולו , כיון שרואה שנתחייב העולם כליה , עומד מכסא הדין ויושב על כסא הרחמים , שלישיות יושב וזן את כל העולם כולו , מקרני ראמים עד ביצי כינים , רביעיות יושב ומשחק עם לויתן , שנאמר לויתן זה יצרת לשחק בו וכו׳ :

"The day has twelve hours. The first three, the Holy One, blessed be He, sits and occupies himself in the law. The second, he sits and judges the whole world. When he perceives that the world deserves utter destruction, He stands up from the throne of judgment, and sits on the throne of mercy. The third, he sits, and feeds all the world, from the horns of the unicorns to the eggs of the vermin. In the fourth, he sits and plays with Leviathan, for it is said (Psalm civ. 26) 'The Leviathan whom thou hast formed to play therewith.'" (Avodah Zarah, fol. iii., col. 2.) In another place we have an account of the manner in which the night is spent:—

ר׳ אליעזר אומר שלש משמרות הוי הלילה ועל
כל משמר ומשמר יושב הקב״ה ושואג כארי שנאמר
ה׳ ממרום ישאג וממעון קדשו יתן קולו שאוג ישאג
על נוהו :

"Rabbi Eliezer says, The night has three watches, and at every watch, the Holy One, blessed be He, sits and roars like a lion, for it is said, 'The Lord shall roar from on high, and utter his voice from his holy habitation: roaring he shall roar upon his habitation.'" (Jer. xxv. 30.) And again, a little lower down, the same assertion is made in the name of two other rabbies, and the cause of God's roaring assigned:—

אמר רב יצחק בר שמואל משמיה דרב שלש
משמרות הוי הלילה ועל כל משמר ומשמר יושב
הקב״ה ושואג כארי ואומר אוי שחרבתי את ביתי
ושרפתי את היכלי והגליתי את בני לבין אומות
העולם :

"Rabbi Isaac, the son of Samuel, says, in the name of Rav, The night has three watches, and at every watch, the Holy One, blessed be He, sits and roars like a lion, and says, Woe is me that I have laid desolate my house, and burned my sanctuary, and sent my children into captivity amongst the nations of the world." (Berachoth, fol. iii., col. 1.) Now we ask every reasonable man whether this is a representation worthy of the Creator of heaven and earth? We are told here, first, that God is like a man in observing day and night—that he has set times for different employments, and a time for amusement. We are told, secondly, that instead of comprehending all things past, present, and to come, at all times, and instead of upholding all things by the continual fiat of his omnipotent rule, that he is obliged to consider each thing in succession; and that, like a poor frail child of man, He can do only one thing at a time. And thirdly, we are here informed, that the Divine Being sits all night, and mourns like a child, over an act which he rashly committed, but now wishes to have undone. Is this a fit representation of Deity, or is it awful blasphemy? How different is the description given by Moses—"Lord, thou hast been our dwelling-place in all generations. Before the mountains were brought forth, or ever thou hadst formed the earth and the world, even from everlasting to everlasting, thou art God. A thousand years in thy sight are but as yesterday when it is past, and as a watch in the night" (Ps. xc. 1—4); and again, that other beautiful passage of the Psalmist, "Of old thou hast laid the foundations of the earth; and the heavens are the work of thy hands. They shall perish, but thou shalt endure; yea all of them shall wax old like a garment: and as a vesture shalt thou change them, and they shall be changed; but thou art the same, and thy years shall have no end." (Ps. cii. 25—27.) In both these passages, unchangeableness, entire freedom from all vicissitude and succession, is presented to our view as the prominent feature in the character of Deity. Whereas, the God whom the rabbies describe, is a being subject to the same alterations as ourselves, and liable to change, in its worst form, that is, to that change of will which ensues on disappointed expectations. They say, that their God destroyed his temple and sent his children into captivity, and that now he is very sorry for it, and vents the bitterness of his grief in lamentations compared to the roaring of a lion. Such a deity is no more like the God of Abraham, Isaac, and Jacob, than Jeroboam's calves. He may not be a graven image, but he is nevertheless an idol, not indeed of gold or silver, but of the imagination. Nothing can be more different than the Being described by the rabbies, and that God declared in Moses and the Prophets. And yet on this very point, where the oral law errs so grievously, Christianity maintains the truth. The New Testament declares unto us the same Being revealed in the Old. It says, " Every good gift, and every perfect gift is from above, and cometh down from the Father of lights, with whom is no variableness, neither shadow of turning." (James i. 17.)

But the rabbies falsely ascribe to God not only variableness, but imperfect knowledge also. They say, that He spends a fourth part of the day in the study of the law. Now either God knows the law, or he does not. If he does know the law, then study is useless; and if he does not, then his knowledge is imperfect, and either supposition is altogether unworthy of the Deity. Indeed it is very difficult to argue against a doctrine so monstrous, or to show the full absurdity where the subject is so grave and sacred. But we put it to the good sense of every Israelite, and ask him whether he can believe that the God of knowledge studies in his own law? Is not such an assertion a blasphemous falsehood, and does it not show that those who made it were themselves utterly devoid of all true knowledge of God? Some persons endeavour to excuse this blasphemy by saying that the words are not to be taken literally, and that the rabbies employed oriental figures. But this will not save the credit of the oral law; for if we admit the figure, we cannot excuse the blasphemy contained in the assertion, that God studies the law one fourth of every day. No man that has any reverence for his Creator would venture to use such language, not even in the way of a parable. It proves in every case that those rabbies were totally devoid of that reverence which is due to God, and therefore most unfit teachers of religion. But, further, if these passages be figurative, what is the real sense? What is meant by studying in the law, or playing with Leviathan, or uttering complaints at the beginning of every watch in the night; or what is intended by ascribing to God one sort of employment in the day and the other in the night? It is not enough to say that these are all figures conveying the most profound wisdom; this assertion must be proved by showing what this wisdom is. Let the Rabbinists explain these figures satisfactorily, and they will then have some chance of being believed, though even that would not amount to a proof, that the authors of these passages intended that they should be understood mystically. It is a certain fact that many of the rabbies have understood these and similar passages literally. In the commentary on the assertion, "That in the second three hours God sits and judges the world," we are told, that some believed this so firmly as to think that on this very account the additional form of prayer, called מוסף, was prescribed:—

יש אומרים כי לכך תקנו בקדושת מוסף לומר
ממקומו הוא יפן כי סתם מוסף בשניות בא ואז הוא
יושב ודן ואנו מתפללין שיפנה מכסא דין לשבת
בכסא רחמים :

"Some say, that on this account the words 'Let him turn from his place,' have been appointed in the sanctification of the Musaph, for this part of the prayer generally occurs in the second three hours, when he is sitting in judgment, and that we pray that he may turn from the throne of judgment, and sit on the throne of mercy." Those who held this opinion plainly thought, that the hours were literal hours, and that the distribution of the day into four different employments was not figurative, but real. These persons, therefore, believed that God studies in the law, that he plays with Leviathan, and observes the distinction of day and night. And it must be confessed that, if they believed in the Talmud, they had good reason for this literal interpretation, as the corresponding passage, respecting God's roaring like a lion at every watch of the night, cannot be explained figuratively, if it be taken in connexion with its context. The context contains a discussion about real, not figurative night-watches. The question proposed by the Mishna is, Until what hour of the night is it lawful to perform the evening-reading of the Sh'mah Israel (Hear, O Israel)? R. Eliezer says, It is lawful until the end of the first watch. The Gemara then considers what the rabbi could mean by this definition—

מה קסבר ר' אליעזר אי קסבר ג' משמרות הוי
הלילה לימא עד ארבע שעות ואי קסבר ארבע משמרות
הוי הלילה לימא עד שלש שעות, לעולם קסבר

שלש משמרות הוי הלילה והא קא משמע לן איכא
משמרות ברקיעא ואיכא משמרות בארעא דתניא וכו׳:

"What did R. Eliezer mean? If he meant that the night
had three watches, he ought to have said until the fourth hour:
but if he meant that the night has four watches, he ought to
have said until the third hour. There can be no doubt that
he meant that the night has three watches, and intended to
say, that there are watches in heaven and watches upon earth,
for the Bareitha says, &c."——And then follows the passage,
saying, that in each watch God roars like a lion. It cannot,
then, be pretended that the night-watches here are figurative
or mystical. It is expressly said that there are the same
watches in heaven and earth, and the whole question is about
the real distribution of time. The following context is equally
unequivocal. R. Eliezer, immediately after saying that in each
watch God roars like a lion, goes on to give the signs whereby
each watch may be recognised even in the dark:—

וסימן לדבר משמרה ראשונה חמור נוער, שנייה
כלבים צועקים, שלישית תינוק יונק משדי אמו ואשה
מספרת עם בעלה:

"The sign of the thing is—In the first watch the ass brays;
in the second watch the dogs bark; in the third watch the
infant sucks at its mother's breast, and the wife talks with
her husband." This is plain matter-of-fact way of speaking,
and proves, beyond a doubt, that the whole passage is to
be taken literally. And if any doubt at all remained, it is
entirely removed, a little lower down on the page, by an
anecdote told by the veracious R. Jose. He says, that he
once went into one of the ruins of Jerusalem to pray, and that
whilst he was engaged in prayer, the prophet Elijah came to
the entrance of the ruin, and very civilly waited for him until
he had concluded, when they had some conversation together.
Amongst other particulars, R. Jose relates as follows:—

ואמר לי בני מה קול שמעת בחורבה זו ואמרתי
לו שמעתי בת קול שמנהמת כיונה ואומרת אוי
שחרבתי את ביתי ושרפתי את היכלי והגליתי את
בני לבין האומות ואמר לי חייך וחיי ראשך לא שעה
זו בלבד אומרת כך, אלא בכל יום ויום שלש פעמים
אומרת כך, ולא זו בלבד, אלא בשעה שישראל
נכנסין לבתי כנסיות ולבתי מדרשות ועונין אמן יהא
שמא רבא מברך הקב״ה מנענע ראשו ואומר אשרי
המלך שמקלסין אותו בביתו כך מה לו לאב שהגלה
את בניו:

"And he (Elias) said to me, What sort of a voice didst thou hear in the ruin? I said to him, I heard a Bath Kol cooing like a dove, and saying, Woe is me that I have desolated my house, and burnt my sanctuary, and sent my children into captivity amongst the nations. And he said unto me, As thou livest, and thy head liveth, it is not at this hour only, but three times every day the voice says these words. And not only so, but when the Israelites enter the synagogues, and the houses of study, and say, 'Amen, may his great name be blessed,' the Holy One, blessed be He, shakes his head, and says, Blessed is the King who is praised in his house; but what profit has the father who sends his children into captivity," &c. Here we have the testimony of R. Jose to the truth of the fact, that God does thus complain in the manner described above, and we have the Prophet Elijah swearing that this happens three times every day. It is plain, therefore, that the authors of the Talmud knew of no mystical interpretation and intended none. It was their simple belief that God observed the three watches of the night, and at the beginning of each roared like a lion. And if this passage must be taken literally, why should the other passage respecting the distribution and employments of the day be taken figuratively? The literal interpretation of the one furnishes a strong argument for the literal interpretation of the other. And it is certainly of no use to ascribe a mystical sense to the one, whilst the other is interpreted literally. The advocates of the oral law gain nothing by it, for the one is not more absurd nor more unworthy of the Deity than the other. Nothing can exceed the folly of representing God as observing the night-watches, and roaring like a lion for grief, because he sent Israel into captivity. Nothing can be more blasphemous than the assertion that God does not foresee the results of his own actions, and that he is afterwards obliged to sit down and mourn over what he has done. This one passage, which cannot be explained away, is quite sufficient to show that the rabbies were utterly ignorant of the nature of God; and that, however they might be acquainted with the letter of the Law and the Prophets, they knew nothing of the real meaning of their writings. This one excess of folly and absurdity entirely overthrows all the claims and pretensions of the oral law in which it is found.

But there is another feature in the passage which we cannot pass without notice, and that is, the total disregard of truth which it manifests. R. Jose's story is evidently a barefaced and wilful lie, unless we say, that when he went into the ruin to pray, he fell asleep, and dreamed that he heard the Bath Kol and had this conversation with Elijah; but either supposition will equally destroy the credit of the Talmud. If it be a lie, it is one of the most profane and wicked lies that can be imagined. We have here a professed teacher of the law telling not only a falsehood about his intercourse with Elijah, but daring falsely to assert that he heard the voice of God mourning over the ruins of the temple. The most profane and wicked lie that can be devised is that which introduces God himself, and trifles with the sacred character of the Deity. If this story be a lie, it oversets the Talmud and the Talmudical religion at once. A religion built upon falsehoods, must itself be necessarily false. But if the other supposition be adopted, that R. Jose mistook a dream for a reality, what shall we say of a religion whose teachers tell their dreams as sacred truths? And what shall we say of the compilers of the Talmud, who were unable to detect the folly and profanity of this narrative, and actually inserted it in their oral law as an undoubted fact? This supposition may save R. Jose from the unhappy character of a liar, but it will not do much towards proving the truth of the oral law; for there it is not given as a dream, but as a fact. R. Jose was silly enough to tell his dream as a reality; and the rabbies to whom he told it were silly enough to believe; and the most learned men of the Rabbinists at that time were silly enough to embody it in their collection of holy and undoubted traditions. We do not mean to ascribe any peculiar degree of folly to the rabbies. Persons calling themselves Christians have been just as foolish, have believed stories just as absurd, and have handed them down as religious truths. But then, we do not receive these legends as a part and parcel of our religion. We are as free to say of them, as of the Talmudic fables, that they are wicked falsehoods. But the modern Jews tell us that the Talmud is a divine book—that it contains their religion, and that without it Moses and the Prophets are unintelligible; and therefore we point out these fables as plain proofs of the falsehood of such an assertion. We wish to direct the Jewish attention to that system which they have called their religion for the last eighteen hundred years, and which they have preferred to Christianity. We desire that they should consider what they have gained, by expelling the family of Levi from the teacher's office and choosing the rabbies as their religious guides. We ask every Israelite of common sense, whether R. Jose and his companions are trustworthy leaders in the way to salvation; and whether they are still prepared to follow the religion of a man who can only be acquitted of being a liar by admitting that he is a dreamer? Or, whether they still choose to worship the Deity proclaimed by the rabbies—a Deity subject to succession of time—imperfect in knowledge so as to require daily study—requiring amusement, and therefore playing for three hours every day with Leviathan—and liable to disappointment, so as to be obliged to spend the night, in mourning over one of his most deliberate and solemn acts?

We are sure that every Israelite would be sadly offended at being told, that he does not worship the God of his fathers, but a strange god, invented by the imagination of the rabbies; and yet, if he worship the god of the Talmud, it is nothing but the truth. The god of the Talmud is certainly not the God of the Bible. Israelites are often shocked at the folly and wickedness of those whom they see falling down before stocks and stones; and yet, if they receive the oral law, and believe in a Deity who plays with Leviathan, &c., the object of their worship is not a whit more rational. They are just as guilty of idolatry, and the only way in which they can clear themselves from the charge is, by rejecting the oral law, and forsaking that superstition which the rabbies have palmed off upon them as the religion of their fathers. It is a most deplorable and melancholy sight to behold that nation, which once was the sole depository of truth, enslaved by a system so senseless; but it is more melancholy still to think, that there is not one among her sons who has the moral courage to denounce its falsehood, and to vindicate the truth as taught by Moses. The priests, the sons of Levi, were once zealous for the honour of God, and united with Moses in destroying the golden calf; but where are they now, and where is there zeal? Alas! they too, are found amongst the worshippers of the Talmudical deity, and uphold the system which has expelled them from their holy office.

No. XLII.

TITLE OF RABBI.

THAT the people, at present scattered over the whole world, and known by the name of Jews, are descendants of the chosen people of God, we freely admit. That the Old Testament contains prophecies of their future return to the God and the land of their fathers, and their subsequent happiness and glory, we firmly believe: but, that the religion which they at present profess is the religion of Moses, we confidently deny. Modern Judaism has not retained the doctrines of Moses; no not even with respect to the fundamental article of religion, the nature of God. Our last number showed how widely the rabbies have departed from the Scripture representation of the divine character, and the number preceding proved that the Jews have not retained even the outward form of the Mosaic edifice. Indeed we know not any problem more difficult of solution than, to assign a reason, why the rabbinic Jews profess any respect at all for Moses, when they have rejected both the form and the substance of his teaching. If they boldly denied his authority, or asserted that the Mosaic law was long since abrogated, and the rabbinic precepts given in its stead, we could, at least, give them credit for consistency; but at present we cannot possibly divine their motives for professing attachment to the lawgiver of their forefathers. Their conduct for ages would appear to indicate a fixed determination to get rid and keep clear of every thing Mosaic, and that for the mere purpose of having something else; for no one can pretend, that the new law and the new teachers, that they have chosen, can lay any claim to superior excellence or antiquity. Of the value of the rabbinic teaching we have given many proofs; and now think of examining a little the *novelty* of the rabbinic order. It is certain that the word, rabbi, does not occur in the law of Moses nor the prophets; it is, therefore, clearly not Mosaic. This one fact does in itself go far to shake the authority of modern Judaism and the oral law. There we cannot go a step without hearing of the rabbies—Rabbi Eliezer said this, and Rabbi Bar Bar Chanah said that. The whole oral law is made up of the sayings of the rabbies, and yet neither their name nor their order was so much as known to Moses our master. The other favourite appellation of the Talmudic doctors חכם *Chacham*, or wise man, does indeed occur, and it appears from the prophets, that there were some even in their time who laid exclusive claim to that epithet, but unfortunately the prophets bring against them the very same charge, which we prefer against their successors, namely, that they had forsaken the law of Moses:—

איכה תאמרו חכמים אנחנו ותורת ה׳ אתנו אכן
הנה לשקר עשה עט שקר סופרים י הובישו חכמים
חתו וילכדו הנה בדבר ה׳ מאסו וחכמת מה להם :

" How do ye say, We are wise (Chachamim) and the law of the Lord is with us? Lo, certainly in vain made he it; the pen of the scribes is in vain. The wise men (Chachamim) are ashamed. They are dismayed and taken: lo, *they have rejected the word of the Lord: and what wisdom is in them?*" (Jer. viii. 8, 9.) The rabbies will scarcely acknowledge that they have succeeded these persons in their office, and yet if they give up such passages as these, they must abdicate all claim to antiquity. Indeed some of them plainly acknowledge that the rabbies are a new order of men, and that the word rabbi was not heard of until less than a century before the destruction of the second temple. Thus the Baal Aruch says—

והדורות הראשונים שהיו גדולים מאוד לא היו
צריכין לרברבם לא ברבן ולא ברבי ולא ברב לא
לחכמי בבל ולא לחכמי ארץ ישראל שהרי הלל
עלה מבבל ולא נאמרה רבנות בשמו, ובנביאים היו
חשובים שנאמר חגי הנביא, לא עלה עזרא מבבל,
ואין מרברבין אותן עם הזכרת שמותיהן ולא שמענו
כי התחילו זו אלא בנשיאים מרבן גמליאל הזקן ורבי
שמעון בנו שנהרג בחרבן בית שני ורבן יוחנן בן
זכאי כולן נשיאים ואף רבי התחיל מסמוכים מאותה
שעה צדוק ורבי אליעזר בן יעקב ופשט הדבר מתלמידי
ר׳ יוחנן בן זכאי ולהלן :

"The first generations, which were very great, did not require the titles of Rabban, or Rabbi, or Rav, wherewith to honour the wise men of Babylon, or the wise men of the land of Israel; for behold Hillel went up from Babylon, but the title of Rabbi is not added to his name. There were honourable persons amongst the prophets, for it is said, 'Haggai the prophet'—'Ezra did not go up from Babylon'—and at the mention of their names the title of Rabbi is not added: neither have we heard that this was begun until the princes Rabban Gamaliel the elder, and Rabban Simon his son, who was killed at the destruction of the second temple, and Rabban Johannan ben Zakkai, who were all princes. Rabbi also began with those who were promoted at the same time, Zadok and R. Eliezer, the son of Jacob, and the thing spread from the disciples of Rabban Johannan ben Zakkai onwards." (Aruch in אביי.) We need not wonder, then, that Moses knows nothing of rabbies, for here is a plain confession, that the name was never heard of until a few years before the last dispersion. It may, however, be said, that the office itself existed, though the name did not, and this is in fact asserted by Rambam, when he says:—

ומשה רבנו סמך יהושע ביד שנאמר ויסמוך את ידיו
עליו ויצוהו, וכן השבעים זקנים משה רבנו סמכם
ושרתה עליהן שכינה ואותן הזקנים סמכו לאחרים,
ואחרים לאחרים, ונמצאו הסמוכין איש מפי איש עד
בית דינו של יהושע ועד בית דינו של משה רבינו :

"Moses our master promoted Joshua with his hands; for it is said, 'and he laid his hands upon him, and gave him a charge.' (Numb. xxvii. 23.) And in like manner with regard to the seventy elders, Moses our master promoted them, and the Shechinah rested upon them; and these elders promote others, and they again others; and thus we have a succession of promoted persons, until the council of Joshua, and until the council of Moses our master." (Hilchoth Sanhedrin, iv. 1.) And so he tells us that—

ודוד המלך סמך שלשים אלף ביום אחד :

"King David promoted thirty thousand persons in one day." According to this statement, it would appear that there had been always a class of persons qualified to be teachers and judges, and a pretty numerous class too, from the time of Moses; but it is very extraordinary that their office should have continued fifteen hundred years without a name, and that the nation should never have felt the inconvenience, nor remedied it until the last few years of their existence; and it is more extraordinary still that so large and important a body should never once be mentioned in the law or the prophets. The land must perfectly have swarmed with them. Thirty thousand would have been a large proportion to the population of the land of Israel; but David made this number in one day; and we cannot suppose that he exerted his right only once in his life, nor that all the other doctors neglected the duty of raising up disciples; and the oral law tells us that before the time of Hillel every one thus promoted had the right of promoting others:—

בראשונה היה כל מי שנסמך סומך לתלמידיו,
והכמים חלקו כבוד להלל הזקן והתקינו שלא יהא
אדם נסמך אלא ברשות הנשיא וכו' :

"At first every promoted person could promote his disciples; but the wise men gave the honour to Hillel the elder, and ordained that no man should promote except by permission of the prince (the Nasi)." According to this, the number must have been very great; and yet that they should have continued so long without a name, and without any mention whatever by any of the inspired writers, is perfectly incredible. But there are in the account itself various particulars which excite suspicion. David's extensive work of promotion in one day entirely exceeds the limits of probability, no matter how the promotion took place, whether by laying on of hands, or by command, or by letter: for if we grant that he devoted the entire four-and-twenty hours of that day to the work, still, in order to make up the number of thirty thousand, it will be necessary to believe that he promoted at the rate of twelve hundred and fifty an hour, or twenty in every minute. One such notorious untruth discredits the whole account in which it is found. But, further, the admission that the right of conferring the dignity of doctor was taken from those who had possessed it, and restricted to those who obtained permission from the prince, shows that the ordinance of promotion was not derived from Moses, but was an invention of men. If it had been of Moses, the wise men could have had no authority to take it away, neither is it at all likely that the numerous possessors of the right, and least of all, the disciples of Shammai, would have quietly resigned it. We must suppose either that the wise men altered an ordinance of Moses, and thereby committed a great sin, or that the ordinance of promotion was a mere human invention. By the latter supposition the whole story of the continued existence of this class of doctors is given up; and by the former supposition the charge of disregard for the law of Moses is fixed upon the wise men, and the value of their testimony taken away. Lastly, the account of the manner of promotion is at variance with the above-quoted assertion of the Baal Aruch. The oral law says that the doctors were promoted in the following manner :—

לא שיסמכו את ידיהם על ראש הזקן, אלא שקורין
לו רבי ואומרים לו הרי אתה סמוך ויש לך רשות
לדון אפילו דיני קנסות:

"They not only laid their hands upon the head of the elder, but also saluted him with the title, Rabbi, and said to him, Behold thou art promoted, and hast authority to judge, even in cases of mulct." Here the conferring the title of Rabbi is made an integral part of the act of promotion, whereas the Baal Aruch says that the title of Rabbi was not in use until after the time of Hillel. The assertion, therefore, that the office of Rabbi existed without the name, even from the time of Moses, is not only unsupported by any proof from the inspired writings, but is inconsistent with other assertions of the rabbies themselves; and is, besides, found very close to a palpable untruth, and is therefore unworthy of credit. Thus the antiquity of the rabbinic office is destroyed, and appears to be a comparatively new invention: so that those who profess the religion of the rabbies cannot pretend to have the religion of Moses or of their forefathers, but that of a new set of teachers, who did not arise until a very few years before the destruction of the second temple. One of the common objections of modern Jews against Christianity is, its novelty. They say that we have got a new religion, whereas they have the ancient religion; that we follow a new teacher, but that they follow Moses. The foregoing examination shows how little ground they have for such a boast. If novelty be a valid objection, they must confess that the religion of the rabbies is false. If the distance of time that elapsed between Moses and Jesus of Nazareth constitute a fair ground of objection, it is as valid against the rabbies as against the Lord Jesus. Nay, if supposed novelty be the reason why they reject Christianity, they must now reject the religion of the rabbies, and embrace that of Christ. We have proved that the religion of the rabbies is a novelty, and every one knows that one peculiar feature in the teaching of Jesus of Nazareth was, that he opposed the rabbinic doctrines, that is, he opposed novelty: this opposition, therefore, is presumptive evidence that the Lord Jesus retained the ancient religion, and has on that very account a claim upon all those who profess to venerate antiquity. At all events the charge of novelty can be as fairly urged against Rabbinism as against Christianity, and every Jew who urges it, is, if he be in earnest about truth, bound to compare Christianity with the law and the prophets, in order to ascertain whether it be a new religion or not. One thing is certain, that the ordinances of no religion can be farther from the Mosaic appointment than those of Rabbinism. The Rabbinists have rejected the religious teachers appointed by Moses, and have chosen others, who cannot pretend even to any degree of antiquity; and not only so, but even when the possibility of having regularly appointed rabbies ceased, they preferred those, who in fact have no authority at all, to those teachers appointed in the law. The oral law makes promotion necessary to the exercise of the rabbinical office, and limits the ceremony of promotion by two conditions, first, that it be conferred with the consent of the נשיא, as we have seen above, and, secondly, that it be performed in the land of Israel :—

אין סומכין זקנים בחוצה לארץ ואע״פ שאלו הסומכין
נסמכו בארץ ישראל, אפילו היו הסומכין בארץ
והנסמך בחוץ לארץ אין סומכין:

" Elders are not promoted anywhere, except in the land of Israel; even although the promoters should have been promoted there themselves. Yea, though the persons conferring the promotion be in the land, if the person to be promoted be outside the land, the promotion is not to take place." Now it is plain that these conditions cannot be fulfilled. The great majority of the present rabbies have never been in the land of Israel; and even if they had been, there has not been a נשיא prince for many a century. For centuries, therefore, there has not been a rabbi promoted to the office as the oral law requires; and yet the Jews, rather than have the priests, the sons of Levi, still keep up the shadow of the rabbinical office. A more determined opposition to the institutions of Moses cannot be imagined. First, the Jewish people rejected the ordinance of Moses, and devised an order of teachers of their own, limited by certain conditions. Then God, in great mercy, made the fulfilment of those conditions impossible. He took away the prince, he drove them out of the land of Israel, to give them, as it were, an opportunity, yea, to compel them to return to his own appointment: but in vain. Although the Jews cannot fulfil the conditions of their own devising, and could fulfil God's appointment, they refuse the latter, and have invented something newer still, and that is, an order of religious teachers, who have not even the qualifications required by the oral law. Truly this is to transgress, for the mere sake of transgressing. How, then, can the Jews pretend to be disciples of Moses, or assert that the Mosaic law is unchangeable? Now, for near two thousand years they have lived in disobedience to one of Moses' simplest commandments, and have changed one of the essential institutions of the law. The most superficial reader of the writings of Moses must see, that a charge of prime importance was assigned to the family of Levi, not only as respected the ministration in the temple, but also with regard to the instruction of the people. God in His providence has deprived them of the former. The Jews themselves, by rejecting the commands of Moses, have taken away the latter office, and thus have destroyed not only the interior, but actually demolished the external form of the Mosaic edifice. It is, therefore, as we have said, a most difficult problem to account for the profession which modern Jews make of zeal for the law of Moses, and one which well deserves the consideration of the Jews themselves. Why should they profess to be disciples of Moses, when they openly trample upon his commands, and reject both the substance and the form of his religion? If they really believe that obedience to the law of Moses is necessary to salvation, they ought instantly to reinstate the family of Levi in their office. But if they prefer the new religion of the rabbies to the old religion of Moses, then they ought honestly to say so; and not go on halting between two opinions. And they ought to do this, not merely to avoid the charge of inconsistency before men, but to satisfy their own consciences before God. How can any man reasonably hope to be saved by a religion whose commands he constantly transgresses, and never intends to obey? And yet this is exactly the case with the Rabbinists with regard to the law of Moses. There have been attempts at reform amongst the Jews, but we have never heard of any who intended to restore the family of Levi to their office; and yet, without this, there is no return to the Mosaic institutions.

A disciple of the rabbies may perhaps think, that he can

retort this argument upon the Christians, and say that Jesus of Nazareth was not of the tribe of Levi. Certainly he was not; but as the Messiah, the prophets foretold that he was to be of the tribe of Judah: and as the Messiah, promised and appointed of God, he has a right to the obedience of all, both Jew and Gentile. If he had been only an ordinary prophet, he would have had a divine right to teach the people and to require their obedience; for, besides the priests, God also appointed prophets, but to the prophetic office the rabbies do not lay claim. The Lord Jesus, on the contrary, claimed not only the prophetic character, but asserted that he was the Messiah, and proved the truth of his claims by exhibiting miraculous powers, and especially by his resurrection from the dead. As a prophet, therefore, and above all, as the Messiah, his teaching in no wise interfered with the office of the priests: and his conduct, as recorded in the New Testament, shows that, though in determined and constant opposition to the Pharisees, the advocates of the oral law, he never lifted up his voice against the office of the priesthood. On the contrary, when occasion offered, he showed a scrupulous regard for the commandments of Moses respecting the priests; as for instance when he healed the leper, he " said unto him, See thou tell no man; but go thy way, show thyself to the priests, and offer the gift that Moses commanded, for a testimony unto them." (Matt. viii. 4.) And this conduct is perfectly conformable to one professed object of the Lord Jesus, which was to vindicate the authority of the law against the unauthorized additions of men. He professed himself the defender of the Mosaic law, and opposed the whole system of the Rabbinists, on the professed ground that they made it void by their traditions. The objections, therefore, which we have brought against the oral law, as overturning the institutions of Moses, cannot be applied to the doctrines or conduct of the Lord Jesus Christ. He never opposed the priests, never interfered with their office, never diminished aught from their authority. In these most important respects, the doctrine of Jesus of Nazareth is necessarily more agreeable to the law of Moses than the traditions of the Pharisees, who have forcibly altered that great institution of Moses, the Levitic priesthood, and have themselves usurped the office and the rights of the priests. Modern Judaism is directly in opposition to the Mosaic law, and has at present no excuse for its opposition. The Jews of the dispersion cannot possibly keep its requirements concerning the promotion of rabbies; their adherence, therefore, to that system has now the appearance of mere gratuitous and wilful hatred to the law of Moses. They profess to know the family of the priests, and could therefore restore them to their office, if they pleased. What is there to prevent them?

Nothing but the want of love for Moses and his institutions. We are convinced that many of the Jews have never considered this matter, or they would not act as they do. The habits of thought induced by early education, the customs of their nation for two thousand years, have drawn a sort of veil over their understandings, so that they have not been able to see the palpable inconsistency of professing a zeal for Moses, whilst they do homage to principles which cut up his institutions by the roots. Until the priests be reinstated in their functions and their rights, as the divinely appointed teachers of religion, the Jews can have no ground whatever to pretend that they are disciples of Moses. They are, at present, nothing but partisans of the sect of the Rabbinists. And if they choose to persevere in their attachment to this sect, they are bound, as honest men, to renounce all profession of regard for the law of Moses.

No. XLIII.

SANHEDRIN.

It is certain that the Jews cannot appeal to the law of the prophets to defend their rejection of the old religion of Moses, and their preference for the new religion of the rabbies. Neither Moses nor the prophets knew anything about the rabbies. They are quite a new order of men, never heard of until the Jewish polity was tottering to its destruction. There is, however, another argument to which they might appeal, in order to justify the reception of new religious teachers, and that is, the existence of the Sanhedrin. It may be said, that when the rabbies arose and taught, both they and their doctrines were approved by this great council, and that this approval is sufficient to establish the justice of their claims, and the truth of what they taught. Indeed, the rabbinists do actually look upon the Sanhedrin as the great foundation on which the oral law rests :—

בית דין הגדול שבירושלים הם עיקר תורה שבע"פ
והם עמודי ההוראה ומהם חוק ומשפט יוצא לכל
ישראל, ועליהי הבטיחה תורה שנאמר על פי התורה

אשר יורוך זו מצות עשה וכל המאמין במשה רבינו
ובתורתו חייב לסמוך מעשה הדה עליהן ולישען
עליהן :

"The Great Council in Jerusalem is the foundation-stone of the oral law, and the pillars of the doctrine: and from them the statute and the judgment goes forth to all Israel. They have the warrant of the law, for it is said, 'According to the sentence of the law which they shall teach thee,' &c. (Deut. xvii. 11); which is an affirmative precept, and every one who believes in Moses our master, and in his law, is bound to rest the practice of the law on them, and to lean on them." (Hilchoth Mamrim, c. i. 1.) Here the indispensable duty of every Israelite to follow the decisions of the Sanhedrin is plainly asserted: it becomes, then, absolutely necessary for us to examine into the nature of the foundation on which claims so unlimited are based. One would suppose that, at the very least, the Sanhedrin was infallible, and could never say or do anything wrong; for if this council was liable to error, and yet undeviating obedience to its decisions required, whenever they went wrong, all Israel must have gone wrong also. But yet, strange to say, the infallibility of the Sanhedrin is not only not asserted, but plainly denied—yea, the possibility of error unequivocally intimated, and even provided for:—

בית דין גדול שדרשו באחת מן המדות כפי מה
שנראה בעיניהם שהדין כך ודנו דין , ועמד אחריהם
בית דין אחר לסתור אותו הרי זה סותר ודן כפי מה
שנראה בעיניו , שנאמר אל השופט אשר יהיה בימים
ההם אינך חייב ללכת אלא אחר בית דין שבדורך ,
בית דין שגזרו גזרה או תקנו תקנה והנהיגו מנהג
ופשט הדבר בכל ישראל , ועמד אחריהם ב״ד אחר
ובקש לבטל דברים הראשונים ולעקור אותה התקנה
ואותה הגזרה ואותו המנהג אינו יכול עד שיהיה
גדול מן הראשונים בחכמה ובמנין וכו' :

"When a great council has decided by one of the rules, and according to the best of their judgment, that the judgment is so and so, and has passed sentence; if there arise after them another council of a contrary opinion, the latter may reverse the sentence, and pass another according to the best of their judgment, for it is said, 'Unto the judge that shall be in those days' (Deut. xvii. 9); thou art, therefore, not bound to follow any other but the existing council. But if a council decree a decree, or ordain an ordinance, or sanction a custom, and the thing has spread in all Israel;

and there arise after them another council, which wishes to abrogate the former things, and to root out that ordinance, decree, or custom, it is not permitted, unless they excel the former in wisdom and in number." (Ibid. c. ii. 1, 2.) According to this doctrine the Sanhedrin in one generation may teach one doctrine, and in the next generation another Sanhedrin may abrogate all the legislative acts of the former, and teach another doctrine, and yet, though one of the two must necessarily be in the wrong, Israel is bound to obey both; and thus the law is made to sanction disobedience to itself. Nay, more, the will of God is made actually to depend upon the wit and the will of man. Instead of being eternal and unchangeable truth, it must vary with each succeeding generation, so that what was truth to a father, might be falsehood to his son; and every new Sanhedrin would, in fact, have the power to make a new law. How, then, can the Jews pretend that the Mosaic law is unchangeable? Here it is asserted, that the Jews are to receive, as the law of Moses, whatever the Sanhedrin may think right to teach—and that every new Sanhedrin may overturn the doctrines of their predecessors, and teach the very opposite; so that instead of being eternal, the law would be one of the most changeable things in the world, and might never last the same for even two generations. But how can any man possibly believe, that a command so preposterous should come from God, or that he would deliver over his people Israel, bound hand and foot, into the power of seventy-one persons, and require unconditional obedience, no matter whether these persons were in the right or in the wrong? Pretensions so extravagant justly excite suspicion, and entirely destroy the credit of those that make them. They betray an inordinate lust of power, and savour far more strongly of ambition than piety. It was no doubt very convenient for the members of the Sanhedrin to be able to reverse the decisions of their predecessors. On these terms, the law could never stand in the way of their own schemes. No matter how it had been explained or understood before, they had the power of giving a new interpretation to suit their own purpose. It is truly wonderful how the Jews can suffer themselves to be deluded by an imposture so exceedingly coarse. A child ought to be able to see, that God could never require a man to renounce his understanding, and to receive two direct contradictions as true.

The manifest absurdity of this doctrine is sufficient to prove that the passage cited from Deut. xvii. is misinterpreted and misapplied; and a little consideration will show that it does not refer to the Sanhedrin at all. In the first place there is no mention of that council, nor any thing that even implies a reference to such a body. The command of God is, "Thou shalt come unto the *priests, the Levites*, and unto the *judge* that shall be in those days, and inquire." It is not said to the judges, but to the judge הַשׁוֹפֵט. To these, and not to the Sanhedrin, Moses requires absolute obedience, and that for a just and sufficient reason, because, as we have shown in Number 2, they had the means of obtaining an infallible answer by means of the אוּרִים וְתֻמִּים Urim and Thummim. It was the privilege of Israel to be able to ask counsel immediately of God; and it was therefore only rational to expect unconditional obedience to the command of the Almighty. Such decisions were absolutely unchangeable as God himself, for "He is not a man that he should lie, nor the son of man that He should repent;" and no man in his senses would have thought of getting a sentence of this kind reversed. These words can therefore by no means apply to a tribunal fallible in judgment, and as changeable in its opinions as in the persons of which it was composed: but if this passage does not apply, there is no other in the Bible which requires us to receive the decision of the Sanhedrin as of divine authority, nor in the oral law either, for it supposes that this council was capable of mistake. Consequently, the Sanhedrin's approval of the new order and new religion of the rabbies is of no weight whatever. The Bible does not command us to believe that they were always in the right; and they themselves tell us that they might be in the wrong, and therefore might be in the wrong in their approval of the rabbies.

But the truth is, that neither the Bible nor history gives us any warrant whatever for regarding the Sanhedrin as a Mosaic institution. In the first place, it is never once mentioned either in the Law or in the Prophets. The word *Sanhedrin* is Greek, and so far as it goes would lead us to suppose that this tribunal was not instituted until some time after the building of the second temple, and after the Greek occupation of the land, when the Jews had become acquainted with the Greek language. This Greek word would lead us even to suppose that the Sanhedrin was instituted by the Greek rulers, and that they gave the tribunal its name. If it had been an old Mosaic institution, the Jews themselves, who hated the Greeks, and that with good reason, would never have given it a Greek name: and even if the Greeks had assigned this name to a Jewish tribunal, which had previously existed, the Jews would not have adopted it. It is true that there is also a Hebrew name for this tribunal, בֵּית דִּין הַגָּדוֹל, "The great house of judgment," but if this had been the original name, it is not at all likely that the Greek name would have supplanted it; whereas if it was a Greek institution, and therefore had a Greek name, it is not to be wondered at that that name should have obtained general currency, or that it should also be translated into Hebrew. The Hebrew name will not do more than the Greek to prove the antiquity of the tribunal, for it never once occurs in the Bible, and it would be very strange, if this council had existed from the time of Moses, that it should never once be mentioned. The High Court of Parliament does not hold a more important place in the history of this country, than the Sanhedrin must have done in the history of Israel, if it had really existed : how then are we to account for the fact, that neither the historians nor the prophets of Israel ever make the most distant allusion to its being ? If the rabbies speak truth, the prophets, the high priests, and the kings of Israel, were mere ciphers compared with the Sanhedrin, for it had supreme power over them all, and could try, condemn, and execute them, and yet they are mentioned again and again, and the Sanhedrin passed by in mysterious ilence! There are two books of Kings, and two of Chronicles, relating the history of the Royal rulers of Israel, but the Supreme Council of the nation, the rulers of kings and priests, the foundation-stone of the law, the pillar of religion, have never obtained even a casual notice ! Is this at all probable ? Would it be possible to write a history of the British Constitution without ever once mentioning the existence of the Parliament? And yet this is what has happened, according to the rabbies, to the essential feature of the Constitution of Israel. Neither the lawgiver, nor the historians, nor the prophets, have said one word about it.

The rabbies have felt the necessity of finding something or other in the written law, that would look like the recognition of the Sanhedrin, and have therefore fixed on two passages which they think will serve their cause. One is that to which we have already alluded, "Thou shalt come unto the priests the Levites, and unto the judge that shall be in those days." (Deut. xvii. 9.) We have already said sufficient to show that this passage is totally irrelevant, and now add one remark more, which is in itself decisive, and that is, that the constitution of the Sanhedrin, as described in the oral law, is altogether at variance with the conditions laid down in this passage. The oral law says—

ומצוה להיות בסנהדרין גדולה כהנים ולוים שנאמר שנאמר ובאת אל הכהנים הלוים ואם לא מצאו אפילו היו כולם ישראלים הרי זה מותר:

" The command is, that there should be in the great Sanhedrin, priests and Levites, for it is said, ' Thou shalt come to the priests, the Levites.' But if they find none. yea, though they be all mere Israelites, this is lawful." (Hilchoth Sanhedrin, c. ii. 2.) According to this the Sanhedrin was to consist of three distinct classes, priests, Levites, and Israelites ; but Moses does not say one word of the Levites, as distinguished from the priests. His words are, "Thou shalt come to the priests, the Levites." He does not say, "The priests *and* the Levites;" but simply, "The priests, the Levites;" from which it is plain that he was speaking only of that one class of the sons of Levi, who had the office of the priesthood; but not of that other class, whose only title was "The Levites." This is the first difference. The second is like it, inasmuch as it is also an unauthorized addition, and that is, that there should be Israelites members of this council, of whom Moses does not say one word more than he does of the Levites. Besides the priests, Moses mentions none but the judge השופט, not the judges, so that if the judge was an Israelite, there could be at the very most be only one Israelite amongst those whom Moses appoints as the highest court of appeal in Israel. But if the judge השופט was himself a priest, then there was not even one Israelite; but the court was composed exclusively of priests. This court cannot, therefore, be the same as the Sanhedrin, which was to be composed of all the three classes. Thirdly, the oral law says, That though the Sanhedrin should not reckon one priest amongst its members, but should consist entirely of Israelites, that still it is lawful; this court can, therefore, never be the same as that of which Moses says, "Thou shalt come to the priests, the Levites, and to the judge." The court which the rabbies have appointed might not have even one priest, and yet they ask us to believe that this is identical with that, which, according to the appointment of Moses, could never have more than one Israelite, but might, and in the days of Eli actually did, consist exclusively of priests. Truly the rabbies must have calculated upon disciples with a most inordinate measure of credulity. The man that would believe this, would believe that black is white; or as Rashi says, that his right hand is the left, and his left hand the right. And this is really what modern Judaism expects, and absolutely commands in so many words. In Rashi's commentary on the words "Thou shalt not decline from the sentence which they shall show thee, to the right nor to the left" (Deut. xvii. 11); which words, as we have seen, the rabbies apply to the Sanhedrin, he says—

אפילו אומר לך על ימין שהוא שמאל ועל שמאל שהוא ימין:

"Yea, though they should tell thee of the right hand, that it is the left, and of the left hand, that it is the right." Of course men that expected from their followers this perfect renunciation of reason, might say any thing they liked, and might therefore ask them to believe that a court consisting of all priests was identical with one from which priests were altogether excluded. But as we are not willing to give up that reason, which we consider a noble gift of God, we cannot help thinking that these two courts are as different as day and night, and that the appointment of Moses does not in the remotest degree serve as a warrant for the appointment of the Sanhedrin. Indeed, the sad perplexity of the rabbies to find out some passage or other on which to father their own inventions, and the desperate necessity which they felt of appealing to this passage, proves to us most satisfactorily, that the Sanhedrin is not a Mosaic institution at all. It is as impossible that there could be two supreme courts, as that a man can have two heads. Moses did appoint a supreme court, from which there was no appeal, as is plain from the words, " Thou shalt come to the priests, the Levites, and to the judge," and we have proved that this court is not identical with the Sanhedrin. But according to the rabbies, the Sanhedrin was a supreme court; if, therefore, it had existed, there would have been two supreme courts, perfectly independant of each other, which is plainly impossible. It never entered into the head even of human lawgivers to be guilty of such absurdity, and it would be an affront to the wisdom of the Almighty to suppose that he had sanctioned it in his own law. This one argument is in itself sufficient to overthrow the doctrine of a Sanhedrin as taught in the oral law. It was not only unknown to Moses, but is directly opposed to his own institution.

This portion of the oral law is, however, most important for proving the total disregard, or rather contempt, which the rabbies had for the institutions of Moses, and the motives by which they were actuated. Moses ordained a supreme court of judicature, to consist exclusively of priests, together with the chief civil governor for the time being. The rabbies not only did not choose to obey the command of Moses, but actually abrogated his institution, and set up another instead of it. They were probably enabled to do this in the time of confusion which followed the Greek conquest. The Greeks, who cared nothing for Moses or his laws, naturally disregarded the priests and the lawful civil governor; and therefore when they conquered the land, sat up a tribunal of their own, composed not of those whom Moses had appointed, but of any whom they could find. Indeed, to secure their own dominion, their natural policy was to exclude those who had previously held the reins of government. To this new tribunal they of course gave a Greek name, and called it in their own language, συνέδριον, or, as the Talmud pronounces it, Sanhedrin. The Jews, whom they appointed members, liked the power which it gave them, and therefore, when the Greeks were gone, endeavoured to perpetuate it; and as they could not find a warrant for it in the written law, declared that the institution was a part of the oral law: and thus, to gratify their own ambition, trampled upon the law of Moses. This is the probable history of the rise of the Sanhedrin ; but however that be, it is certain that it is directly opposed to that supreme court appointed by Moses, and that it was love of power which induced the rabbies to sanction it. They thereby depressed the authority of the priests and the civil governor, and in fact became the dictators of the Jewish commonwealth. A tribunal supported from such motives, and so directly subversive of the commands of Moses, cannot prove to any lover of the old religion the authority of the rabbies. Indeed, the approval of such a body would go far to prove that the oral law and the rabbies were Moses's enemies. The Mosaic law was first pulled down before the Sanhedrin could be built up, and it was founded on the ruins of the Mosaic institutions.

We have not space at present to enter into the other passage which the rabbies cite in proof of the authority of the Sanhedrin, but hope to do so in our next number—not that it is necessary to the argument, but simply because it is our earnest wish that the people of Israel should see how the rabbies are in difficulty to find even a semblance of proof for the foundation-stone of their whole fabric. That one passage from Deuteronomy—" Thou shalt come unto the priests, the Levites, and unto the judge," is quite sufficient to prove that Moses did not institute the Sanhedrin, but that, on the contrary, it must have been established by some determined enemies of the Mosaic law ; and that it was perpetuated by those whose ambition led them to usurp power, which Moses had committed unto others. We have thus another proof that modern Judaism has demolished even the external form of the Mosaic constitution. The rabbies were not content with rejecting the religion of Moses, and casting out the religious teachers whom he had appointed, but have also revolutionized the national polity. Moses ordained a supreme council, consisting of the priests, the Levites, together with the judge, the chief civil governor ; but the rabbies have preferred a tribunal established by idolatrous Greeks, because this Greek institution gave the power into their own hands. No wonder that the God of Moses destroyed their city, and put an end to that delusion with which ambitious and wicked men deceived his people Israel.

No. XLIV.

SANHEDRIN CONTINUED.

THE Sanhedrin is, as we said in our last number, the foundation-stone on which the authority of the rabbies, and the whole fabric of tradition rests. Take away this, and not the shadow of an argument remains to justify the Jews in their rejection of the Mosaic religion, and their demolition of the Mosaic constitution. But this we have done. Enough has already been said to make it probable that the Sanhedrin, with its Greek name, was invented and established by the idolatrous Greeks; and to make it certain that it is subversive of the Supreme Council established by Moses, and that, for that reason, it was not one of his institutions. We have already disposed of one of the passages which the rabbies quote from the Pentateuch, to prove the Divine authority of the Sanhedrin; but, as they have, with much difficulty, found two, we now proceed to consider the second. It is quoted in the following manner :—

כמה בתי דינין קבועין יהיו בישראל וכמה יהיה
מנינן, קובעין בתחלה בית דין הגדול במקדש, והוא
הנקרא סנהדרי גדולה ומנינם ע"א, שנאמר אספה לי
שבעים איש מזקני ישראל ומשה על גביהן, שנאמר
והתיצבו שם עמך הרי ע"א :

"How many councils (or tribunals) ought to be established in Israel, and of how many members ought they to consist? *Ans.* The Great Council in the temple called the Great Sanhedrin, ought to be established first, and the number of its members ought to be seventy-one; for it is said, 'Gather unto me seventy men of the elders of Israel;' and to them Moses is to be added, and as it is said, 'And they shall stand there with thee.' (Numb. xi. 16.) This makes seventy-one." (Hilchoth Sanhedrin, c. i. 2.) Here the rabbies have certainly found the number seventy-one; but to prove that this was the Sanhedrin, they ought first, to show, that these seventy-one persons were not to be scattered through the tribes, but always to remain together as one council; and, secondly, that this council was to be permanent; and, thirdly, that this council did really exist from the time of Moses to the destruction of Jerusalem; and, fourthly, and most important of all, that this was the *Supreme* Council; for even if the other three points could be made out, they would be insufficient without this. The Sanhedrin claims to be the Supreme Council, and, therefore, if it cannot be shown, that the assembly of the seventy elders is identical with the Supreme Council appointed by Moses, this passage is of no more use than the former one. Now, respecting the three first points, nothing whatever is said, either in the Law or the Prophets. And respecting the fourth, even if we grant the three first, we can shew that these seventy elders did not constitute the Supreme Council of the nation. We have proved in our last paper, that the supreme power was vested in an exclusive council composed of the priests, together with the judge השופט, but the seventy elders, here spoken of, were to be chosen promiscuously from the tribes of Israel, and therefore cannot be identical with that exclusive assembly; and therefore did not compose the Supreme Council; and therefore had nothing of the nature of the Sanhedrin, which pretended to be supreme over all. Thus it appears on examination, that there is not one text in the whole law of Moses, which authorizes the establishment of such a council as the Sanhedrin; but that on the contrary, it stands in direct opposition to that order of things prescribed by Moses.

We can, however, go farther, and show that all the particulars which the rabbies detail concerning it are manifest falsehoods; and that, if the Jews choose to believe what the oral law says concerning the Sanhedrin they must not only give up Moses, but renounce all the other inspired writers of the Old Testament. The particular and exclusive duties of the Sanhedrin are thus detailed:—

אין מעמידין מלך אלא על פי בית דין של ע״א,
ואין עושין סנהדרי קטנה לכל שבט ושבט ולכל עיר
ועיר אלא על פי בית דין של ע״א, ואין דנין לא את
השבט שהודח כולו ולא את נביא השקר ולא את
כהן הגדול בדיני נפשות אלא בבית דין הגדול, אבל
דיני ממונות בשלשה, וכן אין עושין זקן ממרא ולא
עושין עיר הנדחת ולא משקין את הסוטה אלא בבית
דין הגדול, ואין מוסיפין על העיר ועל העזרות ולא
מוציאין למלחמת הרשות ולמדידת החלל אלא על פי
בית דין הגדול, שנאמר כל הדבר הגדול יביאו אליך:

"A king is not to be appointed except by the decision of the Great Council of Seventy-one. The minor councils through the tribes and towns are not to be established except by the Council of Seventy-one. Judgment is not to be passed on a tribe that has been entirely seduced, nor upon a false prophet, nor upon a high priest in capital cases, except by the Great Council. (In mere money matters the tribunal of three is competent.) In like manner an elder is not declared rebellious, nor a city dealt with as seduced,* nor the bitter waters admi-

* Compare Deut. xiii. 13, and Hilchoth Accum, c. iv.

nistered to the suspected adulteress, except by the Great Council. Neither is an addition made to the city nor to the courts. Neither are armies led forth to the wars of permission; nor the elders led forth to measure in the case of a slain person (Deut. xxi. 1, &c.), except by command of the Great Council, for it is said, ' Every great matter they shall bring to thee.' (Exod. xviii. 22.)" (Hilchoth Sanhedrin, c. v. 1.) Such is the power and jurisdiction attributed by the rabbies to the Sanhedrin, and which we have now to consider. The mere reading over of these details is sufficient to convince any reasonable man that the whole affair is a waking dream of some man or men, intoxicated with the love of dominion. No man in his senses can believe that God could be the author of a despotism so dreadful over the minds and bodies of men. In the first place, here is an aristocracy of seventy persons, described as having supreme jurisdiction over the King, the High Priest, the Prophets, and the people—possessing the power not only to judge individuals, but to pass sentence on whole cities and tribes, and utterly to destroy them if they pleased—and this without any other law or precedent to guide them than their own will—and, inasmuch as they were self-elective, subject to no control whatever, either of the king or the people. We have heard much of corrupt corporations lately, but any thing at all equal to the self-elective corporation of the Sanhedrin we never heard of, excepting another college of seventy-one, the grand council of another oral law of later date. It is vain to say that this body was controlled by the law of Moses. When the Sanhedrin existed there was no law of Moses, but their own will. They expounded the law as they liked; and as we saw in our last, were not bound even by the decisions of their predecessors: and if any man dared to think for himself or to dispute their interpretation, he was strangled:—

כל חכם שמורה על דבריהם מיתתו בחנק :

" Strangulation was the mode of execution for any learned man, who rebelled against their words. (Hilchoth Mamrim, c. i 2.) They had thus the power to make the law say what they liked: and there was no power on earth to control them. If they had been appointed by the king, or elected by the people, they would have been responsible for the abuse of their power; but they elected their members, and could be deposed by none but themselves. A despotism so complete and so dreadful, so inimical to personal security, and so subversive of all liberty of conscience, could never have been created by God, but must necessarily be the offspring of the distempered brain of man. We can hardly believe that many Jews, except the Talmudistic zealots, who might hope to be made members wish for the restoration of the Sanhedrin; and yet, if they do not, they do not believe in the Jewish religion, for the re-establishment of that Great Council is the consummation of Judaism : and if they do not believe in this religion, can they consider themselves honest men in professing it ?

But we must proceed to consider on what authority the rabbies make these claims to such extensive jurisdiction. One would expect to find some distinct command of God, expressly addressed to the council; but no, their only authority is the words of Jethro to Moses, "Every great matter they shall bring to thee;" a plain confession that there is in the whole Bible nothing to warrant their pretensions, or they never would have taken refuge in words so totally irrelevant. Indeed, we are rather surprised that they appealed to the Bible at all, for such an appeal is fatal to all their pretensions. Just let us examine some of the particulars detailed above, by the light of God's word. The first pretension is, that "A king is not to be appointed except by the decision of the Great Council of Seventy-one." Now is this true? Is it possible to show that any one of the Kings of Israel was appointed by the Sanhedrin? Not one; but it is possible to prove of many that they were appointed without any reference whatever to any such council. Take, for instance, Saul, the first king of Israel; what had the Sanhedrin to do with his election to the kingly office? Nothing at all. So far as man was concerned, Samuel, and Samuel alone, was the instrument of his election. When the people wished a king, they did not go to the Sanhedrin, but to Samuel. He dissuaded them, "Nevertheless, the people refused to obey the voice of Samuel." Would they have ventured to do so if he had been president of so dreadful a council as the Sanhedrin? When Saul was anointed, it was not by the Sanhedrin, nor by their command. No man was present but the king elect and the prophet. ."Then Samuel took a vial of oil, and poured it upon his head, and kissed him, and said, Is it not because the Lord hath anointed thee to be captain over his inheritance?" (1 Sam. x. 1.) And when Saul was solemnly confirmed before the people, Samuel was still the sole agent. "Samuel called the people together unto the Lord to Mizpeh, and said, Now therefore present yourselves before the Lord by your tribes and by your thousands; and Saul the son of Kish was taken." (xi. 17—21.) It cannot be pretended that the Sanhedrin had anything whatever to do with the matter. But let us try another instance. Let us look at the election of David; was he chosen by the voice of the Sanhedrin? Just as little as Saul. Samuel was again the sole agent. "The Lord said unto Samuel, How long wilt thou mourn for Saul, seeing I have rejected him from reigning over Israel? Fill thine horn with oil and go; I will send thee to Jesse, the Bethlehemite; for I have provided me a king among his sons." And so Samuel went and anointed him, without any intervention whatever of the Sanhedrin, or any one else. These two cases are sufficient to prove the falsehood of the rabbinic pretensions; but there is one more decisive still, and that is the case of Solomon. Adonijah had made himself king, and Bathsheba, by the advice of Nathan the prophet, took measures to make her son Solomon king. But to whom did Nathan advise her to go? Did he tell her to go to the Sanhedrin and to seek justice? No, but to go to David the king, and to him she accordingly went, and found him not in council, or surrounded by the members of the Sanhedrin, but with Abishag, the Shunammite, ministering to him; and David, without asking any advice, sware unto her, "Assuredly Solomon, thy son, shall reign after me." The Sanhedrin had nothing whatever to do with the matter. The assertion, then, that "Nothing was appointed except by the authority of the Sanhedrin," is a gross falsehood, and very evidently made by ambitious men, grasping after power to which they had no right.

In like manner, we might appeal to history to show, that the tribe of Dan was judged, and that Saul, David, and the other kings of Israel, waged wars without once consulting the Sanhedrin; but there is one of these pretensions so directly opposed to the plain letter of the Mosaic law, that we prefer noticing it. The oral law says, that the waters of jealousy were not administered except by the authority of the Sanhedrin. But what says Moses? When the spirit of jealousy comes upon a man, does he tell him to bring his wife to the Sanhedrin? No, but to the priest. "Then shall the man bring his wife unto the priest," &c. (Numb. v. 15.) What then is the priest to do? Is he to go first to the Sanhedrin, and get its sanction? No; as soon as the man has brought his wife, and the offering of jealousy, the priest's business is to bring her before the Lord—" And the priest shall bring her near, and set her before the Lord,"—and is then to proceed with all the prescribed rites; and the whole ends with these plain words, "And the priest shall execute upon her all this law." There is not only no mention of the Sanhedrin, but immediate power is unequivocally given to the priest, yea, he is commanded to proceed without awaiting the decision of any other tribunal. Here again, then, the pretenders of rabbinic tradition are in direct opposition to the plain commands of Moses, and are therefore unfounded. It is unnecessary to enter into more of these particulars. The two which we have examined are contrary to truth; and two falsehoods are quite enough to shake the credit of any claims. The only possible way of establishing the authority of the Sanhedrin, in answer to this argument, is, to deny the authority of the Bible. There is no other alternative—either the authors of the Pentateuch, the books of Samuel and Kings, are mistaken, or the jurisdiction of the Sanhedrin is a mere fiction. Moses commands a very different institution, and the historical books represent a very different form of government. He who receives these books as inspired, must renounce the authority of the Sanhedrin, whilst he who maintains it must give up the sacred books.

There is, however, another tribunal mentioned in the above-quoted passage of the oral law which it is necessary to notice, and that is the minor Sanhedrin, or council of twenty-three. It is said, "The minor councils through the tribes and towns are not to be established except by the council of seventy-one;" and elsewhere we read:—

ומעמידין בכל עיר ועיר בישראל שיש בה ק״כ או
יותר סנהדרי קטנה ,וכמה יהיה מנינם כ״ג דיינים :

"In every city of Israel that contains one hundred and twenty Israelites or more, a minor Sanhedrin ought to be appointed, and of how many members ought it to consist? Of twenty-three judges." (Hilchoth Sanhedrin, i. 3.) Now this is another innovation for which there is no warrant whatever in the law of Moses. "Moses chose able men out of all Israel, and made them heads over the people, rulers of thousands, rulers of hundreds, rulers of fifties, and rulers of tens. And they judged the people at all times." (Exod. xviii. 25, 26.) This is the provision which Moses made for the administration of justice, but he says not a syllable about the appointment of minor Sanhedrins of twenty-three, so that in this we have another instance of the effort, which the rabbies made, to get rid of all the Mosaic institutions, and to substitute their own. And also another proof that the laws of the Sanhedrin were not given by Moses, for they require this Council to appoint minor courts, contrary to his ordinances. It appears, then, from what has been said in these two papers, that the Sanhedrin was altogether an unlawful tribunal, and that therefore the oral law can receive no support from its approval: and it appears, further, that modern Judaism has entirely subverted that order of things established by Moses. He ordained the priests, the Levites, as the teachers of Israel. Modern Judaism has turned them out of their office, and substituted the rabbies. Moses ordained a Supreme Council, consisting of the priests and the judge. Modern Judaism has destroyed that Council, and established the Sanhedrin in its place. Moses appointed rulers over thousands, hundreds, fifties, and tens. Modern Judaism has put an end to that order, and erected new tribunals of twenty-three. In fact, if it were possible for the

Jews to realize all the commands of the oral law in their own land, and Moses were to come amongst them again, he could never recognize them as his disciples. He would not find one of his institutions remaining as he left it. It is quite absurd, and if the subject were not so grave, it would be ludicrous to hear the Rabbinists exclaiming that the law of Moses is unchangeable, when they themselves have changed all its main provisions, and made an entirely new religion. But to the Jews it ought to be a matter of very serious enquiry, whether the Mosaic law is unchangeable or not. If the law be unchangeable, then no rabbinical Jew can entertain a reasonable hope of salvation, for he professes a religion which has effected the most extensive changes. In his creed he denies the lawfulness of change, and in his practice he changes without scruple. If the law be unchangeable, it is the bounden duty of every Jew to give up at once the new religion of the rabbies, and to return with all haste to the institutions of Moses. But if he believe that the law is changeable at pleasure, then he ought to renounce that article of his creed which teaches its immutability. In so serious a matter as religion, he ought to endeavour to be consistent, and not halt between two opinions. If Moses be his lawgiver, then let him serve him. But if he be determined to continue in the new religion of the rabbies, he ought to inquire into their character, and the authority and motives which led them to overturn the religion of their forefathers. Is the religion of Moses a bad religion, which it was necessary to renounce? Or, was it only given for a certain period, and when that period had expired, exchanged for a new one? Had the rabbies Divine authority for the changes which they made, or did they change it for their own convenience and interest? The nature of the changes looks very suspicious, they all added to their influence and power. As long as the law of Moses was observed, the rabbies had no power either in Church or State. But by the changes which they made, they became absolute despots over the bodies and souls of all Israel. They had, thus, every possible temptation to reject the one and adopt the other. But is this a reason why the Jewish people should also reject the law of Moses? They gain nothing, and loose everything, both for time and eternity, by the change. By adopting the new religion of the rabbies, they give up the use of that most precious gift, their reason, in all that regards the law and service of God. A Jew, who receives the oral law, can have nothing but a blind faith. He has lost the privilege of considering what God requires of him, and must simply receive what the rabbies choose to prescribe as his duty: and if they should even go so far as to tell him that his left hand is his right, and his right hand his left, he must believe in the decision, and reject the evidences of his senses. Or, if he should dare to doubt, where Judaism reigns triumphant, he must be strangled. There is certainly nothing very inviting in this system, nothing that should tempt a man to prefer it to the just, and equitable, and rational religion of Moses. He gives the law of God into the hands of the Israelite, and says, " Behold I have set life and death before you, choose ye." He deals with men as rational beings, and requires implicit obedience, not to the word of man, but to the oracles of God. He established a supreme council, but did not permit that council to pass off their own opinions as infallible, but commanded them to inquire of Him who alone is free from error. It is truly astonishing that so large a portion of the Jewish people should still prefer the religious despotism of the oral law; and it is more astonishing still, that they should be deluded to believe, that a system, which has subverted all the institutions of Moses, is the Mosaic religion. But the most astonishing circumstance of all is, that those Jews who have detected the grossness of the delusion and have themselves renounced the practice of the oral law, should feel so indifferent about the welfare of their brethren, and so reckless of the interests of truth, as to look on in silence; or even appear to countenance error by joining in the rights and ceremonies of tradition. Even the tribe of Levi itself has lost its zeal, and abdicated the sacred office committed to it by God. For eighteen hundred years there has not appeared in Israel one single person zealous for the law of Moses. All have been content with calling Moses their master, and there the matter ends. The priests and the people all unite in violating his laws, and trampling upon the ruins of his institutions, and then expect other people to believe that they are the faithful disciples of Moses.

No. XLV.

SANHEDRIN CONTINUED.

How a nation, so acute and so fond of learning as the Jews, should ever have been imposed upon by so clumsy an imposture as that of the oral law, is truly astonishing. The exceeding folly of some of its ordinances, the incredibility of the legends with which it abounds, the extravagant pretensions of its doctors, the grinding tyranny of its despotic tribunals, all

seem calculated to awaken doubt in the mind of the most
credulous, and the most ignorant. But the utter want of
evidence to support its claims ought to be sufficient to open
the eyes of even superstition itself. To establish the genuineness of an oral tradition, an unbroken chain of witnesses, from
the rise of the tradition to the present time, is indispensably
necessary. The succession of persons who received it from
their predecessors, and transmitted it to their followers, must
be clearly and accurately made out; and the want of a single
link, or the existence of a single chasm in the chain of transmission is quite sufficient to discredit the whole, and to invalidate the claims to genuineness. To prove the genuineness of
the תורה שבעל פה, oral law, it is necessary not only to
point out a succession of persons, but a succession of Sanhedrins, for, as we have seen, the Sanhedrin was regarded as the
foundation and pillar of tradition. If a single chasm in history exists, where a Sanhedrin cannot be pointed out, or if the
assigned succession be inconsistent with the written and inspired records of the people, the claims of the oral law are
invalidated, and the Jewish nation convicted as the abettors
of a pious fraud, or the unwitting dupes of an imposture.
Now we have already shown that the Sanhedrin was not
instituted by Moses, and was never heard of until after the
Greek conquest of the land of Israel; and hence it inevitably
follows, that the oral law is totally destitute of that chain of
testimony, by which alone its genuineness could be established.
From Moses to the Maccabees there is one continued chasm,
an immense and impassable abyss, which separates between
modern Judaism and truth. But as the rabbies have endeavoured to fill up the yawning gulf, or rather to build a
bridge in the air for the purpose of passing it, we think it
necessary to examine the success of their efforts. They say,
that a chain of testimony, such as is wanted, does actually
exist, and have endeavoured to point out the various links.
If this prove fallacious, then the last and only hope of modern
Judaism is gone; to prove the fallacy does not require much
argument. The chain of testimony as pointed out by the
rabbies themselves, is inconsistent with history, and wants
continuity even at the very commencement. The first part of
the succession is thus described:—

אף על פי שלא נכתבה תורה שבע״פ למדה משה
רבינו כולה בבית דינו לשבעים זקנים ואלעזר ופנחס
ויהושע שלשתן קבלו ממשה , וליהושע שהוא תלמידו
של משה רבינו מסר תורה שבע״פ וצווהו עליה , וכן
יהושע כל ימי חייו למד על פה, וזקנים רבים קבלו
מיהושע , וקבל עלי מן הזקנים ומפנחס:

"Although the oral law was not written, Moses our master taught it all in his Council to the seventy elders; Eleazar also, and Phinehas, and Joshua, all three, received it from Moses. But to Joshua, who was the disciple of Moses our master, he delivered the oral law, and gave him a charge concerning it. In like manner Joshua taught it by word of mouth all the days of his life; and many elders received it from Joshua, and Eli received it from the elders, and from Phinehas." (Preface to the Yad Hachazakah.) Now here the want of continuity begins, immediately after the third link in the chain. That Joshua should inherit the oral law from Moses is very likely, if there was any to be inherited, but who was Joshua's successor the rabbies cannot tell us. It is not enough to say that the elders received it from Joshua; who were the elders, and who was the next president of the Sanhedrin, and who was the president after that? To make out a chain of witnesses, we must at least have their names, but ought to know, besides, their character, their piety, their probity, before we can depend upon their testimony. The absence of this detail shows that the rabbies had no information on the subject, and were merely trying to make up a story to impose upon the credulous. It is self-evident that if they had possessed an accurate detail, they would have given it; but as they do not, we must infer that they had it not; and as the Bible gives no information on the subject, we must assert, that the chain of testimony terminates at the second link. So far are the rabbies from being able to prove a succession of Sanhedrins from the time of Joshua to their own, that they are compelled to make a grand leap from Joshua to Eli, and thus to leave a chasm of more than two hundred years, which of itself is sufficient to overthrow the claims of the oral law, and to stamp the Jews as the most credulous of men if they believe without any evidence. It is true that the rabbies endeavour to stop up this great cavity with a great falsehood. They say that Eli received the oral law from Joshua's elders, and from Phinehas; which assertion implies that all these persons lived to be about three hundred years old! And yet, if it were true, it would not be sufficient to make out the proof, for which the succession of Sanhedrins is absolutely necessary, and especially for this period. From the book of Judges, it appears, that in the interval between Joshua and Eli, and even in the next generation after Joshua's death, the people forsook the law of Moses, even the written law, and gave themselves up to idolatry. Thus we read, "And Joshua the son of Nun, the servant of the Lord, died, being an hundred and ten years old......And also all that generation were gathered unto their fathers: and there arose another generation after them, which knew not the Lord, nor the works which he had done for Israel. And the children of Israel did evil in the sight of the Lord, and served Baalim." (Judges ii. 8—11.) Now, here the inspired writer says that Joshua and all that generation died, which expressly contradicts the rabbinic assertion that Joshua's elders lived to the time of Eli; and, further, he says, that the Israelites turned aside to idols: where was the Sanhedrin at that time? If it existed, why did it not stop the torrent of corruption, and punish the transgressors? And why was it necessary for God to raise up Judges to do the Sanhedrin's work? We do not once read of the Sanhedrin, or any other council, helping Israel. In the book of Judges, deliverance is ascribed solely to the judges whom God raised up. "When the Lord raised them up judges, then the Lord was with the judge, and delivered them out of the hand of their enemies all the days of the judge......And it came to pass when the judge was dead, that they returned and corrupted themselves more than their fathers." (Ibid. 18, 19.) Indeed, that saying so often repeated in the book of Judges, "In those days there was no king in Israel, but every man did that which was right in his own eyes," shows that there was no Sanhedrin either. If any council of the kind, armed with such despotic power, had existed, the children of Israel could not have done that which was right in their own eyes. Whether, then, we look at the Bible or at the rabbinic account, we have a period of more than two hundred years, during which there is no evidence at all either for the existence of the Sanhedrin or of the oral law. The chain of testimony, therefore, offered by the rabbies, is not complete; and is, moreover, unworthy of credit, as it contains a gross falsehood concerning the age to which Joshua's elders lived. A little more examination will show us that it contains more than one falsehood. After telling us that David received the oral law from Samuel and his council, it thus proceeds:—

אחיה השילוני מיוצאי מצרים היה ולוי היה ושמע
ממשה והיה קטן בימי משה והוא קבל מדוד ובית
דינו , ואליהו קבל מאחיה השילוני ובית דינו :

"Ahijah the Shilonite was one of those who came out of Egypt, and a Levite, and he heard the oral law from Moses: but he was little in the days of Moses, and received the oral law from David and his council. And Elijah received from Ahijah the Shilonite and his council." Now, in the first place, this statement is very absurd. To suppose that one, who had heard the law from Moses, should at last receive it from David, is contrary to probability: but to assert that Ahijah was a little boy in the time of Moses, and that he lived until the reign of Solomon, that is, above five hundred years, is manifestly a falsehood, and, whether wilful or not, completely destroys the credibility of this attempt at a succession of witnesses. If involuntary, and the result of error, it shows that the rabbies who have transmitted this story were so weak in intellect as to swallow any improbability; and that as they transmitted one lie, they may have transmitted more. But if voluntary, no one will argue that the testimony of wilful liars is worth much. This last attempt, therefore, to prop up the authority of the oral law is vain.

But this rabbinic chain of testimony goes on to tell us that, amongst others, the oral law passed through Jeremiah the prophet:—

וירמיהו קבל מצפניה ובית דינו , וברוך בן נריה
קבל מירמיה ובית דינו :

"Jeremiah received from Zephaniah and his council, and Baruch the son of Neriah received from Jeremiah and his council." Now, if this means that Jeremiah was the נשיא, or President of the Sanhedrin, it is plainly false. The whole history of Jeremiah shows us that he was not the powerful head of a despotic and irresistible council, but an unprotected and persecuted man. Had he been president of a tribunal so dreadful, and whose sentence of excommunication was in itself sufficient to protect him, the people and the princes would never have dared to reject his words as they did, much less to make an attempt on his life. But if, on the other hand, it be said that Jeremiah's council does not mean the Sanhedrin, then we have another chasm in the succession of Sanhedrins, and consequently the proof fails again. But this chain of evidence is not only contrary to fact, and to the inspired writings of the prophets; it is also inconsistent with the oral law itself, for it asserts that two proselytes form a part of the chain of transmission:—

שמעיה ואבטליון גרי הצדק ובית דינם קבלו מיהודה
ושמעון ובית דינם , הלל ושמאי ובית דינם קבלו
משמעיה ואבטליון ובית דינם :

"Shemaiah and Abtalion, proselytes of righteousness, and their council, received from Judah and Simon and their council. Hillel and Shammai and their council received from Shemaiah and Abtalion and their council." Now, according to the oral law, it is unlawful for proselytes to be members of any council or tribunal. Respecting the Supreme Council, it is expressly said:—

אין מעמידין בסנהדרין אלא כהנים לויים וישראלים
המיוחסים הראויים להשיא לכהונה , שנאמר והתיצבו
שם עמך בדומין לך בחכמה ביראה וביחס :

"None are to be made members of the Sanhedrin except priests and Levites, and Israelites of so good a genealogy as to be fit to intermarry with the priests; for it is said, 'And they shall stand there with thee,' (Numb. xi. 16,) *i.e.* like unto thee in wisdom, in piety, and in genealogy." (Hilchoth Sanhedrin, c. ii. 1.) And even of an inferior tribunal it is said :—

בית דין של שלשה שהיה אחד מהם גר הרי זה פסול :

"A tribunal of three, one of whom is a proselyte, is unlawful." (Ibid. 9.) If then, it was unlawful for a proselyte to be a member of the Sanhedrin, or any other tribunal, how is it that we find two at the head of one of those councils through which the oral law was transmitted? If the decisions of the oral law be valid, that council was illegitimate, and therefore totally incompetent to the transmission of tradition, and then we have a break in the chain of testimony even at that end which is nearest to the rabbies. But if that council be considered competent, then the oral law which condemns it cannot contain the true tradition. But in either case, the genuineness of the law is overthrown.

The sum of what we have said is this :—That even if we were to give up our other arguments against the authority of the Sanhedrin and the oral law, and were willing to rest this question on the testimony of the rabbies themselves, the defectiveness, inconsistency, and falsehood manifested in that testimony, would be sufficient to throw discredit on all their claims. They have not only no proof from Scripture, but are not able themselves to find in tradition an unbroken chain of testimony. They fail at the very outset. After producing two links, they leave a chasm of above two hundred years unaccounted for. When they take it up again, they are convicted of gross falsehood in asserting that men lived, after the deluge, to the age of five hundred years: and are not able even to make out a story that will agree with the oral law itself. The most favourable ground, then, that can be taken for the defence of the oral law proves untenable. But if to this we add the arguments contained in the former papers, and remember that the Sanhedrin is in direct opposition to the law of Moses, is never mentioned in any of the sacred books, nor heard of until the Greek language was spoken in the land of Israel, every support is taken from the oral law, and it sinks down to the level of a mere imposture, of which the Jewish people have been the dupes and the victims. How long they will remain so, it is for themselves to consider. The times of blind faith, such as modern Judaism requires, are gone by; the Jews can therefore no longer remain the blind followers of the superstitious and ambitious rabbies. Either they must honestly confess that they and their fathers have been deceived for the last eighteen hundred years, and earnestly set about seeking that truth which they lost; or they must be content to be regarded either as interested upholders of error, or reckless despisers of truth. No one, who at all knows the nation, will ever believe that they are so weak in understanding as to be unable, under present circumstances, to detect the clumsy pretensions of the oral law. Some Jews may, indeed, still obstinately refuse to investigate the evidences of their paternal religion, and persist in professing Judaism simply because their fathers did so before them: but such persons must be content to acknowledge that their faith is not that of a rational being, or that their religion will not stand the test of reason. All who will take the trouble to investigate, must, if they be honest men, make up their minds to renounce the religion of the rabbies. There is not any one argument, either of internal or external evidence, in its behalf, on which a man of ordinary understanding can rest for a moment. The only shadow of a basis on which to support the oral law is the doctrine of the Sanhedrin, but this, as we have seen, disappears so soon as we approach the illusion. Instead of giving authority to the other parts of the oral law, the doctrine of a Sanhedrin appears one of the most objectionable of its many errors, for it bears upon its front the stamp of selfishness and ambition. It was an invention of men, who aimed not only at a spiritual dominion, but also at a secular despotism. The Sanhedrin was merely the engine whereby the rabbies hoped to get all the power, both of Church and State, into their own hands, and thereby distinguishes the rabbinical religion in the most striking manner from that of Jesus of Nazareth. Christianity contains no apparatus for securing to its teachers the dominion of the world; and therefore the professing followers of Christ, when they aimed at worldly power, were first obliged to invent an oral law of their own. Jesus of Nazareth seeks nothing but the dominion of truth. "When he perceived that they would come and take him by force, to make him a king, he departed again into a mountain himself alone." (John vi. 15.) His doctrine was, "My kingdom is not of this world." And in like manner he taught his disciples not to seek after worldly power. "Ye know that they which are accounted to rule over the Gentiles exercise lordship over them; and their great ones exercise authority upon them. But so shall it not be among you: but whosoever will be great among you, shall be your minister: and whosoever will be chiefest, shall be servant of all. For even the Son of man came not to be ministered unto, but to minister, and to give his life a ransom for many." (Mark x. 42—45.) Jesus and his apostles are perfectly free from the suspicion of making religion subservient to the promotion of ambitious schemes. The teachers of the oral law had, and even now have a temptation to uphold its doctrines, because they make them the absolute rulers of the Jewish people, and this tendency is a strong ground of suspicion. When God sent Moses, he preserved him from all similar imputation, for though he possessed the supreme power during his life, his claims were attested by miracles which could not be denied: and at his decease his children were chief neither in Church nor State. The priesthood remained in the family of Aaron, and the chief magistracy fell to the lot of Joshua. Thus disinterestedness distinguished the characters of Moses and Jesus from those of the rabbies. The doctrine of the Sanhedrin reveals but too plainly the motives by which the authors of the oral law were actuated. Of course we do not mean to ascribe the same motives to all the advocates of the oral law in the present day. Those motives are necessarily confined to those times when Judaism can be realized, and cannot, therefore, be called forth until there is a prospect of restoring the rabbinic polity. Our object is not to condemn the modern Jews, but to open their eyes to a true view of that system by which they have been so long deluded. And if they should ask us, Where, then, is the truth to be found? we reply, in Moses and the prophets. For though we are Christians, we firmly believe that true faith in the Old Testament must terminate in Christianity. The only real obstacle in the way of a Jew's receiving Jesus as the Messiah, is the prejudice, that his fathers, who rejected him, must have been in the right; and this obstacle we are endeavouring to remove. We have already made it appear that they were in the wrong; and our late papers have removed the strongest objection that they urge, namely, that the sentence of the Sanhedrin was decisive against his claims. We have shown that the Sanhedrin was altogether an unlawful tribunal, not established by Moses, but, as its name intimates, by the Greeks, and modelled by artful and ambitious men for their own purposes: and as the tribunal was unlawful, so was the sentence. Indeed the fact that the Lord Jesus Christ was condemned by an unlawful tribunal is a testimony in his favour. It shows that he disapproved of and opposed their unlawful doings. Jesus was not condemned by the friends of Moses, but by his enemies. The religion of Christ was persecuted, not by those who conscientiously kept Moses' commands, but by those who had first defaced every feature of Mosaism. The men who condemned the Lord Jesus were the tyrannical usurpers of an authority which Moses had given to others; and if Moses himself had appeared amongst them, and asserted the rights of the priests and Levites against the rabbies, they would just as readily have crucified him as the

Lord Jesus Christ. The Jews, therefore, of the present day, who approve the condemnation of Jesus, unite with the enemies of Moses; but those who are lovers of the Mosaic law must approve the efforts of Jesus to deliver it from the corruptions of wicked and ambitious men. An unlawful tribunal condemned him for doing what every true Jew must acknowledge to be right. Whether, then, they acknowledge him as the Messiah, or not, they must confess that he died a martyr to his zeal for the law of Moses, and are, therefore, bound to re-consider his claims. Jesus was put to death, not because he violated the Mosaic precepts, but because he reproved others for their transgressions—not because he endeavoured to overturn the religion of Moses, but because he resolutely defended its truth against those who were introducing a new religion upon its ruins.

No. XLVI.

CONTEMPT FOR THE FEMALE CHARACTER.

MODERN Judaism, or the religion of the oral law, cannot bear the slightest investigation. Its existence depends altogether upon a blind faith. As long as a man is willing to deliver up his understanding into the hands of the rabbies, and at their bidding believe that his right hand is his left, as they require; so long he may be a zealous professor of Judaism. But, the moment that he begins to think and to reason, and to compare his traditional faith with the doctrines of Moses and the prophets, he must begin to doubt, and if he really has a love for the law of God, he must ultimately renounce that superstition which caused the destruction of the temple and all the subsequent calamities of his people, and still enslaves the greatest portion of his nation. It matters not at which point he views it—its theoretic principles and its practical effects equally condemn it, and prove that it is so far from being a revelation from God, that it is not even the work of good or wise men. The doctrine of the Sanhedrin, which we lately considered, exhibits it as a spiritual despotism the most intolerable; but the utter contempt with which it looks down upon the female portion of mankind makes it to this hour a positive curse to the daughters of Israel, and proves that it does not proceed from Him who created male and female, and pronounced a blessing upon the one as well as the other. One of the prominent characteristics in every false religion is the degradation of womankind. The Mahometan imposture debases women to the level of the brute creation. Judaism places them in the same category with slaves. In Mahometan countries, women are deprived of all culture of head and heart. Rabbinism, as we saw in No. 3, pronounces that fathers are exempt from all obligation to teach their daughters the law of the Lord: but we must proceed to consider fully *the estimate which Rabbinism teaches the Jews to form of their daughters, their sisters, their mothers, and even the wife of their bosom:* and in doing this we shall not go to the opinions of the ignorant, the vicious, or the superstitious, but to the standard books of the nation. It is not possible to produce in English much of the slanderous assertions contained in the Talmud; many are too bad for translation, but still enough can be brought forward to prove satisfactorily that the rabbies look upon womankind with contempt. It is generally agreed that Rambam, or Maimonides, was one of the most learned and enlightened of the rabbies, and yet the contempt which he felt for the female head and heart appears very plainly in the following passage:—

אל יאמר אדם הריני עושה מצוות התורה ועוסק בחכמתה כדי שאקבל כל הברכות הכתובות בה או כדי שאזכה לחיי העולם הבא, ואפרוש מן העבירות שהזהירה תורה מהן כדי שאנצל מן הקללות הכתובות בתורה או כדי שלא אכרת מחיי העולם הבא, אין ראוי לעבוד השם על הדרך הזה, שעובד על דרך זה הוא עובד מיראה ואיננה מעלת הנביאים ולא מעלת החכמים, ואין עובדין ה' על דרך זה אלא עמי הארץ והנשים והקטנים שמחנכין אותן לעבוד מיראה עד שתרבה דעתן ויעבדו מאהבה:

"Let not any man say, Behold I perform the commandments of the law, and study in its wisdom, in order to obtain the blessings written therein, or to be worthy of the life of the world to come: and I abstain from the transgressions against which it warns, in order to be delivered from the curses written in the law, or that I may not be cut off from eternal life. It is not right to serve God in this way, for he that serves thus, serves from fear, and that is not the degree to which the prophets and wise men attained. No one serves God in this way, except unlearned men (Amharatzin), women, and children, whom they accustom to serve from fear, until their understanding increases, so that they may serve from love." (Hilchoth T'shuvah, c. x. 1.) Here Maimonides sinks women

CONTEMPT FOR THE FEMALE CHARACTER. 359

down to the level of children, and even classes their moral and intellectual faculties with those of the despised *Amharatzin*. We saw in No. 1 that an *amhaaretz* is of so little value, that his life is not considered more precious than that of a fish, and such it appears was Rambam's estimate of the value of a woman. This most learned rabbi considered it impossible for a woman to love God or to serve him aright; and when he wished to warn the Jews against serving God in an erroneous manner, he actually tells them not to serve Him as the women do. A more debasing imputation cannot be cast upon a human being than this, that he is physically incapable of loving God or serving Him aright. If he had asserted that since the fall of Adam, the whole human race is far gone from original righteousness, and that therefore the love of God is not in them, he would have said what is asserted in Scripture: but the opinion that women, that is, one half of the human species, have a physical incapacity to love and serve God; and that we are to regard them as a sort of finger-post for pointing out error, or a notorious example of that irreligion which we are to avoid, is to blaspheme the Creator, and to hold up the whole female sex to the universal scorn of their sons, their brothers, and their husbands. It may be said, in palliation of so foul a libel, that Rambam lived amongst Mahometans, and that he insensibly imbibed the opinions of the followers of the false prophet. Now it is most true that he could never have learned this sentiment from Christians. The New Testament does not teach us to look upon women as Amharatzin, but to regard them as rational and responsible beings, capable of doing God the same acceptable service as men, liable to the same awful judgment, and partakers of the same blessed hope. This apology, if true, would only serve to excuse Rambam: it would not defend the sentiment itself, but on the contrary, stamp it as Mahometan. It is not true, however, that Rambam imbibed this notion from intercourse with Mahometans: he learned it in the oral law, which has such a low opinion of women as to pronounce their testimony invalid.

עשרה מיני פסלות הם, כל מי שנמצא בו אחד
מהן הרי הוא פסול לעדות, ואלו הן הנשים,
והעבדים, והקטנים, והשוטים, והחרשים, והסומים,
והרשעים, והבזויין, והקרובים והנוגעין בעדותן
הרי אלו עשרה :

"There are ten sorts of disqualification, and every one in whom any one of them is found, he is disqualified from giving evidence; and these are they—women, slaves, children, idiots, deaf persons, the blind, the wicked, the despised, relations, and those interested in their testimony—behold these are ten."

(Hilchoth Eduth., c. ix. 1.) Now, it will be observed that these ten classes may be reduced to two—those who are disqualified by physical or intellectual infirmity, as children, idiots, deaf and blind persons; and secondly, those whose moral integrity is exposed to suspicion, as slaves, wicked and despised persons, relations, and those who have an interest in the cause. To one of these two classes women must belong: they are disqualified either because of incapacity, or because their moral feeling may not be trusted, and in either case are treated with a most unmerited contempt. It is true, that the rabbies endeavour to prove that the law of Moses excludes women from giving testimony, saying—

נשים פסולות לעדות מן התורה שנאמר על פי
שנים עדים לשון זכר ולא לשון נקבה׃

"Women are disqualified by the law from giving testimony, for it is said, 'At the mouth of two witnesses,' where the word witness is of the masculine, not the feminine gender;" but this proof is altogether inconclusive; on the same principle it might be proved that women might break all the ten commandments, for they are all given in the masculine gender. Indeed it is self-evident that God could not have given a law so absurd. There are thousands of cases, where, if women could not give evidence, all the ends of justice would be defeated. Take, for instance, the famous judgment of Solomon, where the two women laid claim each to the living child. In this case there could be no testimony but that of the women themselves, and Solomon did not send them away because they were women. Take also the case of Boaz and Ruth. When Boaz wished to marry Ruth, it was necessary first to redeem the inheritance, and for this it was absolutely necessary to prove that Ruth was the wife of Naomi's son. But there was no testimony but that of the women themselves. Elimelech, Chilion, and Mahlon, were all dead, and the marriage had taken place in a foreign land, yet we do not read of any difficulties being raised. Boaz himself, Naomi's kinsman, and the elders of Israel, appear all to have been perfectly satisfied. The disqualification of women, therefore, was not ordained by Moses, but is the invention of the rabbies, and shows that the rabbies had so low an opinion of the intellect or the integrity of women, as to think either that women are so half-witted as not to be fit to give testimony, or so dishonest as not to be trusted in the testimony which they may give.

But this degradation of the female character is not confined to the rabbinic courts of law. They have dared to carry it even into the house of God, and to make it prominent in the public worship of the Creator. The oral law has ordained that no public worship, nor indeed many religious solemnities,

CONTEMPT FOR THE FEMALE CHARACTER. 361

can be performed, unless there be ten persons present, but from this number it has carefully excluded the women, determining that—

ואלה העשרה צריך שיהיו כולם בני חורין וגדולים
שהביאו ב׳ שערות :

"It is necessary that all these ten be free and adult men." (Orach Chaiim, 55.) So that if there should be ten thousand women in the synagogue, they are counted as nobody, and unless there be ten men there can be no service. Hence it is that the daughters of Israel are never suffered to appear as participators in the worship of God, but are compelled to look on from a distance, as if they had neither part nor lot in the matter. Now what reason is there why women should not be regarded as worshippers? Are they not rational beings? are they not creatures of God? are they not heirs of immortality just as well as the men? Will they not join in the praises of the redeemed in Paradise; or is the Mahometan doctrine true, that women have no souls? Certainly, when one looks at the Jewish synagogue, one would think so. Before marriage the women never go there at all, and after marriage how seldom. On the Barbary coast they hardly ever go, and in Poland how common is it, whilst the men are in the synagogue at prayer, to see their wives outside loitering and chatting, as if the public worship of God was no concern of theirs. Even in this country the attendance of females is not at all equal to that of the men. How contrary is this state of things to the command of God in the Psalms, "Both young men and maidens; old men and children; let them praise the name of the Lord." (Psalm cxlviii. 12, 13.) And again, "Let every thing that hath breath praise the Lord." (Psalm cl. 6.) How different is the condition of the Jewish females under the oral law, from that described by Moses :—" When Miriam, the prophetess, the sister of Aaron, took a timbrel in her hand; and all the women went out after her, with timbrels and with dances. And Miriam answered them, Sing ye to the Lord, for he hath triumphed gloriously." (Exod. xi. 21.) Then the women were permitted to unite in the noblest work that can engage the soul of human beings, the praises of our God. But now they are shut out, according to the ordinance of the rabbies—they are not reckoned amongst God's worshippers, and if ten thousand of them should go to the synagogue, unless there should also be a sufficient number of men, a disciple of the rabbies would count them as nobody, and not think it worth his while to read prayers for them. A law like this cannot possibly proceed from God, He makes no such difference between male and female.

לֹא בִגְבוּרַת הַסּוּס יֶחְפָּץ לֹא בְשׁוֹקֵי הָאִישׁ יִרְצֶה:

"He delighteth not in the strength of the horse; he taketh not pleasure in the legs of a man." (Ps. cxlvii. 10.) "The sacrifices of God are a broken spirit; a broken and contrite heart, O God, thou wilt not despise" (Ps. li. 17); no matter whether it be male or female.

But the oral law is not content with degrading women by refusing to number them as a part of the congregation, it actually prescribes a form of daily prayer expressive of their contempt. Every day the men say—

בָּרוּךְ אַתָּה ה׳ אֱלֹהֵינוּ מֶלֶךְ הָעוֹלָם שֶׁלֹּא עָשַׂנִי אִשָּׁה:

"Blessed art thou, O Lord, our God! king of the universe, who hath not made me a woman." Whilst the women are directed to say—

בָּרוּךְ אַתָּה ה׳ אֱלֹהֵינוּ מֶלֶךְ הָעוֹלָם שֶׁעָשַׂנִי כִּרְצוֹנוֹ:

"Blessed art thou, O Lord our God! King of the universe, who hath made me according to his will." (Daily Prayers, p. 6.) The proud benediction of the men is founded altogether on the oral law, which promises rewards not to the state of the heart, but to the external operation of keeping God's commands, and as many of them cannot be kept by the women, intimates that the men will have a greater reward. This prayer, or rather thanksgiving, refers especially to the study of the law, from which they suppose the woman to be dispensed, and for which they expect no small reward in the world to come, and upon which they pride themselves, particularly in this present life. The man who remembers the day of judgment, when the secrets of all hearts shall be revealed, or bears in mind that the distinction of sex, like the difference of rank or office or nationality, is only for this world, will find but little reason for offering up any such thanksgiving. He knows that God will render to every human being, not according to sex, but according to deeds; and feeling that all, both male and female, are sinners, will see that such arrogance is unbecoming at all times, and particularly odious at the moment when he comes to ask pardon of Him "who spieth out all our ways." Instead of despising others, under the pretence of thanking God, the truly devout man will be much more ready to take up the language of David, and say—"Enter not into judgment with thy servant, O Lord; for in thy sight shall no man living be justified."

It appears, from these quotations, that Maimonides did not learn his contempt for womankind from the Mahometans, but from the oral law and the prayers of the synagogue. Modern Judaism disqualifies a woman from giving evidence, shuts her but from the study of God's Word, excludes her from the number of his worshippers, and even in its prayers to God pronounces her as nothing better than a heathen, or a slave: for in the preceding benedictions, the man says first—" Blessed art thou, O God, &c., who hath not made me a heathen;" then, " Blessed art thou, &c., who hath not made me a slave;" and, finally, " Blessed art thou, &c., who hath not made me a woman." Now we ask every Jew and Jewess, into whose hands this book may fall, whether a religion which teaches one-half of the human race to despise and degrade the other half, can possibly come from God? or whether it is not the invention of narrow-minded and vain-glorious men? Even reason itself would tell us that God can never teach us to despise the works of his own hands, and still less to hold up the mother who bore us, or the companion who has shared all our joys and sorrows, to the scorn of a privileged class of human beings. And yet this is what the oral law does, and thereby shows that it does not proceed from Him who inspired Moses and the prophets. The writings of the Old Testament furnish no warrant for female degradation. They commence by telling us that the woman as well as the man was formed in the image of God, and that though woman was first led into transgression, yet that she should have the honour of giving birth to him who should bruise the serpent's head. (Gen. iii. 15.) They tell us further, that when God was pleased to give the commandments from Sinai, that he exacted of all children to honour the mother as well as the father—" Honour thy father and thy mother." But how is it possible for any one to honour his mother who despises her as an inferior being, does not look upon her as fit to give evidence in a court of law, and even makes it a matter of public thanksgiving that he is not like her? Surely such an one is much more like him of whom it is said—

כסיל אדם בוזה אמו :

" A foolish man despiseth his mother." (Prov. xv. 20.) The oral law is, in this respect, altogether inconsistent with the law of God. The former tells fathers to leave their daughters without any religious education, and the latter supposes that they have been so well taught as to be able to teach their sons. Thus Solomon says, more than once, " My son, keep thy father's commandment, and forsake not the law of thy mother," תורת אמך. (Prov. vi. 20.) But how is it possible for those Jewish mothers, in Poland or Africa for instance, who cannot even read themselves, to teach their sons? or, even suppose they could read, how can a son believe in his mother's instruction, when the oral law tells him that she is not qualified to give testimony? But the Bible does not teach us merely to have a respect for our own mother, but shows us generally that God is no respecter of persons, and that he bestows his gifts upon all. It presents to our view many women, as Sarah, Rebecca, Miriam, Deborah, and Hannah, as examples of piety, and informs us that in the time of salvation, he will pour out his Spirit upon all flesh, without any distinction of sex or nation. "And it shall come to pass afterward, that I will pour out my spirit upon all flesh; and your sons and your daughters shall prophesy." (Joel iii. 1. In the English Bible, ii. 28.) Yea, as if to mock the rabbies and the oral law, God adds, that it shall be given even to the male and female slaves.

וגם על העבדים ועל השפחות בימים ההמה
אשפוך את רוחי:

"Yea, even upon the servants and handmaids, in those days, will I pour out my spirit." The two classes of human beings whom, next to the *Amharatzin*, the oral law treats with the most indignity, are women and slaves: but God's thoughts are not like the rabbies' thoughts, and he, therefore, graciously stands forth as the vindicator of the oppressed, and promises even to these classes the gift of prophecy. Here again, then, we see that "as far as the east is from the west," so different is God's law from the present religion of the Jewish people. The religion of the rabbies is a grinding tyranny, oppressive to the Gentiles, to slaves, yea, and to all unlearned Jews, and that does not even spare the wives, the mothers, and the daughters of Israel. Wherever the oral law can have its full sway, as in Mahometan countries, the women are left totally destitute of learning and religion—they are not even taught to read. In not one of those countries is a school for female children to be found. It is only in Christian lands that the daughters of Israel get any education, or ever attain to anything like that station which God destined them to fill. Wherever the light of Christianity shines, however feeble, it ameliorates the condition of the female portion of the Jewish nation, and compels even the disciples of Rabbinism to take a little more care of their souls and their intellects. Jewish females are therefore deeply indebted to the doctrines of Jesus of Nazareth. If he had not risen up against the oral law, they would be universally classed with slaves, idiots, and Amharatzin. He has delivered them from this degradation. Let them then consider the religion of Jesus, and the religion which the rabbies have taught them, and then let them decide which is most beneficial to their temporal and eternal welfare. The religion that comes from God must be beneficial to all his rational creatures. A religion that oppresses or disdains any one class, and deprives them of religious instruction, cannot come from him.

No. XLVII.

POLYGAMY.

GREAT and striking is the difference of position which womankind occupies in Europe and in the countries of the East. In the latter they are men's slaves: in the former his companions. In the latter they are objects of contempt even to their own sons. In the former they are the honoured instruments to impart the first elements of learning and religion. Here in Europe they appear as co-heirs, with man, of reason, of intellect, of liberty and immortality; but there they seem to be an inferior race of beings, at the very most a better sort of domestic animal. That the European state of things is more agreeable to God's intention in the creation of male and female is evident from the consideration, that there one half of the human race is doomed to degradation and misery, whilst here they enjoy a becoming respect, and a much larger portion of happiness; and still more from observing the effects of the two systems. Here the intellectual and moral powers of mankind have far advanced towards perfection, but there the human race is still debased and barbarous. Now that, which makes happy and improves, must necessarily be more agreeable to God's purpose in creation, than that which degrades and makes unhappy; and this argument will also go far to prove that another striking feature of difference, which distinguishes the West from the East, is also more in accordance with the will of God; we mean the fact that here men have only one wife, whilst there they have many. There can be no doubt that this characteristic of European life conduces much to the well-being and the peace of families, as well as to the moral and intellectual improvement of individuals. In these two great advantages and means of happiness the Jewesses of Europe participate. They are not illiterate slaves like their sisters in the East, neither do they divide their husbands' affections with many. Here the Jews, like the Christians, have only one wife. It becomes, therefore, a most interesting subject of inquiry to know to what the European Jewesses are indebted for this superiority of respect and happiness. Is it to their own religion, or to the religion of Christians, that is, is it to Judaism or Christianity? We might answer at once, that Judaism has certainly not produced this salutary difference, for then it would have produced the same effect in Mahometan countries, but we prefer referring to the oral law itself. We have already shown that modern Judaism degrades women to the level of slaves and *Amharatzin:* we shall now prove that *the Jewesses are not indebted to it for the abolition of polygamy.*

When Napoleon assembled the famous Parisian Sanhedrin, he proposed this question to the Jewish deputies, "*Is it lawful for Jews to marry more than one wife?*" To which they returned the following answer :—" It is not lawful for Jews to marry more than one wife : in all European countries they conform to the general practice of marrying only one. Moses does not command expressly to take several; but he does not forbid it. He seems even to adopt that custom as generally prevailing, since he settles the rights of inheritance between children of different wives. Although this practice still prevails in the East, yet their ancient doctors have enjoined them to restrain from taking more than one wife, except when the man is enabled by his fortune to maintain several. The case has been different in the West; the wish of adopting the customs of the inhabitants of this part of the world has induced the Jews to renounce polygamy. But as several individuals still indulged in that practice, a synod was convened at Worms in the eleventh century, composed of one hundred rabbies, with Guerson (Gershom) at their head. This assembly pronounced an anathema against every Israelite who should, in future, take more than one wife. Although this prohibition was not to last for ever, the influence of European manners has universally prevailed." (Transactions of the Sanhedrin, p. 150.) A more evasive, false, and inconsistent answer has rarely been given to a plain straightforward question. First they say decidedly, that it is not lawful for Jews to marry more than one wife : then they spend a page in contradicting themselves, and at last acknowledge that the abolition of polygamy was first owing to the anathema of a rabbi, and that it is now to be attributed to the influence of European manners. But what are European manners? What religion do Europeans profess? Plainly the religion of Jesus of Nazareth, so that here the Jewish deputies acknowledge that if Jewish wives have not got three or four or more rivals shut up with them in the same house, they owe this benefit to Christianity. But we must not rest satisfied with this answer of the Parisian deputies; we must ask the oral law itself, whether it is lawful for Jews to marry more than one wife, and must hear the oral law's reply. It answers thus :—

נושא אדם כמה נשים אפילו מאה בין בבת אחת בין בזו אחר זו ואין אשתו יכולה לעכב, והוא שיהיה יכול ליתן שאר כסות ועונה כראוי לכל אחת ואחת:

"A man may marry many wives, even a hundred, either at once, or one after the other, and his wife cannot prevent it, provided that he is able to give to each suitable food, clothing, and marriage-duty." (Iad Hachasakah Hilchoth Ishuth., c.

xiv. 3.) This is rather different doctrine from that of the Parisian Sanhedrin. Here it is plain that the oral law allows a man to have more than one wife, and does not stint him at all as to the number. The Arbah Turim teaches precisely the same doctrine, except that it advises a man not to marry more than four:—

נושא אדם כמה נשים דאמר רבא נושא אדם כמה
נשים, והוא דאפשר למיקם בסיפוקודהי, ומכל מקום
נתנו חכמים עצה טובה שלא ישא אדם יותר מד׳
נשים:

"A man may marry many wives, for Rabba says it is lawful to do so, if he can provide for them. Nevertheless, the wise men have given good advice, that a man should not marry more than four wives." (Even Haezer, 1.) So far then as Judaism is concerned, poligamy is lawful; and a Jew that would even restrict himself according to the advice of the rabbies, might still have four wives. It is not his religion that teaches him to be content with one: and therefore, we must, further, inquire how it is that the Jews, who consider polygamy lawful, do not indulge in it. The Parisian deputies have already informed us that it still prevails in the East, and that it prevailed in Europe until the eleventh century, when R. Gershom anathematized it. In the place just cited we find a similar statement:—

במקום שנהגו שלא לישא אלא אשה אחת אינו
רשאי לישא אשה אחרת על אשתו, ר׳ גרשון החרים
על הנושא על אשתו אבל ביבמה לא החרים וכן
בארוסה, ולא פשטה תקנתו בכל הארצות, ולא
החרים אלא עד סוף האלף החמישי:

"In a place where the custom is to marry only one wife, it is not permitted to marry more than one woman. R. Gershom anathematized any one that should marry a second, whilst his wife was alive; but this anathema does not extend to the case of the widow of a brother, who has died without children, nor to the case of a woman who is only betrothed. This ordinance, however, does not obtain in all lands, and the anathema was only to last until the end of the fifth thousand years." Hence it appears that before R. Gershom, polygamy was lawful and practised by the Jews in Europe, but that he forbade it except in particular cases; and further, that R. Gershom's prohibition was only temporary, it was to have full force until the end of the fifth thousand years, that is, until the year 1240 of the Christian era. This period is now long past, for the Jews reckon this year 5597, and Gershom's anathema has therefore lost its force; consequently, the only obstacle which their religion opposed to polygamy has been removed, and, so far as conscience is concerned, every professor of Judaism must feel himself at liberty to marry as many wives as he likes. He knows that R. Gershom's anathema has expired, and if he goes to the codes of Jewish law, he finds that it is left doubtful. For instance, the note on the passage just cited says—

ומכל מקום בכל מדינות אלו התקנה והמנהג
במקומו עומד ואין נושאין שתי נשים וכופין בחרמות
ומנדין מי שעובר ונושא ב׳ נשים לגרש אחת מהן
ויש אומרים דבזמן הזה אין לכוף מי שעבר חרם
דר׳ גרשון מאחר שכבר נשלם אלף החמישי, ואין
נוהגין כן :

"Nevertheless, in all these countries the ordinance and the custom remain in force, and it is not lawful to marry two wives; and he that transgresses and does so is to be compelled by anathema and excommunication to divorce one of them. But some say that in the present time he that transgresses the anathema of R. Gershom is not to be compelled, for the five thousand years have been completed long since; but the custom is not according to this." Here then are two opinions. The most strict of the two is, that polygamy is now not lawful, and that he who marries two wives must divorce one of them : but even this cannot be very satisfactory to the woman whom he first married, for it does not define which of the two is to be divorced. It only requires that one of them should be divorced, and leaves it to the man himself to divorce which he pleases. The other opinion is, that polygamy is now lawful, and that he is not to be compelled to divorce either. Hence it appears that it is not Judaism which protects the rights and the happiness of Jewish women, or the peace and comfort of Jewish families. The influence and the laws of Christianity forbid polygamy. To Christianity, then, Jewish females are indebted, not only for the station which they hold in society, but for the peace which they enjoy in their homes. Wherever Christianity has no power, there the Jews may take as many wives as they please: and if ever Judaism should obtain supreme power, Jewesses must expect to be again degraded into the category of slaves and *Amharatzin*, and to have their domestic peace annihilated by the introduction of new wives and families. It may be replied, that this objection applies with equal force to the written law, for that Moses himself allows polygamy. But to this we answer, that Moses only *tolerated* polygamy, but that he shows clearly that it was not the purpose of God, that men should have more wives than one. He found an evil custom existing amongst a people debased by Egyptian slavery, and like a wise reformer, he did not commence his improvements by destroying all that existed, but endeavoured to restrain the evil, to show that it was contrary to God's original institution, and to point out the consequences. He did not immediately pronounce it unlawful, for that would have been attended with serious inconveniences, but by the direction of God gave laws to protect the wives and children. In the beginning of Genesis —he showed that God's will was, that a man should have only one wife, for that he did not create several women, but only one. He gives the words of God, saying, "It is not good that the man should be alone: I will make him an help meet for him עזר כנגדו," where "help" is in the singular number, to show that man was not to have more than one help meet for him. And again, those words, "Therefore shall a man leave his father and his mother, and shall cleave unto his wife," not unto his wives, but to his wife; where it is also to be observed, that God is laying down a law, not for Adam only, but for coming generations. By exhibiting the original institution of marriage in Paradise, whilst man was yet innocent, and stating the original law and purpose of God, Moses plainly showed, that God's will was, that a man should have only one wife. He then goes on to show, that the first who departed from this original institution was Lamech, one of the wicked descendants of wicked Cain. "And Lamech took unto him two wives," (Gen. iv. 19,) whom he held up as a warning, recording of him only that he had two wives, and that he was a murderer. With this he contrasts the conduct of Noah and his sons, who had only one wife each. In the history of the patriarchs he shows the evil consequences of polygamy. He shows that it was not the will of Abraham to take a second wife, but that Sarah in her eagerness to have children misled him, and that discord and domestic trouble soon followed. And by all the troubles which the sons of Ishmael have since inflicted upon the children of Isaac, God has, in his providence, confirmed the moral to be drawn from the Mosaic narrative. Moses then points out the happiness of Isaac, who had only one wife; and the troubles of Jacob, who, not by his own choice, but by the wickedness of Laban and the folly of Laban's daughters, had more than one; and last of all, Moses gave in himself an example of the conduct which he wished Israel to pursue by having only one wife himself. A careful examination, therefore, of the law of Moses will show that he only tolerated polygamy as an existing evil, but that he intended to discourage it, by exhibiting the original institution of marriage, and the many evils that result from a departure from God's purpose. When, therefore, we show that the oral law permits men to have more wives than one, and that consequently it is accountable for all the evil thence resulting, we cannot be charged with reproaching the law of Moses. The oral law says expressly, that a man may marry many wives, even a hundred. The law of Moses nowhere says any thing of the kind. It only legislates in case that such a thing should happen. The oral law plainly advises a man not to take more than four wives. The law of Moses holds up the evil of having more than one. If men would carefully read the law of Moses, they would see that the original intention was, that a man should have only one wife. But if a man follow the oral law, he will be encouraged to take as many as he can support. It is evident, therefore, that if the Jews in Europe do not practise polygamy, their conduct is not to be ascribed to the influence of Judaism, but of Christianity.

It is, further, evident that this Christian practice of having only one wife, cannot be objected to as an unauthorized alteration of the law of Moses. If R. Gershom was allowed to forbid polygamy, and the Jews considered themselves bound to obey him, they cannot reasonably object to the Christian laws on the same subject. Christianity has only effected by its influence what R. Gershom endeavoured to accomplish by anathema. The only difference is, that Christianity was first, and that R. Gershom learnt the evil of polygamy from Christians. If it was lawful for a rabbi, it was still more lawful for the Messiah to restore the original constitution of marriage as established in Paradise, and to deliver Jewish wives and families from all that confusion and discord which results from polygamy. But it is particularly deserving of notice that R. Gershom, by forbidding the Jews to have more wives than one, made a great and decided change in the oral law. That which the oral law allows, R. Gershom forbids. We grant, indeed, that by thus changing the oral law, he approximated to the mind and intention of Moses: but he altered the oral law, and thereby shows us that he himself did not believe that the oral law was to last for ever, or that it is of eternal obligation. If he had considered it unchangeable, he would not have dared to make the change; but by making so important a change as this, to forbid what it allows, he plainly shows it as his opinion, that where there is a grave reason, the oral law may be changed or abolished; and all the Jews who acquiesce in his ordinance, and think it is unlawful to marry more wives than one, consent to the change. But if it be lawful to change in one thing, it must also be lawful to change in another, so that the rabbinical Jews have no reason whatever for reproaching their brethren who renounce the oral law totally. Such persons are only acting upon a principle practically acknowledged by all the Jews of Europe. It may be said that R. Gershom's change was only temporary, and that the present acquiescence of European Jews is only a sort of homage to Christian principles. This is certainly true, and this reply leads us to consider the dreary prospect presented to Jewish females, if ever modern Judaism should obtain power.

The influence of Christian principle would then cease,—polygamy would again be lawful, and the matrons of Israel, who now appear as the participators in the family government and the guides of their households, would again be degraded into one of a herd of female slaves. They might have a hundred competitors and rivals in their husbands' affections, and even if the husband should follow the advice of the rabbies, and take only four wives, they would at least have three. Now, we ask every matron in Israel whether she would wish such a change, or whether she would prefer the present state of things, where a man can have only one wife? If she prefers the present state, then she prefers the Christian principle, and acknowledges that Christianity is better than Judaism. If she does not wish for the restoration of polygamy, then she confesses that the doctrines of Judaism are injurious, and that she does not desire the triumph of her own religion. Then why should she profess a religion which she acknowledges to be prejudicial to her welfare—or why should she reject a religion which protects her peace and comfort? There can be no question, that Christianity has prevented amongst the Jews that practice of having many wives; it has, therefore, been a blessing to Jewish families for centuries; why, then, should they despise or oppose a religion which has been, and still is, a blessing? And we propose this question, not only to Jewish wives, but to Jewish husbands. Is it not a fact, that God's original institution was that a man should have only one wife—does not Moses show that the first polygamist was a descendant of wicked Cain, and, that family discord and unhappiness is the consequence of having more wives than one? Does not reason, and the state of Mahometan countries, show that where there are many wives, woman is degraded, and the education of children necessarily neglected? Is not the moral, the intellectual, and scientific progress of mankind greatly superior in Christian countries, where men have only one wife? Is not, then, the practice of having only one wife a blessing? Has it not been a blessing to Jewish husbands, wives, and children? Are not, then, the Jews deeply indebted to Christianity for that measure of peace and moral improvement which they have derived from this practice? And would not an adherence to their own oral law in the same degree have proved a disadvantage, if not a curse? How, then, can they oppose a religion which has been to them a blessing?—or how can they adhere to a religion which contains principles subversive of their domestic peace, and destructive to the well-being, and the moral and intellectual improvement of one-half the human race? The rabbies say, that the oral law is eternal in its obligation: if so, then polygamy is to be eternal in its continuance, and then men are never to return to that state of perfection which they enjoyed in Paradise. Who is there that does not see that the race of men was most happy when sin was unknown, and most perfect in intellect when he could hold converse with the Deity and dwell in the garden of God? But if Judaism be true, men are never again to enjoy that state, for then polygamy was unknown. Adam had only one wife; and until sin entered into the world, and ripened even into murder, no man had two wives. Judaism is, therefore, opposed to the pure and perfect state of things that existed in Paradise, and favourable to that confusion introduced by the murderous Lamech, the son of murderous Cain—and Christianity resembles, in its principles of marriage, the happy state ordained by God in Paradise. Here, then, we have another and a practical proof that the oral law is not of God. Its authors totally misunderstood the mind and purpose of Moses, the servant of God, and misinterpreted his temporary toleration of an existing evil into a positive permission and sanction for continuing it. We have also another proof of the divine origin of Christianity.

No XLVIII.

DIVORCE.

WHEN God delivered the commandments at Sinai, he placed those which related to himself first, to teach us that our first duty is to love and serve him: and immediately after these he gave the command "Honour thy father and thy mother," to show us that, next to himself, we are bound to reverence, to love, and to obey those to whom we owe our existence. This order of things was not an arbitrary choice, but founded in that natural constitution of creation which God ordained as most conducive to the intellectual and moral well-being as well as to the happiness of his creatures. He does not command us to love and serve Him, and Him only, merely because He has the right on the one hand, and it is our bounden duty on the other; but because a conformity to his will is an approximation both to wisdom and happiness. Neither does he tell us to honour father and mother, because we owe them all such reverence, as from them we have derived our being, and to them are indebted for all the care and affection with which they have tended and watched over our infancy: but because He has himself constituted the relation of parent and child, and ordained parental affection and filial duty as the means of promoting our welfare in time and in eternity. Any religion, therefore, whose tendency is to render obedience to that command impossible, must not only be contrary to the will of God, but to the happiness of man; and this is one of the many reasons for which we think that Judaism must be false. The religion of the oral law has a direct tendency to diminish a son's respect for his mother. We do not mean to say that in this or any other Christian country Jewish sons despise their mothers. The co-existence of Christianity necessarily counteracts the development of rabbinical principles. We intend only to exhibit the natural and necessary consequences, if there were no counteracting force. The contempt which the oral law pours upon women in general, and the encouragement which it gives to polygamy have necessarily the effect of lessening their respect both in the eyes of their husbands and their sons, and this tendency is still more increased by the *rabbinic doctrine of divorce*, which we now propose to consider. The law of Moses permits divorce under certain circumstances. It says, "When a man hath taken a wife, and married her, and it come to pass that she find no favour in his eyes, because he hath found some uncleanness, ערות דבר, in her; then let him write her a bill of divorcement, and give it in her hand, and send her out of his house," &c. (Deut. xxiv. 1.) But this permission, founded on grave and important considerations, the rabbies have perverted into an unlimited licence to divorce on the most trifling pretext.

בית שמאי אומרים לא יגרש אדם את אשתו אלא
אם כן מצא בה ערות דבר דדרשי ליה לקרא כפשטיה
אם לא תמצא חן בעיניו לפי שמצא בה ערות דבר,
ובית הלל סברי אפילו הקדיחה הבשילו דדרשי לקרא
הכי כי מצא בה ערות או ערוה או דבר אחר
שפשעה כנגדו, ור׳ עקיבא כבר אפילו מצא אחרת
נאה הימנה דדריש ליה לקרא הכי והיה אם לא
תמצא חן בעיניו פי׳ חן של נוי או שמצא ערות דבר
והלכה כבית הלל שאם פשעה כנגדו יכול לגרשה:

"The school of Shamai says, A man is not to divorce his wife unless he shall find some uncleanness in her, for they interpret the verse according to its simple meaning, if she find no favour in his eyes on account of his finding some uncleanness in her. The school of Hillel thinks, that if a woman let the broth burn it is sufficient, for they interpret the words, 'a matter of uncleanness,' to mean, Either uncleanness, or any other matter in which she has offended him. But R. Akiva thinks, that a man may divorce his wife, if he only find another handsomer than she is, for he interprets the verse thus, 'If she find no favour in his eyes,' where he explains favour to refer to the favour of beauty, or if he find a matter of uncleanness. But the legal decision is according to the school of Hillel, that is, if a wife sin against her husband, he may divorce her." (Arbah Turim, Hilchoth Gittin., 1.) This monstrous passage is in itself sufficient to shake the authority of the oral law, for in the first place we find three grave authorities, Shamai, Hillel, and Akiva, all differing as to the sense of a most important passage, bearing upon a subject that most nearly affects the happiness and well-being of human society. One of the gravest questions that can be propounded is, When is a man justified in divorcing his wife? If there be an oral law at all, it ought certainly to answer this question clearly, unequivocally, and satisfactorily. The existence of disputation shows that these three rabbies had no authoritative tradition on the subject, but were merely giving their own private opinions: and that therefore the assertion, that an oral law exists, is a mere fiction invented to impose upon the credulous, but insufficient to beget faith in any man or woman that will make use of the reason given by God. The old fable, that God caused a voice to be heard from heaven, saying, when the rabbies differ, " That

אלו ואלו דברי אלהים חיים:

both speak the words of the living God," will not do now. Every one can understand that God does not speak contradictions. No one will believe that the profane sentiment of R. Akiva, That a man may divorce his wife as soon as he finds another who pleases him better, can proceed from the God of holiness and justice. It is true that his opinion is not the law; but the opinion of Hillel, which is the law, is not a whit better. It pronounces that if a woman only spoil the broth she may be divorced : now this interpretation of the words of Moses is plainly contrary to the grammatical sense : עֶרְוַת is in Regimen (סמיכה) and joined to דָּבָר by a munach, and can therefore by no means be separated from it so as to signify " Either uncleanness or some other matter." The words of Moses, the points, and the accents, all decide that there is only one cause for which a man may put away his wife. Hillel and his successors have wilfully passed by the plain sense of the Hebrew words, in their eagerness to obtain a facility for putting away their wives. They were not ignorant of the right sense, for that was plainly asserted by Shamai, but were determined to get rid of it; and such was the state of the Jews at the time, that they had influence enough to turn their false interpretation into law; and such has been the state of the Jews ever since, that it continues law to this very hour. A rabbinical Jew may, according to his religious tenets, turn away his wife, the mother of his children, on a pretext that would hardly justify the dismissal of a servant. He may rudely tear asunder the sacred ties of conjugal affection, and separate between mother and children, if the unhappy woman should only make a mistake in her cookery. One of the worst charges brought against the slave-dealers was, that they had no respect either for maternal or filial affection; that they separated between mother and children. The very same accusation can be brought against modern Judaism, which legitimatizes the very same disregard for the feelings of a mother. Can, then, such a religion, which thus daringly snaps the ties of nature, be from God? Is it possible that God should thus expose one half of his rational creatures to the caprice and the tyranny of those who ought to be their defenders and protectors from every insult and every harm? If the same right were given to women, though the laws would be most contrary to the divine institution of marriage, it would at least have the appearance of justice; but this is denied. The oral law says,—

אם לא תמצא חן בעיניו, מלמד שאינו מגרש אלא ברצונו ואם נתגרשה שלא ברצונו אינה מגורשת, אבל האשה מתגרשת ברצונה ושלא ברצונה:

"The words, 'If she find no favour in his eyes,' teach, that the husband does not divorce except voluntarily; and if the woman be divorced against his will, she is not divorced. But the woman is divorced with or without her will." (Jad Hachazakah Hilchoth, Gerushin, c. 1, 2.) According to this doctrine the happiness of the wife and the children is absolutely vested in the power of the man; and in any paroxysm of ill-humour, he may make them both unhappy for life; he may turn the mother out of her home, drive her forth like a criminal from the bosom of her family, and introduce a stranger. Who does not see that this is a power unfit to be trusted to the hands of any man or any people? We do not mean to impute anything peculiar to the Jews; we believe that as to their natural propensities, humours, and caprices, all men are much alike, and that therefore none ought to have the power of thus lightly breaking up the domestic constitution. It is no answer to this to say, that in this country divorce is not so lightly practised. Thanks to the power of Christian principle and the existence of Christian laws, it cannot be. But every one, who has had much opportunity of seeing rabbinical Jews, knows that divorce is practised amongst them with a facility and frequency that is astonishing. But this is not the question; we are not examining Jewish manners, but the modern Jewish religion; and if divorce had never been practised, we should still pronounce of the oral law, which inculcates such principles, that it cannot be from God; and of its authors that they were bad men, or they would never have thus trifled with God's most holy institution. The truth is, that the rabbies were altogether ignorant of the nature of marriage as God established it. They not only allow divorce on the most trifling pretext, but they sanction the practice of marrying for a given length of time, and, when that time is expired, of dissolving the marriage by divorce:—

לא ישא אדם אשה ודעתו לגרשה, ואם הודיעה
בתחלה שהוא נושא אותה לימים מותר :

"A man must not marry a woman with the intention of divorcing her; but, if he previously inform her that he is going to marry her for a season, it is lawful." (Hilchoth Gittin in Even Haezer, 1.) Now how contrary is such doctrine to the express words of Scripture. "This is bone of my bones, and flesh of my flesh. Therefore shall a man leave his father and his mother, and shall cleave unto his wife; and they shall be one flesh." (Gen. ii. 23.) Here Adam, in his state of innocence, pronounces that the tie of marriage is more sacred and more binding, than even that which exists between parent and child. A man may, and for his wife's sake shall, forsake father and mother, but should no more think of separating from his wife, than from his own bones and flesh. Who would lightly think of parting with a limb, or a portion of his body? Urgent, indeed, must be the necessity that will induce a man to permit the separation of a portion of himself, and equally urgent should be the cause that should move a man to part with her who is bone of his bones, and flesh of his flesh. Such is the Mosaic doctrine of the marriage obligation; but so little did the rabbies understand it, that they permit a man to marry for a week, a month, or a year; and when that season is expired, to tear asunder the sacred ties, and that without any cause whatever. But the evident evil that must result from the rabbinic doctrine of divorce is still more apparent from the first sentence of the passage last quoted—"A man must not marry a woman with the intention of divorcing her." These words show the direct tendency of the doctrine. When power is given to a man to turn out his wife when he likes, a temptation is at once held out to the evil-disposed to marry with the express intention of divorcing. The rabbies, therefore, find it necessary to forbid it; but is it likely that this prohibition will have much force in the eyes of a man who is wicked enough to form the intention? And suppose a wicked man does form the intention, and execute it, what remedy had the poor injured woman? Thus the oral law leaves the daughters of Israel completely at the mercy of the unprincipled, and places them beyond the possibility of obtaining justice.

But the cruelty and total want of feeling which the oral law displays and teaches, with regard to women, appears still more plainly from the following extract:—

מי שנתחרשה אשתו הרי זה מגרשה בגט ותהיה
מגורשת, אבל אם נשתטת אינו מוציאה עד שתבריא,
ודבר זה תקנת חכמים הוא, כדי שלא תהיה הפקר
לפרוצין שהרי אינה יכולה לשמור את עצמה; לפיכך
מניחה ונושא אחרת ומאכילה ומשקה משלה; ואין
מחייבין אותו בשאר כסות ועונה, שאין כח בבן דעת
לדור עם השוטים בבית אחד, ואינו חייב לרפאותה
ולא לפדותה, ואם גרשה הרי זו מגורשת ומוציאה
מביתו ואינו חייב לחזור ולהטפל בה:

"If a man's wife should become deaf and dumb, he gives her a bill of divorce, and she is divorced. But if she become insane, he is not to send her forth until she is recovered: and this thing is an ordinance of the wise men, that she should not become a prey to the immodest, because she is not able to take care of herself. The husband therefore, leaves her where she is, and marries another, and gives her meat and drink out of her own property. But he is not to be compelled to give her food and raiment, and duty of marriage, for it is not in the power of a sane person to dwell in one house with the insane. Neither is he obligated to have her cured, nor to ransom her. But if he should divorce her, then she is divorced, and is to be put out of his house: and he is not obligated to return and take any trouble about her." (Hilchoth Gerushin, x. 23.) Principles more contrary to God's Word, and to the common feelings of humanity, were never inculcated under the name of religion. We have been astonished at the cruelty with which the oral law treats Gentiles—we have been horrified at the coolness with which it speaks of splitting open an *Amhaaretz* —but here it surpasses itself, and out-herods Herod. A man accustomed to judge of his duty by the words of Moses and the prophets, or even to follow the dictates of unsophisticated nature, would conclude that, as he is at all times bound to love and cherish his wife, the obligation is doubly imperative in case of sickness, but especially so when that sorest calamity with which human frailty is visited, insanity, attacks the partner of his life. Then it is that the man, who has one spark of the fear of God or of the love of man, will show all his tenderness, watch over the sufferer with all care and anxiety, and if necessary, devote all his worldly goods to minister to her recovery. No, says the oral law, when the wife of your bosom most requires your attention, then marry another: give her neither food nor raiment, and, if you please, cast her out of your house, and leave her to her fate. The most charitable conclusion would be, to suppose that the men who uttered such sentiments under the mask of religion, were themselves insane. But what are we to think of Israel, that for eighteen hundred years they have been unable to detect so manifest an imposture? And what are we to think of Israel at present, that they sit still and suffer their children to be deluded, by being taught that this most atrocious system of inhumanity, is that pure and holy religion which the God of Israel revealed to Moses? Let not any Israelite mistake us. We do not mean to charge such wickedness upon them. The Providence of God has in a measure delivered them from such an odious yoke. The influence of Christianity has successfully counteracted the full development of these anti-human principles. We only mean to direct their attention to the nature of that religion to which they have adhered so long; and to induce them to consider what would be the state of the world, if Jesus of Nazareth had not arisen to protest against such gross corruptions, and to assert the truth. Just suppose that the traditions had triumphed. The universal law would then be, that men might divorce their wives when they please, and in the time of their calamity cast them forth into the streets. All the bonds of natural affection would be rent asunder. Conjugal affection would cease, filial duty be unknown—no son would honour his mother, for how could a son honour the unhappy being whom his religion pronounces unworthy either of succour or compassion in the time of her utmost need? If such principles had attained dominion, mankind would have been turned into a race of fiends, and this earth have become a hell. What, then, has stopped all this misery? Christianity, and Christianity alone. It teaches very different principles. When a Christian man is married, the vow which he is required to make is this—" Wilt thou have this woman to thy wedded wife, to live together after God's ordinance in the holy estate of matrimony? Wilt thou love her, comfort her, honour, and keep her in sickness and in health; and, forsaking all other, keep thee only unto her, so long as ye both shall live?" This is the doctrine of the New Testament. The Pharisees asked the Lord Jesus, " Is it lawful for a man to put away his wife for every cause? And he answered and said unto them, Have ye not read, that He which made them at the beginning made them male and female, and said, For this cause shall a man leave father and mother, and shall cleave to his wife;

and they twain shall be one flesh? Wherefore they are no more twain, but one flesh. What therefore God hath joined together, let not man put asunder." (Matt. xix. 3—7.) In like manner, Paul teaches, "So ought men to love their wives as their own bodies. He that loveth his wife loveth himself." (Ephes. v. 28.) And Peter teaches in the same spirit, "Likewise, ye husbands, dwell with them according to knowledge, giving honour unto the wife, as unto the weaker vessel, and as being heirs together of the grace of life; that your prayers be not hindered." (1 Peter iii. 7.)

Let any unprejudiced, yea, or any prejudiced, man, if he have only the use of his senses, compare these two doctrines, and say which is most agreeable to the will and character of God, as revealed in the Old Testament—and, which is most calculated to promote the happiness of the human race. The combination of mercy and justice forms a striking feature in the revealed character of God, but is there either justice or mercy in the laws which we have just considered? The happiness of the human race depends, in a more than ordinary measure, upon the right organization of the family relations: but how can there be any such thing as domestic order or peace, so long as the mother is looked upon as belonging to an inferior caste, whom it is permitted at any moment, even in the most afflictive of all visitations, to outlaw, and drive forth from the family circle? The uncontrolled dominion of the oral law would practically annihilate all the sympathies and consolations of the domestic constitution. The husband could not love the wife whom his religion teaches to despise, and forbids to pity. The wife could not love the husband, whom she must suspect not only of being destitute of affection, but devoid of pity; and from whom she could only expect divorce and expulsion in the hour of calamity. The son would learn to despise his mother, whom his religion marks out as a fit object for contempt, and a suitable victim for the exercise of cruelty. The mother, cast out by her own partner, would not even have the consolation of being pitied by her own children. A false religion would have taught them that this unnatural conduct was only obedience to the Divine will. The principles of Christianity, on the contrary, produce and protect all that domestic happiness which distinguishes Christian countries from the rest of the world; and in which Jews participate. The influence of Christianity has prevented that misery of which we have given but a faint outline. Can, then, the Jews deny that Christianity has been, and is, to them a blessing? or that it is, in its principles and effects, more agreeable to the character of God, and more productive of human happiness, and therefore more excellent and more true than modern Judaism.

No. XLIX.

RABBINIC LAWS CONCERNING MEAT.

CONSCIENTIOUS adherence to the dictates of true religion is one of the noblest traits that can adorn the human character, and this trait has appeared in its most vivid light in not a few of the Israelite nation. Elijah the prophet, for instance, is a bright example of religious constancy. At a time when all Israel had forsaken the true God, and zealously professed a false religion, neither the allurements of self-interest, nor the power of universal example, nor the natural desire of self-preservation, could draw him aside from the paths of truth and righteousness. Daniel and his three friends in Babylon exhibit the same unwavering firmness in the assertion of truth. The Royal dainties could not prevail upon them to partake of food offered to idols. The fiery furnace could not terrify Hananiah, Mishael, and Azariah, to commit idolatry; the lions' den possessed no terrors that could move Daniel to omit the worship of his God. But as constancy for the truth ennobles and adorns, in the very same degree an obstinate perseverance in error diminishes from man's moral or intellectual value. It shows either that his moral perception is so blunted as to be unable to discern between truth and error, or his moral taste so perverted as not to care for the difference—or that there is some intellectual deficiency which renders the moral powers inoperative. It leads to the suspicion that there is something wrong either with the head or the heart. There is, however, a class of persons, who persevere in error, not because the head is weak, or the heart sick, but because they have never fairly beheld the light of truth. They have grown up in a mist of error, and circumstances have prevented them from emerging into a purer atmosphere. To this class, we would hope, the professors of modern Judaism belong. That they have been for centuries in error is certain. Many incontestable proofs of this have been already advanced; *The rabbinic laws concerning* שחיטה, *or the slaughtering of animals*, will add another link to the chain of evidence. The Rabbinists have an idea that wherever they may be wrong, in this doctrine they are infallibly in the right; and yet, if the force of education did not afford some aid, it would be impossible to imagine how they can be deceived by a doctrine so manifestly false, and so entirely devoid of Scriptural foundation. In the first place, the slaughtering of beasts is, like eating, of every-day and universal concernment— a matter that affects the poor and unlearned as much as the studious; and yet the rabbinic rules are so many and so intricate that either a man must be learned himself, or employ a man of competent learning, to perform this business; or, he must, in spite of himself, turn Pythagorean and renounce the use of animal food. The oral law gives the following outline of what is to be understood by the word שחיטה or *slaughtering* :—

זביחה זו האמורה בתורה כתם צריך לפרש אותה
ולידע באי זה מקום מן הבהמה שוחטין, וכמה שיעור
השחיטה, ובאיזה דבר שוחטין ומתי שוחטין והיכן
שוחטין וכיצד שוחטין, ומה הן הדברים המפסידין
את השחיטה ומי הוא השוחט, ועל כל הדברים
האלה צונו בתורה ואמר וזבחת מבקרך וכו' כאשר
צויתיך ואכלת בשעריך וכו' :

" It is absolutely necessary to explain the killing (or slaughtering mentioned in the law), and to know, in what part of the beast one slaughters—what is the measure of the slaughtering—with what implement one slaughters—when—where—and how one slaughters—what things they are which invalidate the act of slaughtering—and who is permitted to slaughter. Concerning all these things, He has commanded us in the law where it is said, 'Then thou shalt kill of thy herd and of thy flock, which the Lord.hath given thee, as I have commanded thee, and thou shalt eat in thy gates whatsoever thy soul lusteth after!' (Deut. xii. 21.)" (Jad Hachazakah, Hilchoth Shechitah, c. i. 4.) Here we have at once a list of eight particulars, which must first be known, but then most of these again require a long and learned explanation; for instance the first is thus defined :—

ואיזה הוא מקום שחיטה בקנה משפוי כובע ולמטה
עד ראש כנף הריאה כשרתמשוך הבהמה צוארה לרעות
זה הוא מקום השחיטה בקנה, וכל שכנגד המקום
הזה מבחוץ נקרא צואר, אנסה הבהמה עצמה ומשכה
צוארה הרבה או שאינם השוחט את הסימנין ומשכן
למעלה ושחט במקום שחיטה בצואר, ונמצאת
השחיטה בקנה או בושט שלא במקום שחיטה הרי
זה ספק נבלה :

" On what part of the animal is the slaughtering to be effected ? On the wind-pipe, from the edge of the uvula downwards as far as the top of the extremity of the lungs, as these parts are situated when the beast stretches out its neck to feed : this is the place of the slaughtering in the wind-pipe; and all the part outside which answers to this place, is called the neck. If the beast forces itself, and stretches out its neck much, or if the slaughterer has forced the sinews, and drawn them upwards, and he slaughters at the right part of the neck, but afterwards it is found that the wind-pipe or the œsophagus is not cut at the right place, then it is a doubtful case of carrion." (Ibid. 7.) In like manner, the *measure of the slaughtering* is accurately defined, and must be as accurately attended to, or else the slaughtering must be considered unlawful, and then it becomes unlawful for the Rabbinists to eat it. But the most care is required in examining the knife, which may be of any material that will cut, on condition that there be no gap in it :—

אבל אם היה כמו תלם בחודו של דבר ששוחטין
בו ואפילו היה התלם קטן ביותר שחיטתו פסולה :

"But if there be anything like a furrow in the edge of the implement wherewith the slaughtering is effected, even though the furrow be the least possible, the slaughtering is unlawful." The slaughterer is therefore required to examine the knife before and after the act; for if a gap be found in it after the slaughtering, it is doubtful whether the beast is not be considered carrion :—

לפיכך השוחט בהמות רבות או עופות רבות צריך
לבדוק בין כל אחת ואחת שאם לא בדק ובדק אחרונה
ונמצאת סכין פגומה הרי הכל ספק נבלות ואפילו
הראשונה :

"Therefore he that has to slaughter many beasts or many fowls, must examine the knife after each ; for if he does not, but examines at the end, and the knife is found to have a gap, then all are to be considered as doubtful carrion, even the first." (Ibid. 24.) From these few particulars, it appears that great care, and not a little study and practice, are required in order to slaughter an animal for food according to the oral law, and that it is very easy, by mistake or want of knowledge, to make the meat unfit for rabbinic eating : but then, besides all this, there are the five circumstances which invalidate the slaughtering altogether :—

חמשה דברים מפסידים את השחיטה ועיקר הלכות
שחיטה להזהר בכל אחת מהן ואלו הן שהייה דרסה
חלדה הגרמה ועיקר :

"There are five things which invalidate the slaughtering : and the most important thing respecting the constitutions of slaughtering is, to attend to each one of them, and these are they—1st, If the person makes a stop of a certain length before the act is completed. 2d, If the throat be cut at a single blow, as with a sword. 3d, If the knife enters too deep, and is hidden. 4th, When the knife slips up or down from the right place. 5th, When the wind-pipe or œsophagus is torn and comes out, before the act is completed." (Ibid. c. iii.) These five essentials of rabbinic slaughtering lead again to endless questions and definitions; so that, putting all together, it is much to be doubted whether a beast ever was, or ever will be, rightly slaughtered according to the oral law. And yet these things, of which there is not the slightest mention in the Mosaic law, are tied like a heavy burden about the necks of the poor and ignorant, and are most oppressive to their bodies and their souls. The rich may not, perhaps, feel the oppression, but the poor sigh and groan under the load; and no man considers their sorrow, or stretches out a hand to help them. In the first place, the intricacy of the act always makes rabbinic meat a great deal dearer than other meat, so that the poor man and his family, who can at any time, or under any circumstances, afford to buy but little food, are compelled by the oral law to do with still less, and in many cases to do without it altogether. Let any one visit the haunts of the poor Jews in this city, or enter their abodes, and he will find many a wretched family pining away for want of proper food ; and yet it is too dear to procure a sufficiency ; and if any benevolent Christian should wish to assist them, offer them some of his own, or give them a ticket to some of those institutions which distribute meat to the poor, the starving family would not dare to accept it, even if their conscience allowed them, or if they did, would inevitably draw down upon themselves a storm of persecution, and be treated as if they had committed the greatest crimes: yea, if the oral law had power, the poor starving creatures, that had partaken of Christian bounty, would be flogged for satisfying the wants of nature :—

נכרי ששחט אע״פ ששחט בפני ישראל בסכין יפה ואפילו היה קטן שחיטתו נבלה ולוקה על אכילתה מן התורה שנאמר, וקרא לך ואכלת מזבחו :

"If a Gentile slaughters, even though he does it in the presence of an Israelite, with a proper knife, his slaughtering is carrion ; and he that eats of it is to be flogged according to the written law, for it is said, 'And one call thee, and thou eat of his sacrifice.' (Exod. xxxiv. 15.)" Yea, the oral law goes so far as to extend this rule even to the case of a Gentile who is not an idolater :—

וגדר גדול גדרו בדבר שאפילו גוי שאינו עובד ע״ז שחיטרו נבלה :

"A very strong fence has been made round this matter, so that the slaughtering even of a Gentile, who is not an idolater, is carrion." (Ibid., c. iv. 11, 12.) It is hardly necessary to say, that the above quotation from the oral law is now-a-days altogether out of place. Moses was not speaking of Christians nor of the inhabitants of these countries, but of the nations of Canaan. He had been declaring the words of the Lord, "Behold, I drive out before thee the Amorite, and the Canaanite, and the Hittite, and the Perizzite, and the Jebusite." And then adds, "Take heed to thyself, lest thou make a covenant with the inhabitants of the land, and they go a whoring after their gods, and do sacrifice unto their gods, and one call thee, and thou eat of his sacrifice." (Exod. xxxiv. 11—15.) So then, according to the oral law, because Moses forbade the Israelites to partake of the idolatrous sacrifices of the Hivites and the Jebusites, a poor famished creature here in London is not to touch Christian meat, nor to partake of Christian bounty. A more cruel or oppressive law could hardly have been devised. It is all very well for the rich, but it is very little short of murder to the poor. It binds their consciences with fetters of iron, so that even when relief is offered, many turn from good and wholesome food sent to them by a kind Providence; and if a spark of light has visited the mind of some victim of poverty, and he thinks it lawful to bring home the Christian bounty to save the lives of his starving children, fear prevents him. Perhaps his wife is still enveloped in all the darkness of superstition, and would spurn the proffered relief as an unclean thing, or perhaps his children might innocently betray him, and draw down all the weight of rabbinic indignation. A grosser insult has rarely been offered to the Majesty of heaven, than to call good and proper food, the work of his hands, carrion. A mistake in the slaughtering, an ignorance of the rabbinic art, a Gentile hand, is to be sufficient to turn the bounty of Almighty God into an unclean thing, and to deprive the poor of their daily food. How can the Jews expect God's blessing so long as this state of things continues—how can they be surprised if poverty and want, and wretchedness and scorn, tread close upon their heels, when they themselves spurn God's bounty from them with disdain? As nations deal with God and his word, so he deals with them, מדה כמדה, measure for measure; and therefore, so long as the oral law teaches them to scorn his bounty, and to deprive the poor of their food—so long as the cries of the poor ascend and enter into the ears of the Lord of Hosts, so long must they expect to feel the rod of his indignation. The times of ignorance and superstition God winked at; but those times have passed away. Good or bad, there is a stir in the world—there is a shaking of all old opinions, true and false; and from its effects the Jews have not escaped. There are many who, for themselves and their families, have renounced Rabbinism—who eat Gentile food, and know that in doing so they commit no sin. These are the persons who are most guilty in looking upon the misery of their poor brethren without pity or concern, and without an effort to deliver them. The rabbinic zealot who would persecute his brother for eating meat not slaughtered according to rabbinic precept is in comparison innocent. He conscientiously thinks that he is doing right; but for the man, who himself openly transgresses the oral law, and yet sees the faces of his brethren ground by that system, without a sentiment of pity, there is no excuse. If he had the common feelings of humanity, he would rise up, fearless of all consequences, and cry out with all his might against those principles which have been and are the curse of his nation. He would stand forth as the advocate and defender of the poor—yea, and he would have God's blessing. But so long as this class of anti-rabbinic Jews remain silent, whether from fear or from interest, or from indifference, let them not boast of their superior light. Let them not look with self-complacency on the poor victims of superstition. They are themselves less respectable and more guilty. They are conniving at what they know to be falsehood. They are with their eyes open consenting to oppression and starvation. They are, by their silence, helping to strengthen and confirm a system of anti-social intolerance, which has been the source of all the calamities which their nation has endured for eighteen centuries. What can be more pernicious than to teach the ignorant that the food which their neighbours eat is carrion, so unfit for the nourishment of a Rabbinist that he ought to die, and suffer his family to die of want, rather than eat it? Is it likely to produce kindly feeling on either side, considering that the mass of mankind is not actuated by the dictates of reason or the precepts of the Bible? On the one side it is likely to produce proud contempt, and on the other a spirit of retaliation. Every Jew that wishes well to his nation, and knows that these rabbinic principles are false, is bound to protest against them. He ought not to be a poor selfish thing, insensible to the wants and the sufferings of others, but should do what in him lies, to assert what he knows to be the truth. And is it necessary to remind such of the misery which these rabbinic principles are still working in every part of the world? Here in London the poor are suffering. In the various towns of England many Jews are suffering. In some places a single Jewish family is found, generally poor, and the father ignorant of the rabbinic art of slaughtering: such persons are compelled to abstain altogether from animal food, or to do violence to their conscience. The poor Jews who go out to the colonies to seek employment are in the same case, and are precluded from taking such situations as require them to partake of the food of their employers. Even if they can buy an animal, they are not allowed to kill it for themselves:—

ישראל שאינו יודע חמשה דברים שמפסידין את
השחיטה וכיוצא בהן מהלכות שחיטה שביארנו ושחט
בינו לבין עצמו אסור לאכול משחיטתו לא הוא ולא
אחרים, וחרי זו קרובה לספק נבלה והאוכל ממנה
כזית מכין אותו מכת מרדות:

"If an Israelite does not know the five things which invalidate the act of slaughtering, as we have explained, and slaughters by himself, it is unlawful to eat of his slaughtering, both for himself and others; for this case is much the same as that of doubtful carrion, and he that eats of it a quantity equal to an olive, is to be flogged with the flogging of rebellion." (Ibid., c. iv.) Such is the mercy of the oral law, and such its justice. It punishes the eating of what God has allowed, with the same severity that it would visit a great crime. It makes no provision for those numerous cases of distress which we have mentioned. Whether one of its disciples has or has not food, it never considers. Without reflection and without mercy it sentences every one, who eats meat not rabbinically slaughtered, to be flogged. But, besides the cruelty, what is the effect upon the minds of its votaries? It teaches them that to transgress this mere human observance is a sin of the deepest die, more dreadful far than many which God has forbidden. A Rabbinist would be more grieved to hear that his son had transgressed the law of slaughtering, than to find that he had been guilty of falsehood. Its tendency is directly to draw off the mind from the weightier matters of the law, judgment, justice, and mercy, and to flatter the ill-informed that they are good Jews, if only they abstain from meat not slaughtered according to rabbinic art.

Let not any Jew imagine that we wish him lightly to transgress the law of Moses, or to eat of food which the law of God has forbidden. We now speak of that which Moses has allowed. If a Jew would see meat offered to idols, or be invited to partake of an idolatrous feast, let him abstain—let him refuse, and protest as strongly as he will and can against the sinfulness of such conduct. But where does Moses forbid the poor to partake of meat slaughtered by a Gentile worshipper of the true God, or by an Israelite who has not learned the rabbinic art? Certainly not in that passage to which the oral law refers. Moses gives a general permission to every Israelite, without exception, to kill and eat. "Notwithstanding thou mayest kill and eat flesh in all thy gates, whatsoever thy soul lusteth after, according to the blessing of the Lord thy God which he hath given thee." (Deut. xii. 15.) He makes no mention of any mysteries connected with the art of slaughtering, the ignorance of which would disqualify. Why then should a Jew be prevented from doing what Moses has allowed—why should he be flogged with the flogging of rebellion, or avow that that mode and measure of punishment is impracticable—why should he be persecuted for satisfying the cravings of nature, and endeavouring to supply the wants of his family? There is not room now to show fully how groundless the rabbinic commands are; but the one fact of their cruelty and oppression of the poor is sufficient to show that they are not from God. Is it possible that any man in his senses can believe that God would sentence a poor famishing creature to be flogged without mercy for doing what the letter of the law allows him to do? or, that the All-wise Being, who foresees and foreknows all things, would give a system of laws respecting food, which must expose a large portion of his chosen people to want and starvation? The worshippers of some cruel heathen deity might possibly be led to believe such things, but the disciples of Moses and the Prophets know that God is a God of mercy. Let, then, every one who has got the sacred books contrast their doctrines with those of the rabbies. But, above all, let those Israelites, who reject the rabbinic laws concerning the slaughtering of meat, show that they have not done it from levity nor indifference, but upon principle. Let them explain to their brethren the reasons and the motives by which they are actuated, and let them protest, by word and deed, against such cruelty, oppression, and intolerance.

No. L.

THE BIRTH OF MESSIAH.

This season of the year naturally draws away our thoughts from the subject last under consideration, and reminds us of a remarkable difference between Jews and Christians. The latter are now about to commemorate the birth of the Messiah.* In two days more the voice of praise and thanksgiving will ascend to the Creator and Preserver of men from every part of the world. On the frozen shores of Labrador, and the glowing plains of Hindostan—in the isles of the sea, and on the continents of the old and new worlds, millions

* This number was originally published December 23, 1836.

of Christians will lift up their hands and voices to thank the God of heaven for his unspeakable gift, and this shall be the burden of their song, "Unto us a child is born, unto us a son is given: and the government shall be upon his shoulder: and his name shall be called Wonderful, Counsellor, the mighty God, the everlasting Father, the Prince of Peace." (Isaiah ix. 6.) But amongst the followers of the oral law not a sound of sympathy will be heard. Not a single heart will beat with joy, not a tongue offer up the tribute of praise. Here is a great and striking difference, that should naturally lead both Jew and Christian to inquire, Who is in the right: Those who believe that Messiah is born, and joy in the remembrance of his nativity; or, those who refuse to join in the general rejoicing, and deny that the Redeemer has appeared? The question is whether there is reason to believe that the Messiah was born eighteen hundred years ago? and there are several ways in which it can be satisfactorily answered. An appeal may be made to the predictions contained in the Old Testament, or to the evidence for the truth of the Christian Scriptures—or, it may be shown that the Jewish rabbies have plainly confessed that the time for the birth and appearance of the Messiah is long since past; and this is the mode which we shall adopt at present. The Jews now deny that Messiah is come, and consequently believe that Christians are mistaken as to the time of his appearing. If they had always said so—if they had always assigned a time for the coming of Messiah different from that in which Christians think the Messiah was born, their present assertion would have at least the merit of consistency, and the Jews of the present day might urge that their present belief has been inherited from their fathers, and that Christians have adopted a notion unknown to the nation at large. But, if it should appear that the ancient Jews expected the coming of Messiah at the very time, when, as Christians say, he did actually come, then the ancient Jews testify that Christians are in the right, and that modern Jews are in the wrong, and this is really the state of the case. In the first place, the Talmud contains a general declaration that the time is long since past:—

אמר רב כלו כל הקצין :

"Rav says, The appointed times are long since past" (Sanhedrin, fol. 97, col. 2), where it is to be noted that the word קץ is taken from Daniel, and literally signifies "End," as it is said:—

עד מתי קץ הפלאות :

"How long shall it be to the end of these wonders; and again:—

THE BIRTH OF MESSIAH. 389

ואתה לך לקץ ותנוח ותעמוד לגורלך לקץ הימין :

"But go thou thy way till the end be, for thou shalt rest, and stand in thy lot at the end of the days." (Daniel xii. 6—13.) Rav was therefore of opinion that the period appointed by Daniel the prophet was past. But is it possible to believe that the God of truth would suffer the time, which he had appointed, to pass away without accomplishing what he had promised? When the time which God had fixed for the deliverance from Egypt had arrived, not a single day was lost. "It came to pass at the end קץ of the four hundred and thirty years, even the self-same day,

בעצם היום הזה :

it came to pass, that all the hosts of the Lord went out from the land of Egypt." (Exod. xii. 41.) When the period fixed for the return from Babylon was come, we read, "In the first year of Cyrus, King of Persia (that the word of the Lord by the mouth of Jeremiah might be accomplished), the Lord stirred up the spirit of Cyrus king of Persia, that he made a proclamation through all his kingdom." (2 Chron. xxxvi. 22.) And can we think that the Lord God, who so graciously fulfilled his word on these occasions should break it with reference to the coming of the Messiah? Rav is either right or wrong. If he be right, then the time fixed by God is long since past, and as God cannot break his word, the Messiah must have come long since. But if, to get out of a difficulty, the Rabbinists say, that Rav was wrong, then we have another proof that no reliance is to be placed on the doctors of the oral law; indeed we have a proof that the Rabbinists themselves do not believe it, except when they like; and that therefore they are not thoroughly in earnest about their religion.

But, secondly, the ancient Jews not only believed that the time for the coming of the Messiah was past: they also fixed the exact period:—

תנא דבי אליהו ששה אלפים שנה הוי עלמא שני
אלפים תוהו , שני אלפים תורה , שני אלפים ימות
המשיח :

"Tradition of the school of Elijah. The world is to stand six thousand years. Two thousand, confusion. Two thousand, the law. Two thousand, the days of Messiah." (Sanhedrin, fol. 97, col. 1.) Upon which Rashi remarks—

שלאחר שני אלפים תורה הוה דינו שיבוא משיח
ותכלה מלכות הרשעה ויבטל השיעבוד מישראל :

"After the two thousand years of the law, according to the decree, Messiah ought to have come, and the wicked kingdom should have been destroyed, and Israel's state of servitude should have been ended." Here, then, it is expressly stated, that Messiah ought to have come at the end of the fourth thousand years, that is, according to the Jewish reckoning, fifteen hundred and ninety-seven years ago ; or, according to the Christian reckoning, about eighteen hundred and thirty-six years ago—that is, at the very time when Jesus of Nazareth did appear. We do not quote this tradition because we believe that it is really a tradition of the school of Elijah, but to show what was the opinion of the more ancient Jews, and this it certainly does. If the general expectation of the Jews at that time had not been that Messiah was to appear at the end of the four thousand years, this tradition, whether genuine or forged, could never have obtained currency nor belief. If it be a genuine tradition from Elijah, then the Messiah is certainly come. But if it be fictitious, then it shows the general belief of the Jews at the time, and in every case proves that the modern Jews do not hold the doctrines of their forefathers, but have got a new doctrine of their own. And it further shows, that Christians do not hold any new or peculiar opinion about the time of Messiah's coming, but that they believe, as the ancient Jews believed, that the end of the fourth thousand years is the right time of Messiah's coming.

The only answer that the Jews have, is, that the promise of Messiah's coming was conditional upon their repentance, but that evasion has been long since refuted in the Talmud as contrary to Scripture :—

ר׳ אליעזר אומר אם ישראל עושין תשובה נגאלין
ואם לאו אינם נגאלין, אמר לו ר׳ יהושע אם אין
עושין תשובה אינם נגאלין אלא הקב״ה מעמיד להן
מלך שגזרותיו קשות כהמן וישראל עושין תשובה
ומחזירן למוטב, תניא אידך ר׳ אליעזר אומר אם
ישראל עושין תשובה נגאלין, שנאמר שובו בנים
שובבים ארפא משובותיכם, אמר לו ר׳ יהושע והלא
כבר נאמר חנם נמכרתם ולא בכסף תגאלו חנם
נמכרתם בעבודה זרה ולא בכסף תגאלו לא בתשובה
ומעשים טובים, אמר לו ר׳ אליעזר לר׳ יהושע והלא
כבר נאמר שובה אלי ואשובה אליכם, אמר לו ר׳
יהושע והלא כבר נאמר כי אנכי בעלתי אתכם ולקחתי
אתכם אחד מעיר ושנים ממשפחה והבאתי אתכם
ציון, אמר לו ר׳ אליעזר והלא כבר נאמר בשובה
ונחת תושעון אמר לו ר׳ יהושע לר׳ אליעזר והלא
כבר נאמר כה אמר ה׳ גואל ישראל וקדושו לבזה
נפש למתעב גוי לעבד מושלים מלכים יראו וקמו

שרים וישתחוו, אמר לו ר׳ אליעזר והלא כבר נאמר
אם תשוב ישראל נאם ה׳ אלי תשוב אמר לו ר׳ יהושע
והלא כבר נאמר ואשמע את האיש לבוש הבדים אשר
ממעל למימי היאר וירם ימינו ושמאלו אל השמים
וישבע בחי העולם כי למועד מועדים וחצי וככלות
נפץ יד עם קודש תכלינה כל אלה וגו׳ ושתק ר׳
אליעזר:

" R. Eliezer said, If Israel do repentance they will be re-deemed, but, if not, they will not be redeemed. R. Joshua replied, If they do not repent they will not be redeemed : but God will raise up to them a king whose decrees shall be as dreadful as Haman, and then Israel will repent, and thus he will bring them back to what is good. Another tradition. R. Eliezer said, If Israel do repentance, they shall be redeemed, for it is said, ' Turn, O backsliding children ; I will heal your backsliding.' R. Joshua replied, But was it not said long since, ' Ye have sold yourselves for nought; and ye shall be redeemed without money,' (Isaiah lii. 3.) Where the words 'sold for nought' mean, for idolatry ; and the words 'redeemed without money,' signify, not for money and good works. R. Eliezer then said, to R. Joshua, But has it not been said long since, ' Return unto me, and I will return unto you.' (Mal. iii. 7.) R. Joshua replied, But has it not been said long since, ' I am married unto you, and I will take you one of a city, and two of a family, and I will bring you to Zion.' (Jer. iii. 14.) R. Eliezer said, But has it not been written long since, ' In returning and rest ye shall be saved.' (Isaiah xxx. 15.) R. Joshua replied to R. Eliezer, But has it not been said long since, ' Thus saith the Lord, the Redeemer of Israel, and his Holy One, to him whom man despiseth, to him whom the nation abhorreth, to a servant of rulers, kings shall see and arise, princes also shall worship.' (Isaiah xlix. 7.) R. Eliezer said to him again, But has it not been said long since, ' If thou wilt return, O Israel, return unto me.' (Jer. iv. 1.) To which R. Joshua replied, But has it not been written long since, ' I heard the man clothed in linen, which was upon the waters of the river, when he held up his right hand and his left hand unto heaven, and sware by Him that liveth for ever, that it shall be for a time and times and half a time ; and when he shall have accomplished to scatter the power of the holy people, all these things shall be finished.' Whereupon R. Eliezer was silent." Here then, on the showing of the Talmud itself, the opinion that the coming of the Messiah is dependent upon Israel's repentance, is false ; and consequently it is true, that Messiah was to come unconditionally at the time appointed ; and therefore, as the time is long since past, the Messiah must have come. But the ancient rabbies do not leave us to reason upon their words; on the contrary, they tell us expressly that Messiah was born about the time that the temple was destroyed. In the Jerusalem Talmud, R. Judan tells us a story of a Jew who actually went and saw him:—

עוֹבְדָא הֲוָה בְּחַד יְהוּדָאי דַּהֲוָה קָאִים רָדִי גָעַת
תּוֹרָתֵיהּ קוֹמוֹי עֲבַר חַד עֲרָבִיי וְשָׁמַע קָלָהּ, אֲמַר לֵיהּ
בַּר יוּדָאי בַּר יוּדָאי שָׁרִי תּוֹרָךְ וְשָׁרִי קַנְקַנָּךְ דְּהָא חֲרַב
בֵּית מַקְדְּשָׁא, גָּעַת זְמָן תְּנִיָנוּת, אֲמַר לֵיהּ בַּר יוּדָאי
בַּר יוּדָאי קְטוֹר תּוֹרָךְ וּקְטוֹר קַנְקַנָּךְ דְּהָא יְלִיד מַלְכָּא
מְשִׁיחָא, אֲמַר לֵיהּ אֲמַר מַה שְׁמֵיהּ אֲמַר לֵיהּ מְנַחֵם, אֲמַר
לֵיהּ וּמַה שֵׁם דְּאָבוּי אֲמַר לֵיהּ חִזְקִיָהוּ, אֲמַר לֵיהּ מִן
הָן הוּא, אֲמַר לֵיהּ מִן בִּירַת מַלְכָּא דְּבֵית לֶחֶם יְהוּדָה:

"It happened once to a certain Jew, who was standing ploughing, that his cow lowed before him. A certain Arab was passing and heard its voice; he said, O Jew, O Jew! unyoke thine ox, and loose thy plough-share, for the temple has been laid waste. It lowed a second time, and he said, O Jew, O Jew! yoke thine oxen, and bind on thy plough-shares, for King Messiah is born. The Jew said, What is his name? Menachem. He asked further, What is the name of his father? The other replied, Hezekiah. He asked again, Whence is he? The other said from the Royal residence of Bethlehem of Judah." (Berachoth, fol. 5, col. 1.) The story, then, goes on to tell us how he went and saw the child, but when he called the second time, the mother told him that the winds had carried the child away. We are quite willing to grant that this story is a fable. We do not quote it because we give it the slightest degree of credit, but simply to show that the more ancient Jews were so fully persuaded that the right time of Messiah's advent was past, that they readily believed also that he was actually born. The Babylonian Talmud, also, evidently takes for granted that Messiah is born, as appears from the following legend:—

ר׳ יְהוֹשֻׁעַ בֶּן לֵוִי אַשְׁכְּחֵיהּ לְאֵלִיָּהוּ דַּהֲוָה קַיָּים
אֲפִיתְחָא דִּמְעָרְתָא דְּר׳ שִׁמְעוֹן בֶּן יוֹחַאי אֲמַר לֵיהּ
אָתֵינָא לְעָלְמָא דְאָתֵי אֲמַר לֵיהּ אִם יִרְצֶה הָאָדוֹן הַזֶּה,
אֲמַר ר׳ יְהוֹשֻׁעַ בֶּן לֵוִי שְׁנַיִם רָאִיתִי וְקוֹל ג׳ שָׁמַעְתִּי,
אֲמַר לֵיהּ אֵימַת אָתֵי מָשִׁיחַ אֲמַר לֵיהּ זִיל שַׁיְּילֵיהּ לְדִידֵיהּ
וְהֵיכָא יָתֵיב אֲפִיתְחָא דְּרוֹמִי וּמַאי סִימָנֵיהּ יָתֵיב בֵּינֵי
עֲנִיִים סוֹבְלֵי חֳלָאִים וְכוּלָן שָׁרוּ וַאֲסִירִי בְּחַד זִמְנָא
אִיהוּ שָׁרֵי חַד וְאָסִיר חַד אֲמַר דִּילְמָא מִבָּעֵינָא דְּלָא
אִיעַכַּב אָזַל לְגַבֵּיהּ אֲמַר לֵיהּ שָׁלוֹם עָלֶיךָ רַבִּי וּמוֹרִי

THE BIRTH OF MESSIAH. 393

אמו ליה יה שלום עליך בר ליואי אמר ליה לאימת אתי
מר אמר ליה חיום :

"R. Joshua, the son of Levi, found Elijah standing at the door of the cave of R. Simeon ben Jochai, and said to him, Shall I arrive at the world to come? He replied, If this Lord will. R. Joshua, the son of Levi, said, I see two, but I hear the voice of three. He also asked, When will Messiah come? Elijah replied, Go, and ask himself. R. Joshua then said, Where does he sit? At the gate of Rome. And how is he to be known? He is sitting amongst the poor and sick, and they open their wounds and bind them up again all at once: but he opens only one, and then he opens another, for he thinks, perhaps I may be wanted, and then I must not be delayed. R. Joshua went to him and said, Peace be upon thee, my master and my Lord. He replied, Peace be upon thee, son of Levi. The rabbi then asked him, When will my Lord come? He replied, To-day (alluding to the words of the Psalm, To-day, if ye will hear his voice)." (Sanhedrin, fol. 98, col. 1.) This is evidently a fiction, and a proof how little those doctors regarded truth; but it shows that he who invented it, and those who received it, all equally believed that Messiah was born, and ready waiting to come forth for the redemption of Israel. It does, indeed, confirm the common idea, that Messiah's advent depends upon the repentance of Israel, for it makes the Messiah say that he would come this very day, if Israel would only hear his voice. But if the Messiah may any day, when they repent, come and save Israel, then it is plain that he must have been born long since. The testimony of the ancient Jews, then, goes to establish these points—First, That the time for Messiah's advent has been long past; Secondly, That the end of the fourth thousand years was the time when he ought to have come: and, Thirdly, That at that time he did really come; for about that time, they say, he was born in Bethlehem of Judah. Fourth, That he was taken into Paradise, as Rashi explains the gate of Rome to mean the gate of Paradise opposite Rome; and, Fifthly, That he is waiting to return to this earth for the redemption of his people. Now who is there that does not see at once, that this agrees in the main with the Christian doctrine? We believe that, at the end of the fourth thousand years, the Messiah was born, and at this season of the year we rejoice at the remembrance of the Saviour's birth. The Jews refuse to join with us, but who has the greatest show of right? Not now to speak of the prophecies, and of the historical evidence which we have, we have the testimony even of our opponents to show that we are in the right. The most ancient rabbinical writings unanimously confess, that the time is past, and that the Messiah has been long since born, and thus testify the correctness of our faith respecting the time of Messiah's advent. Christians, however, go on consistently and believe further, that God did not break his word, but performed his promise, and therefore we rejoice. The Jews do not believe, because they are so engrossed with the temporal deliverance of the nation, that they cannot see that another and a greater redemption was necessary. We do not, by any means, wish to deny that Israel is to be restored to the land of promise, and to inherit all the blessings promised in the prophets. On the contrary, we fully believe that the Messiah, who visited this earth, for a short season, will return and re-establish the Theocracy which was once the glory of Israel, and that, in a much more glorious form than Israel ever saw under any of their kings. We heartily wish Israel the enjoyment of every blessing promised; but we cannot help remembering that Messiah has another and more important office than that of restoring the kingdom to Israel, and that is the redemption of the human race. The highest pitch of national glory and earthly prosperity would be as nothing, and less than nothing unless the children of men were delivered from the effects of Adam's sin, and made partakers of a good hope of everlasting life. Even the gathering of Israel from all the ends of the earth would appear but a very insignificant business, if it did not stand in immediate connexion with the eternal welfare of all nations. Many of the sons of men have appeared as conquerors and heroes, and have raised their country to a high degree of glory, and conferred upon them much temporal prosperity; but if Messiah was to be nothing more, we confess we should not think him worth the having. We think of the Messiah as the Being, in whom all the families of the earth shall be blessed, as the restorer indeed of Israel, but also God's salvation unto the end of the earth. This is the doctrine which Christianity teaches, and which is confirmed by the law and the prophets; and therefore we rejoice that this great Deliverer has been born—that He came at first in great humility to bruise the serpent's head, and to lay down his life a ransom for many. We remember that this blessed news, these glad tidings of great joy, were brought to us by Jews; and, therefore, feeling our deep obligations, we desire to show our gratitude by inviting Israel to come and partake in our joy. We feel assured that our joy is no illusion. Even the rabbies themselves bear witness that the Messiah ought to have been born, and was born at the very time in which we believe the Messiah to have been born. But if he was born who was he? What other person can make any claim to the Messiahship, but He whom we acknowledge? Is it reasonable to believe, as the rabbies do, that God actually sent the Great Deliverer down into this wretched world, and then took him away again, without permitting him to accomplish his work? No; if ever he visited this earth—and that he did visit it, both the ancient Jews and Christians assert—he could not have left it again without bestowing upon its inhabitants a remedy for their woes. The ancient rabbies and the Christians both agree as to the time of Messiah's birth, and the fact of his birth in Bethlehem. Indeed the whole nation practically showed their agreement with Christians, as to the time of Messiah's advent, by readily following every military adventurer, who laid claim to the character of Redeemer. Even before the destruction of the temple, multitudes had suffered by their credulity; but immediately after the desolation, the people and the rabbies with one accord followed Bar Chochba, and thereby showed the reality of their belief, that that was about the time when Messiah ought to appear. Judaism, therefore, teaches this doctrine—that God promised the Messiah, that God fixed a time, that that time is past, and yet that God did not keep his promise. Christianity, on the contrary, acknowledges the promise, recognises the time, believes that Messiah was born, but believes further that God fulfilled his word—that Messiah was not carried away into Paradise, until he had accomplished the work that was to be done at his first advent. Then, indeed, we acknowledge that He ascended into heaven, and sitteth at God's right hand, from whence he will come again for the final redemption of his people, and the establishment of the reign of righteousness. The only real difference between us is, as to the VERACITY of God. We believe that God did not, and could not, break his word. Modern Judaism teaches that God broke his promise. It is for rational beings to decide which doctrine is most agreeable to the Divine character. For our own parts, we will rejoice in God's unchangeableness, and say, in the remembrance, that "His truth endureth for ever."

No. LI.

SLAUGHTERING OF MEAT, CONTINUED.

ACCORDING to the confessions of the rabbies themselves, the time for the advent of Messiah is long since past, what is there then that prevents the Jews from believing in him, who came at the appointed time? The grand objection is, that the nation is still in captivity; they say that Messiah ought to have given them liberty. The answer to this objection is, that Messiah was willing, and is willing to this hour, to give them liberty, but that they will not have it. The very first condition of national liberty and independence is moral and intellectual emancipation. No nation was ever yet enslaved until the hearts and intellects of the people had first become the slaves of corruption or superstition—and no nation that hugs to its heart the chains of moral slavery, can ever be made free, nor could it retain its liberty if it got it. When Messiah came, therefore, as he found the Jewish nation already under the Roman yoke, the very first step was to endeavour to emancipate their hearts and minds, and to deliver them from that moral bondage, of which their national degradation was only a consequence. This first step Messiah immediately took—he protested against the superstitions of the oral law, and pointed them to the perfect liberty of God's written Word. But the nation chose to retain the cause of their misfortunes, and to reject the overtures of deliverance. If therefore they are still in a state of national dependence, they must not cast the blame on God, and say that He suffered the time to pass away without fulfilling his promise; nor upon the Messiah, when they themselves refused to receive that without which no national liberty can possibly exist. They chose to give themselves, body and soul, as bond-slaves to the oral law, there was, therefore, no possibility of national redemption. It would require an act of omnipotent coercion, such as God does not employ, to make a nation free against its will. But perhaps the Jews of the present day will deny that they are in a state of moral and intellectual slavery. We refer them, in reply, to the numerous proofs already given in these papers, and especially the laws of שחיטה or *slaughtering*, upon which we have a few words to add. Where in all the world can a more wretched slave be found, than the man, who himself, together with his family, is ready to perish of hunger, and yet dare not partake of wholesome food, offered by the providence of God, because his rabbinical task-masters say, No? But now take another instance:—

כל טבח שלא בדק הסכין שלו ששוחט בה לפני

SLAUGHTERING OF MEAT, CONTINUED.

חכם ושחט לעצמו בודקין אותה, אם נמצאת יפה
ובדוקה מנדין אותו לפי שיסמוך על עצמו פעם אחרת
ותהיה פגומה וישחוט בה, ואם נמצאת פגומה
מעבירין אותו ומנדין אותו ומכריזין על כל בשר
ששחט שהוא טרפה:

"If a slaughterer, who has not had his slaughtering knife examined before a wise man [a rabbi], slaughters by himself, his knife must be examined. If it be found in good order and examined, he is to be excommunicated, because he may depend upon himself another time, when it has a gap in it and yet slaughter therewith. But, if it be found to have a gap, he is to be deposed from his office, and excommunicated, and proclamation is to be made, that all the meat which he has slaughtered is carrion." (Jad Hachazakah, Hilchoth Sh'chitah, c. i. 26.) Here we have the same slavery and the same cruel oppression. In the first place we see the intention to make the Jews entirely dependent upon the rabbies. The Jews are not to eat meat unless it be slaughtered as the rabbies direct, and the slaughterer himself is not even to do that, which he knows to be right according to the oral law, without the express sanction of the rabbies. All are to be in bondage, not merely to the oral law, but to the rabbi for the time being. They are to have no mind and no judgment of their own. In the simplest concerns of life they are to be entirely dependent upon the will and judgment of another. In the second place, we see the determination to maintain this tyranny by the severests punishments. The man who has slaughtered without showing his knife to the rabbi, even though they have no fault to find with him, is to be excommunicated—but if a rabbinic flaw in the knife should be detected, then not only the man himself is to suffer, but those who employed him, and also the Israelites themselves to be deprived of food. All that he has slaughtered is to be declared unfit for use. Who can deny that those who think their consciences bound by such laws are in miserable bondage? Who, that has his senses and God's Word to guide them, can believe that a small gap in a knife is sufficient to make meat unfit for food? Who ever saw a knife, or even the finest razor that ever was manufactured, without a series of such imperfections? Let a rabbi, who has just pronounced, concerning a knife, that it has no gap in it, apply a microscope, and he will soon find out that a knife without gaps never existed. He will be convinced that the oral law requires what is impossible, and therefore cannot possibly be from God. Who then can deny that those who are bound by it, are the slaves of superstition? There never was, and never will be in the world, such a thing as a knife without the least possible gap, and consequently there never was, and never will be, any meat fit for the food of a Rabbinist. The Jews must therefore either give up the use of meat entirely, or they must give up the oral law.

If the oral law were uniformly severe, and everywhere required that its adherents should obtain the best possible evidence that their meat was properly slaughtered: or in case they could not obtain this evidence, that they should entirely abstain from meat, the consistency of the doctrine would in some measure justify, or at least excuse the credulity of the Jews. But this is not the case, its authors felt the inconvenience of their own doctrine, and therefore relaxed whenever it suited themselves. For instance, they say:—

הרי שראינו ישראל מרחוק ששחט והלך לו ולא ידענו אם יודע או אינו יודע הרי זו מותרת, וכן האומר לשלוחו צא ושחוט לי ומצא הבהמה שחוטה, ואין ידוע אם שלוחו שחטה אם אחר הרי זו מותרת, שרוב המצויין אצל שחיטה מומחין הן:

"If we were to see an Israelite at a distance who had slaughtered a beast, and he was to go his way, and we were ignorant of the fact whether he understood the art or not, in that case the meat is lawful. And in like manner, if a man should say to his messenger, Go and slaughter for me, and should find the beast slaughtered, but it should not be certain whether his messenger, or another person, had slaughtered it, this also is lawful, for the majority of persons concerned in slaughtering are skilful." (Ibid., c. iv. 7.) This relaxation shows how exceedingly inconvenient the doctrine was found, and how unwilling the doctors were to bear inconvenience themselves. No doubt cases often occurred in real life similar to those supposed. An Israelite travelling might come to a town in which lived a small congregation of Jews, and might wish to have some dinner, and would of course wish to have it of lawful meat. The only satisfactory way of obtaining it would be to go to the person who had slaughtered it, and examine him as to his competency, but he might be absent, if therefore he should be scrupulous, he would have to go without his dinner; and the same thing would happen to a rich man, who might send a messenger to a neighbouring town to have a beast killed for him. The messenger might send back the meat by some one else, and thus the owner would not have satisfactory evidence, that the rabbinic laws had been observed. Here again the man who was rich enough to do this, might have to go without his dinner, or to wait an inconvenient time. The oral law has therefore provided in this case that the meat is lawful for use without any further scruples. But this decision shows of how little real importance all these precepts about slaughtering are. If it be a sin to eat meat not properly killed, then it is also a sin to eat meat, when there is no satisfactory evidence of this fact. Whenever a man doubts about the right or wrong of any particular action, he is certainly wrong if he does it. But if it be certain that he may either do it or leave it undone without guilt, then that action cannot be sinful. And as the rabbies here affirm, that men may lawfully eat meat, concerning which they have no satisfactory evidence that it has been lawfully slaughtered, it follows that the rabbinic art cannot be of much value. Why then should a poor man be starved if he does not eat, or flogged if he does eat, meat slaughtered by a Gentile, when, if he had money to send a beast to be killed, he might eat what was sent back, even though he had no proof that the laws were kept? Indeed how are the poor and unlearned ever to know, that they eat lawful meat? If they were even to stand by, and see the operation performed, still, as being ignorant of the rabbinic laws, they could not understand, and must therefore take the matter entirely upon trust: and thus the mass of the nation, the unlearned and the women, are made the blind slaves of laws which they neither understand nor know; or rather of those who expound those laws, for how can it be said that a man transgresses that of which he does not know the right or wrong?

If the rabbies were all unanimous in their statement of what is and is not lawful, the unanimity might in some degree excuse the Jews for submitting to a yoke so grievous, and holding it fast round the necks of their brethren. They might urge the uniformity of the tradition as a proof of its genuineness. But this cannot be pretended in the present case. To this very hour the rabbies themselves are not agreed as to what is, or what is not the oral law. We have just seen that if a man send a messenger to have a beast slaughtered, and afterwards find it slaughtered, that he may eat of it without asking any more questions. This is the general principle, but as soon as it comes to be applied in detail the rabbies differ. The Baal Turim thus states the difference :—

וכהב חרמב״ם דוקא שמצאה בבית אבל מצאה
בשוק או באשפה שבבית אסורה וכן כהב בעל העיטור
וא״א ז״ל התיר אפילו באשפה שבבית ולא אסר אלא
באשפה שבשוק וכן הרשב״א:

"Rambam has written expressly, In case that it should be found in the house; but, if he find it in the street, or on the dunghill in the house, it is forbidden. The Baal Haittur has given the same judgment: but my lord my father of blessed memory says, the meat is lawful, even if it be found on the dunghill in the house, and has not pronounced it unlawful, except when found on the dunghill in the street; and Rashba is of the same opinion." (Jorch Deah., 1.) Here, then, we have the most learned of the rabbies, disputing as to what is the law; the one party pronouncing that to be unlawful which the other party declares lawful. What, then, are the unlearned to do in this case? Or how can it be said that there is an oral law which gives the true meaning of the written law? Or, if there be an oral law, what use is it, when it is itself a subject of dispute? Every one who has looked into the oral law knows that this difference of opinion is by no means a rare case; and that it cannot be said that the difference of opinion is in matters of minor importance. Let us, for example, consider the case of an Israelite who is accustomed to eat unlawful meat, and does so to vex Israel—is it lawful to eat the meat which he has killed?

כתב הרשב"א שאין מוסרין לו בתחלה לשחוט
אפילו אם ישראל עומד על גביו, ואם שחט בדיעבד
כשר ע"י בדיקת סכין תחילה או סוף וא"א הרא"ש
ז"ל כתב שדינו כגוי:

"Rashba has written that it is not lawful to give him a beast intentionally to slaughter, even if an Israelite should stand by. But if he has slaughtered the beast, it may be declared lawful by means of examining the knife, either at the beginning or at the end; and my lord my father of blessed memory has written that in the case of such a person the law is the same as in that of a Gentile." (Ibid. 2.) Now the difference here is very great and very important. The one opinion says, that, under certain circumstances, such meat is lawful. The other, that it is unlawful as that killed by a Gentile—that is, what the one allows, the other pronounces to be so unlawful as to deserve the flogging of rebellion, as we saw in No. 49. Here, then, is a case involving severe corporal punishment, and yet the rabbies are not agreed as to which is the law. How, then, can men of sense and reflection give themselves up to a system, the doctors of which cannot agree upon a question so simple as this, What sort of food is lawful, and what is unlawful? and who, nevertheless, require unlimited obedience under the heaviest penalties temporal and eternal? The oral law does not suffer a wise man to be contradicted, and declares that all their sayings are "the words of the living God;" and yet here they contradict one another so widely, that if a man follow the one, he will be sentenced to a flogging by the other—and if from fear of the flogging he should agree with the latter, he will then be contradicting the former, and thereby incur the sentence of excommunication, and even run a risk of losing his soul. But in every case he must give up his judgment and his reason, and submit to be led by those, who are still disputing about the right road: yea, and if he would obey the oral law, must confess that they are both in the right. If this be not moral and intellectual slavery of the worst kind, we have yet to learn the meaning of these words. It will not be a pertinent reply to say that Christians also differ in opinion on important points. We confess that they do, and will continue to do so, as long as they continue to be fallible men: but then these persons do not profess to have an oral law given by God in order to preserve them from a wrong interpretation. There is one Christian Church that has followed the example of the rabbies in this particular, and has therefore fallen into many of their absurdities. Difference of opinion amongst those who make no such pretensions is no argument against the truth of the original records, whence both professedly draw their religion. Two men may differ as to the sense of a verse in the law of Moses, and yet we know that the verse itself contains the truth. But when each of these persons tells us that his interpretation is an inspired tradition, and that both, though contradicting each other, are equally true and correct, then it is evident that they say not only what is false, but what is absurd, and that they are labouring under a delusion. If it be a mere speculative delusion it is to be deplored—but if it be a practical delusion, involving the happiness and welfare of thousands, it must be combated and exposed—and this is precisely the case with the oral law. The particular part of it which we have now been considering seriously affects the temporal comfort of many thousands of the poor in every part of the world. The general principles enslave the minds of the whole nation, and thus prevent the state of happiness and glory which the prophets have promised. The Jewish nation is in a state of dispersion, and in some parts of the world victims of a cruel oppression, simply because they are the willing slaves of superstition. Until an intellectual and moral change is effected, they never can appear as "the peculiar people, the kingdom of priests, the holy nation." High and holy is their destiny, and great is the providential mercy of God in still preserving them, when they refuse obstinately to fulfil it. But neither their destiny nor God's forbearance can be of any avail, until they reassert the glorious liberty of the children of God. The chains of Rabbinism must be broken, and the mild yoke of Messiah taken upon their shoulders, before national independence and liberty can return. How could a nation exist, whose moral and intellectual energies are all crampt by the endless subtleties of the rabbies? How could a people maintain national liberty whilst they are such perfect slaves to superstition as to believe that traditions, which are the curse of the poor, and many of which flatly contradict others, all proceed from the God of mercy and truth? The temple must first be cleansed of all defilement before the glory of God can enter. It is therefore a matter of the first and highest importance, to every Jew who wishes well to his nation, to examine that system, whose constant companion for so many centuries has been misery; and if they are convinced of its falsehood, then to use every exertion to deliver their brethren, from that which is mischievous as well as false. We might urge its tendency to produce and perpetuate an unfriendly separation between the Jews and their neighbours: not that we are ignorant of God's declaration,

הן עם לבדד ישכון ובגוים לא יתחשב :

"Lo, the people shall dwell alone, and shall not be reckoned among the nations." (Numb. xxiii. 9.) We know it and believe it, and are therefore fully convinced, that all the wit and power of man will never be able to effect what some so ardently desire, an amalgamation with the nations where Israel is dispersed. We have no desire to contravene the declared will of God, and to degrade Israel from their position as a holy nation to the rank of an inconsiderable religious sect. But still we might urge against the oral law, that it goes beyond God's intention by producing an unfriendly separation and an estrangement between man and man, which is injurious to the welfare of both Jew and Gentile; we leave this, however, to the consideration of those Israelites who feel, or profess to feel, a love and affection for all men; and content ourselves at present with the indubitable fact, that the laws concerning slaughtering are most oppressive to the poor and enslaving to the minds of all. It is not merely the bodily grievance of starvation to which we now allude, though that is wicked and vexatious to the last degree, and should therefore not be tolerated for a moment by the humane and the merciful. There is something that is worse than any bodily suffering, and that is, to be tempted to do violence to conscience by professing what we do not believe, or by concealing our real sentiments. And yet in many a Jewish congregation this is frequently the case. It pleases God to give to the poor the power of reasoning as well as to the rich, and thus some of this class are occasionally led to see the absurdity of the oral law, and to detest those inventions which doom them and their families to starvation, but yet they would not dare either to avow or to act upon their conviction. To eat any other than rabbinical food would at once cut them off from the bounty of the synagogue, and from the sympathy of its worshippers. To express their convictions would be sufficient to have them numbered with the profane and ungodly, and therefore they conceal their real sentiments, and pretend to be what they are not, that they may not deprive their families of the little assistance which an apparent conformity to rabbinic usages may procure. Here then is another and more unequivocal badge of slavery. The oral law deprives the poor entirely of liberty of conscience. He not only must not eat, he must not think, at least he must not express a thought, no, nor even a doubt, about that system which is the cause of his misery. It is true, that those who profess or suppress religious sentiments merely to serve their temporal interests, are either very weak or very guilty. But we must make some allowance for the infirmity of human nature, and especially in the case of a poor man, who has no bread for his children, and whose mind has been debased from his youth by such bondage. It is to the system that we are to impute these debasing effects. It not only torments the body, but degrades the mind; and, therefore, every Israelite who loves and respects liberty of conscience, should endeavour to procure it for his brethren. According to the law of the land they have it. They are free to worship and serve God as they think most agreeable to his will; but the oral law steps in between, and deprives them of the benefit. The Jewish poor dare not serve God according to their conscience, nor even express the convictions of their heart. All the legislators in Christendom could not set them free. The duty as well as the possibility of delivering them from this bondage rests with their brethren. But they, alas! whatever the motive, decline the glorious task.

No. LII.

LAWS CONCERNING MEAT WITH MILK.

IT is recorded of the Cutheans and those other nations whom the King of Assyria placed as colonists at Samaria, that they endeavoured to combine the service of the true God with the worship of idols. "So these nations feared the Lord, and served their graven images, both their children and their children's children: as did their fathers, so do they unto this day." (2 Kings xvii. 41.) Every one can see that this conduct was as foolish as it was wicked. It was wicked to dishonour the true God by associating him with them that were no gods; and it was foolish to imagine that God could be pleased with a partial homage and a divided heart. Total idolatry would have been more reasonable and less offensive to the Divine Being, for he, whom we acknowledge as God, must necessarily have the whole of our fear, our love, and our obedience. And yet there is perhaps a way of serving God more unreasonable still, and that is by giving to sinful and fallible men the honour that is due to God alone. The Cutheans falsely thought that God was one amongst many; and if they worshipped the many, it was under the impression that they were really gods. But suppose a nation to acknowledge the one true God, and then to fix upon a certain number of men to be honoured and served with the same degree of reverence and obedience; none can doubt that this nation would be far more irrational than that of the Cutheans, inasmuch as to pay Divine honours to a number of our fellow-men is more extravagant still than to worship a plurality of imaginary deities. Some may think that such a degree of absurdity is impossible, but fact shows that it is not only possible, but that it has actually occurred. When men exalt the inventions of their teachers to a level with the known and acknowledged laws of God, and make obedience to these inventions an essential part of their religion, they confer upon men the highest degree of honour and of service that can be rendered to God. The unreserved submission of the heart and conscience to the will of God is the highest act of worship, and when it is given to the will of men, in that degree men are made gods. Whether these remarks apply to those who make the בשר בחלב, הלכות, *i.e.*, " The constitutions concerning meat in milk " a part of their religion, it is for the adherents of the oral law to inquire.

The general principle of these constitutions is thus expressed—

בשר בחלב אסור לבשלו ואסור לאכלו מן התורה
ואסור בהנאה וקוברין אותו ואפרו אסור כאפר כל
הנקברין, ומי שיבשל משניהם כזית כאחד לוקה
שנאמר לא תבשל גדי בחלב אמו, וכן האוכל כזית
משניהם מהבשר והחלב שנתבשלו כאחד לוקה ואע״פ
שלא בשל:

"It is unlawful to boil meat in milk—according to the law, it is also unlawful to eat it; it is likewise unlawful to make any profit by it, and it is to be buried. Its ashes are also unlawful, like the ashes of other things that are buried. Whosoever boils together a quantity of these two things, equal to an olive, is to be flogged, for it is said, 'Thou shalt not seethe a kid in its mother's milk.' (Exod. xxiii. 19.) In like manner, he that eats a quantity of the flesh and the milk, which have been boiled together, amounting in value to an

olive, is to be flogged, even though he did not boil them."
(Hilchoth Maakhaloth Asuroth, c. ix. i.) Here the oral
law determines generally, that it is unlawful to boil meat in
milk, or to make any use of meat so boiled, and sentences
the transgressor to a severe and degrading corporal punishment, and yet this determination is altogether an invention
of men, for which there is not the slightest authority in the
Word of God. The prohibition of Moses is confined to one
single case, which is exactly defined : " Thou shalt not seethe
a kid in its mother's milk," but there the prohibition ends,
for the specification of one particular shows that that alone
is intended, and necessarily excludes all others. To give
some colour to the unwarranted extension, it is asserted that

וגדי הוא כולל ולד השור ולד השה ולד העז עד
שיפרוט ויאמר גדי עזים :

" Kid includes the young of kine, of sheep, and of goats,
so that to particularize, the word goat is added as 'a kid of
the goats.'" And so Rashi also affirms in his commentary.
Aben Ezra, however, has saved us the trouble of giving a
refutation of our own, for he says—

ואיננו כן כי גדי לא יקרא רק שהוא מחעזים ובלשון
ערבי הוא גדי ולא יאמר על מין אחר, רק יש הפרש
בין גדי ובין גדי עזים כי גדי גדול מגדי עזים כי
עודנו צריך היותו עם העזים וככה שעיר ושעיר עזים
וחכמים קבלו שלא יאכלו ישראל בשר בחלב :

" This is not so, for nothing is called kid except the
young of the goats ; and in Arabic the word has the same
signification, and is never applied to any other species. But
there is a difference between *kid* and *kid of the goats*, for
the former is larger, and it is necessary for the latter still
to be with the goats ; and the same thing is true of שעיר,
which is used in the same way. It is by tradition that the
wise men received, that Israel should not eat meat in milk."
(Comment. in Exod. xxiii. 19.) Thus Aben Ezra, himself
a most learned rabbi, confesses that the words of the written
law restrict the prohibition to one particular case, and that
the rest is mere matter of tradition. Of course if it could
be proved that this tradition came from God through Moses,
it would be equivalent to the written law, but there is no
attempt to prove anything of the kind. The authors of the
oral law calculated throughout upon the blind credulity of
their followers, and therefore here, as elsewhere, there is an
entire absence of proof. Indeed, the tradition itself bears
the plain mark of forgery. How can any one possibly be-

lieve that, if God meant to forbid meat and milk entirely, he should first express himself incorrectly, and then leave the correction of the error to uncertain tradition? If the command had only been once noticed, it would have been hard to believe such a thing; but when we remember that this command is thrice repeated, in Exod. xxiii. 19, xxxiv. 26, and Deut. xiv. 21, it is plainly incredible. Thrice is the command written, and thrice it is restricted to one particular case, and yet the rabbies have dared to make unauthorized additions of their own, and their followers to this day exalt them to a level with the laws of God. It cannot be replied that the rabbies would not commit such wickedness as this, for every one who knows anything of the oral law, knows that a great proportion of it consists merely of the *words of the Scribes*, acknowledged as such, and distinguished by that name from the supposed traditions from Sinai. Thus in the constitutions before us, it is plainly confessed that the written law allows the flesh of wild animals and of fowl in milk, and yet the rabbies forbid it :—

וכן בשר חיה ועוף בין בחלב חיה בין בחלב
בהמה אינו אסור באכילה מן התורה לפיכך מותר
לבשלו ומותר בהנאה, ואסור באכילה מדברי סופרים
כדי שלא יפשטו העם ויבואו לידי איסור בשר בחלב
של תורה ויאכלו בשר בהמה טהורה בחלב בהמה
טהורה שהרי אין משמעות הכתוב אלא גדי בחלב
אמו ממש לפיכך אסרו כל בשר בחלב:

" And thus the flesh of a wild animal or of fowl, whether in the milk of a wild or tame animal, is not forbidden as food by the written law, and therefore it is lawful to boil it, and to profit by it. But according to the words of the scribes, it is unlawful to eat it, lest the people should go farther, and be led into a transgression of the written law, and eat the flesh of a clean beast in the milk of a clean beast: for the letter of the written law refers only to a kid in its mother's milk in the strictest sense; therefore the wise men have forbidden all meat in milk." In this there is no equivocation, but a simple confession that the rabbies have taken upon themselves to forbid what God has allowed; and have, without ceremony or scruple, made great additions to his law. It matters little what the motive was, the conduct itself is in the highest degree presumptuous. The pretence, that these additions were made only for the purpose of keeping the people far removed from sin, will not serve as a ground of justification. If God had desired such precautionary measures, as being either necessary or beneficial, he would have prescribed them himself. If he did not prescribe them, and the rabbies themselves confess that he did not, but that they are the words of the scribes, then they can be neither necessary nor beneficial, unless we can believe what it would be blasphemy to assert, that is, that God's law was imperfect until it was mended by the scribes. It is truly astonishing that men professing respect for the law of Moses should treat it with such indignity, and still more so that those who appear so anxious to avoid transgression, should themselves systematically transgress that plain command.

לא הוסיפו על הדבר אשר אנכי מצוה אתכם :

"Ye shall not add unto the word which I command you." (Deut. iv. 2.) But the most extraordinary thing of all is, that the modern Jews should pride themselves on the purity of their faith, and think that they only of all the nations serve the true God and him only, when they are in truth serving the authors of the oral law, and dividing their religious obedience between God and the rabbies. If the rabbinic additions were specimens of profound wisdom in legislation, or had a tendency to promote either the moral or temporal welfare of mankind, there would be some excuse, but what shall we say of those who transgress a plain command for the sake of such an addition as the following :—

הבשר לבדו מותר והחלב לבדו מותר ובהתערב
שניהם ע"י בישול יאסרו שניהם, במה דברים אמורים
שנתבשלו שניהם ביחד או שנפל חם לתוך חם או
צונן לתוך חם אבל אם נפל אחד משניהם והוא חם
לתוך השני והוא צונן קולף הבשר כולו שנגע בו
החלב ואוכל השאר ואם נפל צונן לתוך צונן מדיח
החתיכה ואוכלה :

"The flesh by itself is lawful, and the milk by itself is lawful, but as soon they are mixed together by means of boiling (or cooking) they both become unlawful. In what cases does this hold? When both are boiled together, or when one being hot falls into the other also being hot, or when one, cold, falls into the other hot. But if one of them being hot falls upon the second being cold, then all that part of the meat which was touched by the milk is to be peeled off, and the remainder may be eaten. But if one in a cold state falls upon the other also cold, then that peace is to be washed, and after that may be eaten." (Hilchoth Maakhaloth Asuroth, c. ix. 17.) We have, in the first place, an unwarranted extension of the divine command. God has simply forbidden to seethe a kid in its mother's milk. The rabbies first extend this to the young of kine, and sheep. Then they advance another step and forbid the boiling or cooking of any sort of meat in milk, and now we have seen another advance still, whereby even any mixture of flesh and milk is strictly forbidden. Thus the rabbies aim at universal dominion, and are satisfied with nothing short of an entire subjugation of the heart and conscience. Other tyrants must rest satisfied with the enslavement of the body, but cannot touch the thought. The authors of the oral law attack the liberty of thought, and intrude even into the kitchens of their victims. They are determined that their followers shall not eat excepting as they please, and boldly invade the prerogative of God himself, by forbidding the food which he provides for his people. But this extract presents, in the second place, an outrage on common sense. If milk and meat each be lawful by itself, how can the mixture make them unlawful? Whatever God forbids is unlawful, no matter whether we understand the reason or not. But here the rabbies themselves acknowledge that God has not forbidden this mixture; but that the prohibition is entirely their own invention. We are therefore bound to use our senses, if God has given us any, and to ask a reason why. Then, again, why should that which is lawful when cold, be made unlawful by being hot? It may be said, that this is a matter of little importance. In itself it is; but as a burden on the consciences of men, it is of the very highest importance, and as a cheat upon the ignorant it is more important still. In many countries, these and similar inventions constitute the whole religion of the ignorant, and especially of the women. The oral law affirms that it is not necessary to teach women the law of God, but it is almost a matter of life and death that they should know these rabbinic laws about meat and milk. If a woman is unable to read the Word of God, and is as ignorant as a heathen, of God's will, the rabbies think that is a trifle. But if a woman were, through ignorance to serve up meat with any admixture of milk, the whole family would be in an uproar, and the rabbi himself would have to be consulted about a remedy for so dreadful a calamity. The consequence is, that with the mass of the uneducated, accuracy in these observances passes for piety, and these poor beings hope that they are going straight to heaven, when they are utterly devoid or ignorant of that holiness, truth, and purity, which are the first essentials for admission into the presence of God. Thus the oral law destroys the souls of multitudes, but others will have to answer for their blood. All who uphold the system must share in the responsibility. The rabbies who teach, the learned Jews who aid and abet, the priests and Levites to whom God has committed the pastorship of his people, but who neglect their sacred office, all will have to answer for the souls of the lost. But most of all those who know that these things are wrong, who themselves eat meat and milk, and laugh at rabbinic superstition, and yet are insensible to the miseries of their poor and ignorant brethren. Every one practically acquainted with the working of these laws, knows not only that they beget a false notion of religion, but that they are also a torment in this life. In domestic and culinary economy, accidents will happen. Meat may fall into milk, or milk into a pot of meat. Misery and vexation are the consequence, and if the unfortunate woman to whom the accident has happened cannot get satisfaction at home, she must go to the rabbi to inquire what is to be done. For instance—

בשר שנפל לתוך החלב, או חלב שנפל לתוך
הבשר ונתבשל עמו שיעורו בנותן טעם, כיצד חתיכה
של בשר שנפלה לקדירה רותחת של חלב, טועם
הגוי את הקדרה אם אמר שיש בה טעם בשר אסורה
ואם לאו מותרת ואותה חתיכה אסורה, בד"א שקדם
והוציא את החתיכה קודם שתפלוט חלב שבלעה,
אבל אם לא סלק משערים אותה בששים מפני שהחלב
שנבלע בה ונאסר יצא ונתערב עם שאר החלב:

"With respect to meat which falls into milk, or milk that falls into the midst of meat, the measure is, if it give a taste? How so? If a peace of meat fall into a boiling pot of milk, a Gentile is to taste the contents of the pot: and if he says that it has a taste of meat, then it is unlawful. But if it has not the taste of meat, then the milk is lawful, but that piece of meat is unlawful. In what cases does this hold? In case that the piece of meat has been taken out, before it has emitted the milk which it has sucked in. But if it has not been taken out, then a calculation must be made whether its proportion to the whole is as one to sixty; because the milk that was sucked in, and had become unlawful, has been emitted and has mixed with the rest of the milk." (Ibid.) Now, in the most tolerable case, that is, if the owner of the milk can afford to lose it and the meat too, there is, first, an unnecessary inconvenience and vexation, which no man has a right to inflict upon another. But there is, secondly, and what is of far more consequence, a great sin in wasting good and wholesome, and, according to the written law, lawful food. If the milk tastes of meat, then the milk and the meat are rendered not only unlawful but perfectly useless. How then can the Jews expect peace and plenty, when their oral law teaches them to despise and cast from them with disdain God's blessings? But suppose that the owner of the milk and the meat is a poor man, and that he has laid out his hard and scanty earnings to provide food for his family, an accident of this kind will leave them destitute. Their last hope of support is taken away, and they may die of hunger. If they go to the rabbies, and urge the necessity of the case—plead that they have no more—reason that if meat by itself is lawful, that milk is also lawful—that the law of Moses no where forbids this food—the teachers of the oral law will answer, that their traditions cannot be broken; and the poor people must learn that to eat food permitted and given by God is a sin, but to die of starvation is lawful. How can men with any of the feelings of humanity believe that such a law is from God?—how can men of any common sense suffer the consciences and the bodies of the poor and ignorant to be thus tormented? Above all, how can a nation that prides itself on the purity of its faith yield an idolatrous obedience to cruel and oppressive laws invented by men? It is a vain boast for them to say that they have no images—the oral law and its enactments constitute a whole host of idols. It is an unfounded triumph which they celebrate over the worshippers of Moloch. The oral law is a deity as fierce and as bloody, and to it are daily immolated the souls and bodies of the poor and ignorant. Any homage rendered to falsehood, or to cruelty, is idolatrous; and every thinking man must admit, that the worship of the oral law is of this character. To the Rabbinists themselves we would say, Just think whether it be possible that God would have given a law so oppressive, or whether he can have any pleasure in the obedience which is rendered at the expense of mercy? To those who reject the oral law we would say, You have a duty to perform from which nothing can exempt you—and that is, to rest neither day nor night until Israel is delivered from this idolatrous worship of men, and set free from a yoke so oppressive to body and soul. We grant that Christians have also a duty, and in these papers we endeavour to discharge our share of it. But the duty incumbent upon Israelites is tenfold more imperative. The ties of flesh and blood—their office as a kingdom of priests—the mercy of God in giving them the law as their inheritance—all increase their responsibility and add to the weight of obligation. It would be a shame for Israel to be silent when even the Gentiles cry out for the restoration of the religion of Moses and the prophets. Israelites may have peculiar difficulties. They may be united in commercial relations or by family ties with those who are in bondage to the oral law. They may fear the injury of their worldly prospects —they may dread the frown of relatives and friends. This was also the case of Abraham, when he determined to renounce the false gods of his fathers, and to worship the true God alone; and every one who determines by God's help to follow and assert the truth, must make up his mind to love it even more than life itself. But can a son of Abraham hesitate? Will he forfeit the smile of God to escape the frown of friends?

Nay, if his friends are still in error, is this not a double motive to urge him forward in the overthrow of that error? Must he not be doubly anxious to deliver his father, his mother, his brothers and his sistersfrom such bondage? The first attempt may be difficult—the immediate results may be unpleasant; but if for God's sake he asserts God's truth, he shall have God's blessing, and at last find peace even amongst those who are now offended. As long as the present state of things continues, Israel can never be restored to their ancient position. God in mercy keeps them in dispersion, to prevent the triumph of the oral law. But when is this state of misery to cease? There must be a beginning. Some one follower of Moses must be zealous enough and bold enough to attack the strong holds of superstition, and to rouse his brethren to a sense of their condition—some one who not only professes to be a follower of Moses, but who has imbibed his spirit, and whose trust is in the God of his fathers.

No. LIII.

RABBINISM OPPRESSIVE TO THE POOR.

WHEN God gave Israel the law, by the hand of Moses, he also gave them several tests, whereby they might at all times try themselves, and know to a certainty whether they were really obedient or not—and whether the laws, to which they yielded obedience, were really the laws given by Moses. One of these tests is found in the following words:—" Behold, I have taught you statutes and judgments, even as the Lord my God commanded me, that ye should do so in the land whither ye go to possess it. Keep, therefore, and do them; for this is your wisdom and your understanding in the sight of the nations, which shall hear all these statutes, and say, Surely this great nation is a wise and understanding people." (Deut. iv. 5.) By the help of these words, Israel may know at any time whether they are really keeping the laws of Moses. They have only to consult their own experience, and determine whether they are honoured by all nations on account of their wisdom. Moses promises that a reputation for wisdom, and the honour that accompanies it, shall be the reward of obedience. If therefore the Jews at this present time are obedient, this promise must be in daily fulfilment. But, if they are not honoured and respected for their wisdom, then we must conclude, that they are deficient in obedience, and further, that the laws to which they are at present so devoted are not the laws of Moses. Now it is a certain fact, that admiration for the wisdom of Israel has not been the prevailing sentiment amongst the nations of the world for the last two thousand years. The Jewish people has been most deplorably underrated. Their genius and their literature have been ignorantly undervalued, and the folly of the authors of the oral law has been unjustly visited upon each and every individual of the nation. We grant the injustice and the impiety of such hasty judgments, but cannot deny the fact, and the fact proves that the laws to which Israel now yields obedience are not the laws of Moses. They now obey the commands of the oral law, and the nations have heard of the statutes thereof, but no one says, "Surely this great nation is a wise and understanding people." Some may, perhaps, ascribe this to prejudice, and no doubt there are cases where prejudice has much to do with the decision, but this is not our case. Our prepossessions are all in favour of the Jews, and yet we cannot help questioning the wisdom of those, who make such laws as the following a part of their religion:—

אין לשין העיסה בחלב ואם לש כל חפת אסורה
מפני הרגל עבירה שמא יאכל בה בשר, ואין טשין
את התנור באליה ואם טש כל חפת אסורה עד שיסיק
את התנור שמא יאכל בה חלב, ואם שינה בצורת
חפת עד שתהיה נכרת כדי שלא יאכל בה לא בשר
ולא חלב הרי זה מותר:

"It is not lawful to knead the dough with milk, and if it be done, all the bread is unlawful, lest this should lead to further transgression, and it should be eaten with meat. It is also unlawful to smear the oven with the tail of a sheep; and if it be done, all the bread is unlawful, lest milk should be eaten with it. But, if some change be made in the form of the bread whereby it may be recognized, so as that neither meat nor milk should be eaten with it, then it is lawful." (Hilchoth Maakhaloth Asuroth, c. ix. 22.) We do not wish to persuade the Jews either to knead dough with milk, or to smear an oven with the tail of a sheep, but when we remember all the poverty and want that is in the world, we cannot help asking, What is there so sinful in either of the above actions, as to make such bread unlawful for the use of God's people? Has God forbidden it? or has he so strictly prohibited the use of meat and milk together, as to make this excess of caution necessary? Neither the one nor the other. The law of God as given by Moses, allows the use of meat and milk together. It forbids only one particular case, the boiling of a kid in its mother's milk: and to this the rabbies have, without any authority, added all these other commands, and thus burdened the conscience, and made religion an intricate and difficult science intelligible only to the learned, and not always to them. What wisdom is there in forbidding what God did not think necessary to forbid? What wisdom is there in neglecting or disregarding the revealed will of God, and giving up the conscience to the guidance of weak and fallible men like ourselves? But above all, what wisdom is there in oppressing and tormenting the poor? The oral law says—

מי שאכל גבינה או חלב תחלה מותר לאכול
אחריו בשר מיד.
מי שאכל בשר בתחלה בין בשר בהמה בין בשר
עוף לא יאכל אחריו חלב עד שיהיה ביניהם כדי
שיעור סעודה אחרת והוא כמו שש שעות מפני הבשר
שבין השיניים שאינו סר בקינוח:

"He that eats cheese or milk first, may eat meat immediately after.

"He that eats meat first, whether it be the meat of a beast or of a fowl, must not eat milk after it, until the regular time between two meals, that is six hours, shall have elapsed; because of the meat which remains between the teeth, and which is not got out by wiping." (Ibid., 26, 28.) Now in the case of the rich or the affluent, who can procure a good and sufficient meal of meat, and can therefore wait for six hours, this may be no great hardship, though even in that case, we must protest against the unauthorized burden imposed upon the conscience; but when applied to the needy and the destitute, this law becomes an intolerable yoke. Just suppose the father of a starving family who goes forth to beg assistance from the charitable. He receives a small portion of meat, and hastens back to divide it with his wife and children. They partake of the relief, but it is not sufficient to supply their wants. He therefore goes forth again, and some friend of the poor gives him some milk or cheese, he brings it home with thankfulness, but dare not touch it himself nor give it to his children—they have already fasted many an hour—they are still weak with hunger—a little of the milk or the cheese would recruit exhausted nature—the children cry and entreat their father, but no—they must still endure the pangs of hunger for six hours more, for though God allows this food, the rabbies have forbidden it. Is there wisdom in this? Is God honoured by such a religion, which counts his permission as nothing, and exalts the authority of the rabbies above that of God himself? And may we not ask the same question of the following law?

האוכל גבינת הגוים או חלב שחלבו גוי ואין

חישראל רואהו מכין אותו מכת מרדות׳ והחמאה
מקצת הגאונים התירוה שהרי לא גזרו על חחמאה
וחלב טמא אינו עומד ומקצת הגאונים אסרוה מפני
צחצוח חלב שישאר בה :

"He that eats Gentile cheese, or milk which a Gentile has milked, but the Israelite did not see him, is to be flogged with the flogging of rebellion. But, as to the butter, some of the Gaons have pronounced it lawful, because there is no express decision about it, and because unclean milk will not set. Others of the Gaons, on the contrary, have pronounced it unlawful, on account of the small drops of milk which remain in it. (Joreh Deah, 115.) Here we have the same total want of consideration for the poor, and the same fierce and cruel spirit. Just suppose, again, the case of a destitute Jewish family, where the father is laid on a bed of sickness, and unable to earn daily bread for his children. The mother, weary with tending the sick couch of her husband, and her heart half-broken with the children's cry for bread, goes to solicit help from the almoners of the synagogue. She obtains eighteen pence per month, but finds that on this small sum it is impossible for a family to subsist; she then goes to individuals of her nation, and gets what she can, but still not sufficient to supply the wants of her children, and of her sick husband. In her distress, she goes to some Christian neighbours, who give her some milk and cheese. The pangs of hunger, and the affections of a wife and mother overcome her superstition, she carries this bounty home and partakes of it along with her husband and children. Has she thereby committed a sin; has she violated any one precept of the Mosaic law; has she blasphemed the name of her God? Let reason, let the Law and the Prophets answer, and they will say, No: she has done her duty. But what does the oral law say? It says, that she has committed a dreadful sin. And what is to be her punishment, and that of her husband and children? Flogging—the flogging of rebellion. If the oral law had power, it would lead them forth to the place of execution, and there inflict stripes without number and without mercy. The bystanders, and those attracted by the cries would ask, What dreadful crime has this family committed? and the answer would be, To save themselves from starvation they dared to eat Gentile cheese and milk. Gentiles would ask again, What, is this the law? Does Judaism teach that so innocent an action is to be punished with such severity? and being answered in the affirmative, would go away exclaiming, "What a merciful religion! Surely this great nation is a wise and understanding people!" No: they would retire in horror, thanking God that they are not Jews, and that God has preserved them from so dreadful a delusion, and from such iniquitous cruelty. What, then, do our Jewish readers think of this law, and the religion of which it is a part? It is certain that there are multitudes of Jews in this city who live in the constant violation of this command; who constantly use milk supplied by Gentiles, and yet pretend to profess Judaism as their religion. Let all such ask themselves, by what authority they transgress a command sanctioned by so severe a punishment. Is it because they think it irrational, or unwarranted by the law of Moses? If so, they attack at once the authority of the whole system of Judaism. If the oral law can be proved to be absurd, or unjust, or cruel, in any one particular, its value as a divine tradition is utterly destroyed. Let them, then, be consistent; if they reject Judaism, let them say so, let them not pretend to have the Jewish religion, when they have it not. Let them honestly confess that their reason, directed by Scripture, has led them to reject it; and let them fulfil the consequent duty of endeavouring to deliver their poor brethren from a bondage so cruel. They must know that these laws about milk and butter, and the art of slaughtering, cut off many a poor Jew from the last refuge of the destitute—the poor-house. Many a one who is now starving with his family, would be glad to have the relief which the parish provides, but he dare not accept of it. Either his conscience, perverted by these rabbinical statutes, will not permit him, or he is afraid of his brethren, who would think that in going into such an asylum he had renounced his God. Those who use Gentile milk without scruple, will have much to answer for, if they suffer such oppression and such superstition to continue. It is a vain excuse for any one to say, What can I do? Any one individual, however weak and uninfluential, has it in his power by God's blessing, to deliver the poor. Let him continually protest against such superstition, let him reason with his brethren. Let him determine to take no rest, until the yoke is torn from the necks of his nation. He will ultimately prevail. He will be the instrument in God's hand, of offering a greater deliverance than that from Egypt, inasmuch as the emancipation of the soul is of more importance than that of the body. In this respect, amongst others, Jesus of Nazareth has done more than Moses. If he had not arisen, the oral law would have been universal, and the world have continued either sunk in idolatry or slaves to a cruel superstition. The cruelty of a religion, which commands a man to be flogged for eating that which God permits, is not to be disputed; the prohibition of Gentile bread furnishes another instance of similar inhumanity.

יש דברים שאסרו חכמים אע"פ שאין להם עיקר
מן התורה כמו פת של גוים אפילו אפאו לו ישראל

והשלקות שמבשלין חנוים ואסרו לשתות במסיבתן
אפילו שאר משקין שאין בהן משום חשש יין נסך
וכל אלו דברים אסרו משום חתנות וכו׳ :

"There are some things which the wise men have pronounced unlawful, although they have no foundation for the prohibition in the law, as bread of the Gentiles, even though an Israelite should have baked it for him—and cooked victuals, which the Gentiles have cooked. They have also pronounced it unlawful to drink at a Gentile table, even those drinks of which there can be no suspicion that wine of libation is mixed with them. And they pronounced these things unlawful to prevent the possibility of intermarriage," &c. (Ibid. 112.) There are many remarks suggested by this passage, but at present we limit ourselves to the prohibition of Gentile bread. It is here confessed that there is no foundation for it in the law of Moses, and that therefore the rabbies have no authority for the prohibition; and yet a very little consideration is sufficient to show that great inconvenience may arise. For instance, if a poor Jew is travelling in this country, exhausts his stock of money, and goes to a farm-house to ask relief, he cannot accept any meat—he is not to drink any milk on pain of a flogging. Suppose, then, that the people offer him some home-baked bread, even this is forbidden:—

פת של בעל חבית אסורה לעולם :

"Bread baked by a private house-keeper is eternally forbidden." The poor man, therefore, may starve. But the inhumanity appears still more in the discussion of the question, whether and when it is lawful to eat baker's bread. The rabbies are divided. Some allow it, because the rule is—

מי שהתענה ג׳ ימים מותר בפת של גוים משום
חיי נפש וברוב מקומות גליותנו אין פלטר ישראל
מצוי והוה כאלו התענה ג׳ ימים , ויש אוסרין אותו
אלא א׳כ התענה ג׳ ימים ממש :

"He that has fasted three days may lawfully eat Gentile bread, and as in many places of our captivity there is no Israelite baker, this case is considered parallel to that of him who has fasted three days. But there are others who say that it is unlawful, unless he has fasted three days, in the strictest sense of the word." (Ibid.) One would think that, in a case of doubt, men that had the fear of God would naturally incline to the side of mercy; but here we find teachers of religion forbidding what God has allowed, unless the victim of poverty has first endured the torment of starvation for three days; and in one case actually determining that a fellow-creature shall die of hunger, rather than suffer their unauthorized traditions to be broken. If a Gentile Government should seize on a number of unfortunate Israelites guilty of no crime, and shut them up in a prison, and then leave them to die of starvation, what just indignation would be excited! Every man would protest against such wanton cruelty, and yet this is just what modern Judaism has done. By forbidding Gentile meat, milk, cheese, and bread, it has consigned hundreds to starvation. There are at this moment numbers of individuals, if not families, pining away in want, whose wants could be relieved, if the oral law did not interpose its iron front, and pronounce starvation lawful, and help from Gentiles unlawful; and yet their brethren, who pride themselves upon their benevolence and humanity, leave them to perish, and suffer the system to remain that it may be a curse to coming generations. It is truly astonishing to see the indifference of those who pride themselves upon their emancipation from superstition, and who themselves eat Gentile bread, and milk, and cheese, and perhaps meat, without any scruple. It is more astonishing still, how the nation at large suffers itself to be deluded by men who do not agree amongst themselves as to what the law really is. We saw above, that the greatest of the rabbies, even the Gaons themselves, differ as to the lawfulness of Gentile butter;—here we see that they cannot agree as to the lawfulness of Gentile bakers' bread. How is it, then, that the Jews cannot see that their present religion of the oral law is altogether one of uncertainty and that, therefore, there is no dependence upon it? Here they eat freely, even the strictest, of Gentile bread; but yet, according to some of their greatest men, they are thereby committing a deadly sin. These wise men humanely say, that it is necessary first to fast for three days. Now of what use is an oral law that cannot even tell us certainly what sort of bread it is unlawful to eat? The Rabbinist boast is, that the oral law teaches them the true meaning of the written law, and thus saves them from all doubtful disputation. But how can that be true, when the oral law has not yet settled when it is lawful to eat Gentile bread? If the rabbies cannot agree on so simple a matter, what trust can be placed in them in difficult questions? The Jews cannot even tell, by the help of their religion, whether they are not committing a sin, and leading their children to commit a sin, when they give them a piece of bread and butter. How, then, can they be satisfied with a religion where the simplest concerns of life are still a matter of doubt and disputation; and especially where the poor are made to suffer the greatest hardships, whilst, by keeping to Moses and the prophets, they might find relief? But, above all, how can they believe that a religion is divine, or its authors good and pious men, when an innocent action, nay, the fulfilment of a natural duty, is punished with flogging? There is no punishment of which the oral law is so fond; and it would be a curious and interesting employment to furnish a list of all the offences to which it is annexed. Perhaps in nothing does the Talmud differ more from the New Testament. The New Testament has not, in any one case, prescribed so cruel a punishment. The Talmud and all its compendiums prescribe it on the most trifling occasion. The maxim of the New Testament is that of the Old also, "I will have mercy, not sacrifice." Now, if the practice of mercy be more agreeable in the eyes of God, than even those ceremonial rites which he himself ordained, with what pleasure can he contemplate the religion of the oral law, which punishes, even what God has allowed, with unmeasured cruelty? Aben Ezra supposed that this command, "Not to seethe a kid in its mother's milk," was given in order to prevent cruelty even to the brute creation; if this be true, how does God regard the perversion of his mercy, which pretends to keep this command, to spare the brute creation, by dooming hundreds of mankind to starvation, and by flogging those who endeavour to escape from their misery by eating what he has nowhere forbidden? If God has compassion upon the beasts that perish, what can he think of those teachers of religion who talk with such composure of a fellow-creature's fasting for three days before he may eat bread sold by a Gentile baker, and who absolutely decide that it is his duty to die, rather then partake of bread baked by a private individual who is not a Jew? We appeal to the good sense of every Israelite to answer these questions. Is it not evident that the God of mercy must view with indignation, those teachers who thus misrepresent the nature of revealed religion, and who cause his holy name to be blasphemed amongst the ignorant? But if those men are guilty, a portion of their guilt rests upon all those who aid and abet in upholding the system. There can be but little excuse for those who have the Law and the Prophets in their hands, and who therefore ought to know, that the cruelty of the oral law is as contrary to the character of God, as light is to darkness. And there is no excuse at all for those Israelites who themselves despise these Rabbinical laws, and yet by their silence and indifference leave their brethren still in misery. They are answerable for all the dishonour done to God; for all the misery inflicted upon man; and for all the contempt heaped upon the wisdom of Israel.

No. LIV.

GENTILE WINE.

THE Jews of the present day have got one religion—the Christians have got another. It is much to be desired that all the sons of men should have the one true religion, but, as this is not likely to be the case for some little time longer, it becomes those who differ to examine the nature and grounds of their differences. Whatever Jews may think upon the subject, Christians feel themselves bound to inquire whether they have really erred so grievously as modern Judaism asserts. The oral law brings no less a charge against them than this, That they are guilty of idolatry, and therefore in a worse state than even the Mahometans.

כל גוי שאינו עובד עכו״ם כגון אלו הישמעאלים
יינן אסור בשתיה ומותר בהנאה, וכן הורו כל
הגאונים, אבל הנוצרים עובדי עכו״ם הם וסתם יינם
אסור בהנאה :

"As to those Gentiles who, like the Ishmaelites, are not idolaters, their wine is unlawful to drink, but is lawful for purposes of profit, as is taught by all the Gaons; but Christians are idolaters, and their wine, even such as has not been used as wine of libation, is unlawful even for purposes of profit." (Hilchoth Maakhaloth Asuroth, c. xi. 7.) These words are very plain, and are confirmed by the practice of Rabbinists in every part of the world, who abstain as carefully from the wine belonging to Christians, as their forefathers would have done from the idolatrous libation of the Canaanites. Jews, therefore cannot be astonished if we examine with care a religion that brings against us so grave an accusation, and endeavour to defend ourselves against the charge. We might ask them, whether they behold in our churches any of the emblems of idolatry. We might refer them to the ten commandments written up in the most holy place of our sacred edifices. We might quote from the New Testament many warnings against idolatry as plain and as solemn as any to be found in the law of Moses; but there is a previous question to be considered, and that is, What is the character of that system, which witnesses against us? Is it worthy of credit—can its testimony be depended upon? If the oral law be really from God, and if its teachers should appear as faithful depositories of Divine truth, their testimony would have great weight. But if the rabbies be detected as daring corrupters of Divine revelation, and their religon be proved to be a perversion of the law of

Moses, then this charge must fall to the ground as unworthy of all credit; and this is what we assert. We have already given many reasons in support of this assertion, and now add some more which we find in the laws about יין נסך, "wine of libation," which laws appear to us to be not only unwarranted additions, but unmerciful, uncharitable, and irrational.

We do not mean to deny that it is utterly unlawful to partake of wine that has been consecrated to idols; on the contrary, we would assert this as zealously as any Israelite. Concerning things offered to idols, the New Testament says, "The things which the Gentiles sacrifice, they sacrifice to devils, and not to God: and I would not that ye should have fellowship with devils. Ye cannot drink the cup of the Lord, and the cup of devils." (1 Cor. x. 20, 21.) Let not therefore any Israelite think that we wish to defend what is contrary both to the Old and New Testament. But though fully convinced of the unlawfulness of drinking wine or anything else consecrated to the service of idolatry, we confess that we cannot see why it is unlawful to make use of wine not consecrated to idolatry, simply because it belongs to, or has been touched by, a Gentile; and yet this is the rabbinic law:—

יין הגוים שאין אנו יודעים אם נתנסך או לא
נתנסך והוא הנקרא סתם יינם אסור בהנאה כמו יין
שנתנסך ודבר זה מגזירת הסופרים הוא והשותה
מסתם יינם רביעית מכין אותו מכת מרדות, וכל יין
שיגע בו הגוי הרי זה אסור שמא נסך אותו שמחשבת
הגוי לעכו״ם הא למדת שיין ישראל שנגע בו הגוי
דינו כסתם יינם שהוא אסור בהנאה:

"Wine belonging to Gentiles, of which we do not know whether it has been consecrated or not, and what is called *common Gentile wine*, is unlawful even to make a profit of, just like wine that has been consecrated; and this is by the decree of the scribes. Whosoever drinks so much as one quarter measure of this common Gentile wine is to be flogged with the flogging of rebellion. All wine also which a Gentile touches is unlawful because he may have consecrated it, for the thought of a Gentile is to idolatry. Hence thou hast learned, that concerning wine belonging to an Israelite which a Gentile has touched, the law is the same as in the case of common Gentile wine, which is unlawful even to make a profit of." (Ibid., 3, 4.) Now in this law we have first the unauthorized additions of the rabbies. We have already granted, that wine, and everything else, consecrated to the service of idols is unlawful, but with this the rabbies are not content. They forbid wine that was made by, or ever in the possession of, a

Gentile, or even if a Gentile has touched it, and that not only to drink it, but to make any use of it, or to sell it, or to be in any way employed about it, so as to make any profit by it.

והחמירו חכמים בסתם יינם להיות דמיו אסורין
כדמי יין שנתנסך לעכו״ם לפיכך גוי ששכר את ישראל
לעשות עמו ביין שכרו אסור, וכן השוכר את החמור
להביא עליו יין או ששכר ספינה להביא בה יין שכרן
אסור, אם מעות נתנו לו ישליכון לים המלח, ואם
נתנו לו בשכרו כסות או כלים או פירות הרי זה
ישרוף אותן ויקבור האפר כדי שלא ליהנות בו, שכר
לגוי חמור לרכוב עליו והניח עליו לוגין של יין
שכרו מותר :

"The wise men have been very strict with respect to the common Gentile wine, and have pronounced its price to be unlawful, as that of wine which has been consecrated to idolatry; therefore, if a Gentile have an Israelite to labour with him, in any thing concerning wine, his wages are unlawful. In like manner, if he hire an ass, or a ship, to carry wine, the hire thereof is unlawful: and if it be given to him in money, he is to throw it into the salt sea. But if the hire be given him in clothes, or vessels, or fruits, he is to burn them, and to bury their ashes, that no profit may arise therefrom. But if an Israelite has hired an ass to a Gentile to ride upon, and he lays upon it bottles of wine, then the hire thereof is lawful." (Ibid., c. xiii. 15, &c.) For all this there is no authority whatever in the law of Moses,—it is a pure invention of the rabbies, who had but little respect for the Divine law, and no consideration at all for the necessities of man. It is evident that these additions must, in many cases, become so many impediments in the way of earning a subsistence. The proprietor of a ship, or the owner of cattle, is cut off from one source of employment and profit. Now, even in the case of the rich, though they may feel it less, this is an unjustifiable severity; but in the case of the poor, it becomes a most cruel oppression. In the wine-countries, for example, a poor Jew might perchance find employment with some of the growers of that article; but the rabbies have declared that honest industry, in a matter which God has nowhere forbidden, is unlawful, and the fruits of it so abominable, as to be fit only for destruction. In this city, also, many examples of the absurdity and cruelty of this law might be found. Suppose that a Christian wine-merchant should wish to employ some one or more of those numerous Israelites, who are destitute of the means of earning a livelihood, and should therefore offer him a situation, either in his cellar or his counting-house, the rabbies say that he dare not accept of it: and that it is more pleasing in the sight of God that the man should go about idle, and that his family should starve, than that he should labour honestly, and do what God has permitted. Who is there, except the rabbies themselves, who does not see that such a decision is irrational, oppressive, and unmerciful, not now to speak of its injustice to Christian nations, by classing them with the idolaters of Canaan? But take another case, suppose that some Christian, finding a Jewish family in deep distress, some of the members perhaps recovering from sickness, to whom a little wine might be beneficial, gives them a bottle of wine, What are they to do with it? May they make use of it to strengthen their exhausted frames? The rabbies answer, No. May they sell it, and with the money purchase food, or some other necessary of life? The rabbies answer, No. What then are they to do with it? The rabbies answer, Destroy it; destroy what would recruit your fainting bodies—what would purchase bread for your starving children—destroy what might perhaps save your life, simply because we have forbidden it; and it is more important that our unauthorized laws should be preserved inviolate, than that you should be comforted or strengthened or relieved in your misery. This is the mercy of Judaism. But we have not done yet. Suppose that the mother of the family should begin to reason, and say, This wine would preserve my poor child's life; a little of it would strengthen me, and enable me to tend the sick bed with more alacrity; God has nowhere forbidden it. She accordingly administers to her child, and partakes herself, when some rabbinic zealot enters and perceives what she has done. Now suppose that the ministers of the oral law had the liberty to follow out all its enactments, what would be the consequence? The poor woman would be summoned before a בית דין, a tribunal; the oral law would be opened, and her sentence be, The flogging of rebellion, as we have cited above. Is this merciful, is it just, is it rational? Is there anything like it in the New Testament, or in the religion of Jesus of Nazareth? The oral law says that we are idolaters, but is it worthy of credit? Can any reasonable man place confidence in the teaching of those who are so senseless as to forbid a perishing fellow-creature to make use of proffered relief, and so merciless as to flog him with the flogging of rebellion, if he regards God's permission more than their prohibition? But it is not only absurdity and cruelty, which here are to be noticed, there is also a certain measure of that cleverness which we have remarked on former occasions, which provides for the transgression of the law and the retaining of the merit of keeping it. The above extract says, "If an Israelite has hired an ass to a Gentile to ride upon, and he lays upon it bottles of wine, then the hire thereof is lawful;" and on this principle the owner of a ship or a wagon may let either generally for the transport of merchandize, and provided the word *wine* is not mentioned, the Gentile may transport his wine, and the Jew lawfully receive and use his money, though if the word *wine* had been mentioned, the money would have been so unlawful, that it ought not even be given to relieve the wants of the poor, but thrown into the salt sea. Here the rabbies betray their own insincerity, and their unbelief in their own enactments, by their determination to evade their severity, whenever it interfered with their own interests. But even if there were no cruelty, no contempt for the law of God, and no evasion, the effect of multiplying such observances is to lead away the mind from the weightier matters of religion. The ignorant think, even whilst they are violating the ten commandments, that, if they abstain from Gentile wine, they are fulfilling a most meritorious duty, and making compensation for their other transgressions. Indeed the rabbies themselves are not free from this effect, if we may judge by the following passage:—

זונה גויה במסיבה של ישראל היין מותר מפני
שאימתה עליה ולא תגע אבל זונה ישראלית במסיבת
גוים יינה שלפניה בכליה אסור מפני שהם נוגעין
שלא מדעתה:

"If a Gentile harlot be at an entertainment of Israelites, the wine is lawful, for their fear is upon her, so that she would not touch it. But if an Israelite harlot be at an entertainment of Gentiles, her wine that is before her in her own vessel is unlawful, because they may touch it without her knowledge." (Ibid., c. xii. 26.) Now if men or women are so wicked as to be found in such circumstances, in the open disregard of God's law, is it not deceiving them to tell them, or to lead them to suppose, that there can be any merit in any mere ceremonial observance, even though it should have been ordained by God himself: and is it not straining at a gnat and swallowing a camel, to forbid a poor perishing Jew to taste wine touched by a Gentile, and to allow it to those who are feasting with a harlot? Perhaps some one will reply that it is on account of the idolatry of the Gentile; but we have seen in the first extract given in this paper, that if wine be touched even by a Gentile who is not an idolater, it is unlawful for a Jew to drink it; so that to be a Gentile at all is in the eyes of the rabbies a greater degradation and of more contaminating influence, than to be guilty of gross immorality. Now we appeal to the good sense of every Israelite, whether this is not to exalt vice, and to degrade humanity? God chose a people to himself, Israel is that people; we honour them as such: but, is that any reason why Israel should trample upon the ties of our common humanity, and look upon the touch even of a Gentile who fears God, as so defiling that it makes wine unfit for the use of a Jew? How are peace and charity ever to prevail between Jews and Gentiles, so long as this is looked upon as religion? Yea, and how is true religion and true fear of God ever to prevail amongst the mass of the Jewish community, so long as they are taught that Israelites guilty of immorality are more holy than a Gentile who fears God, and that sin is not so dreadful as uncircumcision? The object of such commands was plainly to prevent all social and friendly intercourse between Jews and Gentiles under any circumstances, and to build up an eternal wall of separation between them. This is very different from that national and official distinction instituted by God himself. The object of God's choice was not to put an end to the practice of love and charity between the Jews and all the other nations of the earth, but to cement the bonds of affection. He made Israel the depository of his oracles, that they might communicate the truth to other nations, and that thus the nations should feel gratitude for the benefit conferred, and the Israelites feel that affection for the nations, which a teacher naturally feels for those who, by his instrumentality, have forsaken error and embraced the truth. The oral law prevents the fulfilment of the Divine law, and cuts asunder also these ties of amity and peace. It makes it impossible for Israel to communicate any blessing, and for the Gentiles to receive any blessing at their hands, and goes far towards throwing suspicion on the Divine law. If there were no other medium of communication, than the rabbies, between the Divine law and the world, the worship of Jupiter and Bacchus and all the other heathen deities would still prevail. How could the nations ever have been converted by those who taught them, in the first place, that God is such a respecter of persons, as to think immorality in a Jew less contaminating than the mere external touch of a pious Gentile? Reason revolts at such profane absurdity, and therefore if God had had no better messengers and representatives of his truth, idolatry would still continue. Some may reply, idolatry does still continue, such at least is the sentence of the oral law, and, though grieved that any should be so blind as to bring such a charge against Christianity, we are by no means angry or offended at it. If the Jews still believe in their own religion, and therefore think that Christians are idolaters, it is their bounden duty to say so. But then we ask in reply, if Christianity be idolatry, how is it that its doctrine is more pure, more merciful, more charitable, and more rational than that of the oral law? Christianity has no ceremonial laws to be observed by those who feast together with harlots—Christianity nowhere sentences the poor to flogging, because they partake of what God allows—Christianity nowhere represents God as an unjust and impartial judge, who looks not at moral good and evil, but at a man's nation. Christianity teaches that true religion is that of the heart—that at the day of judgment mercilessness will obtain no mercy, and that God is the God of the spirits of all flesh. Let then the lovers of the oral law account for this fact, that Christianity, which they call idolatry, teaches a doctrine that glorifies God and benefits all men; whilst Judaism, which they say is the truth, teaches a doctrine dishonouring to God, oppressive to the Jews, and degrading to all other nations. Some Jews will reply, that Christians are not idolaters; then we ask such persons how they can pretend to profess Judaism, which has asserted the contrary for so many centuries, and also acted upon this principle, prohibiting all intercourse, as much as Moses did in the land of Canaan? Either Christianity is idolatry, or Judaism is false; there is no alternative. Every Jew, therefore, who asserts that Christians are not idolaters, pronounces of Judaism that it is false. Let all such persons then deal honestly, let them renounce what they do not believe; and let them denounce to their brethren what they think it necessary to disavow before Christians. They are bound to do this, not only to renounce the injustice with which the oral law treats Christians, but to take away the cruel and oppressive yoke which bows down their brethren the Jews. If Christianity be not idolatry, then all the laws concerning נסך יין, "wine of libation," are utterly out of place in this country. Then poor Jews may accept of Christian bounty, and the offices of kindliness and charity may be practised between Jew and Christian. Those Jews therefore who profess to believe that Christians are not idolaters, are bound, by their obligations both to Jews and Christians, to protest against the oral law, and publicly to disavow all belief in it. So long as they do not make such a public disavowal, their professions of love and charity and respect for the religion of Christians must be looked upon as hollow and insincere. So long as they make such professions, contrary to the oral law, and yet frequent the worship of the synagogue, which asserts the divinity of the oral law, they must be regarded either as persons who have motives for professing what they do not feel, or who want moral courage to renounce what they disapprove. These remarks apply particularly to those Israelites who have practically forsaken Judaism, who associate with Christians, eat Gentile food, and drink Gentile wine, and some of whom perhaps even deal in it as an article of merchandize. Such persons, though Israelites by nation, are not Jews by religion, at least according to that sense in which the word Jew has been used both by Israel and Gentile nations for the last two thousand years. Such persons cannot pretend to be professors of the Jewish persuasion. Any one who is in the habit of drinking Gentile wine has practically forsaken Judaism, just as much as if he had assumed the turban and professed himself a Mahometan. It becomes such persons especially to make a stand against the oral law, and to declare publicly what their religion is, and whether they have any fixed principles at all. They cannot be regarded as Christians, for they have not been baptized; they cannot say that they are Jews, for they have forsaken Judaism; they cannot assert that they have the religion of Moses, for unless that religion be found amongst Christians, it does not exist. There is no body of religionists to be found in this country who profess themselves Mosaists. In the synagogue the oral law is professed; in the Church Christianity is professed; but where is the place of worship frequented by those who have forsaken Judaism without embracing Christianity? Such persons appear in a light that is not at all advantageous to their principles. In private they profess to abhor the intolerance of the oral law, they violate its precepts, and yet on the occasion of the great Jewish fasts and festivals they are to be seen in the synagogue joining in the worship, and observing the rites of the oral law. What then are we to believe concerning such persons? Are they indifferentists, who have no religion at all? or are they secret admirers of the oral law, who, for worldly purposes, deny it when occasion suits, and conform to it when the conscience is uneasy? We are far from pronouncing them either one or the other, but simply propose these questions for their own consideration, remind them of the equivocal light in which they appear, and would give them advice similar to that of Elijah to their forefathers. If the oral law be true religion, profess and practise it. If the oral law be erroneous, superstitious, and uncharitable, renounce it openly and honestly.

No. LV.

MOURNING FOR THE DEAD.

MODERN Judaism, or the religion of the Jews, as it is professed by the majority of the nation scattered through the world, confessedly consists of two parts. The first is composed of those laws which are מן התורה, *i.e.*, which are either really found in the written law, or are supposed to be based upon some passage of it. The second, of those laws which are מדברי הסופרים "of the words of the scribes," and which are, therefore, mere human institutions. Concerning those that were given by God, we readily grant that they can be changed or abrogated only by God himself. But respecting the latter, both reason and Scripture concur in assuring us, that what human authority has ordained, a similar human authority may also abrogate. We grant that so long as the Jewish polity remained, and the scribes were magistrates, their ordinances, so far as they were not contrary to the Word of God, were binding upon the Jews: but even then those ordinances were not immutable. They might have been repealed by the scribes and magistrates who succeeded them. And even then, whenever they stood in opposition to the Word of God, it was the bounden duty of the Jews to refuse obedience. For what reason then do the Jews of the present day still pay the same homage to the words of the scribes that they do to the Word of God? The scribes are not now the civil magistrates of the countries where the Jews reside; their words, therefore, carry with them no authority whatever. The Jews are now in different circumstances—are subject to other magistrates and lawgivers. The magisterial sanction, which the words of the scribes had before the dispersion, has long since been lost; but God nowhere commands the Jews in England to obey laws made by the civil magistrates of Palestine two thousand years ago. There is not a shadow of obligation remaining; and therefore the Jews of the present day have a full right to examine into their tendency and effects, and if they should be found injurious or unsuitable to present circumstances, to reject them. If the words of the scribes be not obligatory by virtue of Divine authority, the only imaginable reason for observing them is the supposition that they are conducive to the welfare and happiness of Israel, but if it can be shown that this supposition is false, then both reason and religion would suggest the wisdom of rejecting them. We have already shown of several such laws that they are alike noxious to man and dishonouring to God, and think now to exhibit a similar result with regard to the *laws concerning mourners for the dead.* Of many of these it is confessed that they are not of God, but simply ordinances of the scribes : thus, of the command to mourn seven days, it is acknowledged, that it is not to be found in the law :—

ואין אבלות מן התורה אלא ביום ראשון בלבד
שהוא יום המיתה ויום הקבורה אבל שאר השבעה
ימים אינו דין תורה :

"The only mourning commanded in the law is that on the first day, which is the day of the death and of the burial. But that of the rest of the seven days is not an ordinance of the law." (Hilchoth Avel., c. i. 1.) And thus with regard to the various things from which the mourner is to abstain during those seven days, it is acknowledged expressly that the command is altogether an ordinance of the scribes :—

אלו הדברים שהאבל אסור בהן ביום הראשון מן
התורה ובשאר ימים מדבריהם אסור לספר ולכבס
ולרחוץ ולסוך ולשמש מטתו ולנעול את הסנדל
ולעשות מלאכה ולקרות בדברי תורה ולזקוף את
המטה ולפרוע את ראשו ולשאול שלום הכל :

"These are the things which the mourner is prohibited from doing, according to the law, on the first day, but according to the words of the scribes on the remaining days—shaving, washing the clothes, bathing, anointing, duty of marriage, putting on shoes, working, reading in the words of the law, elevating the chair, uncovering the head, asking after the peace of any one." (Ibid., c. v.) As therefore the rabbies themselves do not pretend that abstinence from these things during those days of mourning is required in the law; and it is further a matter of fact, that this abstinence is not inculcated by the laws of the land, it naturally becomes a question, Why then do the Jews now observe these rites? Are they conducive to the happiness and welfare of Israel? We might doubt respecting several of them, but one is so obviously oppressive to the poor as to be almost beyond controversy; we mean the prohibition to work during the seven days' mourning. We do not mean to deny, that when death enters a family, it is a providential call to humiliation and serious reflection, and that therefore those who can should withdraw for a while from their every-day occupation, and seek by prayer and penitence to have the affliction turned into a blessing. But to require of those who have not food for themselves or their families to embitter their cup of sorrow by adding the pangs of hunger, is to act the part of an inconsiderate and merciless tyrant, and this is what the oral law does. It says—

כל שלשה ימים הראשונים אסור בעשיית מלאכה,
אפילו היה עני המתפרנס מן הצדקה, מכאן ואילך
אם היה עני עושה בצנעה בתוך ביתו:

"All the first three days it is unlawful to work, even though the man should be so poor as to live on alms. But after that, if he be poor, he may work privately in his own house." Thus, all those whose business lies out of doors, and who are obliged to wander about in order to get a livelihood, are completely cut off from the possibility of supplying the wants of their family. The law was evidently made under very different circumstances from those in which the Jewish people are now found. It presupposes that every one has got some trade or occupation whereby he can earn his bread at home, but this is not the case at present. A large proportion of the people, in every part of the world, now get a living by frequenting the public resorts of men : to forbid these, then, from going forth to their work, is equivalent to forbidding them to eat during seven days. Why then should Israel be bound by these laws, which even, according to the confession of the rabbies, have no Divine authority, and are now only oppressive to the poor?

But it is not merely of inconsideration for the poor that the oral law is guilty: we have more than once remarked the proud contempt with which it treats the poor and the unlearned, and are sorry to find it even in the laws concerning the last sad offices to humanity:—

עיר שיש בה שני מתים כאחד מוציאין הראשון
ואחר כך מוציאין השני, חכם ותלמיד חכם מוציאין
החכם, תלמיד חכם ועם הארץ מוציאין תלמיד חכם:

"If there be two persons dead in a city at once, he that died first, is first to be carried forth to burial, and then the second. But if one of them be a wise man, and the other the disciple of a wise man, the wise man is to have the precedency. If one be the disciple of a wise man and the other an unlearned one (amhaaretz), the disciple of the wise man is to be carried forth first." (Joreh Deah, 354.) We do not here object to the practical result, but to the spirit of the law. God has ordained different ranks and grades of society, and wills, therefore, that honour should be given to whom honour is due, and the common course of the world brings men and things to their level. But the doctors of the oral law were determined not to leave their posthumous honour to the natural course of events, but whilst they lived, took the matter into their own hands, and decreed that the honour paid them in life should also be rendered to their poor bodies after death; and that no plebeian or unlearned person should take precedency, even in the last sad memento of human frailty. After death there is but little difference between the learned and the unlearned, and the real difference is made, not by their previous learning or ignorance, but by their moral worth. An unlearned man may be, and often is, far more beloved by man, and far more pleasing in the sight of God, than the most learned, and therefore, when death has destroyed the imaginary distinctions of time, if religion makes any difference between the dead, it surely ought to make it according to that estimate, which is eternal. But the religion of the oral law cannot forget worldly distinction, even in the solemn moment of death, and therefore commands, that as the unlearned man, no matter what his moral worth may have been, has been despised in his life, he should still bear the marks of dishonour even in his death and burial. But the homage which the oral law pays to wealth and mere worldly distinction, is still more apparent in its commands respecting the measure of lamentation to be dealt out to the deceased. It says, on this subject—

בני עשירים כבני חכמים, בני חכמים כבני מלכים לענין שבח מעשיהם:

"The sons of the rich are to be regarded as the sons of the wise men; and the sons of the wise men as the sons of kings, with regard to praising their deeds." (Ibid., 344.) Here there is no concealment. The learned makers of the oral law choose to have their children honoured with the honours of royalty, and show that, however highly they might prize their learning, they had a due estimate of the value of wealth; and that however they might despise the unlearned, their contempt might be moderated, if the object of it was only rich. In the world we are not astonished at the inordinate homage paid to wealth, but when the teachers of religion bow down before the golden idol, and assign to mere wealth an honour which they refuse to the piety and moral worth of the poor, we cannot help doubting the purity of their professed principles, and questioning the truth of their religious system. The main object of religion should be to raise men above the delusive appearances of this present world—to teach men to look beyond the distinctions of rank, and wealth, and learning, to that eternal distinction which the righteous Judge will make according to man's deeds. And if there be one season more than another where religion ought to disregard the principles and customs of the world, it is with respect to the hour of death and burial. But here the oral law still maintains its love for wealth and worldly distinction, and its haughty contempt for ignorance, poverty, and humbleness of station. If any additional proof is still necessary, it is found in the forms prescribed on the death of slaves :—

העבדים והשפחות אין עומדין עליהן בשורה ואין
אומרים עליהן ברכת אבלים ולא תנחומי אבלים אלא
כשם שאומרין לאדם על שורו וחמורו המקום
ימלא חסרונך כך אומר על עבדו ושפחתו שמתו :

"In the case of male and female slaves, the people are not to stand in a row, nor to say the benediction of the mourners, nor the consolations of the mourners; but, as one says, to a man whose ox or ass is dead, God replace your loss, so one is to say, in the case of a male or female slave who has died." (Ibid., 377.) Volumes could not so clearly set forth the genius of Judaism, and the spirit of its authors, as this one short law. It exhibits the founders of Judaism, not only as void of all true religious sentiment, but absolutely dead to all the natural feelings of humanity. If mourners of any description require sympathy and respect, surely they are the mourning family of a slave, for, excepting crime, there is not anything that can aggravate the bitterness of death more than slavery. Here religion should pour in its oil and wine, and as it alleviated the miseries of life, diminish from the pangs of death. At such an hour, religion should assert the liberty of the soul, and remind the children of pride, that in the life after death the distinction of master and slave is unknown; that there eternal and spiritual liberty awaits all the children of God, whatever their outward condition here. At such an hour, religion should especially console the survivors with the hope, that there is another and better state of existence, where the slave and the freeman are equally regarded, and dealt with according to one eternal rule of justice. But the religion of the oral law, on the contrary, carries the degradation of slavery even down to the grave, and helps it to survive the period of bondage. It ordains that the usual religious rites should not be observed, and places the slave on the same level with the brute that perisheth. It prescribes no consolation for the slave's afflicted family, but ordains that his master should receive the same words of comfort, as if he had lost an ox or ass. The death of the slave is looked upon as nothing; it is only for the slave-owner's loss that the oral law has any consideration. The fact of his having been a human being, an inheriter of God's image, and an heir of everlasting life, is entirely overlooked by the rabbies. He was a slave, and they think, therefore, that as he was treated like a beast whilst he lived, he may be buried like a beast now that he is dead. If these slaves had been Gentiles, it would not have been surprising that the oral law should treat them with such little ceremony. But we must remember that all such slaves were compelled to become proselytes to Judaism. They were, therefore, co-religionists with their masters; but even this could not procure them the respect due to human beings. Because the providence of God had made them slaves, the oral law endeavoured to turn them into beasts. We are sure that many Jews of the present day will revolt with horror from such a doctrine; and acknowledge that it is a libel upon religion. They will be ready to confess, that the poor slave is a fellow-creature, and an expectant of life eternal; but let such persons stop to consider whence they have derived these sentiments, so much more just, more merciful, and more worthy of religion, than those expressed in the oral law. That they have not derived them from Judaism is clear. May they not, then, be indebted for them to the influence and atmosphere of Christianity in which they live? Certain it is, that the New Testament contains very different principles, respecting the treatment of slaves, from those which we have discovered in the oral law. But, further, would it not be well for those who disapprove these rabbinic principles, to ask themselves why they profess the rabbinic religion? If it be true that a slave is something better than an ox or an ass, Judaism, which classes them altogether, must be false: and the men who made such laws, must be confessed to be very unfit teachers of religion. Nay more, Judaism must be acknowledged as a religion most unfit to promote the happiness of the human race. If Judaism should prevail again, and, as its advocates expect, prevail universally, slavery would also prevail in the same degree: slaves would again be compelled to become proselytes, and again be treated as beasts. Such is the great consummation, the regeneration that Judaism promises the world. We therefore ask every Jewish reader, Whether he can pray for such a state of things, and whether he wishes to be thus enabled to degrade and trample upon his fellow-sinners? If he does not, there must be something wrong in the religious system which he professes—and if he only detects this one error, or acknowledges only this one falsehood respecting the classification of slaves with oxen and asses, it is sufficient to shake the whole rabbinic fabric: and if he has any concern for the honour of the Jewish nation, he will endeavour to deliver them from such a foul imputation upon their mercy and their humanity.

But there is one point more in these laws respecting mourners, which it is necessary to notice. The oral law forbids the mourner, as we have seen above, to read in the words of the law for seven days:—

אבל אסור לקרות בתורה ונביאים וכתובים, ואסור לשנות במשנה תלמוד הלכות ואגדות:

"The mourner is forbidden to read in the law, the prophets, and the Hagiographa: it is also forbidden to study in the Mishna, Talmud, Constitutions, and Agadoth." That a mourner would have no great loss in not being allowed to study in the oral law, we can readily believe; but why should he be prohibited from going to the great fountain of consolation—the revealed Word of God? If there be one season of life more fit than another for studying the Word of God, surely it is when death has entered a family, and reminded all its inmates that the wages of sin is death. If a husband or wife be left to mourn over the bereavement of a beloved partner, what consolation can be equal to that which they find in God's promise of a world where there is neither sorrow nor death, and where those who meet shall never part again? If children be left to mourn over the removal of their parents, whither should they flee for consolation rather than to that Word which tells them of him who is the father of the fatherless? Every reasonable person will think also that, when the heart is softened by the paternal chastisement, then is a peculiarly appropriate season for learning his precepts and taking heed to his exhortations— and yet the oral law, with a sort of most perverse ingenuity, has just selected that period of human life, in which the consolations of God's Word are most necessary and its instruction likely to be of most use, to forbid the reading of it altogether. And here, the rabbies have not scrupled to set aside the plain command of God. God says of his law, "Thou shalt meditate therein day and night;" and makes no exception for the seven days of mourning for the dead. In describing the character of the righteous he says, "His delight is in the law of the Lord, and in his law doth he meditate day and night;" and pronounces a blessing upon such a character. But the rabbies, in contempt both of the command and of the promised blessing, forbid the already afflicted mourner to obey the command and to seek the blessing. Even when the scribes and rabbies were in the plenitude of their power as civil magistrates in the land of Israel, obedience to such a command would have been unlawful, as implying disobedience to the command of God. The law of God and the law of man are here plainly in collision; the former commanding Israel to study in his law day and night; the latter prohibiting all study for the seven days of the mourning; but whenever these two authorities are opposed, no rational being can doubt that it is Israel's duty to obey God rather than man. But, in the present day, when the oral law is not the law of the land, when, therefore, the ordinances of the scribes have no authority whatever, it is impossible to conceive why Israel should obey this prohibition, unless they wish, by some public act, to exhibit their determination to transgress the laws of God. Every one who abstains from the study of God's Word for seven days, plainly disobeys the Divine command as given by Moses and the prophets; how then can the Jews of the present day deceive themselves by supposing that they have the religion of Moses? The main difference between Heathenism and the religion of Moses is, that the latter gives a revelation of God's will to guide us in difficulty and to comfort us in affliction. The main difference between a Heathen and a Jewish mourner ought to be, that the Jew flees for consolation to God and his Word, whilst the Heathen indulges in sorrow as those that have no hope. The oral law, however, breaks down with this distinction, and reduces the Jew to the level of the Heathen, by robbing him in his hour of need of God's promises, and commanding him to abstain for seven days from all study of God's Word. These laws respecting mourning, then, as being oppressive to the poor, insulting to the unlearned, degrading to humanity, and contrary to the express precepts of the Divine law, have no intrinsic merit to commend them to Israel, and no claim upon their obedience.

No. LVI.

DISPENSATION FROM AN OATH.

A RELIGION which is plainly contrary to any of the Divine attributes, must necessarily be false. For instance, God is a holy God: a religion, therefore, which would promote unholiness could not have the Holy One of Israel for its author. God is also a merciful and a just God: a religion, therefore, which is characterized by cruelty or injustice, cannot proceed from him; and for this reason, amongst others, we believe that the religion of the oral law cannot be that true religion which God gave to Moses and the prophets. The oral law is most unjust in its laws respecting Gentiles, slaves, and unlearned men, and most unmerciful in very many of its enactments. But if there be one attribute more than another, which is distinctive of the true God, it is truth. In the prophecies of Jeremiah, He is even identified with truth, as it is said:—

וה׳ אלהים אמת :

"The Lord God is Truth." (Jer. x. 10.) And in that prediction, which he put into the mouth of Balaam, he says, that it is by this attribute that he is distinguished from the sons of men. "God is not a man that he should lie; neither the son of man that he should repent: hath he said, and shall he not do it? or hath he spoken, and shall he not make it good?" (Numbers xxiii. 19.) Men may be wicked enough to promise what they do not intend to perform, or after promising, may change their mind, and refuse to fulfil their engagements; but God is too holy to deceive wilfully, or to alter what has proceeded out of his mouth. A religion, therefore, which in any wise tends to lessen our reverence for truth, or encourages men to alter a solemn engagement, or, what is still worse, teaches how to absolve from oaths, cannot proceed from the God of truth; and this is what the oral law does in certain cases. We do not mean to accuse it of teaching, as the religion of Rome does, that dispensation may be had from every kind of oath. On the contrary, the rabbies assume the power of dispensation only in the case of שבועות בטוי, "rash oaths;" but we mean to assert, that even that assumption is contrary to the Word of God, and injurious to the cause of truth; and, therefore, sufficient to overthrow the credit of the oral law as a religion given by God. The doctrine itself is as follows:—

מי שנשבע שבועת בטוי ונחם על שבועתו וראה
שהוא מצטער אם קיים שבועה זו ונהפכה דעתו
לדעת אחרת, או שנולד לו דבר שלא היה בדעתו
בשעת השבועה וניחם בגללו הרי זה נשאל לחכם
אחד או לשלשה הדיוטות במקום שאין שם חכם
ומתירין לו שבועתו, ויהיה מותר לעשות דבר שנשבע
שלא לעשותו או שלא לעשות דבר שנשבע לעשותו
וזה הוא הנקרא היתר שבועות, ודבר זה אין לו עיקר
כלל בתורה שבכתב, אלא כך למדו ממשה רבינו
מפי הקבלה שזה הכתוב לא יחל דברו שלא יחלל
הוא בעצמו דרך קלות ראש בשאט נפש כענין שנאמר
וחללת את שם אלהיך אבל אם נחם וחזר בו חכם
מתיר לו:

"If any man swear a rash oath, and afterwards repent of it, because he sees that if he keep this oath it will cause him grief, and therefore changes his mind; or if something should occur to him which was not in his mind at the time when he swore, and he repent on that account; behold, a person, in such circumstances, is to ask one wise man (rabbi), or three common men in any place where there is not a wise man, and they absolve him from his oath; and then it will be lawful to do a thing which he had sworn not to do, or to leave undone a thing which he had sworn to do: and this is what is called absolution from oaths. *This matter has no foundation whatever in the written law,* but it has been learned from Moses, our master, by oral tradition, that the Scripture, 'He shall not profane his word,' (Numbers xxx. 3, in the English Bible 2,) means, that a man shall not himself profane his word in a way of levity and with a contemptuous mind, according as it is written, 'Neither shalt thou profane the name of thy God' (Levit. xix. 12); but if a man repent and change his mind, a wise man is to absolve him." (Hilchoth Sh'vuoth, c. vi. 1, 2.) Here it is plainly taught, that if a man has reason to fear any personal inconvenience, or even if he changes his mind, he may escape from the most solemn obligation that can be laid upon the consciences of men; and that, after appealing to God in confirmation of his declaration to do or to leave undone some particular action, one or more of his fellow-sinners can remit his duty to his Creator, and give him a license to do the very contrary of that which he had promised before and unto God, that he would do. Now let every Israelite reader first consult his own reason, and reflect whether this doctrine is agreeable to the character of God, as set forth in the Scripture. The God of the Bible is a God of eternal and immutable truth. One of his peculiar characteristics, that he keepeth covenant and mercy. A man, therefore, who breaks his word, and still more so, a man who breaks an oath, is unlike God. Is it probable, then, that God would give a religion with a special provision for making men unlike himself? Again, God is a God of knowledge, and therefore knows that the children of men are in a great degree the children of habit; he knows also that by habit the evil propensities are strengthened, and that there is in men a strong propensity to shrink from their word, if it cause any trouble or damage: is it likely, then, that God would give a law directly tending to strengthen that evil propensity by forming a habit of breaking one's word, even under the solemn circumstances of an oath? Reason decides that such a law cannot proceed from the God of Israel. Has it then any support in the written Word of God? It would be strange, indeed, if the Word of God should contain anything contrary to reason. As revealing the nature of Him who is incomprehensible, it may contain things above our reason: but that in giving laws for man it should give him license to do what his reason tells him is directly opposed to the character of God, is altogether incredible. The rabbies, themselves, however, do not endeavour to justify the doctrine by a reference to Scripture. They say in plain terms, "*This matter has no foundation whatever in the written law,*" and thus acknowledge that it is altogether a matter of tradition, the argument against it, therefore, becomes doubly strong. Every one knows, that a story loses nothing by passing through many mouths, but that in the course of its progress it gets so many additions, and undergoes so many changes as at last to be scarcely recognisable. This circumstance makes all oral tradition uncertain and unsatisfactory, but is particularly suspicious when it appears, not only opposed to the Scripture character of God, but also favourable to the evil propensities of man. If it had exacted a more scrupulous regard to truth and a willing submission to hardship and inconvenience for the sake of truth, then, as opposing the principles of self-interest, it would have been less suspicious; but when it actually tells men that to do what may save them from worldly trouble or personal disadvantage is a Divine institution, one cannot help suspecting that it is an invention of men, who found it convenient occasionally to escape from the obligation of an oath. But after all, the great arbiter must be the written Word of God. The rabbies say, That it has been learned from Moses by oral tradition, that the words, "He shall not profane his word," mean that a man shall not himself profane his word in a way of levity, but that he shall go to a wise man and get absolution; let us then read the whole verse from which those words are taken:—

איש כי ידור נדר לה' או השבע שבועה לאסר אסר
על נפשו לא יחל דברו ככל היוצא מפיו יעשה:

"If a man vow a vow unto the Lord, or swear an oath to bind his soul with a bond, he shall not break his word, he shall do according to all that proceedeth out of his mouth." Now let any man of common sense and honesty say, whether if it had been God's intention to forbid all absolution from oaths, He could have employed words more to the purpose than these; or whether the plain simple grammatical meaning is not directly opposed to the rabbinic doctrine? God says, If a man swear, he shall not profane his word. The rabbies say, he may profane his word. To prevent all mistake, God further adds, "He shall do according to all that proceeds out of his mouth." The rabbies say, he need not do what proceeds out of his mouth; and yet they have the face to tell us, that their doctrine is from Moses, and is the traditional interpretation of words which signify the very reverse of what they say. It is only wonderful that they should have referred to this verse at all, and the fact can only be accounted for by the supposition that this verse was too plain to be got over, and therefore they thought it best to take the bull by the horns, by selecting this very verse as the basis of their interpretation. That this verse in its grammatical construction is directly opposed to the oral law no one can doubt, for it forbids what the rabbies allow, and commands what the rabbies forbid. But the opposition is not found in this verse only. The other verse to which the rabbies also allude is equally plain against it. The words, " Ye shall not swear by my name falsely, neither shalt thou profane the name of thy God. I am the LORD," plainly forbid that absolution from oaths which the rabbies teach not only as lawful, but as of Divine authority. We know that the rabbies make a distinction between שְׁבוּעַת שֶׁקֶר a false oath and a שְׁבוּעַת בִּטּוּי rash oath; but the distinction, as made by them is unfounded. A rash oath, according to their doctrine, is an oath concerning something which it is possible and lawful for a man to do or to leave undone; for as soon as it interferes with the fulfilment of a Divine command, it belongs to that class of oaths which they call שְׁבוּעוֹת שָׁוְא vain oaths. If, therefore, a man swears to do what is both lawful and possible for him to do, and afterwards draws back and does it not, what man in his senses can doubt, that that individual, no matter what the pretext for not keeping the oath, is guilty of having sworn falsely? What is it to swear falsely, if voluntarily to refuse to do what a man had previously sworn to do, constitute not that sin? A sinful falsehood is a wilful departure from truth; here there is that wilful departure: who, then, will dare to affirm, that such conduct is not contrary to the express command of God? Rabbinists sometimes say, that though the oral law sometimes commands more than is commanded in the Scriptures, it never allows what God has forbidden; but here we have a plain example of the contrary. Here the oral law allows false swearing, which God has positively forbidden. The doctrine of absolution from oaths teaches men to transgress three מִצְוֹת לֹא תַעֲשֶׂה negative precepts. The man who swears to do anything and then does it not, because he has got absolution, violates, first, the negative precept, "He shall not profane his word;" he violates, secondly, the negative precept, "Ye shall not swear by my name falsely;" and, lastly, he violates a negative precept more important than either of the others; and that is, "Neither shalt thou profane the name of thy God." Any man, pretending to religion, who should act upon these principles, first swear and then obtain absolution from his oath, would expose his religion to the contempt and indignation of all honest men, and thereby do all that in him lies to profane the name of his God. Let, then, every Israelite who thinks that the negative precepts are more important than the affirmative, remember, that in this one instance the oral law teaches him to violate three such precepts; and let him reflect further, that the upholding such a law as this is to profane the name of the God of Israel before those who are ignorant of the Scripture.

But the rabbinical doctrine does not stop at prospective absolution, it goes so far as to absolve from the guilt of perjury actually committed:—

מִי שֶׁנִּשְׁבַּע שְׁבוּעָה בִּטּוּי לְהָבָא וְשִׁקֵּר בִּשְׁבוּעָתוֹ,

DISPENSATION FROM AN OATH.

כגון שנשבע שלא יאכל פת זו ואכלה, ואחר שאכלה
קודם שיביא קרבנו אם היה שוגג, או קודם שילקה
אם היה מזיד, נחם ונשאל לחכם והתירה לו הרי
זה פטור כין הקרבן או מן המלקות, ולא עוד אלא
אפילו כפתוהו ללקות ונשאל והתירו לו קודם שיתחילו
להלקותו הרי זה פטור:

" If a man swear a rash oath concerning the future, but lies in that which he has sworn, as, if he should swear not to eat this bread, and afterwards should eat it; and if, after he has eaten it, before he brings his sacrifice, in case he did it ignorantly, or before he is flogged, in case he did it presumptuously—he repent and ask a wise man, and he absolve him, behold such an one is exempt from the sacrifice or from the flogging: and not only so, but if they had actually bound him in order to flog him, and he ask a wise man, and he absolve him before the flogging has commenced, he is exempt." (Ibid. 18.) In this rabbinic decision there are two cases, and both contrary to the Word of God. First, we have the case of the man who has broken his oath ignorantly, and respecting whom God has decided in the following words: " If a soul swear, pronouncing with his lips to do evil, or to do good, whatsoever it be that a man shall pronounce with an oath, and it be hid from him; when he knoweth of it, then he shall be guilty in one of these. And it shall be, when he shall be guilty in one of these things, that he shall confess that he hath sinned in that thing: and he shall bring his trespass-offering unto the Lord for his sin which he hath sinned," &c. (Levit. v. 4, &c.) Here God positively commands, first, that he should confess his sin, and secondly, that he should bring a sacrifice in order to obtain forgiveness; and, by the above law, the rabbies as positively declare that obedience to these commands is superfluous. A man need only say that he has changed his mind, and get a rabbi to absolve him, and then he can set the Word of God at defiance, he need neither confess his sin, nor bring the sacrifice. How can the men who profess such a religion pretend to have any regard for the law of Moses, or how can they with any consistency reproach Christians with the non-observance of the ceremonial precepts, when they themselves profess religious principles which unceremoniously subvert such plain commands? The second case is, however, far more flagrant. It supposes a man to have sworn that he would not do a certain thing, but afterwards wilfully to have done it—that is, it supposes a man to have been guilty of wilful perjury, and yet declares that he may be delivered both from the guilt and the punishment, by going to a rabbi and getting absolution. This oral law, which would flog a poor starving creature for eating Gentile food, or meat and milk together, devises an expedient for delivering him who is guilty of the grave crime of perjury —that is, though cruel to the poor, it is merciful to the criminal. If this be not to violate the laws of God with a high hand, then we know not what sin is. Here both classes of the precepts, negative and affirmative, are treated with the same contempt; both equally trampled under foot. The guilty are absolved, not only from doing what God commands, but from the penalty of actual transgression. The rabbies presume not only to absolve a man from doing what he has sworn to do, but also to turn perjury actually committed into innocence. They have assumed the high prerogative of God, have abrogated his laws, and taught the guilty to set his threatenings at defiance. We verily believe that the mass of the Jewish people have been ignorant of this gross contempt for the Mosaic law, or they could never have continued so long in such a system, nor so long have suffered the name of God to be profaned by the attempt to pass off such a religion as proceeding from Him. Now, then, we call on every reader of this paper to decide whether the oral law can really be from God? Has this doctrine of absolution from oaths anything resembling the character of the Divine Being as a God of truth? Is it possible that God should give an oral law directly subversive of that which he has given in writing; or will any one dare to say that the Almighty, when he wished to give a law permitting absolution from oaths, knew so little of the Hebrew language as to enunciate it in words which directly forbid it? Let no one misunderstand us, as if we applied the passages quoted from the oral law generally to the case of all oaths, or as if we attributed this doctrine of the oral law to all Israel. We do neither the one nor the other; in a future number we hope to consider the case of an oath between man and man, and at present our only intention is to show that the oral law is dishonouring to God, subversive of the commands given by Moses, and injurious to the best interests of the Jewish people; nay, that it is actually a libel on the children of Abraham; and that, therefore, if they have any love to God, any reverence for Moses, and any respect for themselves and their brethren, they are bound publicly to renounce the principles which it inculcates, and by which they have been deluded for so many centuries. It is possible to do one of two things—either to approve the doctrine of absolution from oaths, or to disapprove of it. Those who approve of it will, of course, endeavour to uphold it, and will thereby continue the profanation of God's name; and, so far as they can, stamp dishonour upon the religion of Israel. Those, who disapprove the idea of a rabbi's absolving from a solemn oath, and think that oaths are not to be tampered with, are bound not only to protest against this particular abuse, but to reject the whole oral law. The rabbies declare that this doctrine is not an ordinance of the scribes, but an oral tradition from Moses; if then it be false, the rabbies are again convicted of passing off an invention of their own as an ordinance of God, and are therefore wholly unworthy of credit. The oral law depends altogether upon the validity of the testimony, and if the witnesses can be proved, in any one instance, to have spoken falsehood, the credit of the whole is destroyed. Now this is eminently the case, for not only have they said what is false, but have endeavoured to establish a principle subversive of all reverence for truth. It would be difficult for any man, who was known as one in the habit of getting dispensation from oaths, to find belief or credit in the world, and he would scarcely be admitted as a valid witness in a court of justice; but the man who propounds dispensation from oaths as a religious doctrine, and teaches it systematically as agreeable to the will of God, is a more suspicious person still, and such are the authors of the oral law. The former might be regarded as a deluded person, who only broke his oaths when he got dispensation, but the latter would be considered an artful underminer of principle, and a wilful despiser of truth; his testimony would, therefore, have no weight. Now, it is upon the testimony of such persons that the authority of the oral law entirely depends. It is confessed, that until the Mishna and Gemara were compiled, there was no written record of its contents, but that it was propagated from mouth to mouth. If, therefore, it appear that those who transmitted it were men whose love for truth was equivocal, we cannot be sure that they did not transmit a forgery. The doctrine, which we have just considered, shows that they did not love truth, and that they have actually libelled the memory of Moses, the servant of God, by asserting that he taught them how to get absolution from oaths. It is for the Jews to consider whether they will still be deluded by such incompetent witnesses, and still, even silently, uphold a doctrine so dishonouring to their religion.

No. LVII.

DOCTRINE OF OATHS, CONTINUED.

EVERY one naturally thinks that his own religion is the true one. The Mussulman thinks thus of Mahometanism, the Christian of Christianity, and the Jew of Judaism, and yet it is plain that they cannot all be right—two out of the three must necessarily be in error. What then is to be done? Are they all to go on in listless and lazy indifference, and leave it to another world to find out whether or not they have been in the right, or are we to lay it down as a maxim that every one is to continue in that religion in which he was born, whether right or wrong, and that therefore the Turk is to remain a Mahometan, and the Hindoo an idolater, to his life's end? There are very many in the world who seem to think so, and who adhere to a religion simply because it was the religion of their forefathers. Now we grant that no man should carelessly or lightly abandon the religion of his childhood, and have no scruple in saying that he who changes his religion as he would his clothes must be a fool, or something worse. But we must say, at the same time, that he who retains his religion, merely as a matter of prejudice or interest, is not a great deal better, and can hardly be considered as a rational being. Every being, whom the Creator has endowed with reason, ought to have a religion and to know why he prefers it to all others. But perhaps some reader will say, I have a religion—I am a Jew, and I prefer this religion to all others, because God himself gave it to Moses on Mount Sinai. To this we reply, But how do you know that you have got the religion of Moses? If you really had Moses' religion you could not be wrong, but how can you prove that the religion which you now profess is really that true religion? Your fathers in the times of old often forsook Moses and the Prophets, and taught their children a false religion, how, then, can you be sure that this is not the case with what you have got at present? Certainty can be had only by examination and comparison. The Judaism of the present day must be compared with the Law and the Prophets. If it agrees with them, then the Jews have reason to believe that they are in the right; but if not, then they must be in the wrong. Our own firm conviction is, that modern Judaism is altogether spurious, and plainly opposed to that religion which God gave to your fathers. The doctrine of dispensation from oaths is sufficient to prove this, as was shown in the last number. But we have more objections still to make against that doctrine, and all confirmatory of the conclusion to which we have come. We saw in our last, that if a man swear an oath to himself only, where others are not concerned, he can have absolution, but we now come to consider the case of an oath made to another person, respecting which the oral law teaches us as follows :—

ראובן שהשביע לשמעון וענה אמן או קבל השבועה
ונחם שמעון על שבועתו ונשאל עליה אין מתירין
לו אלא בפני ראובן שהשביעו, וכן אם נשבע ראובן
או נדר שלא יהנה משמעון או שלא יהנה בו שמעון
ונחם ונשאל לחכם אין מתירין לו אלא בפני שמעון
שנדר ממנו הנאה ואפילו היה שמעון קטן אוי גוי אין
מתירין לו אלא בפניו כדי שידע הנידר שהתיר זה
נדרו או שבועתו ולפיכך יהנה ממנו או יהנה לו:

"If Reuben should adjure Simeon, and he answer Amen, or accept the oath; and afterwards Simeon should repent of his oath, and ask concerning it, he is not to be absolved except in the presence of Reuben who adjured him. In like manner, if Reuben should swear an oath not to receive any profit from Simeon, or that Simeon should receive no profit from him, and afterwards should repent and ask a wise man, he is not to be absolved except in the presence of Simeon, concerning whose profit he had vowed: yea, even though Simeon were an infant or a Gentile, he is not to be absolved except in his presence, in order that he, with respect to whom the vow was made, may know that the other has got absolution from his oath or vow, and that therefore he may receive from or confer profit upon him." (Hilchoth Sh'vuoth, c. vi.7.) Now in considering this doctrine, we must not withhold that measure of approbation which is due to the rabbies. There is here a certain degree of honesty and plain dealing. The rabbies have determined that where one man swears to another, he is not to be absolved, except in the presence of that other, and are in so far vastly superior in morality to those who hold and teach, not only that all oaths may be absolved, but that they may be absolved secretly, so that he who is most affected by the dispensation, knows nothing about it. Bad as the oral law is, it does not descend to such a depth of hypocrisy and profaneness. Another trait which deserves notice is, that it does not teach that no faith is to be kept towards those who have got another religion, but expressly determines, that if a Jew swear to a Gentile, he is not to be absolved without that Gentile's knowledge. We readily admit that this is greatly superior to a doctrine of dispensation, taught and practised by some who call themselves Christians; but, having made this admission, and given the rabbies their due, we must also say, that the doctrine of absolution here taught is plainly contrary to reason and Scripture, and if extensively practised, would destroy all confidential intercourse or dealings between man and man. Just suppose that the law of this country was, that any one who had entered into a solemn engagement with another, could be enabled to break it, simply, by calling up the person to whom he had made the promise before a magistrate, and by declaring, in his presence, that he repented of what he had done, who would ever trust another, or value even an oath? Not only would the commercial transactions of the country be at an end, but the very bonds of society would be rent asunder. The existence of human society depends upon that measure of confidence which a man can place in his brother, but if the rabbinical doctrine prevailed and were acted upon, there could be no confidence more. A man's oath would be good for nothing, and if so, the value of his word still less. But, besides this, the doctrine that a rabbi may absolve Simeon from his sworn obligation to Reuben, is absurd. If Simeon swear to Reuben a lawful oath, no one on earth but Reuben can release him; but here we are told that a rabbi, who has nothing at all to do with the matter, may remit the obligation. He might, with as much reason and with less profanity, undertake to absolve Simeon from his pecuniary debts. That the dispensation must take place in the presence of the party to whom Simeon swore, is but poor satisfaction, and would not remove the inconvenience, nor diminish the guilt. Suppose, for instance, that Simeon should promise Reuben with an oath, that within a given time he would complete certain business, or lend him a certain sum of money, or anything else of the kind, and that Reuben should arrange his affairs in dependence upon this oath, what satisfaction would it be to Reuben to be present at the absolution! It would not remove the inconvenience nor indemnify him for the loss to which the non-fulfilment of the oath exposed him, nor abate the vexation and sorrow which he must feel to see a teacher of religion trampling upon the most solemn sanction with which religion guards the intercourse between man and man. For, after all, the main objection to the doctrine is, that it allows what God forbids, as we showed in the last number, and under the pretence of religion, makes perjury systematic.

But to estimate this doctrine fully, and also the character of the men with whom it originated, we must look at the original passage in the Talmud, on which the above-cited decision is founded:—

המודר הנאה מחברו אין מתירין לו אלא בפניו
מנהני מילי אמר רב נחמן דכתיב ויאמר ה' אל משה
במדין לך שוב מצרימה כי מרו כל האנשים אמר לו
במדין נדרת לך וחתר נדרך במדין דכתיב ויואל
משה אין אלוז אלא שבועה דכתיב ויבא אותו באלה

DOCTRINE OF OATHS, CONTINUED. 445

וגם במלך נבוכדנצר מרד אשר השביעו באלהים חיים
מאי מרדותיה אשכחיה צדקיהו לנבוכדנצר דהוה
קאכיל ארנבת חייא אמר ליה אישתבע לי דלא מגלית
עלוי ולא תיפוק מילתא אישתבע ליה לסוף הוה קא
מצטער צדקיהו בגופיה איתשיל אשבועתיה ואמר שמע
נבוכדנצר דקא מבזין ליה שלח ואייתי סנהדרין
וצדקיהו אמר להון חזיתין מאי קא עביד צדקיהו לאו
הכי אישתבע בשמא דשמיא דלא מגלינא אמר ליה
איתשלי אשבעתיה ואמר ליה מתשלין אשבועתא]
אמרי ליה אין אמר להו בפניו או שלא בפניו אמרי
בפניו וכו' :

"He that has a vow upon him, with respect to profit from his neighbour, is not to be absolved, except in that neighbour's presence. How is this proved? Rav Nachman says, it is proved by the words, 'And the Lord said unto Moses, in Midian, Go return into Egypt; for all the men are dead which sought thy life;' he said to him, In Midian thou hast vowed, go and get absolution from thy vow in Midian, for it is written, וַיּוֹאֶל מֹשֶׁה, 'And Moses was content.' (Exodus ii. 21.) Now this word means nothing else but swearing, as it is written, 'And he took an oath of him.' (Ezek. xvii. 13.) It is further proved by the words, 'And he also rebelled against King Nebuchadnezzar, who had made him swear by God.' (2 Chron. xxxvi. 13.) What was the nature of his rebellion? Zedekiah found Nebuchadnezzar eating a live hare, whereupon Nebuchadnezzar said to him, swear to me not to reveal this, nor to report the matter. Zedekiah swore, but afterwards he was grieved, and went and got his oath absolved and told. Nebuchadnezzar heard that they despised him, and sent and fetched the Sanhedrin and Zedekiah, and said to them, Ye see what Zedekiah has done, although he swore by the name of God not to reveal the matter. They said to him, He got a dispensation from his oath. He said, Is it lawful, then, to get dispensation from an oath? They said, Yes. He said again, Is this to be done in the other's presence or absence? They say, In his presence," &c. (Nedarim, fol. lxv. 1.) Now this passage not only illustrates the doctrine of dispensation, but throws much light upon the character and knowledge of the men from whom the tradition is derived. In the first place, it shows a strange confusion of mind to derive וַיּוֹאֶל, "he was willing,' from אלה, "he sware;" but it is stranger still out of this mistranslation, to invent a story of Moses having sworn and got absolution; but the most strange of all is, that any one should be found who can believe this a sufficient warrant for the doctrine of dispensation from an oath made to a fellow-creature. If even it were true, as the rabbies say, that Moses had sworn to Jethro not to return into Egypt, still this is not a case in point; for Moses did not get absolution from any third person, but received express permission from Jethro himself to return, as we find in the chapter referred to, where it is said, "And Moses went and returned to Jethro, his father-in-law, and said unto him, Let me go, I pray thee, and return unto my brethren which are in Egypt, and see whether they be yet alive. And Jethro said to Moses, Go in peace." (Exod. iv. 18.) If there was any oath, we see that it was dispensed with, not by a wise man, nor by any third person or persons, but by him to whom the oath was made. This passage is, therefore, decidedly against the rabbinic doctrine, and therefore the rabbinic doctrine cannot be true. The second case cited by the Talmud is still stronger, as a testimony, both against the system and the men. It tells us that Zedekiah swore to Nebuchadnezzar not to betray him in a certain matter, which no law, either of God or man, compelled him to divulge —that he swore by the name of the God of Israel, and yet that, after this most solemn transaction, he did what he had sworn not to do. He betrayed a man from whom he had received kindness, and equally disregarded the obligations of gratitude and the sacred ties of an oath—in short, that he committed perjury. This is in itself bad enough; but the Talmud proceeds further to tell us, that this was not his own individual act, but the solemn decision of the Supreme Council of the Sanhedrin. Zedekiah did not perjure himself without having advice. He went to the Sanhedrin, and they absolved him from the obligation of the oath, and that contrary to their own maxim, that an oath sworn to a neighbour cannot be absolved, except in his presence. Here, then, the Talmud plainly confesses that the Sanhedrin did wrong, in fact, that they were aiders and abettors in Zedekiah's perjury; that, therefore, they were men who had no regard to truth, and no fear of God; and, consequently, that no man of any common sense would believe a single word that came out of their mouths. What, then, becomes of the whole fabric of Jewish tradition? It depends altogether upon the unimpeachable character of the various Sanhedrins through whose hands it passed. If, therefore, we should find that any one Sanhedrin consisted of notorious liars, the genuineness of the oral law is at an end. But here the Talmud itself tells us that even before the deportation of Zedekiah, the Sanhedrin consisted, not of common liars, but of false swearers, of men who had so little regard for the name of the Lord, as to absolve a solemn oath of which that name was the safeguard. If they had done this in accordance with their traditions, there would be some appearance of consistency, but they did it in the face of the tradition, which says, that when an oath is sworn to another person absolution cannot be given except in his presence. When Zedekiah demanded absolution, they should have refused, and told him that it was contrary to the oral law; but, whether from fear or from self-interest, they acceded to the king's wish, and helped him to commit perjury: and these are the men who have handed down the oral law; what trust, then, can be placed in their word, when they disregard an oath? The story is either true or false. If true, then all the members of the Sanhedrin were guilty of perjury,—if false, then the Talmud has handed down a falsehood as truth, and in neither case is it worthy of credit. Surely it is time for the chosen people of God to use the reason which God has given, and to examine the grounds upon which they profess Judaism. The ignorant and the thoughtless may retain their profession as a mere matter of prejudice, but it would be very strange if any, who think religion worth a thought, should still adhere to a system for which there is not only no evidence, but against which there is evidence so satisfactory. According to the Talmud itself, and on its own showing, the persons whose office it was to guard the traditions in the days of Zedekiah were men who transgressed those traditions, and made themselves guilty of perjury; what warrant, then, have the Jews for believing that those men did not change the traditions, and hand down mere inventions of their own? What was there to restrain them from such conduct, if they could free themselves from the obligation of an oath by the name of the God of Israel?

But as the men who handed down the traditions are described by their own successors as wicked and ungodly persons, so the traditions which they have handed down are of the same character, and, as we have said, if generally acted upon, would rend asunder all the ties of human society, and beget universal distrust and suspicion. The oral law plainly and unequivocally allows a man to swear to his neighbour that he will do or leave undone something that his neighbour requires, and then to get absolution from that oath and do the contrary. It is true that it requires this to be done in the presence of the other person, but that does not much alter the matter. Whether Zedekiah divulged what he had sworn to Nebuchadnezzar to keep secret, in his presence or behind his back, is a thing of very little consequence; the oath is just as much and as really broken, and the results might be just as pernicious and injurious. Take, for example, the case of a manufacturer who communicates to his servant some important secret in his trade, and for his own security binds him by an oath not to divulge it. In a little time, the servant, for some reason or other, finds it convenient or profitable to make this secret known, and goes to a wise man, summons the manufacturer to be present, gets absolution, and then divulges what he had sworn to keep secret,—where is the difference as to all practical purposes, or as to the actual guilt of perjury? But again, suppose that the wise man was to act as the Sanhedrin did, and absolve the man without summoning the person to whom he swore, it is a question whether the servant would then be bound. Zedekiah evidently thought not. All he was concerned about was to have absolution, and if there was any sin in giving it, he evidently thought that the onus rested upon those who gave, and not upon him who received it. According to the oral law, the Sanhedrin was wrong in giving absolution under the circumstances: but, according to the same oral law, Zedekiah was right in obeying their decision. Implicit and universal obedience to the words of the Sanhedrin and wise men is required by the Talmud; and, therefore, if a wise man give absolution, even though he give it unlawfully, it is still the duty of him who is absolved to obey his decision, and act upon it. A Rabbinist is not allowed to reason; but as we have seen on a former occasion, to believe that his right hand is his left, and *vice versa*, if the rabbies say so—and, consequently, if a wise man absolve him, he is not to trouble either his conscience or his reason as to the right or the wrong; his duty is not to dispute, but to receive the determination as the words of the living God. The provision, therefore, that if Simeon swear to Reuben he is not to be absolved, except in Reuben's presence, affords but little protection. If it was possible for the Sanhedrin, a body consisting of seventy-one persons, to disregard it, it is surely possible that any other wise man might disregard it also, and absolve Simeon, even in Reuben's absence. Now the bare possibility of such occurrences would make all promises, whether sanctioned by oaths or not, of no value, and have the most pernicious effect as to the practice of speaking truth. Men might reason from the greater to the less, and say, If it be lawful, by means of absolution, to break an oath, וחומר קל, *à fortiori*, it is lawful to break one's word without absolution; and, at all events, those to whom the promise was given would be likely to reason thus, and say, If we cannot depend upon this man's oath, much less can we place confidence in his word. But what is worse still, such a doctrine is calculated to make men despise all religion, and to render them a prey to infidelity. The thoughtless and the rash are very likely to say, If this be religion, better far to be without it; or, to conclude that as such doctrine cannot possibly be the offspring of the Divine mind, all revealed religion is a mere imposture. In every case it is a reproach to the good sense and piety of Israel to profess such a doctrine; or, if they do not believe it, to remain silent, and suffer mankind to suppose that this is the religion of the children of Abraham. So long as they profess that the oral law is the source of their religion, so long are they responsible for the doctrines which it teaches; and so long as they abstain from a public renunciation of the oral law, they must be considered as believers in its authority. It will not do to renounce one particular doctrine, whilst they profess faith in the general system. The body of traditions is a whole which cannot be parted. They have all come down, resting on the same evidence; if, therefore, the evidence be invalid in any one case, it is invalid in all; and if any one admits its validity in some cases, he cannot, if a reasonable man, deny it in others. He may dispute about the conflicting opinions of the rabbies, but if he admit any one of those doctrines which are called traditions from Sinai, he must admit them all, and, consequently, this which professes to be one of them. It remains, therefore, for the Israelites of the present day to choose, whether they will still retain the system of the oral law, and thereby sanction the dispensation from oaths, or whether they will repudiate this doctrine, and thereby renounce the whole oral law.

No. LVIII.

MERITORIOUSNESS OF CIRCUMCISION.

WHEREVER there is an internal principle of religion, it will, like all other principles, manifest itself in external acts, and in an external form of rites and ceremonies. It is just as impossible for a living man to continue without giving any signs of life, as for the religious principle to exist without an outward expression. It is the universal law of creation that every vital principle should manifest itself, and therefore, when the Creator himself was pleased to give a religion, he ordained certain rites and ceremonies to give notice of its existence, and to serve as the body in which the soul should reside. Rites and ceremonies, therefore, are not to be despised, even when devised by man, for they are demonstrations of an internal life from which they proceed; but when instituted by God, they are doubly important, because besides being a sign, they have all the authority of a Divine command. False religion, however, is not satisfied with this acknowledgment, nor this measure of reverence. It goes still further, and elevates the external sign above the thing signified, by making the external rites the great essentials of religion. Thus, in the time of the Prophet Isaiah, the Israelites thought that the act of sacrifice, and the external observation of the Sabbath and holidays, formed the substance of religion, and therefore God told them, that even these things, though ordained by himself, were not pleasing in his sight, unless they proceeded from the living principle within. "Bring no more vain oblations: incense is an abomination unto me; the new moons and Sabbaths, the calling of assemblies, I cannot away with; it is iniquity, even the solemn meeting." (Isaiah i. 13.) And again in a subsequent chapter he says, "They seek me daily, and delight to know my ways, as a nation that did righteousness and forsook not the ordinances of their God: they ask of me the ordinances of justice; they take delight in approaching to God." (lviii. 2.) And yet at the same time he shows that this was all mere outside work, and displeasing in his sight. Wherever, therefore, we find a religion, which places external observances above the moral duties, we may be sure it is not of God; and for this reason, amongst others, we believe that the oral law is the invention of men. We had an instance in the subject last considered, the dispensation from oaths. The rabbies disregard the moral obligation, but make the mere form of going to a rabbi to get absolution an essential requisite. Another proof is furnished by their doctrine concerning *The meritoriousness of Circumcision*, which is set forth as follows:—

מצות עשה לכל אדם מישראל שימול את בנו
וגדולה היא משאר מצוות עשה שיש בה צד כרת,
וגם נכרתו עליה שלש עשרה בריתות בפרשת מילה,
ולא נקרא אברהם שלם עד שנימול ובזכותה נכרתה
לו ברית על נתינת הארץ והיא מצלת מדינה של
גיהנם כמו שאמרו חכמים שאברהם אבינו יושב
בפתחה של גהינם ואינו מניח ליכנס בו לכל מי
שנימול, ומאוסה היא הערלה שנתגנו בה הגוים
שנאמר כי כל הגוים ערלים, וכל המפר בריתו של
אברהם או שמושך ערלתו אע״פ שיש בידו תורה
ומעשים טובים אין לו חלק לעולם הבא:

"It is an affirmative precept, binding on every man of Israel, to circumcise his son; and this is greater than any of the other affirmative precepts, for there is a threat of excision attached to it; and further, on account of it, thirteen covenants were made, as is recorded in the chapter of circumcision. Abraham was not called perfect until he was circumcised, and by the merit of circumcision, a covenant was made with him respecting the giving of the land. It also delivers from the judgment of hell, for the wise men have said, that Abraham our father sits at the door of hell, and does not suffer any one that is circumcised to be cast into it. Uncircumcision is despised, for the Gentiles are reproached with it, as it is said, 'All the nations are uncircumcised' (Jer. ix. 25); and every one who breaks the covenant of Abraham our father, either by not being circumcised or by becoming uncircumcised, has no part in the world to come, even though he possess a knowledge of the law and good works." (Joreh Deah., 260.) Here we have the very same misconception, which God reproved by the mouth of Isaiah; an external act is preferred to holiness of life, and a mere preparation of the body to purity of heart. It is gravely and solemnly asserted that the precept concerning circumcision is greater than all the other affirmative precepts, that is, it is exalted above our duty to God and our duty to our neighbour. The command

ואהבת לרעך כמוך

"Thou shalt love thy neighbour as thyself," is an affirmative precept, and is therefore one of those to which circumcision is preferred. The command

כבד את אביך ואת אמך

"Honour thy father and thy mother," is an affirmative precept, and has a promise of long life in the land attached to it. It concerns our duty to those, to whom, under God, we owe our existence, and yet the oral law teaches that obedience to it is not so important as to the precept concerning circumcision. We do not mean to deny the scriptural importance of circumcision, nor of any other of the Divine institutions, but we do mean to appeal to every Israelite of understanding to judge, which of these commandments is of most importance. Can an Israelite, merely because he is circumcised, though he has no love to his fellow-men, and no reverence for his parents, be acceptable in the sight of God, or can he be more acceptable than a Gentile who obeys these commands? But the sweeping declaration of the oral law, not only teaches men that circumcision is more valuable than love to man, but exalts it even above love to God. The commandment, "Thou shalt love the Lord thy God, with all thy heart," &c., is an affirmative precept, and is consequently included amongst those which are stated to be inferior to circumcision. This conclusion seems so monstrous, that one is almost afraid of having misunderstood the sense; but Rashi, who must be acknowledged as an authority, goes still farther, and endeavours to prove that circumcision is equal in importance to all the other commandments put together.

שהיא שקולה כנגד כל המצוות שבתורה :

"It is equivalent to all the commandments which are in

the law." (Nedarim, fol. 31, col. ii.) So that there can be no doubt that this is the doctrine of the oral law. Now just let the reader consider the nature of circumcision. It is, in the first place, an external act,—it is, in the second place, an act performed without the will of the infant, and at a time when he can exercise no act of moral responsibility, and yet the mere act is placed above the highest perfection of a created being, love to God and his fellow-creatures. But the oral law does not merely assert this doctrine, but gives its proofs, and the first is, that to the precept of circumcision the threat of excision is annexed. Of course, we admit the fact, for it is plainly said, "The uncircumcised man-child, whose flesh of his foreskin is not circumcised, that soul shall be cut off from his people; he hath broken my covenant" (Gen. xvii. 14); but we deny the consequence. There is nothing peculiar to circumcision in the annexed threat of excision. God has pronounced the same threat against every presumptuous sin, as it is written, "But the soul that doeth ought presumptuously, whether he be born in the land or a stranger, the same reproacheth the Lord; and that soul shall be cut off from among his people. Because he hath despised the word of the Lord, and hath broken his commandment, that soul shall be utterly cut off; his iniquity shall be upon him." (Numb. xv. 30, 31.) Here we see that presumptuous transgression of any one of God's commandments will be visited with the same punishment denounced against the omission of circumcision, so that the annexed threat is far from proving that this precept is superior to all the other affirmative commandments. On the contrary, it shows that God does not judge by the external act, but by the state of the heart, and that presumptuous disobedience of any commandment, as demonstrating an utter want of love to him, will be visited with the severity of his wrath. It is further alleged, "That Abraham was not called perfect until he was circumcised,"—and this is proved in the Talmud, by the words, "Walk before me, and be thou perfect." But these words do not prove that, even after his circumcision, Abraham was called perfect; they are a command to be perfect, but not a declaration that he was so; and it cannot be urged that by being circumcised he obeyed this command, and thus became perfect, for this would open an easy way of attaining perfection to the most abandoned of mankind. Besides, it is easy to prove that this word "perfect" is also given to the uncircumcision. Long before circumcision was given, it was applied to Noah. "Noah was a just man, and perfect in his generations, and Noah walked with God" (Gen. vi. 9), where that which is only commanded to Abraham, is asserted to have been found in Noah. God commanded to Abraham to walk with him, and to be perfect; but he declares of the uncircumcised Noah, that he was perfect, and did walk with him. In this respect, therefore, even if the rabbinic interpretation of the words were correct, circumcision has no superiority over uncircumcision. The next proof, namely, "That by the merit of circumcision a covenant was made with Abraham, respecting the giving of the land," is equally inconclusive. Long before the covenant of circumcision God had promised the land to Abraham, and that repeatedly; and not only had promised it, but had actually made a covenant with him respecting the gift, as we read, "In the same day, the Lord made a covenant with Abram, saying, Unto thy seed have I given this land, from the river of Egypt unto the great river, the river Euphrates." (Gen. xvi. 18.) This covenant was made before the birth of Ishmael; and when Ishmael was born, Abraham was eighty-six years of age; consequently, it was at least fourteen years before circumcision, so that the assertion that the covenant respecting the land was made on account of the merit of circumcision is altogether false. God made the covenant, not because Abraham deserved it, but according to his own grace and mercy, when Abraham had no bodily mark to distinguish him from the surrounding nations. Here again, then, the oral law asserts what is false. But the rabbies were not contented with Scripture proof; they felt that the letter of Scripture was against them, and therefore had recourse to their own invention, and have devised the fable that "Circumcision delivers from the judgment of hell, for that Abraham sits at the door of hell, and does not suffer any one that is circumcised to be cast into it." That this is a regular and wilful falsehood, no one that has reason, and takes the Scripture to guide it, can possibly doubt. It implies that many who are circumcised deserve the punishment of hell, and are led to the very door, but that Abraham interferes, and delivers them from their just punishment. If they did not deserve it, and were not liable to it, there could be no necessity for Abraham's sitting in so unpleasant a situation. The guilt of these persons is, therefore, fully admitted, and yet the wise men say, that out of regard to the mere external token of the covenant, God gives up his attribute of justice, and acquits those who deserve punishment. But it implies further, that God does not deal thus to the Gentiles—that to them he exercises all justice, and shows no mercy. Abraham looks on with unconcern when a Gentile is brought to the place of the damned, feels no compassion and exercises none, and the Divine Being himself is made a party in this injustice, and want of compassion. Religion is misrepresented as a mere system of favouritism, and the Judge of all the earth as a doer of wrong. That this is the plain drift of the story is plain from what follows: "Circumcision is despised, for the Gentiles are reproached with it, as it is said, 'All the nations are uncircumcised.'" Here the rabbies plainly tell us, that God despises the works of his own hands, that he disdains the overwhelming majority of his rational creatures, and that not because of their wickedness, or their cruelty, or their idolatry, or their profanity, but because they have not got a commandment which He never gave them. The rabbies themselves will admit that God never gave the Gentiles the commandment of circumcision, how then is it possible that he should blame them, or despise them, or treat them with unmitigated severity, because they have not got what He never gave them? If it had been offered to them, and they had refused, there would have been some ground for such a representation, but at present there is none. It is not true that God reproaches the Gentiles in the words, "All the nations are uncircumcised;" on the contrary, He is reproaching Israel. The context is, "Behold the days come, saith the Lord, that I will punish all them which are circumcised with the uncircumcised; Egypt, and Judah, and Edom, and the children of Ammon and Moab, and all that are in the utmost corners, that dwell in the wilderness; for all the nations are uncircumcised, and all the house of Israel are uncircumcised in the heart." (Jer. ix. 25, 26.) This is very different doctrine from that of the rabbies. God declares that the mere outward sign of circumcision shall not save from punishment; that he makes no difference whatever between the uncircumcised and the circumcised, but that he looks upon the heart, and deals out to all evenhanded justice. He says, that he will punish the idolatrous nations, whom he has enumerated, but declares that he will punish the sinners of Israel along with them, and then to obviate the very objection which the oral law urges, and to take away all false confidence in circumcision, he adds, "The nations are uncircumcised, and all the house of Israel are uncircumcised in heart;" as if he would have said, Do not deceive yourselves, thinking that your circumcision will save you: there is a worse uncircumcision than that of the flesh, the uncircumcision of the heart. This is doctrine worthy of the Divine Being, consistent with his attributes of justice and holiness, and consolatory and encouraging to all his rational creatures; whereas the rabbinic doctrine is dishonouring to God, and contemptuous to all the Gentile nations. If it were believed, no Gentile would have any motive to serve or honour the true God, from whom he could expect neither justice nor mercy. It is equally pernicious and destructive to the moral and spiritual welfare of the Israelites themselves. Any man who believes that his circumcision will save him from hell, will feel himself at liberty to violate other commands without fear. Why should he be holy, or chaste, or honest, or true? His father Abraham is sitting at the gate of hell waiting for him, and will deliver him from the just reward of his delinquencies. We do not mean to attribute such reasoning to all Israelites—far from it; but it is certain that on the minds of the ignorant and superstitious this doctrine must have this effect. Those who are acquainted with the Word of God, or know how to reason, must believe that it is false, but then it is their duty not only to disbelieve it in their hearts, but to renounce it publicly, and to teach the ignorant and uneducated that it is false. Israelites often feel justly indignant at the want of due appreciation which characterizes public opinion with regard to the nation, but let them reflect on the causes, and they will cease to wonder. Mankind in general does not distinguish between the Jews and Judaism, but erroneously attribute, without any discrimination, the errors of the system to the men; and how can they do otherwise, so long as the oral law is still upheld as a Divine code of law? Let Israel renounce the errors publicly, and all the causes of misconception will be removed.

But we would ask our readers to go a little farther, and compare the doctrines of Christianity on this subject with those of the oral law. They will find that where the rabbies have erred, the disciples of Jesus of Nazareth have taught the truth. St. Paul admits the importance and the privileges of circumcision. He asks, "What advantage then hath the Jew? or what profit is there of circumcision?" And answers, "Much every way: chiefly, because that unto them were committed the oracles of God." (Rom. iii. 1.) He does not undervalue God's mercy to Israel, but at the same time he honours God's justice and holiness, by declaring that "God will render to every man according to his deeds: to them who by patient continuance in well doing seek for glory and honour and immortality, eternal life: but unto them that are contentious, and do not obey the truth, but obey unrighteousness, indignation and wrath, tribulation and anguish, upon every soul of man that doeth evil, of the Jew first, and also of the Gentile; but glory, honour, and peace, to every man that worketh good, to the Jew first, and also to the Gentile: for there is no respect of persons with God." (Romans ii. 6—11.) This exactly agrees with the words of Jeremiah, and with the character of God, as set forth by Moses and the Prophets, and must commend itself to the mind of every reflecting person. Let then those who reject Christianity account for the fact, that where the rabbies are wrong, the preachers of Christianity are right. If all truth come from God, and unassisted human reason must go wrong, how is it that

God should have helped Christians to the truth, and left the Jews in deadly error for so many centuries?

Judaism teaches that the Gentiles are despised, simply because they have not got an outward sign, which God never intended they should have. Christianity proclaims that God is a just Judge. It says, "Circumcision verily profiteth, if thou keep the law; but if thou be a breaker of the law, thy circumcision is made uncircumcision. Therefore if the uncircumcision keep the righteousness of the law, shall not his uncircumcision be counted for circumcision?" Judaism teaches that Abraham sits at the gate of hell to deliver even the wicked, if they be only circumcised. Christianity teaches that Abraham has no respect to the outward sign, unless it be accompanied by purity of heart. "There was a certain rich man, which was clothed in purple and fine linen, and fared sumptuously every day: and there was a certain beggar named Lazarus, which was laid at his gate, full of sores. And it came to pass that the beggar died, and was carried by the angels into Abraham's bosom: the rich man also died, and was buried; and in hell he lifted up his eyes, being in torments, and seeth Abraham afar off, and Lazarus in his bosom. And he cried and said, Father Abraham, have mercy on me, and send Lazarus, that he may dip the tip of his finger in water, and cool my tongue; for I am tormented in this flame. But Abraham said, Son, remember that thou in thy lifetime receivedst thy good things, and likewise Lazarus evil things; but now he is comforted, and thou art tormented. And beside all this, between us and you there is a great gulf fixed: so that they which would pass from hence to you cannot; neither can they pass to us, that would come from thence. Then he said, I pray thee therefore, father, that thou wouldest send him to my father's house: for I have five brethren; that he may testify unto them, lest they also come into this place of torment. Abraham said unto him, They have Moses and the prophets; let them hear them. And he said, Nay, father Abraham: but if one went to them from the dead, they will repent. And he said unto him, If they hear not Moses and the prophets, neither will they be persuaded, though one rose from the dead." (Luke xvi. 19—31.) Let the reader compare this with the rabbinic doctrine, and then explain why it is that where the oral law errs, God has given the truth in the New Testament.

No. LIX.

CRUELTY TO THE UNLEARNED.

THE great object of these papers has been to compare Judaism, as it at present exists, with the religion of Moses and the Prophets, and thus to ascertain whether the Jews of the present day walk in the good old paths pointed out to their forefathers. We have endeavoured to give our reasons for believing that the Jews have been imposed upon by the inventors of the oral law, and have now got a religion diametrically opposed to that which was revealed to them by God. More than a year has elapsed since the first of these papers was published, and yet no answer has appeared. This silence may be attributed to one of three causes. Either there has been a want of sufficient zeal on the part of those who profess Judaism—or, prudence has suggested that the system would not bear discussion—or, these papers have been thought unworthy of notice. It is for the Jewish people at large to consider, which of these three reasons have influenced the champions of the oral law. The Jews certainly have a right to some explanation from those, whose learning and station point them out as the natural defenders of Judaism. Every reflecting man must be staggered by the fact, that a strong case has been made out against the oral law—that, contemporaneously with the publication of these papers, strong symptoms of dissatisfaction with certain parts of Judaism have been manifested in one of the most respectable synagogues in London—and yet, that nothing has appeared, either in the shape of defence or explanation. That this silence has not proceeded altogether from contempt is made probable by another fact, and that is, That it is confidently asserted that a public answer was given orally to the first number, and that this answer was satisfactory to those who heard it. It is much to be regretted that the answer was not made known generally, so as to afford the same satisfaction to others. For ourselves, we should have been most happy, if convinced of error, to have retracted any erroneous charge. We have, in the interval, frequently considered the subject which is said to have been answered; and now consider it our duty, before closing this series, to make known our reasons for still believing, that that one topic is in itself sufficient to prove that the religion of the oral law is a system of error. Our arguments were simply these. A religion which despises and insults the unlearned cannot be from God. The oral law does despise and insult the unlearned, for it commands its disciples not to marry the daughters of the unlearned on the ground that they are no better than beasts. There-

x

fore the oral law cannot be from God. Secondly, a religion which makes the murder of an unlearned man lawful, cannot be from God. The oral law does make it lawful, for, as we showed in No. 1, Rabbi Eleazer says, That it is lawful even on the most solemn day of the Jewish year, to kill an unlearned man without observing any of the technicalities of the rabbinic art of slaughtering; or, as another says, to rend him asunder like a fish. Therefore the oral law cannot be from God. We now proceed to show why we still think that that line of argument is valid.

The first step is, to establish the meaning of the expression עַם הָאָרֶץ *Amhaaretz*, which we translated "an unlearned man." The literal English of this expression is, "People of the land," it might therefore signify the inhabitants of Canaan, but in the Bible it is more commonly used of the mass of the Israelitish people, as for instance:—

וכל עם הארץ שמח ותוקע בחצוצרות :

"And all the people of the land rejoiced, and blew with trumpets." (2 Kings xi. 14. See also verses 18—20.) Here the expression is opposed to king and princes, and evidently means the mass of the population, or, as some would say, "The common people." And, again, to give an example from the Prophets:—

ועתה חזק זרבבל נאם ה׳ וחזק יהושע בן יהוצדק הכהן הגדול וחזק כל עמי הארץ :

"Yet now be strong, O Zerubbabel, saith the Lord; and be strong, O Joshua, son of Josedech, the high priest; and be strong, all ye people of the land." (Hag. ii. 4.) Here, also, the expression is opposed to the governor of Judah and the high priest, and plainly signifies the mass of the population. In the oral law, it has much the same signification; it stands for those who are not counted amongst the learned, nor the great men of the time, nor the almoners, nor the schoolmasters, as appears in the extract given in page 7, with this difference, that in the oral law the want of learning is a prominent idea, and the expression may therefore be applied to a high priest if he be unlearned. In further proof we might appeal to the common parlance of the Jews, even at this day, for they commonly call an unlearned man an *Amhaaretz*. We prefer, however, giving one or two extracts more from the laws, where the expression *Amhaaretz* is put in opposition to "The disciple of a wise man," that is, to a learned man. We read, for instance, that in a court of justice,

דין תלמיד חכם קודם לדין עם הארץ :

"The cause of the disciple of a wise man takes precedence of the cause of an Amhaaretz." (Hilchoth Sanhedrin, c. xxi. 6.) Again,

וכן אסור לו לנהוג בהן קלות ראש אע״פ שהן עמי
הארץ, ולא יפסיע על ראשי עם הקודש אע״פ שהן
הדיוטות ושפלים בני אברהם יצחק ויעקב הם:

"In like manner, it is unlawful for an elder to behave with levity to the congregation, even though they be Amharatzin. Neither let him behave haughtily to the holy people, for although they be common and humble persons, they are children of Abraham, Isaac, and Jacob." (Ibid., c. 25.) Again,

לפיכך כשמלמדין את הקטנים ואת הנשים וכל
עמי הארץ אין מלמדין אותן אלא לעבוד מיראה וכדי
לקבל שכר וכו׳:

"Therefore, when children and women, and the whole genus of Amharatzin, are instructed, they are to be taught to serve God only from the motive of fear, and the desire to receive a reward until," &c. (Hilchoth T'shuvah, c. x. 5.) In these passages, and many, many more may be added, *Amhaaretz* plainly signifies an unlearned man, and it does not appear from any one, that there is any crime to be laid to his charge. He may appear as suitor in a court of law; he is considered as a son of Abraham, Isaac, and Jacob; he is put on a level with the children and the women of Israel. The only disparagement is, that he has not been brought up at the feet of a learned rabbi, and, therefore, cannot be reckoned amongst the disciples of the wise men.

The next thing to be established is, that the oral law despises and insults those whose misfortune it is to be unlearned; and here, in addition to the complement paid to their wives and daughters, noticed in No. 1, we bring, as a proof, the general rule which is given respecting their treatment:—

תנו רבנן ששה דברים נאמרו בעמי הארץ אין
מוסרין להן עדות ואין מקבלין מהן עדות ואין מגלין
להן סוד ואין ממנין אותן אפוטרופוס על היתומים
ואין ממנין אותן אפוטרופוס על קופה של צדקה ואין
מתלוין עמהן בדרך וי״א אף אין מכריזין על אבדתן:

"Our rabbies have handed down as a tradition, that six things are said with respect to Amharatzin. Testimony is not to be given to them, nor received from them. A secret is not to be revealed to them. They are not to be appointed as guardians to orphans, nor to an alms-fund. One is not to bear them company in the way. And some say, that if they have lost any thing, and it is found, no public notice is to be given respecting it." (Pesachim, fol. 49, col. 2.) Here, then, the unlearned are branded as liars, whose word is not to be depended upon—as rogues, unfit to be trusted with property—as murderers, with whom it is unsafe to walk by the way-side. Can contempt or insult add more? Yes; rabbinic contempt had one insult more galling than these, and that was to put them on a level with Gentiles, and this it has done by forbidding public notice to be given, if any thing which they had lost should be found. Now, we fear not to assert, that this one passage is fatal to the claims of the oral law. There is not a particle of resemblance in it to the merciful and just religion made known by Moses. It is the effusion of a mind intoxicated with self-conceit and arrogance. The authors of the oral law were determined, so far as they could, to lay it down as a maxim, not only that no wisdom, but no truth, no honesty, and no humanity, was to be found, except amongst themselves, and their disciples; they wished to have the monopoly of all moral virtue, as well as of all learning. We ask both the learned and the unlearned, whether it be possible that such a law could have emanated from the God of Israel? But there is not only excessive arrogance, there is also gross injustice in their law. It is ordained, first, that in a court of law, the cause of the learned is to be heard before the cause of the unlearned; this is in itself most unjust, but is not to be compared with what follows. The oral law forbids the appointment of an unlearned man as guardian to orphans; can any thing be more oppressive? Suppose that an unlearned man, on his death-bed, thinks of a guardian for his orphan children, and looks to a brother, or an intimate friend, as unlearned as himself, but whose worth, and honesty, and affection, he has long known and valued; the oral law forbids him to make such an appointment; and if he has no learned friend—and how, where such a law exists, is it ever possible that the learned and the unlearned should be friends?—he must die with the agonizing thought, that his children must be left to the guardianship of a perfect stranger. Is it possible to conceive anything more oppressive, unjust, or cruel? But the oral law is not content with this; it will not permit an unlearned man, even in his lifetime, to recover property that has been lost. Whoever finds it may keep it. The law for other people is, that if any thing be found, the finder is to have proclamation made in the city, or, if the majority of the inhabitants be Gentiles, in the synagogue, that the loser may hear of it. But the poor Amhaaretz is excluded from the benefit of this command. It may, however, puzzle the reader, how the finder is to know whether the thing which he has found belongs to a learned or an unlearned man. One of the commentators has solved this difficulty in the following manner:—

CRUELTY TO THE UNLEARNED. 461

ואיה מאין יודע שהוא של עם הארץ ואמר ר׳
יצחק כגון ששיירא של עם הארץ עוברת וראינו
שנפל מהם :

"If you ask, How is the finder to know that the thing found belongs to an Amhaaretz? R. Isaac says, it is in such a case as when a crowd of Amharatzin is passing, and we see that it fell from them." (Ibid.) So that, according to this interpretation, the disciples of the wise men are positively allowed to retain what they know does not belong to them, if they only see that it does belong to an unlearned man; and yet these are the men who are so afraid of the dishonesty of the unlearned, as to forbid their appointment to the office of guardian to orphans, or treasurer to a charitable fund. Let any man of common sense decide, whether this law is honest or dishonest, and then let him decide, whether it can come from God, and whether such a religion is fit for an honest man?

The most important point, however, remains, and that is, the permission to kill an unlearned man, or to rend him like a fish. We have been told that this is merely figurative language, but the context is not such as to lead to this conclusion; on the contrary, the passage itself, and all that precedes and follows, leads us to believe that it was meant literally. In the first place, it is said, that it is lawful to kill an Amhaaretz without observing the rules of שחיטה slaughtering, and when the disciples ask the reason, R. Eleazar replies, Because these rules would require a benediction to be pronounced, whereas he would not have an Amhaaretz treated with such respect. Let any man explain the figurative meaning of all this. Secondly, R. Samuel, to take away all ambiguity, says, in the name of R. Johannan, that it is lawful to rend him as a fish. Now it is known that, with regard to fish, the rules of שחיטה or slaughtering, are not observed. All ambiguity, therefore, as to R. Eleazar's meaning, is here removed. Thirdly, it is evident that the rabbies looked upon the unlearned as nothing better than beasts. They say, that the daughters of the unlearned are an abomination, and their wives vermin: yea, that their daughters are beasts. Now, when men are so wicked as to use such language concerning their fellow-creatures, are we to be astonished that they should draw the conclusion that necessarily follows from such premises, and that they should allow these beasts and vermin to be killed? When we see that these rabbies allow an unlearned man to be robbed with impunity of that which he has lost, what principle of conscience or justice is there left to prevent them from killing him whom they have robbed? If all the other principles of these rabbies were just, honest, upright, and merciful, we might be tempted to suppose, that in these words they enveloped some mystical sense. But when we see that the principles which precede and follow are an outrage upon humanity, justice, and mercy, no such supposition is necessary.

But, after all, how did the commentators understand the passage? If we, as Gentiles, are accused of misrepresenting the sense, what did the rabbies, who succeeded, make of this passage? The commentary from which we have just quoted, after saying, that if a crowd of Amharatzin let any thing fall, it is lawful to keep it without giving public notice, adds, that this is to be understood strictly of what is lost, but that it does not warrant the learned to rob them by force; upon which the following difficulty is started:—

אמאי ממונו אפור השרא גופו מותר שמותר לקרעו
כדג וכו׳ :

"Why should it be unlawful to deal thus with his money, when it is lawful to deal violently with his body, for it is lawful to rend him as a fish." (Ibid.) Now here this rabbi evidently interpreted the permission to kill literally, and he naturally asks, If it be lawful to take away a man's life by violence, why should it not be lawful to take away his money? If the words had been taken figuratively, there would have been no room for this question. We have, therefore, neither misunderstood nor misrepresented the meaning. The oral law allows the murder of an unlearned man, and that with as little ceremony as it permits the killing of an unclean animal, or a fish. We therefore repeat our assertion, that the oral law cannot be from God. One such passage is quite sufficient to discredit the whole, not only because of its intrinsic wickedness, but because it displays the character of those men with whom the oral law originated. Superabundant self-conceit, cold-blooded cruelty, and unrelenting enmity, are the striking characteristics of those men, who, by dint of force and fraud, gradually enslaved the minds of the Jewish people. It appears from these passages, and from the plain confessions of the rabbies in the context, that the common people struggled hard before they submitted to the yoke of the oral law. The attempt to impose such a burden, evidently produced the most bitter animosity between the rabbies and the people. The people were ready, as one of the rabbies says, to kill all the wise men, and these, in return laid down the principles of retaliation which we have just considered, and which are a disgrace to the name of religion. These principles, however, would not have triumphed if the rabbies had not got the whole power of the State into their own hands. By means of that unlawful and heathenish tribunal, the Sanhedrin, they were able to coerce the people, and to kill all who refused to submit. Judaism, therefore, as it at present exist, is a religion which was originally forced upon the Jewish people against their will, and therefore has no claims upon their reverence or gratitude. By the dispersion, God has removed the main difficulties in the way of their moral and spiritual emancipation. Christianity is in the ascendant, and will not permit any "wise men" to kill the unlearned without ceremony. The people may, therefore, assert their religious liberty in perfect security, and without any fear of the Sanhedrin. We tell the Jews, even on the admissions of the Talmud itself, that their present religion is not even the object of their choice, and much less the religion given by God, but that it was imposed upon the consciences of their fathers by force; and, therefore, ask the Jews, Whether they still wish to continue slaves to superstition and cruelty, when God has, in his providence, arranged the means of their delivery? The Jewish people have often had reason to complain of the injustice, contempt, and cruelty of the nations amongst whom they have been scattered; but we ask them, Have the most barbarous nations ever treated them with more contempt, injustice, and cruelty than that which we have just found authorized by the oral law? Ignorant and superstitious Gentiles have turned the holy name of Jew into a term of reproach, but where was it ever known or heard of, that the most ignorant and most superstitious called the Jews vermin, or compared the wives and daughters of Israel to beasts? It is Judaism, and Judaism only, that utters this foul and inhuman slander. In seasons of popular tumult, mobs have risen and plundered the Jews; but where is the nation, or the religion, which has made a law that it is lawful to keep the lost property of a Jew? Judaism, and Judaism alone, is guilty of this injustice. Prejudice has unjustly assailed the character of the Jewish people, but what sect or party of Christians ever thought of branding them as liars, whose evidence is not to be received; as rogues, unworthy to be appointed as guardians to orphans or property; as murderers, with whom it is unsafe to walk by the road-side? Yet this is the deliberate sentence of Judaism respecting the unlearned; that is, respecting the great mass of the Jewish people. Just suppose that the Parliament of England was to pass a law, declaring that the Jews are to be considered incompetent to give testimony, or to be guardians of property, warning people to beware of walking with a Jew, and permitting men to kill them, or to rend them like a fish; would not the Jewish people perceive in a moment the injustice and the cruelty of such legislation? Would they not have just reason to complain of the blind prejudice which possessed the minds of the legislators? And yet, this is only what the rabbies have done. If Judaism be true, then the mass of the Jewish people are liars, rogues, and murderers; for this is what Judaism asserts; and if the Jewish people consent to its truth, they are stamping themselves, their wives, and their daughters with infamy. The truth or falsehood of the oral law is not simply a speculative question, or a question relating to their eternal interests in another world; it is a question deeply affecting their characters and their welfare at present. It simply comes to this, are all unlearned Jews, that is, the overwhelming majority of the people, to be considered as utterly destitute of truth, honesty, and humanity? If Judaism be true, the answer is, Yes. Let, then, every Jew, rich or poor, learned or unlearned, consider whether he will still profess a religion that defames and insults the mass of his countrymen. The character of the nation is foully attacked, defamed, and vilified, but not by Gentiles, not by Turk, Infidel, or Heretic, but by the Talmud and the Rabbies. The only way in which this calumny can be met and wiped away, is, by a renunciation of that system which has dared to utter it. If there live a Jew who has the slightest regard for the honour of the nation, he is bound to protest aloud against the falsehood of the oral law. That it is false, requires no great stretch of argument to prove. Every unlearned Jew, who is conscious that he is not a liar, a rogue, and a murderer, has the proof in his own breast, that Judaism is false. Every unlearned Jew, who duly honours and respects his wife and daughters, and believes that they are neither vermin nor beasts, is a witness against the truth of the oral law. Every one who believes that dishonesty is contrary to the will of God, and that the murder of the unlearned is unlawful, has the proof that that system which was imposed upon his fathers, is not from God.

No. LX.

RECAPITULATION.

HAVING, by the help and mercy of God, brought these papers to the last number, we propose here to sum up their contents, and to give a review of the arguments which have been urged. The topics discussed have been very various, but the object in all has been the same,—To show that Judaism, or the religion of the oral law, is not the old religion of Moses and the Prophets, but a new and totally different system, devised by designing men, and unworthy of the Jewish people. That Judaism is identical with the religion of the oral law was proved in the first number by an appeal to the highest possible authority, the Prayer-book of the synagogue, which is not only formed in obedience to the directions of the oral law, but declares expressly that the Talmud is of Divine authority. So long, therefore, as that Prayer-book is the ritual of the synagogue, the worshippers there must be considered as Talmudists, believers in all the absurdities, and advocates of all the intolerance of that mass of tradition. That this is no misrepresentation and no unfounded conclusion of our own, appears from the latest book published in this country by a member of the Jewish persuasion. Joshua Van Oven, Esq., has, in his "Introduction to the Principles of the Jewish Faith," a chapter, headed JUDAISM, which begins thus,— "The Jewish religion, or Judaism, is founded solely on the law of Moses, so called from its having been brought down by him from Mount Sinai. With the particulars of these laws he had been inspired by the Almighty during the forty days he remained on the mount, after receiving the Ten Commandments; these he afterwards embodied in the sacred volume, known and accepted as the written law, and called the Pentateuch, or the Five Books of Moses, contained in the volume we term the Bible. *We also, from the same source, receive, as sacred and authentic,* a large number of traditions not committed to writing, but transmitted by word of mouth down to later times; without which many enactments in the Holy Bible could not have been understood and acted upon; these, termed traditional or oral laws, were collected and formed into a volume called the 'Mishna,' by Rabbi Jehudah Hakodesh, A.M. 4150. In addition to this, *we are guided* by the explications of the later schools of pious and learned rabbies, *constituting what is now known by the name of the Talmud, or Gemara.*" *

Nothing can be more explicit than this avowal. A learned and pious Jew of the nineteenth century honestly avows that Judaism is the religion of the Talmud; and upon this principle we have examined Judaism, and compared it with Moses and the Prophets, and the result of this comparison is—

I. THAT JUDAISM IS A FALSE RELIGION.

The premises, from which we draw this conclusion, are—

I. *That the oral law is altogether destitute of external evidence.* To establish the authority of the oral law, it is absolutely necessary to prove a succession of Sanhedrins from the time of Moses to that of Rabbi Jehudah, or at the least an unbroken chain of tradition. But it has been proved, in Nos. xliii. and xliv., that there was no such thing as a

* "A Manual of Judaism," by Joshua Van Oven, Esq., M.R.C.S.L. London, 1835. Page 22.

Sanhedrin until after the Greek conquest of Judea, and in No. xlv., that there is no continuous chain of tradition. The only evidence, therefore, which could beget faith in the mind of a reasonable man is wanting.

2. *The oral law itself is full of manifest fables.* This has been proved almost in every number, but particularly from Nos. xvii.—xxi., where the fables selected are such as are particularly noticed in the prayers of the synagogue. No one can doubt that the stories about Leviathan and Behemoth—of Adam's singing the 92d Psalm after a conversation with Cain—of the river Sambation—of the experiment made by Turnus Rufus to raise his father—of Mount Sinai having been turned, like a tub, over the Israelites—of the descent of 600,000 angels to crown the Israelites—of the people's travelling 240 miles backwards and forwards during the delivery of the Ten Commandments, &c., &c.,—are all downright fables, not a whit more authentic than similar stories contained in the Koran, or the Arabian Nights' Entertainments. Any one fable would be sufficient to overturn the credit of the oral law, but what are we to think of the host of downright falsehoods here enumerated?

3. *It is directly subversive of the state of things established in the written law.* Moses appointed the priests, the sons of Levi, as the religious teachers of Israel. The oral law has ousted them altogether from their office, as was shown in No. xli.

4. *The oral law encourages those Heathen superstitions expressly forbidden by Moses and the Prophets*, such as magic, astrology, amulets, and charms, as is shown from Nos. xxii. —xxvi.

5. *The oral law loosens the moral obligations.* It teaches men how to evade the Divine commandments, as was shown in Nos. xi., xiv., and xv. It allows dispensation from oaths, as proved in Nos. lvi. and lvii. It allows men to retain what they know does not belong to them, if it only belongs to a Gentile (p. 18), or to an unlearned Jew, as appears from No. lix. It sanctions the murder of the unlearned.

6. *It leads men to put trust in mere external acts as a compensation for moral delinquencies.* The washing of hands (No. x.)—the external sanctification of the Sabbath (No. xxix.)—the blowing of the cornet at the new year (No. xxxiv.) —the rite of circumcision (No. lviii.), &c., &c., are represented as sufficient to save wicked men from the just punishment of their misdeeds.

7. *Though called an oral law, because not written with ink, it is really written in blood.* For the most trifling offences it sentences the offender to be flogged (Nos. xiii. and liii.)—for the transgression of the rabbinic commands respecting the Sabbath, it awards the sentence of death (No. xxvii.)—and,

by its laws respecting the killing and cooking meat (Nos. xlix.—liv.), it prevents the poor from getting food for themselves and their children.

8. *It degrades the female sex*, by permitting polygamy (No. xlvii.)—by permitting divorce on the most trifling pretext (No. xlviii.)—by declaring women incompetent to give evidence—by excluding them from the public worship of God —and by teaching that they are under no obligation to learn the revealed will of their Creator (No. iii.).

9. *It oppresses and insults slaves*, by forbidding them to be instructed in the law (No. iii.), and by placing them, when dead, on a level with brutes (No. lv.).

10. *It is a persecuting and intolerant system.* It gives every rabbi the power of excommunicating the Jews (No. xxxi.), and it commands the conversion of all the Gentile nations by the sword (No. vi.).

11. *It forbids the exercise of the commonest feelings of humanity to those whom it calls idolaters.* It will not permit a drowning idolater to be helped, nor a perishing idolater to be rescued, nor an idolatrous woman in travail to be delivered (Nos. iv. and v.).

12. *It leaves those Gentiles who are not idolaters without religion.* It teaches that they are not commanded to love God, and breaks up all the happiness of domestic life, by asserting that amongst Gentiles there is no such thing as marriage (No. viii.). For these and other reasons which might be adduced, we believe that Judaism is contrary to the religion of Moses and the Prophets—that it has not proceeded from God, but is the mere invention of men, and therefore false.

II. From these premises we have concluded, secondly, THAT JUDAISM HAS FOR ITS AUTHORS WICKED MEN, UNWORTHY OF CREDIT. One of the most daring acts of wickedness, that can be committed is to invent laws and principles, and pass them off as the laws of God. Every degree of wilful falsehood is sinful; but to forge Divine laws, and impose upon the consciences of men, is the most daring of all wickedness, for it not only deceives men, but it dishonours God. The Divine Being is represented as the author of principles and practices which are abhorred by the good even amongst men. Is it possible that those men could be good, who invented the fables of which we have spoken above—or who overturned the Mosaic constitution for the purposes of personal aggrandisement—or who teach that oaths may be broken with impunity —or that men may keep what does not belong to them—or that unlearned men may be murdered without ceremony—or that it is lawful to look upon the agonies and pain of an idolater without rendering him any assistance or feeling any pity? If falsehood, perjury, dishonesty, cruelty, and inhumanity, constitute men wicked, then the authors of the oral law are wicked men, and altogether unworthy of credit. And therefore we conclude—

III. THAT THEIR TESTIMONY AGAINST CHRISTIANITY IS OF NO VALUE. Many Jews of the present day reject Christianity simply because the rulers of the nation rejected the Lord Jesus Christ. But the discoveries which we have made of the principles and practices of these men show, that there is no force whatever in this argument. Their testimony against Jesus of Nazareth is not to be trusted any more than Mahomet's testimony against the fidelity of the Jewish nation in preserving the Scriptures. This impostor says, that the Jews have corrupted the Old Testament, but no one believes the charge, because he has been convicted himself of forging revelations and laws. The authors of the oral law have been convicted of the same offence, and their testimony must be rejected for the very same reason. They have passed off their own inventions as Divine laws—they have taught their absurd legends as undoubted matters of fact—they are plainly convicted of falsehood, and the only alternative is to say that these falsehoods are wilful, and then the men who witness against Christianity are wilful liars, or to confess that the authors were mad, and therefore incompetent to give any testimony. In every case they must be regarded as propagators of falsehood. But falsehood is not the only trait in their character; they were interested in their testimony against Jesus: they were his personal enemies, because he opposed their pretensions and condemned all their inventions. They had, therefore, a strong motive for condemning him, and there is nothing in their character to lead us to suppose that their love of justice would prevail over their private feelings. When the general tenour of a man's conduct is evidently the result of upright principle, it is possible to believe that he would be just even to an enemy. When a man's whole life has been distinguished by tender compassion, it is possible to believe that he would not be cruel even to a foe. But neither supposition holds good with respect to the authors of the oral law. They do not even profess integrity, for they teach that it is lawful to defraud an unlearned man—they declare, by their permission to kill an Amhaaretz, that they had no value for human life. If they were capable of murdering in cold blood a man who had never offended them, simply because he did not belong to their party, is it to be wondered at that they should endeavour to destroy one who who was a direct opposer? The condemnation of the Lord Jesus Christ by such men is not only no argument against his character or claims, but even an argument in his favour. It is a decisive proof that he did not belong to their party, and that, therefore, there are not the same objections to his testimony as to theirs. The Jews of the present day, therefore, must find some other reasons for rejecting Jesus of Nazareth. The conduct of their great and learned men at the time can supply no warrant for unbelief at present: it is, on the contrary, a sort of presumptive evidence that He was a good man. And this presumption is much strengthened by comparing the oral law with the New Testament, whereby we learn—

IV. THAT IN ALL THOSE POINTS WHERE THE ORAL LAW IS WEAK, THE NEW TESTAMENT IS STRONG. In the first place, it is entirely free from all fabulous additions to the Old Testament history. It recognises the authority, and frequently cites the writings, of Moses and the Prophets, but it is never, like the Talmud, guilty of forgeries. Neither Jesus nor his disciples pretended to have an oral interpretation of the law, unknown to the people at large, and therefore capable of being twisted to their own purposes. They referred simply to the written word, and by it desired to have all their doctrines judged. In the second place, it is free from all superstitious doctrines concerning magic, astrology, and other heathenish arts. It does not allow absolution from oaths, nor mark out any class of society as the lawful victims of fraud and violence. It is merciful to the poor and to slaves. It teaches that the souls of women are as precious in the sight of God as those of men. It forbids polygamy, and allows divorce only in one case where it is necessary, and thus protects the weaker sex, and guards the sacredness and the happiness of domestic life. It differs especially from the oral law in its estimation of external rites, and thus gives the strongest evidence of its Divine origin. If there be one sign of true religion more satisfactory than another, it is the placing of holiness of heart and life as the first great requisite, at the same time that it does not undervalue any of God's commands. Now this mark Christianity has, and Judaism wants. The former teaches expressly, That without holiness no man shall see the Lord, and that for the want of it no external ceremonies can compensate. Further, Christianity knows of no violent methods of propagating the truth. It nowhere tells its followers, when they have the power, to compel all men to embrace its doctrines, or to put them to death if they refuse. It has not a criminal code written in blood, and prescribing floggings of rebellion, or even death, for a mere ceremonial offence. It does not allow each individual teacher to torment the people by excommunication and anathema at his pleasure. And lastly, it does not misrepresent God as an unjust and partial judge, who confines the benefits of revelation to one small nation, and sentences the overwhelming majority of mankind to unholiness and unhappiness. If ever Judaism should attain to universal dominion, and the principles of Judaism be brought into action, the whole Gentile world would be doomed to misery and ignorance. By pronouncing that amongst Gentiles there is no marriage-tie, it would rob them of all domestic peace. By sentencing every Gentile reader of the Bible to death, it would deprive them of all the consolations and instructions of the Word of God, and by forbidding them to keep a Sabbath, it would, so far as it could, annihilate every token of God's care and loving-kindness. The triumph of Christianity, on the contrary, and the full development of all its principles, would fill the world with peace, and joy, and happiness. The fundamental principles of Christianity, namely, that the Messiah has died for the sins of the whole world, sets forth God as the tender father who cares for all his children, and therefore teaches all men to regard one another as fellow-heirs of the same eternal salvation. It does not deny that Israel has peculiar privileges as a nation, but fully acknowledges that "they are still beloved for the fathers' sakes," and that they are yet to be the benefactors of the human race as they were of old. But it asserts, at the same time, that God is not the God of the Jews only, but of the Gentiles also, and thus makes it possible for Jew and Gentile to love each other. The only foundation for the peace and unity of all nations is the recognition of God as the Father of all, and this foundation is the very corner-stone of Christianity, whilst it neither does nor can form any part of the fabric of Judaism. Christianity teaches that the first and great commandment is, Thou shalt love the Lord thy God with all thy heart; and the second is, Thou shalt love thy neighbour as thyself; and teaches, at the same time, that all men are our neighbours. Judaism teaches that circumcision is the greatest of all the commandments, and that none but Jews and proselytes are neighbours. Thus Judaism divides, whilst Christianity tends to unite, all the children of men in the bands of peace. It has only one principle of God's dealings to men, and that principle is love; and one principle for the guiding of man's conduct to men, and that is love also. Let not the Jewish reader think that we Gentiles wish to ascribe any merit to ourselves, as if by our own wit or wisdom we had found out a religious system superior to anything that Israel had been able to devise. Far from it; we acknowledge again, as we did in the first number, that we are only disciples of one part of the Jewish nation. From the Jews Christianity came to us. It has been a light to lighten us Gentiles, but we acknowledge its Divine Author as the glory of his people Israel. All we mean by instituting the comparison is, to show those who still adhere to the oral law, that there is another Jewish religion infinitely superior, and more like that of Moses and the Prophets. And we appeal confidently to every reader of these papers to decide whether the New Testament or the Talmud is the better book, and to say which is the most agreeable to the will of God as revealed to their forefathers. We earnestly call upon them to make the decision, and to deliver themselves from that unmerited weight of odium which has rested upon them for centuries; and from that still more dreadful evil, the displeasure of Almighty God, which has followed them ever since they forsook the Old Paths wherein their fathers walked.

It is time for those, at least, who profess to abhor certain parts of the Talmud and oral law, to justify their professions by consistent conduct. If they wish people to believe them when they profess love and charity towards all men, they must begin by repudiating the authority of the oral law, and renouncing the worship of the synagogue. How can we possibly believe that those are sincere in their professions to men, who declare that they are insincere in their worship of the heart-searching God? Every man who uses the prayers of the synagogue, there confesses himself to God as a believer in the oral law, and consequently ready to execute all its decrees of cruelty, fraud, and persecution—ready, when he has the power, to convert all nations with the sword. That is his profession in the synagogue; when, then, he comes forth from the solemn act of Divine worship, and tells me that he is liberal and charitable, and that he abhors persecution, how can I possibly believe him? There is falsehood somewhere, and the only possible mode of removing this appearance is by a public renunciation of the oral law, and an erasure of those passages in the public prayers which affirm its Divine authority. This all truly liberal-minded Jews owe to themselves, to the Christian public, to their brethren, and, above all, to their God. To themselves they owe it, because so long as their words and their deeds contradict each other, a mist hangs over them. To the Christian public they owe it, for they must naturally desire to know the principles of those with whom they are connected. To their brethren they owe it, for this is the only way of delivering the nation from the calamities of centuries. To their God they owe it, for by the blasphemies of the oral law, His character is misrepresented, and His name blasphemed.

THE END.

INDEX.

Abarbanel, 124
Aben Ezra, 123
Abraham at the door of hell, 450
Adam, 136
Agadah, recognized in Jewish Prayer-book, 3
Ahijah, the Shilonite, fable about, 352
Almsgiving, Rabbinic, 302
───────, merit of, 307
Amhaaretz, meaning of the word, 458
───────, disqualifications of, 459
───────, may be robbed and slain with impunity, 461
───────, lawful to kill, 6
Amulets, virtues of, 183
Angels carry up the sound of the horn at new year, 267
Angels, of the waves, 197
Angel, evil, 229
Angels ministering, 164
Apostates, to be killed, 36
Arbah, Turim, 112
Astrology, taught and practised, 175
Atonement, day of, 279
───────, itself an atonement, 279
───────, repentance an, 279
───────, a cock killed as an, 283
───────, death an, 299
Baptism necessary to a proselyte, 304
Bar Kochav, 222
Bechai, 142
Behemoth, legend of, 128, &c.
Bither, the city of, 216
Cain, 138
Catechism, Bavarian Jewish, 25
───────, gives a false view of Judaism, 26
Charity, Rabbinic, 112
Charm, Rabbinic, for a bleeding of the nose, 192
─── for the bite of a mad dog, 193
─── for a storm at sea, 196
─── for the bite of a scorpion, 200
Charms allowed on the Sabbath-day, 200
Charm for bed time, 201
Christianity, a Jewish religion, 1

Christianity, the religion of the New Testament, 2
Christians considered as idolaters, 419
─────── not counted amongst the pious of the nations, 4
─────── not in a state of salvation, 4
Circumcision equivalent to all the commandments, 451
───────, meritoriousness of, 450
Cock, killing a cock as atonement, 283
Commandments, 442; 162
Cruelty, Rabbinic, 8, 99, 209
───────, to women, 377
Dead, Rabbinic mourning for, 428
───, prayers for the, 295
Death, an atonement, 299
Demons, asking counsel of, 203
Deniers of the law, three classes of, 4
Deputies, French Jewish, 24
Deuteronomy xvii. 8, &c., explained, 11
Dispensation, Rabbinic, from oaths, 434
Divorce, Rabbinic, doctrine of, 373
Drunkenness allowed on feast of Purim, 47
Edomites, Christians called, 123
Eleazar, Rabbi, 6
Elijah, the Prophet, conversation of, with R. Jose, 323
Epicureans, 4
───────, to be killed, 36
Epicurean, reader in synagogue suspected of being, 127
Evasion, Rabbinic, 80, 83, 107, 225, 235
Excommunication for not washing hands, 75
───────, Rabbinic, 239
───────, laws concerning, with respect to the unlearned and learned, 239
───────, injustice of, 239
Fast on the ninth of Av, 216
Fasting, merit of, 264
Fire, not to be extinguished, 102
Flogging of rebellion, 99, 211, 228, 383, 386, 420
Friday, Good, 87

Gentile, who studies the law, guilty of death, 22
——, who keeps a Sabbath-day, guilty of death, 22
——, good advice not to be given to, 33
—— woman not to be helped in childbed, 33
——, not neighbour, 34
——, lost property not to be restored to, 35
——, Daniel punished for giving good advice to, 33
—— who wishes to turn Jew, 63
——, a Jew not publicly to receive alms from, 306
——, Sabbath not to be profaned to save a Gentile's life, 212, 214
—— food regarded as carrion, 383
—— food not to be eaten, 383, 416
—— wine unlawful, 419
——, he that steals from, only to pay the principal, 34
—— wine, to drink, worse than fornication, 424
Gentiles, idolatrous, to be exterminated, 42
—— to be converted by force, 42
——, idolatrous, not to be suffered in the land of Israel, 28
Gentile, drowning, not to be delivered, 30
Gentiles, duties towards, 24
—— not brethren, 26
—— not neighbours, 26
—— not to be greeted except from fear, 10, 26, 28
—— condemned for transgressing the command about tabernacles, 288
—— still have the defilement of the serpent, 156
——, cursing the, on the feast of Passover, 120, 121, 122
——, no pious, now, 67
——, marriage of, not binding, 58
—— and dogs, 107
Gershom, R., anathema by, 366
Hands, laying on of, 328
——, washing of, 71
Heathen, who are not in a state of salvation, 5
High Priest, an unlearned man, 7
Hilchoth Accum, 28, 33
—————— Avadim, 21
—————— Avel, 428
—————— Berachoth, 71, 73
—————— Deoth, 113
—————— Genevah, 34
—————— Gezelah, 34
—————— Girushin, 375
—————— Gittin, 374
—————— Iom Tov, 116
—————— Ishuth, 366
—————— Issure Biah, 64
—————— Kiddush Hachodesh, 100
—————— Maakaloth Asuroth, 419
—————— Mamrim, 335
—————— Matt'noth Aniim, 304

Hilchoth Megillah, 48
—————— Mikvaoth, 72
—————— M'lachim, 22, 25
—————— P'riah u'r'viah, 7
—————— Rotzeach, 32, 33
—————— Sanhedrin, 172, 342
—————— Sh'vuoth, 436
—————— Taanith, 216
—————— Talmud Torah, 17, 148
—————— T'phillah, 2, 128
—————— T'shuvah, 4, 247
Hillel, the elder, 187
Holyday, how to make fire on, 106
Holydays, additional, prescribed by the rabbies, 98, 101
Jeremiah unjustly condemned, 13
Jewish-German, 283
Jews persecuted in Spain and Portugal, 42
Illegitimate, a learned man takes precedence of High Priest, 7
Intolerance, Talmudic, 28—39
Ioma, 19
Jonathan, son of Uzziel, 187
Jost's history, 125
Isaac, merit of offering, 271
Jubilee, year of, 66
Judaism the religion of the oral law, 2
—————— and of the Jewish Prayer-book, 2
—————— and Christianity cannot both be true, 3
—————— a false religion, 465
——————, its authors wicked men, 467
Judgment, Rabbinic, idea of the final, 287
Karo, R. Joseph, 17
K'hillath Shlomoh, 282
Kiddushin, 19
Kimchi, 93
Leaven, putting away of, 80
Legends, 127—167
Levi, family of, still known, 312
——, privileges of, in the synagogue, 313
——, David, 134
Leviathan, legend of, 128, &c.
Levites, scriptural privileges of, 311
Liberty, religious, first taught by Jesus Christ, 46
Luck, good, 182
Magic allowed by Talmud, 168—174
Maimonides, 25, et passim
——————, intolerance, 26
Meat, lawful and unlawful, 397
—— in milk, laws concerning, 404
—— contrary to Scripture, 404, 405
Medrash Rabba, 153
Merit of ancestors, 285
Merit, doctrine of, 247, &c.
Messiah, already come, 387
Miracles, Rabbinic, 203
Mishna, recognised in Jewish Prayer-book, 3
Mixture, Rabbinic, command of, 116
Muktzeh, 103
Napoleon, 24
New Year, Jewish, 247

INDEX.

New Year, judgment at, 247
———, prayers for, 264
———, merit and advantage of blowing the horn on, 266
Noachidæ, 25, 41
———, who they are, 55
———, seven commandments of, 56
———, may transgress commandments, 57
———, murderer of, not to be put to death, 62
———, unintentionally killing a Jew, to be put to death, 61
———, when received, 67
———, how received, 68
Oral law opposed to the Word of God in duty to parents, 9, 10
———, a mixed system of good and evil, 16
———, how much time to be devoted to the study of, 16
———, women and children not to study, 18
———, perpetual and unchangeable, 53
———, precepts of, given to Moses, 161
Oaths, Rabbinic dispensation from, 435, 450
Parable of Good Samaritan illustrated, 29
Parents, if in captivity, to be redeemed after the Rabbi, 9
———, duty to, according to oral law, 9
Passover, rites of, 79
———, Christ our, 91
———, four cups of, 96
Pentecost prayers, 145
Pesachim, treatise, 6
Pharisees, enemies of the Lord Jesus, 9
———, bad men, 8
Physician, Jewish, not to cure idolaters, 33
Pirke, Eleazer, 137
Planets, 175
Polygamy, allowed, 366
Poor, Rabbinic, oppression of the, 97
———, Rabbinic religion not for the, 237
———, Rabbinic cruelty to, 414, 429
Power, Rabbinic, to excommunicate, 239
Prayer-book, Jewish, acknowledges and teaches the authority of the Talmud, 2, 3
———, Jewish, full of legends, 127—167
Priests, scriptural office of, 310
Proselytes, sojourning, 26
———, how to be instructed, 63
———, baptism of, 304
Purgatory, Rabbinic, 296
Purim, feast of, 47
Rabbi, duty to, goes before duty to parents, 9, 10
———, fear of, as the fear of God, 11
———, reverence due to, 15
———, whosoever despises a, to be excommunicated, 15

Rabbi, not to forgive a public affront, 243
———, method of creating a, 328
Rabbies not agreed, 399, 400
Rabbinic charity, 112
———, evasion, 107, 110
———, order, novelty of, 328
———, power to excommunicate, 239
———, acknowledgments that Messiah is born, 389—393
Ramban, 142
Rome called Edom, 123
Rosh Hashanah, 298
Saadiah Gaon, 162
Sabbath, unlawful for a Gentile to keep a, 22
———, laws of, 104, 114—119
———, spirits cannot be cited on, 141
———, damned have rest on, 141
Sabbath-day, amulets on, 184
Sabbath, laws concerning, 285—230
———, lamp, reward for, 229
———, moving things on, 232
———, merit of keeping the, 224
———, jurisdictions, 232
Salvation, who are excluded from, by the oral law, 4
Sambation, 139
Sanhedrin, not infallible, 8
———, great council of, 168
———, members of, magicians, 168
———, understood seventy languages, 168
———, all handsome men, 171
———, pillar of the oral law, 335
———, a later, may reverse the decision of a former, 335
———, not a Divine institution, 337
———, of Greek origin, 341
———, greater and lesser, 343
———, business of, 345
———, death to those who rebelled against, 344
———, contrary to Scripture, 345
———, Parisian, 366
Satan deceived by the blowing of the horn in the month of Elul, 266
Scapegoat, 280
Schoolmasters, Rabbinic, 315
Scripture, women not bound to study, 18
———, not to be studied so much as the Talmud, 16
———, when not to be studied at all, 17
Sepher Jetzirah, 181
Schulchan Aruch, 7
Sinai, 163
Slaughtering, laws concerning, 380
———, laws of, 396
Slaves exempt from the duty of studying the law of God, 17
———, unlawful to teach, 21
———, regarded as beasts, 431
Souls of all Israel at Sinai, 152
Sotah, 76
Stars, influence of, 175

Study of the law equivalent to all the commandments, 51
Tabernacles, feast of, 287
———, merit of, 287
———, prayers for the feast of, 295
Talmud, recognised in Jewish Prayer-book, 3
———, legends of, 128, 167
Tradition, Rabbinic argument for overthrow, 11
———, no unbroken train of, 350
Treatise, Avodah Zarah, 291
———, Bava Bathra, 187
———, Berachoth, 161
———, Gittin, 192
———, Moed Katon, 175
———, Shabbath, 157
———, Succah, 180
———, Z'vachin, 150
Turnus Rufus, 140, 216
Unlearned man, lawful to kill, 6
———, the wives and daughters of, not to be taken as wives, 6
———, to be accounted as beasts, 6
———, man, unlawful for, to eat meat, 7
Van Oven, Joshua, Esq., Manual of Judaism, 465
Venus planet, 177

Washing of hands, 71
———, to neglect, as bad as fornication, 76
———, who neglects, excommunicated, 75
Wine, Gentile, unlawful, 419
Woman, insane, to be turned out, 377
Women, exempt from the duty to study the law, 17
——— do not receive the same reward as a man, 18
——— not to be taught the law, 18
———, minds of, not equal to the study of the law, 18
———, command of Moses, respecting, 21
———, duties of, prescribed in New Testament, 22
———, Rabbinic degradation of, 359
——— cannot give testimony, 360
——— not regarded as part of the congregation, 361
World to come, who are excluded from, 4
———————, all Israel has a share in, 64
———————, Rabbinic opinions about, 129

www.ingramcontent.com/pod-product-compliance
Lightning Source LLC
Chambersburg PA
CBHW051232300426
44114CB00011B/706